THE
ROCKY
RIOTER
TEARGAS SHOW

THE ROCKY RIOTER TEARGAS SHOW

THE INSIDE STORY OF THE 1976 SOWETO UPRISING

PAT HOPKINS AND HELEN GRANGE

Published by Zebra
an imprint of Struik Publishers
(a division of New Holland Publishing (South Africa) (Pty) Ltd)
PO Box 1144, Cape Town, 8000

First edition 2001

10 9 8 7 6 5 4 3 2 1

Publication © Zebra 2001
Text © Pat Hopkins and Helen Grange 2001

Cover photograph © Peter Magubane

PUBLISHING MANAGER: Marlene Fryer
MANAGING EDITOR: Robert Plummer
EDITOR: Frances Perryer
COVER DESIGN: Christian Jaggers
TEXT DESIGN: Beverley Dodd
TYPESETTING: Monique van den Berg

Reproduction by Hirt & Carter (Pty) Ltd
Printed and bound by CTP Book Printers, Caxton Street, Parow, 7500

ISBN 1-86872-342-9

For Megan, Tiffany, Chelsea
Valerie, Jack and Leilah Natasha

CONTENTS

Photographs and documents between pages 116 and 117

In October 1976 Naomi Nconjwa collapsed and died after hearing that her sons, Henry and Gavin, who had been arrested during the Soweto Uprising, were refused bail. After her death, Reverend S Nkoana, the dean elect of the Anglican Diocese in Johannesburg, tried to persuade the police to allow the boys to attend her funeral, but failed.

This book is dedicated to Naomi and all the mothers of South Africa traumatised by the madness that was our past.

AUTHORS' NOTE

What is the single most important moment in South African history?

Within 100 kilometres – plonked in the African veld – are three human creations that appear at odds with their surroundings and with each other. To the north is the elegant city of Pretoria; in the centre is the frenetic commercial metropolis of Johannesburg; and to the south-west of that, the matchbox sprawl of Soweto. Each appearing isolated, different in character and in people, yes, but undoubtedly intertwined because what happened in one held far-reaching implications for the others. Theirs is the story of South Africa.

The march to Orlando Stadium by students in Soweto on the cold winter's morning of 16 June 1976 forever altered the balance of that interrelationship – and, in so doing, changed the course of South African history. Over a million pages of newspaper reports, commission of inquiry notes and personal reflections were generated. This is as it should be, with an event of such historic and symbolic significance. Because of this rich source, we should know everything – yet we know nothing, as each page appears to be describing events on a different planet. The upshot is that the event is shrouded in a myriad interpretations and contradictions – fertile ground indeed for fanciful claims and mythology.

The event came to be known as the Soweto Riots, the Soweto Uprising, 16 June, the Language Riots and the 'Children's War'. It was all of these, and none of them. It was not a riot, it was an uprising. The language issue was a symptom, not the cause. It was most certainly not a 'Children's War': Children were involved, often at the forefront, but many adults gave direction. Reference to children also represents a fundamental misconception about black education under apartheid, where scholars in high school were often aged between 18 and 22 – hardly children. It was also not confined to 16 June 1976, nor was it restricted to Soweto. The flames engulfed the whole country until the New Year and limped through to 19 October 1977 – 'Black Wednesday' – when the government banned all but the most compliant black organisations in the biggest crackdown on dissent since the Sharpeville massacre in the early 1960s. For the sake of clarity, however, we will bring the curtain down on the scholar-inspired disturbances at the end of 1976 and refer to them as 16 June or the Soweto Uprising.

Blacks, over the time frame of this book, were referred to as Africans, Natives, Bantu and Plurals: we use black, but, where quotes or excerpts are used, we remain with the original. Likewise, Boer and Afrikaner are used to describe Afrikaans-speaking people at various times: we prefer Afrikaner, but use Boer either when quoting or when referring to the citizens of the two Boer republics that existed before the Anglo-Boer South African War (also known by many titles, the most common being the Boer War). We also encountered difficulties with people's names whose spelling has changed over the years – Prime Minister Hans Strijdom's surname is now commonly spelt Strydom, but we stick with Strijdom. In like manner, Zolile Hector Peterson's surname has been spelt Pieterson, Pietersen and Petersen, but we choose the former because phonetically it is the truest. And, Chief Mangosuthu Buthelezi of the Inkatha Freedom Party was known as Chief Gatsha Buthelezi in the mid-1970s, but we use Mangosuthu because he is still actively involved in South African political life.

We have also taken the liberty of simplifying the staggering array of political, cultural and social organisations – ranging from the African National Congress to the Zealous Azanians – that abounded during apartheid. Many small or splinter groups ultimately owed allegiance to or broadly identified with a national organisation. Where this is the case we refer to them under the umbrella movement or simply as a community or student leader.

A great number of people and friends contributed time or gave us encouragement – we thank you all. In particular, this book would have been impossible without the invaluable efforts of the researchers at De Waal and De Waal and the ever helpful staff at the State Archives who helped us access classified papers and documents never seen by the public. We are also indebted to Michele Pickover, Carol Archibald and Kate Abbott of the University of the Witwatersrand (Historical Papers); the staff of the Johannesburg Library; Megan Hopkins, Vicky Canning, Frances Perryer, Justin van Dooren and Gail Gerhardt; and Marlene Fryer, Georgina Hatch and Marika Truter at Zebra.

In answer to the question, 'What is the single most important moment in South African history?' we believe it was the instant the first shot was fired on 16 June 1976, because it effectively killed the dream of grand apartheid. The traumatic death throes would last for many more years, but the beast was mortally wounded. Many of the events and tactics employed in the 1980s during the final thrust also find their roots

in the Soweto Uprising. Moreover, it inspired blacks countrywide, motivated workers, boosted liberation movements, forever changed the perceptions of white South
Africa and sowed the panic in Afrikaner ranks that would place them on the defen-
sive and keep them there.

ABBREVIATIONS

ANC	African National Congress
ARM	African Resistance Movement
AWB	Afrikaner Weerstandsbeweging (Afrikaner Resistance Movement)
BC	Black Consciousness
BCM	Black Consciousness Movement
BOSS	Bureau of State Security
BPA	Black Parents' Association
BPC	Black People's Convention
CI	Christian Institute
FRELIMO	Front for the Liberation of Mozambique
MPLA	Popular Movement for the Liberation of Angola
NGK	Nederduitse Gereformeerde Kerk (Dutch Reformed Church)
NICRO	National Institute for the Prevention of Crime and Rehabilitation of Offenders
NUSAS	National Union of South African Students
OAU	Organisation of African Unity
PAC	Pan Africanist Congress
PUTCO	Public Utility Transport Company
SABC	South African Broadcasting Corporation
SABRA	South African Bureau for Racial Affairs
SACC	South African Council of Churches
SAIRR	South African Institute of Race Relations
SANNC	South African Native National Congress
SASM	South African Students' Movement
SASO	South African Students' Organisation
Spro-Cas	Special Project for Christian Action in Society
SSRC	Soweto Students Representative Council
UBC	Urban Bantu Councils
UDF	United Democratic Front
UN	United Nations
UNITA	National Union for the Total Independence of Angola
WCC	World Council of Churches
WRAB	West Rand Administration Board

PART I

A TALE OF THREE CITIES

1 ■ THE BROTHERHOOD

Those whom the gods wish to destroy they first make mad.

'Let us build a monument of united Afrikaner hearts stretching from the Cape to Pretoria,' urged Henning Klopper, a founder of the Afrikaner Broederbond (Brotherhood), as the *Eeufees Trek* (Centenary Trek) got under way on 8 August 1938. 'We trust the wagons will be the means of letting Afrikaner hearts, which today may not beat in unison, beat as one again.'

It was a masterstroke: the nation thrilled as the lead wagon, with Oswald Pirow perched on the *wa-kist*, creaked away from the statue of Jan van Riebeeck in Cape Town and through the cheering streets on the first leg of an epic journey north – *Die pad van Suid Afrika* (The South African road). Wagons named after Boer heroes and accompanied by mounted commandos separated outside the city to lumber along routes mapped to take them through every town and *dorp* to Pretoria – Canaan, the heart and soul of Afrikanerdom – where they would converge on 16 December (the centenary of the Battle of Blood River) to be led triumphantly in procession to Monument Koppie for the laying of the foundation stone for the Voortrekker Monument.

Among them, the Magrieta Prinsloo trekked through the Western and Northern Cape and the Hendrik Potgieter passed through the Eastern Cape and Orange Free State. 'Of all the trek wagons now gradually converging on Pretoria,' reported a *Sunday Express* correspondent, 'the Johanna van der Merwe has been confronted by difficulties more closely in keeping with the conditions under which the Great Trek was completed than any of the symbolic vehicles. This wagon, which left Moorreesburg in the middle of September, has followed the *thirstland* route through the sterile countries of Namaqualand, Bushmanland and Griqualand, and the drivers and oxen have encountered some of the difficulties which the pilgrims of 100 years ago had to face. The wagon itself was built 90 years ago, and is the oldest in use on all the treks.'

Along the way, wagons were met by bearded, grizzled men dressed in corduroy *klapbroeke*, flowered waistcoats, heavy jackets and *veldskoene* and women wearing

bonnets and flowing black cloaks who had travelled many miles to touch the
vehicles, pray with the occupants or listen to readings of poetry:

> Ah, she is worn out now and old;
> Her back is bowed, her hands are cold,
> My Mother.
> I know not what to do or say;
> I can but send a kiss each day
> To Mother,
> My Mother.
> And wheresoe'er my footfall lands,
> There is but one who understands:
> My Mother.
> I know my Mother prays for me.
> Oh God, look down in sympathy
> On Mother,
> My Mother.
>   – BB Keet: 'My Mother'

And everywhere they went, welcoming committees ceremoniously renamed streets,
buildings and town squares in honour of the Trekkers.

'There was something strangely symbolic in the spirit of the new trek,' continued
the *Sunday Express* correspondent, 'something in the creaking of those wagon
wheels across the face of South Africa; a refrain of national unity, swept into an
unprecedented wave of national fervour every mile of the epic journey.

'As these kakebeen wagons, and their little commando raised new dust-clouds on
Die Pad van Suid-Afrika, a new realisation dawned. Everywhere the wagons rumbled,
all sections of the community rushed to greet and salute them, to give them a friendly hand on their way northwards. Sentiment cast aside political argument. The
homage was sincere. The people of South Africa were not allowing the memory of
the hardy Voortrekkers to be sullied by racial and political differences. This was the
year of homage, they argued; the greatest centenary in South African history.
December 16 would see the crescendo of that racial harmony for which every South
African was hoping and for which so many were striving.'

When the Johanna van der Merwe, led by four women carrying Vierkleurs and hailed by a scattered volley of rifle fire from the 300-strong mounted escort, entered Johannesburg it was met by throngs that included old men in bath chairs and cripples leaning on crutches. 'The contrast between the old and the new was vivid,' commented the *Sunday Express* reporter, 'as primitive ox-wagons of 100 years ago rolled on tarmac streets through towering avenues of sky-scrapers.'

On the same day, Dr DF Malan, leader of the right-wing opposition Purified National Party, which had broken away from General Barry Hertzog's National Party in 1933, was milking the situation for all it was worth. 'We are recalling the century which is past and looking forward to the century which is coming,' he told a packed gathering at Redelinghuis. 'If we wish to keep burning the light which was lit a century ago, until 2038, it will depend upon us and generations which are to come. The time has come to consider what heritage will be left to posterity. Everything will depend upon courage and conviction, and the great question is, whether the Afrikaner, a century hence, will still believe in God.'

By 13 December there were already 10 000 camped at Monument Koppie and by the 15th their number had swollen to 200 000 to witness the 'river of flame'. 'The two torches brought by relays of Voortrekkers from Cape Town and Dingaan's Kraal (Blood River, site of the defining Boer victory of 16 December 1838), arrived in the valley below the monument tonight,' recalled TC Robertson in the *Rand Daily Mail*. 'Three thousand boys and girls, carrying torches, met them on the hill above the aerodrome. They marched down towards the camp like a winding river of fire more than a mile long. There the crowd stood waiting in silent amazement.

'Then as the chain of light wound past them, they started cheering – more lustily and enthusiastically than I have ever heard a South African crowd cheer. Women rushed forward and burned the corners of their handkerchiefs and *kappies* in the flame of the two torches, to keep as mementos of the great event.'

General Chris Muller led the wagons, on 16 December, from the centre of Pretoria to Monument Koppie. 'General Muller had one of the most distinguished and meteoric careers on commando,' explained the *Sunday Express*. 'Beginning as a corporal of the Boksburg Commando at the time of the Jameson Raid, he rose to the post of General. During the guerrilla warfare in the Transvaal, General Muller received a "clairvoyant leg". If the enemy advanced or moved up in his direction, his leg would begin and keep on paining just above the knee. When they fought and his calf began paining, the enemy either fled or retreated. Of such infinite help was this clairvoyant leg, that the enemy never surprised him.'

The cheering could be heard all along the route as the wagons completed their journey, after which the foundation stone of the Voortrekker Monument – 'a monument that in its colossal massiveness would symbolise the courage, morale, piousness, unshakeable faith and daring of the Voortrekkers to inspire great deeds for ever more' – was laid. 'A score of women knelt in silent prayer in the darkness round the bare foundations of the Voortrekker Monument tonight,' reported TC Robertson as the festivities drew to a close at the end of the day. 'I saw the outlines of their *kappies* silhouetted against the brilliant lights of Pretoria – the Voortrekker city – in the valley below. The action of these 20 women was characteristic of the reverent spirit that is prevailing at the Monument. Although a soft rain was falling they climbed the steep slopes of Monument Koppie through the thick growth of protea bushes and long grass. From the camp the echo of the massed choirs singing hymns could be heard. In the south the lights of the city of gold, where the modern Voortrekkers are fighting their battle, could be seen twinkling over the hills.'

Pretoria was chosen as the site for the Monument because it was here that the deeds of the Voortrekkers were given form. When the first whites visited it in 1829, the region where the city now stands was occupied by Mzilikazi, a breakaway Zulu chief who founded the Matabele nation. Between then and 1854, Boers settled the area that was to become Irene and in that year Commandant-General Marthinus Wessels Pretorius, the son of the hero of Blood River, Andries Pretorius, purchased land at Elandspoort for a *kerkplaas* (church square) to serve the central Boer Zuid-Afrikaansche Republiek, commonly known as the Transvaal Republic.

Within a year a town had developed round the church square and it was christened Pretoria Philadelphia – in honour of the Pretorius family and the brotherhood of Voortrekkers – but later shortened to Pretoria. For the next three decades it was to remain a poor town trapped in a centuries-old racially exclusive lifestyle – a place so puritanical that the clock on the tower of the Dopper church had no hands.

'Pretoria is a little town,' wrote novelist Anthony Trollope in *South Africa*. 'The streets lie in holes, in which when it rains the mud is very deep. In all such towns as these mud assumes the force of a fifth element, but in spite of this Pretoria is both picturesque and promising.'

'The prettiest of the South African towns, with its red and white houses, its tall clumps of trees and pink lines of blooming rose hedges,' added Rider Haggard in *Jess*.

And Pretoria would have remained a small, poor town had gold not been discovered 80 kilometres to the south on the Witwatersrand in 1886, heralding the greatest gold rush ever. While the pious Boers in the capital looked on in horror as a veritable Gomorrah mushroomed on their doorstep, the wealth generated allowed them to transform Pretoria into the elegant city it is today.

'As Pretoria was approached the country became very pretty,' wrote Lady Sarah Wilson, the hated aunt of Winston Churchill, in *South African Memories* in the mid-1890s. 'Low hills and many trees, including lovely weeping willows, appeared on the landscape, and away towards the horizon was situated many a snug little farm; running streams caught the rays of sun, and really rich herbage supplied the pastures for herds of fat cattle. In the town itself an imposing space called Church Square was pointed out to us with great pride by the Dutch gentleman who did ciceron. There we saw the little primitive "Dopper" church where the president always worshipped, overshadowed and dwarfed by the magnificent Houses of Parliament, built since the Transvaal acquired riches, and by the no less grand Government Offices.'

But the new wealth brought with it turbulence and insecurity as imperial Britain cast a rapacious eye over the goldfields – often with comic consequences. Dr Jan Gunning, director of the State Museum in Pretoria, was planning to remove his menagerie to the farm *Rus in Urbe* on the outskirts of the city, where he intended to establish a zoological garden. While attending the South African Congress in Cape Town in September 1899 he struck up a conversation over lunch with Cecil John Rhodes that culminated in Rhodes offering the director a lion, Fanny, to add to his collection.

Gunning, while eager to accept the gift, was keenly aware of the political tensions of the time and the implications of accepting a gift from the man branded 'an enemy of the state' by the Transvaal. He tactfully suggested to Rhodes that Fanny be exchanged for a silver pheasant and two eagles. The deal was struck and all would have turned out well had someone not sent a mischievous telegram to Pretoria to the effect that 'Dr Gunning was bringing up the "British Lion"'.

'Nearly 100 people were on the railway station to meet Dr Gunning and Fanny,' wrote Lesbury Roberts in a newspaper article. 'Fanny had been placed in a trolley for removal to the museum, when a telephone message came from Mr FW Reitz (the State Secretary), saying the animal was on no account to be kept on Government property. Failing a more suitable place, she was put for the time being into a backyard belonging to one of Dr Gunning's friends. Shortly afterwards Mr Reitz brought a message from President Paul Kruger, ordering the return of Fanny to Cape Town. Mr Reitz added that if Mr Gunning was not satisfied he could "go with Fanny".'

The lioness was sent back to Rhodes, who shipped her to the London Zoo after penning an indignant letter to Gunning: 'I see no connection between a zoological garden and your Government's present differences with Her Majesty's Government. It is the first time that *lions and politics* have been mixed up.'

Shortly after, the region was drawn into the cataclysmic conflict now known as the Anglo-Boer South African War. But Gunning, furiously establishing his zoo, would hardly have noticed. When Field-Marshall Lord Roberts entered Pretoria at two o'clock on the afternoon of 5 June 1900 and tore down the Vierkleur, the city was unscathed. 'There was no ruin of streets,' wrote Prevost Battersby, the *Morning Post* correspondent, 'no cringing people, no debris of an army, none of the very needful adjuncts of success.' The fall of Pretoria, however, did not herald the end of the war, but rather the start of the guerrilla phase – one that would bring 'the very needful adjuncts of success' as General Lord Kitchener, Roberts's successor, climaxed the Afrikaners' 'Century of Wrong' with his scorched-earth policy and concentration camps.

'And to Fanny, the political lion?' wrote VC Malherbe in the *Cape Argus*. 'Transplanted to London she was renamed "Beauty" – whether through somebody's whim or a kindly desire to conceal an unfortunate past, who can say? But fate had in store a delightful ironic denouement. When the war was over, the political lion was returned to Pretoria where, as Beauty, she lived in Dr Gunning's zoo until her death in April 1916.'

While the Great Trek and the Anglo-Boer South African War left deep scars and formed the core of future introspective nationalist philosophy and mythology, they might never have found currency but for Alfred Lord Milner's aggressive post-war anglicisation policy. To the humiliation of defeat was heaped the indignity of a 'superior English civilisation' that recognised only one language in the civil service and forced children to wear placards declaring 'I am a donkey' should they dare use Dutch in school. It was the perfect hook for General Hertzog. 'Had it not been for Milner and his extreme measures,' commented General Jan Smuts, 'we Afrikaners would probably all quite happily have been speaking English by now. By his opposition to our language, he helped create it.'

'That General Hertzog should choose the language as the starting point of his struggle for Afrikaans survival was the logical development of his belief that language was much more than a means of expression,' explained his official biographer. 'It was a vehicle of a people's distinctive culture and separateness.'

Afrikaners, frustrated at being refused permission to teach their children in their mother tongue, began, in September 1903, to establish private Afrikaans schools – the forerunners to the Christian National Education that would blossom in the latter part of the twentieth century. And as the Afrikaner phoenix was resurrected by language, so flames of revival began to nourish the ravaged political and cultural wasteland. Military leaders like generals Louis Botha, Jan Smuts and Barry Hertzog started to reorganise their people, while poets such as Eugène Marais, Totius and C Louis Leipold began the painful process of rebuilding Afrikaner dignity.

'Seek therefore all that is good and beautiful in the past,' Paul Kruger had advised, 'and build on it your ideal and strive to realise that ideal for the future.'

Afrikaner revival received a huge boost from its arch foe, the English, after the war. The British were concerned with two things – to rebuild the agricultural capacity of a scorched land and return the gold-mining industry to full production as soon as possible, so that the enormous debts incurred by the war could be settled and southern Africa be reconstructed as a Greater Britain in the veld. To achieve this, it was necessary to reconcile with the Boers and sacrifice Britain's black allies.

By 1905 the political direction South Africa was taking was becoming clear. The British imperial government, to reconcile with the former Boer republics, was anxious to grant them responsible self-government as soon as possible. And this meant segregation – a policy overwhelmingly favoured by local whites, both Boer and colonial – to maintain white economic and political domination. And a key element of this thinking was separation of black and white land. Blacks, whose place it was to provide labour for the mines and farms, would be confined to 'reserves' where they could fulfil their political aspirations.

'The Bantu's condition after war has grown worse and worse every year,' wrote Dr Modiri Molema in *The Bantu: Past and Present.* 'Their rights, never many or mighty, have been curtailed systematically from then to now and the future is dark and dreary.'

Moreover, Britain believed its long-term interests in southern Africa would be preserved by the four colonies coming together in union. To achieve this, the British were forced to choose between the demands of their racist white kin and the future of their black friends. They chose family and, as a result, there was no place even for the extension of the limited non-racial Cape franchise to the rest of the country, let alone 'equal rights for all civilised men'. The draft South Africa Bill, negotiated between white South Africans and the British imperial government, provided no effective black representation. The other three colonies would have rejected union had this issue been forced on them.

The South African Native Convention held in Bloemfontein from 24 to 26 March 1909 was called so that black South Africans could present a united front to the grave danger inherent in the proposed union. Out of this convention grew the South African Native National Congress in 1912, which would become the African National Congress in 1923.

Black protest had little impact, and union became a reality in 1910 under a South African Party government led by General Louis Botha and including Smuts and Hertzog. 'The Imperial Government,' snarled Sol Plaatje, 'after conquering the Boers, handed back to them their old republics, and a nice little present in the shape of the Cape Colony and Natal.'

While the seat of Parliament was Cape Town, Pretoria was selected as the executive or administrative capital of the new union. In mark of this honour the streets were planted with avenues of alien jacarandas, and Herbert Baker, the celebrated architect, was commissioned to find a suitable site and design and build a grand edifice. 'I was given a free hand in suggesting sites in and around the city,' he wrote in *Architecture and Personalities*. 'I was shown the block of land which the government had bought in the centre of the city. But with the high ideals we all had at the time I thought this site unworthy of the capital buildings of a United South Africa. So I explored the surrounding kopjes.' He eventually settled on Meintjeskop, on which he constructed a semi-circular colonnaded acropolis that incorporated a natural amphitheatre. Today it is regarded as an architectural triumph; then, however, it was criticised as 'ponderous and stony'.

At first it appeared that the government would take a soft line with regard to blacks, and false optimism was raised when Botha appointed Cape liberal Henry Burton as Minister of Native Affairs. But the Prime Minister was being squeezed at the hustings. From platform and pulpit and in the press he was derided by Afrikaners for being pro-English and weak on blacks. And the Cape liberals were as trapped as Botha. Each action that appeared soft on blacks was pounced on by General Hertzog, the leader of a faction that was to become the National Party, who was calling for tougher 'native policies'.

Afrikaner nationalism was growing, and the balance of power soon reflected this by shifting increasingly to the more conservative, racist northern provinces. Soon bills such as the Native Labour Relations Act, which tightened control on black labour, and the Mines and Works Act, which reserved certain categories of work for whites, were passed into law. The central issue after Union, however, remained segregation – a desire that was to become law with the passing of the Natives Land Act of 1913. This cynical piece of legislation – in which Britain acquiesced – was drafted to satisfy white aspirations for segregation while satisfying the labour needs of farmers and mine owners. And with it the foundation for apartheid and the mass exploitation of black South Africans was laid.

The Land Act sought to deprive blacks of the right to acquire land, by purchase or leasehold, outside demarcated areas of occupation referred to as 'Scheduled Native Areas'. J Keyter, the MP for Ficksburg, in a speech in support of the legislation, said that it was necessary to tell blacks that South Africa 'was a white man's country, that he was not going to be allowed to buy land there, and if he wanted to be there he must be in service'. What Keyter did not mention was that, in effect, the Act was designed by enfranchised whites to steal the country and virtually enslave the unrepresented: its core purpose was the provision of cheap labour. This was accomplished by allocating 7.3 per cent (later increased to 13 per cent) of the country's land surface to 80 per cent of the population. It was obvious that this was not sufficient to support the blacks in South Africa and would immediately throw more than a million souls into the deep end of the labour pool.

'Awakening on Friday morning, June 20, 1913,' declared Plaatje, 'the South African native found himself, not actually a slave, but a pariah in the land of his birth. For to crown all our calamities, South Africa has by law ceased to be the home of any of her native children whose skins are dyed with pigment that does not conform to the regulation hue.'

The effects of the Act, passed in the middle of one of the coldest winters on record, were devastating. Desperate peasant families were forced to submit to conditions of labour provision at derisory compensation or abandon homes that had belonged to ancestors. Roadsides were filled with animals, children, the old and the sick. They could not stop, not even to bury the scores of elderly and children that perished, for if they did they were arrested and charged with vagrancy. And if their cattle or livestock became sick or starved they were criminally charged for that too. 'It was a sickening procedure of extermination,' said Plaatje, who witnessed this outrage and regarded it as an act of war.

If there was one bright spot for blacks in the Act, it was the galvanisation of the African National Congress to action. And while it appears implausible that it could have been anything other than beneficial for all whites, catering as it did to predominantly Afrikaner farmers and English mining and business, there was a growing band of white Afrikaners severely threatened by its consequences. Drought, rinderpest, locusts and the inability to adapt to new farming methods had all taken their toll on these Boers, who had been driven in ever-increasing numbers to the cities to seek employment.

These impoverished, unskilled people, living in wretched shanties on the outskirts of towns or in slums in the cities, faced serious competition from blacks prepared to work for lower wages and take on tasks poor whites believed to be beneath their dignity. The Land Act, by forcing many blacks to the cities, exacerbated the problem. Though political power was theirs, urban Afrikaners remained economically oppressed – subjugated by the old foe, the English, who controlled the economy, and by the hordes of blacks who marginalised them by taking most jobs. And it was utterly inconceivable to these supremacists that urban blacks were in the same boat as them and thus potential and powerful allies in their struggle. What they *were* receptive to was the message that they were a people chosen by God and had been severely wronged. The ground was fertile for mythology – a brooding fiction focusing not on triumph but on the suffering wrought by the Great Trek and war against the English. It was a tale weaving the threads of a tormented history to create a sacred epic that would unify and mobilise the *volk* to real power and ultimate freedom.

While Botha and Smuts, the leaders of the South African Party, saw whites 'as children of one family' of South Africans, a growing number of Afrikaners led by Hertzog and Malan believed their people had to be separated even from the English until such time as their culture was strong enough to stand on its own. Their great fear was the swamping of the *volk*. 'Let the Afrikaans language become the vehicle for our culture, our history, our national ideals, and you will also raise the people who speak it,' thundered Malan. 'The Afrikaner language movement is nothing less than the awakening of our nation to self-awareness and to the vocation of adopting a more worthy position in world civilisation.' And it was this need for isolation that the National Party, formed in 1914, used to hammer away at the policies of the government, claiming it harmed Afrikaners in its quest for conciliation with the English. It was a message with a growing audience.

On the night of 17 April 1918 a National Party meeting in Johannesburg addressed by Malan, the Cape leader, was broken up in a free-for-all in which party members were assaulted. The following day three teenage Afrikaners, Henning Klopper, Danie du Plessis and HW van der Merwe, who attended the meeting, vowed to form an organisation that would fulfil Afrikaner dreams. On 5 June the group met again at Du Plessis's house at 32 Marathon Street in Malvern, Johannesburg, with a select party and there formed a secret society called Jong Suid Afrika – later to become the Afrikaner Broederbond.

'A nation is born when a few people decide it should be,' declared Benjamin Arnold in *Imagined Communities*. While the Broederbond started out as an organisation concerned with the cultural and economic upliftment of urban Afrikaners through the creation of a powerful Afrikaner middle and entrepreneurial class, its aim was political power in a republic. 'Let us bear in mind the fact that the main point is for Afrikanerdom to reach its ultimate goal of dominance in South Africa,' wrote Professor JC van Rooy, a later chairman of the Broederbond, in a circular to members. 'Brothers, our solution for South Africa's troubles is that the Afrikaner Broederbond must rule South Africa.'

The society grew rapidly, its members carefully selected from 'Afrikaner-speaking Protestants of good character'. Soon, 800 cells were infiltrating members into all levels of society – permeating school boards, town and city councils, the press, industry and agricultural unions. One of its fiercest opponents, however, was Hertzog, who predicted that their 'Afrikaner jingo self-glorification' would eventually lead to the downfall of Afrikanerdom. But the National Party split in 1933 when Hertzog joined Smuts to form the United Party and Malan founded the Purified National Party – thereby creating an opportunity for the Brotherhood to become the power behind the throne if they could bring about Afrikaner unity. That chance came with the Broederbond-inspired *Eeufees Trek* of 1938 – a cultural event with decidedly political undertones that would contribute greatly to Malan's triumph a decade later.

In those 10 years the Broederbond laid the foundation for South Africa's future obsession with racial affairs. 'Without giving an exposition of different points of view regarding the native question, we want to state our own point of view briefly, and thereafter the basis on which it rests,' read a circular to members. 'Total segregation should not only be the ideal, but the immediate practical policy of the State. The purchase and separation of suitable and adequate areas of habitation by native families, and tribes living on farms and smaller reserves, should take place at any cost.

'The opportunity should be provided for different tribes to gather in separate areas. Then it should be made compulsory for these groups of natives to return to these areas. Here they can become co-operative and separate landowners. But the land should be purchased by the natives from the State through a form of taxation such as a hut tax, or occupied in freehold from the State. In these areas, greater degrees of self-government can be granted after some time. This should be in line as much as possible with the native's history and traditional forms of government. Areas should be under control of specially trained white commissioners directly answerable to the Minister of Native Affairs.

'Here the native can fulfil himself and develop in the political, economic, cultural, religious, educational and other spheres. In these areas whites cannot become landowners, and whites who settle there as traders, missionaries, teachers, etc. will have no political rights there.

'A native who has reached a stipulated age will be allowed, with the permission of his tribal chief and the commissioner, to go temporarily to white areas to work on farms and in towns and cities. But he will not be allowed to take his family.

'The detribalised native must as far as possible be encouraged to move to these native areas. Those who cannot do so must be housed in separate locations where they will enjoy no political rights and own no property because they will be viewed as temporary occupants who live in the white areas after having been allowed a reasonable time to obtain work.'

This document sought to extend the restrictions of the Natives Land Act in providing for urban blacks. Not only were blacks to be pariahs in the land of their birth, they were now also to be foreigners housed in specially established compounds. And while this was theory, it formed the foundation for apartheid – the absolute segregation of South Africa.

Over the next 15 years these ideas were to be fine-tuned and theologised, but there was always the suspicion, as with the Land Act, that massive fraud lay at the heart of the philosophy. While Afrikaners claimed God's will, and other lofty principles, they were concerned with giving their own an unfair advantage over the disenfranchised. And while the English scoffed at the crudity of it, they were quite happy to profit from the potential for exploitation. 'Christian guardianship' was the guise. As stated by Ben Schoeman, a future Minister of Labour, the reality was quite different: 'Apartheid means that non-Europeans will never have the same political rights as the Europeans; that there will never be social equality; and that the Europeans will always be *baas* [boss] in South Africa.'

The problem was that DF Malan, with the support of the Broederbond, pulled off a surprise victory in the 1948 general election that allowed this fanciful brand of national socialism to be given effect. There were many reasons why the Nationalists triumphed: they offered a package of promises that appealed to white workers, farmers, professionals and intellectuals; they benefited from the weighting of the rural vote; and they exploited white fears attendant on black mass urbanisation, while the governing United Party led by an elderly Smuts seemed increasingly out of touch with local sentiment. But, more than anything else, they offered apartheid in simple, easy-to-grasp terms. 'Any party that shouts "Keep the Native down" long enough and often enough will prevail,' commented Dr Edward Roux.

'The outcome of the election has been a miracle,' gloated Prime Minister Malan on 1 June 1948. 'No one expected this to happen. It exceeded our most optimistic expectations. Afrikanerdom has lived under a dark cloud and the future has been black for many years. We feared for the future of our children. But the cloud has disappeared and the sun is shining once more. In the past we felt like strangers in our own country, but today South Africa belongs to us once more. For the first time since Union, South Africa is our own. May God grant that it always remains our own.'

Immediately after the election result became known, Malan rode a 'victory train' from Cape Town to Pretoria, stopping at every station to greet the Vierkleur-waving, cheering people. And at the Union Buildings a hymn-singing crowd gave thanks for the dawning of the long-awaited Afrikaner revolution.

The triumph was God's will, but, to make absolutely sure, the Nationalists consolidated their base by bringing in six MPs (all National Party supporters) from the South West Africa protectorate, removing coloureds from the common voters' role and banning the Communist Party, which included barring communist MPs from Parliament. Further, they moved quickly to impose tight controls over civil society, cracked down on extra-parliamentary opposition and trade unions, loaded the civil service, police and army with reliable Afrikaners, and introduced Christian National Education in government schools.

'I declare that the Nationalists subscribe to the Christian National Education System with a view to eventually establishing Dutch Reformed schools,' said B Coetzee, a leading National Party spokesperson.

'How parallel the system is to some of the worst features of the Nazi system!' stated the Anglican dean of Johannesburg. 'The cold-blooded attempts to capture the children and the country in the interests of the state recall Hitler's phrase "a religion peculiar to our race".'

To give effect to the philosophy of apartheid, the South African Bureau for Racial Affairs (SABRA) was launched in 1948. Its 'scientific study' led directly to the Prohibition of Mixed Marriages Act, introduced in 1949, which outlawed marriages between white and non-white; the Immorality Act of 1950, which made sexual relations across the colour line illegal; the Population Registration Act, which assigned every person within the borders of South Africa to one of four broad racial categories (white, black, coloured and Asian) and governed how each would be organised and administered; and, the 'very essence of apartheid', the Group Areas Act, which enforced separate urban areas for each race group.

'We had endured Botha, Hertzog and Smuts,' wrote Chief Albert Luthuli, the president of the ANC. 'It did not seem of much importance whether the whites gave us more Smuts or switched to Malan. Our lot had grown steadily harder, and no election seemed likely to alter the direction in which we were being forced. Nevertheless, I think it is true that very few, if any, understood how swift the deterioration was destined to be. I doubt, too, whether many of us realised at the time that the very intensity of nationalist oppression would do what we had so far failed to achieve – awake the mass of Africans to political awareness, goad us finally out of resigned endurance and so advance the day of our liberation.'

'The rest of the world do not know what it means to live with a people that are consumed by hate,' added Nelson Mandela's wife Winnie, some years later, 'a people who are so petrified of domination, who feel that if they share power, it means they will lose their identity. The Afrikaners' neurotic desire to keep their purity as a race is something like what Hitler must have had in mind when he flung the rest of the world into a state of chaos, with millions losing their lives because of their race.'

The Nationalist election victory celebrations culminated with the opening of the Voortrekker Monument on 16 December 1949. Among the 3 000 people who gathered at the massive shrine ringed by 64 granite ox-wagons and designed by Gerard Moerdijk in the fashion of the Volkerschlacht-Denkmal at Leipzig was the people's wrestling idol Manie Maritz, selling copies of his father's anti-Semitic, anti-English work, *My Lewe en Strewe* (My Life and Struggles). At noon, a shaft of sunlight pierced the eye of the dome and lit up the words *Ons vir Jou, Suid Afrika* (We for Thee, South Africa).

'Back to your people,' trumpeted Malan to the faithful, 'Back to the highest ideals of your people; back to the pledge that has been entrusted to you for safe-keeping; back to the altar of the people on which you must lay your sacrifice and, if it is demanded of you, also yourself as a sacrifice; back to the sanctity and inviolability of family life; back to the Christian way of life, back to the Christian faith; back to the church; back to your God.'

Back at the Prime Minister's office, questions were being asked as to how long it would take to implement 'complete' apartheid. Professor AC Cilliers of Stellenbosch University thought it would take about a century, maybe sooner if nine million blacks could be shifted to Central Africa; Dr Donges, the Minister of the Interior, believed five years sufficient; and the ever-pragmatic Dr EG Jansen, the Minister of Native Affairs, suggested it should be allowed to happen 'in its own time and fashion'. But there was a nagging feeling that while urban blacks could not be accepted as inhabitants of European areas, as this 'must inevitably lead to his adoption as fellow citizen in the political sphere', it would be counterproductive to send them all back to wherever they came from, as this would remove all the cheap labour. It was these imponderables that gave hope that sense would prevail and that Malan and his successor Hans Strijdom would shelve the more extreme ideas of apartheid – and they probably would have, had the fanatical Hendrik Frensch Verwoerd not been chosen to succeed Strijdom in 1958.

The rugged, tall Verwoerd, with a high-pitched unimpressive voice and unruly lock of hair that continually fell over his right eyebrow, was not a South African – thus breaking the tradition of prime ministers having impeccable Great Trek and Anglo-Boer South African War ancestry. He was born on 8 September 1901 in Amsterdam and arrived in southern Africa with his parents two years later. At school in South Africa and Rhodesia he was regarded as lonely and aloof, but by the time he reached the University of Stellenbosch he was showing leadership qualities and was elected chairman of the Union Debating and Philosophical Society and chairman of the Students' Representative Council.

In the 1920s he studied at three German universities and came into contact with fanatical Nazi ideology – ideas he brought back with him to Stellenbosch in 1928. He would probably have remained in academia completing theses like the one that earned him his PhD – *Experimental Study of the Blunting of the Emotions* – had not the 'wild men of the north' under Strijdom decided to wrest control from the Cape Nationalists by establishing a competing mouthpiece to the 'moderate' Nationalist-supporting newspaper *Die Burger*. These initiatives led to the establishment of Voortrekker Pers, with Verwoerd as the first editor of its radical *Die Transvaler*, which sprang to notoriety during the British royal family's visit of 1947, when the only coverage he gave the event was a solitary paragraph prior to their visit to Johannesburg: 'The presence of certain visitors today will cause some dislocation to the traffic.'

During his 11-year editorship, Verwoerd established himself as a powerful force in the Broederbond and in the 'back room' of the National Party. In 1948 he was the only senior Nationalist not to win his constituency, but he was brought into Parliament via the Senate and in 1950 took over the small portfolio of Native Affairs from Jansen. The zeal he brought to this department was to transform it into a super-ministry with tentacles that would touch the lives of all South Africans and earn him the title 'Architect of Apartheid'.

In the mid-1950s the Tomlinson Commission – an initiative of the Ministry of Native Affairs – issued a report that would form the basis for the Promotion of Bantu Self Government Act, which created eight ethnic bantustans, later called homelands, and became the foundation for grand apartheid. 'Under the new policy,' wrote Nelson Mandela in *Long Walk to Freedom*, 'even though two thirds of Africans lived in so-called white areas, they could have citizenship only in their own "tribal home-land". The scheme gave us neither freedom in white areas nor independence in what they deemed "our" areas.'

The central premise of the homeland policy was that there was no black majority, but, rather, groups of ethnic minorities of which whites were one. In any case, only the whites were South Africans, as all the black splinter groups belonged in clearly defined areas to be excised from South Africa and eventually given 'independence'. 'These were the areas of South Africa where the Bantu had always lived and which belonged to them,' claimed school textbooks, contradicting all archaeological evidence. Blacks suddenly faced the prospect of becoming 'temporary sojourners' in the land of their birth. 'Where the imperialist regime robbed Africa of Africans,' wrote a bitter journalist, 'the new one is in the process of robbing Africans of Africa.'

Whatever the morality – and the Nationalists claimed divine intervention – the real purpose was to create a chain of 'labour reservoirs' in the most infertile parts of South Africa to which all blacks would belong, depending on their roots. In the economically viable 87 per cent that belonged to whites, blacks were to be foreigners with no rights to live with their families, own property or become citizens. And to ensure that they didn't stay longer in the white areas than their labours warranted, a string of laws and regulations to control their influx was promulgated. Blacks, oppressed for centuries, began to experience the most appalling cruelty as they were brutally hounded in pass raids, beaten or jailed for the simplest and most bizarre reasons, while their families lived in dire poverty in the homelands.

With grand apartheid, its structure founded on the need to keep blacks out of South Africa, came the petty apartheid that ensured they did not mix with whites when they had to be in the country to work. Post office and bank queues were segregated, as was all public transport. Hotels could not rent rooms to blacks, nor could blacks buy liquor in the same bars as whites or in the same stores. Park benches and beaches carried signs specifying who could sit on them and heavy fines were imposed on transgressors.

Here is a selection of some of the insanities of petty apartheid, extracted from the *Cape Times* and *Argus* of the 1950s:

- 'Does he not know that the question is so acute that large sections of the European population, especially European women in the Peninsula,' said Malan in reply to a question in Parliament, 'refuse to travel in the trains or buses any longer simply because frequently Natives and coloured people deliberately seat themselves next to the white women, and next to other Europeans, simply to show that they stand for absolute equality and social equality. This intolerable state of affairs has led to European women resorting to the use of motor cars in the Cape Peninsula that has not only imposed a large additional burden on their shoulders but contributed to the traffic congestion in Cape Town.'
- 'A European child, deeply sunburnt after a month's holiday at Muizenberg, was ordered out of a "Europeans-only" coach by a train conductor this week.'
- 'The police report of the Paarl Liquor Licensing Board issued yesterday emphasises that in all cases glasses for Whites and non-Whites are to be washed separately and kept apart. Separate cloths must also be used for drying the glasses and kept apart.'
- 'At a cost of several thousands of pounds a new subway for railway workers has been built to connect Salt River station with Salt River Railway workshops. It will enable White workers and non-White workers to arrive at the workshops and leave them through different subways. But having arrived through their different subways, White and non-White workers will continue to work side by side inside the workshops.'

The lunacy did not stop there. A township to be called Waay Hoek, on the outskirts of Ladysmith, was proposed for the 23 000 Zulu workers in Johannesburg, some 400 kilometres away. The idea – and the Johannesburg City Council voted revenue toward the scheme – was that these workers would be whisked by high-speed trains to Johannesburg on a Sunday and back on a Friday so they did not darken the city over weekends. 'Conditions may become so attractive in Ladysmith,' enthused one of the planners, 'that many of Johannesburg's Zulus would voluntarily move permanently from Soweto.'

And *Black Beauty* was banned.

Verwoerd was fired by another Afrikaner dream – that of breaking all ties with Britain to become a republic. After consulting the Broederbond, he announced that a referendum would be held on the matter in October 1960. The outcome was no sure thing and he had clearly staked his future on it. To ensure a 'yes' vote, Nationalists hit the streets to intimidate opponents and woo the English with promises of unity and security.

As part of this campaign, Verwoerd attended the Rand Show on 9 April 1960. 'Dr Verwoerd entered the parade ring and inspected some of the champion cattle and congratulated their owners,' reported the *Sunday Express*. 'Then he returned to the president's box. Dr Verwoerd sat down. The would-be assassin walked up to Dr Verwoerd, bent forward and said: "Verwoerd ..." Dr Verwoerd turned his face towards the man. The man had a .25 revolver in his hand and he placed it against the Prime Minister's head. Two shots were fired. Mrs Verwoerd, sitting behind her husband, screamed and jumped to her feet. She lunged towards Dr Verwoerd as the shots were fired. Dr Verwoerd slumped forward, his head between his hands. Blood oozed between his fingers.'

Verwoerd survived the attack by wealthy farmer David Pratt and – helped by increasing numbers of English votes – triumphed in the referendum. Both, he was convinced, were acts of God, or else the Lord would have ensured a different outcome.

'A crowd of more than 40 000 gave Dr Verwoerd the most emotional welcome ever witnessed in Pretoria when he arrived for a "thanksgiving service" at the Voortrekker Monument yesterday afternoon,' reported the *Sunday Express* on 16 October 1960. 'Waving Vierkleurs, they stood to their feet and cheered him with cries of "Die Leier" (the leader) and "Die Republiek" (the Republic) as he marched down the steps to the rostrum to speak.

'Dr Verwoerd said that many people were now writing to him suggesting names for the new republic. Among the suggestions was that it should be called the

"Republic of Good Hope." He was not looking for a new name for the republic he said, but he merely mentioned the point to emphasise how great were expectations for the future. The mood of the crowd was one of triumph and jubilation. Sabre jets wrote "Ons vir Jou" (We for Thee) in smoke trails in the sky. Choirs of schoolchildren sang the national anthem and chanted poems in Afrikaans.

'In his speech Dr Verwoerd said: "The English-speaking and Afrikaans-speaking South Africans have now become like the bride and groom entering life in love to create together and to live together as life's partners." Cynics point out that South Africa has one of the highest divorce rates in the world.'

In another speech to celebrate the referendum victory, he said: 'I have in my hands here a dove, which I now send out into space as a symbol of peace and prosperity, which we wish all peoples on earth. It will be our messenger of goodwill.' At that moment, the Prime Minister threw the bird in the air, but, instead of soaring, it plummeted to earth. Another message from God?

It poured with rain on 31 May 1961, the day South Africa officially became a republic, but crowds still flocked to Church Square to witness the inauguration of the figurehead state president, 'Blackie' Swart. 'Scores of people gathered round the foot of Paul Kruger's statue to watch the inauguration,' reported the *Sunday Express* 'As the State President, Mr Swart, stood on the platform he faced directly the statue of Kruger, the last president of the South African Republic. Officials had asked the crowd not to cheer Mr Swart when he mounted the platform, but to wait until after the 21-gun salute was over. But when Mr Swart walked to the centre of the dais and raised his top-hat in a gesture to the people, the moment was too great for most of the crowd – and, with wild flag-waving, they let out a mighty roar.'

Among the crowds entertained by marching children wearing commemorative medals and carrying banners proclaiming 'Keep the heritage of our fathers' and 'Be faithful, maintain your own' were Boer survivors of the Anglo-Boer South African War. 'When the old Republic ended,' said one, 'so did winter rain. Over the years we came to believe that the next winter rain would fall on the birth of the new Republic. It did rain a bit in winter after the National Party retained power in 1953 and we took it as a good sign. This rain is surely a good omen in our future.'

'Today's inauguration of the new Republic of South Africa is yet another of those curious and vaguely unhappy occasions with which we are familiar,' commented Laurence Gandar in the *Rand Daily Mail*, 'an event which the members of one race group in this country celebrate with great fervour and deep reverence while the members of all other race groups look on awkward and uncomprehending, with little or no sense of participation.'

There had been dire predictions and uncertainty in the lead-up to the events. Natal had threatened not to join the Republic and hordes of professional people applied for passports. Harold Macmillan had warned of a 'wind of change' and economists forecast doom. All were wrong and South Africa entered a decade of sustained growth that was the highest in the world – one that attracted huge international investment. The boom was based on the virtual slave labour conditions of grand apartheid and the increasingly harsh repression of trade unions and dissent that brought the hard-line Minister of Justice, BJ Vorster, increasingly to the fore.

On 6 September 1966 a group of children sat down in the front row of the parliamentary public gallery at 2:15 pm to witness the day's proceedings. An attendant asked them to make room for the Prime Minister's bodyguard. One of the children jokingly remarked: 'What use is the bodyguard up here if something happens down there?'

Below, division bells rang to summon members of the House to their green leather benches as messengers completed their duties before the Speaker's procession entered the chamber. Verwoerd was going through his notes when Dimitrios Tsafendas, a messenger, approached him. 'When he was two or three feet away from Dr Verwoerd, he lifted his hand,' recalled 17-year-old Magda Strydom, who was in the front row of the gallery. 'I saw a dagger flash in the dim light below. As he stabbed him he grabbed hold of Dr Verwoerd's jacket and pulled it back. His hand plunged downwards a couple of times. Dr Verwoerd sagged backwards, his face grew deathly pale. Even now if I close my eyes I can see his face before me.'

The bells were still ringing when Verwoerd died and white South Africans went into mourning – even if they still did not know the man they wept over. 'Verwoerd was the most unknown man in world affairs,' wrote Gary Allighan in one of the most brilliant descriptions of the man in *Verwoerd – The End*. 'For that matter, he was, even to South Africans, their least-known Prime Minister; so little did they know about him that, as a person, he almost had no existence. There was no political leader named Verwoerd; there seemed to be no individual, no human being, of that name. What their Prime Minister really was, as a man – what constituted life for him – what, in brief, "made him tick", was a tightly-closed book, as if he had resigned from the human race. When an individual becomes a public figure, he becomes public property, but to that generally-accepted rule the first Prime Minister of the Republic of South Africa was a conspicuous exception.'

Today it is fashionable to refer to Verwoerd as mad. Yet, white South Africans loved and admired him – even most English-speakers. And if he was mad, then surely they must have been too?

'Yesterday, in Heroes' Acre in the Old Pretoria Cemetery,' commented the supposedly liberal *Sunday Express*, 'a man was buried who has indelibly left his mark on the pages of this country's history.

'A leader.

'A statesman.

'A man of vision

'Controversial, as all politicians and world figures are.

'Dedicated, as only a few who have a sense of destiny are.

'Mourned, as only a man of stature can be.

'In life, few people knew him well.

'In death, all grieve his passing.

'Thus did Hendrik Frensch Verwoerd leave his country's scene, his towering physical and intellectual presence removed by the hand of an assassin, his achievements, his devotion to ideals and his love of country a source of inspiration to those who remain and who are to follow. Indeed, at the very time that his policy was broadening into a grand design for the subcontinent, a black and white checkerboard in which independent States could live in peace and fulfilment, he was lost to South Africa, the subcontinent, and the great land mass of which they form part.

'It is left to his successor to pursue this policy, if he so wishes, with its promise for the future. But it will be no easy task, since Dr Verwoerd showed a vision and sense of history that was peculiarly his own. Thus passes a great South African, the granite man of Africa, the astute politician, the brilliant statesman, the wise Prime Minister. He was one of the ablest White leaders that Africa has ever produced. He rests today in Heroes' Acre and a nation mourns.'

The *Sunday Express* was not out of step; in fact, this drivel was some of the least sycophantic from the English press. What it does show, however, is how far the National Party had been successful in transforming the idea of Afrikaner exclusivity into a unifying issue involving all white South Africans. The assassination of Verwoerd also highlighted another subtle change that had been taking place in white politics. The ascension of Verwoerd had brought the somewhat doe-eyed innocence of thinkers like Malan to an end – and with the elevation of Vorster to Prime

Minister, at the tender age of 51 ended whatever morality might have underpinned Afrikaner nationalism.

While analysts suspected that Verwoerd's 'spiritual home was nearer Berchtesgarten', there was no doubt that the hard-drinking, bushy-eyebrowed John Vorster was a Nazi. He grew up near Stellenbosch and studied psychology under Verwoerd and law under Donges. And, like Verwoerd, his heart was not in the more 'moderate' Cape, but in the Transvaal. During World War II, as a general in the radical Ossewabrandwag, he was interned at Koffiefontein – a restriction he considered a deep injustice.

Improbable as it may appear, after the war the National Party had found him too extreme and refused him membership. In the 1948 general election he was forced to stand as an independent in Brakpan and nearly caused an upset by falling short by two votes. By the 1953 general election he had settled his differences with the National Party and entered Parliament as the member for Nigel. He was grim and dour – when a press photographer once pleaded with him to smile, he shot back: 'I am smiling' – but blessed with a biting, nimble tongue and a talent for fierce debate that fast brought him to the attention of the party leaders and eventually the Justice portfolio in 1961. From this position he began to build the security apparatus that would rapidly transform South Africa into a notoriously repressive police state.

'I realised that if the security forces had to play according to the rules it would be like fighting an implacable and vicious enemy with one hand tied behind their backs,' he commented. 'I was not going to send my men into battle with one hand tied behind their backs. I saw very clearly right from the outset because my own experiences during the war had given me clear insight into the whole thing from both sides – from the inside and from the outside.'

He was applauded for his success in crushing the African National Congress and Pan Africanist Congress underground movements in the early 1960s. Dissenters, trade unionists and student leaders were terrorised or rounded up and incarcerated and tortured for increasingly lengthy periods without trial. On more than one occasion, reports surfaced of Vorster visiting detainees late at night with his drinking buddies. However, the National Party was, and remained, extremely sensitive to criticism of its methods and, rather than change them, clamped down on the press and branded all but the most timid opposition as communist.

In 1962 the *Sunday Times* named Vorster their 'strong man of the year' and credited him, in a single year, with placing 18 South Africans under house arrest, banning

103, listing 437 as communist, outlawing the Congress of Democrats and closing the *New Age* newspaper. During his time as Minister of Justice, General Hendrik van den Bergh, an old Ossewabrandwag crony, became his closest advisor. After becoming Prime Minister, Vorster created the Bureau of State Security (BOSS), under Van den Bergh, to co-ordinate the activities of the security police and intelligence departments of the military, and this effectively became his power base.

Vorster, however, was not as extreme an Afrikaner as Verwoerd, and he was able to lure the growing numbers of English-speakers who were increasingly alarmed at what was happening in the rest of the continent as the colonial powers scrambled out of Africa. They liked his tough persona and the fact that the economy continued to boom after he became Prime Minister. He was getting things done. The Xhosa of the Transkei, with the Tswana of Bophuthatswana to follow, were soon to be hived off and given 'independence' as the homelands scheme began to reach a climax that would strip citizenship from millions of blacks and leave those who did not apply for citizenship of these regions stateless.

Further afield, the Department of Information was achieving success with the policy of 'détente' – which sought to counter the 'hate South Africa' crusade by seeking out African governments willing to co-operate with Pretoria. President Kenneth Kaunda of Zambia was moved to remark that Vorster had become 'the voice of reason for which Africa had been waiting'. Though these relationships within Africa were largely forged through bribery, they did instil fear within the exiled ANC that it would be excluded from operating in many African states south of the Sahara.

But it was the calm before the storm. The economy began to collapse in the early 1970s and it entered a prolonged recession in the wake of growing inflation and the culmination of many of the deferred costs of grand apartheid. Blacks, appallingly oppressed and crushed in the 1960s, were beginning to stir to the message of Black Consciousness (BC), and the growing number of recently decolonised African states represented in the United Nations began a clarion call to isolate South Africa – beginning with South Africa's suspension from that body in 1974 and a bar on sporting contact.

A combination of two factors, one influencing the other, elevated the problems to a crisis. Behind the scenes there was an internecine succession struggle in the Cabinet between Connie Mulder, under whom the Department of Information fell, and Minister of Defence PW Botha – and Mulder was undoubtedly the crown prince. Secondly, white South Africa had largely been buffered from black Africa by the

Portuguese colonies of Angola and Mozambique and the illegal Rhodesian regime of Ian Smith. A coup in Portugal in 1974, however, led to the decidedly hostile Samora Machel, leader of the FRELIMO liberation movement, taking power in Mozambique, while in Angola competing groups struggled for ascendancy. Botha, in a disastrous move in August 1975, clandestinely committed the South African army to support the UNITA movement of Jonas Savimbi. South Africa had been promised assistance by the Central Intelligence Agency of the United States of America, but this was not forthcoming: the country faced the superior Soviet weaponry and Cuban forces that supported the MPLA faction alone and was forced into a humiliating withdrawal.

The upshot was that all South Africa's traditional defences altered and she suddenly faced serious security threats over a wide front. 'Police are holding 15 FRELIMO soldiers in Nelspruit after two border incidents,' reported *The World* on 24 March 1976. 'In one clash, yesterday afternoon, shots were exchanged over the border. Eight of the FRELIMO troops were seized on Sunday when they pursued a group of fleeing white Mozambicans across the Border into the Kruger National Park. Seven more were captured at the same spot – south of the Olifants River – yesterday afternoon. Three of the group, who managed to get back into Mozambique, shot at South African Police, who fired back.'

In April, guerrillas 100 kilometres north of the border post at Beit Bridge shot three young white South African holidaymakers in Rhodesia. Vorster, together with American Secretary of State Dr Henry Kissinger, dealt with the crisis in his usually enigmatic way by attempting to pressure Smith into compromising. 'South Africa will continue its efforts to bring the parties together again around the conference table,' he said. 'The alternative is too ghastly to contemplate.' He also attempted to get the détente programme, in ruins after the incursion into Angola, back on track.

'There are hints at the United Nations that South Africa has embarked on a new diplomatic offensive in Africa to bolster détente in the aftermath of the war in Angola,' reported *The World*. 'According to African diplomats, visits to African countries by the Prime Minister, Mr Vorster, and other government leaders, are part of the latest moves. They also say that Mr Vorster is anxious to re-establish his bona fides with African leaders such as President Leopold Senghor of Senegal and President William Tolbert of Liberia who have recently expressed misgivings about détente.'

Vorster attempted to soften aspects of petty apartheid by removing regulations regarding park benches. But each action had to be countered with a step back to pacify an extremely edgy and powerful right wing in the National Party. Dr Andries

Treurnicht, a disciple of grand apartheid and leader of the conservatives, was pro-moted to Deputy Minister of Bantu Education and Training – a position that gave him power over the destiny of millions of blacks. In other moves, the government announced plans to outlaw sex and marriage between blacks and coloureds, banned leggy black American singer Brenda Arnau from touring South Africa, arrested a white barmaid for serving a black journalist in a 'Whites-only' pub and removed a Soweto actress, Cecilia Motsie, from the *Dingleys* TV show because she shared a table with white cast members in the white canteen of the South African Broadcasting Corporation.

The mood in Pretoria, however bleak, was lifted by the arrival of Andy Leslie's 1976 All Black rugby team, and the hottest debate in town – not dissimilar to the one behind the scenes in National Party circles – was who should lead the Springboks. Some said it should be Western Province's Morné du Plessis, others argued for Northern Transvaal's Thys Louwrens. The one thing they all agreed on was that the All Blacks were an ugly bunch. 'The All Blacks have already earned an unenviable tag,' commented Ray Woodley in the *Sunday Express*. 'They are the ugliest sporting team to visit South Africa. There were gasps of "yugh!" instead of "oohs" and "aahs" when the pictures were printed. This was the immediate reaction of some women readers when they studied individual pictures in last week's *Sunday Express*. I must admit that a handful of tourists looked particularly villainous. The sort of blokes I would hate to face in a loose ruck or scrum.'

For the moralistic, Calvinist-inspired chosen race, there was something better to feast the eyes on a few hours away in neighbouring Lesotho. 'Doors Smit had his first taste of heaven on Friday night,' reported Clare Stern in the *Sunday Express*. 'He found out that the Garden of Eden was not strewn with koeksusters and konfyt, but baubles, bottoms and boobs. It was all too much for poor Doors. He had never seen a strip show, let alone had so many women fanning his perspiring pate with frillies and feathers. The audience of Strip Spectacular 1976 in Maseru's Holiday Inn theatre rolled in their seats, while Doors blushed bright as a beetroot. Stripper Danielle smothered him in kisses and tried to entice him to join her act. Doors managed to keep his shirt on. But he lost his head when she whipped his specs off his quivering nose. After dropping her black bra and corset at his feet, she invited him to undo her G-string. Unable to see what he was doing, he grappled for five minutes. "Jislaaik," he gasped as it snapped in his sweaty palms.

'The crowd that paid R15 a head to see the show went wild when Miss Swaziland

1976, Tzatza Vinah, and Busty Beebe did a dual Zulu dance and stripped out of their bear skins into their bare skins. Those *oomies* [uncles] were tickled pink by the multi-racial contest, but one of the entrants withdrew in protest against a decision to include Blacks.'

'I come from the newly discovered goldfields at Kliprivier, especially from a farm owned by a certain Gert Oosthuizen,' declared George Harrison on 24 July 1886 in an affidavit to the Pretoria Mines Department. 'I have a long experience as an Australian gold digger, and I think it is a payable goldfield.'

The featureless highveld grassland expanse, dotted with a few thorn trees near the Bezuidenhout homestead and a cluster of bluegums on the bank of a small lake on the farm *Braamfontein*, was broken by the ridges of the Witwatersrand, which form the watershed between the Indian Ocean in the east and the Atlantic in the west. Below this fairly ordinary surface, however, lay reefs of ore containing massive reserves of gold. Their discovery heralded a rush of English, German, American, French, Australian, Portuguese, South American, Turkish and Jewish fortune-seekers, who swamped the local Boer population. And with them came blacks and coloureds in search of work as well as the normal cast of characters – hoteliers, barmaids, shopkeepers, gamblers and enough prostitutes to service every need of a predominantly male community.

Within months the landscape was strewn with wagons and tents organised in camps along streams and interconnected by a wagon trail that would later become Commissioner Street. 'And what are we going to call this new dorp?' asked President Paul Kruger of Johan Rissik, acting surveyor-general of the Transvaal, and his colleague Christiaan Johannes Joubert.

'I believe it is possible to see Johannesburg as it really is only when we view it as a place of mystery and romance, as a city wrapped in mist,' wrote pre-eminent South African storyteller Herman Charles Bosman in *Johannesburg* in the 1940s. 'Is there any other city that is less than sixty years old – and the origin of its name already lost in the shadows of time?

'People who were present at the Christening of Johannesburg say that the town was named after the second baptismal name of President Kruger. Others with equal authority say it was called Johannesburg after Johan Rissik. Other candidates – and in each case their names are put forward on most excellent authority – include Christiaan Johannes Joubert, Veldcornet Johannes Meyer, Johannes Lindeque and Willem Gerhardus Christoffel Pelser (the latter, possibly, because his seemed to be the only set of names that didn't have Johannes in it).

'There are at least another dozen claimants. And you need have no hesitation in supporting any one of them. The evidence in each case is indisputable.'

The mining camps soon began to take on a more permanent air as reed and clay huts, galvanised iron shacks and buildings – including clubs and a stock exchange – sprang up. In the middle of the main camp, and a block north of the wagon trail, was the busy, unpaved Market Square, filled with dust, open wells and the stench of animal droppings. This square, lit only by the lamps advertising pubs and various other entertainments, was a haven for muggers at night.

'You can still come across lots of people who can tell you about the spirit that prevailed here in the early days when Johannesburg was a roaring, wide open mining camp, in which every citizen was imbued with the one laudable desire of making all the money he could in the shortest possible time,' continued Bosman. 'It was an all-in scramble with no holds barred. The place teemed with short cuts to a gaudy opulence. Adventurers from all parts of the world heard that there was money going in Johannesburg, and they flocked here to get some. And through some of the quaint whimsicalities of the Roman-Dutch law, which was the basis of legislation in the Transvaal Republic, some ways of making money were regarded as less legitimate than others.

'Thus when members of a spirited fraternity, hailing in the main from Australia, alighted at Park Station and started getting busy with their luggage, their activities gave rise to a good deal of unfriendly comment. For the sole luggage that these gentlemen had brought with them were home-constructed sandbags which they wielded on the populace, left and right, with a singular effectiveness.

'The members of this fraternity, perhaps not unjustly, resented the discouraging attitude which officialdom adopted towards their industry as an unfair discrimination, based on the fact that they were newly arrived immigrants who still had to ask passers-by the way to the Stock Exchange or Rand Club, when they wanted to go and look for customers. The point of view of the authorities seemed to be, "you can see for yourself that we impose no restrictions. You can do anything you like to a man in order to take his money off him. Only you must not hit him with your luggage."

'Even today this seems an unreasonable sort of distinction to make. Not allowing a man from foreign shores to contribute his luggage to the building up of a new nation and a new culture.'

Johannesburg, in the first few years, was regarded as an eldorado – a temporary mining camp where you got rich quickly before the gold petered out as it had done everywhere else. As mining required large amounts of development capital, the shares of some 450 gold-mining companies were furiously promoted by stockbrokers – called, by the Cape politician John X Merriman, 'bummers seeking to sell you "the best claims on the Main Reef"'. Most of these hucksters plied their trade in Simmons Street, between Commissioner and Market Streets – an area closed to traffic by means of chains slung between metal posts that became known as 'Between the Chains'. They were renowned gamblers, the favoured wager being 'tempting the fly', where a lump of sugar was placed on a gold sovereign and the owner of the coin on which the first fly landed scooped the pool.

In 1889, as anticipated, it was found that the character of the ore at a depth of about 100 metres changed and traditional forms of gold recovery were no longer effective. This was all the news needed: the gamblers dumped their claims and deserted the workings in droves, causing shares to drop by an average of 75 per cent. This crisis caused the collapse of the Union Bank in Cape Town, which had advanced too much against the security of 'sound' mining shares, and resulted in the ruin of many families. But, thanks mainly to the effectiveness of the MacArthur Forest process of cyanide extraction and advances in technology to permit deep-level mining, Johannesburg was able to bounce back. This required even more financing, and the pioneers of yore were quickly replaced by engineers and other professionals, giving the fledgling city a more settled character. Even so, it was unable to shake its frenetic here-today-gone-tomorrow image.

No city on earth grew faster: within six years it was the largest in southern Africa, with a population of over 30 000 that mushroomed to 100 000 in a decade. As fast as buildings went up, so they were torn down to build even better and higher ones. 'I wander down Commissioner Street,' said WC Scully, 'past the Corner House, the Standard Bank, the Stock Exchange, and many other exaggerated human ant-hills throbbing with energy. It is all a gloomy inferno of stone – a series of linked Babylon-towers of masonry heaped menacingly against the almost obliterated heavens.' And its vertical development was matched only by its sprawl, which would eventually encompass an area of 500 square kilometres.

'Johannesburg is a colonial city,' commented author John Buchan, 'full of the exaggerated independence of the self-made. The fastidiousness that comes from culture and tradition, the humour that springs from unshakeable confidence must necessarily be absent in a municipality which is still diffident, still largely uneducated.'

The wealthy – a mix of some old money and many nouveaux riches – built gabled, palatial homes on the ridges to the north of the town. Among these mansions was Hohenheim on Parktown Ridge, which belonged to Percy Fitzpatrick. To the west of this property lived the Dale Laces, who ignored the Fitzpatricks until Percy was knighted. Cecily, Fitzpatrick's daughter, remembered the Dale Laces calling soon after in a horse-drawn cab pulled by two black horses and followed by their aristocratic Afghan hounds: 'I watched from my bedroom window as the horses swept through our gates. Now my father had about 27 dogs of difficult-to-define breeds. Many were from the bushveld. As soon as they saw the Afghans, who they must have mistaken for buck, they gave chase. It was a day or so before they were all rounded up.'

As for the rest, the upper-middle-class, predominantly English-speaking residents settled in the near east, west and northern suburbs, close to their places of work, where they constructed Victorian cottages of burnt clay bricks, suspended wooden-strip floors and pressed iron ceilings. The predominantly Afrikaans lower-middle class occupied Brickfields and Braamfontein, where they lived in mainly semi-detached accommodation. Black migrant labourers were enclosed in single-sex hostels and compounds attached to mines and factories. And the hordes of poor, black and white, were left to fend for themselves in locations or slums just north of Fordsburg, noted for poor living conditions. Some loved it, others hated it.

'For the first time in South Africa I saw life,' enthused Lady Sarah Wilson. 'Cape Town, with its pathetic dullness and palpable efforts to keep up a show of business; Kimberley with its deadly respectability – both paled in interest beside their younger sister, so light-hearted, reckless, and enterprising. Before long, in spite of gloomy reflections on the evils of gold-seeking, I fell under the fascination of what was a wonderful town, especially wonderful from its youth. The ever-moving crowds that thronged the streets, every man of which appeared to be full of important business and in a desperate hurry, reminded one of the City of London. Smart carriages with well-dressed ladies drove rapidly past shops cunningly arranged with tempting wares.'

'Hideous and detestable,' commented journalist Flora Shaw after visiting Johannesburg, 'luxury without order; sensual enjoyment without art; richness without refinement; display without dignity.' Olive Schreiner, the writer, needed only one word to describe it: 'Hell!'

Within six months of the discovery of gold there were three newspapers servicing the mining camp – the *Standard and Diggers' News*, *Witwatersrand Advertiser* and *Transvaal Mining Argus*. Others came and went – including *Nugget*, *Burlesque*, *Tatler* and *Judge*, which was edited from Douglas Blackburn's bedroom in the Grand National Hotel – but only the *Eastern Star*, which was to become *The Star*, survived.

In the early years there was much to report on. Insurrection was in the air and dissatisfaction with Kruger's government culminated in a plot by Johannesburg mining personalities to overthrow him. Weapons were smuggled into the city in oil drums by Rhodes's De Beers and stashed at the Standard Bank while Leander Starr Jameson prepared to ride from Pitsani near Mafeking to assist the plotters. The Jameson Raid was high farce, but the fallout was so intense that war became inevitable, leaving many newspapers with the dilemma of which side to support. Those that championed the Boers found favour until the occupation of Johannesburg in May 1900 by the British, who shut them down. Among the casualties was the *Standard and Diggers' News*, owned by Emmanuel Mendelssohn.

One afternoon in June 1902, Mendelssohn was having a drink with friends at Heath's Bar and bemoaning the fact that he was still burdened with the printing press. Freeman Cohen, one of the group, offered to purchase it and immediately accepted the price suggested by Mendelssohn.

'What do you intend to do with it?' asked Mendelssohn.

'Now that I've got it,' replied Cohen, 'I'll start my own newspaper.'

'How can you start a paper without an editor?' enquired Mendelssohn.

'Oh, I hadn't thought of that.'

'I think I can help you,' suggested Mendelssohn as he spotted a young man entering the bar. After a brief discussion with the man he returned with him to the table and introduced him to Cohen. 'Here's your editor. His name is Edgar Wallace.'

'Excellent,' said Cohen.

And so was founded the *Rand Daily Mail*. This was followed by the *Sunday Times* in 1906 and the *Sunday Express* in the 1930s. Though regarded as liberal, all these major newspapers were owned either by the Randlords or the mining houses and danced to their tune. It would remain that way, too.

While Johannesburg's population remained a colourful mix of blacks, British colonials, Afrikaners, Europeans and Asians, its life was dominated by businesses whose mindset was largely that of imperial Britain. Thus, the power behind Johannesburg was held by people convinced of the natural superiority and intellectual distinction of their kind. At the other end of the scale of human development were 'childlike' blacks. It was the 'white man's burden' to care for these 'perpetual juveniles'. But this 'noble' calling was corrupted by the demands of commerce – one of the pillars of imperialism – and the exploitation of blacks was elevated to an art form. The English-speakers, however, were convinced of their calling, and Johannesburg became the home of a quaint form of liberalism that was human, tolerant and just – as long as it did not interfere with the whims of capital and big business when they conspired in and funded the subjugation and disenfranchisement of blacks in their pursuit of maximum profits.

'In so far as the future of the British in South Africa is linked with the exploitation of the mines,' commented JA Hobson, 'there is, unfortunately, at present little reason to believe that the kind of man who will control the industry, and the profitable ends he has in view, will in any way contribute to the elevation of the native races which he professes to have at heart.'

While profoundly contemptuous of crude Afrikaners and their nationalism, the English-speakers of Johannesburg were in fact the flip side of the coin. 'In a crisis you only have to scratch the Afrikaner to find a Boer,' wrote Adamastor in *White Man Boss*. 'If you scratch an English-speaking South African on any race issue involving colour you will make the same discovery.' Dr EG Jansen, some years later, added: 'It has always suited the English to make use of Afrikaans-speaking leaders to carry out their imperialistic colour policy.'

'Like many white South Africans,' wrote Diana Russell in *Lives of Courage: Women for a New South Africa*, 'we were raised with and by servants who were black indigenous South Africans. This institutionalised form of racism was, I believe, my major instructor in racial prejudice.

'When the power structure is as firmly in place as it was in my family, statements like "Don't let me catch you playing with a kaffir" didn't need to be made. A system of apartheid reigned in my world before the term was coined, and before the laws were passed to keep it that way.'

Blacks, like white fortune-seekers, were originally attracted to Johannesburg by short-term financial gain. Here the similarity ended. The whites naturally assumed they were masters and blacks the servants – a convenient belief when it is considered that cheap labour, possessing no rights and forced to work long hours to extract low-grade ore deep below the surface, was essential to profitability. Blacks were not free to move about either: after working all day in oppressively dangerous, dirty, dusty and noisy conditions they were herded into single-sex compounds that contained hundreds of concrete bunks separated from each other by only a few inches.

From the very first it was taken for granted that these men would be migrant labourers who worked for a short period before returning home.

But not all employers were able to house their workers on the premises, and many moved into servants' quarters in the backyards of white areas, specially laid-out locations close to the centre of town such as that at Klipspruit, adjacent to the sewerage works, and the rat-infested inner city slums that teemed with the poor. These slums were not only home to blacks, but to whites – particularly Boers forced from their lands who now faced the prospect of competing for jobs with blacks who were often more skilled and prepared to work longer hours for less pay. Strikes in protest against the use of cheap labour erupted in 1904, 1907, 1911 and 1913–1914. These culminated in the Rand Revolt of 1922.

In December 1921, gold miners were informed that 2 000 semi-skilled jobs held by whites were to be taken over by blacks. In January 1922 the workers of the South African Industrial Federation declared a strike, and commandos were formed to thwart police action and break 'scab labour'. Police captain Jock Fulford, faced by a mob of strikers, ordered his men to kneel and fire one round each. Three strikers died, but Fulford was exonerated – a decision that outraged the strikers. A general strike was called.

The situation soon turned ugly. An observer, who watched a women's worker commando dragging out the occupants of a telephone exchange, wrote: 'A little hello-girl first knew of something having gone amiss by a frowsy amazon biting her arm. She retaliated by hitting her over the head with a receiver.' Elsewhere, William Urquart witnessed rebels surging into various mine buildings: 'Shouting and yelling, slogging with the butts of their rifles, wielding clubs and whirling lengths of chain, the Reds fell on the men at the mine with the utmost ferocity and barbarity.' By 10 March the situation was so out of control that martial law was declared and Sir Pierre van Ryneveld had Benoni bombed by the fledgling South African Air Force.

Nearly 700 were killed or injured in the uprising and the anger of workers led directly to Smuts being swept from office to be replaced by General Hertzog's National Party, which settled the issue by introducing a formal 'colour bar' in mining and industry to protect white workers. From now on, the development of black skills was to be subordinated to the needs of white labour. This was quickly followed by regulations forcing municipalities to apply residential segregation. While no money was made available to achieve this, Johannesburg appointed a 'Director of Native Affairs' in 1927, and in 1931 unveiled a competition to design South Africa's first 'native township' to which blacks could be removed. The winning submission, which included a vast expanse of uniform matchbox houses without community services, formed the plans for Orlando – the core around which Soweto was to develop.

After the Great Depression the city experienced a fervour of building activity. Old structures were once more razed to make way for art deco ziggurat skyscrapers that had many referring to Johannesburg as the 'Wonder of Empire'. 'With its skyscrapers, Johannesburg is today no mean city,' wrote Bosman in *Johannesburg*. 'These tall edifices of concrete and steel would look highly imposing anywhere, leave alone just being dumped down in the middle of the veld. But we still bear one or two traces of our mining-camp origin. For instance, there is the public library.'

But as South Africans – English, Afrikaans and black – went off to fight in World War II, so a corresponding shortage of skilled and semi-skilled labour occurred that created opportunities for blacks. And the South African economy boomed because its raw materials and cheap labour were ideal for mass-production industries feeding the war machine – which, in turn, created greater labour shortages. Restrictions were temporarily relaxed, and blacks streamed to Johannesburg to take advantage of the situation.

These workers, however, were also ripe for exploitation, and they became increasingly dissatisfied and strident:

> Growl more softly, you machines;
> Because the white men are as stone,
> Can you, of iron, not be gentler?
> Hush your roaring in the mines
> And hear what we would say to you
> Or else we may not care for you
> When that far day, now hidden, dawns,
> And we, at last, will cry: 'Machines!
> You are ours, the black men's, Now!'
> – B Wallet Vilakazi: 'In the Gold Mines' (1945)

And as more skilled and semi-skilled blacks entered the shop floor, so the predominantly white Afrikaans worker felt increasingly threatened, and the white farmer more dissatisfied as his labour pool shrank. Added to this was the confusion caused by returning black soldiers who believed they had earned the right to share in the new democratic world they had fought for, and by white troops filled with more enlightened ideas.

'We started what we called a Union of Soldiers,' wrote Fred Carneson. 'Then we heard about the Springbok Legion that had started almost simultaneously, from servicemen who for one reason or another found themselves back in South Africa, and from then onwards we were busy recruiting for the Springbok Legion. It became the vehicle in the South African Army for a lot of progressive thinking, on the race issue as well, amongst white South African soldiers.

'It's funny, you seldom heard anti-black sentiment amongst the white soldiers. If you're in the army and a man's on your side, you respect him, you see. They saw people of different races fighting together on the same side against a common enemy. This couldn't but have had an effect on their general thinking. How long it lasted after the war, I don't know, but I'm sure a hell of a lot of it stuck.'

Not actually. Soldiers returned to unemployment, housing shortages, food rationing, high prices and an increasingly militant black workforce. It was a time of intense contradiction, and the Smuts government dithered between continued persecution and reform. The message from the opposition National Party was clear: keep the black in his place to protect the white way of life.

As the Nationalists moved to crush black defiance, so they waged a war on the more radical elements of English liberalism. The Liberal Party folded in the face of the onslaught, as did the short-lived white African Resistance Movement (ARM), which was crushed after a bomb exploded at the main Johannesburg railway station on 24 July 1964. 'I stood in a hospital ward in Johannesburg yesterday and marvelled at the courage of the victims of the petrol-bomb explosion at the city's railway station concourse,' wrote a reporter in the *Sunday Express*. 'Danie Gerber, 17, peered through slits in the bandages that covered his face, held up two bandaged hands, and said: "I don't mind the bandages so much, but I wish they'd let me smoke a cigarette." Then he added: "They certainly have some pretty nurses in this hospital."

'All he remembers of the explosion is a tremendous crash and a blinding sheet of flame. "The next thing, my clothes were on fire," he told me. "Without knowing what I was doing, I began to run, trying to remove my jacket at the same time. I was held fast by a railway policeman, who beat out the flames."

'Next to him in the ward, offering him sympathy, was his brother-in-law, Pieter Koekemoer, his hands swathed in bandages, his face carrying the yellow marks of burns and blisters. "When the explosion took place, I remember running a few paces forward automatically," he said. "Then I turned and saw my three-year-old daughter, Cornelia, lying on the ground, her body covered in flames. I ran to her and beat out the flames with my hands." Cornelia is in the Johannesburg Children's Hospital, seriously ill.'

John Harris, a former chairman of the South African Non-Racial Olympic Committee and a member of ARM, was arrested seven hours after the blast. He was sentenced to death and the rest of the movement were either arrested or forced to flee into exile. This left only the National Union of South African Students (NUSAS) and the University Christian Movement to carry the liberal flame. For the rest, the white English-speaking residents of Johannesburg left politics to the Nationalists and retreated to the laager of money-making, funding the distasteful things it was essential for the politicians to do.

One thing was certain in a city built on the sweat of black men – and that was that blacks were incapable of governing themselves, let alone the country. Harry Oppenheimer, the mining magnate and doyen of Johannesburg liberals, while calling for the softening of labour laws – not their complete overhaul – stated that giving power to blacks would ferment chaos in southern Africa. 'In a major preview of the country's future,' reported the *Sunday Express*, 'made before the London Stock Exchange this week, the chairman of the Anglo American Corporation, Mr Harry Oppenheimer, says there is today a sharpened understanding that our present situation is dangerous and unjust. There is, he believes, a "new determination to put things right". But, with most whites apparently ready to accept change, the real problem is that they see majority rule in terms of a one-party state headed by an authoritarian left-wing government determined to destroy the free enterprise system. And he adds that the real anxiety felt by white South Africans is that the removal of discrimination against blacks might in present circumstances involve the destruction of the free enterprise system and of normal parliamentary government.' On another occasion Oppenheimer said: 'Black nationalism and majority rule is a major danger to the security and prosperity of the country. I advocate a system which denies uncivilised blacks the vote.' Nothing, therefore, seemed capable of removing entrenched attitudes of white superiority – and it was doubly difficult because it was profitable too.

During the 1960s the South African economy boomed – driven by the Johannesburg engine room. As the economy became more sophisticated it required less unskilled labour and more semi-skilled workers, which resulted in growing demands for the relaxation of apartheid laws that restricted the mobility, employment and training of blacks. This flourish, however, was built on the shaky foundations of heavy government subsidies, the inflow of foreign capital and cheap migrant labour in an economy targeted at the small white market. More skilled workers demanded more pay, and industry became less competitive. Add to this the world's growing rejection of apartheid and the subsequent closing of the doors to nearly everything South African other than raw materials, and it was not difficult to predict impending economic collapse.

The boom, however, had a completely unpredictable consequence. It naturally provided more and better work for blacks, and their growing affluence allowed them to get a better education for their children, with a resultant increase in blacks attending universities. These students, without their own political structures, initially gravitated to the white liberal student movements. It was not long before they saw through the patronising façade.

'The black–white circles are almost always a creation of white liberals,' wrote Steve Biko, the founder of the Black Consciousness Movement (BCM) and initially a member of NUSAS. 'As a testimony to their claims of complete identification with the blacks, they call a few "intelligent and articulate" blacks to "come around for tea at home", where all present ask each other the same old hackneyed question "How can we bring about change in South Africa?" The more such tea parties one calls the more of a liberal he is and the freer he shall feel from the guilt that harnesses and binds his conscience. Hence he moves around his white circles, whites-only hotels, beaches, restaurants and cinemas with a lighter load, feeling that he is not like the rest of the others. Yet at the back of his mind is a constant reminder that he is quite comfortable as things stand and therefore should not bother about change.'

'One expects black power to sneer at white liberals,' retorted author Alan Paton in *On Turning 70*. 'After all white power has done it for generations. But if black power meets white power in headlong confrontation, and there are no black liberals and white liberals around, then God help South Africa.' What Paton did not see, or refused to acknowledge, was that the extremists of right and left alike objected to any group in the middle that might dilute the rabid perception of their opposition. It was precisely the point: liberals had to go.

The seeds were sown, but in the meantime it was business as usual. The massive investments that flowed into Johannesburg in the 1960s were pumped into building a 'City of Towers' – or, rather, a Gotham interconnected by tunnel-like arterial roads.

In 1972 the Carlton Centre was opened and in the same year major parts of a free-way connecting suburban peripheries to the city were commissioned. But whites had grown weary of the increasing numbers of blacks in the city centre and retreated to the suburbs for everything other than employment.

As a result, Hyde Park Corner Shopping Centre opened in 1969, to be followed by the Rosebank Mall in 1976. Lifestyles also changed: rather than 'go into town' for entertainment, the residents of Johannesburg found recreation at places such as the Zoo Lake and the botanical gardens. While news abounded of growing black activism and trouble in neighbouring countries, their most serious concerns revolved around the recession and the effects it was having on their quality of life.

Black wages continued to increase, and domestic servants began to demand a minimum wage of R60 per month. 'The day I have to pay R60, I'll do without help,' fumed a housewife. The question loomed of who would do the work of these high-ly exploited people. 'How much is your wife worth in cash?' asked the *Sunday Express*. The answer was R780 per month – with a rider that caused some difficulty: 'Bedtime comforts are a debatable point. In a marriage these would presumably not be charged for, on the assumption that partners give as much as they take. But if the wife was to be replaced in this role, one member of our panel estimates it would cost a man R300 a month to get all-night, professional bedtime services.' The maid stayed, but if she dared demand a minimum wage she was summarily dismissed without benefits and immediately replaced by someone prepared to accept a lower wage.

It was a depressing time. And because the English-speakers of Johannesburg were morally superior to their Afrikaner country cousins, they could hardly enliven the moment with a trip to Maseru to take in a strip show. Or were they better? The antics of former Miss World Anneline Kriel, photographed skinny-dipping with Ray MacCauley by former Mr World Roy Hilligenn at his Vaal Dam retreat, caused a sen-sation. And society was aflutter at the news that Jack 'The Priest' Bouillon, South Africa's most notorious brothel keeper, had written a book in prison and was threat-ening to reveal all. It was all more exciting than the 'horrible mediocrity' dished up by the recently launched television channel, as the *Sunday Express* reported: 'Speaking to John Bishop on the programme, "Galaxy", Trevor Philpot – one of the world's top documentary producers – explained that good television production did not depend on its tools for success. "Even with marvellous tools a man can make lousy furniture." And he added that the South African Broadcasting Corporation did have marvellous tools.'

3 ■ SHANTY TOWN

From the hearts of starving children
To the malnutrition bound
From the banned on Robben Island
To the chained in Africa
We will always stand united
To the call of our FREEDOM
We will fight for our dignity
We will stand up for our rights.

We will never be subservient
To the things that hold us down
We will fight for all BLACK people
Africa; our dear land.

– ANON: 'THE ROOTS'

'The history of South Africa cannot be understood outside the history of Soweto,' wrote African National Congress stalwart Walter Sisulu in his foreword to *Soweto: A History*. 'The development of the township, and the trials and tribulation of its people are a microcosm of the history of this country. Industrialisation, apartheid policies and the struggle of South African people all find expression in that place called Soweto.'

Matters for blacks in southern Africa had been complicated by the overwhelming changes wrought in the last three decades of the nineteenth century by the discovery of diamonds and gold. Prior to 1870 most South African blacks lived in independent chiefdoms; by 1899 none did. And as blacks were absorbed by either the British or the Boers, they lost their freedom, their lands and their ability to support themselves independently. The only options, for most blacks, as they were deprived of their domains, were to starve or offer their labour cheaply either to white farmers or to white mine owners. Add to this the fact that whites believed they were natural masters and that blacks were born labourers, and it is not difficult to discern the yoke of impending slavery.

Even if the options – working for white farmers or white city businesses – were highly unattractive, the opportunities offered in the cities, and by the mines in particular, were preferable. A male farm worker was expected to provide the white farmer with six months' free labour – in which time he toiled seven days a week and 14 hours a day – as well as the services of his wife and children, for the right to work a patch of land he could not call his own and which was insufficient to provide for his family's most basic needs. And his bondage was made worse by strict, often violent discipline. Cities, on the other hand, proffered cash wages that could be repatriated to rural communities and an escape from the drudgery of farm life.

But those blacks drawn by the riches of Johannesburg faced an entirely different set of prospects than white fortune-seekers. Most were prohibited from bringing their families with them and were obliged to enter into short-term contracts, after which they were required to return home. Moreover, they were made to reside in squalid single-sex hostels surrounded by high walls, and forced to carry passes, detailing their work contract, that could be demanded at any time by the authorities.

As Johannesburg grew and began to take on a more settled character, so more and more blacks were required for domestic work and labour in the industrial sector that mushroomed to support gold mining. Domestic workers, so that they could be at the beck and call of their employer, normally lived on the premises in a servant's shack in the backyard. And labourers took up residence in one of the three locations established some distance from the city by the Transvaal government, or in one of the inner-city slums.

'One man, one family driven from the land,' wrote John Steinbeck in *The Grapes of Wrath*, his story of Californian migrant workers. 'I lost my land. I am alone and bewildered. And in the night one family camps in a ditch and another family pulls in and the tents come out. The two men squat on their hams and the women and children listen. Here is the node, you who hate change and fear revolution. Keep these two squatting men apart; make them hate, fear, suspect each other. Here is the anlage of the thing you fear. This is the zygote. For here "I lost *my* land" is changed; a cell is split and from the splitting grows the thing you hate – "We lost *our* land." The danger is here, for two men are not as lonely or perplexed as one. And from this first "we" there grows a still more dangerous thing: "I have a little food" plus "I have none". If from this problem the sum is "We have a little food", the thing is on its way, the movement has direction. Only a little multiplication now, and this land is ours. This is the thing to bomb. This is the beginning – from "I" to "we".

'If you who own the things people must have could understand this, you might preserve yourself. If you could separate causes from results, if you could know that Paine, Marx, Jefferson, Lenin were results, not causes, you might survive. But that you cannot know. For the quality of owning freezes you forever into "I", and cuts you off forever from the "we".'

Within the burgeoning black community of Johannesburg was a small but dynamic black intelligentsia. Drawn from all over South Africa, they were the elite who had passed through the mission schools – mainly Lovedale College and Healdtown Institute – and occupied the prime positions open to blacks. In 1899 this group in particular was deeply conscious of the growing tensions between Boer and Briton and supported Britain on the far-fetched idea of a united non-racial society where the quality of individuals rather than the colour of their skin was the determinant. The British fraudulently encouraged this confidence, leading many blacks to fall into the trap that the coming war was a just crusade to bring about equal rights. It was absolutely and utterly inconceivable that, at the end of the war, their champions would prefer their white enemies to their black supporters.

But in 1902, the British and Boer representatives signed the Treaty of Vereeniging, which finally brought peace to a subcontinent that had been engulfed by three years of devastating war, but in which the matter of rights for blacks was deferred. In essence, blacks were to receive no political reward or recognition for their services or support for the British imperial government. What little they had was continually eroded. All-white juries increasingly passed biased decisions in cases involving blacks, the English press was becoming decidedly illiberal, and there was a yawning gap between the theory and practice of British rule. It appeared the new masters were trying to out-Boer the Boers.

'The benefits of the Pass Law,' thundered Sol Plaatje in a newspaper column in response to the British policy of continuing to enforce this inheritance from the Boer republic, 'is that thousands of useful, unoffending black men, than whom His Majesty has no more law abiding subjects, are daily sent to prison, without having done harm to anybody, and they die as regular gaol-birds even though they have never, during their lifetime, dipped the tips of their fingers in criminality.'

When gold mining resumed after the British occupation of Johannesburg in 1900, there was a rapid influx of blacks and Boers driven from the land by Britain's 'scorched-earth policy' employed during the guerrilla phase of the war. These people crammed into inner-city slums which a report by the Johannesburg council described as consisting of 'narrow courtyards, containing dilapidated and dirty tin huts without adequate means of lighting and ventilation, huddled on an area and constructed without any regard to sanitary considerations of any kind. In the middle of each slop-sodden and filth-bestrewn yard there is a well from which people get their water supply and they choose this place for washing purposes and urinals. It is as crowded as a rabbit warren. I shudder to think what would occur if plague or cholera broke out in that place. These places are dark dens.'

But it was not the health risks so much as different groups 'living on friendly terms' that concerned the authorities. An outbreak of bubonic plague in 1904 gave them the excuse to burn down the 'Coolie Location' of Nancefield and remove the 1 358 black residents 13 kilometres from Johannesburg to Klipspruit, which would later become Pimville and eventually Soweto. 'I saw misery and hardship which attended the enforcement of the measure,' wrote Sol Plaatje, who witnessed the action, 'and heard native viragoes loudly lamenting the fall of Kruger and cursing the new administration, which they termed "remorseless tyrants".'

On another occasion he noted that Transvaal blacks 'unanimously declare that they were far better off under the Field Cornets of the late Government than what they are under the Sub-Native Commissions. We are sure that never was the name of her late Gracious Majesty, Victoria, dragged in the mire like now, when the cruelty of those officials drives it into the minds of the black people, who lost their life and property to establish British rule in their country, that her reign is worse than Krugerism.'

As the realisation dawned that the new Union of South Africa only meant worse was to come, in 1911 the South African Native Convention began discussing the formation of a new organisation to represent blacks. Envisaged was a movement that would unite politically active black organisations, bring in the chiefs as representatives of traditional society, and promote the aspirations of emerging black leaders. This was easier said than done, because politics can be as much about personality as about policy. Personal rivalry, past slights, competing ideals, ambitions and self-interest all required attention before agreement could be reached on the necessity to establish a single, national political organisation.

By late 1911 it was finally agreed that all parties were ready to hold an inaugural conference and its date was set for 8 January 1912. The atmosphere on that day, among the large number of political and traditional leaders who attended, was pervaded by a sense of optimism that the way was being cleared for the formation of a body capable of attending to black grievances. After the singing of the hymn *Nkosi Sikelel' iAfrika* (God Bless Africa), Pixley Seme, an attorney, opened the convention by explaining its purpose: 'Chiefs of royal blood and gentlemen of our race, we have gathered here to consider and discuss a theme which my colleagues and I have decided to place before you. We have discovered that in the land of their birth, Africans are treated as hewers of wood and drawers of water. The white people of this country have formed what is known as the Union of South Africa – a union in which we have no voice in the making of laws and no part in the administration. We have called you, therefore, to the conference so that together we can find ways and means of forming our national union for the purpose of creating national unity and defending our rights and privileges.'

Seme concluded by proposing that a permanent congress be established. The motion was unanimously accepted with a standing ovation and cheering that went on and on. The Reverend John Dube was elected president and Sol Plaatje the first secretary-general of what was christened the South African Native National Congress (SANNC) – to be changed in 1923 to the African National Congress (ANC).

The leaders of the SANNC still believed that the time-honoured methods of lobbying, petitions and delegations would be effective in the new dispensation of Union. Thus, there was no question, at this point, of the SANNC working in any way other than within the constitutional framework. Even its modest objectives reflected the desire to foster a greater understanding between black and white in South Africa.

But these were weighty matters, especially when the primary concern for most blacks was simply staying alive. Thus, the concerns of the growing township of Klipspruit would be more local and immediate. By law, no blacks were permitted to live in Johannesburg after the founding of this township, situated in the bowl of the municipal sewerage works (cynically chosen because it was the one piece of land that would be of no interest to whites). The stench, particularly in summer, constantly permeated the A-frame galvanised huts, built with no foundations. So unhealthy was the environment that infant mortality was five out of ten. Add to this rent, hut taxes, transport difficulties and frequent police raids and it is not surprising that blacks still resident in inner-city slums resisted every effort to move them.

In 1923 the Smuts government passed the Native Urban Areas Act in an attempt to keep blacks out of city confines other than when it was necessary for them to be there to minister to white needs. But the council lacked funds and feeble attempts to implement this legislation were largely ineffective.

While life may have been rough and tough in the slums, they did offer the attraction of a buzzing, creative vitality inspired by the many cultures resident in them. The prohibition of the sale of liquor to blacks led to the formation of shebeens (after the unlicensed Irish liquor houses, *sibins*), which illicitly sold alcohol from private houses. And a new music tradition, Marabi, which incorporated aspects of black, white and coloured musical forms, flourished. 'Marabi was either organ but mostly piano,' explained jazz saxophonist Wilson 'King Force' Silgee. 'You get there, you pay your ten cents, you get your share of whatever concoction there is and you dance. It used to start from Friday night right through to Sunday evening.'

The Great Depression again forced large numbers of rural blacks and Afrikaners to the cities, placing increased pressure on the slums. 'And then the dispossessed were drawn west,' wrote Steinbeck on the situation in California, 'families, tribes, homeless and hungry. They streamed over the mountains, hungry and restless – restless as ants, scurrying to find work to do – to lift, to push, to pull, to pick, to cut – anything, any burden to bear, for food. The kids are hungry. We got no place to live. Like ants scurrying for work, for food.'

The Depression, relieved by a rising gold price, was replaced by rejuvenated industry hungry for land close to the city centre – and it was not long before rapacious eyes fell on the slums. In response to pressure from industrialists, the government began enforcing the Urban Areas Act. In the 1930s the George Goch and Prospect slums were cleared and the black inhabitants forcibly removed to the farm Klipspruit No. 8, on which a township, Orlando East (named after the first chairman of the Johannesburg Native Affairs Committee, Councillor Edward Orlando Leake), had been built for a 'better-class black' in the middle of present-day Soweto.

'Each house has a neat verandah and either two or three airy apartments, such as many Europeans would not despise,' enthused *The Star*. 'This will undoubtedly be somewhat of a paradise,' added the *Bantu World*. 'And to a greater extent will enhance the status of the Bantu within the ambit of progress and civilisation.'

It was anything but paradise. The monotonous, matchbox township was 15 kilometres from the centre of Johannesburg and serviced by public transport that was both expensive and unreliable. The town had no community facilities or shops, and the dusty roads were unpaved, with only one tap per street. The unplastered houses, on minute stands, had grass floors and no internal tap, electricity or sanitation other than a bucket. And the community spirit was so dead that Orlando became known as 'the place of hunger'.

'As far as I could see, stretching interminably away into the dusk, the houses of this township lay there blankly,' wrote author Jan Morris. 'A few candles flickered here and there. It is the deliberate impersonality of the location that is most terrible and you cannot escape the suspicion that this severe barracks-like order is intended to subjugate the African, to impress upon him his inferior status, to prove that he is not in white South Africa by right, but only by sufferance.'

Again slum-dwellers resisted efforts to move them. But, during World War II, Johannesburg experienced another mass influx of black people lured by the relaxation of restrictions to encourage labour to booming industries. No new houses were built to accommodate them, and the city fairly burst at the seams, forcing the over-flow to crowd into Orlando. Soon there was an extensive waiting list for homes. Add to that the fact that many of those attracted by the wartime boom were black women who did not qualify for housing, and the sum was a chaotic situation perfect for the political ambitions of a flamboyant, messianic character such as James Sofasonke Mpanza.

Mpanza, a small, shrill man who loved sport and women, had converted to Christianity and begun preaching to fellow prisoners while serving a 15-year sentence for murder. 'Many people thought I was arrested, and yet I was not,' he claimed. 'The same as with Jesus.' In the 1930s he had been elected to the township advisory board, which had no powers but was a conduit for criticism from home-owning res-idents to the authorities. What was soon apparent to Mpanza was that the most stri-dent complaints originated not from home owners, but from the predominantly female masses who had no roof over their heads or were crammed into existing accommodation as sub-tenants. Moreover, women were a constituency largely ignored by the main black political party – the ANC.

Mpanza, through his Sofasonke Party, decided to force the Johannesburg City Council's hand through confrontation – in a move in which he likened himself to Moses leading the children of Israel across the River Jordan. ' I am a messenger sent by God,' he declared in an affidavit. 'The municipality has taken on the duty of pro-viding us with houses. But it has not carried out that duty. There are no houses for us. We can no longer wait for them to put a roof over our heads. I am taking possession of the authorities' vacant land.'

Seated on his horse, on 20 March 1944, Mpanza led a group of women and sub-tenants to a vacant strip of council land in Orlando West where they set up shacks. This settlement, which became known as Masakeng, or simply Shanty Town, grew at an average of 300 families per day until there were over 4 000 shacks policed and administered by Mpanza.

'Situated on the slopes of a hill about ten miles outside the city of Johannesburg is a township whose expanding dimensions should soon entitle it to the prestige of being termed a city, also,' wrote Herman Charles Bosman in an article titled 'Shanty Town'. 'Shanty Town today contains several thousand shacks, each consisting of a rough framework of poles covered over with sacking and each housing a native family. Here let it be explained that our visit took place in bright sunshine. It was a pleasant morning and as far as the writer was concerned the visit was not made in any spirit of sociological crusading, which seems to demand of the individual a preconceived righteous indignation against the existing economic order – so that whatever is experienced and observed gets fitted into appropriate and ready-made emotions.

'Consequently, where this picture of actual conditions in Shanty Town may appear to fall short will be in respect of its deliberate avoidance of the obvious. Stories of squalor, told with a consistent drabness in grey shadows unrelieved by the light of imagination, tend, in their ultimate, to pall. The heart gets tired of the same old note struck over and over again. It is not human nature for one's feelings to be kept at the same pitch of intensity – whether the feelings are of pity or of righteous wrath – all the time. There is such a thing as tedium. And if it is not polite to yawn at a platitude it is, at all events, natural.

'For this reason this article will be confined to an objective description of an interesting little town, healthfully situated on a hillside, and it will be left to the reader to make his own comment, such as "dastardly" or "delightful", depending alike on his own subjective reactions and his capacity for reading between the lines.

'What first struck the writer, who has considerable practical knowledge of constructive engineering, was that two distinct types of building material are employed in the erection of the shanties. Most of the residential abodes are covered over with mielie sacks. A few – and these belonging obviously to the more aristocratic section – have their walls and roof constructed of sugar pockets bearing the trademark of Messrs Hulett. Close examination shows that the hessian in a sugar pocket is of finer texture and better woven than that in a mielie bag, and is consequently a better building material. It keeps out the elements better.

'Each shack is numbered in some dark-coloured paint. These numbers are run into thousands, thereby affording a rough-and-ready means of computing the population of the place. It also makes it easier for the postman on his round to deliver correspondence and newspapers. One does not imagine that the residents of Shanty Town get troubled much with tradesmen's circulars, however. Although an enterprising house agent can, if he so desires, strike an incongruous note by circularising the area with printed literature about "Why pay Rent?" "Let Us show You how to Build Your Own House."

'There is little about these hessian-covered shacks that is in conflict with the fundamental laws of architecture, which are that a building should be planned in accordance with the purpose for which it is required, that it should carry no ornamentation that is outside of this purpose, and its design should be guided by the type of material that is employed. From an aesthetic point of view the architecture of Shanty Town can therefore be described as not undignified. About none of these shacks is there that false attempt at drama that makes Park Station an eyesore.

'And when a native woman told us she was suffering from chest pains as a result of her hut being drenched during the recent rains, and that most of the people there were suffering from various illnesses contracted through sleeping under soaked blankets, her complaints were not based on artistic grounds but on the simple scientific fact that sacking is porous and lets in the water in the rainy season.

'But from the point of view of pure architecture there is not much wrong with these dwellings. The washed-out yellows of the hessian roofs and walls blend prettily with the grass of the South African veld in mid-winter. Washed-out yellow against bleached fawn. Pretty. And veld-coloured huts built close to the soil seem much more appropriate for South African conditions than skyscrapers and blocks of flats. The shacks in the main street of Shanty Town seem to express the true spirit of Africa in a way that the buildings in Eloff Street do not.

'But all these things are merely by the way. For that matter, one feels that if a number of Kalahari Bushmen were brought to Johannesburg on a visit to a fashionable block of city flats they would go back to the desert with strong feelings about the white man's degradation. "Like living in an anthill," they would say. "Squalor." "Unhygienic." "Like Pigs." "And you ought to see some of these pictures they hang on their walls ... just too awful."

'What was most interesting about Shanty Town was its human side. One felt in the place the warmth of a strong and raw life. Deplorable though their economic circumstances were, there was about these men and women and children a sense of life that had no frustrations in it. A dark vitality of the soil. An organic power for living that one imagined nothing in this world could take away. Was there anything about us, about this party of white visitors, that the residents of Shanty Town could genuinely envy? In our hearts the answer was, no.

'The replies which the natives returned to our questions were prideful. Their attitude was a lesson in breeding. They resented our presence, in the way that any proud person resents the intrusion into his affairs of curiosity or patronage. And they received us with that politeness that shames. We wanted to know what had happened to Mpanza and they informed us, with grave dignity, that "he was not there." Although everybody knew, what we subsequently learnt from a policeman, that Mpanza was in gaol.

'Whatever information we got we received from the policeman: from the side of the authorities and not from the side of the residents. And when we left, a native woman asked if we were going to send blankets. It was a perfect snub, whose imputation could not be lost even on the most obtuse. A duchess could not have administered it better.

'Whatever ill effects detribalisation may have had on the natives, it has done nothing, judging from what is happening in Shanty Town, to the stateliness of their aristocracy. Living under what are nothing less than ghastly conditions, deprived, apparently, of even the barest necessity of human existence, the inhabitants of Shanty Town are displaying, in the face of adversity, a sublime courage that goes far beyond questions of economics and sociology.

'If life is spirit, what the natives of Shanty Town bear about them is not poverty but destiny.'

'The houses of hessian are arranged side by side with no lines of demarcation,' added the *Umteteli wa Bantu*. 'It is one big family united by a strong will to see their struggle through to the bitter end.

'Here, on this patch of ground, in the midst of the noise of grinding wheels of trains carrying thousands of African workers into the city, a few miles away is a village where life is different. Water is drawn from a nearby stream; the sanitary arrangements are quite primitive; there is no individuality, all is communal. Below the dwellings, where the stream is wider, is the communal washing place. On either side of the stream, on the clean grass, are spread yards and yards of white linen and other articles of clothing.

'In the centre of the settlement is the communal fuel depot. Yes! There is enough coal and wood for everybody. Shanty Town is properly administered. It has its Headquarters in the tent over which James "Sofasonke" Mpanza presides.

'James Mpanza is an elderly man, with an oval, emaciated face. He speaks with a chronic hoarse voice. There is a perpetual glimmer of light in his eyes. Around him centres the whole business concerning Shanty Town. It is to him that more than 10 000 look for leadership; it is to him that they owe their newly found freedom, for these houses of hessian have given the occupants a sense of proud ownership. As one resident said: "I'd sooner have my own place here, than be crowded in one room over there," indicating the place where he was living before coming to Shanty Town.'

The Johannesburg City Council, caught off guard, was incensed. 'Mpanza was a criminal; he was a thug,' recalled Wilhelm Carr, the council's manager of Non-European Affairs. 'He extorted money from every possible source he could. He was a man of very bad character. He fathered more illegitimate children in that part of the world than anybody before or since. He stole money. He was always drunk. He was an unmitigated pest. He had nothing, nothing, nothing, to do with the subsequent development of the area.'

But this is not true, because there is currency to the claim that Mpanza was the 'man who founded Soweto' – and if not, he certainly gave it shape. The authorities initially attempted the tried-and-tested 'strong display of force', but squatters would merely pack up their shacks and meagre possessions and move a few hundred metres. Then, to sabotage Mpanza, the council began doing what the people wanted in the first place – building houses. Shelters were built on council land at Jabavu and Moroka and offered to family men who could prove they were employed. Many migrant workers took up the offer and either brought their wives to live with them or abandoned them and married city women. These townships, with their nine-metres-squared shacks that had no toilets and were plagued by thuggery, were the new slums, but, importantly, they provided a legal home for many workers and their families. And even though Mpanza was outmanoeuvred, he had proved that mass-based community rebellion was an effective political strategy.

At the same time that Mpanza was making political capital out of a constituency largely ignored by the ANC, an Africanist faction within the movement was also becoming increasingly discontented at the inability of the party to mobilise the masses – an incapacity they feared would marginalise the ANC. Included in this group were the young activists Walter Sisulu, Peter Mda, Anton Lembede, Oliver

Tambo and Nelson Mandela, who formed the Congress Youth League – with Lembede as president and Mandela as an executive member – which was approved at the ANC annual congress in Bloemfontein in December 1943.

'Anton Lembede,' wrote Mandela in *Long Walk to Freedom*, 'said that Africa was a black man's continent, and it was up to Africans to reassert themselves and reclaim what was rightfully theirs. He hated the idea of the black inferiority complex and castigated what he called the worship and idolisation of the West and its ideas. The inferiority complex, he affirmed, was the greatest barrier to liberation. He noted that wherever the African had been given the opportunity, he was capable of developing to the same extent as the white man. "The colour of my skin is beautiful," he said, "like the black soil of Mother Africa." He believed blacks had to improve their self-image before they could initiate successful mass action. He preached self-reliance and self-determination, and called his philosophy Africanism.

'Lembede declared that a new spirit was stirring among the people, that ethnic differences were melting away, that young men and women thought of themselves as Africans first and foremost. He had taught for years in the Orange Free State, learned Afrikaans, and had come to see Afrikaner nationalism as a prototype for African nationalism.'

In 1944 the ANC Youth League issued its manifesto: 'To mislead the world and make it believe that the Whiteman in South Africa is helping the African on the road to civilised life, the Whiteman has arrogated to himself the title and role of Trustee for the African people. The effects of Trusteeship alone have made the African realise that Trusteeship has meant, as it still means, the consolidation of the Whiteman of his position at the expense of the African people, so that by the time national awakening opens the eyes of the African people to the bluff they live under, white domination should be secure and unassailable.

'These conditions have made the African lose all faith in all talk of Trusteeship. He now elects to determine the future by his own efforts. He has realised that to trust to the mere good grace of the Whiteman will not free him, as no nation can free an oppressed group other than the group itself. Self-determination is the philosophy of life which will save him from the disaster he clearly sees on his way, disasters to which Discrimination, Segregation, Pass Laws and Trusteeship are all ruthless and inevitably driving him.

'The formation of the African National Congress Youth League is an answer and assurance to the critics of the national movement that African Youth will not allow the struggles and sacrifices of their fathers to have been in vain. The Congress Youth League must be the brains-trust and power station of the spirit of African Nationalism, the spirit of African self-determination, the spirit that is so discernible in the thinking of our youth.'

'The basic policy of the league did not differ from the ANC's first constitution in 1912,' explained Mandela. 'But we were re-affirming and underscoring those original concerns, many of which had gone by the wayside. African nationalism was our battle cry, and our creed was the creation of one nation out of many tribes, the overthrow of white supremacy, and the establishment of a truly democratic form of government.'

And the constituency of this group was those in the sprawling townships where life was uncompromisingly harsh and tough. Many were battling with the transition from a rural to an urban life, high costs associated with living far from their places of work, and brutal and uncaring white masters who harassed and exploited them without providing any education or health services in return. This spawned an entrepreneurial 'culture of survival' that encouraged a heightened sense of collective hospitality, escapism to relieve the sombre atmosphere, and systems to impose order.

'In the evening a strange thing happened,' wrote Steinbeck, 'the twenty families became one family, the children were the children of all. The loss of home became one loss, and the golden time in the West was one dream. And it might be that a sick child threw despair into the hearts of twenty families, of a hundred people; that a birth there in a tent kept a hundred people quiet and awestruck through the night and filled a hundred people with its birth-joy in the morning. A family which the night before had been lost and fearful might search its goods to find a present for a new baby. In the evening, sitting about the fires, the twenty were one.'

In the townships to the south-west of Johannesburg, evangelical churches featuring revivalist meetings and faith healers became big attractions in a community plagued by severe health problems. Businesses such as the use of large American cars as taxis, to provide an alternative form of transport to that offered by the state-owned railway and the Public Utility Transport Company (PUTCO) bus service, were launched and laid the foundation for commercial giants. Shebeens flourished, as did methods of avoiding official detection; 'people's courts' (*makgotla*) were established to mete out quick justice, and social institutions of mutual sharing and support were created that helped build a powerful community spirit. The toe-twitching, hip-swaying township jazz of musicians such as Tshooks Tshukudu and his Elite

Swingster Band, the Manhattan Brothers, and Philip Thabane's Malambo Jazz Makers provided a nightlife, and soccer and boxing inspired passion. 'Sport in the townships is neither a pastime, nor a form of recreation, nor a kind of entertainment,' commented sports writer Ali Gu Twala. 'It is all these things together and more. It is township food for thought and body, but most of all it is part of the townsman's way of life, and he gets hooked on it like junkies get hooked on pot.'

In soccer, the Moroka Swallows, Pimville United Brothers, Kaizer Chiefs and Orlando Pirates – the Mighty Bucs – drew thousands of cheering supporters to games, particularly local derbies. The very essence of township soccer was its carnival, frenetic pace – and it was the same in boxing. 'It's left, left, right, head, stomach and to-the-chin stuff we demand from our boxers,' declared one commentator. 'In the township we are born fighting,' added boxing enthusiast Elijah Msibi. 'Yes man, you grow up fighting poverty, fighting ignorance and fighting a feeling of ignorance that seems to haunt you. So township boxers were fighters first and boxers later. Tough like hippo hide and never believing they've been licked even if they've been KO'd. Man, those boys and hundreds like them are what we call pure township stock.'

There was, however, a flip side: the brutality of black existence transformed townships into what Jan Smuts called 'universities of crime'. Dehumanising and overcrowding, with sometimes 20 people sharing a four-roomed house, created the perfect environment for child abuse and rape. Frustrations also found outlets in street fights, bloody assaults and one of the highest murder rates in the world, which four police stations were powerless and disinclined to control. But worst of all was the growth of gangs.

Family discipline was naturally lax in a society where both parents were forced to work long hours at places far from their residence. Compounding the problem was a gross shortage of schools: fewer than half the township children were accommodated, and even these educated kids faced bleak prospects of employment. The result was that the community's youth gravitated to crime and delinquency in gangs such as the XYs, the Spoilers and the Americans. Commuters were favourite targets, and greenhorn migrant workers were particularly vulnerable. Attacks on the latter led directly to the formation of ethnic gangs – such as the Basuto-blanket-clad Russians, formed by Sothos to protect migrants – that later branched into more lucrative crime.

'The hand of the pickpocket does not probe so expertly as to be unnoticed by most of the people in the commotion,' wrote Berung Seluki in *Dumani* on the gangs operating on commuter trains, 'but even though they are aware of what is going on in their pockets they will keep mum for fear of the worst. The victim will stand stiff and straight until the thugs are through with him, while others will watch the episode frozen by the knowledge that their turn is either just past or still coming. These hooligans also drag women and girls at knife-point into the open veld. They rape the expectant mothers to be. They even rape old women of their grannies' age and little schoolgirls.'

The obsession of white rule in the twentieth century was not crime prevention in black townships, but what to do to control the 'necessary evil' of the influx of blacks to urban areas. Most whites conveniently believed that blacks were natives of clearly defined geographic homelands and that urbanisation was alien to them – even if more and more were attracted to the cities for the very same reasons European rural folk were attracted to urban areas during the Industrial Revolution. While the concept of townships was well established before the National Party election victory in 1948, social engineering after this time gave them a more sinister and brutal air.

'The apartheid policy of the National Party is nothing new,' commented Dr Xuma, the ANC president, on hearing the election results, 'and should be nothing surprising to any honest and serious student of colour relations. It is a mere elaboration, a natural and logical growth of the Native Policy.'

But it was more than that – more complex, more ferocious, more impersonal and more insane.

The Nationalists believed that if they ordered the urban population through a policy of divide and rule they could realise their dream of a white South Africa in which blacks were present only as providers of labour. The first step was to categorise blacks into four distinct groups – urban, immigrant, migrant and labour tenant. The first two were the only categories allowed to live with their families in townships – which were further split into zones to represent different ethnic origins where mother-tongue schooling and so on were provided. The third group was forced to live in heavily policed and dehumanising single-sex hostels specifically constructed for men of one tribe in the corresponding ethnic township. Dube Hostel, in the Zulu sector of Soweto, for example, was reserved for Zulu migrant workers, and Nancefield Hostel, in the Sotho sector, for Sotho migrants. These people were not allowed to receive visitors or take up permanent residence in the township unless they had worked for 15 years in the same area, 10 of them for the same employer. To make matters worse, they were preyed on by gangs and treated as country bumpkins by permanent township residents. The fourth category was to prevent labour tenants from leaving farms; they were absolutely forbidden to live in townships under any circumstances.

All these categories and statuses were recorded on passes – known as the *dompas* – that were administered from 80 Albert Street on the outskirts of the Johannesburg city centre. The Minister of Native Affairs, in 1956, proudly announced that this single office had turned away 25 331 people seeking to live in Johannesburg. Once refused permission to remain, or 'endorsed out', as the regulation stated, the person was placed in a 'kraal' to await shipment back to his or her point of departure. So traumatic was this banishment that it was not uncommon for victims to commit suicide.

The overriding philosophy, and everything hung on this, was that townships were places that housed black temporary sojourners, of varying status, from rural areas while they performed necessary services for whites. After this usefulness, they had to leave, irrespective of their status. It was absolutely inconceivable to the whole scheme of things to admit the permanency of urbanised black people, because this would have been an admission that some black people were not foreigners in white South Africa. Townships, in effect, became labour compounds, and the Nationalist government clearly resolved to forcibly remove all urban blacks to them so they could be better controlled through tougher pass laws.

This required the provision of more township housing. 'The most pressing single need of the native community is more adequate housing,' commented Dr Werner Eiselen, the secretary for Native Affairs, in 1951. 'Only by provision of adequate shelter in properly planned native townships can full control over urban natives be regained because only then will it be possible to eliminate the surplus natives who do not seek or find an honest living in cities.' The problem of providing these displaced persons with housing was partially solved through leasing land to them. On this land they could build homes according to uniform plans provided by the council. Other regulations taxed employers per head of labour to provide revenue for the provision of services. As part of this overall scheme, 10 000 serviced sites were released in Soweto in 1955.

'To possess your own lavatory pail might not seem to be the ultimate in human ambition,' reported *The Star*. 'Nevertheless on yesterday's smiling, sunny Sunday, a pail and dustbin presented to each of 12 Bantu families by the superintendent of Jabavu Township, represented a passport to a new life and a new hope. Pail in hand, the Bantu clamoured onto a lorry that held all their possessions and were taken to their new stands on Johannesburg's first site-and-service scheme at Moroka North. On each site they saw a "little house" that was for the exclusive use of their family. Proudly each family put the new pail into it.

'Then they walked round the boundaries of their sites, exclaiming at the size. The 40 ft by 70 ft stands seemed so vast after the pocket-handkerchiefs of land from which they had come. These pioneers on site-and-service in the Johannesburg area came from a miserable unserviced squatter camp in the Moroka area oddly known as 'New Look'. These nearly 200 families had been paying 23s a month for the privilege of living on a bit of land without tap water and without latrine.'

Much of the development of the township in the first decade of National Party rule was further made possible by low-interest loans from members of the Chamber of Mines to the Johannesburg City Council. The largest of these loans came from an initiative from the Anglo American Corporation as a direct result of Wilhelm Carr inviting Sir Ernest Oppenheimer to visit Moroka. 'There were only three of us,' recalled Carr, 'it was Boris, I and Sir Ernest. It was quite amusing. We went out in the morning in Sir Ernest's Rolls Royce. Now the roads were pretty well non-existent. And the very first dip and this thing was grounded and couldn't go. So the rest of the day we rode around in my Ford. Everybody treated it like a joke. And we took the old boy to show him the Shanty Town and he didn't say much; he was never a man who talked a great deal. But it was obvious that he was deeply moved by what he had seen.'

Oppenheimer arranged a loan of £3 million to be repaid over 30 years, and a massive housing programme was launched – which coincided, conveniently enough, with the clearing of the freehold townships of Sophiatown, Martindale and Newclare to the west of Johannesburg, as well as the Western Native Township. By 1957 the drab, monotonous, regimented townships of Tladi, Zondi, Chiawelo, Senoane, Dlamini, Jabulani, Naledi and Piri had been laid out. These townships round Orlando and the others that had preceded them were known as South Western Bantu Townships, but they had no official name until Carr launched a competition in 1959. Thousands of entries poured in and the debate raged for four years until, in 1963, the name Soweto – an acronym of South Western Townships – was settled on.

The thinking behind townships and divide and rule was an extension of the broader scheme to deny the existence of a group of South Africans that was neither rural nor tribal. That is not how it worked out in reality. Instead, the Nationalists sowed the seeds of revolution by forcing large numbers of disgruntled, exploited and harassed people together. It was this that would contribute to making Soweto the symbol of the struggle for freedom.

The National Party, soon after coming to power, introduced Bantu Education, which was placed under Hendrik Verwoerd's Ministry of Native Affairs. While this schooling was intended for a broader base than anything preceding it, it was appallingly sub-standard – designed only to provide the most basic numeracy and literacy skills necessary for the increasingly technical demands of modern industry. There was, according to Verwoerd, no other purpose in educating blacks: anything more would merely show them the green pastures of European society in which they were not allowed to graze. But, while whites received free education, black parents were forced to pay for their children's textbooks and schooling in overcrowded, ill-equipped institutions where the teachers were unqualified. 'Education for ignorance and for inferiority in Verwoerd's schools is worse than no education at all,' declared ANC leader Professor ZK Matthews. Nevertheless, black school enrolment was so overwhelming and schools so overcrowded that even rudimentary standards could not be maintained.

There were a myriad other oppressions and repressive measures. It was a crime to strike and the freedom of speech and movement was severely curtailed. 'It was a crime to walk through a Whites Only door,' wrote Mandela, 'a crime to ride a Whites Only bus, a crime to use a Whites Only drinking fountain, a crime to walk on a Whites Only beach, a crime to be on the streets after 11 pm, a crime not to have a pass book and a crime to have the wrong signature in that book, a crime to be unemployed and a crime to be employed in the wrong place, a crime to live in certain places and a crime to have no place to live.'

It was fertile ground for the more radical ANC Youth League, which appealed in particular to the hundreds of thousands of educated urban black youths. And with each slight, injustice and indignity to blacks it gained a wider following. To counter white repression it advocated a Plan of Action that included boycotts, passive resistance, strikes, civil disobedience and work stayaways. It was through this campaign that the leaders of the Congress Youth League changed the direction of the ANC to that of a mass-based movement intent on liberation. As the defiance campaign escalated in response to increasing discrimination, so repressive measures intensified.

Because of the support these campaigns received from other sections of the community, in the 1950s many of the Youth League leaders – including Tambo, Mandela and Sisulu – began to have second thoughts about Africanism. This group, increasingly embracing multiracialism, moved away from the positions still held by die-hard Africanists like Zeph Mothopeng and Robert Sobukwe. The matter reached a head at the all-race Congress of the People organised by the ANC and held at Kliptown in Soweto in June 1955, where a charter of demands – the Freedom Charter – was adopted on behalf of the disenfranchised black population. The charter reaffirmed the ANC's multiracialism, and the Africanists, with a goal of non-racialism, broke away to form the Pan Africanist Congress (PAC) in 1959.

'Against multiracialism,' wrote Sobukwe, 'we have this objection that the history of South Africa has fostered group prejudices and antagonisms, and if we have to maintain the same group exclusiveness, parading under the term of multiracialism, we shall be transporting to the new Africa those very antagonisms and conflicts. Further, multiracialism is in fact pandering to European bigotry and arrogance. It is a method of safeguarding interests irrespective of population figures. In that sense it is a complete negation of democracy.'

In 1958 the ANC launched an anti-pass campaign targeting the most hated symbol of apartheid, the *dompas*, which annually made criminals of up to half a million people. 'You would leave Braamfontein station to find hidden behind the building, a squad of cops, who would line up thousands of blacks and check their documents,' recalled Soweto community leader Dr Nthato Motlana. Those caught without papers or with documents that were not in order faced imprisonment that included being hired out to employers or farmers as forced labourers.

Dompas!
I looked back
Dompas!
I went through my pockets
Not there.

They bit into my flesh (handcuffs)

Came the kwela-kwela
We crawled in.
The young men sang.

In that dark moment
It all became familiar.
  – Mafika Gwala: 'Kwela-Ride'

'I saw things in jail that I never expected to see there,' said ANC leader John Nkadimeng. 'It was terrible. I was absolutely angry. I was sick because I knew I had not committed any crime. Knew that I had not done anything wrong! Except this bloody rubbish of the pass! And they took me to jail for such a long time and got me mixed up with terrible criminals! The campaign of the ANC against pass laws attracted me because I thought that was an evil law. I thought that the only thing I could do was to work to obliterate that law, to get rid of it, get it out of the way. So I joined the defiance campaign. We wanted to go out in the street to sing and walk about in town without any documents so that we could court arrest. The police spotted us during the day when we were singing and so we didn't really defy, we just walked into the police van.'

The ANC, as part of its overall campaign against passes, organised a defiance action to commence on 31 March 1960. The PAC refused to participate and in response called its own protest for 21 March. 'Sixty nine Africans were shot dead and at least 180 wounded when police opened fire at Sharpeville on Monday,' reported *The World*. 'The police used their rifles and Sten-guns when stone throwers demonstrated outside the police station at the opening of the Pan Africanist anti-pass campaign.

'The Sharpeville shootings took place in the afternoon. The police were putting up loudspeakers to address the crowds in the square when young people started shouting, singing and throwing stones. The police opened fire and the square was littered with dead and wounded. African car owners rushed many of the wounded to hospital. Ambulances led by motorcycle traffic police raced through the area with sirens screaming. Casualty wards were soon full and wounded people were laid on the verandah and in the hospital grounds, crowds of relatives came to the hospital. It was impossible to let them in.'

Protests flared across the country and an outraged international community censured South Africa at the United Nations. 'There was a time we could shoot as many people as we liked and the world did not seem to care,' lamented Cabinet minister FC Erasmus. The Johannesburg Stock Exchange once more collapsed as capital fled the country and English-speaking whites made plans to emigrate. On 8 April, to stem the panic, the government declared a state of emergency and banned the ANC and the PAC. The ANC responded by going underground and establishing an armed wing, Umkhonto we Sizwe (Spear of the Nation), which was to be responsible for a number of acts of sabotage against government installations.

'We had no alternative to armed and violent resistance,' wrote Mandela. 'Over and over again, we had used all the non-violent weapons in our arsenal all to no avail, for whatever we did was met with an iron hand. A freedom fighter learns the hard way that it is an oppressor who defines the nature of the struggle and the oppressed is often left no recourse but to use methods that mirror those of the oppressor. At a certain point, one can only fight fire with fire.'

As part of the few cosmetic reforms that followed, Urban Bantu Councils (UBCs) – promoted as democratic forums but known in Soweto as 'Useless Boys' Clubs' and 'United Black Crooks' – replaced the township advisory boards. Whatever was done to improve the system, for blacks, was undone by harsher repression. The false calm created by this situation allowed the economy to recover and the most fanciful aspects of grand apartheid to be imposed.

The 1960s were a boom time in South Africa, and the residents of Soweto enjoyed some benefits. 'The debate about African wages in South Africa highlighted the facts about race discrimination, African poverty and the large gap between black and white wages in South Africa,' wrote Merle Lipton, a visiting research fellow at the School of African Studies of Sussex University. 'But it also reinforces the erroneous belief that Africans have gained little from South Africa's rapid growth rate and recent research shows that real wages of many Africans have risen markedly.'

Many immersed themselves in escapism. 'In those days,' commented jazz musician Hugh Masekela in *Drum*, 'a man was known and recognised by the kind of label that was attached to his clothes. We used to spend hours cleaning our shoes, and then go to the cinemas, very early, just to show off.'

He wears
the latest Levison's suits
'Made in America';
from Cuthberts
a pair of Florscheim shoes
'America's finest shoes',
He pays cash

that's why
he's called Mister.

...

He knows
he must carry a pass.
He don't care for politics
He don't go to church
He knows Sobukwe
he knows Mandela
They're in Robben Island
'So what? That's not my business!'
  – Oswald Mbuyiseni Mtshali: *from* 'The Detribalised'

As blacks remained quiet, the designs of grand apartheid reached a crescendo under Verwoerd, then Vorster. From the mid-1960s the provision of housing for blacks in townships stopped and all resources were channelled into homelands. The government even insisted that a major portion of the enormous profits realised by the Johannesburg City Council through control of township beerhalls be diverted towards funding this policy rather than being spent on maintaining or upgrading local services. And homelands were fast becoming a reality, because the government had co-opted a sizeable black petty bourgeois through bribery and the promise of unimagined power and riches. 'A R1 639 000 official residence,' reported *The World*, 'including banqueting hall and wine cellar, was being built outside Umtata for the future head of state of the Transkei, the Minister of Bantu Administration, Mr MC Botha, disclosed in the Assembly yesterday.'

The government, to rid South Africa of all blacks, ordered that home leasehold rights be terminated if they did not take out homeland citizenship – thus denying urban blacks any claims to their homes; that urban residents unemployed for a month or longer be denied permission to remain in that urban area; that widows, unmarried mothers, divorced women and deserted wives be removed from waiting lists for accommodation; that migrant workers be forced to return to their place of origin to renew their work contract, so as to deny them permanent status; and that black professionals be prevented from practising in any area other than 'their homeland'. 'Ensure that non-Europeans who render professional services (lawyers, doctors etc.) are not granted office accommodation in Bantu residential areas,' instructed a directive to local authorities in 1969. 'The Bantu should be persuaded to offer their services in the Bantu homelands. Professional services in urban Bantu residential areas should be rendered by whites. Those who already had such premises should be persuaded to move and establish themselves among their own people in the homelands.'

Worse was to come. The Bantu Homelands Citizens Act of 1970 compelled all blacks to become citizens of a homeland corresponding to their ethnic group even if they had not been born there or ever set foot there. 'The government this week published legislation setting out terms for the Transkei's independence,' reported *The World*. 'A schedule to the Status of the Transkei Bill makes it clear that more than 3 million Xhosa and Sotho-speaking people with even distant links to the Transkei will automatically lose their South African citizenship and become Transkei citizens on Independence Day.'

'No amount of reassuring talk will convince urban blacks that there is a moral justification for them to take out homeland citizenship,' commented *The World*. 'Neither will the "bribery" tactics which the South African government now wants to employ. For, is it not bribery to say that blacks who take out homeland citizenship will be given preferential treatment in employment contracts, housing, hospitalisation and generally in other ways? And is it not holding blacks to ransom to require that they take out homeland citizenship before they can get leasehold rights in the urban areas? There can only be one reason for this attitude on the part of the government: If all blacks in urban areas associate themselves with homelands, the government can claim an all round success of its grand apartheid design. Technically, the government would have succeeded in making greater South Africa white, and all blacks present in South Africa would be foreigners who could lay no claim to any rights in 87 percent of the country.'

'They should be witness to this – all our homeland leaders,' wrote journalist Aggrey Klaaste in *The World*. 'They should be witness to the impotent anger in the eyes of fathers, the sad resignation in the care-worn eyes of mothers, and the bewilderment in the frightened eyes of little boys and girls. All homeland leaders should be witness to this, for they have betrayed their people.

'Betrayal started when leaders thought of opting for the distasteful expediency of homeland politics. Today, with the stroke of a pen, Xhosas who have never been in the homelands and whose parents have never been there, are being deprived of homes, jobs and a future. The betrayal is becoming so monstrous that people who are not even Xhosa are caught in the widening strands of this frightening web. There is the case of Mr Elijah Moremi who is not even Xhosa, but his mother was, and his mistake was to use his mother's surname when he went for a pass book. This proved to be an inexcusable oversight he later tried to rectify. Now he has to pay, and the payout is as real as the spectre of being endorsed out of his area, to a place he hardly knows, a place in which he is most likely to be met with hostility.

'The historical national suicide of the Ama Xhosa is going to be something of a picnic if all urban Xhosas have to be declared citizens of an over populated undeveloped area like Transkei. Soon it will be the Tswanas, then the Vendas and Shangaans, the Pedis and almost inevitably the Zulus. There is no escape, not for a single black-skinned man and woman in South Africa. In power politics, this is called the grand-design, friends, the grand design of separate development, invoked by the nationalists with divine guidance, the trap was sprung with the idea of homelands. Do not be lulled into security by talk of a new deal for blacks. We are still temporary sojourners for the South African government is going to deliver its divinely inspired goods, if it kills them or us. They are going to deliver the goods if it means making the majority of the people in this country citizens of 13 percent of the land.'

And what could not be accomplished through bribery was achieved by increased repression. The Terrorism Act, which provided for indefinite detention without trial, was added to the battery of security legislation. The Bureau of State Security (BOSS) was established with lavish budgets to safeguard the internal security of the country and an army of informers recruited to infiltrate and sow fear in all organisations opposed to the state. 'I believe in the supremacy of the white man in his territory,' declared Prime Minister Vorster, 'and I'm prepared to maintain it by force.'

Behind the calm and prosperous façade, however, a spark was lit by the economic boom that would cause the whole edifice to implode. 'Blacks in South Africa must grasp education with both hands and hand it to the younger generation like a torch of life,' said M Rantho, president of the National Institute for the Prevention of Crime and Rehabilitation of Offenders (NICRO). 'Education is an important asset for the black man, with it all the doors to success stand open.'

'Young black South Africans should plan their futures to suit their needs and the progress of the country,' added Percy Qoboza, editor of *The World*. 'The day will come when the black people of South Africa will be called on to participate in the wealth of the country. For this reason the young black child should arm himself or herself with every possible material of commerce and other professions he or she could lay hands on, economy is the backbone of each and every country. Fighting for political power without knowledge of economy will get us nowhere.'

It was the common refrain – get yourself an education, and rights and respect will follow. In this call, black leaders had an unexpected ally, but for different reasons. Before the 1960s, secondary schooling was even worse than primary schooling, as the government believed that what blacks needed to know was adequately catered for in primary school (and, in any case, they were focusing on constructing schools in the homelands to force parents to send their children away from the townships). But the economic boom created a shortage of skilled labour and a demand from business for improved secondary schooling. In a short time, the standard and number of secondary schools began to improve. This is not to imply that the quality of this improved schooling was anywhere near adequate or approached what was offered to whites for free.

Parents were still required to pay fees they could not afford for facilities that were appalling: there were insufficient teachers and their training was derisory; teacher–pupil ratios averaged 53:1 (in some schools it was 150:1); enrolment was eight times available space; and the conditions under which scholars were forced to study were shocking. 'Black children live in overcrowded houses,' wrote Joyce Harris, regional chairperson of the Black Sash, 'for the most part without electricity, and with no study aids whatsoever. Many of their parents are relatively uneducated and cannot provide them with the cultural background which facilitates learning. The only contribution they can make is to work and scrimp and save in order to finance their children's education, for it is not free for them as it is for white children.'

'Effective teaching and learning are adversely affected where the teacher–pupil ratio is as high as it is in black schools,' added RN Gugushe, general secretary of the Advisory Board for Bantu Education. 'The size of the classes teachers have to cope with tends to sap their enthusiasm and frustrates them, especially when written work is given and has to be marked. The temptation to use the "chalk and talk" method is consequently greater and active class participation through discussion, discovery and inquiry is relegated to the background. Thus the whole teaching programme from the sub-standards up to the secondary school classes, with very few exceptions, tends to be dull and uninteresting to the average pupil. Consequently, the bright pupils get thoroughly bored, hence the high dropout rate in black schools.

'The current high teacher–pupil ratio has apparently also come to be a repellent to teacher recruitment on a qualitative basis. Amongst the students who proceed to college or to university for teacher training there is only a thin veneer of academic or intellectual ability. It would appear to have become a "last resort" profession to most black students today.'

If this were not enough, some children were taught in the open, others in shifts, while many were not permitted to graduate from primary school because no positions were available in secondary schools. There was danger too – children attending school adversely affected gang recruitment, and this created serious conflict between scholars and gangs. 'A Soweto student was this week brutally killed when he was attacked by thugs on his way home after a day at the Dube library,' reported *The World*. 'Edward Ndodeni was a Form Three student at Mncube Secondary School. According to reports, Edward had left the library at 6:30 pm. As he went past the Bantu Affairs Department offices, thugs attacked him. One of them stabbed him with a knife. He screamed that he was being killed and crossed the busy road. A car missed him by inches as he stumbled across the road. He was rushed to hospital by an ambulance, but died on the way.'

While parents saw education as a passport to a prosperous life, students flocked to schools for another reason – the opportunity for solidarity and the sharing of ideas for liberation. 'The students share the same fundamental political aspirations as their parents,' commented Temba Nolutshungu, a youth organiser with the Institute of Race Relations. 'The only difference between the youth and their parents is that the parents are basically political negotiators while the students are political activists.

'The parental generation still adhere to the doctrine of passive resistance. They go to church on Sunday and pray for change. They read the newspapers, complain about the spiralling costs of foodstuffs, cry about ridiculous wages and protest verbally at pass law arrests and general harassment. They have their own description of what a parent is and the students have their own description of themselves. To the parent a student is someone who goes to school, does his homework, endorses Bantu education and bothers about nothing but his career.

'The students, however, see themselves as people to whom education is a means to an end. The end being the ultimate realisation of the political aspirations of the people. The students regard going to school as a means of preparing themselves to serve their people. It means being vested with responsibilities towards their people. They look at past graduates of Bantu Education and find many of them snugly settled in enviable positions. They don't want that to happen to them. They regard it as immoral.'

To weep is a waste of glorious time.

Time to grab arms,

And aim them at

The blue-eyed enemy

Lurking in the bushes.

   – Anon

This growing awareness, activism and sense of destiny was further fuelled by the growing philosophy of Black Consciousness (BC).

The hard-living, tall, charming and charismatic Steve Biko had enrolled at the Wentworth Medical School in 1966. At that time the white-dominated National Union of South African Students (NUSAS) was leading any struggle against apartheid and black liberal students, including Biko, gravitated to it. But trouble within the ranks soon flared. 'In the NUSAS conference of 1967 the blacks were made to stay at a church building somewhere in the Grahamstown location,' wrote Biko, 'each day being brought to the conference site by cars etc. On the other hand their white "Brothers" were staying in residence around the conference site. This is perhaps the turning point in the history of black support for NUSAS. So appalling were the conditions that it showed the blacks just how valued they were in the organisation.'

The honeymoon was over. 'Basically the South African white community is a homogenous community,' wrote Biko in 'Black Souls in White Skins'. 'It is a community of people who sit to enjoy a privileged position that they do not deserve, are aware of this, and therefore spend their time trying to justify why they are doing so. We are concerned with that curious bunch of nonconformists who explain their participation in negative terms: that bunch of do-gooders that goes under all sorts of names – liberals, leftists, etc. These are the people who argue that they are not responsible for white racism and the country's "Inhumanity to the black man". These are the people who claim that they too feel the oppression just as acutely as the blacks and therefore should be jointly involved in the black man's struggle for a place under the sun. In short, these are the people who say that they have black souls wrapped up in white skins.

'The role of the white liberal in the black man's history in South Africa is a curious one. Very few black organisations were not under white direction. True to their image, the white liberals always knew what was good for the blacks and told them so. The wonder of it all is that the black people have believed in them for so long.'

'South African black nationalists took the line that the moment to distrust the white man most was when he stretched out his hand in friendship,' added Jordan Ngubane in *An African Explains Apartheid*. 'They agreed that they could collaborate with him on specific issues, but they would not identify themselves with him. They feared that he would either betray them to his government or would be unwilling to bear the suffering that had always been part and parcel of the African's fight against white supremacy.'

Black liberals broke away from NUSAS in an acrimonious split and launched the BC-inspired South African Students' Organisation (SASO) at the University of the North in July 1969. In 1972 this organisation, together with black religious and education leaders, formed the Black People's Convention (BPC) – the political arm of BC, with Biko as its spokesman.

'We have in our policy manifesto defined blacks as those who are by law or tradition politically, economically and socially discriminated against as a group in the South African society and identify themselves as a unit in the struggle towards the realisation of their aspirations,' wrote Biko. 'This definition illustrates to us a number of things: Being black is not a matter of pigmentation – being black is a reflection of a mental attitude; and merely by describing yourself as black you have started on a road towards emancipation, you have committed yourself to fight against all forces that seek to use your blackness as a stamp that marks you out as a subservient being.

'From the above observation, therefore, we can see that the term black is not necessarily all inclusive, i.e. the fact that we are all *not white* does not necessarily mean that we are all *black*. Non-whites do exist and will continue to exist for quite a long time. If one's aspiration is whiteness but his pigmentation makes attainment of this impossible, then that person is a non-white. Any man who calls a white man "Baas", any man who serves in the police force or Security Branch is *ipso facto* a non-white. Black people – real black people – are those who manage to hold their heads high in defiance rather than willingly surrender their souls to the white man.

'Briefly defined therefore, BC is in essence the realisation by the black man of the need to rally together with his brothers around the cause of their oppression – the blackness of their skin – and to operate as a group in order to rid themselves of the shackles that bind them to perpetual servitude. It seeks to demonstrate the lie that black is an aberration from the "normal" which is white. It is a manifestation of a new realisation that by seeking to run away from themselves and to emulate the white man, blacks are insulting the intelligence of whoever created them black. BC therefore, takes cognisance of the deliberateness of God's plan in creating black people black. It seeks to infuse the black community with a new-found pride in themselves, their efforts, their value system, their culture, their religion and their outlook on life.'

'My contact with whites was always the kind of contact where I saw myself as inferior,' said student leader Seth Mazubuko. 'This white was a boss, no matter how young or old he was. My grandmother was called a "girl" by her employers. The sight of a white person in the township used to scare me a great deal and I used to ask myself why was I so scared? The concept of BC like "Be Black and Proud", "close ranks and fight", "Black man, you're on your own", built something in all of us. It was able to say to us, "Stand up, Resist!" BC became a way of life. It caught up with the youth of the time. It came to cure a person who'd been in this trance of fear.'

> Brother and sister never cease
> To feel that you are Black
> Your Blackness is yourself
> It is your humanity
> Your true-self.
>
> Cease only to feel that Blackness
> Then, you start to be indifferent
> Not only to yourself but your community
> Feel Black then you know
> It's nothing to lose Brothers and Sisters.
>
> You possess nothing Brother
> You possess nothing Sister
> Death or prison you lose nothing
> Feel Black. Black. Real Blackness.
>   – Seeiso Lenkoe: 'A sense Of Persecution'

While the roots of BC lay in white liberalism, it was defined by the American Black Power movement, which had similarities to Afrikaner nationalism. 'Like Afrikaner Nationalism,' commented the *Rand Daily Mail*, 'BC was the product of a culture under siege and was characterised by exclusiveness, dogmatism and movement towards a closed system.' Biko and the proponents of BC often faced attacks from liberals and were regularly accused of also being racist – to which they responded: 'We are collectively segregated against – what can be more logical than for us to respond as a group.'

Jesse Jackson, Shirley Chisolm, Eldridge Cleaver, James Farmer, Malcolm X and the writings of Stokely Carmichael and Charles Hamilton on Black Power heavily influenced Biko. 'No *sane* black man really wants integration!' thundered Malcolm X. 'No *sane* white man really wants integration! No sane black man really believes that the white man ever will give the black man anything more than token integration. No! The honourable Elijah Muhammad teaches that for the black man in America the only solution is complete *separation* from the white man!'

'The concept of integration,' wrote Biko, 'whose virtues are often extolled in white liberal circles, are full of unquestioned assumptions that embrace white values. It is a concept long defined by whites and never examined by blacks. It is based on the assumption that all is well with the system apart from some degree of mismanagement by irrational conservatives at the top. If on the other hand, by integration you mean there shall be free participation by all members of a society, catering for a full expression of the self in a freely changing society, as determined by the will of the people, then I am with you.' For him that integrated society would be African in nature – it would have to be because of its location. 'We are aware that the white man is sitting at our table,' he wrote. 'We know that he has no right to be there; we want to remove him. Strip the table of all trappings put on by him, decorate it in true African style, settle down and then ask him to join us on our own terms if he wishes.'

SASO and the philosophy of BC made some inroads into the black adult community – particularly through their Black Community Programme, focused on literacy, adult education, health and employment designed to show solidarity with the masses. Their message of being proud to be black struck a chord, but it was also true that most of the older generation found them too radical and still firmly supported the broad-based ANC. Among the school-going youth, however, it was a different matter.

In 1968 high-school scholars established the African Students' Movement to give voice to their grievances. This body was soon exposed to SASO and the BC ideology and in 1972 it disbanded and reconstituted itself as the South African Students' Movement (SASM). To avoid harassment from the Security Branch, this group kept the flame of protest flickering through inter-school debating tournaments, church youth clubs and secret meetings held at the homes of sympathetic adults.

Two events, above all others, defined and boosted the fledgling scholar organisation. In 1973 leading SASO figures staged a walkout of black universities and many took up posts in schools as teachers, which gave them intimate contact with scholars and their leadership. The following year FRELIMO won the first democratic election in Mozambique – bringing hope that the shackles of white rule were being cast off. Pro-FRELIMO rallies were organised, at which demonstrators chanting 'Viva!' (long live) clashed with police. There was a new spirit of enthusiasm and confidence sweeping through the youth, and this was particularly passionate at Soweto schools – such as Morris Isaacson, Naledi High, Orlando High, Sekano Ntoana High and Orlando West High – that had supportive headmasters.

At the beginning of 1976, while there was widespread student and scholar disenchantment, it was generally believed that trouble – if there was to be trouble – would flare on the labour front, which was being buffeted by continued exploitation and an economy in full recession. 'Widespread black labour unrest, which could cripple South Africa's economy,' reported *The World* in April, 'is imminent unless immediate steps are taken to strike a "new deal" with black workers. Time is running out fast. And black worker power – and militancy – are on the march. These stark warnings came from leading trade unionists, politicians and economists in the wake of the disturbances at the Heinemann Electrical factory where police baton-charged 300 workers recently. The experts voiced fears that by failing to recognise and negotiate with black trade unions the South African Government – and "short sighted" employers – were creating a "highly explosive" situation which could seriously bedevil race relations and damage the economy.'

For the rest of the Sowetans, 1976 appeared little different from any other year. The roads continued to deteriorate, PUTCO raised its fares, the cost of school books increased and the housing crisis worsened. This last was highlighted by the fact that the Broederbond-controlled West Rand Administration Board (WRAB), which had taken control of Soweto from the Johannesburg City Council in the early 1970s, budgeted that year to spend 40 times more on its salaries than on providing houses.

Insidious crime continued to plague the township. 'A well known Soweto socialite and funeral parlour owner was brutally killed at the weekend when he was tied to the bed and stabbed in the chest a number of times after being found in a house with a woman,' reported Thami Mazwai in *The World*. 'Mr Andrew "Boy" Thekiso, the owner of the Ma-Afrika funeral parlour in Moletsane, was found with five stab wounds in the chest at a house in Mapetla Extension. His death has stunned Soweto's social scene and was being discussed at all "five star" shebeens over the weekend.

'According to reports, Mr Thekiso and his woman friend had arrived at the Mapetla house on Friday afternoon. At 6 pm more than eight men arrived at the house. They strapped the two people to beds by tying them with thin ropes. Mr Thekiso struggled to free himself and then untied the woman. But they could not escape as they were locked in and all windows had burglar proofing. After 15 minutes the group returned and entered the house. Thekiso struggled with the men and they again tied him to the bed. The woman was taken to another room. The men with Thekiso then stabbed him in the chest. One of the wounds pierced his heart. The men then left, leaving the woman with Mr Thekiso, who bled profusely as he died.'

'Death at the hands of thugs has become so commonplace in Soweto that its million inhabitants have come to accept it as a way of life,' commented Langa Skosana in *The World*. 'People in this crime ridden complex live in fear of attacks during the day and night even when they are locked up in their houses. Last weekend alone, 16 people were murdered, 12 women raped and 23 robberies committed. Those crimes bear testimony to the social problems experienced in black townships.

'A Johannesburg lawyer, Mr Martin Mabiletsa, put his finger on the pulse of the problem when he told a seminar of NICRO at the weekend that some of the causes of crime amongst blacks were overcrowded housing, lack of home ownership, poor educational facilities, iniquities in migratory labour and discriminatory wages. He also blamed the pass laws as being directly responsible for the escalating crime rate because they denied blacks freedom of movement to seek employment. He cited an observation by Mr Justice Hiemstra, who after visiting Soweto, criticised the painful lack of facilities there. "It is difficult to expect people living in these circumstances to have a loyalty towards themselves and their community," the judge remarked. Community leaders have shown their concern at the dramatic rise in crime. As a result, vigilante committees, popularly known as makgotla, have mushroomed in the township in a bid to help police in their battle against criminals. But the makgotla have not been effective enough because thugs often pose as members of these vigilante committees to rob and kill residents.

'Mr M Khumalo, a lecturer in African languages at the University of the Witwatersrand, said at NICRO's seminar that the problem of crime among blacks was directly and indirectly related to politics. "The black man has become so emasculated to the extent that he has become impotent, is helpless and tells you that his son has beaten him, his daughter is incorrigible and that he has no will to live. Is this not fertile ground for escalation of crime?" he asks. He concludes by saying that blacks need to share in the government or govern themselves to make laws in order to have the power and authority to enforce legislation which would serve to save them from the system under which they are forced to live.'

Irrespective of these problems, 53 per cent of readers of *The World*, in an opinion poll in February 1976, 'expressed the opinion that the leadership of South Africa was in the right hands'. If nothing else demonstrated the yawning gulf between adults and the youth, this did. 'Mr Vorster, in Parliament, responded that he did not regard this as a triumph personally,' commented *The World*, 'because a leader could not be divorced from his party or the policies of his party. Mr Vorster said he would not go so far as to say that South African blacks were living in a paradise. But their position compared favourably with that of blacks elsewhere. Mrs Suzman (Progressive Reform Party) interjected to ask: "When were you last in Soweto?" To which Mr Vorster replied: "When did you last read *The World*?"'

'In many ways, Soweto's residents enjoy, as is claimed, a far higher standard of living than most blacks in other African urban centres on the continent,' wrote Harry Henzerling in *The Scotsman*. 'But Soweto is also a symbol of South Africa's policy of apartheid, which refuses to accept mixing of races. The blacks have been relegated to Soweto, a "city" with only two cinemas, two banks and no supermarket. It is to the advantage of white businessmen that blacks should shop in Johannesburg.

'The lack of electrical power in so many of the homes is a major cause of frustration. It means no electrical appliances, no heaters in the cold winter, or lights, forcing many students to study by candlelight. A black Rhodesian journalist who recently visited Soweto gave these impressions: "I remember the first night I was driven into Soweto – a backyard of Johannesburg. Rows of monotonous, bare brick matchboxes suddenly appeared behind the mine dumps to the south-west of the city. A huge blanket of overpowering coal smoke which hangs over the township greeted us. My heart sank."

'Most of the residents of Soweto, I found, proudly carried stab marks or have been clubbed at one time or another by thugs. Between 1 July 1974 and 30 June 1975, police reported 701 murders, 12 096 cases of rape and 8 118 reports of assault. Much of this is blamed on excessive drinking. Constance Khuziwe Ntshona, a community leader and businesswoman, gives this description: "Soweto is the black city, proud, tidy, humble, poor, occasionally rich, soccer-crazy, pulsating and church-going."

'Official figures show there are at least 167 churches in the township plus an esti-mated 900 sects. "You may ask why there is so much violence," she said. "One rea-son for it is a definite reaction to a continual suffering and a crying need to say, 'take notice of us, we are people'."'

Life was brutal and ironic in Soweto, but the show went on. Afro hairstyles were the rage, as was the music of Burning Spear. The Staple Singers sang to packed hous-es and a new act, Jonathan Clegg and Sipho Mcunu, shattered the country's segre-gation laws with their Zulu folk guitar. Not so successful was the Black Mikado, which was cancelled because the Department of Community Development refused to issue it a permit to play before black audiences.

On the sporting front, Soweto golfer Vincent Tshabalala won the French Open and much was expected of him in the British Open. In boxing, the exploits of Elijah 'Tap Tap' Makhatini and Norman 'Pangaman' Sekgapane were big news, as was the international heavyweight fight between George Foreman and Joe Frazier. In soccer, the continuing saga of the shenanigans in the National Professional Soccer League made headlines, as did the 5–0 victory of South Africa's first multiracial national team over the visiting Argentine Stars XI. 'All five goals were slammed home by black play-ers,' reported *The World*, 'with no less than four coming from the boot of Jomo "Troublemaker" Sono and the fifth by Patrick "Ace" Ntsoelengoe. It was indeed a night to remember as apartheid soccer took a body blow from which it will never recover.'

4 ■ WAG THE DOG

'The broad masses of Soweto are perfectly content, perfectly happy,' *commented Manie Mulder, the chairman of the West Rand Admin-* *istration Board, in an interview with the* Rand Daily Mail *in May 1976.* *'Black–white relationships at present are as healthy as can be. There is* *no danger whatever of a blow-up in Soweto.'*

As if blacks were not already suffering enough, in 1974 the government decided to convert Broederbond thought into policy and enforce a 1955 Bantu Education ruling (not implemented before because of a lack of funds), making it compulsory for black schools in white South Africa to teach half the subjects after Grade 3 in Afrikaans and the other half in English. Until this time, black children had been taught in their mother tongue for the first three years of school and beyond that in one of the offi-cial languages – English or Afrikaans – selected by the relevant ethnic school board.

As part of the government's divide-and-rule strategy of splitting townships into trib al sectors, each zone had a school board – answerable to the Department of Bantu Education – made up of members of that community. These boards, until 1974, were mainly responsible for implementing government education policy, but had certain limited powers, the most important being the right to choose which official language was to be used as a medium of instruction after the first three years of schooling. Tswana children, for example, would initially be taught in Tswana and later in either English or Afrikaans, based on a decision made by the school board – in Soweto's case, the Tswana School Board in each Tswana-designated sector. Standards aside, blacks were generally in favour of receiving education in a second language because of the problems associated with living in a multilingual society where the obvious solution was a common language through which all could effectively communicate. The Afrikaners' gripe was that the choice was invariably English. This was, however, not the primary reason for enforcing the 50:50 rule – the straw that broke the camel's back.

It appears inexplicable that Afrikaner nationalists, born as they were out of Lord Milner's anglicisation policy, should attempt to force their language on other people – but the issue becomes clearer when one peers behind the scenes at the heart-and-soul internal battles taking place in the upper echelons of the National Party between

the *verligtes* ('enlightened') and *verkramptes* (conservatives). The issue was complicated by an intense succession struggle between the right, which championed Dr
Connie Mulder, and the 'left', which supported PW Botha.

After Verwoerd's assassination these differences became more apparent.
Externally, increased pressure was being placed on the government to abandon its
race-based policies and practices. Internally, business was beginning to feel the same
chill that had already nearly totally isolated sporting and cultural contacts between
South Africa and the rest of the world. Survival, according to the *verligtes*, required
more pragmatism and a move from Afrikaner exclusivism to policies that would
appeal to most white South Africans – thus, they favoured enough reforms to attract
English-speakers. The right, however, felt that the dilution of Afrikaner nationalism
and any move from grand apartheid spelt doom. It was all or nothing, and these arch-
conservatives opposed every attempt to change, even going so far as pushing for the
removal of English as an official language.

The first major battle during Vorster's era was with Barry Hertzog's fiery son,
Albert, who had been Minister of Posts and Telegraphs since 1958. This culminated
in Hertzog's dismissal from the Cabinet in 1968 and his expulsion from the party in
1969. (The SABC had fallen under Hertzog's portfolio and he had resisted the introduction of television to South Africa, believing it the instrument of the devil and a
serious threat to the purity of Afrikaans. With his departure the way was cleared
for the introduction of television in January 1976.) It was expected that some 40
National Party members of Parliament, including Dr Andries Treurnicht – a leading
Broederbond member – would follow Hertzog into his Herstigte Nasionale Party.

A split in the party was averted by Broederbond appeals for unity. While this
patched up the differences, it perpetuated the paralysis in the party caused by the
pull of opposing forces. As part of the payoff, the Broederbond undertook to pay
increased attention to the question of the primacy of the Afrikaans language and
began to formulate strategies in this regard – paying particular attention to the tendency of blacks to prefer English as a second language. In September 1968 it distributed a secret circular to members titled 'Afrikaans as a Second Language for the
Bantu'. 'Two years ago in our monthly circular we drew the attention of members to
the importance of using Afrikaans to Bantu,' it stated. 'That idea created widespread
interest and as a result most right-thinking Afrikaans-speakers today concentrate on
addressing Bantu in Afrikaans whenever they meet them.'

There was no hint that the Broederbond wished to create hordes of black

Afrikaners or even endear the language to them. 'He can be our cultural servant as well as our farm servant,' said one Afrikaner, reflecting on the thinking behind the issue. The position of blacks in the economy required that they speak at least one of the two official languages so that they could understand instructions. Blacks preferred English because it was a universal language, much to the chagrin of Afrikaners who believed that their language should be favoured because it was also an African language. Moreover, most of the whites with whom blacks came into direct daily contact were white Afrikaners: 'the police, with whom the Bantu make a lot of contact, are almost all Afrikaans speaking,' noted the circular.

The Broederbond thus became obsessed with 'establishing Afrikaans as the predominant second language, after the mother tongue, among as many Bantu as possible', and black schools were the most obvious starting point – especially considering that the Department of Bantu Education was riddled with members willing to cooperate in implementing this policy. The realisation of this plan was designed to coincide with the introduction of television to allay the fears of those still deeply fearful of the effect it would have on Afrikaans.

In 1972 Treurnicht, now the leader of the arch-conservative faction within the National Party, became chairman of the Broederbond. From that time, Punt Janson, the Deputy Minister of Bantu Education (which fell under MC Botha's portfolio of Bantu Administration and Education), began to receive a flood of instructions from the person who was effectively the power behind the throne.

In 1974 policy guidelines were issued by the Department of Bantu Education enforcing the 50:50 rule from 1975 for black children up to Grade 7, to be naturally extended to Grade 8 in 1976, and so on. In response, WC Ackerman, the Southern Transvaal regional director of Bantu Education, under whom Soweto fell, immediately issued a peremptory circular headed 'Uniform Approach in Schools', which made it obligatory for science and practical subjects to be taught in English and mathematics, arithmetic and social studies (history and geography) in Afrikaans. The only deviation that would be considered was if individual teachers made applications to the circuit inspector to teach the subject in the vernacular because they experienced difficulty with the set language. While the issue of having Afrikaans 'pushed down our throats' caused deep anger in 1975 among pupils, teachers, parents and school boards, it only became a crisis in 1976 when it entered the high schools and became a rallying point for student leaders – most of whom were in higher grades and would never be affected by it.

'We have a situation where once again the whites are deciding arbitrarily what is best for a black man – even in the matter of how his children should be taught,' commented *The World*.

'No,' responded Punt Janson, 'I will not consult the African people on the language issue. An African might find that "the big boss" only spoke Afrikaans or only spoke English. It would be to his advantage to know both languages.' Other officials explained that, because these facilities were in white areas, whites had the right to choose the language of instruction. Finally, blacks were insensitively told that if they did not like it they could remove their children from school, as education for blacks was not compulsory. But blacks were having none of it.

'You only need to look at school results to appreciate that for black children the killer subject is Afrikaans,' commented one outraged teacher. 'And the principals can tell you what a sweat it is to get teachers willing to offer Afrikaans, let alone being capable and qualified to teach it.'

'The kids were mad about this thing,' added Dr Nthato Motlana, a Soweto community leader. 'They would tell me what it was like to be taught by a black teacher who did not know Afrikaans himself.'

'By what right do the powers that be take it upon themselves to ordain that black children shall be educated in their mother tongue in primary school, and shall be obliged at a later stage to cope with the demands of higher education and to study difficult matric subjects in both official languages, neither of which is their mother tongue?' demanded Joyce Harris of the Black Sash. 'Black children already have sufficient obstacles to overcome and there can be no justification for compounding that handicap by insisting that they, and only they, be obliged to study in three languages. White children are educated in their mother tongue, and the second language is taught separately as a subject. Black children must write their examinations in English and Afrikaans. Parents have indicated that they take the strongest exception to this ruling.'

'The National Party has, over the years and ever since they came into power, strongly opposed dual medium instruction in white schools,' wrote Dr EG Malherbe, former principal of the University of Natal, in an article in the *Pretoria News*. 'Their objection was particularly against Afrikaans-speaking children receiving instruction in some high school subjects through the medium of the English language – "The language of the conqueror". They frequently used the slogan: "The language of the conqueror in the mouth of the conquered is the language of slaves." Ironically, the same slogan was used when referring to Afrikaans by Soweto pupils in an essay competition. Their expression of aversion to Afrikaans was because of its association with an oppressive and discriminatory authority. The Soweto pupils were predominantly English-speaking and so were their teachers. Nearly all who taught high-school classes had had their training in English-medium institutions (Afrikaans institutions refused to have them).

'The English-speaking children of Soweto had to learn Afrikaans as a subject. That was difficult enough – but it was pedagogically stupid and politically insensitive to have inflicted upon them Afrikaans as a medium of instruction. In doing so, the government was arrogantly forgetful of South African history of 30 and 40 years ago. At that time the Broederbond had no scruples about calling for a general strike by Afrikaans pupils and students against the use of English as a supplementary medium at high school level. Ironically, it was Mr MC Botha who called for the strike in a memorandum dated 11 October 1943. "It is sacrificing Afrikanerdom on the altar of British–Jewish imperialism," it read. "Afrikanerdom has suffered enough under the British yoke and the introduction of the second language as a medium in certain subjects is just a part of the old Milner policy that wanted to Anglicise and de-nationalise the Afrikaner."

'The strike, however, did not materialise as the plan was exposed before it got under way. Nevertheless the Broederbond was so strong that ultimately when the National Party came into power, dual medium as well as parental choice of medium was abolished and, wherever possible, children were segregated into separate single-medium schools. In this way it was felt that Afrikaans children could be better indoctrinated and, being in the majority, the Afrikaners would ultimately rule South Africa.'

School boards reacted by forming the Federated School Boards to petition government to change the policy. At a meeting with the secretary for Bantu Education in January 1975 it was suggested that those who felt they could not implement the policy should apply for exception. However, in response to the flood of applications from Soweto, 17 requests were refused and the rest ignored. During the same month the African Teachers' Association of South Africa sent a memorandum to Vorster asking that schools continue to be allowed to choose a single language of instruction.

'The memorandum made it clear the choice of English was not motivated by an anti-Afrikaans bias and went out of its way to emphasise it believed Afrikaans should be taught as a subject.' explained Leslie Xinwa in *The World*. 'It stated that ideally pupils should be taught through the medium of their mother tongue right up to matric, as was the case in white schools, but accepted that for various reasons, black pupils should be instructed through a European language from standard two. "Once a European language has been selected, it is completely unnecessary – indeed it may even be gratuitously unjust – to compel the use of yet another foreign language as a medium and in that way double the burden," the memorandum said.'

Vorster forwarded the memorandum to the Department of Bantu Education, which chose to reject the request and issued two circulars on the same day. The first stated that the policy would not be reversed and the second warned school boards that they had no right to decide the medium of instruction, only to follow orders. All further attempts to discuss the matter with officials were refused. The association then sent a representative to South African embassies abroad to impress on them that trouble was brewing – also to no avail.

The 1976 school year for blacks in Soweto, as expected, opened to chaos. Some teachers tried to translate history, geography and mathematics textbooks from English into Afrikaans, and students had not the slightest idea what they were trying to say. Others showed solidarity with scholars by refusing to teach in Afrikaans, even though examinations were to be in Afrikaans and questions would have to be answered in that language. To make matters worse, Janson was cynically replaced by Treurnicht in a Cabinet reshuffle – and it is not difficult to appreciate the intentions of the Broederbond in engineering this move. The hard-headed Treurnicht quickly made his intentions clear.

'Dr Treurnicht said that in the white area of South Africa, where the government provided the buildings, gave the subsidies and paid the teachers, it was "surely our right to determine the language dispensation",' reported *The World*. 'This was in schools where there was no compulsory education. "Why are pupils sent to schools if they do not like the language dispensation?" he asked.'

'Who said Lord Milner was dead?' quipped Andrew Pyper, the opposition education spokesperson. 'He is alive and well and at the helm of Bantu Education. As an Afrikaner, Dr Treurnicht should be ashamed of himself. His attitude – that we built the schools, we know what's best for you and if you don't like it you can stay at home – is a disgrace. A more irresponsible attitude is hardly conceivable. Just as Lord Milner did untold harm to the English, Dr Treurnicht, a present day Lord Milner, hangs like an albatross around the neck of the Afrikaner. I as an Afrikaner object most strongly.'

On 20 January the Meadowlands Tswana School Board met at the Moruto-Thuto

Lower Primary School, where they were addressed by the circuit inspector, Thys de Beer. The inspector, in response to a question regarding how black taxes were utilised, informed the board that all direct taxes paid by blacks were repatriated to the homelands for education purposes there. 'In the urban areas the education of a black child is being paid for by the white population and therefore the secretary for Bantu Education has the responsibility towards satisfying these white people,' he told the incredulous gathering. De Beer did not stop there: he continued to trot out the normal response that school boards could not make decisions on the medium of instruction and if they wished they could apply individually for relief. The inspector then left the meeting, and the board, in angry defiance, accepted a proposal by K Nkamela, seconded by SG Thwane, that only English be used as a method of instruction in secondary schools in Meadowlands.

Ackerman reacted to this challenge by dismissing two board members, Joseph Peele and Abner Letlape, and the rest resigned in protest. 'Parents are threatening to remove 14 000 children from school in support of the protest resignation by the Meadowlands Tswana School Board,' reported Nat Serache in the *Rand Daily Mail* as the matter escalated. 'There is talk that Tswana school boards in other parts of Soweto may also take action – so far unspecified – in support of the Meadowlands board.'

When Serachi first contacted Ackerman for comment he was referred to Dr AB Fourie, the department's director of control, who referred him back to Ackerman. Ackerman, when the reporter phoned again, at first refused to speak to him – then, in frustration, enquired 'Are you a Tswana?' before hanging up.

In an attempt to resolve the matter at the beginning of March, the Chief Minister of the Bophuthatswana homeland, Chief Lucas Mangope, appealed to Vorster, who indicated that permission would be granted for Tswana schools to teach in the language of their choice if they applied to the Department of Bantu Education. The department, however, refused to back down unless the Meadowlands Tswana School Board rescinded its decision to instruct school principals to teach only in English. 'Here we are already in March and I'm utterly confused about what to do,' said one exasperated principal when asked about the stalemate. Even the National Party-supporting *Beeld* newspaper called for a return to sense, also to no avail.

In other parts of Soweto, rows were brewing. At Thomas Mofolo Secondary School in Naledi, the principal had fired Ribbon Moshodi for refusing to teach in Afrikaans, and schools under the jurisdiction of the Mashangaan School Board dismissed three principals for their stand against Afrikaans. 'About 1 000 pupils at two schools in Soweto under the Mashangaan School Board went on strike yesterday in protest against the sacking of their headmaster,' reported Nat Diseko on 9 April in the *Rand Daily Mail*. 'The sacked headmasters are Mr GJ Nkuzana of Tiyani Higher Primary School in Diepkloof and Mr Edward Sono of Mawila Higher Primary in Meadowlands. No reasons have been given to them for their dismissals. Yesterday, pupils milled around the school premises and most played games. Teachers were idle. There were no lessons going on.

'On Wednesday, pupils at Ngungunyane Higher Primary School in Chiawelo, went on strike and demanded the reinstatement of their headmaster, Mr A Tlakula. Ngungunyane is also under the Mashangaan School Board. There were unruly scenes as Mr B Mdaka, chairman of the board, addressed the pupils who had locked the school gates preventing him from leaving the school yard until he had reinstated Mr Tlakula. "We want our Tlakula back," read one placard. Yesterday, things were back to normal at the school following the reinstatement of Mr Tlakula.'

When Mdaka addressed scholars at Mawila Higher Primary on 12 April he was hit on the head with a half brick, and the tyres of his kombi were deflated. Police were eventually called in to quell the near riot as Mdaka was again forced to yield and reinstate the principal.

Most of the protest until April was adult led. That, however, changed in May as mid-year exams – half of which were to be written in Afrikaans – loomed and scholars began to agitate more vociferously for change. Those who wish to relegate or dismiss the importance of the Soweto Uprising often point to the fact that it was confined to students and school issues – not the broader struggle for liberation. This is nonsense, conveniently ignoring the fact that the students who fuelled the growing crisis were not, and never would be, affected by the Afrikaans ruling. What they were influenced by were calls by BC leaders to blacks to stand up and cast off their oppression and by the challenge thrown out by Winnie Mandela for student leaders to pick up the language issue as a rallying point.

Student concerns were thus broader and more radical than those of adults. And as they became enmeshed, so they took the struggle away from their moderate, despondent parents. 'Our parents are prepared to suffer under the White man's rule,' wrote a student in a letter to *The World*. 'They have been living for years under these laws and they have become immune to them. But we strongly refuse to swallow an education that is designed to make us slaves in the country of our birth.'

The point of no return was reached soon after students became involved. 'Students threatened to beat up their headmasters and threw textbooks out of class-room windows in a demonstration against being taught some subjects in Afrikaans,' reported Willie Bokala in *The World* on 18 May. 'The 600 students at Phefeni Junior Secondary School in Orlando West, then went on strike and refused to attend any classes. In a violent display of pupil power yesterday, the pupils also demanded the reinstatement of Mr Mahlangu, chairman of the school board, whom they claimed had been sacked because he was against using Afrikaans for teaching.'

'The strikes by some Soweto students over the use of Afrikaans as a medium of instruction are growing to alarming proportions,' commented *The World* a few days later in response to other schools striking in solidarity with Phefeni. 'While we do not dismiss the claims of the students that they are being frustrated by the insistence on Afrikaans we do believe it is the duty of the parents to protest against this move rather than the students, who should get on with their studies. There have been accusations and counter-accusations while the strike has been going on. Tape recorders were seized by students because of feelings that a vice-principal was an "informer". That vice-principal himself has accused a teacher of inciting the kids into seizing the recorder. And all the time, students are wasting valuable time.

'The students point out that they have expressed the desire to use English as the medium of instruction, and nothing has been done. This, they claim, is why "Pupil Power" took over. Is this not, perhaps, a reflection on school boards, committees, and parent associations? Surely the parents who pay hard-earned money to keep the kids at school, must have a strong voice in determining the future of their children but all these bodies are toothless.'

'Have you ever heard of 13-year-old children striking?' snorted circuit inspector De Beer. 'The public do not realise that there are many who want to spread unrest in South Africa. I don't know who is behind the strike – but it is not the children.'

The question of whether the students acted on their own or were under the control of those De Beer claimed wanted 'to spread unrest in South Africa', has long been an issue of debate – particularly now that it is fashionable to claim ownership of this iconic event. Rebellious young students, especially highly politicised ones such as those in Soweto, can generally be relied upon to be anarchic – something tempering any analysis of outside influence.

Most proprietary claims to the Soweto Uprising are so fanciful they can be dismissed. SASO and the BPC probably have the strongest case, but they always played down their role – saying only that they had expressed their moral support for the students' actions. But they were closest to the South African Students' Movement (SASM) in spirit, and continually urged the striking scholars to fight the Bantu Education system. The scholar leadership also needed vast amounts of funding in the build-up to the uprising and during its course, and most of this originated from church groups and was channelled through the BC movements.

The most controversial claimant is the ANC, which recently 'revealed' that the exiled leadership had actively participated in the planning and execution of the event. All evidence suggests the opposite. Joe Nzingo Gqabi, an underground ANC member at the time, was issued instructions by the exiled leadership to 'normalise' the situation, and Motlana – an old ANC supporter – received a message to persuade the scholars to call off their actions as they did not fit in with broad ANC plans. In fact, the ANC was particularly worried about being upstaged by the proponents of Black Consciousness and again felt the threat of marginalisation. However, there is one ANC figure, more than any other non-scholar participant, who was part of the planning and never far from the action – Winnie Mandela. And while it is impossible to assess her precise involvement, it was substantial. Therefore, it is true that while the ANC-in-exile's claims are extravagant, members of the internal underground wing played a crucial role. It is also correct that in the escalating crisis the students aligned themselves with individuals whom they believed felt as they did, rather than with broad organisations.

'The Soweto strike against tuition in Afrikaans has now spread,' reported Rosemary Northcott in the *Sunday Express* at the end of May. 'With the half-year examinations due in two weeks, almost 2 000 children are now striking. A serious element of violence has crept into the impasse and teachers and principals fear the situation can get worse. Already this week, Mrs Karabo Tshabalala, an Afrikaans teacher at the Pimville Higher Primary School, was stabbed in the back with a screwdriver – and when police tried to arrest the culprit, a pupil, they were stoned by his friends.'

De Beer took a hard-line stance. He decreed that children absent from school would be expelled and their schools closed. 'If you want to learn English, then go to England,' he declared. 'The voters have ordered that you must learn this way.' At first he refused to address the students, who had declared him Public Enemy Number One. Then he made an appearance at Phefeni where he again threatened scholars with expulsion. On that visit he noted that the school still had no textbooks for the subjects to be taken in Afrikaans. Two days later, books arrived, only to be torn up and 'barbecued' by the students.

At the end of May the South African Institute of Race Relations (SAIRR) sent an urgent telegram to member of Parliament René de Villiers asking him to approach Treurnicht about the volatile situation. Treurnicht informed De Villiers that the problem was not serious, but that he would enquire into the cause of the strike.

'Detectives were stoned and their car overturned and burnt yesterday in a riot at a Soweto school,' reported Nomsa Msibi in *The World* on 9 June. 'The riot – which ended only after police using teargas dispersed the students – started at Naledi High School in Soweto when two detectives tried to arrest a student, Enos Ngutshana. Another student said later: "Two detectives came to the school during the lunch hour. They parked their unmarked car in the yard and then arrested a young student – we don't know why. As they were walking back to their car students started to stone them. They let go of the boy they had arrested and fled to the principal's office, where they locked themselves in. Then the students went across the yard and overturned their car before setting it on fire. A little later three more policemen arrived with dogs, but they were also driven away with stones. The students only dispersed after more policemen arrived and used teargas on them."'

'In another incident,' reported the *Rand Daily Mail* on the same day, '15 boys from Thulasizwe Higher Primary School, also of Soweto, were taken to Orlando Police Station yesterday for questioning after allegedly disrupting classes at the school. The boys were apparently unhappy when other pupils decided to end the strike over the use of Afrikaans as a medium of instruction for mathematics and social studies.'

The strike, even if some students wanted to return to classes, had majority support. 'Every morning all the pupils turn up and after assembly they refuse to go into class and hold their own meetings from which we are banned,' said one teacher.

'The issue has become, in a way, a symbol of resistance among the youth to white oppression and white authority,' commented educationalist B Ngakane in the *Sunday Tribune*. 'The children have learned that they can defy their principal, they can defy the school board, they can defy the inspectors – and they have in the process learned the lesson of solidarity. Their solidarity has succeeded in sharpening their hatred of the white man and white authority. It has been a political lesson to them. The children show no sign of breaking and there is the danger that the strike will spread. The children, aged between 13 and 18, have the sympathy of their parents and teachers, although not active encouragement. The pupils don't trust their parents on this. They think they'll send them back to school before they've won their point. Order in the schools should be maintained without the interference of the police. They are just hardening attitudes. The situation is potentially explosive.'

Inspired by the action against the police at Naledi, the students at Morris Isaacson High School hung a notice on their gate warning: 'No Special Branch allowed. Enter at risk of your skin.' And SASM called a secret scholar meeting for Sunday, 13 June.

It was obvious that matters were spinning out of control. Again the SAIRR sent De Villiers a telegram: 'Situation Soweto schools over Afrikaans as medium apparently deteriorating daily. Violence has already occurred and can easily be repeated. Sincerely trust Dr Treurnicht fully informed on matters.' Clearly he was not, or he chose not to be, because he informed De Villiers that the matter was only serious enough to be dealt with at a lower level. The following day his boss, MC Botha, told Parliament five more schools had been refused permission to deviate from the language-medium requirement. Both Botha and Treurnicht appear to have been blind to the rising anger, relying instead on department reports that downplayed the matter.

On the same day, the Meadowlands Tswana School Board were finalising summonses to be sent to Ackerman the following week regarding the issue of Afrikaans and demanding their reinstatement. Over the weekend, the Soweto Urban Bantu Council called an urgent meeting to discuss the issue – and even this puppet organisation issued a dire warning to the government. 'Councillor Leonard Mosala warned that enforcing Afrikaans in schools might result in another Sharpeville shooting incident if the matter is not dealt with immediately,' reported Willie Bokala in *The World*. 'Mosala said Soweto was heading for "very ugly scenes that will come through our children, who are tired of being made to accept what they don't like".'

At the student meeting that Sunday, some 400 students arrived at the Donaldson Community Centre and proposed that an Action Committee be formed under the leadership of 19-year-old Morris Isaacson student leader Tsietsi Donald Mashinini and Phefeni leader Seth Mazibuko. Mashinini proposed a mass demonstration against Afrikaans for Wednesday and the suggestion was greeted with wild cheering.

'Mashinini is the second eldest of the 13 children of a Johannesburg chauffeur, Mr Joe "Sonny Boy" Mashinini,' wrote Martin Schneider in the *Sunday Express*. 'Tsietsi means "danger" in Sotho. But friends, relatives and acquaintances say that Mashinini is a non-violent man. Tsietsi can also mean a "riddle" or a "puzzle". And if ever there was a young man who is an enigma in South African society, then it must be Tsietsi Mashinini.

'He seems to have made a particular impression on fellow pupils and teachers as an avid drama student with considerable acting flair. One of his teachers at Morris Isaacson High School, Mrs Bernadette Mosala, recalls his portrayal of Cassius in a school production of Julius Caesar in 1973. "He had real potential in the theatre," she said. "After I stopped teaching and opened a community centre in Soweto, he often came to me for assistance with his own productions." Mrs Mosala says Mashinini had high aims for himself and would refuse to play second fiddle. "He is a very attractive, handsome young boy. I know the girls loved him and he was very confident with them."'

In 1975 he joined a local branch of SASM and his charisma soon ensured his election as regional president. Abraham Tiro, a SASO and BPC leader, was briefly one of his teachers and Mashinini borrowed many books on Black Consciousness from his mentor, even though he preferred reading Alastair MacLean and Enid Blyton. He was a stylish dresser, preferring the American hippie fashions to the Afro-American style that was so popular.

The thinking behind the proposal for a march was to parade as a large group to place pressure on the authorities to introduce changes. One of the great myths of the Soweto Uprising is that this meeting and the planned march were a secret that was kept faithfully until that Wednesday. "What was interesting about 13 June,' remarked Sibongile Mkhabela, 'was that students had a pact that parents should not be involved. Given the multitudes of students who were there, it was actually surprising that we all went home and kept quiet.'

This was not so. Lekgua Mathabathe, the headmaster of Morris Isaacson, disclosed on Monday, 14 June, that scholars intended holding a protest march on the Wednesday. Aubrey Mokoena, a BPC leader, was with Mashinini, Naledi High School leader and SASM executive member Tebello Motapanya, and other student representatives at Winnie Mandela's house on 15 June discussing what action police might take against the marchers. 'Motapanya said that the police may use dogs, teargas and rubber bullets to disperse the crowds,' said Mokoena in an affidavit. 'Mandela said that students must use stones – the African bomb – to defend themselves. This was her instruction. Mashinini went on to state that the march would start in Naledi for all those schools in that area and that Naledi High School would lead them from that point of departure. That column of the march would then come down to Morris Isaacson, collecting all the students on the way. The schools in the Meadowland area would come alone and join up with the column at Phefeni School. They would then proceed as a main column to Orlando Stadium, which was going to be their destination. He said that schools in the Orlando East complex would culminate with the others at Orlando Stadium. Mandela praised the students and said they were brave and courageous.'

Murphy Morobe, a student leader who was also at the meeting, claimed that Winnie Mandela urged them to fight the police and target government buildings and white property such as delivery vans and PUTCO buses. Aaron Matlhare, a community leader, insisted he had noticed Mashinini, Morobe, Mokoena and Motapanya on numerous occasions prior to the meeting of 13 June and after. 'After work, on Tuesday, 15 June 1976,' declared Matlhare, 'I passed Winnie Mandela's house and I saw Aubrey Mokoena's van parked outside with another car. I paid no further attention to it and drove on home. At about 2:30 am that night I was called out to a patient. As I later drove back home I passed Winnie Mandela's house. I noticed people coming out of her gate. I switched my bright lights on and saw Mokoena and Tsietsi Mashinini very clearly in my lights. They were in the company of Winnie Mandela. There were also a few others whom I did not see clearly. A few minutes after I arrived home I received a phone call from Mandela, asking me to send her some tablets which I refused to do.'

Kenneth Hlaku Rachidi, a BC leader, and probably also Biko were informed of the plans in King William's Town by Rodney Rammekoa, a SASM leader, who drove from the meeting on Sunday and returned to Johannesburg that Tuesday. The student leaders also contacted members of the press – an organisation notorious for infiltrators – and invited them to cover the event.

On 15 June a meeting was held at Naledi High School where particulars of the march were given to student leaders, who were also instructed to ensure placards were brought. Following this meeting, a source, at 4 pm, informed Major Viljoen at Jabulani Police Station of the student plans. At the same time, a black policeman relayed the same information to Colonel Kleingeld at Orlando Police Station. Kleingeld again received information about the march later that night.

So much for secrecy.

The reason this myth of secrecy continues to receive currency is because it suits all sides. It adds a romantic air to the students' endeavours while emphasising their solidarity. For the police, it was important to cover up their gross incompetence in not acting on information presented to them.

The die was thus cast for the event that would set off a chain reaction to eventual liberation.

PART II

THE GREEN CAR

5 ■ THE YOUNG LIONS

White man! Call yourself a hate
teacher
You! Have invented the hate
Call yourself a racist
You have invented racialism

Whitey! You an imperialist
You come from doom
And you'll end in hell

Why not call yourself a Murderer
How many Africans did you kill?
Since your white supremacy
You're war-mongers
extremists and opportunists
your Afrikanerdom
Vorsterism
Krugerism
is doomed

The black community
has banned you
from their motherland
Including Africa as a whole

Whitey! You an imperialist
You come from doom
And you'll end in hell
- ANON: 'HATRED HATRED'

At 7 am on the frosty morning of Wednesday, 16 June 1976, the last commuters, the steam of their breath like cotton against the grey smog and gloom of the winter's morning, hurried to catch the taxis, buses and trains that would deliver them to their places of labour in Johannesburg. When they returned that evening their world would be changed forever.

Before most reached their destination, the bell for morning assembly would be ringing at schools throughout the township. But the scholars did not gather as usual; they assembled in school grounds to sing *Nkosi Sikelel' iAfrika* and protest songs. After this they chanted '*Amandla!*' (Power!) and unfurled banners and placards that read 'Afrikaans means confine to South Africa', 'Away with Afrikaans', 'Afrikaans the most dangerous drug', 'The Department Of Bantu Education is formed of ignorant fools', and 'It happened in Angola. Why not here?'

Tsietsi Mashinini enthusiastically led the singing at Morris Isaacson, while at Naledi High, Tebello Motapanya addressed the students and outlined the route they were to follow to Orlando Stadium. The vice-principal tried to address the scholars, but was driven away. The headmaster at Orlando West High School, Mashumi Mzanduma, having heard that the marchers were to congregate at his school and fearing they were planning to coax away his students, who were in the midst of writing exams, telephoned the Orlando Police Station. Colonel Kleingeld, in response, ordered all available policemen to be on standby and sent a black sergeant to investigate. He returned at 7:45 am and notified the commanding officer that scholars were marching from north to south along Xorile Street. Five minutes later, Brigadier SW le Roux, the divisional commissioner for Soweto, instructed six station commanders to send out patrols.

Motapanya, flanked by knobkerrie-wielding scholars, led the swelling Naledi High column down Mphatlalatsane Street and over the stream that separates Naledi from Tladi. Then the procession snaked across the veld and eastwards into Ligwale Street, where three police cars waited to escort the marchers. The cars turned left at a T-junction and the protesters lost them by turning right into Zola Street towards Moletsane. The scholars by this time were becoming emboldened and were forcing motorists to give the Black Power salute or have their cars struck with open hands until they did. In another part of Soweto, DD Smit, an inspector of schools, was attacked by a group of students in Maputu Street and narrowly avoided serious injury by fleeing into the nearby Jabulani Police Station. It was 8:10 am and reports were flooding in of police vehicles being stoned in various parts of the township. At the same time crowds were pouring on to the streets – attracted by the songs, chants and the excitement that permeated the air.

'Are you going to kill our children?' asked a woman bystander of a police sergeant who strode by.

'No,' replied the policeman. 'There'll be no shooting. The children are not fighting anybody, they are only demonstrating.'

Meanwhile, Motapanya's marchers had passed Malopo Junior Secondary School, where they collected that school's marchers, and gone through Jabavu towards Nancefield Station, where they would swing towards Vilakazi Street and Phefeni Junior Secondary School, where all the other marchers were congregating. Also converging on Phefeni was Mashinini's growing column, which had passed Sizwe Stores and schools along the route. It was now 8:30 am and vehicles were being overturned and some set alight.

When groups converged on Phefeni they were wildly cheered and welcomed by a throng that would grow to 15 000 students. 'I couldn't get over their size,' wrote journalist Lucy Gough Burger in *The Star*. 'The boys bulked out of their school clothes, the girls, legs like sturdy tree trunks beneath their gyms, squarely stood their ground. It was pupil power in the most terrifying sense of the word.

'Approaching Orlando West by car with the aim of reaching Phefeni Junior Secondary School which had been the focus of pupil power for a month, from far off we could see striking school children bunched together on open ground. Then like disturbed ants they activated, running in all directions from what turned out to be police. A policeman stood with a Sten-gun cradled and a van full of dogs next to him.

'Approaching Phefeni School by a back route we parked at a crossroads crowded with pupils, girls and boys, armed with "kerries" (knobkerries). A teacher from the school came up to us: "Get that car out of here – they're coming!" he urged.

'On the brow of the hill, in a great dusty whirlwind, a phalanx of chanting high school kids surged down the road in thousands. Below us, pupils from Phefeni began running to meet them. "Hurry!" cried the teacher.

'Timothy, the *Star* driver, turned into the deserted long drive of Orlando West High School. The river of placard and stick-waving pupils outside the school's mesh fence converged like two rivers of protest in an emotional embrace. That was the moment they saw me snapping away from behind a tree. With my camera behind my back, it was the longest walk back to a car I have ever experienced. I pushed the camera in through the car window just as the mob reached us. A black youth of about 15 years of age with a 2 metre long saw blade, thrust his face close to mine. Another pinioned me against the car.

'"What do you want?" they screamed. I mouthed something, but nobody heard. All about were menacing clenched fists and shouts of "Black Power".

'"Get off the ground now," roared a youth waving a whopping big stick. "This is black property. Get out!"

'"Get out white woman," they chanted.

'It was driver Timothy – cool, wise Timothy! – whose words in that split second while the mob hesitated, saved me. "Leave her alone. She is from a newspaper. She is not from the Department of Bantu Education," he pleaded.

'"All right Daddy, take your car and get her out of here!" The youth with the saw blade cleared the way like a cop while the pupils fell back a few centimetres and continued thumping on the windows of the hemmed in car. At the gate, the escort ceased.' It was 9:15 am.

Not far from there, about an hour later, 'Tiny' Peterson was searching for her younger brother, Hector. 'He was a shy child, but funny and full of tricks,' she told Clare O'Donoghue in an interview in *Marie Claire* magazine. 'We called him "Chopper" because of his square haircut. He loved karate and was always asking for a few rands to go to bioscope. He had a naughty streak – he'd ride trains without a ticket – and would giggle when he got into trouble. Most of the time, he liked to play alone. Even though I was the eldest and he was the youngest, we were very close.

'At assembly, the students were already singing protest songs. Through the window, I saw a large crowd walking down from Morris Isaacson. Their faces were very serious, and they wanted us to join the march. I thought it would be fun – we were going to express ourselves. And because there were so many of us I thought we'd be okay.

'More kids joined. When the police cars arrived we never expected anything bad. But at Orlando, the police had guns. They told us to disperse, threw teargas and let the dogs loose. There was utter confusion, and we ran to hide. I remember thinking: "What's going on?" When I got teargas in my eyes, my friend Maggie pulled me into the shrubbery of a nearby house. The police were on the opposite corner.

'Minutes later, some students came out. Maggie said, "Look who's coming." I turned and saw Hector walking towards me down the street. He saw me and I called, "Hey, what are you doing here?" He just put his head on his shoulder and smiled. I told him to stay at my side.' Hector, however, joined several thousand scholars led by Hastings Ndlovu on a rocky knoll. Facing them were Colonel Kleingeld and a patrol consisting of 48 policemen (40 of whom were black), with four police cars, three anti-riot Hippo vehicles and two vans carrying dogs.

Sections 7 and 8 of the Riotous Assemblies Act of 1956 laid down clear guidelines for police to follow in dispersing gatherings – the commander of the police squad was first required to order the group to disperse in a specified time, and, if that failed, to use force proportional to the circumstances. As far as firearms and weapons were concerned, less dangerous weapons had to be used before proceeding to those likely to cause serious injury or death. The intention was clear: deadly force was to be used only as a last resort.

Kleingeld had been informed of the march twice the previous day, yet had no loudhailer with him, even though it was generally accepted that being able to communicate with large groups – in particular, being prepared to listen and promising that grievances would be conveyed to the relevant authorities – was probably all that was necessary. The colonel was thus reduced to waving his hands and shouting at the top of his voice: 'Get away from here. I'm giving you three minutes to disperse!' If anyone was able to hear him, they did not respond. He then ordered teargas to be fired into the crowd of pupils, but only one canister exploded. He then attempted a baton charge, which was even less spectacular. With each effort, however, he succeeded in inflaming the students, who pelted his squad with stones – one hitting him on the leg – and began advancing on his position. The commander then released dogs.

'The mistake the police made was to release the police dog – it injured one of our students,' recalled Paul Ndaba. 'The students decided to kill the dog.' Another dog was also killed – doused with petrol and set on fire. 'For us in the black community,' explained Sifiso Ndlovu in *The Soweto Uprising*, 'the dog was a symbol of police power, brutality and of the contempt of white supremacists for black people's dignity and life.'

What happened next is the subject of intense dispute. Kleingeld claimed he fired five shots over the heads of the scholars and, when they still did not disperse, 'fired 20 rounds into the ground in front of them with a Sten-gun – because it has a more demoralising effect than a pistol shot.' Without receiving an order to shoot, members of his squad then opened fire. However, most witnesses – including journalist Sophie Topsy Tema and photographer Sam Nzima of *The World* – dispute the assertion that he fired any warning shots and claim he aimed directly at the crowd and fired two shots.

'A white policeman in uniform pulled out a revolver and aimed it at the students,' recalled Tema. 'A colleague of mine said: "Look at him. He's going to shoot at the kids."'

Most evidence points to this, even though the later inquiry and cover-up absolved Kleingeld. There is, however, another point that exposes the apparent falsity of the claim, and this opens another issue of controversy – who was the first scholar killed in the uprising? Kleingeld's account suggests warning shots and then a random firing by policemen in panic – if this were true then probably the two fatal bullets would have hit random targets. As part of basic anti-riot training, police were taught that if deadly force was to quell a mob, the quickest solution was to take out the leader first – in this case Ndlovu. It was thus highly likely that Kleingeld fired two shots, as witnesses stated, and that the first hit its intended target – Ndlovu – and the second Hector Peterson. In any case, Kleingeld's testimony contradicted an interview he gave the *Rand Daily Mail* when he said: 'We fired into them – it's no use firing over their heads.'

'Suddenly I heard a gunshot,' continued Hector's sister. 'We raced back to hide. I looked around and asked "Where's Hector?" It suddenly went quiet. Then there was another shot. My heart was beating so fast, I couldn't speak. I kept looking for Hector. Then I noticed a ring of boys, carrying another boy, moving towards me. I was shivering and I didn't know why. As they passed I saw blood on the boy's shoe, which I recognised as Hector's. I shouted: "That's my brother." Then Mbuyisa Makhubu came from nowhere, pushed us out of the way, grabbed Hector and started running. I'd never seen him before but I ran next to him, screaming.'

The photo of that instant, taken by Sam Nzima, would be flashed round the globe before the day was out and would come to symbolise the Soweto Uprising and the agony of apartheid. From here Sophie Tema took the boy, who had blood frothing from his lips, to the Phefeni Clinic, but he was dead on arrival.

Back on the knoll, it took a dumbfounded moment for the enormity of the brutal police action to sink in – then all hell broke loose.

Some children fled, others dived to the ground for cover, the rest stood petrified in their tracks. Soon, however, rage replaced terror, and bricks, stones and bottles were hurled at the police, who climbed into their vehicles and retreated to the open ground across the Klip River, which flows between Orlando West and Orlando East.

One black policeman who did not withdraw fast enough was chased, cornered and handcuffed with his own handcuffs. When Tema returned from the clinic she saw his body lying on the ground covered with a piece of paper.

'In me,' said student leader Seth Mazibuko, 'there was this thing that now, good Lord, I have called these students out of their classrooms into the streets and here were now bullets and teargas and all those things. I didn't expect that to happen.'

'We were inadequately prepared to deal with the situation once those shots were fired,' added Murphy Morobe. 'The only thing on our minds was to disperse everyone as soon as possible. We went back to the area to try to do that, but it was difficult. The first questions people asked us was: "If you say we must go away, where must we go to? If these policemen come to Soweto, where must we go because this is where we stay?" We were entirely out of our depth in terms of what to do.'

And in that vacuum of leadership, with emotions overflowing, the pupils went on the rampage. PUTCO buses and government buildings, the symbols of apartheid, were obvious targets – in particular, the WRAB-controlled beerhalls and liquor outlets that many students associated with the enslavement of their parents. Even municipal libraries did not escape. 'Two factions of rioters argued for several minutes before setting fire to the Dube Library in Soweto,' reported Vin Mvelase in the *Sunday Express*. 'The argument centred on whether the library should be burned down because it was the "white man's property" or kept because it was a place of learning.

'"That's a place that can help our people become educated," said one man. "Let's not burn it." "No," another rioter insisted, "the library must go. It's white man's property." "But there's not many Afrikaans books in there," said the first man. "Let's take them out and burn them and leave the library alone." For a while it looked like the pro-library faction had won. The mob moved away to the Dube Post Office and burnt that down. But they came back and set fire to the library.'

As the riot escalated, so student anger increasingly focused on whites – the oppressors and the perpetrators of the outrage on Ndlovu and Peterson – who happened to be in the township at the time. A white woman welfare officer was dragged from her car and beaten before being rescued by police. In another incident, two elderly brothers, Joseph and Israel Kruger, were returning to Johannesburg from delivering furniture in Meadowlands when scholars at a red robot confronted them. The *Rand Daily Mail* carried the story: 'At first I thought it was some kind of a game and smiled at them as they approached us,' recalled Joseph Kruger, who was driving.

'Then all of a sudden I realised that they were out to kill us as half bricks began smashing into the windscreen. It was the most horrifying moment of my life as all those youths seethed around the truck like ants. With blood pouring down my face and my brother almost senseless in the seat next to me, I put the truck into gear and did the only thing I could – force a way through the crowd. Fortunately for us we didn't hit anyone in doing so, and so avoided enraging the mob any more than they were.'

'I've just had my car fixed,' said Arthur Judge, surveying the wreckage of his vehicle in Orlando. 'I was just lucky.'

Not so lucky was WRAB official JNB Esterhuizen, who was driving along Khumalo Street in Orlando when his van was attacked by a mob. A stone shattered the windscreen, forcing him to stop, and he angered the group further by attempting to draw his handgun. The mob dragged him into an alley where he was beaten to death and his body forced into a dustbin, where pupils attempted to set it alight.

In the most significant incident of black-on-white violence, Dr Melville Edelstein, WRAB's chief welfare officer, who planned soon to emigrate to Israel, was trapped with RE Hobkirk and a black worker in the Youth Centre in Jabavu. The black worker suggested to Edelstein that he hide under a table while the worker tried to persuade the advancing mob that the whites had already left. The scholars remained unconvinced and set fire to the building, whereupon Edelstein – probably in the belief that the students would recognise and protect him – rushed out towards the attackers, who pelted him with stones before stabbing and hacking at him. Hobkirk escaped to safety out the rear. It was noon.

'Dr Melville Edelstein, the prominent Johannesburg sociologist murdered in Soweto on Wednesday, died in a situation he foresaw more than four years ago,' commented Peter Bunkell in the *Sunday Express*. 'Furthermore, he was probably killed by a mob of enraged schoolchildren, the very people who told him way back in 1972 that they did not approve of Afrikaans.

'Dr Edelstein was awarded his master's degree for a comprehensive survey on the attitudes of adolescent blacks in Soweto. Most important findings to emerge from his thesis was that young Africans were hostile towards Afrikaans-speaking whites and preferred to be taught in English. Although Dr Edelstein did not predict the outbreak of destructive violence, he did identify and isolate its cause. It was a warning that could and most certainly should have been heeded. It was ignored.

'The 120-page thesis compiled by Dr Edelstein is called "What do Young Africans

Think?" Ironically, it begins with the words: "And seek the peace of the city ... And pray unto the Lord for it, for in peace therefore shall ye have peace." The survey canvasses the attitude of 200 matric pupils from eight Soweto schools. Its primary function is to ascertain the pupils' views and attitudes towards other South African ethnic groups. The Afrikaans language was rejected by the schoolchildren. Almost 90% opted for English rather than Afrikaans as a language of instruction. Dr Edelstein believed there were several reasons for the hostility and he felt additional research was needed to establish the causes. He felt the antagonism could have been due to the fact that policemen and other officials who had to enforce unpopular laws were predominantly Afrikaans-speaking. "These are the Afrikaners with whom young urban Africans come into contact. They rarely meet Afrikaners on a non-official level and this lack of knowledge might have something to do with their hostility."

'The Government, too, which was responsible for laws regarded by Africans as discriminatory in the economic, social and educational spheres, was identified by them as "Afrikaans". The events in Soweto – specifically Dr Edelstein's death – seem to show, however, that young blacks today see all whites as part and parcel of the system of oppression. Dr Edelstein's greatest wish, and one he expressed constantly in his thesis, was that his work would contribute to a better understanding of the South African racial situation. "This study then," Dr Edelstein said, "is an attempt to fill the gap in race attitude studies in South Africa. It is hoped that, perhaps, through this study, more knowledge and understanding of Bantu attitudes can be gained, some prejudices can be dispelled, and the gate opened for an improvement in race relations among all the ethnic groups of South Africa."

'Dr Edelstein was a man who cared. He was concerned about the welfare of black South Africans and he devoted his energy to the alleviation of problems. But little importance seems to have been attached to Dr Edelstein's findings and nothing has been done to remove potential sources of friction. He saw the warnings and he cried wolf. Unlike the boy in the well-known story, he did not deserve to be ignored.'

'He may have felt immune; after all the main protagonists on the pupils' side all knew him and the work he did,' added journalist Jon Qwelane in *Tribute* magazine. 'It was not to be: He realised too late that, no matter what good he might have done for the township, he remained a white man and as a white man he would die -- cut in his final flight as he tried to make a dash for it, his body a mangled and bloody heap between two offices, butchered by the same unchannelled energy of the same youths on whose side he campaigned. An unkinder twist of irony would be hard to imagine.'

The initial reaction of the white English press to Edelstein's death, reflecting the feelings of English-speaking residents in Johannesburg, can be found in one word – 'murdered' – in the tribute by Peter Bunkell. Across at *The Star*, Don Mattera was handed Sam Nzima's photograph of Hector Peterson and instructed to write a caption. 'They told me a child had been killed but I said he was murdered,' he said in an interview with Clare O'Donoghue in *Marie Claire*. 'They insisted that I write "killed". I refused to write the caption and threw the photograph back at them.' It finally appeared captioned 'died'. This may appear to be making a mountain out of a molehill, but it is not. The insinuation in one is of premeditated savagery, while in the other it is the inevitable consequence of looking for trouble. One implies guilt, the other unquestioning absolution. It is the biased terminology on which oppression was based.

Nzima, incidentally, was experiencing his own problems as his photograph, which would win the Best News Feature of the Year Award, was appearing on the front pages of newspapers the world over. A policeman telephoned *The World* and ordered that they immediately send Nzima to the notorious John Vorster Square Police Station to explain the unfavourable image he was portraying of South Africa. He did not go and was forced into hiding.

Many whites who inadvertently found themselves in the township that Wednesday morning, however, were saved by brave blacks who risked their own lives for them. A white woman student and the black woman social worker she was accompanying were stopped by a mob on Phefeni Bridge and the white woman dragged from the car. A number of scholars rescued her and placed her in the care of a black priest who shielded her in the face of life-threatening danger. In another incident, a group of 10 construction workers were led to safety through the back routes of Soweto by a black man. 'Good Samaritan blacks have saved the lives of dozens of whites trapped in angry mob riots,' reported Melanie Yap in the *Sunday Times*. 'They have risked their lives to hide and smuggle out whites whose presence invited immediate attack from stone-throwing crowds. Sowetan Ben Sibaya, former president of the Johannesburg Bantu Football Association, rescued an unidentified Swiss immigrant being chased by an angry crowd. He pushed the dazed, middle-aged man into his car and drove off while people flung stones at them. Johannesburg pest control officer Mr TD Beebe was sheltered in a black family's home and later smuggled out of the township.' And Father Giovanni Marino, parish priest of Meadowlands, was taken in by one of his parishioners.

As Edelstein died, Tsietsi Mashinini addressed scholars at Morris Isaacson and ordered them to remain away from school for the rest of the week and await further instructions to be issued over the weekend. By now the army had been placed on standby, helicopters were buzzing over Soweto and dropping teargas on groups of students, and the notorious Riot Squad, dressed in camouflage uniforms and led by Colonel Theunis 'Rooi Rus' Swanepoel, had arrived. The commander and his trigger-happy unit were to become renowned for their brutality and they did much to increase temperatures. As Jon Qwelane quipped: 'It was difficult to tell who was actually rioting, the pupils or the police.'

As the situation accelerated into chaos, concerned adults held an emergency meeting to attempt to form a single organisation to regain control from the scholars. Dr Nthato Motlana of the Parents' Vigilante Committee approached Dr Aaron Matlhare of the Soweto Parents' Association and suggested they join hands with the Black Women's Federation, headed by Winnie Mandela. It was agreed they would meet at 9 pm at Matlhare's rooms. While Motlana and Matlhare were discussing a meeting, another was taking place elsewhere in Soweto. 'The Urban Bantu Council (UBC) in the face of such an explosive issue,' commented *The World*, 'treated us to shocking scenes, turning the Jabulani Council Chamber into a battlefield, with a name plate flying and abuse the order of the day. What is more, when they finally got round to appointing a delegation to see the government on the Afrikaans issue, they engaged in debates on the legalities of such a delegation on which they could not even agree. Indeed, talk about castrated bulls!'

As these crisis meetings continued, so did the violence, and many photographers were attacked. 'Press photographers trying to cover disturbances,' reported journalist Chris Smith, 'were attacked by bands of rioting students who seemed to resent the publicity. Alf Khumalo, a *Sunday Times* photographer, was covering the march before violence erupted. As young Africans clashed with police he was dragged down by students who objected to him taking photographs. "A boy next to me was shot," said Mr Khumalo. "Students started crying. One grabbed my camera and a lens. As I was being hit, another student dragged me away. He had a knife and he told those hitting me to stop." Mr Khumalo said he saw about four young boys shot and a white man killed.

'André de Kock, a photographer for *Beeld*, an Afrikaans morning newspaper, drove close to the hub of activity. The front side window of his car was smashed and a stone hit him on the side of his head. "We just drove out as quickly as possible," he said. Peter Magubane, a *Rand Daily Mail* photographer, was attacked and his clothes torn. One of his cameras was snatched. "I was photographing the parade," he said. "They told me to stop, and I tried to sneak some pictures. Then another group approached. One camera was grabbed and I ran away. My clothes were torn as I jumped a fence."'

While perilous for some, the situation proved an opportunity for others. Looters and gangsters – armed with knives, shovels, pickaxes, iron bars and sticks and shouting '*Amandla!*' – joined the fray. They wandered along main roads indiscriminately smashing and burning vehicles and taking whatever they could lay their hands on from gutted buildings and shops – particularly liquor outlets. Near Uncle Tom's Hall in Orlando, looters set up a roadblock and plundered delivery vans – including one of a baker and another carrying condensed milk. Pupils also got in on the act. 'Students stopped an oncoming truck and told the old man in there – who happened to be black – to take the money and use it for his children,' said Seth Mazibuko. 'They told him they wanted what was in the truck – yoghurt, milk, sour milk, buttermilk. "We are hungry and we just want to eat," they said.'

Black workers in Johannesburg had been informed of the uprising and many businesses had closed early to allow people to get home. But transport was seriously disrupted and most only made it to the burning township after nightfall. And if getting there was a problem, getting about was downright dangerous in the chaotic conditions. As the sun set, the balance of power in the poorly electrified township shifted from the police to the students, and returning commuters ran the gauntlet of student road blocks, looters and gangsters on one side, and police vans driving this way and that while shooting at random.

'On Wednesday,' wrote Vin Mvelase in the *Sunday Express*, 'I got home from work two hours later than usual, long after sunset. The portion of the main street in Dube where I live was in total darkness. People stood in little groups in the street or in the yards of their homes watching the superintendent's office being destroyed by fire.

'My own home looked deserted. Inside a candle flickered. In a far corner, sat my wife with our baby daughter on her lap. Our other two girls were huddled together on a mat in another corner. They were all terrified. Because, maybe, the police would come and stray bullets would begin whizzing through our windows. Or the riot mobs who had burned down the superintendent's office and were now starting on the bank opposite us, might next turn their attention to this house.'

'The Soweto riot has shown how deep the antagonism already is but it has also demonstrated the ferocious intent of the Soweto youth to change his environment,' commented Tony Duigan in *The Star*. 'The youth's parents have also been watching and they too have been drawn into the controversy. Their turn is still to come and in the mood that presently prevails the parents could grasp at the strength they have in numbers to form a power block that could wring meaningful concessions from the government.'

But the parents were hampered, and would remain weakened, by a lack of cohesion. On the one side was the conservative UBC and its supporters, on the other the plethora of organisations that catered to a myriad interests. At 9 pm the meeting arranged earlier for more progressive adults – including church leaders, educationalists and community leaders – took place at Matlhare's rooms. From this group would emerge the Black Parents' Association (BPA), with Dr Manas Buthelezi of the Lutheran Church as chairman, and including Matlhare, Motlana, Aubrey Mokoena and Winnie Mandela on the executive committee – most of whom would be sympathetic to the ANC, though riven by philosophical differences, jealousies, competing agendas and mutual suspicions.

Winnie Mandela and Mokoena were actively involved with the students and would have been unwilling to dilute their influence by supporting motions to bring the scholars under the control of a parents' committee; Motlana and Matlhare were terrified of the effect student power would have on traditional black political movements and were desperate to regain authority and return community life to normal. Some favoured negotiation with the government, others believed that speaking with the enemy would confer on it a legitimacy it did not deserve. Matlhare was suspicious of Winnie Mandela (stating in an affidavit that she had had affairs with Motlana and photographer Peter Magubane, and that she had come on to him with some decidedly unpolitical intentions). He also stated that he could not trust Motlana because he had approached Matlhare to warn him about Winnie Mandela ... and so it went on. It is thus not surprising that the only thing this group could resolve at that first meeting was to raise funds to assist the 250 injured and pay for a mass funeral for the 35 dead on Sunday, 20 June.

While the BPA would become more influential, it would remain largely irresolute, because when it tried to negotiate with the government the authorities undermined it, believing it was too radical, while the students objected to an organisation that professed to negotiate on their behalf with a government they wanted to destroy, not speak to. On top of this, it was continually undermined by internal rivalries. This allowed Justice Minister Jimmy Kruger constantly to reject calls to talk with the BPA because he could not be sure who its leaders were.

'The orgy of rioting, arson and pillage that swept Soweto, carried on throughout the night,' reported *The World* on 17 June. 'At dawn today the violence continued in some areas as workers streamed out of the "shadow city". Rioting mobs, who during the night had burnt municipal offices, school buildings and bottle stores, were finally brought under control in the early hours of this morning.

'Soweto residents struggled to make their way to work this morning because trains into Soweto did not start running until after sunrise. PUTCO buses were also not running their usual routes, but were turning around well clear of the night's trouble spots. On the old Potchefstroom Road, buses were going in only as far as Baragwanath Hospital. It was also reported that nine PUTCO buses had been burned out and five are reported missing.

'From just before sunrise police manned roadblocks at all entrances to Soweto and stopped all whites from entering the township. Hundreds of pupils in uniforms were flocking to school this morning in spite of the closure of all Soweto schools ordered by Minister MC Botha.'

For Soweto, 17 June was probably worse than 16 June. 'From the air Soweto looked like a festering sore,' reported *The World.* 'Smoke and flames were pouring out of at least 15 buildings and some vehicles throughout the area. Scattered groups of 50 to 60 people were roaming the streets in most areas and one group was seen running from a "Hippo" anti-riot personnel carrier, into a side street. They hid from view behind some houses. Crowds milled around smouldering and burning buildings, some of whose roofs had collapsed with heat and disintegration of the girders. One building, which looked like an office, was spitting flames through the windows and doors. What was probably a bus was smouldering on the side of one main road – its roof a scorched rib cage of burnt metal. Two large trucks have presumably collided at a junction in the township and their cargoes of boxes of paper have swamped the intersection. What looked like a beer hall or club set among lawns, tall trees and with a swimming pool and marquee was on fire as well.'

There was an angry mood among the groups of youths that manned barricades or roamed the streets demanding a Black Power salute from passers-by as their passport to safety. And their slogans and placards contained wider political messages than those of the previous day: 'These honkies are provoking the black community',

'Homeland leaders are bloody sellouts', 'Release all detained people', 'Arrest us all please', 'Afrikaans is terrorism.' Whenever Mashinini arrived to issue orders, however, their humour improved and they bore him aloft on their shoulders.

Journalists and photographers remained in the firing line. 'A concussed TV cameraman whose vehicle stalled in the face of a rock hurling mob, broke the ignition key in his terror and haste to get away,' reported the *Rand Daily Mail*. 'TV news reporter Mr Freek Robinson said he had to pull his struggling colleague, cameraman Mr Chris Schutte, from the car and drag him down the road behind him. "He fought to get away from me because he thought I was leading him to his death," Mr Robinson said.

'Mr Robinson described how, minutes earlier, Mr Schutte's skull had been smashed by a rock hurled through the window of their car as they approached an angry mob. "Chris was concussed and had no idea what was happening. The car went out of control and veered off the road towards some trees," he said. "I grabbed the wheel and told him to accelerate, but the car stalled. The crowd began to run towards us, shouting and hurling rocks. I told Chris to get the car started because there was no time to lose. He couldn't so I pushed him out of the way and found the key had broken off in the keyhole. He must have done it in his terror and haste. I don't know how he managed it, it must have taken considerable power."

'Mr Robinson then dragged the struggling cameraman from the car. "I had to force him to come with me because he didn't know what was happening and there was no time to explain. He thought I was leading him to his death," he said. Mr Robinson described how, at one stage, Mr Schutte broke loose and tried to head back to the car. "I ran after him to stop him, but the hail of rocks from the mob forced him back."

'Mr Robinson described how he tried to stop passing cars so they could escape. "The crowd was approaching from all sides and some drivers were as terrified as we were. They jumped out of cars and fled. Suddenly, I noticed a car coming out of a side street. It moved slowly, with the back doors open. We dashed after it and as we got in, it accelerated and sped us out of the area to safety."'

The police, too, were more resolute, and any squeamishness about shooting people – including children – had disappeared. 'Police convoys moving around Soweto fired several bursts of automatic fire today at rioting mobs,' reported the *Rand Daily Mail*. 'Bursts of fire could be heard from Orlando Police Station on several occasions, but the pall of smog over Soweto was too heavy to see any crowd movements. Mr David Silumo, a Diepkloof resident, said he saw policemen fire into a mob of youths in his area. "The police opened fire without warning, and I saw several people fall."'

Bullets also came from above. 'Shortly after being scared by a helicopter above him, 16-year-old Enoch Nunu Follie dropped dead while others in his group ran for cover in the streets near Rockville,' reported the *Rand Daily Mail*. 'Nunu dropped after he had been hit by three bullets – two in his chest and one in his back. His friends carried him home dead. Giving an eye-witness account was Madoda Mdluli, 16, "Nunu was in our group who stood chatting about the events of the day when suddenly a helicopter flew above our heads. We were scared but did not move. Minutes after we heard gun shots and I saw Nunu drop and we ran for cover. From where I stood looking back I saw Nunu crawl on all fours then drop to the ground. When all was quiet and after the helicopter had gone, friends ran back and found Nunu dead." When his father, Mr Reggie Follie, returned home from work, he was met with the news of his son's death by the mourners who had already gathered at his house.'

A new horror also arrived in Soweto that morning – the green car. Policemen in camouflage uniforms would prowl the streets in this Chevrolet and fire from the car window at random – often killing small children. Whenever the number plate was noted and reported to police, either nothing would be done or it would prove to be a false registration plate.

Police also resorted to using automatic weapons, which greatly increased the chances of innocent bystanders being hit by stray bullets. 'Soweto was in the grip of terror as we toured flashpoints,' reported Jan Tugwana and Nat Serache in the *Rand Daily Mail*. 'In Meadowlands and Rockville we saw police in camouflage suits opening fire with automatic weapons. From Orlando East, Jabavu and other areas came reports of more firing. An unknown 14-year-old boy was shot dead in front of us at Rockville. He had tried hiding in a yard not far from the bottle store where the police were firing on looters. We saw him stagger and collapse on the doorstep of a house. "I couldn't bring myself to look at him as he lay there," wrote Tugwana. "All I could see at a glance, was a pool of blood covering the area where he lay."'

Lily and Martha Mithi, walking with their mother in Soweto, were both hit by random bullets – eight-year-old Lily fatally. And so it continued. 'In Meadowlands,' wrote Tugwana and Serache, 'we saw two boys shot ...'

As news of the uprising spread, solidarity with Soweto began to be displayed in other centres. Buildings at the University of Zululand were set alight, and in Durban

87 black students from the University of Natal were arrested out of a group of 200 marchers carrying placards that included: 'Don't start the revolution without us', 'Soweto is our blood' and 'White pigs, bastards, snobs, murderers.'

'An 18-year-old girl told how she was escorted through a mob of stone-throwing students to fetch her pet cat during the riots at the University of Zululand yesterday,' recounted the *Rand Daily Mail*. 'Miss Shuan Warriker, daughter of a university building inspector, said she had been told early yesterday by a family servant, she named as Simon, that she must leave because the students were "cross and are going to kill white people."

'"He grabbed my arm with one hand and in the other one he carried a panga. He took me to Mr J Snyder, a family friend, who lived about a block away. I suddenly realised I had left my Siamese cat, 'Kishe', at home. So Simon escorted me back through the mob again to fetch her. Simon said that as we had always treated him well he would defend me with his life."'

Barricades were erected in the township of Alexandra to the north of Johannesburg. On the West Rand, incidents were reported from Chamdor, Kagiso, Krugersdorp and Munsieville; on the East Rand from Tembisa, Vosloorus and Boksburg; and from the University of the North in the homeland of Lebowa. But the most serious confrontation with police on the second day of the uprising occurred in the centre of Johannesburg.

'Streetfighting erupted in central Johannesburg and Braamfontein yesterday afternoon when multiracial mobs of students and workers battled police and self-styled vigilantes,' reported the *Rand Daily Mail*. 'The first outbreak happened when a placard-wielding group of about 200 University of the Witwatersrand students and 400 black workers who had joined them were set upon in Jorissen Street by almost 100 whites using makeshift weapons. Suddenly police vans swept in and without warning the officer in charge gave the command: "*Gaan vat hulle*" (Go and get them).

'Policemen swarmed from the trucks. The crowd panicked and fled, screaming. Batons flashed and people fell. Girls were beaten and pulled over railings. Others scrambled over the railway embankment in terror only to be forced back by white railway workers. One man jumped from the railway bridge and lay critically injured and unconscious below. Those who tried to escape the way they had come were stopped by scores of plainclothes policemen blocking the street. Many fell to the ground. Some were kicked and punched. Several students were taken away in police vans. Most were warned and released but two were charged.

'One of the self-styled vigilantes told afterwards how he and other whites were drawn into the disorder. "We grabbed anything at hand – I had a piece of steel piping – and laid into them, the students were no problem, but some of the blacks gave us a bit of trouble."' Though these vigilantes were part of the disturbance, none was arrested or charged.

The uprising was not restricted to South Africa. In New York a black man and a companion targeted South African Airways' Fifth Avenue office. As he destroyed a computer terminal, ripped out telephones, flung freight packages about and smashed windows and a cocktail cabinet, his companion recorded the devastation on film. Both fled before police arrived to seal off the building and search for a bomb that was reported to have been planted. No bomb was found and the staff returned four hours later.

On Friday, 18 June, Soweto remained a no-go area and it was again a day of tragedy for bystanders. 'Soccer fans and officials throughout the country are mourning the death of school teacher and Kaizer Chiefs star Ariel "Pro" Kgongoane, who was killed by a stray bullet while driving his car,' reported *The World*. 'Mr Washington Mposula, chairman of Orlando Pirates, in paying tribute to Kgongoane yesterday, said: "We have lost a professional man whose contribution to the children in the classroom and to football made him an asset to the nation."'

Unrest continued in all the centres that had experienced it the previous day and spread to another 10 townships on the Witwatersrand, and also to Witbank, the University of Cape Town and Bothaville. 'In Bothaville a riot broke out – not in support of the Soweto students – but because a provincial traffic officer stopped a film show,' reported the *Rand Daily Mail*. 'The trouble started during a double-feature show when the traffic inspector – in his capacity also as an entertainment tax inspector – stopped the show and confiscated money, tickets and projectors. The enraged crowd then proceeded to stone cars and set alight a beerhall and administration offices.'

The most serious uprising, however, in which 24 died, was in Alexandra, where many believe the fighting on that single day was more intense than anything that occurred in Soweto during the first two days. 'I was in Alexandra township at the height of the bloody violence and looting,' wrote Ray Joseph in the *Sunday Express*. 'From early morning, frenzied mobs, drunk on stolen beer and Black Power, roamed the dusty roads in a wild orgy of arson, looting and death. The area around the police station bristled with policemen. Many of their weapons looked new and still had official armoury tags hanging from the barrels. I was to see some of these weapons in use before too long.

'With a heavily armed platoon from the Riot Squad, I was allowed to enter the heart of the township and the eye of the violence. Rocks thrown by the mobs bounced off my car as I followed the police in convoy and screams of "Black Power!" and "Amandla!" rent the air. Then it happened. My escort suddenly swooped on an Indian shop where six people had barricaded themselves in a house at the back. Police opened fire on the looters and they scattered across an open field. But an African woman who fled from the shop, her arms filled with loot, fell dead in the road as a bullet hit her. Another two died in the yard of the shop. "Rather kill three now than 10 next week," a policeman told me.

'As our convoy crawled through the smoke and chaos, an African interpreter screamed at looters through a megaphone to "stand or we'll shoot!" Few heeded him. I watched as another five tried to escape rather than stand and be arrested. They all died.'

Police feared the battles might spill over into the exclusive nearby town of Sandton, and set up patrols to protect it. The residents were less concerned and arrived in droves at the outskirts of Alexandra to view and take pictures of the clashes. 'Some had children with them,' said a traffic officer, 'They behaved as though it was a picnic in there. Naturally we turned them back.'

Saturday 19 June, concluded Joseph, 'I travelled with the same unit through many of the same streets. The fires had burned down. Only razed shops, buses and cars were left. Blacks still lined the streets. But the shouting and the stone throwing was over. Alexandra was sullen and subdued.'

It was the same in the other strife-torn areas, which were experiencing an uneasy calm after three days of bloody war. It was time to count the cost of the violence in lost lives, human suffering and property damage. The toll was now 140 dead, with over 1 000 injured and a financial cost in excess of R30 million. Included in the accounting were 8 702 rounds from automatic rifles, 732 rounds from .38 revolvers, 1 750 rounds from .32 firearms, 2 650 rounds from 9 mm weapons and 2 529 rounds of shotgun fire. And Soweto faced an additional burden. 'After a week of riots, some Soweto residents are now faced with the problem of survival,' reported *The World*. 'In the wake of the student protest and the violence which followed, the halting of food supplies by city businessmen – a number of whom became victims of looters at the height of the rioting – the means of sustaining life in Soweto have been diminished. Deliveries have come to a halt. Already a number of commodities have run out. These include bread, milk, butter, flour, sugar, tea, paraffin, and many others. And these shops which have sufficient stocks for the next few days may soon start charging black market prices. Not only foodstuffs are affected. There is also transport. Yesterday many mourners had to walk to funerals because there were no buses available to carry them.'

In fact, all the machinery to keep a vibrant city running was gutted. It was estimated that it would take at least three months to restore vital services. Three of the 10 clinics were in ashes and the others, including baby centres, closed. 'The loss of the three clinics means there will be a tremendous gap in the provision of preventative health services for the people of Soweto,' warned Johannesburg's chief medical officer, Dr Alexander Smith. 'The baby clinics are a fundamental service and without them we could revert to the high infantile mortality rate of 25 years ago. At that time 500 babies in every 1 000 died by the age of one year.'

It was also a time for parents to search for children who were missing. 'Demonstrations, shootings and arrests have taken such prominence in our lives lately,' wrote Carol Mathiane in *The World*. 'But whoever thinks of the mothers of the victims. Children are arrested at all times, in many places – at home, at school and while demonstrating. Nobody ever explains the disappearance of a child – it's not necessary. The mothers know that things are happening, but don't know what or when. And the mothers are torn. On the one side is pride – pride in the courage of the children, and hope for the future. On the other side there is sheer stark fear which every mother must face. Will it be my child's turn for a bullet or a pick-up van...?

'A child is arrested or killed next door. Friends and neighbours offer sympathies and cheer the family up. It is all very well while they are around, telling you it will be over soon and that there are so many of them they'll pull through. Such words give you strength and like all other women in that position, you push back the tears and be brave. But then comes the night. You go to bed and hope sleep will come soon, but it doesn't. All that friends said during the day goes overboard. After all, it so happens that this is your child and not someone you read about in the newspapers. You're now faced with reality. YOUR child is not home tonight. All kinds of pictures come to your mind. You remember him as a baby. The problem of bringing him up. His first day at school. What a proud mother you are – he's doing well at school and you have high hopes, when suddenly Black Power strikes.

'Imagine the anguish of an ordinary woman whose life has been void of politics.

A life she's never questioned before; politics was for the educated elite. But when her child is picked up she is exposed to the cruel life of searching, seeking, wondering. Where is he? Is he alive? Is he well? And the fear. Fear every minute of the day, every day of the week. This goes on and each dawn you hope there will be some ray of sunshine. The mother visits the police station. Together with women in the same predicament they plead to see their children. Sometimes they never see them. Some are told their children have been transferred to faraway cells. Some cry while others have run out of tears.

'You return home without even saying "hello" only to be accosted by the younger ones at home wanting to know how you fared. What do you tell them? Somewhere along the street you recognise a figure of a man in his teens. He happens to be a man simply because he is no longer at school. He used to be your child's friend from crèche to high school. He also wants to know how his friend is. You envy his freedom. You wish your child had also left school – but it was not to be. You had high hopes of your son. You wanted him to be a doctor or a teacher, but it was not to be, so ... you wait.'

'Crowds of people have been flocking to the Johannesburg Mortuary in Hillbrow to identify relatives and friends killed in the bloody riots of the past few days,' added Thami Mazwai in *The World*. 'Some families left weeping, others were told to come back when more bodies were received. Armed police stood by. "You see what trouble the children have caused the parents," commented a nurse.'

Late on Saturday, 19 June, the barricades were lifted and delivery vans re-entered bearing relief for the battle-weary residents. 'The bitterly cold winds were keeping the streets fairly clear of pedestrians but apart from the upturned, burnt-out cars that litter the streets, everything looked normal,' wrote Mike Dutfield in the *Rand Daily Mail*. 'The only other signs of the tragedy of the riots were the flimsy barricades African children set across the roads to slow down traffic. The barricades have now been pushed aside along with the rubble. The massive police presence that gathered at Orlando Police Station at the height of the riots has been sharply reduced. For the people of Soweto themselves, life is getting back to normal.'

'Any peace now evident in Soweto is "superficial",' warned the Anglican dean of Johannesburg, the Very Reverend Desmond Tutu, in a BBC interview with David Dimbleby.

The implications of the initial salvo in the first battle of the final push for liberation were immediate and far-reaching. South Africa, black and white, would never be the same again. The country, simply, was faced with the realisation that its very future was at stake.

'Wednesday's tragic events will probably go down in history as the beginning of an era where whites no longer hold exclusive control over political power in our country,' commented Dr Erich Leistner, the Deputy Director of the Africa Institute. 'This does by no means say that henceforth the South African scene will be radically different from what it was before the riots. However there can be no doubt that in future the views and aspirations of blacks and more particularly of urban blacks, will increasingly become a factor circumscribing the freedom of white South Africans' political decision-making. In practice this will mean that whites can no longer alone decide the lot of blacks and that decisions will have to be taken with full regard to the black's viewpoint.'

Internationally, Soweto joined Sharpeville as an abhorrent symbol of apartheid as news of the event flashed round the world. 'The black political demonstrations in Soweto are certain to emblazon the name of that teeming black township on the consciousness of the world's peoples,' commented the *Washington Post*. 'For the South African government, which has long and smugly insisted that apartheid served the black majority's interests and commanded its approval, the demonstrations have come as a tremendous shock. The embarrassment to Pretoria's foreign policy is only a small part of it: South Africa's efforts to make itself an accepted partner of its black neighbours has been undermined, and in its dealings with non-African countries like the United States, South Africa has lost the confidence and strength that comes from demonstrating competence and command at home.'

In the United States there were calls for tougher action against South Africa as the uprising became a factor in the presidential race between Jimmy Carter and Gerald Ford. Protests and marches, which included a rally in London, were organised throughout Europe in solidarity with the people of Soweto. The net result of this intense pressure was that governments reassessed their relationships with South Africa. 'South Africa's closest allies – the Americans, the British, the French and the Germans – are slowly redefining their attitudes towards Africa and the Republic,' wrote Martin Schneider in the *Sunday Express*.

If the West was finding it increasingly difficult to defend South Africa, the Organisation of African Unity (OAU) and the United Nations (UN) revelled in the opportunity to attack. The UN Security Council backed a resolution condemning South Africa for 'Massive violence against and killing of African people, including schoolchildren and students and others opposing racial discrimination'. The resolution, further, described apartheid as 'a crime against the conscience and dignity of mankind that seriously disturbs international peace and security' and recognised the 'legitimacy of the struggle of the South African people'. The Soviet Union, backed by most African delegates, suggested a full trade embargo be imposed on the country to isolate it.

At the annual summit of the OAU, held in Port Louis in Mauritius at the end of June, calls were made to increase the pressure on South Africa through greater support for liberation movements to remove the remaining shackles of colonisation, apartheid and discrimination. 'The OAU must now extend the frontiers of freedom to the southernmost part of the continental land mass of Africa,' urged Liberian Cecil Dennis. The call had clearly changed from a negotiated settlement to a military solution. It was also declared that 16 June would be remembered by member states as the 'Day of the Soweto Massacres'.

While white South Africa celebrated a Springbok victory over the All Blacks in the first rugby test, the tour was souring fast as African nations boycotted the Olympic Games in Montreal because of the tour and New Zealand's participation in the games. 'Sports and politics are these days like the body and soul,' thundered a Kenyan official. 'You cannot separate the two. Our decision was taken on principle and in accordance with the majority views and agreement of the UN. We shall use all means available to us, including sports, to put pressure on South Africa until apartheid is wiped out and freedom achieved in the whole of South Africa.'

White South Africans took some pleasure in witnessing the disruption of games from which they were excluded, but were soon outraged when expelled from the International Amateur Athletics Federation. A walkout threatened the Miss World competition over the participation of 18-year-old Lynn Massyn and 21-year-old Rozette Motsepe from South Africa (as discrimination laws outlawed joint contests, South Africa was permitted two entrants – a white Miss South Africa and a black Miss Africa South). The noose was tightening.

While the world was expressing solidarity with Soweto, any unity the townships may have had was showing serious strain. The students had proved that they could be determined and assertive. 'The boldness, dedication, sense of purpose and clarity of analysis of the situation – all these things are a direct result of Black Consciousness ideas among the young in Soweto and elsewhere,' commented Steve Biko. But while students were emboldened, they were also inexperienced, and wildly inconsistent demands led to splits and acrimony in the ranks. If their relationship with their peers was cool, that with their parents was a yawning divide – as was the split between the BPA and the UBC. 'When the clouds of discontent were building ominously in our schoolyards,' wrote Aggrey Klaaste in the *Weekend World*, 'we shook our heads and clicked our collective tongue. Then the kids boycotted classes. Still we shook our collective head lethargically and hummed our collective disquiet. We were frightened. We were shocked. But all we did was despair. My language spells it very clearly – "*Singa Magwala*" (We are cowards).'

Affairs within the BPA were not much better. At its first full meeting Winnie Mandela attempted to have Aubrey Mokoena elected chairman and Matlhare opposed this because he suspected her of trying to establish an organisation over which she effectively would have control. Further, Motlana took issue with a journalist for not having informed him of the march planned for 16 June, and Motapanya accused Motlana of refusing to attend to scholars injured in the uprising. Matters would not improve. To add to these stresses, the new-found celebrity of Soweto was fertile ground for the political aspirations of a host of black politicians such as Chief Mangosuthu Buthelezi who descended on the township take advantage of the situation.

In one of the rare incidents of co-operation, the BPA and student leaders applied for permission to hold a mass funeral for the Soweto dead on Sunday, 20 June. This was declined by the chief magistrate of Johannesburg. 'We are getting sick and tired of trying to tell the Prime Minister that the present South African way of life is unholy and oppressive,' responded a frustrated Tutu. Permission was eventually given for funerals to be held in Alexandra and Soweto on 3 July.

'In Soweto dozens of heavily armed riot squad police manned roadblocks at the main entrance of the city and barred whites from entering,' reported Daniel Mothabela and Vin Mvelase in the *Sunday Express*. 'The uniformed police kept away from the funerals, although black plainclothes policemen mingled with mourners. At least 50 000 people attended the funerals of 18 victims in Soweto. Most of the funerals were held at the Avalon Cemetery at 30-minute intervals. There were emotional scenes at the graveside as women fainted and mourners sang freedom songs and Nkosi Sikelel' iAfrika. As they sang they raised their hands in Black Power salutes and shouted "*Amandla awethu*" (Power is ours). Among the funerals was that of Hector Peterson. In Alexandra Father SS Meje urged the people not to be discouraged but to gain more determination and understanding – "like the Jews when they were in Egyptian Bondage".'

The dead were hailed as heroes who had not died in vain, and poets recited poems at the graveside:

> Our spears are immersed in blood
> We are on the warpath
> Of blood river
> The distance is long
> But the courage is thriced
> We are the elephant
> We are the warrior
> Transformed to a guerrilla
> The spirit of Sharpville
> Emerges from the present
> Wearing a new mask
> Soweto, Soweto, Soweto
> History repeats itself
> We are the elephant
> We move the way of no return.
>   – Lefifi Tladi: 'Our Spears Are Immersed In Blood'

For many black parents, the dilemma was witnessing children ruling Soweto, not knowing what to do, and interminably squabbling over inconsequential matters. 'At a time when the country is virtually aflame,' commented journalist Obed Kunene, 'and faces a real crisis when issues are clearly drawn and black/white relations are nowhere near as placid as some would have us believe, the last thing black people can afford is division within the ranks.'

An example of the problem could be found in the deliberations of the BPA. Some, like Manas Buthelezi, wanted to establish 'machinery for dialogue' so that discussions could be held with government and student grievances placed on the table. Students rejected adults speaking on their behalf and certainly opposed working within the system. And Winnie Mandela opposed discussions with the authorities and placed the responsibility on white shoulders to end the crisis: 'It is purely and simply the white man's problem,' she said. 'Not only does the government know what needs to be done, all white people know what must be done. It is in their hands. It is the government that must change the situation. They must do what is right. They know what to do. They don't need to be told. My only plea to them – and I imagine this is the plea of all black people – is please save our country.'

But the whites did not have a clue what to do, and if they did they lacked the courage or imagination to do it.

If blacks were divided by the events of three days in June, it was nothing compared to the complete disarray within Afrikaner, Broederbond and Nationalist ranks. What had started out as a cynical move in the game of succession had left the dream of grand apartheid in tatters, and the soul-searching was bitter, acrimonious and traumatic. The Afrikaner monolith had experienced crises before, but now, for the first time, it faced the real threat of implosion. And the Nationalists were so struck with panic that they caused greater confusion. They gave with one hand and struck out with the other, made wild promises and issued dire threats – the result being greater alienation on all sides.

In the immediate firing line were the *verkramptes* – MC Botha, Treurnicht and Jimmy Kruger. But the most serious casualty was the aura of regional statesman Vorster had attempted to create. The timing of the uprising could not have been more disastrous: he was scheduled to meet American Secretary of State Henry Kissinger the week after to discuss the Rhodesia question. 'The Soweto riots have come as a dramatic moment of truth for Mr Vorster before his meeting with Kissinger in West Germany this week,' commented the *Sunday Express*. 'For it now seems inevitable that they will influence the whole course of the discussions. Initially it was widely assumed that Dr Kissinger's chief interest in the talks would be Rhodesia. African leaders had emphasised to him during his recent tour that Mr Vorster held the key to a peaceful settlement in Rhodesia. Therefore the speculation was that Dr Kissinger's main purpose at the meeting would be to try to persuade Mr Vorster to put pressure on Mr Smith to reach a settlement with Rhodesia's black nationalists and there were rumours of various things he might offer on a quid pro quo basis, such as a softer line on South West Africa (Namibia).

'But now Dr Kissinger's interest is likely to focus more on South Africa itself than on Rhodesia. For suddenly the country which has been negotiating with Western powers and African states for peace in southern Africa has itself become a major flashpoint in the overall crisis. The Soweto riots will underline the vital message Dr Kissinger will be handing Mr Vorster. It is a message US officials believe the South African government and its supporters can no longer afford to ignore, no matter how distasteful it sounds to them. And this message is the same the German and French

THE

ROCKY RIOTER TEARGAS SHOW

SPECIAL LUNCH HOUR SHOW

2nd great week!
It's a knockout!
Already half of C.
stoned!

See stone throwing schoolgirl choir clubbed
down by sex crazed riot policemen!

Lotsa blood and violence!

Surging crowds and clouds of teargas!

(A REAL TEAR JERKER - BRING YOUR OWN STONES AND KLEENEX!)

16

GREAT SONGS!
Including ...

"Burn Baby Burn"
"Black is Black"
"Light my Fire"
"Teargas keeps falling on my Head"
"Banned and on the Run"
"O Darling (Street)"

Music by:-
S.A.P. Siren.

Special appearance
Lt. van der Merwe
on his loudhailer

In Black and White
(Censors slash multi-colour version)

NOW SHOWING FROM 80

The previous page shows the satirical pamphlet drawn up by a Cape Town protest theatre troupe at the time of the Soweto Uprising.
SOURCE: State Archives

The photographs on the following 11 pages are held in the State Archives in Pretoria. Recently unclassified, they have never been seen by the public before. They were taken during the second half of 1976, and show the tragedy and destruction that occurred in Soweto and other centres of unrest.

The following nine pages show previously classified documents held in the State Archives.

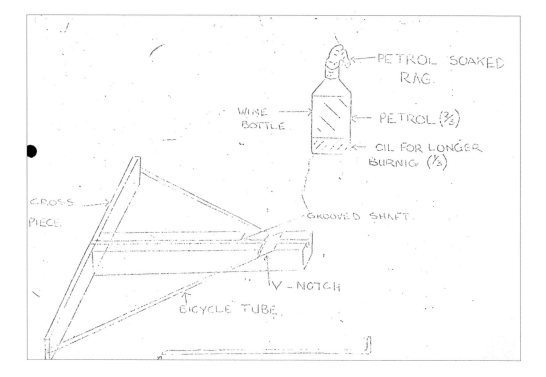

ABOVE: Instructions to make a petrol bomb.

OVERLEAF: A pamphlet urging scholars to stay away from their schools in August 1976.

STUDENTS ARE DEMONSTRATING
AND HAVE BEEN KILLED THROUGH-
OUT SOUTH AFRICA. WHY?

1.BECAUSE THEY RESENT AFRIKAANS
BEING FORCED UPON THEM. TO BLACKS
IT IS THE LANGUAGE OF THE OPPRESSOR
AND A SYMBOL OF THEIR OPPRESSION.

2.THEY HATE THE INFERIOR EDUCATION AND
OPPRESSIVE LAWS WHICH GOVERN THEIR
EVERYDAY LIVES.

IS IT NOT THEREFORE NATURAL THAT THEY
WISH TO ELIMATE THESE INJUSTICES?

RECENTLY STUDENTS AT U.W.C., TRAINING
COLLEGES AND SCHOOLS IN THE CAPE HAVE
DEMONSTRATED AND BOYCOTTED CLASSES IN
SUPPORT OF THEIR FELLOW STUDENTS IN
SOWETO. AND ELSEWHERE IN THE COUNTRY.
AND 'WHY NOT YOU?

THIS IS YOUR CHANCE TO SHOW SOLIDARITY

STAY AWAY FROM YOUR SCHOOLS
FROM TUE. 16TH AUG TO FRI. 21st AUG

UNITE! STAND FIRM! TO HELL
WITH WHITE BAASKAP. AND
RACIAL OPPRESSION.

The following three pages show a letter written by Soweto Students'
Representative Council leader Tsietsi Mashinini.

We the SSRC (Soweto Students Representative Council)
condem
1. Police action in Soweto by irresponsibly
shooting out students on their way
to school or black children playing
in the location as it has been
reported in the newspapers. We
see it as an unofficial declaration
of war on black students by
our "peace-officers"

2. The statement by Mr Gert Prinsloo
that the racist regime will not
"succumb to the demands of a
handful students". instead we are
the voice of the people and our
demands shall be met

3. The response by Jimmy Kruger that
he will not accept the B.P.A.
as the authentic body representing
us. We see no peace and
order if our demands are
not met

4. The statement by the Prime Minister that the racist regime "will not panic". We do not anticipate panic but expect responsible ACTION from the leaders of this country.

5. The action of elements burning schools we believe that is no black man's action.

6 The brutality experience by students in police hands especially those who have been recently arrested and released.

7. The abuse of power by security officers to refuse relatives to see detainees and demand a just investigation in the suspicious conditions in which Mr Mapetla Mohapi died and we are afraid the same may befall our people

detained in connection with the so called "riots"

* I ~~do~~ Tsietsi Mashinini appeal on students to report back to school and notify the authorities of any injured dead or missing students. We still have our end exams to write and we must have our priorities sorted.

⑧ We lastly condem the detention of B.P.A. members and see it as an unwarranted move by the system. We never meant them to meet Mr ~~Kgt~~ Kruger in detention

Ours is a peace-ful struggle whith only the racist regime can curb by a dialoque with our leaders.

Tsietsi Mashinini
(Chairman)

The Cabinet minutes of 10 August 1976 end with the proposal 'that the movement [the Soweto Students Representative Council] be broken and the police should take more drastic and harsh action that will lead to more deaths.' The word 'goedgekeur' (agreed) is appended to the document.

10.8.76   Onluste in Soweto
duur nog voort. Die kinders
in Soweto is goed opgelei.
Die konflik van so met wie
Men Samesprekings, het probeer
aanmerk, maar daar is klaarblyklik
teenaksie. Die leerlinge/studente
het Studenteraad gestig. Die
basiese gevaar is groeiende
onverwerkheid, en die
om die insidente te voorkom,
Wat met militêre presiesheid
waarmee hulle optree.
Men stel voor dat hierdie
beweging gebreek moet word, en
dink polisie moet miskien 'n bietjie meer
drasties en hardhandig moet optree wat
meer sterftes meebring.   Goedgekeur

The following thee pages show disinformation pamphlets distributed by the police. They urge Sowetans not to strike, but to stay at work.

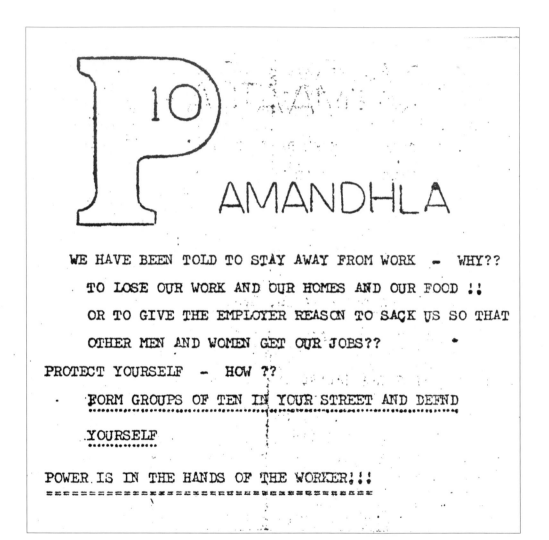

AMANDHLA

WE HAVE BEEN TOLD TO STAY AWAY FROM WORK - WHY??

TO LOSE OUR WORK AND OUR HOMES AND OUR FOOD !!

OR TO GIVE THE EMPLOYER REASON TO SACK US SO THAT

OTHER MEN AND WOMEN GET OUR JOBS??

PROTECT YOURSELF - HOW ??

FORM GROUPS OF TEN IN YOUR STREET AND DEFND

YOURSELF

POWER IS IN THE HANDS OF THE WORKER!!!

STRIKE ??

THE PEST IN OUR MIDST

THE PEST THAT KEEPS US FROM OUR WORK

THE PEST THAT KEEPS THE FOOD FROM OUR MOUTHS

THE MARCH TO "FREEDOM" IS A MARCH TO HUNGER
AND TO A JOBLESS SOCIETY

ALL BLACK PEOPLE SUFFER UNDER THE BURDEN OF
JOBLESS HOOLIGANS

A STRIKE WILL NOT HELP US - IT WILL ONLY MAKE IT
HARDER TO FIND A JOB, AND FOOD, AND A HOME

A SACRIFICE NOW MAY BE A SACRIFICE OF THE
FREEDOM OF FUTURE GENERATIONS

IF YOU STRIKE YOU STRIKE A BLOW AT YOURSELF AND YOUR FAMILY

VUKANI - AWAKE

Mothers Awake!

You have given birth to MA-AFRICA!

You carried this responsbility with love and care and devotion!

CHILDREN ARE HUNGRY AND SICK!

WHY?

Our men are kept away from work by children.

Our men allow youngsters to burn our Clinics.

WHAT has become of our men, the fathers of our children!

The men who should support, guide, educate and initiate the sons of Africa towards responsble manhood.

WHERE are the men who should feed, clothe and protect us!

ARE OUR MEN STILL MEN?
They are dictated to by children.

WOMEN OF AFRICA - AWAKE!

Let us take the trousers from our men and put them on!

Jacki Selebi

Horst Kleinschmidt

Beyers Naudé

Billy Lesedi Masethla

Barney Pityana

Murphy Morobe

Daniel Sechaba Montsitsi

Nthato Harrison Motlana

governments are impressing on Pretoria with increasing urgency. Simply put, it is this: Pretoria must help the West to help South Africa by relieving the tensions which have reached breaking point in the country.'

Not only was Vorster's international star plummeting, but his reputation at home for decisiveness was severely dented as he dithered while Soweto burned. At first his silence was deafening; then, when he did speak, it was to offer a mixture of red herrings and strong talk about order being restored at any cost. The general image was one of an embattled man with clay feet facing a tide of violence with a momentum beyond his grasp or control.

The consequences of the threat to Afrikaner nationalism were most acutely felt in the Broederbond – the body that had promoted the issue of Afrikaans in black schools in the first place. The first order of business was thus to divert attention from the language question. Over the next few weeks Cabinet ministers would be heard spouting nonsense such as: 'Black Power Nazis fuelled the uprising'; 'Black school principals gave children dagga [marijuana] to make them fearless'; 'Black children were looking for any excuse not to sit their exams'; 'Emotions' were to blame, as were NUSAS, the French Revolution, gangsters and, of course, the press. And the media were not only responsible for the riots; the photos of atrocities they published were doctored to create a 'disgusting misrepresentation'. What it was not was the 'communist plot' that was the favourite refrain, because, as US congressman Andrew Young pointed out, the Nationalists were too good an agent for communism for the communists to want to get rid of apartheid.

In the most extraordinary exercise designed to demonstrate that race problems and race riots occurred all over the globe, the Broederbond involved the Department of Information in a worldwide analysis of racial friction – at the taxpayers' expense. And this department, which fell under Connie Mulder (whose supporters in the succession race were the ones feeling the heat), was only too willing to oblige. Research was conducted into the student riots in Paris in May 1968, as well as civil disorder between Canadian immigrants and native Canadian Indians, labour unrest in Argentina, underground movements in Italy, white Americans attacking an African American in Washington Square, Israeli–Arab conflicts, the oppression of Aborigines in Australia, the carnival riots in London's Notting Hill, and troubles in Cyprus, Lebanon, Greece, Turkey, India, Pakistan, the Soviet Union and Brazil. The conclusion: 'There are worse disputes in other parts of the world.'

Afrikaans academics and newspapers were having none of it, however, and were making their voices heard over the unacceptable issue of having 'blood on their language'. The clarion call from this sector was that blacks needed to be treated with greater sensitivity, Treurnicht was the wrong man for the job, and, most of all, Afrikaners were feeling threatened. 'In what must be the most outspoken criticism of his own people any leading Afrikaner has ever made, a member of the academic elite has warned that his volk's days are numbered,' wrote Hugh Murray, political correspondent for the *Sunday Express*. 'This, he says, is because "the Afrikaner has betrayed his own fatherland to ensure his own survival – not as a volk but as a ruler". In the process he has excluded and estranged the English-speaking South Africans. He has caused blacks and coloureds to regard Afrikaans as the language of the oppressor, so that when South Africa becomes integrated – as it inevitably must – Afrikaans will be eliminated. And he has become a crass materialist who uses "church and political contacts to make money around the corner" – so destroying his integrity. The man who makes this powerful but deeply concerned criticism of his own people is Professor Dreyer Kruger, professor of psychology at Rhodes University.'

There were, however, contradictory calls coming from the Afrikaner on the street – and their message was simple: flog the troublemakers. The head and the heart of Afrikanerdom were obviously pulling in different directions, and these conflicts were felt between the left and right in the Cabinet in a fury known as the 'new Boer War'. The government could not resolve the issue, deciding to maintain the appearance of unity at all costs, and thus crudely attempted to pander to the right while pacifying those clamouring for change.

The first call was for a commission of inquiry, and Kruger wasted little time in appointing the Transvaal judge president Justice Cillie as a one-man commission to investigate the causes of the Soweto Uprising. Dr Percy Yutar, the attorney who had so vigorously prosecuted Nelson Mandela and others at the Rivonia Trial, was selected to aid him. So far so good, but the Nationalists were not going to rock an already troubled boat. Both the commissioner and his assistant were very friendly to the Nationalist cause, and when they did show independence they could easily be misled. The report they eventually produced would run to hundreds of pages, with thousands more in support documents – it was so corrupted, however, that its findings were of little weight other than as a minute-by-minute record of incidents.

Blacks were refused permission to sit on the commission, and when two blacks involved in the disturbances appeared before it they were arrested by the security police, which put paid to any further input from that quarter. The police responded by claiming that the pair were arrested for other incidents related to the uprising and not for the matters about which they were giving evidence – either way, the message was clear: 'We do not want to hear evidence from the "wrong" people.' With that problem out of the way, the commission was manipulated by the government as a vehicle to absolve the police of any wrongdoing, and in this it did a sterling job. All bystanders' and press evidence of the first shot fired on 16 June were rejected in favour of the police version. Thousands of police affidavits were submitted on all incidents in which people were injured or killed. None of these was investigated further and no comment was made on the remarkable coincidence that certain policemen were confronted with the identical situation in different parts of the country and reacted in the same fashion to each of them. For example, in Alexandra, a policeman claimed that he fired a shot into the ground as a warning to a fleeing person to stop and that unfortunately the bullet ricocheted and hit the person in the middle of the back, killing him instantly. The identical situation occurred in Soweto, but the commission made no comment on this or other glaring coincidences. Every case of police brutality was swept under the carpet and everything other than the government line rejected.

For the rest it was pure political circus. Kruger urged black leaders to talk to him, then claimed there were none to speak with. 'We used minimum force,' he told one group, but to the other, he said, 'I've had enough. It is my duty to maintain law and order and I shall do so.' 'Rubber bullets were not used because they have proved to be ineffective in riot situations,' he told a foreign journalist, and 'We did not use rubber bullets because it made people tame to the gun,' he told the *Sunday Times*. His colleagues were not to be left out: No you may not perform mass burials, yes you may; Soweto residents will receive more powers, the lot of urban blacks will not change; blacks will be better represented, no they may not sit on the administration boards; we are considering home ownership for township residents, it's full steam ahead for the homelands; a better deal for black schools, black schools will remain closed until blacks show a willingness to use schools for the right purpose; mixed schools to get government go-ahead, we will act against Roman Catholic schools that opened their doors to black students in the wake of the uprising; compulsory free education for blacks may be considered, parents will be held responsible for riot damage; and a new multiracial sports deal on the cards, but no, blacks may not travel on white buses.

The ambivalence did not end here. There was brutal oppression. Dozens of children and students were arrested and held in police cells without their parents being informed; people already banned, like Beyers Naudé, had their conditions made more onerous; while others, such as Fatima Meer in Durban, had fresh banning orders slapped on them. Then there were concessions. While the Broederbond claimed Afrikaans had nothing to do with the uprising, MC Botha dropped the issue on 6 July and reinstated the right of school boards to choose the language of instruction. 'They all say it was my fault,' responded Thys de Beer, the circuit inspector. 'I'm just a public servant. Personally I couldn't care less: Let them have all their schooling in English if that is what they want. But professionally I must tell them that is not in the children's best interests.' And, in response to pressure, Ackerman and his entire staff of circuit inspectors were transferred and the two sacked Meadowlands Tswana School Board members were reinstated – the stable door now securely fastened after the horses had bolted.

Reacting to the announcement that the 50:50 rule was to be dropped, TW Kambule, the principal of Orlando High School, said 'This was to be expected.' But he went on to warn that the inspectorate would use other ways to promote Afrikaans in black schools and that many principals who were known for their habit of trying to 'curry favour' would attempt to maintain the 50:50 rule. 'If they do,' he said, 'they must know that the students will quickly intervene.'

Whatever concessions were made, one thing was clear: government was not going to take bold steps. Rather, airy proposals of a change in the form of government – away from the Westminster system to a canton style with an executive president – began to surface. Much of this initial thought formed the basis of the changes introduced in the 1980s, but there was no mention of blacks being given a say because no change was anticipated for the homeland system other than that it was to be speeded up. 'All Mr Vorster was able to tell Dr Kissinger is that he will review measures which have become outdated, but will not bring about the rapid, radical reforms the West believes are vital for peace,' reported Martin Schneider in the *Sunday Express*.

'South Africa is unwilling to make any drastic changes to the broad concept of separate development at a time when the policy is coming to fruition,' responded Foreign Minister Hilgard Muller. 'This is a prescription for disaster,' replied the *Financial Mail*. 'The fruits of the policy of apartheid are frustration, injustice and hatred. Among its latest consequences are arson, rioting and slaughter. If it is continued, the end result may well be revolution.' The Nationalists, however, were not taking note.

In Johannesburg there was a mass wringing of hands among the English-speakers. Those who could emigrate reached for their passports again, but their wealth was devalued as the Stock Exchange fell further and house prices plummeted. 'The beautiful homes of Johannesburg's Beautiful People are selling at basement prices,' reported the *Sunday Express*. 'They make up a spectacular list of some of the most impressive homes in and around the city. In the middle of this price range is one of Johannesburg's finest houses at Khyber Rock, owned by Mr Harold Myhill, former managing director of British Tyre and Rubber. It is offered for R325 000. But, says the *Financial Mail* this week, the market expects it to go for about R180 000, while the replacement cost for the house is estimated at half a million. Another spectacular bargain is John Schlesinger's Hyde Park mansion, Summer Place. He had invested R1 million in it – and sold it to top businessman Neels Swart for only R275 000. Johannesburg property agent Don Martin, who specialises in high-priced houses, sums it up like this: "You can't replace them at double their cost. But you can't sell them off at half their cost."'

Something had to be done, but what? The country was at a crossroads – but which route to take? The hard-line speeches were a comfort, but those poor blacks, the English-speakers agonised. Groups were established to promote a better understanding between the races and relief funds were raised: the mayor of Johannesburg, Monty Sklaar, established the Mayoral Soweto Fund, which aimed to raise R100 000; the Women for Peaceful Change Now group was launched; and the Anglo American Corporation's Chairman's Fund provided the salaries for eight social workers to be employed at black schools in Soweto. But why, they asked, did blacks always destroy the things given them? 'Blacks do not destroy facilities,' replied Obed Kunene, the editor of *Ilanga*. 'They destroy symbols of the entire system devised by whites for them. It is a system that has virtually ruined the fabric of black society, especially in the urban areas. It is abhorrent, resented, despised and hated almost to pathological limits. And the blame is squarely on the whites who consider it their divine right to order and regulate the lives of black people.' It is unlikely that many heard him.

In the suburbs the disquiet was palpable. Mandy Den Dulk, a resident of Melville, had just given birth. 'At the time you have a baby, you're so elated the whole world could explode around you,' she said. 'But afterwards I worried about bringing our baby into this situation. It's especially worrying when you have little girls, they're so vulnerable. The only thing that could guarantee a safe future for my children is for South Africa to be a mixed society. We can't just stay white and push the blacks down. I suppose it would be nice if things stayed as they are, only more peaceful.'

English-speaking politicians were thinking the same way. NUSAS, the rejected wishy-washy liberals, proposed a 'white Africanism' whereby whites would become a little more African. The fragmented parliamentary opposition tried to unite to form a united front with progressive Afrikaners, which came to nothing. And Helen Suzman suggested it would be acceptable to her to live under a government led by a responsible black person such as Chief Mangosuthu Buthelezi or his cousin, Manas Buthelezi. They certainly were not going to go as far as novelist Alan Paton suggested:

'South Africa: where are you going? This question is not original. It was first used, if I remember rightly, by Prof BB Keet of the Stellenbosch Seminary, more than 20 years ago. The flood of racial legislation of the new National Party Government appalled him, and he wrote it all down. The laws were to him a denial of the Christian religion, which he took seriously. This did not make him popular, but he did not write for popularity. He wrote for justice and righteousness, and he wrote for us too, us, all the people of South Africa.

'I am not writing for all the people of South Africa. I am writing for its white people. White people cannot write for black people any more. Yet, in a way, I too am writing for us all. What do we, the white people of South Africa, after that week of desolation, do first? The first thing we do is to repent of our wickedness, of our arrogance, of our complacency, of our blindness.

'There has been much evil in Soweto. The killing of Dr Melville Edelstein, friend and servant of Soweto, was evil: the killing of Hector Peterson, 13-year-old schoolboy, was evil. The burning of schools, crèches, nurseries, clinics, shops, universities was evil. The hatred for whatever cause, was evil. And behind all this evil stand we, the white people of South Africa. The tsotsis [thugs] are evil, but we made them. They are the outcasts of our affluent society. And unless we can understand our guilt, we shall never understand anything at all.

'The compulsory teaching through the medium of Afrikaans (the language of the white descendants of Dutch settlers) is the immediate cause. But the deeper cause is the whole pattern of discriminatory laws.

'Who are the agitators? They are the discriminatory laws.

'Who are the polarising forces? They are the discriminatory laws. It is fantastic that a minister should accuse anonymous polarising forces. They are not anonymous, they can all be given names. They are the Group Areas Act, the separate universities, the

Mixed Marriages Act, the abolition of parliamentary representation for African and coloured people and a dozen other laws. That there are human agitators as well, no one can doubt. But their weapons are the discriminatory laws, the laws of apartheid.

'Do you think that our immutable doctrine of the separation of the races has brought peace and concord to South African? Do you as Christians believe that the poor should pay for the poor, that you should spend between R400 and R500 a year on the education of each white child, and between R30 and R40 on each black child? Do you as Christians believe that white industry should be maintained at the cost of the integrity of black family life? Do you believe that your separate universities have encouraged the growth of wholesome national identities, co-operating gladly with others in a multinational country? Do you believe that you can move away from racial discrimination until you repeal discriminatory laws?

'There are other questions but these are enough. The blame does not lie wholly with the Nationalist Government. It lies with us all. The English-speaking people are also responsible. But the greater portion of the blame, and the greater portion of the responsibility, lies with the National Party. They have the power. They are the ones who have exalted law and order above justice. And by law and order they mean that kind of law and order which keeps them in power.

'I am not going to suggest what our rulers should do now. They are intelligent enough to know, even if they are at the moment psychologically incapacitated. I shall ask one question instead. Right Honourable the Prime Minister, a great responsibility lies on you. But if you regard yourself as first and last an Afrikaner, you will not save our country. You will not even save Afrikanerdom. You must be able to transcend your racial origins in a time of crisis, such as this undoubtedly is. Instead of declaring that you are determined to maintain law and order, could you not assure us that you are determined to find out – without prejudgement – why law and order have broken down, and to put the wrong things right?

'After repentance comes amendment of life.'

6 ■ METHODS OF BARBARISM

As a result of the massive crackdown on dissent and the closure of schools in June by Jimmy Kruger, matters appeared to return to something approaching normality. Students fell back to seething, black adults reverted to worrying about how they would educate their children and whites quickly lapsed into memory loss, pretending that nothing had happened and that it was business as usual. As the weeks passed, matters proved somewhat advantageous to the government: whatever loss of favour it suffered from the 'searchings of heart' on its left was more than made up for by a massive growth in support from the man in the street, petrified about security and threats to his way of life. It was in fact so good that Kruger could take the holiday Helen Suzman had suggested he needed.

While on vacation, and a week after schools should have reopened after the mid-year recess, Kruger received an urgent call from WRAB chief director JC de Villiers requesting he meet with delegates from the Urban Bantu Council – which he did on 21 July. At that meeting he extracted a promise from the black councillors that they would take responsibility for order in return for schools being reopened. 'I was surprised by the co-operation and assurances of Soweto leaders,' commented Kruger at a press conference after the meeting when he announced that schools would be allowed to open the following day. 'These Soweto leaders were also bitter that there had been so much burning, which they blamed on Black Power. Black Power is a snake in the body of South Africa which must be removed root and branch – it is a negative emotion which is nihilistic, destructive and undemocratic. On the other hand, black nationalism, which we support with our homelands policy, is good. It means a man will have a bath every day, keep himself healthy and work hard. That's nationalism.'

Confusion reigned the following day. 'Hundreds of kids were not aware that the schools were due to reopen today,' reported *The World*. 'As a result some schools were still deserted by 8 am when they were supposed to start. Even teachers were conspicuous by their absence. There were no incidents apart from two schools being set alight last night by vandals. The schools are Isipho School in Dlamini and Phakamani in Mofolo North. Meanwhile parents and civic leaders have welcomed the decision by the Minister of Justice to reopen schools.'

The problem of the first day's low turnout was solved by headmasters agreeing to start lessons in earnest only on Monday, 26 July. 'After poor attendance last week,' reported Willie Bokala in *The World* on 26 July, 'large crowds of people turned up at their Soweto schools this morning. Lower and higher primary schools drew the largest crowds while higher and secondary schools were not yet filled to pre-riot levels. Schools started late and classes were still empty at 8:00 am as children awaited the arrival of teachers. In some cases large crowds of children were seen standing in the streets outside their schools. A teacher at one of the schools said he hoped that by the end of the week conditions would be back to normal.'

It was not to be.

The reopening of schools gave students the opportunity to regroup and reappraise the situation. While the Afrikaans instruction issue had disappeared, it was replaced by anger over the large number of scholars who had been arrested and detained without trial. Moreover, the students had experienced power, and narrow concerns about their quality of education were replaced by a desire to change the political lot of people of colour. And, while Soweto schools were generally calm when they reopened, scholars were soon energised by reports of renewed unrest filtering through from the rest of the country. Included in these flare-ups were incidents at the University of Fort Hare and Lovedale College in the Eastern Cape, Mhluzi and Lynville townships in the Middelburg/Witbank area and Boipatong township near Vanderbijlpark, and the destruction of local government offices and a beerhall in Motshiwa township near Mafeking.

The boycotts soon resumed, and by the end of the first week school attendance had dropped dramatically. 'Soweto faces serious social problems created by the refusal of a group of students to go back to school,' reported *The Star.* 'About 50 percent of secondary and high school students have gone back with another 50 percent roaming the streets apparently for no reason. Parents and headmasters see the latter 50 percent as likely to create serious social problems because of their apparent recalcitrant attitude.

'They say there are already new gangs in the township that are terrorising innocent people parading in the name of "Black Power". A number of people have been stabbed, axed and robbed. Last week alone, 15 people were murdered in Soweto and scores of rapes and robberies were reported at various police stations. One headmaster, who does not want to be named, said some students who "bunked" classes were a menace because they abducted young girls and kept them "captive" at their hide-outs during the day until parents returned from work. There was no way of parents finding this out because the "captives" were threatened with violence if they reported the matter. Licentiousness in these days was commonplace, he asserted.

'Another problem that will face the Sowetan of tomorrow is that these pupils will swell the already high drop-out rate in the area causing untold socio-economic difficulties in future. Why are these pupils refusing to go back to school? One disgruntled youth said it was useless to start all over again at such a critical time of the year. A student in Orlando West, Soweto, said: "Our struggle is not only against the use of Afrikaans as a medium of instruction in black schools. We are aiming at changing the entire Bantu Education system – which means equal education for all."'

To make matters worse, a group of vandals, operating at night, set fire to schools. 'Fear and confusion still gripped Soweto today as most pupils stayed at home following the burning of four more schools there during the night,' reported *The Star*. 'There are now indications that the tsotsi [gang] element has taken control and instituted a reign of terror over both parents and children in the township. Colonel JP Visser, head of the Soweto CID, said he believed the tsotsi element was responsible for the disruption of classes at Soweto schools since they reopened. Last night and yesterday afternoon four schools in Soweto were damaged by fires started in classrooms. The Soweto police, who believe one gang is responsible for all arson attempts in Soweto, have offered a R500 reward for information that will lead to the gang being smashed.'

While the police blamed gang members for school burnings, all evidence suggests that the police were themselves responsible, because they had the most to gain. Any trouble gave them an excuse to maintain a heavy presence at schools, thus placing them in a position to quell any new uprising among scholars. And considering this heavy round-the-clock presence, it is highly suspicious that they were incapable of apprehending a group of 'youthful vandals' operating at will.

The police presence also contributed to class boycotts. 'The head of the Soweto CID this morning rejected claims by school principals that the low attendance in schools was caused by police patrols in streets,' reported *The World*. 'This allegation was made by school principals at a meeting held at Morris Isaacson. The principals said "continued police patrols in Soweto" were frightening many children into staying away. The fact that the police were heavily armed aggravated the situation. The meeting unanimously agreed that the police should be withdrawn immediately. Colonel Visser said he completely rejected this and said the police were instead there to protect the students and not harm them. "We are there to protect them against intimidation from people who do not want the children to go back to school."'

The school burnings were certainly not organised by the scholars. The Action Committee, which organised the 16 June march, was increasingly concerned as the situation reverted to anarchy – and it too suspected that the police were behind the chaos and were irresponsibly inciting tension 'for the ends of the fascist regime'. At an Action Committee meeting on 2 August, at Morris Isaacson, it was felt that more co-ordination was needed to protect the residents of Soweto from youth gangs. It was decided that each school would nominate two student leaders to sit on a council. This group was christened the Soweto Students' Representative Council (SSRC) and Tsietsi Mashinini was elected as its first chairman. The SSRC urged that scholars return to school and resolved that on 4 August students would march from Soweto to security police headquarters at John Vorster Square in Johannesburg to demand the release of all schoolchildren in detention. This demand was to be backed by calling on workers and parents to observe a three-day stayaway from 4 to 6 August.

Again, Winnie Mandela – at a time when many BPA members were trying to rein in the scholars – appears to have played a role in this plan. 'In July, Tebello Motapanya, Tsietsi Mashinini and I had a discussion with Winnie Mandela,' stated Murphy Morobe at the time. 'She told us that the "system" was now desperate; she said that this was because they had never thought that kids can do what they did on 16 June. She said that the government had killed so many people and were now arresting people at random. She further said that the students must never retreat, but must go on with what they are doing. She mentioned that as soon as schools reopen, the students must do something about some of their colleagues who have been detained. She then said to us that the sooner students do something again then she can be very happy, because we must maintain the spirit which prevailed on 16 June. We did not go further than this because she then said to us that we should not frequent her house because she suspects that "they" could have started to watch her house again.'

While Winnie Mandela urged further action, the idea for the stayaway came from the BC-supporting trade unionist Kyalushi Drake Koka, also known as the 'Godfather'. According to Morobe, Koka suggested a stayaway to him 'as a project that would put the whites into trouble'. At a subsequent SSRC meeting, Morobe was told by another student that Mashinini had also been to see Koka and had received the same advice.

Police quickly pounced on the idea of a stayaway, pointing out that boycotts were a favoured tactic of the banned ANC, and vowed to do all they could to maintain 'law and order'. 'Colonel Visser said that the police were aware of a protest march planned to take place between Baragwanath and Johannesburg,' reported the *Rand Daily Mail.* '"We will take the necessary steps against such an illegal procession," he said. Soweto's divisional commissioner of police, Brigadier le Roux, said the police were ready for anything. "Students gathered in Soweto decided on certain actions," he said. "We don't know what they plan to do – there are only rumours to depend on – but it appears they are not going to school. But we are prepared for anything and I don't think their plans will work."

'In Cape Town a mass meeting of University of Cape Town students decided to propose a one-day boycott of classes. A pamphlet circulated said: "Wednesday [4 August] has been called a day of solidarity with children of Soweto and with those detained."'

On 4 August police mounted a massive blockade to contain the 20 000 who gathered to march on Johannesburg. Frustrated, the protesters turned on anyone not heeding the stayaway call – PUTCO buses were commandeered and set alight, trains were stoned and sections of track lifted, and cars were harassed and drivers threatened. While the march was prevented, with four people killed in the process, job absenteeism reached nearly 70 per cent. 'Wednesday was the first day of the first big stayaway by the black worker,' wrote Martin Creamer in the *Sunday Times.* 'Johannesburg – though not seriously disrupted – had its first taste this week of doing without the services of the black man. His stayaway coincided with the second round of violent and deadly Soweto rioting in under two months.

'The rioting, however, confined as it has been so far to the townships, has not directly affected the lives of the city and suburban white. The last riots proved that. No sooner had they died down than South Africa was back to braaivleis, rugby and sunny skies. But Wednesday's big stayaway introduced a new dimension to the black unrest. Whites found themselves having to drive delivery vans, sell newspapers and work in the kitchens of restaurants. The black man's absence was being felt.

'While Johannesburg survived surprisingly well, employers were beginning to conceive what a prolonged stayaway could do to their comforts, their businesses and the sensitive economy, and hoping that it was not an omen of things to come. Industrialists are already warning that worker-absence of long duration will be bad for business. "If it's just a day or two, I won't worry, but longer than that and we will be badly affected," said the managing director of a big Johannesburg firm.

'Blacks should have no illusions: The stayaway will hit them just as hard as anyone else, perhaps even harder. Employers would not go on paying workers for services they had not rendered. The black worker, who by-and-large cherishes his job, would also not be happy to take home a pay packet even smaller than the one he can already hardly come out on.'

The students, delighted at the blow they had rendered the government and big business, again called for scholars to return to school and committed the residents of Soweto to another stayaway from 23 to 25 August. 'The SSRC has appealed to students to go back to school,' reported the *Rand Daily Mail*. 'In a press statement the council chairman, Tsietsi Mashinini, asked that principals make sure lessons are held "because examinations are going on which we regard as our major priority". Students were asked to be alert for elements attempting to exploit their unity and to take their instructions from their leaders and from no one else. The statement said: "We honour our parents' support and our voice is one with theirs. Our struggle is peaceful and only the elimination of our grievances can bring about peace and order, and not the perpetuation of this country's Draconian laws. We condemn the police action for turning our peaceful efforts into a bloody confrontation, as we are unarmed.

"'Be ashamed to die until you have

"'Won some victory for humanity.'"

The government was again in panic – particularly as the unrest now threatened to immobilise an already fragile economy fatally. Because of this the Cabinet conspired in a criminal decision – and because it was criminal it marks all the members individually as criminals. At a Cabinet meeting on 10 August it was unanimously agreed 'that the movement [Soweto Students' Representative Council] be broken and the police should take more drastic and harsh action that will lead to more deaths'. Murder was clearly the intention, and the word '*goedgekeur*' (agreed) is appended to the document.

When detention without trial became legal in 1963, it had the effect of removing political prisoners from society and holding them in filthy cells, where they were fed terrible food and were not allowed visits, legal representation or a change of clothing. Here, in an effort to extract information or to force the signing of confessions, the most appalling tortures were practised. Beatings, starvation, sleep deprivation, cigarette burns, acid burns, suffocation, partial drowning, electric shocks, and, for women, rape and the insertion of live rats into their vaginas were commonplace. And when detainees died under these circumstances the police gave cynical reasons such as 'slipped on a piece of soap in the showers', 'removed the bars from prison cell and leapt to his death', or, simply, 'suicide'.

'Since September 1963, when Looksmart Ngundle, a 90-day detainee, was found hanging in his cell, 35 others have died,' wrote Jennifer Hyman in the *Sunday Express*. 'Of all the detainees' deaths, 18 have been officially described as "suicide", though inquests are pending in some cases. The Minister of Justice, Jimmy Kruger, explained this high figure by saying ANC members were under communist orders to die rather than give information. With this prior knowledge, says the Institute of Race Relations, "It is cause for grave concern that known hardcore ANC members should be so loosely guarded in prison that they find the opportunity to commit suicide." The commissioner of police, General Gert Prinsloo, said that in light of the known suicide instruction, police did all they could to prevent detainees from taking their lives, short of "slapping them in chains". We asked Mr Kruger to release the ANC document containing the suicide instruction but received no reply.'

From 16 June to 10 August the police indulged in their normal brutality. Of the hundreds of scholars – some as young as 10 years old – arrested during the initial uprising, many were forced to exercise to the point of exhaustion before being made to load corpses in a van, which were then placed in a helicopter and dropped in Avalon Cemetery. 'When I was collected for interrogation one of the policemen cracked a joke and I laughed,' stated a pupil of Morris Isaacson. 'He said I was laughing at him and I was taken to an empty room with one chair, and beaten up by five white policemen. They said to me that I wanted to overthrow the government. They kept on beating me. They asked me about prefects at the school. Then they asked me about meetings I attended at the school. I told them I hadn't attended any meetings. Then they beat me up. I was screaming. They put a newspaper inside my mouth. They also asked me about Khotso [Khotso Seathlolo – a student leader]. I told them I'd never seen Khotso. Then they beat me up. They said they would give me five minutes to think about it. They came back and asked me the same question. Again I denied it. They beat me up again. They told me to go out. Then one policeman followed and beat me on the back with a stick. From there I was taken to another room to wait for my colleagues. From there I was taken to another police station. The riot police came in every half-hour during the first night and ordered us to stand up and hold meetings in the cells. We got no sleep. After three days we were taken back to Protea Police Station. One riot policeman told another that they were taking us for a beating and then they would bring us back. Twenty-eight of us, including teachers, were put into a room. They made us stand. They took me to an interrogation room. They told me to take my clothes off. I took them off and then they told me to sit on a chair behind the door. Then they fastened me to the chair by my wrists. Then they put something on my head, like a cap. I didn't see what it was. Then they came with a wet cloth and put it inside my mouth. Then I felt electric shocks going through my body. After five minutes the shocks stopped and they asked me if I would tell them the truth. I said I would tell them the truth.'

Stories began to surface that police were aiming shotguns at children's heads with the intention of blinding them. 'Hospitals cannot comment officially on allegations that black children were blinded when police fired birdshot,' reported Mike Dutfield in the *Rand Daily Mail*. 'Mr Sybrand van Niekerk, the administrator of the Transvaal, said yesterday that the allegations related to the riots and that therefore only the police could release details. We then asked senior police officers to confirm or deny allegations made by a doctor at St John Eye Hospital, Baragwanath. General Dawie Kriel, deputy commissioner of police, had not received any complaints about the use of birdshot. He added that birdshot had been found to be one of the gentlest methods in dealing with violent riots.'

Any gentleness disappeared after the Cabinet meeting of 10 August. Police action also became more sinister. The green car became a more frequent visitor to the streets of Soweto. In one incident, a woman saw the car cruise down the street with riot police pointing rifles from the window. They killed two boys, aged between eight and nine, who were playing soccer. 'A student was shot dead and five others injured when police in a green car opened fire at different spots in Soweto yesterday,' reported the *Rand Daily Mail* on another occasion. 'The car was driven by two white policemen in camouflage kit. It is the car that is frequently on the scene in Soweto. I was travelling with a *Rand Daily Mail* photographer along the Mofolo Golf Course at 11:00 am yesterday when I saw a group of students running across the course. Some were carrying schoolbooks. Three shots rang out from the green car. A boy fell near a small donga after the shooting. When we went to investigate after the police had left, we discovered the schoolboy was dead.

'Minutes later we were told that another boy had been injured during the same shooting. He had already been taken to hospital in a private car. Earlier on, police in a green car had opened fire on a mob at Meadowlands and later on the same happened at Mofolo Central. Another boy was reported shot yesterday in Mofolo Village.'

'We continue to receive startling reports from Soweto residents alleging indis-criminate police action,' added the *Sunday Express*, 'as well as emphatic denials from the police themselves that there is any such campaign. The *Express* has been unable to verify the allegations that have been made to it and to other organisations. In sum-mary these are the allegations made: Men in camouflage uniforms are conducting raids and arrests in a commercial van with "Simba Chips" lettered on the sides; A white Valiant Regal car – registration TJ165-237 – occupied by men in camouflage uniform cruises through the township conducting raids and in one incident, auto-matic rifles are said to have appeared from the windows and shot seven youths in Mda Street, Orlando West; a green Chevrolet, which changes number plates or car-ries none at all, is also said to conduct raids in Soweto. Last Sunday, men in camou-flage uniforms are said to have shot a youth dead from the Chev's windows.

'Mr Sipho Mthunzi, 20, an employee at a leading Johannesburg hotel, said he was playing soccer with eight other youths outside his home in Mda Street. "I saw a white Valiant turn the corner into our street," he said. "Three white men in camouflage were inside the car. Suddenly rifles appeared out of the windows and moved up and down the block shooting." Mr Mthunzi and six other youths were shot, two of whom died instantly. He was shot in his right foot. The *Express* checked the registration with the Licensing Department of the Johannesburg City Council, and found that the car is reg-istered as a police vehicle.

'Mr Patrick Muse, 20, a student of Diepkloof, told the *Express* he was in the yard of his home when a youth he knew only as Lawrence walked past in the street. A green Chevrolet, which he described as a LTD model, approached, occupied by four white men in camouflage uniforms. Rifles appeared from the windows and "a lot" of shots were fired. Mr Muse said that Lawrence tried to run, but dropped to the ground "about five metres" from where he was standing. The car stopped. The men got out. One of them took an axe from the boot and dropped it on the ground next to Lawrence. Mr Muse said he heard one of the men using the words "Black Power". As the car drove away, he approached Lawrence and found he was dead.

'The Rev Cornelius Mphaki, of Dube Village, told how his 12-year-old son, Leonard, was wounded outside of the gate of his home. A friend Leonard had been talking to died in the shooting. The Rev Mphaki said police had opened fire on Leonard and three others. The boys tried to run away, but Leonard and one of his friends were felled by bullets. "When I tried to go and help my son, one of the police-men threatened to shoot me," he said. Leonard had bullet wounds in the head and back. He spent six weeks in hospital. His speech is affected and he is still going for treatment.

'Mr Gabriel Madingwane and Mr David Moeketsi, both of Zone 3, Diepkloof, gave an account of how Mr Madingwane's 11-year-old son, David, was killed after police had opened fire while they were standing inside his yard. The shots were being fired by policemen in two cars. People in the yard ran into the house, but heard someone outside shouting about a child. Mr Madingwane went outside to investigate and saw David on the ground. By the time he had been taken to hospital he was dead.

'The strangest of all the reports was one by numerous residents claiming that the police were using vehicles with "Simba Chips" lettered on the side to conduct raids and arrests in the township. The van has been seen in different places and at different times, and independent reports claim it is always occupied by men in regular or camouflage uniform. Mr A Greyvenstein, group-managing director of Simba-Quix, the company which markets Simba Chips, denied that any of his company's vehicles could be used by police in Soweto. "I am shocked at these reports," he said. "All our trucks are accounted for, even those we sell."'

So it went on. A 10-year-old girl was shot dead, as were youths fired on with shotguns from a decoy car. A Cabinet minister might as well have shot them, because this was the interpretation of the decision taken on 10 August. But it backfired, because it added to the grim image of the police – equating them with shooting and death – and increased the politicisation of blacks.

'You are either alive and proud or you are dead, and when you are dead you can't care anyway,' said Steve Biko in an interview with a United States businessman. 'And your method of death can in itself be a politicising thing. So you can die in the riots. For a hell of a lot of them, in fact, there's really nothing to lose – almost literally, given the kind of situation that they come from. So if you can overcome the personal fear of death, which is a highly irrational thing, you know, then you're on the way.

'And in interrogation the same sort of thing applies. I was talking to this policeman, and I told him: "If you want us to make any progress, the best thing is for us to talk. Don't try any form of rough stuff, because it just won't work." And this is absolutely true also. For I just couldn't see what they could do to me which would make me all of a sudden soften to them. If they talk to me, well, I'm bound to be affected by them as human beings. But the moment they adopt rough stuff, they are imprinting on my mind that they are police. And I only understand one form of dealing with police, and that's to be as unhelpful as possible. And I told them this: "It's up to you."

'We had a boxing match the first day I was arrested. Some guy tried to clout me with a club. I went into him like a bull. I think he was under instructions to take it so far and no further, and using open hands so that he didn't leave any marks on the face. And of course he said: "I will kill you." He meant to intimidate. And my answer was: "How long is it going to take you?"'

'We see it as an unofficial declaration of war on black students by our "peace-officers",' declared Mashinini, whose stature as a hero grew with each outrage committed against blacks.

Mashinini became the 'Scarlet Pimpernel' – the chief voice of the rebellion. 'In the weeks following 16 June he never slept in one place for more than a night,' recalled his brother Mpho. 'He appeared mostly at meetings where he could not stay longer than 10 minutes. Even though our home was like a police station because of all the police hanging about, he still managed to come home by jumping over a neighbour's fence. Twice he came disguised as a woman.'

At first the police appealed to him to hand himself over – warning that a group wanted to kill him. 'The warning came after the comparative calm of Soweto in the past few days was broken last night when six classrooms at the Orlando High School were burnt out,' reported *The Star*. 'The school was the pride of Soweto and students described the burning as stupid. Police have been trying to get hold of Mr Mashinini for several weeks. Colonel JP Visser, of the Soweto CID, appealed to him to hand himself over, saying he risked being killed by a group of angry hostel dwellers who were disturbed by the recent unrest. They were blaming Mr Mashinini for it. Colonel Visser said it would be best if Mr Mashinini was brought to him by his parents.'

A day later, however, Visser showed his hand by placing a R500 reward on the head of Soweto's most wanted man. 'We believe that Mr Mashinini is active and moving about Soweto and other townships, but we have been unable to locate him,' he said. 'If you spot him or know where he is you must report his presence to the nearest police station.'

There is debate about how organised or spontaneous the uprising of 16 June was. What is not in doubt is that the events of August and September were well planned and well financed – allowing leaders to remain in hiding and to travel to other centres. At the time there was intense speculation about the source of this financing. Mashinini approached Nthato Motlana for money, but was sent packing. The figure of Winnie Mandela and SASO members loom large – and it was probably through them that funds were channelled. Seven years later it surfaced that these grants originated from the South African Council of Churches (SACC). It was this mobility that helped spread the rebellion to nearly every centre in the country – including Cape Town.

On Wednesday, 11 August, 500 scholars from the adjacent Cape Town townships of Langa and Guguletu marched on the Guguletu Police Station, apparently in a show of sympathy for the residents of Soweto. The police gave the crowd eight minutes to disperse before firing teargas at them and arresting 19 pupils. That afternoon, a crowd of 5 000 adults and children marched on the police station to demand the release of those detained. The police intercepted the procession and released dogs into the crowd.

'The protest was peaceful till the police appeared,' said a middle-aged resident of Langa. A man from Guguletu added that he did not think the police were interested in negotiating. 'It is only a pity that the police fired on the mobs because the people then adopted a militant stand,' he said. 'When young kids are shot you cannot keep your cool. I saw people fleeing in panic and being shot as they ran away.' Seven people died in the ensuing disturbances as protesters played cat and mouse with the riot police – being dispersed here only to reappear there. The following day trouble spread to other black townships in the Peninsula and to the University of Cape Town, where police broke up a student demonstration. By the end of the week, 27 were dead and dozens injured – with rumours circulating that as soon as the wounded at Groote Schuur, Tygerberg and Conradie hospitals were stitched up they were handed over to police and taken away.

'As this is written, some measure of peace and calm had returned to the troubled Peninsula townships,' wrote political commentator Gerald Shaw. 'But there is no certainty that it would stay that way. If any good is to result from the events of the last few days, it is because traumatic happenings of this sort bring with them a heightened receptivity in public opinion and, briefly at least, the possibility of securing public support for far-reaching reform. If the heightened awareness of public opinion is to help bring about change, sufficient people must make the effort to reflect in calm, detached fashion on what is happening in South Africa.

'The first thing to consider is that the country has in fact reached the point of crisis which people have feared and predicted these many years past. This is THE crisis and it is right upon us, internally and externally. Mr Vorster might choose to regard things as serious rather than grave or critical, but anyone whose business it is to be informed is aware that things will never be the same again. If anyone still finds it hard to understand why people should burn down "their own" schools, clinics, libraries and so on, I would offer the explanation that what is happening is that people are venting rage and resentment at what they regard as symbols of an oppressive and hateful system – one which they have had no hand in shaping and in which they have no say whatsoever. The fact that most wage-earners and breadwinners are doing their best to battle through to work should not be taken as an endorsement of the system. It is not.

'What is happening in South Africa at the present time is that the black masses, through their articulate and rebellious younger generation, are rejecting the system out of hand. If this is what Black Consciousness means, we are going to have to get used to the idea. The party is over. The system, as at present devised and executed, is never going to work again with real efficiency. Soweto was not just a series of incidents in and around African townships: Soweto represents a change of political atmosphere; it is a condition, not something that has happened and will go away again.'

But the government was not listening, and the SSRC proceeded with plans for the 23–25 August stayaway. This involved a massive campaign by scholars to urge their parents to heed the call; a large-scale distribution of pamphlets to publicise the boycott; and a door-to-door drive to politicise and convince residents. In an oversight that reflected the students' lack of organisational maturity, little effort was made to enlist the support of migrant hostel dwellers.

'There are 10 hostels in Soweto, accommodating 36 000 inmates,' wrote Martin Creamer in the *Sunday Times*. 'By and large these hostels are little pieces of rural South Africa transplanted into the city, for living in them are predominantly contract workers from various homelands who come to town on a temporary basis. They leave their families – and often their hearts too – in the homelands and have to live a bachelor-type life in austere, single-sex hostels. They share neither the political aspirations nor, in most instances, the social life of the black city slicker. They tend to be looked down on by city blacks, who regard them as unsophisticated and lacking in education. The rural blacks in turn show tendencies of being not over-fond of the city blacks whom they regard as being too smart by half.

'Many of the hostel dwellers, being semiliterate or illiterate, are not given to much newspaper reading, relying mainly on the (government controlled) radio for information. Because of this many have been unaware of the real issues involved in the recent township rioting. They do not have children at school in the cities so they have never shared the feelings behind the schools' unrest which started the 16 June disturbances. Life in the city for the hostel men centres largely on work and earning a living. Keeping them from their jobs therefore meets with resistance particularly as hostel people were not well aware of what it was all about.'

'They don't have the same sort of stake in the urban area and are by and large not as politically orientated as the large population of Soweto people,' added Sean Maroney of the Institute of Race Relations. 'They condemn young politically minded city blacks who try to keep them from earning a living. They see the issues of urban black life in the short term.'

'The government should never have built hostels in the township,' said Soweto resident John Mahlanga. 'What happened is that the townships are now crammed with rural men who are starved of women and who regard city dwellers as weaklings. It is like putting tigers and lambs together in the same kraal – something terrible is going to happen.'

The poor planning with regard to enlisting the backing of migrant workers was exacerbated by Mashinini's dash into exile, buried in a coal truck, on the eve of the stayaway. The SSRC chairman made his way first to Botswana, then to Tanzania and on to Britain, where he was given asylum. At first he was toasted as a heroic celebrity and many organisations competed for his time and endorsement, but his star soon waned. He involved himself with British Trotskyists, severely irritated the ANC by claiming the organisation was corrupt and that it spent huge sums of money on trifles in the name of a liberation struggle, and, in a South African government set-up, gave a boastful interview to the Department of Information–sponsored *Pace* magazine. He later married and divorced a Liberian beauty queen, with whom he had two children, before moving to live with Miriam Makeba in Conakry, Guinea, where he died in 1990 of unexplained causes.

Within a day the SSRC named one of its youngest members, 18-year-old Sydney Khotso 'Tiny' Seathlolo, its new chairman. While the diminutive Seathlolo, a matric student from Naledi High, possessed none of Mashinini's charisma, he was a tactician of note. 'Seathlolo,' commented the *Weekend World*, 'like the leaders who came after him, had one strong factor running in his favour: the desire for leadership was so great, the need for organisation so strong, that the vast majority of Soweto students would follow the line he set without question. His election itself confirmed the SSRC's absence of democracy – or, at least, the absence of formal democracy. A British prime minister once said of the Conservative Party in England: "Its leaders are not elected:

they emerge." So it was with the SSRC. Tsietsi himself was never formally elected, though he was clearly a popular choice. Neither was Khotso elected by any sort of normal vote.

'When Tsietsi skipped the border, students generally expected that his deputy, the quiet and scholarly Murphy Morobe, would take his place. But at the tension-filled emergency SSRC executive meeting called after Tsietsi's departure, it was decided that a leader wouldn't be elected. Instead, he would "volunteer". Khotso volunteered. This procedure has caused some people to complain that the Council is imposed on Soweto students, rather than being placed in power by them. Council members themselves deny this. They admit that the system is not democratic in the formal sense, but say that in fact the chosen leaders always have the support of the people they represent. For example, they say if Khotso had not held the inward support of the executive members, his volunteering would have been ignored.'

The security police were not idle in the build-up to the stayaway. They countered it with a door-to-door drive, warning residents to go to work, and their own pamphlet campaign:

> AMANDHLA
>
> We have been told to stay away from work – why?
> To lose our work and our homes and our food
> Or to give the employer reason to sack us so that
> Other men and women get our jobs??
> Protect yourself – How??
> *Form groups of ten in your street and defend yourself*
> *Power is in the hands of the worker!!!*

There was, however, a certain smug confidence in a warning issued on 22 August by the security police's Major-General Mike Geldenhuys. In it he said the mood of black adults was changing and that they were getting sick of 'these people [students] and because of this the police are not worried'. While there is no direct evidence to suggest the police were instrumental in convincing hostel dwellers to ignore the boycott, there were numerous reports about outside attempts to organise workers against students before the stayaway. And subsequent events strongly suggest that the Security Branch had identified the pupils' Achilles' heel and acted on it – hence Geldenhuys's conviction, which flew in the face of police experience from 16 June.

'Industry and commerce in the Johannesburg area were hit by a massive stayaway by Soweto workers, ranging from 30 to 100 percent of labour and staff,' reported Clive Emdon and Mervyn Rees in the *Rand Daily Mail*. 'Mr Jimmy Kruger appealed to black workers not to give in to intimidation, and to get on with the job. The minister said he was prepared to hold another round of talks with black leaders, although it was difficult to determine who the leaders were at this stage. The Johannesburg Chamber of Commerce reported yesterday that the extensive stay-away hit industrialists, retailers and insurance companies. "Either nobody turned up on the black staff or considerable numbers stayed away," said Marius de Jager, the Chamber of Commerce director.'

But, while residents appear to have heeded the call overwhelmingly, migrants generally reported for work. There is little doubt that migrants were aggrieved at not being consulted and were angered by intimidation. Two Zulus were thrown from a train near New Canada Station by groups of students while others were taunted and stoned when returning from work. In the ensuing battle, two students were killed by migrants near the Meadowlands Hostel (known as the Mzimhlope Hostel), which was the biggest Soweto hostel, with 10 316 inhabitants, mainly of Zulu origin.

The following day, someone lured hostel residents of Mzimhlope with disinformation that other migrants were being intimidated by students at the station. The residents armed themselves with sticks and pangas and rushed to assist. While they were away, rooms were set alight. 'When we came home we found the whole place was a mess,' said migrant worker James Shika. 'The bar, beer lounge and butcher were all destroyed. The corrugated iron walls were removed and the place was left naked. We did not know who had caused the whole thing. We had been to work – we had no idea what started it all.' The police pointed fingers at scholars, but there is no evidence of this – and, in any case, migrant workers were unlikely to fall for a trick by the group they distrusted most. There were numerous reports, however, of specially convened meetings between security police and hostel leaders, and it is not far fetched to detect once again the criminal mischief of the security police, who were desperate to break any unity between township residents and migrants. Whatever the case, mayhem ensued.

'Hundreds of Soweto's Zulu hostel dwellers banded into a massive impi late yesterday afternoon and, armed with sticks, assegais and pangas, charged through the streets breaking into homes and attacking householders,' reported the *Rand Daily Mail*. 'Unconfirmed reports said six people were killed by the mob, and that at

Baragwanath Hospital more than 100 people, mostly teenagers, were treated for bullet, stab and other wounds.

'As the chanting impi surged through Orlando West, men, women and children fled through Meadowlands towards Dobsonville where they sought refuge. Scores of women and children camped outside the Meadowlands Police Station, asking for protection. By late last night, fierce street fighting was going on between the hostel Zulus and residents of Meadowlands who bonded together in an effort to protect their property.

'Police are reported to have watched from their anti riot Hippo vehicles without taking action as the "warriors" rampaged through the Mzimhlope area of Orlando West, scouring streets and homes in search of "cheeky children". Other reports claimed that police had taken the side of the Zulus against the township residents.

'After the Zulus poured into the streets, they were addressed by police through an interpreter from a Hippo vehicle. The Zulus then broke into war chants, turned and ran, brandishing assegais and sticks, witnesses said. Mr A Mabokela, who took his children to Dobsonville from Meadowlands, said: "The Zulus were massed behind the police. When the police fired shots, residents ran into their homes. Then the Zulus chased the residents, burnt their houses and attacked them." Two of the children known to have died are Gideon Mankayi and his younger brother, Arthur.

'An eye-witness to the mob rampage, Mr Moffat Makaga of Meadowlands, described how black attacked black as dusk settled over Soweto. "Screaming women ran from their houses clutching infants and were chased down the streets by armed young men. When I left the scene at least 50 houses had been smashed. The mob was worked up to a frenzy and bellowing out war songs as it charged through the streets," he said. Mr Makaga estimated the impi to be "about 1 500 strong and armed with every conceivable weapon except guns".

'*Rand Daily Mail* photographer, Peter Magubane, encountered a group of 150 armed Zulus outside Phefeni Station. "I watched as a car with two white policemen in camouflage dress in the front seat drew up outside the Merabe Hostel. Then three African men got out of the back seat, and joined the mob of Zulus."'

The *Star* reporters confirmed the complicity of police in siding with hostel dwellers. One staff reporter on the scene wrote: 'Men carrying butcher's knives, pangas, tomahawks, sharpened spikes, knobkerries and stones started chasing people around. What amazed me was that as they assaulted people, heavily armed police stood by and did nothing to protect the residents.'

A police spokesman, however, responded that the incidents involving migrant workers and residents were 'minor'.

One of the 'minor' incidents involved Samuel Mohlomi. 'A schoolboy was dragged from a church in Dobsonville and beaten to death by a gang of Zulus,' reported Steve Kgama in the *Rand Daily Mail*. 'The Reverend A Mataboge of the Nederduitse Gereformeerde Kerk in Afrika said the boy, Samuel Mohapi Mohlomi, 16, a pupil at Samuel Mangala Higher Primary School, had sought refuge in his church from a gang that was chasing him. "But the Zulus, wielding sticks, burst into the church and Samuel rushed into my arms," said Rev Mataboge. The priest said he pleaded with the men not to harm the boy. "But they threatened to kill both of us," he said. "They snatched the boy from my arms and dragged him away. Samuel's last words to me were 'Thank you, father, you tried to save my life.'" He watched the gang from the church as they took Samuel away. "They were not far from the church gate when I saw sticks rise and fall – blow after blow landing on the boy's head. He fell and the men marched away. I found Samuel was dead."'

Running battles and terror continued throughout the night and into the next day. 'The Mzimhlope hostel area of Soweto was still in a state of high tension after a day of violence in which at least 20 bodies were found in the township – 13 of them from panga wounds,' reported the *Rand Daily Mail*. 'As night fell residents grouped together to organise their defence against an expected assault by hostel inmates on their houses and families and donned white headbands to identify themselves. The residents' preparations came after repeated clashes with hostel inmates over the past 36 hours and the evacuation of many of the women and children to the comparative safety of other Soweto townships.

'Early in the day two African *Rand Daily Mail* reporters overheard police encouraging the hostel workers to take action against troublemakers but not to attack official property. One reporter, who had hidden away in a coal box near the hostel, heard a man say in Zulu: "We didn't order you to destroy West Rand Administration Board (WRAB) property. You were asked to fight people only." The second reporter heard a similar instruction after he had entered the hostel. A policeman in camouflage uniform addressed workers through an interpreter: "You were warned not to continue damaging the houses because they are the property of WRAB. If you damage houses you will force us to take action against you because you have been ordered to kill troublemakers only."'

'Utter nonsense,' responded General Gert Prinsloo, the commissioner of police.

When Meadowlands residents, on the afternoon of 25 August, formed into a group of about 1 000 to raid the Mzimhlope Hostel to free dozens of women taken hostage by the migrants, the police suddenly swung into action to protect the hostel dwellers and dispersed the crowd. But the tide had turned against the migrants and many began packing and leaving the hostel for fear of further reprisals. The death toll by now was 35, with 350 wounded.

Reports that desk officers at police stations refused to assist residents who wished to lay complaints also flooded in. In one instance, a resident of Soweto was informed that she would only be attended to if she undertook to take action to control the children. Another was told that if there was any terror in Soweto, the children caused it and the problem would be solved by proper discipline.

The reason for the police action in inciting migrants and siding with them was because they believed black-on-black confrontation would encourage a backlash that would divide blacks and make it easier to restore order. 'I frankly think the situation will calm itself now, once black people realise there is a strong backlash,' commented Kruger.

But, rather than split blacks, the clash brought them together. Township residents began to question their attitudes to their rural kin, and Chief Mangosuthu Buthelezi flew into Soweto to pacify his Zulu supporters. 'For the first time since the flare-up between people living in Mzimhlope and the hostel residents, people from both factions were able to sit together as they listened to Chief Buthelezi who on Friday called for peace and the healing of wounds,' reported Lucas Molete in the *Sunday Times*. 'He said blacks in the country needed to have a common strategy when it came to mass action. "We need to co-ordinate efforts instead of playing a game of political one-upmanship."

'Chief Buthelezi said young people had a right to demonstrate peacefully against the imposition of Afrikaans on them. "We taught them we want freedom," he said. But it was regrettable that so much violence followed the peaceful demonstration. Chief Buthelezi said they must learn from the Mzimhlope flare-up, when blacks attack blacks, that "we must spend time and energy in organising ourselves into a cohesive force before attempting any mass action. My appeal therefore today is that we must heal the wounds we have inflicted on each other in the past few days. We dare not play the game of turning against each other."' Buthelezi then turned on the police and confirmed their complicity, much to the outrage of the force.

Peace did not return immediately. Sporadic clashes continued into the next week, leaving a further 35 dead. But students and hostel leaders held regular meetings and eventually resolved that a solidarity stayaway be called for mid-September, which was the most successful of all the strikes.

And as the drama played itself out in Soweto, incidents flared round the country. Towards the end of August the last piece of the puzzle of the uprising fell into place as coloured townships on the Cape Peninsula joined the struggle. 'Riot squad police opened fire on rioters in Cape Town township areas last night,' reported the *Rand Daily Mail*, 'killing at least one man and injuring several as unrest flared. The coloured area of Bonteheuwel was totally sealed off at 10:00 pm with two buildings set alight. Ambulances were not entering Bonteheuwel last night and patients were picked up from police on the outskirts. Late last night, the situation in Bonteheuwel was described as a "battlefield" by a police spokesperson. Police said action had been taken against rioters when stoning, arson and violence spread throughout Bonteheuwel and spilled into Klipfontein Road, Athlone, and even Settlers Way – the main route to DF Malan Airport.'

Trouble in coloured townships on the Peninsula continued into September and they actively supported the mid-September stayaway. The uprising also spilled into white Cape Town suburbs for the first time. 'Cape Town has changed overnight into a frightened city,' commented Diana Powell in the *Sunday Express*. 'Fear has become a tangible thing which walks side by side with hatred in the streets. The violence of the past fortnight has had a profound effect on Cape Town. When I arrived back this week after a month out of the country, it wasn't the same city. Gone was the camaraderie between white, brown and black which, in spite of apartheid, was part of the Cape way of life. For the first time, real racial tension could be felt in the one part of the country where people of all colours have always more or less got along with one another. And for the first time, people are running scared. White people are frightened of coloured people, coloured people fear the violence and deaths.'

The government was again caught in a vice. The right clamoured for more oppression, the left for more reform. Promises were made: urban blacks would be given more say in their own affairs, the migrant labour system would be investigated, full home-ownership rights would be extended and township services would be improved. 'There is no doubt that South Africa is suffering from an epidemic of change,' commented Percy Qoboza, editor of *The World*. 'The prime minister, Mr Vorster, says that the "necessary" changes will be effected to meet the new South African situation. The minister of the interior, Dr Mulder, also says that changes are coming. Everybody, but everybody who matters, has jumped on the bandwagon of change. In fact, listening to the enthusiasm of the changing world of apartheid, one would easily be convinced that a new political dispensation is on the way.

'But what about the people of Soweto? Do they see change? They just do not be-lieve it. Past experiences have made them sceptics, and as long as they do not be-lieve the good faith of white South Africa to make meaningful and positive changes, I am afraid we have a permanent crisis on our hands.'

But Vorster was not convinced that there was a crisis. When he ended another long silence on the disturbances, he stunned the country by telling a meeting in Springs that there was not even an emergency. All he would concede was that the country was having a problem economically and internationally – a reference to the condemnation in the UN Security Council, this time supported by Britain and the United States. 'But it's really child's play when compared to some other countries,' he concluded.

'I think the honourable gentleman has totally lost his grip,' commented the opposition United Party's general secretary, Senator Bill Horak.

The government, however, showed how seriously it regarded the matter with the most brutal crackdown to date. Security policemen round the country began a systematic rounding-up of black leaders, arresting nearly 300 in one day. Most of these were detained without trial and would be subject to inhuman treatment and torture. 'Black Consciousness movements have been virtually silenced by the continuing round-up by security police,' reported the *Sunday Times*. 'Most have been held under the new Internal Security Act. Among those held are Mrs Winnie Mandela, Mr Steve Biko, Dr Aaron Matlhare and Mr Aubrey Mokoena.'

Those against whom the police had watertight cases were tried and imprisoned on Robben Island. 'These young men were a different breed of prisoners from those we had seen before,' wrote Nelson Mandela in *Long Walk to Freedom*. 'They were brave, hostile and aggressive; they would not take orders, and shouted "*Amandla!*" at every opportunity. Their instinct was to confront rather than co-operate. The authorities did not know how to handle them, and they turned the island upside down. During the Rivonia Trial, I remarked to a security policeman that if the government did not reform itself, the freedom fighters who would take our place would some-day make the authorities yearn for us. That day had indeed come on Robben Island.'

Thousands, however, avoided the dragnet and fled the country – where the ANC and PAC were waiting to recruit them in Botswana, Lesotho, Swaziland and Mozambique. 'It is tragic enough to have parents subjected to the agony of seeing their children flee their country,' commented *The World*. 'The Government, with its usual lack of foresight, has chosen to disregard, has chosen to ignore, one of the dangers of this mass exodus. It is no good people sitting down and saying good riddance. Far from that, it is our experience that with the strong commitment these children have – to destroy once and for all the injustices perpetrated against their parents – they will come back with an added incentive. This will be for the destruction, along with the government system, of the system of free enterprise. They will be bent on imposing a socialist order.

'We have in the past emphasised that far from protecting the interests of the West and the free world, South Africa's racial policies are in fact playing into the hands of the communists. They are the communists' biggest and most active public relations officers. The more our people look at the supposedly democratic and Western-orientated system as practised in South Africa, the bigger becomes the temptation to look elsewhere for freedom from the yokes and burdens of discrimination. We now believe that most Western countries are beginning to read the situation as we do. This is why we are convinced that unless this country heads for meaningful changes at great speed, it will find itself increasingly isolated in a hostile world.'

Kruger's only reaction was to offer a week's amnesty for those who had left, but he refused to guarantee that they would not be arrested for other matters on their return. No one took up the offer.

If the government was not listening, nor were English-speakers – who today lament that they knew nothing. Nonsense. The press was crammed with information, albeit cursory analysis, and people such as Dr Beyers Naudé, director of the Christian Institute, continually warned of the need for meaningful change and dialogue – but, he added, whites refused to listen or learn 'that proximity without communication always leads to confrontation'. He suggested that the very least employers could do was be sensitive to the needs of their workers and permit them to vent their feelings. Business, however, retreated into a laager of worrying about the bottom line, threatening workers that if they stayed away they would be dismissed or have their pay cut.

The second phase of the Soweto Uprising also witnessed a hardening of the divisions between black urban leaders. 'In Soweto two factions are competing for leadership,' commented Patrick Laurence in the *Rand Daily Mail*, 'with neither being able to establish its authority completely. On the one side is the conservative UBC; on the other is the radically inclined BPA. Although both factions have denied that there is a rivalry between them, their denials are belied by concrete facts.

'The BPA has minced no words in condemning members of the UBC and rejecting their claims to lead the people. In the eyes of the association, the officially created council was specifically established by Pretoria to "misrepresent" the people. The UBC faction has distanced itself from the association – largely because it thinks too close an identification would shut off its access to ministers like Kruger and MC Botha. The rivalry was manifest on 1 August when both groups held separate meetings in Soweto immediately before the second round of township unrest flared up. Soweto has experienced a partial paralysis of leadership as a consequence.'

There is enough evidence to suggest that the government was employing the old divide-and-rule tactic with the Soweto adult population. On the one hand, it promoted the UBC by granting its leaders interviews and concessions, while, on the other, it harassed the BPA and refused to grant it an audience. Strangely, Kruger's assertion that he could not identify the BPA leaders to talk to was forgotten when he needed to arrest and detain them. But Kruger was playing a dangerous game, because this machinated inertia only served more radical Black Consciousness movements which continued to gain credibility as the real opposition to apartheid.

The students too had lost some lustre with the Mzimhlope massacre, and Seathlolo had his work cut out in its aftermath. The people of Soweto blamed the SSRC for the debacle and its inability to control what it had started. Moreover, the students were humiliated to find Buthelezi – whom they deeply mistrusted because of his closeness to both the government and white liberals – restoring peace. If that was not bad enough, most of the scholar leaders were in prison or had fled. The new chairman wisely decided it was time for a change of course and ordered a return to school, but with exams to be boycotted, and a period of mourning. Act three envisaged a 'Black Christmas'.

7 ■ BLACK CHRISTMAS

When mama asked
Are you attending the funeral
I said that I couldn't
Then she was disappointed
Splash came the reprimand.

A mixed emotion engulfed me
True I felt like weeping
Same as I felt like dancing
Weep for my losing you
Dance that mama's also concerned.

Alas … sorry no laments
Bravo … yours was redemptive
Yes I mean your suffering
And more so your death
No different from that of Christ.
- XOLA NUSE: 'BIG IS THE BOY'

Initially, the SSRC-inspired 'three months of mourning' was conceived to allow a peri-od for regrouping while keeping the flame of rebellion alive. This was to be achieved through a variety of tactics, starting with turning the funerals of students into politi-cal events. The slogan was 'For freedom we shall lay down our lives – the struggle continues', and the first targeted burial was that of 16-year-old Isaac Dumisani Mbatha, who died after two days in police detention.

'Mbatha's death saw the opening of a new phase in the student campaign – the mass funerals,' recalled the *Weekend World*. 'The SSRC called for all students to attend the funeral and thousands responded. This funeral thus became the first of many to take a totally unconventional nature. Dirges were replaced by freedom songs. The condolences of the ministers who conducted the services were overshadowed by calls to keep up the struggle and by exaltations of the dead as martyrs.'

Mbatha's funeral began in the early morning of Sunday, 17 October, as 15 000 pupils from all over Soweto congregated outside his home in Emndeni Extension. From here they marched or were transported in commandeered cars, taxis and buses to Avalon Cemetery. Most of the graveside proceedings were conducted by student leaders who delivered fiery political speeches punctuated with shouts of *'Amandla!'* and followed by freedom songs. As the grave was being filled with soil, angry scholars broke away and rampaged through the surrounding areas, causing extensive damage to government property and vehicles.

Following the political success of this funeral, the SSRC extended its mourning period to include a ban on frequenting white-owned stores, parties, Christmas celebrations, weddings and shebeens – shebeens being the most important target because many of the Black Consciousness students regarded liquor as a major contributor to blacks' perceptions of themselves as inferior. 'Our daily experiences,' commented the SSRC, 'is that nothing good has ever come out of shebeens. Many of our black sisters have been raped and murdered by drunkards and thugs from shebeens. Shebeens have become houses of vice and immorality. We cannot tolerate to see our fathers' pay packets being emptied in shebeens. Shebeens must go.'

On Saturday, 23 October, pamphlets, calling on the residents of Soweto to align themselves with the mourning period by observing these bans, were distributed at the second funeral – that of 17-year-old Anna Mkwanazi. Evidence that police intended taking a hard line at burials began to surface here as they burst into her parents' house, interrupted the service and dispersed all but relatives and friends.

The following day, between 4 000 and 5 000 students began congregating at Doornkop Cemetery on the outskirts of Soweto for the funeral of former University of Zululand student Jacob Zungwane Mashabane, who police first claimed had died in detention of natural causes, then alleged that he had committed suicide by hanging himself. 'When the funeral procession arrived at the graveyard, police cars were already positioned at various points outside the cemetery,' reported the *Rand Daily Mail.* 'Shortly after, mourners gathered at the graveside and immediately young mourners began raising fists and singing freedom songs. About 3:10 pm several police cars drove to the graveside, while others remained outside. Policemen got out of their cars and shouted to the people to disperse. Then there was general panic as the police began firing. There was no warning.

'The Doornkop nightmare had started. The crowd scattered as police continued to fire. The shooting seemed to last for several minutes, and many people fell, only about 10 people stood, transfixed at the graveside, while the family of the dead student huddled together in the mourners' car, sobbing bitterly. Scores of screaming people managed to scurry through the fence and run for safety in the veld, while others battled through a swamp just outside the cemetery. Several youths were held by the police and marched to a waiting van. After the shooting, Doornkop was like a battlefield, with the dead and several seriously wounded.'

Major-General Kriel, the deputy commissioner of police in charge of riot control, described reports that police had fired without warning, in an outrage that killed seven and injured 51, as 'ridiculous'. But every other reporter on the scene confirmed that no warning was given. 'One moment we were together then pandemonium broke loose,' wrote Nat Diseko and Langa Skosana in *The Star*. 'Everyone scattered as the shooting began. Before the shooting started, no warning was given. Even at the graveside there was no warning.'

Funerals would remain an integral feature of South African political protest throughout the liberation struggles. The immediate effect of the massacre was to boost support for the students and inflame black anger. 'We strongly deplore this killing of black children and adults,' declared the Black Peoples' Convention. 'Blacks cannot even get a chance to bury their dead peacefully. The police are plunging the country into violence and bloodshed. We call upon the government to put a stop to this kind of violence. We demand our rights which we will have. Black people will be liberated.'

The Doornkop shooting galvanised the students, and they redoubled their vigilance regarding the 'period of mourning'. One of the most successful of their boycott campaigns was that against shebeens, set to run from 22 October until the New Year. 'Parties that used to go on throughout the weekend have ceased,' wrote Martin Mahlaba in the *Rand Daily Mail*. 'Some shebeens have given up selling, some sell "take away" while others only serve known customers. Drunkenness has almost disappeared, not so much because of the lack of liquor but the threats of what will happen to one who is seen staggering in the streets. Rumour has it that drunks will be forced to point out the place where they have been drinking.

'At the start of the call for general sobriety – as a mark of mourning for those shot during the unrest and for those detained without being charged – township people felt the students were carrying things too far, but it soon became apparent who had the upper hand. Residents had seen a number of buildings go up in flames in the townships. No one wanted to risk having his coveted property burn because he ran a shebeen.'

Less successful was the 'buy black' strategy that called on Soweto residents to purchase only from black-owned stores, and for these shops to shut early as a sign of mourning. The problem was obvious: black-owned stores only operated in townships because of trade restrictions under apartheid; they offered a limited range of goods; and they were forced to close before residents returned home. So the students quickly recanted the 'close early' demand, but enforced the rest of the drive. Residents returning from work with shopping bags were stopped and searched by roving groups of students and either were warned or had their purchases destroyed. At the same time, the students attempted to ease the burden by holding discussions with the Soweto Traders' Association to attempt to get them to reassess their product lines and range and to ensure they did not take advantage by charging exorbitant prices.

The 'buy black' move, while unpopular with adults, certainly had a sobering effect on white-owned businesses in Johannesburg, and many complained bitterly that they had always provided good service to their black customers and that it was unfair for them to be punished. But it was a bonus for black business people who helped lay a strong foundation for an emerging group of traders. 'I saw an interesting price survey the other day,' commented Carol Mathiane in *The World*. 'It showed the price for various items in Soweto shops and in city supermarkets – and, as you can guess, the prices in Soweto were very much higher than they are in the supermarkets. I know that some people will simply say that our businessmen are crooks. But I won't say that. It's just that I have some good friends who are Soweto businessmen, and who I know are honest and decent people.

'The reason I won't cry "Crooks!" is because I know that many of them are NOT making huge profits from us – their problem is a lack of organisation and expertise, combined with small turnover. I am nothing like an expert in business economics, it is easy for fools to rush in where angels fear to tread, but it seems to me that there must be ways of solving this problem. I am sure you will agree with me that it is absolutely necessary that the problem is solved. Surely it is ridiculous that we never do anything to generate any wealth within our own, black community?

'We earn our wages by helping our white employer to become rich and when we are paid we go straight to white shops and help the white shopkeeper to become rich too. It would be so nice if part of this river of money could be channelled into our own hands. But as long as we can buy the things we need for half the price in the city than they would cost in Soweto, it is not surprising that we continue to use the city shops.

'Isn't it possible for our own black shopkeepers to form a syndicate so that they can buy at lower prices? Isn't it possible that such a syndicate could arrange contracts whereby factories would supply them at low prices? If they do, and if it turns out that black shops can sell as cheaply as white ones, then we should all support the black shops.'

The call to 'buy black' may not have been a roaring success, but it did highlight and boost an idea whose time had come. And even though its effects were limited, the 'buy black' campaign was the one that eventually caught the attention of white English-language dominated business – *The Star* went so far as to label it a 'Dangerous Weapon'. The newspaper, in an editorial, warned of further black unemployment as white-owned businesses were driven to bankruptcy – as if corresponding employment opportunities would not arise through the black-owned businesses. But the newspaper also acknowledged that the complacent white community of Johannesburg was now listening, and urged the government to speed up reforms to trading rights.

The SSRC, however, experienced complete failure with its call for another stayaway from Monday, 1 November. 'Thousands of workers this morning ignored the five-day stayaway call by the SSRC and made their way to the city as usual,' reported *The World*. 'The stayaway had been planned to start today and go on until Friday. But early this morning, workers left their homes and went to work as usual. Buses, taxis and trains all ran normally. There were no incidents reported.'

'Johannesburg's strong black workforce, which was urged to stay away from work, defied the call,' commented *The Star*. 'They did this fully aware of the risks involved in defying the call by the students, whose apparent aim is to disrupt the country's economy. The students also want the workers to stay away from work as a sign of mourning for the hundreds of schoolchildren and adults killed since the disturbances broke out.

'During the past weekend, workers had an agonising decision to make – to go to work or not. Many decided to go. Staying at home would probably result in wages being docked or being fired. Even more distressing was the possibility of finding one's home razed on returning from work. There was also the stark possibility of being assaulted or having one's car smashed or burnt when coming home from work.

'So with all these risks the question is, WHY did the workers defy the call when on two previous occasions they responded to the call to strike? Firstly, it seems, the duration of the stay-at-home was too long. Secondly, employers' attitudes hardened after the last strike and many boycotters found themselves without jobs. Thirdly, some people say the demands of the pupils are many and incessant and seem to lack direction. And fourthly, there were rumours that if people stayed away, police would raid homes and demand to know why the heads of families were not at work. Migrants had also heard that if they stayed away they would be "repatriated to their homelands". The big question stemming from this massive defiance of student power is whether future stayaway calls will be resisted in the same concerted manner.'

Opponents of the SSRC gleefully pounced on this setback, and questions were raised in many quarters as to whether this was the end of student power. It certainly was evidence that adults were tiring of the constant demands on them in a war many believed was being fought over narrow student concerns, rather than broader community issues. It was also the first clear indication of the effects of the police war of attrition on a scholar leadership that was appearing decidedly weak. Seathlolo was quick to realise this, and inspired a campaign to counter perceptions that the students had nothing to offer other than negativity and destruction.

The biggest threat Soweto faced in October 1976 was the near collapse of its infrastructure. The destruction of clinics and the breakdown in refuse removal made the threat of killer diseases more acute as summer and the rainy season approached. 'We could have 300 cases of paralytic poliomyelitis, 300 of diphtheria and about 600 additional cases of measles there within weeks,' said Dr Alec Smith, Johannesburg's chief medical officer of health. 'There is also the possibility of a massive increase in infant mortality from gastro-enteritis.'

The main culprit was the lack of refuse removal, which left huge heaps of rotting garbage strewn in the streets and in turn contributed to an increase in rodents that brought further health hazards. It was an opportunity not to be missed, and the SSRC launched a highly effective 'Clean-up Operation' that began in the Mzimhlope area.

'The SSRC must be congratulated for the launching of their "Clean-up Operation" in which they have called on all students to take off their jackets and get down to the business of cleaning up Soweto of the dirt and filth the township complex is swimming in at the moment,' commented *The World*. 'They launched the operation following various warnings by health authorities that diseases and epidemics are threatening Soweto unless some action is taken to clean up the township. In our opinion the action of the students is a positive one – one which must go a long way towards dispelling the widely held view by certain people in official quarters that Soweto students were nothing but a bunch of revolutionaries.'

So successful was Seathlolo's drive to improve Soweto that police began to regard him as more dangerous than Mashinini, and they increased the tempo of oppression and dirty tricks in an attempt to divide students and adults. They set fire to Morris Isaacson High School and Aaron Matlhare's consulting rooms, and blamed students. Men in balaclavas accompanied police on pass raids and terrorised householders with pangas. And parents of wanted children, even those who had fled the country, were arrested and held in detention until their children gave themselves up.

Then there were the inexplicable events – ones that had the signature of the security police all over them – designed to sow terror among whites and keep them in the fold. Three children sitting in a car in Durban while their parents shopped were abducted by a black man who returned them safely to a nearby spot a little while later. A Piet Retief farmer and his wife were attacked in their home by men in disguise shouting Black Power slogans and demanding cash and weapons – only to leave without taking what was on offer. And a number of crude pamphlets 'accidentally' began finding their way into white suburbs. These highly effective pieces of anti-propaganda were clearly intended to enter the grapevine and, while there were many variations, all had as their central theme an order by black students to their comrades to murder whites. 'Black people are not butchers, but responsible fighters for liberation,' responded Seathlolo in an attempt to calm hysterical whites.

The clean-up was a public relations coup for the SSRC, but it remained beset by other problems as the year drew to a close. School burnings continued and police blamed the student movement. While the council protested its innocence, the allegations did affect its credibility. Other organisations, many sponsored by the police, were also springing up and issuing pamphlets and statements with abandon. To make matters worse, SSRC members displayed their indiscipline by making individual announcements at will and the executive were hard put to decide what was issued from their camp and what was not. Rumours began to surface that a split in the council was imminent.

While Seathlolo was cleaning up Soweto, the political profile South Africa would take over the next two decades was taking shape. Transkei was given 'independence' in October in an act designed to strip some four million blacks of their rights in South Africa. Chief Kaizer Matanzima, the 'president', lost no time in taking on the airs of his masters by threatening to hang anyone who cast doubts on the sovereignty of this 'nation'. While this was happening, the parliamentary opposition, in an attempt to acquire relevance, was holding secret talks with Chief Mangosuthu Buthelezi, who was simultaneously involved in discussions to form a united black front. This prompted Aggrey Klaaste to comment in *The World*: 'There was a time when Chief Buthelezi was looked upon as the Zulu oracle who had come to set his people free. Those days are sadly gone, but the Chief still has the aura that generates controversy every time he opens his mouth. And he does that with painfully strident regularity.'

An integral part of the SSRC 'period of mourning' campaign was the boycott of end-of-year examinations, and this was the most successful of all its actions. While many whites criticised the SSRC as 'irresponsible' for this stand, the students had real concerns that, under the circumstances, examinations would be meaningless. There had been the Afrikaans issue at the beginning of the year, severe disruption in the middle of the year, and now students attending schools ran the risk of being harassed or detained by police, who maintained a heavy presence. When examinations commenced on 2 November there was near total absenteeism throughout the country. The authorities first threatened those who failed to write examinations that they would be forced to repeat a full year at school, then backed down and rescheduled examinations for March 1977.

Another key call by the students was for a 'Black Christmas'. They had insisted that Soweto residents not celebrate Christmas, but mourn those killed in the uprising and reflect on those held in detention. Specifically, no parties were to be held or liquor consumed, and no new clothes or presents bought. Though white-owned retail outlets experienced a massive decline in sales, the campaign was not a severe hardship for blacks. 'Blacks mostly look on Christmas as an imported feast,' explained Percy Qoboza in *The World*. 'It is a foreign and usually varied experience, depending on whether it is associated with an all-out slog to cater for madam's feast, time to drink excessively, be with the family or to celebrate the birth of Jesus Christ with a fervour whites have lost.'

The effectiveness of the 'Black Christmas' strategy is difficult to measure. 'The mourning plea, which fell more and more into the limelight as the Christmas season drew closer, had brought with it its own tensions,' reported the *Weekend World*. 'The plea was widely accepted by Soweto people. At least, it was accepted in spirit – but not as widely in practice. Those who had lost relatives and friends – and there were many of them – were in full agreement with the general proposal for a mourning period. But there were many who drew the line at the total absence of festivities which the SSRC was demanding.'

The SSRC, while not dead, appeared to be exhausted and its authority was waning. 'The struggle is ours,' declared Seathlolo, 'the ball of liberation is in our hands.' But he lacked conviction, and it was time to pass the ball.

Christmas also brought something new – something Qoboza had warned of – the clandestine return of those who had fled in the wake of the September crackdown. Four ANC leaflet bombs exploded in Cape Town, blasts damaged the Jabulani Police Station and UBC chambers in Soweto, grenade attacks were reported in Northern Natal and the Eastern Transvaal, and arms caches were found in the same areas. In the most serious incident, a man had his hands blown off when he walked into a crowded restaurant in the Carlton Centre in Johannesburg carrying what appeared to be two sticks of smouldering dynamite. 'Patrons scattered from Fontana Restaurant in the Carlton Centre when a loud blast shook windows and broke glasses,' reported the *Rand Daily Mail*. 'A waiter was temporarily deafened but no guests were hurt. Two women noticed the man pacing up and down outside the restaurant. He was unconcernedly swinging two smouldering sticks, apparently undecided whether to throw them. One woman ran to alert the security guards, screaming that a bomb was about to go off. The man then entered the restaurant holding the explosive device behind a shopping bag. There was a "tremendous explosion," said an eyewitness. The man fell unconscious, his right hand blown off and his left arm injured. He had multiple flesh wounds on his chest and legs.'

'The Carlton Centre explosion underscores the possible existence of highly motivated underground recruiting and indigenous arms supplies inside South Africa, a top expert has warned here,' reported *The World*. 'Dr Peter Janke, a full time researcher at the Institute for the Study of Conflict, made it clear in an interview that the attack could well spell the start of a new terrorist thrust. Dr Janke said that a high degree of motivation lay behind it. "Obviously there is recruitment and technical knowledge," he said, "but what motivates a young man to launch an attack that would result in either his death, imprisonment or execution?"'

The Carlton Centre explosion was the next salvo in an intensified campaign against apartheid, marking the moment when the ANC regained the initiative from the young pretenders, who had breached the Bastille and prepared the ground for the future. But much of the rejuvenation of the liberation movement, in turn, can be attributed to its ranks having been swollen by brave and zealous youths who had fled the country and were now itching to get back and take up the battle on another front. Not only did the ANC benefit from this influx, it actively targeted the youth leaders still in the country. In December, for example, Billy Masethla – a leading ANC underground operative – arranged for Murphy Morobe and other student activists to receive training in Swaziland secretly.

For the shell-shocked residents of Soweto, liberation must have seemed far off as Christmas approached, and many must have questioned whether it was worth the sacrifice. The Nationalists were still firmly in power, albeit on the back foot, and whites, rather than embracing reform, were becoming more reactionary and brutal. 'June 1976, like Sharpeville, was another turning point where South Africa did not turn,' commented John Kane-Berman of the Institute of Race Relations. Moreover, the economy was in tatters and Soweto parents' relationships with their children forever changed. For the majority, though, amidst the anger and despondency, there was a new confidence. Qoboza spoke for most blacks when he addressed his readers at Christmas with a plea titled 'Think how you can save your white brothers'.

'For the first time in many years, I cannot wish you a Merry Christmas. We are all in a state of mourning and because of the gloom and despondency existing in our townships, it will be very difficult indeed to wish it is going to be a merry Christmas season. Maybe it is a good thing, I think it will have served a worthwhile purpose if all of us can take advantage of a sane and sober weekend to contemplate the situation in our country. To talk to our friends and neighbours about the state in which we would like the country to be, and relationships with other people. I am convinced that we have a role to play in shaping a new and dynamic nation in which all her people – black and white – can develop an acceptable formula for a peaceful and harmonious co-existence.

'Strange as it may sound, I believe it is within our power to save our fellow white South Africans from the self-destroying dangers facing them as a result of pursuing futile political policies. Many of them are suffering from a fear and guilt complex as a result of years in which they preserved privileges for themselves while you were labouring in the depths of deprivation, ignorance and hunger. They do not as a result believe that you are capable of forgiveness and reconciliation. I know for a fact that you are. I know for a fact that you sincerely believe from the bottom of your hearts that they have a future in our common country provided they deviate from the path of political domination and economic privilege.

'I know that the last thing you want to see is a confrontation between the races in our country. I know that you have been sickened by the bloodshed and the violence we experienced in the past few months. I know you are keen to see the end of it all. I know that you are hoping that valuable lessons have been learned from these experiences in which those in power will reflect on effective means of bringing you into the decision making machinery of our country, thus avoiding the recurrence of the past few months.

'This much I know and more. I know, for instance, about the deep-rooted resentment and bitterness when people discriminate against you on the basis of your colour. I know that you are proud to be black because black is beautiful. I know that you know that black is not inferior but equal to white, yellow or what-have-you provided there are equal opportunities for showing what black can do and achieve when given those opportunities. I know you have always wondered what would happen if people got to heaven and found God is black. I know you have always wondered how people could possibly go to church on Sunday and sing "in Christ we are one" when they spend six days of the week furiously turning the unity of brotherhood into shambles by hammering away at those things that divide us instead of unifying us.

'I know it has amazed you to find people paying lip service to the sanctity of the rule of law, when their everyday actions – like detention without trial and bannings – are a prostitution of every cardinal principle of the rule of law upon which our Western system of democracy is based. By attacking certain churches and church leaders and organisations like the Christian Institute and others. I know they surprise you because they are bent on destroying the only institution where the spirit of brotherhood and reconciliation can actively be promoted.

'I know you are tolerant people. I know you are beautiful people. I know you love your country passionately. I know you have the capacity to pursue the truth, no matter how bitter it may be. Finally, in the words of the late Dr Martin Luther King, "I know you shall overcome, deep in my heart, I know we shall overcome." And in the same vein that great civic leader also echoed your sentiments correctly when he also added: "Not only will we win our freedom, we shall so appeal to your hearts and consciences we will win you in the process. And your victory will be a double victory."

'So when you reflect this Christmas, think of how you can save your white brothers from the chains of fear. Take them along to a new South Africa where man will be man irrespective of the colour of his skin or the colour of his eyes. Or the length of his hair. They need your help. They need your guidance. Help them, for your children's sake.'

And they did need help. While the uprising in Soweto was taking a different direction, violence inspired by 16 June was still spreading throughout the country – even to places with no history of black political activity – in solidarity with the township. But most of it was focused in the black and coloured townships round Cape Town, which continued to flare through October and November and climaxed in December over Christmas, with a replay of the Mzimhlophe affair. This time the police encouraged Xhosa migrant workers in Nyanga to refuse to go into mourning for the Soweto dead over the Christmas period. As expected, this resulted in clashes between migrants and students.

'The police were more provocative than preventive,' commented a local priest. An eyewitness claimed that when residents tried to protect their property they were fired upon by police who stood idly by when migrants attacked. A document presented to the UN by the Ministers' Fraternal of Langa, Guguletu and Nyanga included the following account: 'On Sunday afternoon, 26 December 1976, I was in my backyard when five vans with riot police came into 5th Avenue, Nyanga. I saw a riot policeman sitting in front of the van on the bonnet. He shot at an elderly man who was carrying no weapon and intended no harm. After the shot the man fell, bleeding at the stomach. I saw the riot policeman beckon with his arm, and a large group of migrants came running. The riot policeman pointed them to the man on the ground and then left, as the migrants came and killed him with their weapons.

'The migrants carried sticks and axes. Some had petrol bombs, and I saw them throwing them into houses, setting them alight. The riot police never made any attempt to intervene and stop the violence, instead they came in with guns and opened the way for migrants, instigating a group of them to attack us.' In one of the most senseless outrages, two babies were burnt alive in a house while migrants prevented their mother from going to their assistance. At the end of it, 26 were dead and over 100 injured, bringing the toll for the year to 499 dead with more than 1 000 hurt. It was a black Christmas, made worse by a new wave of detentions.

'The whites will rule and let there be no mistake about that,' declared Vorster in his New Year message. Then, in a strange twist, as if he had the faintest glimmer of comprehension, he added, 'The storm has not yet struck. We are only experiencing the whirlwinds that go before it.' And he was right, because the Soweto Uprising, unlike the Sharpeville massacre that heralded the end of a phase in the struggle for liberation, marked the beginning of the final battle for freedom.

PART III

DAWN

8 ■ HOMECOMING

In the agonising wait between SABC-TV's link with its crew outside Victor Verster Prison, in Paarl at 3 pm on 11 February 1990, and the 50-metre walk to freedom by Nelson Mandela at 4:16 pm, South Africa was treated to a spectacle of how apartheid had drained the creative energy from white South Africans. While the rest of the world was enthralled by extensive background reporting on all aspects of the Mandela story together with analysis of State President FW de Klerk's unbanning of the ANC, the PAC, the South African Communist Party and scores of outlawed organisations the week before, the country squirmed as anchor Clarence Keyter battled to make time go by: 'Here we stand outside the most beautiful prison in the world.' 'The sun is baking down on us – the sun, not only needed for growing grapes, but for growing South Africa.' 'The people are getting a bit impatient – but are waiting patiently.'

'It was only a few steps beyond the gate that marked the entrance to Victor Verster Prison, and a brief gesture with one fist in the air, but it is likely to change the course of South Africa's future,' wrote Gavin Evans in a special edition of the *Weekly Mail*. 'The release of the world's most famous prisoner could be South Africa's equivalent of the fall of the Berlin Wall – an event of singular importance which represents a turning point for a nation. It is one of those decisive moments in history which arise out of the accumulation of a thousand pressures on a system and sometimes lead to the creation of a thousand new ones.

'The release has massive symbolic importance. Mandela is the man who has come to embody South Africa's fight against minority rule and for non-racial democracy. To have him walk the streets is the most visible evidence so far that years of stagnant minority rule have given way to a situation of flux and dynamism. But its importance is not only symbolic. It is also an event of direct political importance, because by releasing Mandela the government has unleashed a force that it can no longer control. Mandela's international stature and his local popularity, the force of his personality assures that he will never be leashed again.'

In Johannesburg a hooting, whistling procession passed through Hillbrow and in Soweto a 35 000-strong crowd in Jabulani Stadium watched the TV broadcast of Mandela's release. Afterwards, crowds danced in the streets, drank shebeens dry, and marched to Mandela's home where they prepared to camp until his return. 'I'll sleep outside his house, because all I want to see is him,' said one ecstatic man.

De Klerk claimed he had freed Mandela because he was convinced that Mandela was committed to peace. But he was forced to, because his choices had narrowed to either negotiation or apocalypse. South Africa was totally isolated, the pariah of the world, and its state machinery could no longer cope with the boycotts, strikes, stay-aways and incursions by freedom fighters. Either way, De Klerk faced the wrath of right-wing Afrikaners.

'Stayaways, calls for resignations from Parliament, appeals to police to join the struggle, vows to cripple essential services, threats to take up arms ... such was the stuff of extra-parliamentary groups this week,' reported Gavin Evans in the *Weekly Mail*. 'So what's changed? What's changed is that the calls are coming from an angry and desperate far right, incensed with the scale of FW de Klerk's concessions and ready to go to war.'

'Mandela is making a deadly mistake if he thinks he can rob the *volk* of its rightful land and freedom by involving himself in President FW de Klerk's government,' fumed ultra-right-winger Robert van Tonder. 'He is a Xhosa and he must concentrate his energy only on furthering the wellbeing of the Xhosa nation.'

On the evening of 12 February, Mandela flew into Lanseria Airport outside Randburg from where he was whisked to a secret destination before his address to the residents of Soweto at Soccer City, scheduled for the next afternoon, and his return home.

'There were 150 000 dreams at Soccer City on Tuesday,' wrote Thami Mkhwanazi in the *Weekly Mail*. 'The dreams unfolded, in broad daylight, amid the strains of muted jazz trumpet, screams, chants and poetry.

'Little Boitumela Sisulu had been sleeping on the lap of a woman in the grand-stand as the dream unfolded. A massive balloon of black, green and gold colours stood in the air above the pitch as the girl slept soundly. She is the daughter of Sheila and Mlungisi Sisulu, son of Walter Sisulu. She and throngs of South Africans of all hues had come to see Nelson Mandela make a triumphal return to his home town. The sea of people from all segments of South African political opinion occupied every single space in the stadium, which was already bursting at the seams two hours before Mandela was scheduled to arrive. Many were to remain outside and hear their idol speak. The crowds outside jostled for entry at the gates outside the stadium. In the process some children were almost crushed.

'There was self-discipline and order enforced, not by the police, but by South African Youth Congress marshals. The marshals enforced order on the police too. I saw a contingent of policemen being led in convoy into the open parking area by a marshal, who held a large ANC sign high. I'm not sure how committed they were to the struggle, but the convoy too shouted "Viva Mandela" as they followed the grinning marshal.

'Two helicopters landed on the pitch. The stadium thundered with screams of "Viva Mandela", followed by "ANC, ANC, ANC" chants. Then Mandela arrived, followed by fellow African National Congress leaders Walter Sisulu, Andrew Mlangeni and Ahmed Kathrada. Next came Winnie Mandela, Albertina Sisulu, June Mlangeni and Caroline Motsoaledi, as well as Rivonia Trial lawyers Arthur Chaskalson and George Bizos. As the party took their seats, the crowd stood up and cheered. Then they sang: *Somlandel' uMandela* (We'll follow Mandela). Sisulu then presented Mandela to his followers. They rose again and 150 000 fists punched the air as the throngs sang the people's national anthem.

'Mandela spoke: "We are going forward. The march towards freedom and justice is irreversible ... Your struggles, commitment and discipline has released me to stand before you today ... We call on the police to abandon apartheid and serve the interests of the people ... Our victory must be celebrated in peace and joy ... Join our march to a new South Africa."

'We again sang the national anthem. The helicopter returned. The drum majorettes in their black, green and gold uniforms did their bit. Mandela and his entourage sauntered towards their aircrafts, amid the strains of Miles Davis' muted trumpet.

'"It is a dream," said pop singer Mercy Pakela, as the chopper rose and disappeared in the blue sky.'

It was the dream of a free South Africa – one that would not have been realised but for the sacrifices made on 16 June 1976.

9 ▪ M E M O R I E S

A book that concentrates on a single event runs the risk of isolating that incident from the greater historical context. We concluded the narrative of 16 June round the time that the ANC began to reclaim the initiative as the leading force for liberation in South Africa. But that was an arbitrary decision based on our belief that by then the spirit of the story had been told. In this chapter we profile some of the people who shaped this episode – and, in doing so, we intend to tie up loose ends and give the Soweto Uprising a more complete perspective.

These profiles, apart from the one on Theuns 'Rooi Rus' Swanepoel, who is dead, are based on recent interviews. We commented in the Authors' Note at the beginning of this book that the event we now know as the Soweto Uprising is shrouded in a myriad interpretations and contradictions – with everyone remembering the event from their own viewpoint. The occasion has also assumed such symbolism that memories are often tainted with romanticism. This is clearly reflected in individual accounts – but we allow this, even welcome it, because it proves that history is not sterile, but full of lively interpretations reflecting the fact that it means different things to different people.

DANIEL SECHABA MONTSITSI

On Friday, 7 January 1977, Khotso Seathlolo and two SSRC companions were returning from Johannesburg when they noticed they were being followed by the green car. They first tried to speed off, but could not shake the tailing vehicle, so they pulled up and tried to make a dash for safety in the Mzimhlophe area. Bullets buzzed round them and Seathlolo was hit in the arm, but pulled to safety. Within a week he fled to Gaborone in Botswana and was replaced as SSRC chairman by Daniel Sechaba Montsitsi, 20, a matric student at Sekano Ntoana High School, who immediately declared, 'The struggle goes on and we the students are going to fight until the end.'

Montsitsi had entered student politics in 1973 when he became a member of SASM. 'While student leaders were more politicised than their followers, the conditions in 1976 were ripe for mobilisation and the response was tremendous,' he said. 'But none expected what happened on 16 June – the students weren't prepared. We expected loudhailers and batons, but there were just bullets and bullets.'

Montsitsi is one of those surprised at ANC claims that it was behind the Soweto Uprising, but he did receive weapons training in late 1976 from ANC operative Billy Masethla. 'I remember Dan was quite religious,' said Masethla. 'He was distinctly uneasy about the arms and ammo part of the training.'

The continuing struggle Montsitsi alluded to in his opening address as chairman of the SSRC was to be anything but plain sailing. When he took the reins he ordered that schools be boycotted; he reversed an earlier instruction that the writing of examinations be left to individual student consciences and insisted that scholars not sit them – claiming that it had transpired that the majority of students opposed examinations. 'Under the circumstances,' he said, 'it was evident that the SSRC had to take a stand and we decided to revise our earlier position and place a blanket ban on all examinations.' But more and more students streamed back to school, vowing they would write their examinations. Ugly confrontations developed between the students and the SSRC, which claimed to represent them – notably at Morris Isaacson and Naledi High, the two driving forces behind the SSRC.

It appeared the soft-spoken, reserved leader would be the one to preside over the death of the SSRC. In the following weeks, however, he searched for new issues and his decision to involve the student movement fully in non-student community affairs in April 1977 marked him as the most effective of the SSRC chairmen. In May he brought the students out in protest against WRAB-proposed rent increases and forced WRAB to back down. Following this success, he concentrated such scholar pressure on the Urban Bantu Council that this puppet body collapsed in June. Shortly after, a dozen Security Branch vehicles surrounded a house in Diepkloof and arrested 21 people, including Montsitsi and 16 members of the SSRC. This effectively broke the organisation, even if it did limp on for some time under the chairmanship of Trofomo Somo.

'Major Visser, who was in charge of the investigation, warned me that if I didn't co-operate he had medicine for me,' said Montsitsi. 'The police used brutal force to extract information. They squeezed my testicles with pliers, gun-butted my face, punched me and beat me with rubber truncheons.' So brutal was his torture that rumours surfaced in July that he was in a critical condition in hospital. Montsitsi would successfully sue the Minister of Justice for his treatment in detention, but the information extracted would still be used to convict him of sedition. 'When handing down his sentence,' wrote Jonathan Ancer in the *Mail & Guardian*, 'Judge H van Dyk referred to Montsitsi as having behaved "seditiously" from the first day of unrest. "I didn't know what the hell sedition was, but if it meant organising the students to fight against Bantu Education then, *ja* [yes], the judge was right, I behaved seditiously." Montsitsi received four years in prison. "I expected Robben Island to be a place of dark horror, but when I arrived I discovered a political institution. Walter Sisulu gave lectures on the struggle of the workers and [Govan] Mbeki Snr was an expert on the development of capitalism.'"

'My understanding of the Freedom Charter had not been that thorough before,' Montsitsi told Shaun Johnson of the *Weekly Mail*. 'It was on the island that we could look back and learn from our history. One was able to put into correct perspective those pieces of the jigsaw puzzle which had been missing all along. We began to understand that we young people were not the first to take this kind of action. We found out about the old ANC Youth League, and the African Student Organisation.'

'Murphy Morobe and I made a noise when we came out,' said Montsitsi after his release in July 1983. 'When we addressed rallies we would say, "No, it's not me speaking, it's Mandela." Through us, people could see Mandela and Sisulu were alive.'

A few weeks after being freed, Montsitsi was thrown out of Natalspruit Hospital in Germiston while recovering from a knee operation. 'Do you know the background of this man?' responded an incensed Dr AF Chemaly, the hospital superintendent, to questions put to him by the *Sowetan* newspaper. 'We are dealing with an agitator, the man who took over student leadership when his friend, Tsietsi, fled the country.'

Montsitsi returned to his roots on release and joined the ranks of the Soweto Youth Congress, one of the early affiliates of the United Democratic Front (UDF) established to tackle apartheid. In 1984 he was elected to the UDF executive as a youth officer and during a flare-up between the UDF and Black Consciousness camps the following year, he helped restrain UDF youths from revenge attacks. In December 1987, Montsitsi, now serving as a committee member of the Soweto Civic Association, was 'picked up somewhere on the streets' and held for 14 months – only being released when he and fellow inmates embarked on a much-publicised hunger strike, which caused the authorities considerable discomfort. 'Montsitsi is known as a sober and reflective person,' wrote Joanne Collinge in *The Star*. 'On a public platform he is more apt to lecture than rabble-rouse. Knowing this, his family are deeply disturbed by the do-or-die attitude they have seen in him in recent weeks.'

Before the first democratic election in 1994, Montsitsi worked as a co-ordinator at Matla Trust, a voter education group. In 1996 he entered Parliament as an ANC MP.

MAFISON MURPHY MOROBE

The Ermelo-born Murphy Morobe, a Morris Isaacson matric student and member of the Action Committee formed on 13 June, was the brains behind Tsietsi Mashinini. But early on 16 June 1976 he was not feeling very clever. With his placard 'Away with Afrikaans' under his arm, he was delayed and when he reached school it was to find that the scholars had left without him. As he traced their movements he was decidedly uneasy. 'I felt cold droplets of sweat trickling down my spine,' he recalled. 'But somehow I was already on auto-pilot, and there was no stopping the adrenaline rush that kept propelling me forward. As the distance between our humble abode and me increased, I realised what was really troubling me. Was this to be the last time I was to wake up from my bed and walk through those gates on my way to and from school? Perhaps I might end up in jail, I thought, but that was the worst I expected.' He eventually caught up with the column in Dube. By the time they reached the rendezvous, information had reached Mashinini and Morobe that there was a large police presence in the area.

Morobe was an ANC supporter, a member of SASM since 1973 and a student activist. 'It was part of our adventure as youngsters,' he said. 'The 1970s were not long after the major student uprisings in Europe, France and the Civil Rights and Black Power movements in the United States.' For him, there was nothing spontaneous about 16 June: he believes the events that led to it can be traced to the ANC defiance campaigns of the 1940s and 1950s, and were boosted by the Portuguese withdrawal from Angola and Mozambique in 1974. He strongly feels that the issue of spontaneity is a red herring fabricated by those who wish to devalue the uprising as an accident of history.

The enigmatic Morobe, circumspect and precise, was the perfect foil to the charisma of Mashinini, and after 16 June the two leaders played cat and mouse with the police. 'I remember trying to organise a meeting when many people were on the run, with police all out to detain us,' he recalled. We all pretended to be swimmers and had the meeting at the swimming pool in Orlando dressed only in bikinis and swimming trunks. I must say it wasn't the most comfortable way to have a serious meeting.' During his time on the run he would receive weapons training from Mosima Tokyo Sexwale of Umkhonto we Sizwe and hold clandestine meetings with the ANC in Swaziland.

On New Year's Eve 1976 his luck ran out: he found himself in the wrong house at the wrong time, was arrested with Billy Masethla and Supa Maloy and taken to

John Vorster Square. 'The first thing they did was to tell me what actually happened and where I fitted into that,' said Morobe. 'I had to fit into their scheme as to why 16 June happened, why the rest of the things happened, and what our role was in that. Clearly, the government did not believe that the uprisings were a result of their policies.'

From John Vorster Square, Morobe was removed to the equally notorious Leeuwkop Prison, where he was held in solitary confinement and subject to 'the usual torture'. 'You knew you would get electrocuted,' he said. 'You had a wet sack tied around your head and electrodes were put on your body and you were shocked. Then they used to sit with you for hours and I had to weigh the options. You had to say to yourself, if I say yes now and turn once I am in the witness box, is the punishment going to be worse than if I say no? I decided I must tell them no.' This remark is typical of the focused and intricately thought-out approach so characteristic of the man.

When the state finally formulated a case, he was tried and convicted for sedition and sentenced to three years in prison. 'Sedition,' he said: 'I think the charge had last been used at the beginning of the century in the Bambata Rebellion. There was nothing that pinned us to any incident, but because we had organised rallies, we were held responsible for the violence of the uprising.'

'Morobe gives the impression of quiet strength, of a man well centred and dependable,' wrote Amma Ogan. 'He describes his sojourn on Robben Island where he completed matric and went on to read his undergraduate degree, as the "cherry on top of the cake".'

On his release from Robben Island in 1982, Morobe joined the General and Allied Workers' Union before going on to be appointed publicity secretary of the UDF in 1985. During the height of State President PW Botha's 'total onslaught' against democratic forces, Morobe, together with a core of committed UDF activists, held the organisation together – spending much of his time living underground in a variety of disguises ranging from priest to labourer. Once again, in 1987, police caught up with him and jailed him in Diepkloof Prison for 14 months. Then, in a dramatic turn of events, Morobe, together with Mohammed Valli Moosa and Vusi Khanyile, sneaked away from police guards at the Johannesburg Hospital and holed up in the American consulate in Johannesburg. Known as the 'Kine Three', they stayed there for more than a month to draw attention to the plight of hundreds of detainees – some of whom had been in jail for more than two years without trial. 'That was one of the highlights of my life,' Morobe recalled with a smile. 'We grow up seeing these things in movies. It never occurred to me that one day I would be one to jump prison walls and dash for safety.'

The three men were freed in October after receiving assurances that no action would be taken against them. But the UDF was becoming increasingly suffocated by the weight of repression, and a new opposition force, the Mass Democratic Movement, emerged with Morobe as spokesman. One of the most publicised actions of this new organisation was its condemnation of the 'reign of terror' unleashed on Soweto by Winnie Mandela and her Mandela United Football Club. While many regarded Morobe's actions as highly principled, he was ostracised by the broader ANC movement and he left the country to study at Princeton in New Jersey.

He returned in 1991 and entered business before being re-embraced by the ANC. He formed part of their pre-1994 negotiating team and after the election held various government posts until appointed chairman of the Financial and Fiscal Commission established under the Constitution. 'He has the persuasiveness, patience and diplomacy to control meetings,' commented a colleague, 'and the political legitimacy to command respect.'

A nature lover and keen hiker, Morobe keeps 16 June 1976 close to his heart: 'It was bequeathed to future generations as a day deeply etched with the blood of my comrades. It lives forever in my memory as a day not only of pride but also of shame at a society that allowed its young to be brutalised for what they believed was right.'

DR NTHATO HARRISON MOTLANA

On 16 June Dr Nthato Motlana's consulting rooms in Dube were busy as usual when an approaching ominous drone was heard. The doctor, wearing white shorts and a white jacket, shut his rooms and went out into the streets to witness horror and courage that etched itself into his memory forever. 'I'll never forget seeing those kids, especially the girls, confronting the police dogs,' he recalled. 'The girls were more courageous than the boys, shouting *"Asibasabi!"* (We are not afraid of you!).' Motlana immediately went to Dr Aaron Matlhare's rooms and they arranged to hold a meeting with other Soweto leaders that night.

That afternoon, the 52-year-old Motlana's rooms were converted into a makeshift casualty ward for children who had been shot, and he and his staff worked into the night extracting bullets and stitching torn flesh. He had been instructed by the police to record the names and addresses of the injured, but refused. While he worked, he was continually haunted by the idea that if adults, particularly those belonging to his Parents' Vigilante Committee, had been more assertive in dealing with student concerns in the build-up to 16 June the crisis might have been averted.

Motlana has a long political history. He came to prominence in the early 1950s as Transvaal secretary of the ANC Youth League and stood trial with Nelson Mandela and others during the defiance campaign – for which he received a five-year banning. Though he studied medicine, his ambition was business. He clearly remembers waiting for a tram in Sophiatown and seeing Asian and white people driving past in their fancy cars. 'I realised then that to get money one had to either have a fat government job or go into business.' He first dabbled in business in 1960, at the age of 35, when he and some friends launched Phakame Africa Commercial Enterprises, but they lacked the business skills and access to finance, and the venture failed. Undeterred, they launched Africhem, the first African chemical company, which is still in existence.

During the 1970s, as resistance to the government grew, Motlana became a vital cog in the Soweto community. He was constantly developing plans for relief, self-help projects to reduce unemployment, mobile kitchens to provide food to schools and the underprivileged. Politically, he founded the Soweto Civic Association to fight for political rights for the disadvantaged, and the Parents' Vigilante Committee.

The arranged meeting at 9 pm on the first day of the uprising led to the foundation a few days later of an association of progressive parents. 'As parents,' commented Motlana, 'we could not allow a situation in which our children were dying. I mean, they died in their thousands; we believe the figures given by the government were way off the mark. And therefore we could not allow that kind of thing to happen, to go unchecked. We had to be seen to be involved with our children in the ongoing struggle. And we decided there and then to form a committee which could talk to the children, talk to the authorities, form a bridge between the warring factions, which were the police, the state and the children. It was called the Black Parents' Association.'

But the association was beset with problems: internally it was riven by competing agendas, and externally the authorities undermined it and the students opposed the idea of a parent body speaking on their behalf. 'The parents weren't in agreement with some of the methods the students were using,' he commented, 'while the kids, on the other hand, had the courage to die.'

With the collapse of the UBC in 1977, progressive Soweto leaders attempted to fill the void by creating the broad-based Soweto Local Authority Interim Committee, popularly known as the Committee of Ten. 'The Committee of Ten,' wrote Thomas Karis and Gail Gerhart in *From Protest to Challenge*, 'was formed at an extraordinary meeting of 61 representatives of Soweto organisations held in late June at the offices of *The World*.' This committee, with Motlana as chairman, included BC militants, former UBC member Leonard Mosala, journalists and prominent businessmen. Most importantly, it received the endorsement of the SSRC. 'This intergenerational alliance was to be a distinctive feature of the post-Soweto period,' continued Karis and Gerhart. 'While the 1976 uprising had certainly given many older Africans a new respect for the courage and dedication of youth, the crushing of the revolt had also brought home to younger people the necessity for forging co-operative relationships with older leaders who were capable of drawing vital adult constituencies – workers, parents, consumers – into united action. In this sense, the emergence of the Committee of Ten represented a return of authority, by mutual consent, to Soweto's parental generation.'

Whatever the mandate, the government was still not listening, even though it is known that some Cabinet ministers favoured discussions with the committee. It was banned on 19 October and its leadership detained. 'Motlana was a tower of strength in prison because he stopped people from smoking,' recalled his friend, Aggrey Klaaste. 'He was a healthy guy and got many people to start jogging.'

Surprisingly, for such an amiable and effusive man, Motlana generates a huge amount of debate – particularly about his leadership abilities. John Kane-Berman, of the Institute of Race Relations, claimed he was 'Soweto's most popular civic and political leader'. 'The truth is that Motlana was equivocal a lot of the time,' countered Lindi Myeza of the Christian Institute. 'It was his position that lifted him up. He was more of a supporter than a leader. In fact his wife was the leader.'

By 1980, Motlana had served two short prison sentences, been banned twice and prohibited from leaving the country for 32 years. Long convinced that the only real power for blacks lay in economic upliftment, he turned his attention more and more over the next two decades to big business. This did not mean, however, that he abandoned the political stage: he remained at the forefront of the political struggle during the turbulent 1980s. He was a key figure in the Soweto Parents' Education Crisis Committee, which in 1985 lobbied for an end to school boycotts and demanded a 'single education department', and in 1986 led a campaign to boycott township service payments.

Because of his entrepreneurial spirit and political reputation, he was an obvious candidate to spearhead transformation in the predominantly white-owned corporate sector. By 1993, at 68 years of age, Motlana was one of South Africa's most active community organisers and corporate board members, tending to his business concerns in the mornings and his patients – including the Mandela and Tutu families – in the afternoons. Despite unspectacular business success, few businessmen, black or white, have served on as many boards and this has attracted its fair share of scepticism. 'Dr Motlana is a medical doctor, a decent soul, a man with the best intentions,' wrote Patti Waldmeir in the *Sunday Times*. 'But his record as a businessman can scarcely explain the large infusion of corporate powers he has received from white business, eager to divest itself of peripheral assets in the name of black economic empowerment.'

Among Motlana's current civic positions is chairmanship of the Soweto Heritage Trust, which is building a monument to Hector Peterson. For him, this memorial will be a symbol of the courage of youth in changing the perception of adults that apartheid was an overwhelming problem. He is married to Sally and they have six children and 12 grandchildren.

KYALUSHI DRAKE KOKA

It was around midnight on 17 June when Tsietsi Mashinini knocked on 43-year-old Kyalushi Drake Koka's door. The schoolboy was still in shock over the bloodbath the day before and needed counselling – some assurance from the energetic older man that it was not all in vain, together with guidance on the way forward.

Koka, at the time under house arrest and serving a five-year banning order, rose immediately to the young student leader's request. He had, after all, become known to the scholars in 1976 as the 'Godfather', a role he would continue to fill for another two decades while in exile. Until then, and for months afterwards, the Pietersburg-born Koka – a teacher, Roman Catholic layman, trade unionist and the first general secretary of the Black People's Convention (BPC) – had ghost-written numerous pamphlets on behalf of the South African Students' Movement calling for a rejection of Bantu Education.

Koka had displayed his rejection of the appallingly discriminatory nature of Bantu Education in 1971 by resigning his post as a schoolteacher and immersing himself in the growing Black Consciousness Movement, which functioned from the Black Allied Workers' Union office he ran. A year later, at a meeting convened by MT Moerane, then editor of *The World* newspaper, the BPC was born and Koka was elected general secretary.

'We set up offices in Eloff Street,' he recalled. 'As blacks we weren't allowed to rent office space, so we went to Joubert Park and found some white hobos, bought them beers and got them to sign their names on the papers. Our headquarters was called Downing Mansions, and we'd joke about it being 10 Downing Street.'

Because of police harassment, Koka became adept at disguising his movements, adopting pseudonyms where necessary. 'If I were writing a letter to Dr Asvat, for instance, I'd be Reverend Kahn. If I was booking into a hotel, I'd be Reverend Mayson after my friend Reverend Cedric Mayson.'

Koka developed a strong bond with 'student daredevils such as Mashinini and Murphy Morobe' in the build-up to 16 June. 'I gave them guidance because they were our children,' he recalled, 'and they needed political education.' Koka insists that even though he was aware of the student leadership's movements, they organised the march of 16 June on their own.

After the uprising, Koka spent his weekends – despite the restrictions of his banning order – organising the resistance undercover with the aid of an old battered Volkswagen Beetle borrowed from his Catholic priest friend, Father Cosmas Desmond. 'He would just give us that old car,' laughed Koka, 'and never ask questions about what we did with it. We'd be driving all over the townships with it to keep contact with the kids and arranging escapes for hunted youngsters to Botswana. On Sundays we'd just return it again.'

Among those he helped flee was Mashinini, but soon after that he too began to feel the heat when the security police came for him. 'When they came to my home in Soweto, I happened to be out, but they went through every part of the house and found all my pamphlets in a hole I had dug where the dog slept,' grinned the old stalwart. 'I'd actually bought that dog from the security cops so it would frighten people off!'

Koka fled South Africa in November 1976 with the help of Mayson – who was also a pilot and who would secretly fly many refugees to Botswana from Grand Central Airport.

'Mr Drake Koka, well-known Soweto trade union leader, is alive and safe in Botswana where he is a political refugee,' reported *The World*. 'The soft-spoken trade unionist left home on November 7 for Botswana. Earlier that morning his home had been raided by police. They searched the house and left with a typewriter and several documents. Mr Koka returned later that morning, but then disappeared. On Tuesday, November 9, two policemen from Orlando visited his home and told his wife that he had not reported to the police as he is supposed to do every Monday. They left a message that as soon as he returned he must report to Orlando Police Station.'

In Gaborone he hooked up again with Mashinini and within months the pair were travelling extensively to muster support for the anti-apartheid struggle under the BC banner. 'Two South African refugees, Mr Drake Koka and Mr Tsietsi Mashinini, have been involved with talks in Gaborone between different factions of the BC movement aimed at creating a "third force" in external South African politics,' reported *The Star*. 'These talks are designed to unite movements that do not fall under the sphere of the PAC and the ANC.'

Because of the better organisation of the ANC, Koka's efforts were largely fruitless and he settled in England where he lectured on African history at the University of Leicester. Here, and in the rest of Europe, he became a familiar face at worker-organised rallies and conferences – platforms he used tirelessly to call for disinvestment and solidarity with South African unions, now emerging as potent vehicles for disruptive mass protests against apartheid. 'I found the international community was generally supportive of our cause, though those with heavy investments in South Africa, like Britain, were reticent,' he said.

Koka, however, never forgot the kids and he continued to play a critical first-contact role for new refugees from South Africa. 'Ideology, for me, did not matter,' he commented on the differences between him and the two main liberation movements. 'What mattered was that these were my children. I would get calls from all over the world from kids stranded, crying for help.' In his 15 years in exile he never lost his political sense of purpose and maintained good relationships with other parties. 'What bound us was that we were all South Africans who believed we'd return to a changed country.'

As a result of the new political era ushered in by FW de Klerk, Koka finally returned home in 1991. The 64-year-old, now grey, but sharp as ever, again took up the cudgel for his old union, the Black Allied Workers' Union. 'Remember the little man with a goatee who wore colourful caftans and showed up at most political events in the township in the 70s?' wrote journalist Nomavenda Mathiane. 'Well Drake "the Godfather" is back. Except for the grey Afro, a tribute to the hard years of life as a refugee, Koka has not changed one bit.'

But what had changed was South Africa. 'The country had been devastated by the apartheid government,' he commented. 'Because of this we entered a tough period.'

Koka continued lecturing empowerment politics, and does so to this day, protesting simultaneously that he's an old man and 'retired'. 'I was trying to drill into the youth the importance of taking the task of leadership into our own hands,' he explained. 'But again the inferior education system was mesmerising their minds, numbing them. That is still the case, even today. Soweto 76 dispelled our fears and proved we could succeed; now black people need to realise themselves – to look at their objectives and actualise them. If we don't we will have no one to blame and will not be capable of reconstructing this country.'

Since his return Koka has been made honorary president of the Socialist Party of Azania, and has served on the technical committee that drafted the Bill setting up a commission for the promotion and protection of the rights of cultural, religious and linguistic communities. He lives with his wife and family in Noordwyk, Midrand.

BRIGADIER THEUNS 'ROOI RUS' SWANEPOEL

One of the most frequently used newspaper photographs of the late Brigadier Theuns 'Rooi Rus' Swanepoel depicts him glaring stony-eyed into the distance, his jaw jutting, holding a 9 mm Beretta pistol with an outsized right hand unflinchingly poised to squeeze the trigger. During the *Sunday Star* interview when the picture was taken, the cantankerous Swanepoel fired nine shots into the grass, uncontrollably incensed by his own tales of the 'communists' and 'terrorists' he had despised throughout his blood-and-guts career as a policeman.

On joining the Oudshoorn police at the dawn of apartheid in 1947, the 19-year-old Afrikaner showed a remarkable aptitude for the job of killing – proving to be a lethal embodiment of the bilious anti-communist propaganda fermenting inside the security forces at the time. Indeed, it was his self-proclaimed knowledge of 'communism, terrorism, sabotage and explosives' that earned him his nickname 'Rooi Rus' (Red Russian). 'The communists gave it to me because they feared me,' he once laughed.

His quaint views on the insidious threat of communism and its infiltration of black American civil rights movements were very popular with the government. It was a short step from there to seeing the Black Power salute used by opponents of apartheid in South Africa as evidence that Black Consciousness was a front for the 'communist-tarnished' ANC – a belief that was anathema to Africanist-inclined BC proponents. It was, however, a common and convenient flaw in government think-ing at the height of the Cold War to label all its enemies as communists – including those who wore blue jeans and sported peace signs.

Swanepoel earned his fearsome, cold-blooded reputation as commander of the notorious police anti-terrorist unit and as one of the security police's most infamous interrogators – he once hung Mac Maharaj out of a seventh floor window by his ankles. 'He was absolutely notorious,' wrote Hugh Lewin in *The Star*, 'the most feared of the sixties people, a mixture of total thuggery and terrifying intelligence, the epit-ome of a Nazi thug.' Another of Swanepoel's torture victims, former political prison-er Indres Naidoo, bolstered this assessment by telling the *Sunday Independent*'s Pippa Green and Adele Sulcas that Swanepoel had a fearsome intelligence and ded-ication to his cause, albeit manifested through torture and the barrel of a gun.

By the time of the Soweto Uprising, Swanepoel was a thickset 48-year-old who had an ANC bounty of R50 000 on his head – a fact he always jocularly dismissed. 'They drafted me to Soweto,' he told Philip van Niekerk of the *Weekly Mail*, 'because Soweto at that time was completely under-policed. They could not control the riots so outsiders were called on to send in task forces.' When the call came alerting him to the swelling student march in Soweto, he grabbed the first 60 men he could enlist and headed for the township that would come to know him as the 'Beast of Soweto'.

Far from the remorse some of his colleagues felt afterwards for firing randomly at juvenile protesters, Swanepoel always felt that the police should have taken stern-er action. 'The police did not use enough force and in the end the unrest spread all over the country,' he told Gerard van Niekerk of the *Sunday Star*. 'If the police had enough men available on the 16th and used sufficient force – irrespective of the num-ber being killed – we could have stopped them. I'm not going to go into if we had killed a thousand or ten thousand that day – I'm saying if we used enough force that day we could have stopped the riots in Soweto and they wouldn't have spread throughout the country. It's not a question that the police could not deal with the sit-uation. It is my honest opinion some of our officers were dragging their feet. They were not scared but they were reluctant.'

On 18 June Swanepoel was hit in the eye by a bottle that caused permanent dam-age – and fired him to even greater atrocities. So effective was he in dealing with the uprising in Soweto and Alexandra that he was placed in charge of the Riot Squad operating in the Johannesburg area. He was convinced that the uprising was 'clever-ly organised by the South African Communist Party' (and thus the ANC). As proof of this he cited certain hand signals used by agitators to signal the formation of an ox horn flank advance to engulf the foe in the centre. 'This, says the colonel, is a well-known communist signal and a well-known communist attack formation,' wrote Donald Woods in the *Rand Daily Mail*. 'And perhaps he is right. But I remember from my childhood in Transkei that one of the most familiar tribal gestures of aggression in a stick-fight or a faction-fight was precisely the ox horn signal described by Colonel Swanepoel. What is more, the wide-flanking attack formation is as old as any recorded tribal battle. Chaka's Zulu armies employed this formation as long ago as 1821. It was even called the ox horn formation.

'The gesture is also used at sports gatherings – for example, to urge a boxer to get stuck in. Disturbingly, most rugby referees make something approximating to the ox horn signal when they indicate a penalty kick at the posts. Referee Gert Bezuidenhout did so several times at Ellis Park during the fourth test against the All Blacks. And what's more he was wearing a red jersey.

'He says he learnt all about communism while investigating offences under the Suppression of Communism Act. It is interesting to hear that this Act actually has something to do with communism, because up to now the only link I have ever been able to detect between communism and the Suppression of Communism Act is the Russian-like approach of punishing people without trial. We live and learn. These are mind boggling times, especially if people were to insist that old tribal gestures come not from the kraal, but from the Kremlin. Oh, well, as we say in the Transkei, behind every ox horn is an awful lot of bull.'

In the 1980s, as head of the Crime Prevention Unit and the Johannesburg Riot Squad, he would invariably pop up when protest marches became volatile, particularly at schools or university campuses. His appetite for arresting and detaining activists remained insatiable, drawing comment from Methodist clergymen at the church's annual synod in 1980 that in his actions he was 'irresponsible', 'unapproachable' and 'uncouth'. 'Somehow I think he enjoys arresting people,' remarked Reverend Cecil Begbie. To which Swanepoel bombastically replied: 'I've detained thousands in my time. I'd happily detain ten times more.'

Two years after his retirement in 1982, after 35 years in the force, Swanepoel made a bizarre comeback as a water diviner – a gift he claimed was God given. Swanepoel's wife, Sarah, advertised him in a farmer's magazine as the 'greatest water diviner Africa has ever seen'. He told the *Sunday Times*'s Savvas Georgiades that he first discovered his talent while serving on the border in 1971 during a critical shortage of water. Out of desperation, he picked up a forked stick and before he realised what was happening, the stick started quivering.

In the 1987 general election he re-emerged as the Westdene candidate for the Conservative Party, campaigning against the National Party's Pik Botha. At one political meeting he called politicians 'a lot of chattering monkeys sitting at the side of Table Mountain' and promised that if elected he would give the security forces the power to do what they were trained for – kill ANC members and communists.

Having lost the election, Swanepoel found a new political home as security chief of the ultra-right-wing Afrikaner Weerstandsbeweging (AWB). But, while he always complained about being held back by his seniors in the police force, he was strangely subservient to orders in the AWB and faded from the news to a quiet death, which passed almost unnoticed, of a heart obstruction in 1998. Swanepoel left his wife, two daughters and two teenage grandsons.

DR BEYERS NAUDÉ

In early May 1976 Dr Beyers Naudé's Christian Institute (CI) report on detentions in South Africa was receiving widespread international publicity. The front page of *The Times* of London declared the document 'one of the most damning indictments ever to be published in South Africa of the government's Draconian security apparatus'. At the same time the churchman approached member of Parliament René de Villiers. 'I asked him to please get in touch with Andries Treurnicht and warn him not to continue enforcing Afrikaans as a medium of instruction because the suppressed suffering and rage in black communities was likely to explode in bloodshed and violence.'

'Treurnicht is a hard-headed Afrikaner,' replied De Villiers, after raising these concerns with the deputy minister. 'My impression is that he'll continue with his policy.'

'When news of the shooting began to filter through on 16 June it was painful,' recalled Naudé. 'How could the Afrikaner, considering his history, have tried to impose Afrikaans with such insensitivity and lack of understanding? Do we never learn?'

'The CI last night called the protest of the Soweto pupils an issue of national importance surpassing the Sharpeville "massacre",' reported the *Rand Daily Mail*. '"In expressing our solidarity with the students of Soweto we confess the truth of their complaint," said Dr Beyers Naudé, director of the CI. "Not only the government but also the parents and the churches did little to support the students' claims, mediate in their dispute or prevent its escalation into violence."

'The CI called upon the government to remove enforced instruction through the medium of Afrikaans and to convene a national conference of black and white leaders. "For a very long time the CI has warned South Africa of the serious dangers created by the racial policies which have been forced upon our population and the enormous tension which they have generated among blacks," said Dr Naudé.'

The government, however, was not listening: on 18 June 1976 it served orders on Naudé in terms of the Riotous Assemblies Act, warning him to dissociate himself completely from the 'situation of unrest'. Treurnicht was not the only hard-headed Afrikaner in a people renowned for their obduracy; Naudé, the government's *bête noire*, could match and better him in stubbornness.

Naudé was born to fervent Nationalist parents in 1915. His father had been a chaplain during the Anglo-Boer South African War and a founder member of the Afrikaner Broederbond. For his first 45 years Naudé appeared to be following in his father's footsteps – Stellenbosch University, rapid advancement to the moderature of the Nederduitse Gereformeerde Kerk (NGK), membership of the Broederbond and, ultimately, selection as minister of the elite new NGK congregation of Aasvoelkop in Northcliff, Johannesburg. But the 1960 Sharpeville massacre changed all that and he began seriously to doubt the moral code of both his community and his church.

The turning point came that December, at the World Council of Churches conference in Cottesloe, when he defied NGK authority by refusing to repudiate decisions that championed the basic rights of all. Over the years that followed, Naudé sought vainly to help his church see the light and move away from apartheid within its ranks. In 1963, when he founded the Christian Institute – an ecumenical, non-racial organisation opposing apartheid – retribution orchestrated by the Broederbond was swift and punitive. He was deprived of his status as a minister and constantly vilified by his fellow countrymen – at one point being labelled 'the most unpopular person in South Africa' by the *Vaderland* newspaper.

'The outstanding merit of Beyers' life and work lies in the fact that he blazed the new trail almost entirely alone,' commented his brother-in-law and former chief executive officer of the NGK, Dr Frans Geldenhuys. 'It is no easy decision for an already accepted and honoured young leader among his own people to break with many of the traditions of the past and move out into a broader South Africanism.' But the more he split with the past, the more his uncompromising integrity and willingness to assist young black activists won him respect among apartheid's opponents. In conferring an honorary doctorate on him in 1974, the University of the Witwatersrand declared him an 'international figure, an embodiment of the liberal spirit in this land.'

'Here was somebody who was an Afrikaner,' remarked ANC chairman Mosuioa 'Terror' Lekota of Naudé. 'I mean, I'd just known Afrikaners to beat us up and all. It was quite clear that there were Afrikaners who were evil, but there were many who were not like that.'

'We were very grateful for whites like Beyers Naudé and Cedric Mayson,' added Kyalushi Drake Koka. 'They helped the struggle immensely – in whatever way they could.'

On 'Black Wednesday', 19 October 1977, the government had had enough and outlawed numerous organisations, banning Naudé for seven years. But they could not break him. 'Fortunately I could use those years to reflect on many issues,' he told *The Star*. 'I especially invited young black people to come and discuss with me the issues of the day, to open their hearts – so that I could understand what went on in the hearts of millions of young blacks in our country.'

Until his banning order was lifted in 1984, Naudé lived under constant scrutiny. 'My wife, Ilse, and I had to live with the awareness that our letters were regularly opened, our phone was tapped and our home was under surveillance.' Soon after the banning order was lifted, the 79-year-old Naudé was appointed general secretary of the South African Council of Churches as successor to Archbishop Desmond Tutu, and again he took a vociferous platform against apartheid. From 1985 the tireless octogenarian also established an ecumenical advice bureau in Braamfontein to cope with the stream of visitors seeking his advice and help, became patron of the United Democratic Front and involved himself in numerous bridge-building initiatives.

The security establishment always suspected Naudé of close involvement with the ANC, but the extent of that involvement only became clear in 1995 when he published his autobiography. Rumours that he helped the ANC smuggle weapons into the country, he said, were completely untrue, though he participated in smuggling people out of the country, assisted underground ANC members who illegally entered the country, and distributed banned ANC pamphlets. 'I was convinced by activists who came to see me that there was no other way the political situation could be resolved other than for them to go away and join the military,' he said. 'I knew that to be true. My father eventually took up arms against the British and when I compared the two historical scenarios, I could not see any difference. Although I wasn't a member of the ANC, I fully identified with its goals.'

Though he was not a member of the ANC, the movement honoured him in 1990 by including him in its delegation for pre-negotiation talks with the National Party government. The only person not enamoured with his contribution was himself, and in 1997 he atoned before the Truth and Reconciliation Commission 'for not having done enough' during the apartheid years. 'I could have started earlier in my preaching to indicate to my congregation my deep concern. It is true that I did that two or three times at Aasvoelkop, but I could have done more. I could have mobilised more people to express concern,' he told the commission.

Today, Naudé – recovering from an operation for thrombosis in his leg – is still pondering South Africa's future, and his words are again ominously laced with warnings. 'I'm deeply concerned about the growing gap between rich and poor,' he said. 'A big question is how we are going to divide property in South Africa. If you look at the Free State, not a single square metre is owned by blacks. Like the rebellion in Soweto in 1976, there is a groundswell of anger and bitterness about this inequitable situation that must be addressed if history is not to be repeated.'

Dr Beyers Naudé lives in Northcliff with his wife, who has always been at his side, continually nagging him to get some rest. That appears unlikely. He is a patron of Transparency International SA and continues to work for political unity and economic upliftment through the SACC. He is also working towards forging unification of all NGK churches across the racial spectrum.

HORST KLEINSCHMIDT

In April 1976, South African newspapers were making a feast of Namibian-born Horst Kleinschmidt's mysterious disappearance. The young CI deputy to Beyers Naudé, who a year earlier had spent 72 days in prison under Section Six of the Terrorism Act, had fled his Melville home. Feverish speculation ended two weeks later when he telephoned his then wife Illona from Botswana. He was lying low, she told the *Rand Daily Mail*, because 'he fears being blown up by a parcel-bomb'. Within a fortnight he was in Holland announcing that he would continue the fight against apartheid as the European representative of the CI.

Kleinschmidt, in the 1960s, was a student at the University of the Witwatersrand and NUSAS vice-president. He first encountered Steve Biko in 1967 when he noticed him defiantly sitting through the singing of the national anthem, *Die Stem*, at a NUSAS conference. Kleinschmidt later travelled to Durban to forge a friendship with the young firebrand.

After graduating, Kleinschmidt joined the CI in 1972 and as director of Spro-Cas (the Special Project for Christian Action in Society, later the Programme for Social Change) began recording the disappearances of detainees, establishing their condition and acting as a link for the families desperate to find them. His damning reports about the ruthless treatment of prisoners, and the resultant negative press internationally, were a constant thorn in the government's side. Kleinschmidt, however, felt that even though it was the government doing the jailing on behalf of white South Africans, it was the whites who were in prison. In one of his 1973 essays, published in a booklet titled *White Liberation,* which he edited, he wrote: 'Unknown to himself the white man has placed himself in a racial jail – his own racial jail which has become so much part of him that he is no longer aware of it, or of the need to free himself.'

Kleinschmidt was finally arrested in 1975 on a spurious allegation and spent the following three months in solitary confinement in Pretoria. 'Those were lonely days,' he recalled. 'There was a lot of self-doubt because the CI, other than Naudé, felt I'd gone too far. I also had very little support because we weren't linked to the bigger movement of the ANC.' A few months after his release, Kleinschmidt, with the help of Cedric Mayson, silently fled a country in the grip of seething discontent and ominous calm.

Kleinschmidt's primary concern when he first arrived in Holland was the South African government's continued confrontation with churches and their blocking of visiting church leaders' visa applications. But then came 16 June – whose roots he believes lay in the Black Consciousness philosophy in general, though he feels the event itself was spontaneous. He clearly recalls the moment: 'I was visiting Amnesty International in London that day, and I had an appointment to see the Chancellor of the Exchequer, Dennis Healey, that evening. Then reports came through of Hector Peterson being shot and I started getting calls from Beyers Naudé. He was saying, "This is big, very big. We must tell Dennis Healey this has much wider implications."'

Naudé's concern about getting across the message of 'wider implications' was an oblique reference to the skewed coverage by the 'liberal' South African press, which he felt could diminish the importance of the uprising. But it was bigger than that. 'The shock-waves of 16 June were felt the world over and caused the Western world to condemn apartheid in more significant terms,' said Kleinschmidt. 'The ANC had already mobilised the Eastern bloc, but '76 touched a moral note in the West and there was a huge growth of anti-apartheid organisations.'

That September, three months after the start of the uprising, Kleinschmidt launched a stinging attack on the media's treatment of the unrest before the American Senate – accusing it of censoring itself and misrepresenting the facts. 'The press tried to suggest there was a division between young and old and later that various groups had turned against each other and were killing each other,' he told Senator Dick Clark's African Subcommittee. 'The way in which these arguments were willingly believed spelt out some of the crude racism of the whites, who wanted to hold their prejudiced view that the blacks were initially instigated to riot, and later turned against each other due to tribal differences.'

Even though the West was distancing itself from South Africa, it would take years for it to accept the ANC as a legitimate vehicle of the struggle against apartheid. Kleinschmidt was also having problems with the CI, which continued to view him as a radical because of European church threats to have nothing to do with him if he continued to take the ANC line. In 1979, amid mounting internal tensions over his views, Kleinschmidt closed down the European office of the Christian Institute – then banned in South Africa – and joined the International Defence and Aid Fund for Southern Africa in London as its director.

In 1991, a year after Nelson Mandela's release, Kleinschmidt returned to South Africa after 14 years in exile to attend a conference on repatriation – only to leave again with disheartening views that despite important developments, apartheid was anything but dead. 'It appears there has been a new wave of detentions,' he told *The Star*. 'Violence seems more vicious than at any period I have known. Those in power continue to use violence to maintain its supremacy.' He added that he would recommend to anti-apartheid organisations that they maintain pressure until fundamental changes were made.

But it had felt so good to be back that, in December, Kleinschmidt returned for good. After a short stint at Lawyers for Human Rights, he joined Kagiso Trust – later founding its investments unit before leaving the institution in 1999. His political path since has thrust him into yet another cauldron of conflict, one he is distinctly uneasy about. As the Cape Town-based deputy director-general of marine and coastal management under the Ministry of Tourism and Environmental Affairs, Kleinschmidt has the unenviable task of rooting out decades of corruption in the fishing quota system, traditionally weighted in favour of affluent white businessmen. 'It's extraordinarily tense and difficult, and I've already been taken hostage once,' he smiled. 'I'm a bit old to go through this kind of stuff again.'

JACKIE SELEBI

Jackie Selebi, currently national police commissioner, tells some of the most compelling subterfuge stories of the 1970s when he was an operative for the ANC underground in South Africa. Among these is an anecdote about his regular Sunday visits to detained comrades in prison to discuss strategy while the police – many of whom work for him today – scoured the country for him. He was able to do this because of the number of policemen recruited as spies and allies. 'Nobody ever won a war without recruiting a sector of the security establishment,' he commented. 'We would start by paying them until they became committed to the cause.'

Soweto-born Selebi began his political apprenticeship with the ANC in the early 1970s while a teacher at Orlando West High School. Fired in 1975, 'because I was politicising the kids at every opportunity', he immersed himself deeper into the hidden matrix of the struggle, where, as the regional director of SASO, he worked closely with youth leaders such as Billy Masethla, Supa Maloy and Zwelise Zane. 'These leaders and the organisations they represented were strongly aligned to the ANC and played a pivotal role in leading the student resistance,' he said. 'Tsietsi Mashinini and Murphy Morobe were in fact Zane's recruits. Tsietsi was elected into a leadership role and Morobe briefed to organise.'

Selebi is adamant that the more militant agents of the ANC underground, as opposed to BC proponents, planned and steered the events that culminated in the Soweto Uprising – but, he admits, the uprising itself and its aftermath were not expected. 'It came as an opportunity, a challenge to the ANC organisation,' he said. In the weeks and months that followed, the 28-year-old Selebi and his colleagues were hard at work capitalising on the gains of 16 June. Having undergone short training stints outside South Africa in propaganda/intelligence techniques and the basics of guerrilla warfare, the young Jackie spent his days making pamphlets, detonating pamphlet bombs, recruiting new agents, setting up units and cells, planning the exodus of students on the run, mobilising the public and convening secret ANC underground meetings that were vital in maintaining unity, morale and direction following the rebellion. Former Christian Institute staffer Lindi Myeza recalls the young Selebi as a quiet but potent force at these political meetings: 'His eyes were very sharp, focused. He'd be less vociferous, but quick to call people to order.'

While it was deemed necessary for a number of the students of 1976 to leave for military training outside the country, Selebi, a vital cog in the underground structures, was instructed to stay behind. In the mass detentions of October 1977, he was held in Modderbee Prison. There he belonged to a radical group that advocated Marxist theory and he christened his prison cell 'Vietnam'. When he was released he continued his underground activities until ordered by the ANC to leave in 1979. 'The reason I left was because the risk was too high of me being caught and compromising other detainees, who would have had to turn state witness against me,' he said. His flight via Lesotho and Mozambique signalled a 20-year exile during which he would undergo further military training in Moscow, Tanzania and Angola, and lead the ANC Youth Sector for young members in exile. In 1987, having completed a four-year stint as representative of the World Federation of Democratic Youth in Budapest, Hungary, Selebi, at 36 years old, was elected onto the ANC's national executive as its youngest member.

Formidable in both physique and temperament, Selebi, the war veteran, finally returned home in 1990 after the ANC's unbanning. Convinced of the pivotal importance of the youth, he immediately set to work with Peter Mokaba to amalgamate the South African Youth Congress and the South African Youth Sector to relaunch the ANC Youth League. 'The youth have always been in the front trenches of political warfare and they are going to play a vital role in determining the future of South Africa,' he said at the time. Before succeeding Winnie Mandela as head of the ANC's Social Welfare Department in 1992, he also directed the repatriation of exiles.

In 1995, after a year as an ANC member of Parliament in South Africa's first democratically elected government, Selebi was appointed ambassador to the UN in Geneva – a move that would mould him into a highly effective diplomat. Here he built an unassailable reputation, first as chairman of the Oslo International Conference to ban anti-personnel landmines, and then as chairman of the UN Commission on Human Rights. The experience was a huge personal and political challenge: 'It was the first time a South African had been placed in a position to direct and bring about an international treaty,' he said. 'So there was a lot of pressure on us.'

While his experience at the UN did much to blunt the ragged edges of the soldier in him, it did little to alter his pugilistic style, and he shook the traditional debating style of the UN. 'With his boxer's physique and the conviction of a man of faith,' commented *Le Temps*, a Swiss newspaper, 'Jacob Selebi owes more to the charisma of Cassius Clay in his youth than the traditional profile of a diplomat.' That said, he was the obvious choice as director-general of Foreign Affairs to succeed Rusty Evans in 1998 – an appointment that heralded the start of another intense period of adjustment. When he entered the Union Buildings, he recounted, he was shocked not so much by the politics of the old guard he inherited, as their deference to rank and power. 'When I walked down the passage, they would turn and face the wall as if I was some kind of strange animal.'

He coped so impressively with the new portfolio that Minister of Foreign Affairs Alfred Nzo remarked, 'He displays an in-depth understanding of the challenges facing South Africa as it consolidates its international position.' A year later, the government, under growing pressure to get rampant crime and corruption under control, appointed the 49-year-old warhorse to succeed George Fivaz as national police commissioner. While many were surprised at his selection, given his inexperience in domestic law and order issues, he had proved himself competent and successful in diverse assignments and it was felt his robust, no-nonsense style was what was needed to shake the police force out of its impassivity. 'I never thought I'd put on a uniform again,' he said. 'But I've grown up in the ANC and the organisation has taken care of me ever since I can remember. It has been my family and my guardian, and if I was issued an order, I would follow it without question. It was decided I should take this position, so here I am.'

The police soon felt the heat of his volcanic eruptions of temper in the face of apathy and inefficiency, in what became a highly publicised affair, when he called a woman sergeant in Pretoria's Brooklyn Police Station a 'fucking gorilla'. For the rest he has focused intently on crushing 'high-flying' crime syndicate bosses.

BILLY LESEDI MASETHLA

'Billy's attitude is that of a turret of a tank,' said Thele Moema of his friend Billy Masethla, 'he can adjust and move fast when required to.' Another friend, Murphy Morobe, added, 'He belongs to the nothing-is-impossible brigade.'

The Alexandra-born Masethla, along with Jackie Selebi and a handful of other activists, had long been a member of a loosely connected, militant and rebellious ANC underground cell when the Soweto Uprising started. At the time, he was a 22-year-old student at the Teachers' Training College in Heilbron and secretary-general of the South African Students' Movement (SASM). Every weekend he travelled to Soweto to help launch branches of the movement and he recalls that in 1976 the township 'was becoming really explosive'. He was preparing for a SASM conference when news first reached him of 16 June: 'When I got calls that students were dying, it really shook me. I was feeling guilty and anxious about who had got killed.'

Like Selebi, Masethla is adamant that the ANC was responsible for the build-up to the Soweto Uprising – and he is scathing of Tsietsi Mashinini, whom he dismisses as an 'eloquent decoy'. Masethla had attempted to recruit Mashinini to SASM structures, but the Hero of Soweto had resisted all overtures. Mashinini was not only a wild card, he was also a loose cannon whose growing prominence worried the ANC as it tried to harness and direct the rebellion. Nonetheless, Masethla's unit agreed to let Tsietsi's star rise. 'His visibility would detract from the rest of us in the underground,' he said. 'None of us wanted to be identified.' But Mashinini's antics, which sent South African government temperatures soaring, placed underground ANC cells at growing risk in the ensuing crackdown. Masethla's unit, eventually, were able to get him out the country – but the hothead Mashinini continued to bad-mouth and bruise the ANC.

Tenacious and hard-working, Masethla was a strong organiser, and in the months that followed he introduced hand-picked students, among them Murphy Morobe and Paul Langa, to cursory training sessions in the use of firearms, AK-47s and grenades, conducted by Mosima Tokyo Sexwale. He was also heavily involved in co-ordinating the Black Christmas campaign towards the end of 1976.

One of Mashinini's most publicised outbursts against the ANC concerned its security: he claimed that the organisation was so heavily infiltrated that it could not be trusted and advised fleeing scholars to avoid it. It was counsel that would haunt Masethla. On New Year's Eve, based on leaked information, Masethla and the rest of his cell were arrested in a massive security swoop. Masethla refused to testify against his comrades and six of them were released, but the rest were to spend over a year languishing in Modderbee Prison. Despite the hardships of life in an apartheid jail, Masethla has some fond memories of that time: 'I remember sympathetic warders used to smuggle in newspapers and gin and tonic for Percy Qoboza. I was in a way excited because I was with my friends.'

Released in January 1979, Masethla hit the ground running and quickly picked up where he had left off. He was instrumental in establishing the ANC-inspired Congress of South African Students and the Azanian Students' Organisation. He soon re-attracted the attention of the Special Branch and was forced into hiding. In May he received the ANC orders he was dreading – it was time to leave the country. Contrary to instruction, the young Masethla, with Supa Maloy in tow, went and visited his mother for a last home-cooked dinner and to say his goodbyes – but the police were keeping the house under surveillance and he found himself behind bars again.

This time his detention was mercifully brief, and on being released he left for Botswana – heralding an 11-year stretch away from home during which he would receive intensive military intelligence and combat training in Angola, East Germany and Zambia. Disciplined, focused and a vital ANC operative in the shadowy world of espionage, Masethla was an ideal candidate to oversee wider intelligence-gathering operations: in 1988 he was appointed deputy chief representative of the ANC's intelligence office in the UK and Ireland. 'You needed to be smart,' he remarked about his experience in this position. 'You needed to be a gentleman playing a very dirty game. I was travelling extensively, recruiting heads of states, prime ministers, kings. In any conflict on the continent, we knew the players on both sides. It was a big challenge – and extremely dangerous. On one occasion one of our big chiefs misused information and my mole got arrested as a result.'

In 1990 the 36-year-old Masethla returned home a seasoned freedom fighter. He was appointed a leader of the ANC's task team to re-establish youth and student structures and he played a key role in launching the provisional National Youth Congress – the forerunner to the ANC's reformulated Youth League. But Masethla really wanted to be in intelligence and in 1996 was made director-general of the South African Secret Services. He and his deputy, Barry Gilder, told the media they wanted to be called 'democratic spies' because of the unenviable task of amalgamating the operatives from the liberation movements, the homelands and the old National Party secret service into a single unit. 'He is a very energetic person, very disciplined, with good leadership skills and a commitment to measured, achievable transformation,' remarked one of his colleagues. To this the *Mail & Guardian* added: 'Despite his background, he is able to carry all sectors of the service behind him – which is a very necessary skill in this period.'

In 1999 he was reassigned to the moribund and corruption-riddled Home Affairs Department as its director-general. Eyebrows were raised by the move because the dislike of his political boss, Chief Mangosutho Buthelezi, was no secret. Even Masethla asked: 'Why me?' The job is an enormous strain, but he remains undeterred by the incompetence and skulduggery in the department he runs. He seldom leaves his office before 9 pm, trying to cope with an endless stream of 'urgent crises' arising over migration red tape, endless bungles and, his biggest challenge, complaints against his staff.

PETER SEXFORD MAGUBANE

One of Peter Magubane's photographs, published in his book *June 16, 1976 – Never Never Again*, depicts the back of the notorious 'green car', the driver pointing his firearm out of the window towards the pavement where a lone woman is standing. 'I would follow that car around,' he said. 'It was driven by two white policemen and they would go around shooting people indiscriminately – women, children, men. If a person was badly wounded, I would take them to the clinic.'

Thousands upon thousands of such images are stacked in the photographer's personal archives. It took just a few, though, to turn the Vrededorp-born Magubane into a living legend. He has exhibited extensively all over the world and won so many awards he's lost count. A bear of a man, with a shock of white hair and sensitive down-turned eyes, Magubane has been obsessed ever since he was a young man with freeze-framing township life, and his works are irrefutable documents that will remind generations to come of the terrible price black South Africans had to pay for their freedom.

Like all his old Sophiatown contemporaries, Magubane was swept up into a historical torrent from a world of innocence, replete with fashion copied straight from American men's magazines. An old colleague, Bridgeman Stukuni, in a 1996 report in *New Nation*, remembered the young Magubane: 'Cripes! Peter, at that young age was such a fancy and colourful a dresser that I dubbed him several nicknames. They were of Spanish origin and suited his sartorial flamboyance. Pedro Gonzales or Pancho Sebura and don't ask me why! When he appeared along Troy Street next to Samkay House, he was a sight in scarlet or magenta-coloured pants, multicoloured Jantzen skipper, two-toned Robblee mesh-nylon shoes, mustard cardigan and, I forget his headgear. It might have been a tartan tam-o'-shanter cap or an eight piece Ayres and Smith cap and a Paris belt. All American *Esquire* magazine image.'

In 1954 the young Magubane started working at *Drum* magazine as a driver. Whites were not allowed into townships, so drivers would also play the role of reporter and photographer for their publications. Within six months Magubane had his first camera – a Yashika Flex bought for him by his fruit-seller father – and one of his first subjects was Nelson Mandela. With the camera came creative awakening and a powerful new political consciousness. Magubane would walk the streets until the 9 pm curfew and spend nights on the darkroom floor.

After a couple of years Magubane moved to the *Rand Daily Mail*, South Africa's most rebellious newspaper at the time – and his images of apartheid's merciless scourges in everyday township life were everywhere. 'In those days it was easy,' said Magubane. 'We were all in our way fighting against apartheid. In the 50s and 60s black people were treated like animals; it was our task to show the rest of the world.'

These images made him a worldwide phenomenon, garnering a string of local and international awards, and his daring became the stuff of legend.

He was the first African to hold a one-man exhibition – a collection of graphic shots of a riot during the 1957 Treason Trial, taken with a camera concealed in a milk carton. He burst through the police cordons and braved batons to get the best pictures of the day. 'The more difficult it was to take a picture, the more exciting he found it,' wrote Nat Nakasa, a fellow pressman.

His pictures, which documented 'the social conditions which surround African life', found their way into *Life* magazine, the *New York Times* and the *Observer*. But he was to pay a heavy penalty in a country desperate to conceal the horror of life under apartheid: Magubane got his first taste of the inside of a prison cell in 1956. Incarceration, detention without trial and bannings were to become a regular feature of his life. After a banning order was lifted, wrote Erica Rudden in the *Sunday Express* in September 1975, 'He spent the first day threading through the crowds in Johannesburg, shooting lovers, the Carlton Centre, people on park benches, a messenger on a bicycle.'

Nine months later he was focused on the Soweto Uprising. Two photographs – one of a small naked boy, teargassed and yelling in shock, being doused with water by a bewildered and frightened older schoolgirl; and another of a pair of screaming girls, one of them lifting her sweater to expose a stomach ripped open by a police bullet – capture the full horror of the time. But it was not only about pain and death; he also captured the ecstasy, euphoria and excitement – conveying the image that this was the day of the youth. For Magubane, 16 June was the seminal event of our time: 'One child was killed and South Africa was never the same. It exposed the cracks in the wall of apartheid. Without '76, without the courage of those schoolchildren, we wouldn't be where we are today.'

'That day was the first time I'd seen a police vehicle burning,' he added. 'Sharpeville came and went, but it was nowhere near as explosive as 16 June. I'd never felt such anger before. The situation was extremely volatile and at one point the kids confronted me for taking pictures. I had to convince them that their resistance to oppression had to be recorded for the world to know about apartheid. That saved my skin. But Soweto was nothing to what happened in Alexandra on the Friday. There the police went on a mission to kill. I saw a man shot dead while he was on the toilet. A policeman fractured my nose that day when he hit me with a baton. But the most painful blow was being forced to open my camera and expose my film.'

Two months after the start of the Soweto Uprising, Magubane was detained for the fourth time – on this occasion under the draconian Internal Security Act. He was released, without being charged, after 123 days. While in detention he received the Stellenbosch Farmers' Winery Award for Enterprising Journalism. 'There is little doubt that 1976 will go down as the year of the black journalist,' commented *The World*. 'It was our moment of glory, in which we had the opportunity to show what we can give the news, given the opportunity. For Peter, the prize was well deserved. He showed great courage, endurance and dignity in the execution of his duties. Not only that, he suffered the supreme penalty for his dedication – being arrested and detained without trial. He was also harassed, his cameras were wrenched from him, he was assaulted and his clothes were left in undignified tatters. But Peter had a job to do and he did it without fear or favour.'

Violent conflict continued in townships throughout the country and Magubane recorded it until 1980 when he decided to leave the country and further his studies at the New York Film School. He returned in 1985 when 'things got hot again' and soon came the closest he'd ever been to being killed – being hit 17 times below the waist with police buckshot in the East Rand township of Natalspruit. He was left for dead, but a group of children pulled him to safety. The experience didn't deter him and in 1990 he was shot again, this time with birdshot, as he photographed the shootings in Sebokeng, which left 11 dead. But the worst was yet to come. In 1992 his son, also a photographer, was killed and his body dumped near a hostel in Dube. 'Violence is not exclusive and it has claimed many victims at random,' remarked Magubane. 'My son was hacked and shot in the head like an animal.'

That same year Magubane received the Missouri Honour Medal for Distinguished Service in Journalism from the Missouri School of Journalism – an honour previously conferred on Winston Churchill and Walter Cronkite. His work, from here, took him on assignment to Somalia and Ethiopia for the UN High Commission for Refugees – and a *National Geographic* assignment on the Ndebele that was the beginning of a passionate interest in traditional tribal life and the vanishing indigenous cultures of South Africa. In 1997 he received the Mother Jones/Leica Lifetime Award in New York, where some of the world's top news photographers and executives paid tribute to him.

Now retired from hard news photography, but still passionate about the camera's ability to hold a moment, Magubane believes it was his destiny to record history in the way he has. He has produced 15 pictorial books on the history of South Africa.

BARNEY NYAMEKO PITYANA

The turning point for the affable, irascible Barney Pityana was when, as a teenager, he arrived at the Holy Rosary Convent in Port Elizabeth to request maths and science tuition, only to be angrily turned away by a nun thinking he was a beggar because he was black. The 'Cheeky Bantu' immediately put pen to paper and wrote a letter to the local newspaper, signing it 'Beggar Man'. The school apologised, but never bothered to help. It was a case of 'black man, you are on your own', which would become a Black Consciousness rallying call – one attributed to Pityana.

That fire would again be evident when black students were slighted by NUSAS, and he and Steve Biko began laying the foundation for SASO and BC. As president, then secretary-general of SASO, fired by the teachings of Malcolm X, he ran the gauntlet of the security fraternity as he travelled extensively from meetings to conferences. 'We all worked like mad,' he told Mathatha Tsedu of *The Star*. 'We would wake up in Johannesburg and have a meeting, drive to Durban for another meeting, then back to Johannesburg, and leave immediately for Port Elizabeth and Cape Town. One time we were driving Harry Nengwekhulu's battered Peuguot, I think, from Durban, and when we arrived in Johannesburg, I collapsed. I was rushed to hospital, unconscious, and it was discovered that the car had been tampered with, and a pipe inserted into the exhaust and back into the car, bringing in carbon monoxide.'

After he was expelled from the University of Fort Hare for participating in a student strike against the inadequate skills of the staff foisted on black students by the state, he immersed himself in the work of Black Consciousness. And the message had a ready audience among black students. 'The response was fantastic,' he said. 'Some students were nervous that joining SASO might affect their university careers, but they accepted it as the kind of organisation through which they could express themselves because there was a general feeling that multiracialism was proving very ineffective.'

Pityana's radical ideas soon brought him to the attention of the security police and by the end of the 1960s he had been arrested and tortured – further politicising him and inflaming his anger against racism. He was banned in 1973, along with Biko and other BC leaders, and when Soweto ignited he was restricted to Port Elizabeth. Keeping a low profile, he completed his law articles in his home community of New Brighton. 'We'd expected it,' said Pityana, intimating that senior BC members were aware of the planning of the 16 June march.

The following year Biko was murdered by policemen while in detention. 'I am not pleased nor am I sorry,' responded Justice Minister Jimmy Kruger on hearing the news. 'Biko's death leaves me cold.' If that statement was not enough, National Party MP FJ le Roux added that he would have liked to have killed Biko himself, and added: 'In South Africa, when a man disturbs law and order the way Steve Biko did, he should be killed. I went so far as to get it from the Bible that if one man destroys law and order then this is what should happen to him.'

The ensuing storm made it necessary to shoot the messenger. On Wednesday, 19 October, sweeping bans on *The World* and 17 other organisations – including SASO – and the detention of scores of dissidents were announced. This left only a handful of cultural organisations, government-approved bodies and homeland political parties still functioning. Among those arrested was Pityana, to be held for one year without trial. When released in 1978 he was placed under 24-hour house arrest and continual harassment left him 'a nervous wreck'. The risk of being 'permanently eliminated' was too high and one night he, his wife Dimza and their seven-year-old daughter sneaked past a police car containing a sleeping security officer and fled to Lesotho. 'A sympathetic magistrate issued us false travel documents,' he recalled, 'and we flew out three weeks later to London on a plane chartered by Peter Bruce (now *Financial Mail* editor – then a student activist on the run from military conscription). On arrival in the United Kingdom, Pityana was elected UK chairman of the BC movement.

His role in exile with BC was short lived. Pityana, studying theology at London University, was soon deeply dissatisfied with the lack of unity and flagging morale in the movement. It was a rudderless ship, paralysed by deep debate: 'Discussions were frequently bogged down in ideology and rhetoric,' said one report. In 1979 he resigned both as the chairman and as a member of the organisation. Within a year he was talking to the ANC and in 1982 announced he had joined the organisation. It was a bitter pill for his contemporaries to swallow, but he downplayed the shift: 'It's important to understand that in joining SASO, I never renounced my commitment to the ANC. I never saw BC as a substitute and I believed in its legitimacy even when I left. But at the time a lot of BC people were dispirited and hostile to the ANC and I didn't think it was healthy. There was a need to develop a relationship with other liberation movements, a unity and a modus operandi with the ANC, so I made my own decision to quietly leave BC and join the ANC.'

Now an ordained Anglican priest, Pityana plunged headlong into the political machinations of the church with his appointment in 1983 to Geneva as director of the World Council of Churches (WCC) unit overseeing the provision of grants for combating racism. 'Fighting racism had been a lifelong thing for me,' he said, 'but here I found another cauldron of discrimination. During most of the 1980s the ANC was hardly even recognised by the South African Council of Churches. The churches had never really had serious discussions about the race issue. The first time the liberation movements got on an equal footing here was during a church convention in Lusaka in 1987, where it was finally resolved that the armed struggle was indeed justifiable. Beyers Naudé was a key person in that convention.' At the time of his WCC directorship, Pityana told the *Guardian* newspaper that he included even Archbishop Tutu among the church leaders who dragged their feet.

Returning to South Africa in 1992, Pityana joined the religious studies department of the University of Cape Town as senior research officer, and in 1995 was admitted to the Supreme Court as an attorney. A year later he was appointed head of the Human Rights Commission – an organisation he has kept in the limelight with his indicting, fire-tipped words, first labelling law professor Dennis Davis a racist and refusing to back down, then instituting an inquiry into racism in the media. His supporters laud him for his courage and tenacity in exposing and rooting out the deep racism that still exists in South African society, which at the end of the day is the job he is employed to do. His detractors accuse him of being stubborn, defiant and blinkered – even racist. 'It's not that I hate white people,' he said. 'I have white friends. But this doesn't mean we mustn't talk about and deal with racism.'

GLOSSARY

Afrikaner Weerstandsbeweging – Afrikaner Resistance Movement

assegai – short Zulu spear

bioscope – cinema

dompas – pass book

donga – gully, ravine

Dopper – a conservative branch of the Dutch Reformed Church

dorp – small town

impi – Zulu military regiment

jislaaik – exclamation expressing surprise

kaffir – derogatory term for black people

kappie – bonnet

klapbroeke – trousers closed with a flap

knobkerrie – fighting stick with a knobbed head

koeksuster – deep-fried twisted doughnut dipped in syrup

kombi – minibus

konfyt – fruit preserve

kopje – small hill

kraal – animal enclosure

laager – self-isolating group, named after the protective circle of ox wagons used by early
   Afrikaners

Nederduitse Gereformeerde Kerk – Dutch Reformed Church

Ossewabrandwag – literally ox-wagon sentinel: a pro-Nazi paramilitary movement during
   World War II

panga – large broad-bladed knife

robot – traffic light

veldskoen – handmade shoe made of animal hide

Vierkleur – literally 'four colour': the flag of the Transvaal Republic

volk – nation

wa-kist – wooden chest on an ox wagon, used as a seat for the driver

BIBLIOGRAPHY

Heribert Adam and Hermann Giliomee, *The Rise and Crisis of Afrikaner Power*. Cape Town: David Philip, 1979.

Adamastor, *White Man Boss*. London: Gollancz, 1950.

Gary Allighan, *Verwoerd – The End*. Cape Town: Purnell, 1961.

Peter Becker, *Tribe to Township*. St Albans: Panther, 1974.

Steve Biko, *I Write What I Like*. Randburg: Ravan, 1978.

Philip Bonner and Lauren Segal, *Soweto – A History*. Cape Town: Maskew Miller Longman, 1998.

Herman Charles Bosman, *A Bosman Treasury*. Cape Town: Human and Rousseau, 1991.

Luli Callinicos, *A Place In the City – The Rand on the Eve of Apartheid*. Johannesburg: Ravan/Maskew Miller Longman, 1993.

Michael Chapman and Achmat Dangor (eds.), *Voices from Within – Black Poetry from Southern Africa*. Johannesburg: Ad Donker, 1982.

William Cobbett and Robin Cohen (eds.), *Popular Struggle in South Africa*. London: James Currey, 1988.

Max Coleman (ed.), *A Crime Against Humanity – Analysing the Repression of the Apartheid State*. Cape Town: Mayibuye Books/David Philip, 1998.

RM de Villiers (ed.), Better Than They Knew, Vol II. Cape Town: Purnell, 1974.

John D'Olivera, *Vorster – The Man*. Johannesburg: Ernest Stanton, 1977.

Julie Frederickse, *The Unbreakable Thread – Non-Racialism in South Africa*. Johannesburg: Ravan, 1990.

Denis Herbstein, *White Man, We Want to Talk to You*. New York: Africana Publishing Company, 1979.

Heidi Holland, *Born in Soweto*. Johannesburg: Penguin Books, 1994.

Muriel Horrell, Tony Hodgson, Suzanne Blignaut and Sean Morony (compilers), A *Survey Of Race Relations In South Africa*. Johannesburg: South African Institute Of Race Relations, 1977.

Johannesburg – One Hundred Years. Johannesburg: Chris van Rensburg Publications, 1986.

Peter Joyce (ed.), *South Africa's Yesterdays*. Cape Town: Readers' Digest, 1981.

Thomas Karis and Gail Gerhart, *From Protest to Challenge – Nadir and Resurgence, 1964–1979*. Pretoria: Unisa Press, 1997.

Tom Lodge, *Black Politics in South Africa Since 1945*. Johannesburg: Ravan, 1983.

Peter Magubane, *June 16 1976 – Never Never Again*. Johannesburg: Skotaville Publishers, 1986.

Nelson Mandela, *Long Walk to Freedom*. Randburg: Macdonald Purnell, 1994.

Jean Marquard (ed.), *A Century of South African Short Stories*. Johannesburg: Ad Donker, 1978.

N Mokgatle, *The Autobiography of an Unknown South African*. London: C Hurst & Co, 1971.

SM Molema, *The Bantu – Past and Present*. Cape Town: Struik, 1963.

M Mutloase (ed.), *Forced Landing Africa South – Contemporary Writings*. Johannesburg: Ravan, 1980.

M Mzamane, *Children of Soweto – A Trilogy*. Johannesburg: Ravan, 1982.

Sifiso Mxolisi Ndlovu, *The Soweto Uprisings – Counter-Memories of June 1976*. Randburg: Ravan, 1998.

Jordan Ngubane, *An African Explains Apartheid*. London: Pall Mall, 1963.

Dan O'Meara, *Forty Lost Years – The Apartheid State and the Politics of the National Party, 1948–1994*. Randburg: Ravan/Ohio University Press, 1996.

Sol T Plaatje, *Native Life in South Africa* (4th ed.). Kimberley: Tsala ea Batho, 1916.

Barbara Rogers, *Divide and Rule – South Africa's Bantustans*. London: International Defence and Aid Fund, 1980.

Diana Russell, *Lives Of Courage – Women for a New South Africa*. London: Virago, 1989.

Themba Sono, *Reflections on the Origins of Black Consciousness in South Africa*. Pretoria: Human Sciences Research Council, 1993.

Allister Sparks, *The Mind of South Africa*. London: Arrow, 1997.

John Steinbeck, *The Grapes of Wrath*. London: Pan Books, 1939.

Ivor Wilkins and Hans Strydom, *The Super-Afrikaners – Inside the Afrikaner Broederbond*. Johannesburg: Jonathan Ball, 1978.

Brian Willan, *Sol Plaatje – A Biography*. Johannesburg: Ravan, 1984.

Brian Willan (ed.), *Sol Plaatje – Selected Writings*. Johannesburg: Witwatersrand University Press, 1996.

Lady Sarah Wilson, *South African Memories, Social, Warlike and Sporting, From Diaries Written at the Time*. London: Edward Arnold, 1909.

INDEX

Poetry sources

Anon, 'Hatred Hatred', and Lefifi Tladi, 'Our Spears are Immersed in Blood' from Philip Bonner and Lauren Segal, *Soweto - A History*, Cape Town: Maskew Miller Longman, 1998. Mafika Gwala, 'Kwela-Ride', and Oswald Mtshali, 'The Detribalised' from Michael Chapman and Achmat Dangor (eds.), *Voices from Within - Black Poetry from Southern Africa*, Johannesburg: Ad Donker, 1982.

PRETRIAL

M&B

PRETRIAL
Fourth Edition

THOMAS A. MAUET

Director of Trial Advocacy
and Riepe Professor of Law
University of Arizona

ASPEN LAW & BUSINESS
A Division of Aspen Publishers, Inc.
Gaithersburg   New York

Library of Congress Cataloging-in-Publication Data
Mauet, Thomas A.
      Pretrial / Thomas A. Mauet. — 4th ed.
         p.   cm.
      Includes index.
      ISBN 0-7355-0052-5 (alk. paper)
      1. Pre-trial procedure—United States.   I. Title.
KF8900.M386   1998
347.73'72—dc21   98-41825
                                                                      CIP

About Aspen Law & Business
Legal Education Division

In 1996, Aspen Law & Business welcomed the Law School Division of Little, Brown and Company into its growing business—already established as a leading provider of practical information to legal practitioners.

Acquiring much more than a prestigious collection of educational publications by the country's foremost authors, Aspen Law & Business inherited the long-standing Little, Brown tradition of excellence—born over 150 years ago. As one of America's oldest and most venerable publishing houses, Little, Brown and Company commenced in world of change and challenge, innovation and growth. Sharing that same spirit, Aspen Law & Business has dedicated itself to continuing and strengthening the integrity begun so many years ago.

ASPEN LAW & BUSINESS
A Division of Aspen Publishers, Inc.
A Wolters Kluwer Company

This book is dedicated to my father,
Rudolf B. Mauet

SUMMARY OF CONTENTS

CONTENTS

III.   LEGAL INVESTIGATION

IV. CASE EVALUATION AND STRATEGY

PART B
CONDUCTING THE LITIGATION   109

V. PLEADINGS

VII. MOTIONS

VIII.   PRETRIAL CONFERENCES AND SETTLEMENTS

APPENDIX

PREFACE

New litigation lawyers are quickly faced with an uncomfortable reality: Civil litigation is vastly different from studying civil procedure in law school. For civil litigators the procedural rules are primarily functional tools that regulate the pretrial stage of the litigation process. The new litigator's primary concern is not to "miss the boat."

Helping that litigator not to miss the boat is this book's purpose. Whether a third-year law student in a clinical program or a litigator in the first years of practice, you must approach every lawsuit systematically to make sure that you think through the important considerations and take all timely steps during the investigation, pleading, discovery, and motion practice stages of the pretrial process. Only then have you adequately prepared for settlement or trial.

This text approaches litigation the same way. It presents a methodology for preparation, and reviews the procedural rules and thought processes a litigator should utilize before and during each stage of the process. In addition, it discusses and gives examples of how these litigation skills translate into pleadings, discovery, and motions. In litigation, as in trials, there is no one "right way" to litigate. Consequently, while the text presents standard ways of drafting pleadings and motions and of conducting discovery, there are actually numerous ways of effectively conducting pretrial litigation. The examples set forth in the text are only one approach and are there to illustrate how these steps, in recurring situations, can be accomplished.

This text is of necessity an overview of the basic steps in the civil litigation process. Because any single-volume work must limit how much space can be devoted to any specific topic, compromises and hard choices were inevitable. In making them, I followed a basic rule: Provide an overview that gives inexperienced litigators the basic information they need to handle routine civil cases. What they *need* was arrived at by reflecting on my beginning years as a litigator and by discussing the book's scope with a number of inexperienced litigators. Sometimes their suggestions were surprising. For example, almost all recommended an overview of joinder, jurisdiction, and venue, since these are such complex, technical areas. They did not mean to suggest that some topics were more important than others, rather these inexperienced litigators felt they were weak in some areas and stronger in others. In many ways their suggestions corresponded with my experiences and account in large measure for the text's coverage.

The text focuses on federal district court practice and the Federal Rules of Civil Procedure. This is done for two reasons. First, the federal rules have been adopted by many state jurisidictions. Most other states have modern code pleading rules that are very similar to the federal rules. Second, solid planning, investigation, and drafting are essential skills regardless of the particular jurisdiction, and the text's emphasis is on those skills. Hence, the book is designed to be a basic resource regardless of where a case is to be litigated.

Rather than using case references, this text cites the treatises commonly used by litigators. These are Wright; James & Hazard; Friedenthal, Kane & Miller; Moore's Manual; the Manual of Federal Practice; Moore's Federal Practice; and Wright & Miller. The citations to these treatises should be much more useful in researching legal issues that may arise than individual case citations. Most topics discussed in this text begin with a footnote that provides citations to the relevant portions of these treatises. The citations generally appear in this order.

As always, a book is the result of much more than just the author's efforts, and this one is no exception. Instrumental in creating this text were my editors at Little, Brown and Company, who for a long time encouraged me to write this companion to my other text, Trial Techniques. Also of considerable help were Gloria Torres, John Thomas, Abby Jones, and Merle Turchik, who reviewed the text and made numerous constructive suggestions. Finally, I must thank my former students at the University of Arizona College of Law who researched, edited, and provided suggestions. I owe a great deal to them all.

What's New in the Fourth Edition

Several trends in civil litigation continue. First, case volume and case complexity continue to increase, while court resources have not kept pace. The response has been to give courts a more active role in case management, reflected in changes to Rules 16 and 26. Second, "discovery abuse" remains a concern. The response has been to give courts more control over discovery, as well as to limit the amount of discovery, reflected in changes to Rules 26, 30, and 33. Third, summary judgment as a method of case resolution has been revitalized, principally through Supreme Court cases on the proper application of Rule 56 and on the admissibility of expert testimony based on scientific tests. Finally, there is a trend toward non-uniformity in federal court litigation, as many districts have opted out of the initial disclosures of Rule 26(a), local rules become more important, and congressional intervention in the litigation process becomes more common.

This fourth edition reflects these trends, since enough time has passed since the significant rules changes in 1993 to assess how these changes affect litigation practice. The text also expands the treatment of several topics, such as attorney-client agreements and settlements. The text more thoroughly cites to and discusses the application of ethical rules and concerns at the various stages of the litigation process. Finally, the text more systematically covers common mistakes inexperienced litigators make as they carry out litigation tasks.

This fourth edition now comes with a floppy disk version of my companion book, *Materials in Pretrial Litigation.* This makes it much easier to use both books for a course in pretrial litigation.

As always, comments from judges, litigators, instructors, and students continue to be helpful and have resulted in numerous changes in the text. My thanks again go to those who have contributed their thoughts and ideas over the years.

Thomas A. Mauet

Tucson, Arizona
October 1998

CITATIONS

For ease in citing, the text uses the following abbreviated citations:

Wright
Law of Federal Courts, Charles Alan Wright (5th ed. 1994)

James & Hazard
Civil Procedure, Fleming James, Jr., Geoffrey C. Hazard, Jr. & John Leubsdorf (4th ed. 1992)

Friedenthal
Civil Procedure, Jack H. Friedenthal, Mary Kay Kane & Arthur R. Miller (1993)

Moore's Manual
Moore's Manual—Federal Practice and Procedure, James W. Moore, Allan D. Vestal & Philip B. Kurland (supplemented annually)

Manual of Federal Practice
Manual of Federal Practice, Richard A. Givens (4th ed.), which is part of Trial Practice Series (supplemented annually)

Moore's Federal Practice
Moore's Federal Practice, James W. Moore, et al. (2d ed.) (supplemented annually)

Wright & Miller
Federal Practice and Procedure: Civil, Charles Alan Wright & Arthur R. Miller (supplemented annually)

PRETRIAL

Part A
INVESTIGATING AND PLANNING THE LITIGATION

I
INTRODUCTION TO LITIGATION PLANNING

§1.1. Introduction

You have just been called into the office of a partner in the firm that recently hired you. The partner tells you that a prospective client will be coming to the office shortly who has a "problem" that might lead to litigation. The partner tells you that this problem appears to be just right for you to manage. With a smile, he hands you a note containing the prospective client's name and appointment time. Apprehensively you walk out of his office, thinking: "My God. What do I do now?"

What you do, when you do it, how you do it, and why you do it is what this book on civil pretrial litigation is all about. This first chapter is an overview of the litigation process, and discusses how to organize a coordinated litigation plan. Each step in the plan will be discussed in detail in the other chapters.

§1.2. Organizing litigation planning

Litigation planning deals with two basic questions. First, what overall litigation strategy will best serve the client's realistically attainable goals? Second, how does each piece of the litigation plan contribute toward achieving those goals? Addressing these two questions early, and constantly keeping the answers to them in mind, will do much to develop and implement an intelligent, realistic litigation plan.

An effective litigation plan obviously requires structure. That structure should trigger the important thinking, at the right times, so that you will not "miss the boat" during any step in the litigation process. The basic steps in this plan are listed here followed by a discussion of each step.

1. Establish the terms of the attorney-client relationship
2. Determine the client's needs and priorities
3. Determine the elements of potential claims, remedies, defenses, and counterclaims
4. Identify likely sources of proof

5.   Determine what informal fact investigation is necessary
6.   Determine what formal discovery is necessary
7.   Identify solutions
8.   Devise a litigation strategy
9.   Devise litigation cost and timetable estimates
10.   Organize a litigation file system

1.   Establish the terms of the attorney-client relationship

The first step in any litigation plan is to formally establish the attorney-client relationship. This is best done through a written agreement, unless the client is a regular client with whom you have an established business relationship, because an attorney-client agreement is a contract between the attorney and client, and general contract principles apply.

The agreement should spell out who the client is, who will do the work for the client, what work will be done, how you will be compensated, and when the client will be billed for costs and legal work. All too often either a clear understanding with the client is never reached or all likely issues are not covered, causing serious problems later. Representing a client in litigation is difficult enough without having client relationship problems adding to the difficulties.

Before entering into an agreement, of course, you must first decide if you should take the case. In a simple case you can frequently make an intelligent decision after interviewing the potential client and reviewing available records. For example, in a personal injury case arising out of an automobile accident, you can probably determine whether the client's case has merit by interviewing the client to get the history of what happened, and by reviewing available records, such as police reports and medical records. In more complicated cases, substantial factual and legal investigation may be necessary. For example, in a medical malpractice or product liability case, the common practice is to send all the records about the patient or product to an appropriate expert for evaluation before deciding whether to take the case.

Establishing the attorney-client agreement is discussed in §4.3.

2.   Determine the client's needs and priorities

People seek out lawyers when they have problems that need to be managed and solved. The lawyer, therefore, should first identify the client's problems and needs, viewing them broadly. The client's needs, seen from his perspective, may well be in conflict with possible solutions; however, finding out what the client wants to have happen is the beginning step in dealing with the problems that brought him to a lawyer in the first place.

Keep in mind that the client's needs must be considered in the long-term as well as the immediate sense. Clients often demand a lawsuit against every imagined wrongdoer, when any lawsuit may be against the client's best interests. You need to assess what can be gained by a lawsuit, and then see how a suit would affect the client in the long-term. For example, consider the frequently encountered situation of a client who wishes to sue another party with whom there is an ongoing business relationship. While the particular matter may have merit, suing the other party may put in jeopardy that valuable relationship and adversely affect current deals with that party. A lawsuit that may vindicate the client on one deal may not make sense when viewed in light of the overall picture.

You will also need to assess the client's priorities. Clients rarely get everything they want, so they must develop a scale of priorities that will help you fashion the litigation strategy. For example, suppose your client wants to sue another party over a contract dispute. Does she want a quick, inexpensive resolution to preserve an ongoing relationship? Does she simply want the other party to live up to the agreement, or is she primarily interested in money damages because she considers the relationship destroyed? These possibilities must be arranged to reflect their relative importance to the client before you can sensibly decide how best to help that client.

Determining the client's needs and priorities is discussed in §2.3.

3. Determine the elements of potential claims, remedies, defenses, and counterclaims

The initial client interview will often identify the legal areas involved. At this early stage, however, it is better to think expansively and consider all legal theories that might apply to the case. For example, while a "contract case" will obviously involve contract claims, it might also involve UCC claims, state and federal statutory claims such as securities and product safety statutes, and business torts. It's best to include all of them in your initial thinking.

After you have identified the possible applicable legal theories, determine what the legal requirements are for each theory. This is best done by looking at the applicable jurisdiction's jury instructions. Most jurisdictions have approved pattern jury instructions for commonly asserted claims and defenses. These will tell you what the required "elements" are for a particular claim or defense. If pattern instructions are unavailable, you should consult practice manuals that cover the particular field or research the cases and statutes to learn the elements for the applicable law.

The same type of analysis must be made for remedies. The availability of remedies is related to the choice of claims, and some remedies are broader than others. For example, in a contract dispute, contract damages will be an available remedy. However, if the dispute has fraud aspects, you may be able to bring a business tort claim and have broader damages rules apply. In litigation, particularly complex litigation, the nature of the remedies is frequently a compelling reason a particular claim is, or is not, raised in the pleadings.

Potential counterclaims must also be considered. Before bringing a lawsuit, always check on what the other side has against your client. This is particularly important in commercial litigation, where the parties have dealt with each other many times over a period of time. There is little point in starting a lawsuit if it succeeds in provoking a large, previously dormant counterclaim.

Evaluating potential claims, remedies, defenses, and counterclaims is discussed in §3.3.

After you have identified the possible applicable legal theories and the elements for each of them, it's best to set up some type of litigation chart, or diagram, to list the theories and elements. For experienced litigators planning routine cases, this may not be necessary. New litigators, however, should develop a chart system to systematically analyze cases from the beginning by correlating the elements of claims and defenses, sources of proof, informal fact investigation, and formal discovery. When fully developed, the litigation chart will form the basis for your trial chart, should the case eventually go to trial.[1] For now, the chart will be the basis for your strategic litigation planning. Litigation charts are commonly organized like the one below.

Example:

You represent the plaintiff in an automobile negligence case.[2]

LITIGATION CHART

Elements of Claims	Sources of Proof	Informal Fact Investigation	Formal Discovery
1. Negligence			
(a) negligence			
(b) causation			
(c) damages			
(1) lost income			
(2) med. expenses			
(3) disability			
(4) pain and suffering			

Developing a litigation chart is discussed in §2.2.

4.   Identify likely sources of proof

Most litigation involves events or transactions that have occurred in the past. The likely sources of proof will be centered on those witnesses who

1. See T. Mauet, Trial Techniques §10.3 (4th ed. 1996).
2. The elements of negligence claims are duty, breach of duty, proximate cause, injury, and damages. Duty is a legal question, however, so the terminology used here fits more to the trial proof.

have some knowledge of, and exhibits that contain information about, past events or transactions.

The usual witness sources include your client, other witnesses to the events or transactions, the opposing parties, witnesses who have no direct knowledge of the events or transactions but may have useful circumstantial information, and experts. Exhibit sources include physical objects, photographs, police reports, business records, transaction documents, and any other paperwork that has a bearing on the events or transactions involved. At this stage it is best to think expansively. Develop a long, thorough list early and refine it over time.

Finally, list the likely sources of proof of the elements of each possible legal theory on your developing litigation chart.

Example:

LITIGATION CHART

Elements of Claims	Sources of Proof	Informal Fact Investigation	Formal Discovery
1. Negligence			
(a) negligence	plaintiff police officers bystanders defendant		
(b) causation	plaintiff defendant treating doctors police officers police reports		
(c) damages			
(1) lost income	plaintiff employer employment records		
(2) med. expenses	med. bills treating doctors pharmacy bills		
(3) disability	plaintiff treating doctors employent records		
(4) pain and suffering	plaintiff treating doctors		

Identifying the likely sources of proof is discussed in §2.2.4.

5.   Determine what informal fact investigation is necessary

Once you have identified the likely sources of proof, you then need to decide how to acquire information from those sources. Your choices are two-fold: informal fact investigation and formal discovery.

Inexperienced litigators frequently use formal discovery as the principal fact-gathering method. This is often a serious mistake. It is vitally important to acquire as much information as possible *before* filing suit while formal discovery methods usually are unavailable. As a defendant, you will most likely begin the investigation after the suit has been filed, but you should still consider informal sources of proof. Rule 11 of the Federal Rules of Civil Procedure requires that a lawyer make a "reasonable inquiry" to determine if a pleading is well grounded in fact before signing the pleading.

Informal fact investigations are principally conducted by interviewing witnesses and obtaining documents, records, and other data from willing sources, and getting expert reviews of the case. These investigations have advantages and disadvantages. On the plus side, they are relatively quick and inexpensive and can be done without other parties being present. This is important because evidence can become lost unless identified and obtained quickly. On the negative side, while such investigations can yield important information, it is usually not developed in a way that makes it directly admissible at trial. For example, taking a written statement from a witness during an interview does not normally create a statement that is admissible as an exhibit at trial. At best, the statement is useful for impeachment.

When you have identified the witnesses and exhibits that are best reached through informal investigations, note on your litigation chart how you plan on getting the necessary information from those sources.

Example:

LITIGATION CHART

Elements of Claims	Sources of Proof	Informal Fact Investigation	Formal Discovery
1. Negligence			
(a) negligence	plaintiff police officers bystanders defendant	interview interview interview	
(b) causation	plaintiff defendant	interview	
	treating doctors police officers police reports	interview interview request letter	

(c) damages			
(1) lost income	plaintiff employer employment records	interview interview request letter	
(2) med. expenses	med. bills treating doctors pharmacy bills	pl. possession interview pl. possession	
(3) disability	plaintiff treating doctors employment records	interview interview request letter	
(4) pain and suffering	plaintiff treating doctors	interview interview	

Informal fact investigations are discussed in Chapter 2.

6.   Determine what formal discovery is necessary

Formal discovery can ordinarily be used only after suit has been filed. For that reason, it is the last stage of the fact-gathering process. It also has benefits and risks. On the plus side, it is usually the only way to get information from the opposing party and other hostile or uncooperative witnesses. In addition, the information is often in a form that makes it admissible at trial. For example, obtaining business records from an opposing party or a nonparty will generate an exhibit that will usually be admissible at trial. On the negative side, formal discovery is time consuming and expensive. In a case with a modest litigation budget, formal discovery may be substantially curtailed because of its cost.

Once you have decided which witnesses and exhibits must be reached through formal discovery, you have to decide which of the discovery methods are best suited to obtaining the necessary information. Each of the formal discovery methods—initial disclosure, interrogatories, documents requests, depositions, physical and mental examinations, and requests to admit facts—is particularly suited to obtaining certain types of information. To be both effective and cost efficient in obtaining the missing information, the methods must be carefully selected and used in the proper sequence.

Formal discovery serves two purposes: obtaining information you need to get but don't have, and pinning down your opponent and other witnesses on facts you already have. You will need to use formal discovery to obtain missing information from your opponent and uncooperative witnesses and other sources. You will want to pin down your opponent to learn where the key factual disputes in the case will be and to make your proof easier if the case later goes to trial. Although there is some overlap, each discovery method is particularly suited for certain kinds of information.

Initial disclosures govern four categories of information: the identity of persons likely to have discoverable information; the production of documents, data compilations, and tangible things; a computation of claimed damages; and the production of insurance agreements. This discovery device applies unless a district has "opted out," which many have. Initial disclosures are automatic and do not require a request or any action from the other side.

Interrogatories are most effective for obtaining basic factual data from other parties, such as the identity of proper parties, agents, employees, witnesses and experts, and the identity, description and location of documents, records and tangible evidence. They are also useful in obtaining other parties' positions on disputed facts, and experts' opinions and bases for opinions. On the other hand, interrogatories are not usually effective instruments for getting detailed impressions and versions of events.

A request to produce documents and tangible things is the discovery method by which one obtains from another party or a nonparty witness copies of records, documents, and other tangible things for inspection, copying, and testing. Such a request also permits an entry on another person's land or property to inspect, photograph, and analyze things on it. This is the only discovery device that forces another person actually to produce records and things or to permit entry onto his property to copy, photograph, or study evidence found there.

Depositions can be used on nonparty witnesses as well as parties. They are most effective in tying down parties and witnesses to details and in discovering everything they know pertinent to the case. It is the only discovery vehicle that permits you to assess how good a witness a person is likely to be at trial. It is an excellent vehicle to secure admissions or other evidence favorable to your side. Further, a deposition is the only method that preserves testimony if a witness becomes unavailable for trial.

A physical and mental examination of a party can be obtained by court order when the physical or mental condition of that party is in issue, a situation most common in personal injury cases. While other discovery methods can be used to get records of past examinations, this is the only means of forcing a party to be examined and tested prospectively. For that reason it is the best method for evaluating a party on such damages elements as permanence and extent of injury and medical prognosis.

Finally, a request to admit facts is the method that forces a party to admit or deny facts or a document's genuineness. Requests to admit are used principally to pin down the other party to specific facts to learn what facts will be conceded or disputed at trial. An admitted fact is deemed conclusively admitted for the purpose of the pending trial. This method is effective if limited to simple factual data, such as someone's employment on a specific date, or the genuineness of signatures on a contract. It is not a good method for dealing with opinions or evaluative information.

When you have identified the witnesses and exhibits that must be reached through formal discovery methods, note on your litigation chart what discovery methods you plan to use to obtain the missing information. You might also annotate your litigation chart by putting question marks next to topics that you are unsure of or by writing in numbers to reflect your planned discovery sequence.

Example:

LITIGATION CHART

Elements of Claims	Sources of Proof	Informal Fact Investigation	Formal Discovery
1. Negligence			
(a) negligence	plaintiff police officers bystanders defendant	interview interview interview	deposition? deposition & interrog- atories
(b) causation	plaintiff defendant treating doctors police officers police reports	interview interview interview request letter	deposition deposition?
(c) damages			
(1) lost income	plaintiff employer employment records	interview interview request letter	request to admit
(2) med. expenses	med. bills treating doctors pharmacy bills	pl. possession interview pl. possession	deposition? request to admit
(3) disability	plaintiff treating doctors employment records	interview interview request letter	deposition?
(4) pain and suffering	plaintiff treating doctors	interview interview	deposition?

Formal discovery is discussed in Chapter 6.

7. Identify solutions

There are many ways to deal with conflict, and litigation is only one of them. Before a decision to litigate is made, a client's problems should be considered in broad terms to determine what approach will best serve the client's immediate and long-term interests. The best approach must be arrived at through discussion with the client, with whom the decision about what to do ultimately rests. There are several basic possibilities:

1. Do nothing
2. Seek an informal resolution
3. Seek formal dispute resolution
4. Litigate

1. Doing nothing should always be considered. The case may simply be a high-risk case. The amount realistically recoverable may not be enough to justify the financial cost of seeking it. In addition, the noneconomic costs should always be assessed. Your client may not have the resolve to get involved in a lengthy fight. He may not want to take his time, and that of others, away from other pressing concerns. He may have more important ongoing business, professional, or personal relationships with the adversary. Finally, negative publicity surrounding the disputed matter may make litigation prohibitive. If you decide nothing should be done, let the client know and get his agreement in writing so you can formally end the case.

2. If your client decides to push ahead, you should always consider resolving the dispute informally. Your adversary may also wish to avoid a lengthy, expensive battle. He may admit liability, and dispute only damages. It is always worthwhile to look at informal solutions before battle lines are drawn.

3. If informal solutions are impossible, think next about alternative dispute resolution, such as mediation, arbitration, and summary trials. These can be relatively quick and inexpensive, and frequently are required in commercial contracts. By getting an impartial, experienced outside party involved, the adversaries can frequently get advisory opinions or binding decisions on both liability and damages.

4. The last possibility is formal litigation. Keep in mind that litigation is expensive and time-consuming and that a litigant is rarely made whole. These realities must be driven home to the client. The worst thing that can happen is for a lawyer to quickly yield to a client's insistence to sue, only to have that client become disinterested, then uncooperative, as the realities of litigation set in. The only safe way to do this is to develop a litigation strategy, litigation budget, and litigation timetable and have your client approve them before starting the lawsuit.

Identifying solutions is discussed in §4.5.

8.   Devise a litigation strategy

Up to now you have been thinking expansively, to ensure you are not "missing the boat" on anything that might influence the case. If you and the client have decided that litigation is the only solution, it is time to focus your thinking and begin making choices.

Assume that your client has valid claims, that attempts to resolve them informally have failed, and that the client agrees that the only recourse is formal litigation. What do you do now?

Everything you do in litigation must have a purpose. A common mistake inexperienced litigators make is to conduct litigation mechanically so that it becomes an end unto itself, rather than becoming a means to an end. Always ask yourself two questions. What are my client's goals in this lawsuit? How does each thing I do help achieve those goals? Only if you constantly focus on the desired result will the individual steps in the process help achieve it. Perhaps the easiest way to think of litigation strategy is to consider its principal parts:

1.   What claims, defenses, or counterclaims should I plead?
2.   How extensive should discovery be?
3.   What motions should I plan?
4.   When should I explore settlement?

First, how "big" a lawsuit do you want? This decision, of course, comes at the pleading stage. There is a world of difference between a simple contract case involving two parties and a complex commercial case involving multiple parties. You have to keep in mind the consequences of your pleadings. Multiple claims frequently require multiple parties, which in turn usually generate extensive pleadings, discovery, and motions; just because the claims are there does not necessarily require that you assert them. Also, litigation must be cost conscious. Inexperienced litigators sometimes allege every conceivable claim, with the result that the client becomes immersed in expensive, time-consuming litigation, which may not be in his best interests. This is the time to review your litigation chart, see which claims and remedies are the most meritorious, and structure a lawsuit that will serve the client's interests, and that is feasible in light of the client's economic resources.

As plaintiff, when you have decided on appropriate claims and remedies, you must determine where, and against whom, you can bring the suit. In federal district court, as well as in state court, there are several procedural issues that must be considered:

1.   What parties must or can I join?
2.   Will I have subject matter jurisdiction over the claims?
3.   Will I have personal jurisdiction over the parties?
4.   Where will proper venue lie?

Asking and answering these questions is critical because they determine what actions can properly be brought in a particular court. The questions are interrelated. For example, choosing the claims and parties is affected by whether you have subject matter jurisdiction over these claims in a particular court. The choice of parties is necessarily related to the question of whether you can get personal jurisdiction over them. These decisions in turn influence the determination of where venue is proper. In short, each of these questions is to varying degrees dependent on the others.

Second, once you have decided on the pleadings, you need to select the discovery that is appropriate for your case and your purposes. What do you need to know that you don't already know or can find out through informal fact investigation? What witnesses do you need to pin down with depositions? What are your cost constraints? What order, and when, should you engage in formal discovery? How extensive should each discovery method be? Again, many inexperienced litigators mechanically begin a standard discovery sequence—initial disclosures, interrogatories, documents production, depositions, physical examination, and requests to admit—without a clear idea of what information is needed and how best to get it. Without a consistent overall litigation strategy, the case then bogs down as discovery assumes a life of its own.

Third, what motions should you plan? Your motions strategy must be part of, and coordinated with, your overall litigation plan. For instance, if you plan on moving for summary judgment on some counts, or some issues, your discovery must be focused on getting the facts that will support your motion. Now is the time to plan on making those dispositive motions and to make sure that your litigation plan, principally the pleadings and discovery, is thought through to support those motions.

Finally, when should you explore settlement, if your opposing party doesn't? Since over 90 percent of civil cases are settled before trial, you need to think through what your position on settlement should be at those points when the issue is likely to come up. This includes assessing the "value" of the case at various times, as well as the financial and emotional benefits of settlement. The likelihood of a settlement, particularly an early one, will also affect your handling of the litigation and the relationship with your adversary.

Devising a litigation strategy is discussed in §4.5.

9.   Devise litigation cost and timetable estimates

A litigation cost estimate is something every litigator should make in every case. The client, particularly a sophisticated one, will always ask: "How much is this going to cost me?" All clients, except those whose cases are on a contingency fee basis, will ask this question sooner or later. You should give your client an estimate of likely costs *before* starting the litigation and get the client's approval, keeping in mind that you are dealing with an estimate, not a guarantee, and that you do not have complete control over costs.

Creating a litigation budget forces you to develop a realistic litigation plan and assess the tasks required at the beginning of the case. Over time, you will become more accurate in estimating how much time and cost the various parts of the process will likely require in a particular type of case. Many law firms have task-based litigation software that does this systematically, and many sophisticated clients will expect such an analysis when they send out requests for proposals to law firms interested in handling a substantial matter.

The cost estimate should be broken down by basic litigation categories. For example, in a simple personal injury case your estimate may be as follows:

Litigation Cost Estimate

Fact and legal investigation	15 hrs.
Pleadings	5 hrs.
Discovery	50 hrs.
Motions	20 hrs.
Pretrial memorandum and settlement	20 hrs.
Trial preparation and trial	60 hrs.

The total estimated time before trial totals 110 hours; trial preparation and trial will add another 60 hours. As defense counsel, if you are billing at $100 per hour, the likely cost if the case settles after the pretrial conference is $11,000; a trial will add another $6,000. Expenses, such as for experts, depositions, and travel costs, might add a few thousand dollars.

The client may not like the estimated litigation costs, but what they are and whether your client wants you to cut costs (for example, by restricting formal discovery) must be discussed before plowing ahead. Explain the assumptions on which the cost estimate is based, and emphasize that it is only an estimate based on facts presently known.

As plaintiff's lawyer, even though you will usually handle a personal injury case on a contingency fee basis, preparing a cost estimate is still useful to determine if taking the case makes economic sense to you.

The last step in the litigation plan is to create a realistic timetable that will control the litigation. As plaintiff, you have substantial flexibility. Unless there is a statute of limitations problem, a short notice of claim period, or a particular reason to file suit quickly, you will have the advantage of time to think through your litigation plan before filing the complaint. Once the complaint is filed, the litigation timetable is largely controlled by procedural rules and judges' practices. Judges will usually hold a scheduling conference after the pleadings are filed to establish a timetable for discovery, motions, and the final pretrial conference. For example, a judge may order that all discovery be concluded within 6 months and that any dispositive motions be filed within 30 days of the discovery cut-off date, and then schedule a pretrial conference 60 days later. Even where the judge does not establish a timetable, every jurisdiction has an informal set of expectations in routine cases that you should usually follow.

When you have structured a realistic timetable for your litigation plan, it is best to plot it out on a calendar to ensure that you don't omit any steps or lose track of when particular steps should be taken.

Example:

Litigation Timetable

1/1 (today)	Client interview
by 2/1	Interview bystander witnesses Get pl.'s medical records Get pl.'s employment records Get police reports Interview police officers
by 3/1	File complaint
by 4/1	Interrogatories to def. Documents request to def. Deposition notice to def.
by 5/15	Depose def.
by 7/1	Depose other witnesses? Depose physicians?
by 8/1	Requests to admit to def.
by 10/1	Prepare pretrial memorandum
11/1	Pretrial conference
12/1	Anticipated initial trial date

Every client will ask: "How long is my case going to take?" Keeping in mind that your timetable is an estimate, not a guarantee, you should let the client know what your best estimate is, revising it later if necessary.

Devising a litigation timetable is discussed in §4.5.8.

10. Organize a litigation file system

The last step is to develop and use a system for organizing your litigation files. There is no magic in doing this. Most law firms have systems for the types of cases they routinely handle. The important point is that your system must be logical and clearly indexed to reflect the kinds of materials your cases will generate. It should be in place when litigation starts.

Litigation files are usually divided into several categories. The files should have tabbed dividers for each category. In larger cases, categories may be further divided. For example, discovery is frequently divided into initial disclosures, interrogatories, documents requests, depositions, and requests to admit facts.

The following file organization and categories are commonly used in routine civil cases:

1. Court documents
    a. pleadings
    b. discovery
    c. motions
    d. orders
    e. subpoenas
    f. pretrial memoranda
2. Attorney's records
    a. chronological litigation history
    b. case summary
    c. retainer contract, time sheets, bills, costs
    d. correspondence
    e. legal research
    f. miscellaneous
3. Evidence
    a. bills, invoices, statements, receipts
    b. correspondence between parties
    c. business records and public records
    d. photographs, diagrams, maps, charts
    e. physical evidence (need to be safeguarded in secure location)

Certain paperwork, such as pleadings, orders, and correspondence, should be clipped together in chronological order with the most recent on top. Original evidence, such as bills and correspondence, should be put in clear plastic sheet protectors so that the originals will not be marked during the litigation process.

§1.3.   Conclusion

This overview chapter has discussed the basic sequential steps in litigation planning. The critical concept is that every step of that plan is interdependent with every other. Each step you take influences what happens later, and the various steps you take will make sense only if they are part of an overall plan. When you are immersed in the technical details of any particular step in the process, it is easy to lose sight of that overall plan. Consequently, before doing anything, always ask yourself two questions. Why am I doing this? How does it promote my overall litigation plan? If you never lose sight of the big picture and keep your long-term objectives in mind, you will have a much better chance to conclude your litigation with satisfactory results.

II
INFORMAL FACT INVESTIGATION

§2.1. Introduction

Preparation and planning for litigation are the critical initial components of the litigation process. Too many lawyers, however, rush to court and file a complaint to get the process started without thoroughly investigating the facts and the law and without devising a coordinated litigation strategy. Small wonder, then, that the results are frequently disappointing.

Most cases are decided by facts, not law. Litigation outcomes are usually decided according to which party's version of disputed events the factfinder accepts as true. Hence, litigators spend much of their time identifying and acquiring admissible evidence that supports their contentions and evidence that refutes the other side's contentions. That evidence at trial will be witness testimony and exhibits. Hence, the fact investigation principally involves finding and acquiring "people and paper," which means following the people trail and the paper trail. The party that is more successful in doing this will have a better chance of convincing the factfinder that its version of the facts is what "really happened."

§2.2. Structuring fact investigations

There are two ways of "getting the facts." You can get the facts informally before filing suit, and you can get them through formal discovery after suit is filed. A common mistake inexperienced litigators make is using the informal investigation, such as an initial client interview and the reviewing of an accident report, only to decide whether to take the case, and using formal discovery methods as the principal fact-gathering method. This is a serious mistake. First, information is power, and the party that has a better grasp of the favorable and unfavorable facts is in a stronger position to accurately evaluate the case. Second, information obtained early on, particularly from witnesses, is more likely to be accurate and complete. Third, information sought before the action is formalized is

19

more likely to be obtained, since a lawsuit often makes people cautious or uncooperative. Fourth, information obtained before suit has been filed is less expensive to acquire. Formal discovery is the most expensive way to get information. It is usually more effective and less expensive to use informal discovery before filing suit, and to use formal discovery methods to obtain missing information, pin down witnesses, obtain specific information and records from the opposing party, and for other such focused purposes. Fifth, Rule 11 of the Federal Rules of Civil Procedure requires that a lawyer conduct a reasonable inquiry into the facts to ensure a pleading that is well grounded. Finally, you can get information informally without the opposing parties participating, or even being aware that you are conducting an investigation. For all these reasons, then, you should use informal discovery as much as possible.

1. When do I start?

The best time to start is immediately, particularly in cases that are based primarily on eyewitness testimony. For example, a personal injury case should be investigated as soon after the accident as possible. Witnesses forget, or have second thoughts about being interviewed; witnesses move away and disappear; physical evidence can be lost, altered, or destroyed. In this type of case, where liability will be determined largely by eyewitness testimony, it is best to start quickly.

On the other hand, an immediate investigation is not always required. For example, in contract and commercial cases, where the evidence will primarily consist of documents, correspondence, and other business records, and there is no danger that records will be lost or will disappear mysteriously, a prompt fact investigation may not be essential. Contract and commercial cases may have complex legal questions that must be researched and resolved before you can start an intelligently structured fact investigation. In addition, delay sometimes helps. For a defendant who expects to be sued, starting an investigation may only serve to stimulate the other side into investigating the case. Unless the defendant needs to investigate an affirmative defense or counterclaim, a sound approach may be simply to wait for the other side to do something.

2. What facts do I need to get?

Your job as a litigator is to obtain enough admissible evidence to prove your claims and disprove the other side's claims. Therefore, you need to identify what you must prove or disprove. This is determined by the substantive law underlying the claims, remedies, defenses, and counterclaims in the case. However, how do you research that law if you do not yet know what the pleadings will allege? What do you research first, the facts or the law?

There is no easy answer here. In litigation, the facts and law are intertwined. The investigation of one affects the investigation of the other. You will usually go back and forth periodically as you develop your theory of the case.

Example:

You have what appears to be a routine personal injury case. From your initial interview of the client it appears to be a simple negligence case against the other driver. You do preliminary research on the negligence claim to see if the damages are sufficient to warrant litigation. You then continue your fact investigation and discover that the defendant is uninsured. Because of this, you start wondering if there may be a claim against the municipality for not maintaining intersection markings and safe road conditions. Of course you need to research the law here. If there is a legal theory supporting such a claim, you then need to go back and see if there are facts that support that theory. Back and forth you go between getting the facts and researching the law until you have identified those legal theories that have factual support. This process, going back and forth between investigating the facts and researching the law, is ongoing, and is how you will develop your "theory of the case," what really happened from your side's point of view.

3. How do I structure my fact investigation?

The easiest way to give structure to your investigation is to use a system of organizing the law and facts based on what you will need to prove if your case goes to trial. In short, this is a good time to start a "litigation chart."[1] A litigation chart is simply a diagram that sets out what you need to prove or disprove in a case and how you will do it. The chart is a graphic way of identifying four major components of the litigation plan:

1. Elements of claims, remedies, and defenses
2. Sources of proof
3. Informal fact investigation
4. Formal discovery

Start with the "elements" of each potential claim, remedy, and defense in the case. Most jurisdictions have pattern jury instructions for commonly tried claims, such as negligence, products liability, and contract claims. The elements instructions will itemize what must be proved for each claim, remedy, or defense. If pattern jury instructions don't exist, more basic research will be necessary. If the claim is based on a statute, read the statute and look at the case annotations that deal with elements and jury instructions. If the claim is based on common law, consult treatises covering the claim and research the recent case law in the applicable jurisdiction. Regardless of where the applicable law is, you must find it and determine what the specific elements are. When you have done this you will have completed the first step on your litigation chart.

to find the law & elements

---

1. The litigation chart will become a "trial chart" if the case is ultimately tried. See T. Mauet, Trial Techniques §10.3 (4th ed. 1996); F. Lane, Goldstein Trial Technique Chs. 2-4 (3d ed. 1986).

Example:

You represent the plaintiff in a potential contract case. Your client says she obtained goods from a seller and paid for them, but the goods were defective. From your initial client interview, and from reviewing the documents and records she provided, you decided to bring a contract claim against the defendant. Your jurisdiction's pattern jury instructions for contract claims list the elements you must prove to establish liability and damages.

LITIGATION CHART

Elements of Claims	Sources of Proof	Informal Fact Investigation	Formal Discovery
1. Contract			
(a) contract executed			
(b) pl.'s performance			
(c) def.'s breach			
(d) pl.'s damages			

This approach should be used for every other possible claim. For example, since the contract is for the sale of goods, a claim based on UCC warranties may be appropriate. If so, you should put the elements of this claim on your litigation chart.

The litigation chart has two principal benefits. First, it helps you identify what you have to prove or disprove so that you can focus your fact investigation on getting admissible evidence for each required element. Second, a litigation chart helps you pinpoint the strengths and weaknesses of your case as well as your opponent's case. In most trials the side that wins is the one that convinces the factfinder to resolve disputed issues in its favor. The litigation chart will help you identify the disputed matters on which you will need to develop additional admissible evidence to strengthen your version and rebut the other party's version.

4. What are the likely sources of proof?

Facts come from five basic sources: the client, exhibits, witnesses, experts, and the opposing party. Of these categories, most can often be reached by informal investigations. The client, of course, must be interviewed. Whenever possible obtain exhibits in your client's possession, and other evidence such as physical objects, photographs, documents, and records in the possession of third parties. Witnesses can frequently be interviewed. You can hire consulting experts to help analyze and prepare your case.

On the other hand, formal discovery may sometimes be the only way to get essential information. For example, important witnesses may be uncooperative and need to be deposed. Exhibits in the possession of uncooperative third parties may need to be subpoenaed. Information from the opposing party can usually be obtained only through initial disclosure, interrogatories, depositions, and other discovery methods. However, it is always worthwhile to try the informal approach first, since it is quicker, less expensive, and may be more accurate and complete.

The only exception concerns other parties: Ethics rules forbid you to make direct contact with an opposing party whom you know is represented by counsel.[2] You must deal with the other party's lawyer. What constitutes a "party," however, is an imprecise thing. Many lawyers feel that any employee of a corporate party, and any expert employed by a party, are included in the rule that prohibits an interview without the lawyer's permission. This position is supported by the Federal Rules of Evidence, Rule 801(d)(2)(D), which makes statements of agents and servants, concerning a matter within the scope of their agency or employment, made during the existence of the relationship, an admission that is admissible against the principal. Model Rule of Professional Conduct 4.2 also bars a lawyer from communicating with employees having a managerial responsibility within the organization that is an adverse represented party, and with any other person whose statements may constitute an admission on the part of the organization.

While informal fact investigations should always be conducted, their usefulness depends significantly on the particular case at hand. Some cases can be almost completely investigated through informal means, while others must rely principally on formal discovery. For example, in a routine personal injury case based on an automobile accident, you should be able to get all the basic information informally, since the principal sources will be your client, police officers, police reports, medical reports, and disinterested nonparty witnesses. By contrast, in a products liability case brought against the manufacturer of a consumer product, most of the information about the product's design, manufacture, distribution, and safety history will be in the possession of the defendant manufacturer and can be obtained only through formal discovery methods.

Regardless of the type of case, you must first identify the likely sources of proof, then decide how that proof can be obtained. The second step on your developing litigation chart is to list the likely sources of proof and correlate them to the required elements of the claims.

---

2. See Model Code of Professional Responsibility, Rule 7-104(A)(1); Model Rules of Professional Conduct, Rule 4.2. The rule is silent as to former employees, and states differ on whether and under what circumstances they can be interviewed. (Note that Model Rule 4.2 was amended by the ABA House of Delegates in 1995 to apply to a "person," not just a "party." Although this broader wording has been infrequently adopted by states, a number of states have broadly interpreted the present rule to apply to non-parties.)

Example:

In a contract case, determine the witnesses and exhibits that will provide the facts about the case. Your client, the plaintiff, is an obvious witness, and the contract is a central exhibit. Other than these obvious sources, where else can you go for proof? For example, what proof is there that the plaintiff performed his obligations under the contract? The plaintiff is again a source of proof. In addition, the plaintiff may have business records showing his performance. The defendant may have written letters acknowledging the plaintiff's performance. The defendant may have business records proving performance. There may also be nonparty witnesses who have knowledge of the plaintiff's performance.

Continue this type of analysis of each element of every claim you are considering, and put those sources on your developing litigation chart.

Example:

LITIGATION CHART

Elements of Claims	Sources of Proof	Informal Fact Investigation	Formal Discovery
1. Contract			
(a) contract executed	plaintiff defendant contract pl.'s secretary		
(b) pl. performed	plaintiff pl.'s records def.'s records		
(c) def. breached	plaintiff pl.'s correspondence def.'s correspondence pl.'s records def.'s records experts		
(d) pl.'s damages	plaintiff pl.'s records replacement vendor replacement vendor's records experts		

The third step is to determine whether these sources of proof can be reached by informal fact investigation and, if so, what method is best suited to getting the necessary information. Witnesses can be interviewed; exhibits in your client's possession should be obtained and reviewed; exhibits possessed by nonparties can frequently be obtained from friendly or neutral nonparties simply by requesting them; experts can be interviewed, and you can sometimes obtain their reports. Once again, think expansively here, since obtaining information informally is quicker, less expensive, frequently more candid and accurate, and can be obtained without the opposing party participating or perhaps even being aware that you are investigating the case. Put the methods by which you plan to obtain the information on the litigation chart.

Example:

LITIGATION CHART

Elements of Claims	Sources of Proof	Informal Fact Investigation	Formal Discovery
1. Contract			
(a) contract executed	plaintiff defendant contract pl.'s secretary	interview obtained from pl. interview	
(b) pl. performed	plaintiff pl.'s records def.'s records	interview obtained from pl.	
(c) def. breached	plaintiff pl.'s correspondence def.'s correspondence pl.'s records def.'s records experts	interview obtain from pl. obtain from pl. interview	
(d) pl.'s damages	plaintiff pl.'s records replacement vendor replacement vendor's records experts	interview obtain from pl. interview request letter interview	

The last step is to decide what to use formal discovery methods for, and how and when to use them. These considerations are discussed in Chapters 4 and 6.

5.   What is my litigation budget?

You can't buy a Cadillac on a Ford budget, and the same holds true for litigation. The client's financial resources are an important consideration. The "value" of the case, the amount you can reasonably expect in a jury verdict, is another. The amount of work the case requires for adequate preparation is a third consideration. Consequently, you need to estimate how much work the case will require, and see if it is feasible that you can accomplish the work given the resources involved. You need to prepare a litigation budget.

How do you do it? First, you need to estimate how much time you can devote to the case and whether the case can be adequately handled within that time. If a client has a limit on what she can spend, that is the outside limit. Simply divide your hourly rate — if you are billing by the hour — into the fee limit, and you will know the total number of hours you can devote to this case. If your fee is a contingency fee, you can still do the same type of calculation. Start with the dollar amount of a reasonably expected verdict after a successful trial. Reduce that amount by the likelihood that liability will not be proved. For instance, if you have a 50 percent likelihood of proving liability, reduce the expected verdict by that percentage, then divide that dollar amount by your usual hourly rate, and you will again determine the total hours you can devote to the case and still reasonably compensate yourself. Once you determine the total hours, estimate the time you will need to spend on each part of the litigation process: preliminary investigation, pleadings, discovery, motions, and trial.

Think you can't do it? You'd better start. Insurance companies and businesses, knowing that litigation makes sense only if it is cost-effective, regularly require lawyers to prepare detailed litigation budgets. Keep in mind that your time *estimates* are only that, and it is sometimes appropriate to have a range for your estimates.

Example:

You represent the plaintiff in an automobile accident case. Your fee is one-third of any recovery. Assume that if you win at trial, your client can realistically expect a verdict of about $90,000. However, you estimate your chances of proving liability at 50 percent. This reduces the "value" of the case to about $45,000, of which you will earn $15,000. Your time is presently billed at $100 per hour. This means you can devote up to 150 hours on the case and still be paid a fee equal to your hourly rate.

The case will take approximately two days to try and require about four days of trial preparations, for an estimated total of 48 hours. How do you allocate the remaining 102 hours? Your prefiling investigation — client interviews, witness interviews, exhibits acquisition, legal research, and just plain thinking about the case—may require about 25 hours. Preparing and responding to pleadings may take about 10 hours. Preparing and responding to discovery will require the largest amount of time, approximately 50 hours.[3] Making and responding to motions may take another 15 hours. Preparing pretrial memoranda and attending pretrial conferences may require 15 hours. How does your budget add up?

Investigation	25 hrs.
Pleadings	10 hrs.
Discovery	50 hrs.
Motions	15 hrs.
Pretrials	15 hrs.
	115 hrs.

You didn't come within the allocated 102 hours, but your initial time estimates are reasonably within range. With experience, you will become more accurate in estimating time requirements of particular cases and in estimating the likelihood and amounts of a recovery. This will help you determine if you should take a case to begin with, and, if you do, how much time you can realistically expect to devote to the various stages of its preparation and trial.

However, always keep in mind that your ethical obligations to the client must ultimately control your handling of the client's case. You have an obligation to handle the case competently: your performance is determined by the requirements of the case, not the anticipated fee.[4]

6. What sources should I investigate?

The basic sources for informal investigations are four-fold: the client, exhibits, witnesses, and experts. Your litigation chart will provide the directions for your informal fact investigation. That investigation should focus on obtaining basic facts—favorable and unfavorable—about the case, and identifying credible, admissible evidence for each claim you are considering.

How extensive should your fact investigation be? It needs to be thorough enough to fill out your litigation chart, to the extent that you can do so through informal fact investigation, while meeting the cost constraints you have established. Practically, this means several things. First, the client must be interviewed as often as necessary to learn everything she knows about the case. You will also need to interview her periodically as you gather additional information from other sources.

Second, you should try to obtain all key documents, records, and other exhibits. In a personal injury case, this includes the police accident reports, hospital and doctor's records, insurance claims records, and employment history. These can often be obtained informally, and many ju-

3. Determining how to allocate these 50 hours among the various discovery methods is discussed in detail in §6.3.
4. See Model Rules of Professional Conduct, Rule 1.1.

risdictions have statutes that require they be released to the client on request. In a contract case, this includes the contract, correspondence, invoices, shipping records, and related business records. Where physical evidence is important, it should be safeguarded or photographed before such evidence is altered or possibly lost.

Third, witnesses usually need to be identified, located, and interviewed, although what you do will depend on the particular case. In most cases, what witnesses say is critical. For example, in a personal injury case, where the plaintiff and defendant are likely to have contradictory versions of how the accident happened, the testimony of neutral witnesses will frequently control the liability issue. You need to identify, locate, and interview them whenever possible. On the other hand, witness testimony is not invariably critical at trial. For example, in a contract or commercial case, the issues are frequently decided by the documents, records, or substantive law. In such a case there may be no advantage in interviewing witnesses quickly.

Finally, in some cases you will need to consult appropriate experts early in your investigation. For example, in medical malpractice and products liability cases, plaintiff's lawyers usually have the case reviewed by a physician and a technical expert before filing suit. You might as well see what a qualified expert thinks of the strengths and weaknesses of your case now.

§2.3. Client interviews[5]

The initial meeting between client and lawyer may be the most important event in the client's life. How it goes will largely determine the nature of that relationship during the course of the litigation. Understanding what is involved in that meeting is critically important.

Client interviewing has two components: what information to get, and how to get it. What to get will be determined by your litigation chart. How to get it is based on interviewing techniques that must be fully understood in order to get the important information from the client.

1. Client attitudes and disclosure

The typical client is unsure of his rights and obligations, and a lawyer's office is an unfamiliar, imposing environment. The lawyer who empathizes with the client's psychological needs and knows the factors that promote and inhibit client disclosure will be more sucessful in getting an accurate picture of the problems that brought the client to a lawyer in the first place.

5. There are several excellent texts that discuss and illustrate in detail the dynamics of client interviewing. See, e.g., D. Binder & S. Price, Legal Interviewing and Counseling (1993); K. Hegland, Trial and Practice Skills (2d. Ed. 1994).

A client comes to a lawyer to determine if there are actual legal issues relative to his problems and, if so, how to deal with them. The lawyer needs to interview the client so she can identify the legal issues, get all relevant available information, and discuss with the client how the problems can best be handled. How does a lawyer go about getting that information from the client?

There are several factors that can inhibit a client from a full disclosure of information. First, a client being interviewed often feels that he is being judged. This causes the client to withhold or distort facts that may create negative impressions about the client or his case. Second, a client being interviewed often tries to satisfy what he feels are the lawyer's expectations. This causes the client to tell the lawyer what he thinks will be a pleasing story and, again, to withhold negative and contradictory facts. Third, a client may have a variety of internal reasons, such as embarrassment, modesty, and fear that, once again, prevent him from disclosing all information.

On the other side, there are positive factors that promote full disclosure. First, a client is more likely to disclose fully if he feels that the lawyer has a personal interest in him. A friendly, sympathetic lawyer is more likely to get "all the facts" from a client. Second, a client is more likely to disclose fully if he senses that the lawyer is identifying with him. The lawyer who lets the client know that "she's been there too," or is familiar with and understands the client's situation, is more likely to draw out all the facts. Third, some clients enjoy being the center of attention. Supplying critical information makes the client feel important and may stimulate his supplying more information. Fourth, a client enjoys feeling that he is doing the right thing. The lawyer who can instill the feeling that full disclosure is the proper, decent approach is more likely to achieve it.

Lawyers will obtain the fullest possible disclosure by stressing the positive psychological influences and by understanding and minimizing negative influences that inhibit disclosure. Lawyers who create a comfortable physical environment and show an understanding and appreciation of the client will be more successful in obtaining "all the facts," both good and bad. This sensitivity will establish a positive context for client relations during the course of the litigation process.

2. Interview environment

Creating a positive interview environment has several components. What kind of physical setting should you have? How will you record what the client says? What should the client do to prepare for the interview? What topics will you cover during the actual interview?

Many clients will be uncertain and insecure during the interview. After all, it may be the first time they have ever been to a lawyer's office. A physical setting that is informal, friendly, and private will help make a client feel relaxed and comfortable. A lawyer's private office is a good place to conduct an interview; a small conference room is another.

Strive for informality. Sit in a place other than behind your desk, have coffee and soft drinks available, perhaps play quiet background music. Avoid interruptions. Leave the telephone alone, and close the door to keep others out. Schedule the interview so that you will have enough time to accomplish what you have planned. An interview with a client can easily take one or two hours, but perhaps much more. If possible, schedule client interviews as the last appointment for the day, provided you are still mentally sharp at that time. This will allow you to continue the interview without running out of time because of other appointments.

A principal function of a client interview, in addition to establishing rapport and gaining the client's trust, is to obtain information. This information needs to be recorded and there are several ways to do this. First, you can take notes yourself. This has the advantage of allowing for privacy, but has the disadvantage of interfering with your interview. Second, you can have someone else, a secretary, clerk, or paralegal, take notes. Here the advantage is that you are relieved of note-taking, but it puts a third person into the interview environment, which may be an inhibiting influence, particularly during the client's first interview. Third, you can tape-record the interview with the client's permission. Here the advantage is completeness. However, you will still need to make a summary of the interview, and many clients are uncomfortable having their statements recorded. Fourth, you can avoid taking notes altogether and dictate notes immediately following the interview. This has the advantage of conducting the interview without distractions, but has the disadvantage that your notes of the interview may not be as complete as they otherwise would be.

The paramount consideration is creating an atmosphere in which the client feels comfortable and tells everything she knows about the problems that brought her there. Most lawyers conduct the initial part of the interview without note-taking. After the client becomes comfortable with you and the interview environment and you begin to get the details of her story, you can discuss the need to record what she says and then ask her if she will feel comfortable with the method you suggest. Once you explain why it is so important for you to have an accurate record of what she says and how the attorney-client privilege will prevent anyone else from getting it, the client will usually agree.

What can you have the client do to prepare for the first interview? First, the client should be told to collect all available paperwork, such as letters, documents, bills, and other records. Second, many lawyers ask the client to write down everything she can remember about the legal problems, particularly if they involve a recent event. If the memo is directed to the lawyer, and no one outside the lawyer's staff is permitted to see it, the memo should be protected by the attorney-client privilege, even though the attorney-client relationship may not yet formally exist.[6] The records and memo should be brought to the initial interview.

---

6. See Wright & Miller §2017; McCormick on Evidence §§88-89 (4th ed. 1992); Fed. R. Civ. P. 26.

Some lawyers, particularly plaintiff's personal injury lawyers, frequently use paralegals to screen prospective clients by conducting the "intake interviews." The interviewing techniques discussed here obviously have equal applicability regardless of who does the initial client interview.

3. Initial client interview

The initial client interview should have several objectives, although accomplishing all of them may require more than one session. First, conduct yourself in a manner that establishes a good working relationship. When the client arrives at your office, don't make him wait. Greet him personally. Have the client make himself comfortable in your office or conference room, and spend a little time making small talk — about traffic or the weather, for instance. Offer him coffee or a soft drink. Remember that the client is sizing you up both as a lawyer and as a person. Second, spend a few minutes learning about the client's background. This shows the client that you see him as a human being and not just as another case. It also helps you evaluate the client as a witness and provides important biographical and financial information. Third, let the client know what is going to happen during the interview, what you need to accomplish, and the reasons for it. Explain that you need to get all the important facts in order to intelligently identify and analyze his legal problems. Stress the importance of candor and completeness. Give the client an overview of the litigation process and why this interview is an important part of it.

Fourth, have the client identify the general nature of his problems. You will usually have a general idea — a "car accident," a "contract problem" — when the client makes the appointment. However, it is always useful to have the client initially tell his story his own way, without interruptions, sizing him up as a trial witness. You may also discover facts you might never otherwise have stumbled upon, and it allows the prospective client to get the matter off his chest in his own words. These considerations are well worth "wasting time" on, even if the client talks about seemingly irrelevant things. The usual way to get the client to tell the story his way is to ask open-ended, nonleading questions. For example, simply asking "I know you were in an accident. Why don't you tell me what happened in your own words?" will usually get the client started. While the client tells his story, listen not only to what he says but also note things he omits, things that would usually be mentioned. When the client is done, you can paraphrase what he has said. This serves as a check on accuracy and shows the client that you have been listening carefully.

Fifth, after the client has told his story, you need to get a detailed chronological history of the events and other background facts. It is frequently advantageous to make an outline or checklist so that you do not overlook important topics. Your litigation chart, setting out the elements of the claims you are considering, should provide a start. Get a set of your jurisdiction's uniform or pattern interrogatories for this kind of case. (These will be sent to your client to answer after the lawsuit is filed, so you might as well get the information you will need to answer them now.) It is sometimes useful to look at deposition checklists for this type of case and witness.[7] These may help you develop ideas for the topics and necessary detail as you go through the history of the case. However, don't use a checklist as a questionnaire, since your interview will quickly lose the personal touch. The standard method is to use the chronological story-telling approach. Most people think chronologically, and that is usually the best way to elicit details. While your checklist should be tailored to fit the particular case involved, you will usually cover the same basic topics regardless.[8]

Sixth, you need to ask follow-up questions on potential problem areas. Here it is best to use specific, focused questions that bear on potential claims, remedies, and defenses (although most lawyers avoid aggressively cross-examining clients during the first meeting). A client naturally wants to impress his lawyer and convince her that the case is a good one, so he will often give only "his version" of what are disputed facts and omit altogether the unfavorable ones. It is always better to get the bad news early. Remind the client that your job is to get all the facts, both good and bad, so you can accurately assess the case and represent him effectively.[9] Remind him that the opposing lawyers will discover the bad facts soon enough, so it is better to deal with them now. This will usually keep him from adopting an "I thought the lawyer was on my side" attitude.

Where do you probe? Look for information that might adversely affect the client's credibility. Are there problems with the client's background? Is there a spotty work history? Are there prior convictions or other such trouble with the law? Clients frequently omit negative facts in their background. Therefore, you should be looking for the gaps and asking what the client has left out of the story. For example, in an automobile accident case, has the client omitted the fact that he was given a traffic citation? Was driving with a suspended license? Was drinking? Had just left a bar before the accident happened? Or was using a car without permission? A useful device in getting out these kinds of facts, without directly suggesting to the client that you don't believe his story, is to get the client to be a kind of devil's advocate. Ask him what the other side is probably going to say to his lawyer about the event. This will frequently draw out the "other side's version" of the disputed facts. Keep in mind that under Rule 11 it is at your peril that you accept your client's version of the facts. The client needs to be pushed, probed, even cross-examined to test the facts he gives you. You may need to verify his version of the facts with an independent examination.

The usual topics you will need to discuss with the client during the initial interview include the following.

---

7. See, e.g., D. Danner, Pattern Discovery (series 1981-1996).

8. See D. Baum, Preparation of the Case §§1.10-1.21 (Art of Advocacy Series 1984); J. DeMay, The Plaintiff's Personal Injury Case: Its Preparation, Trial and Settlement (1977); R. McCullough & J. Underwood, Civil Trial Manual II 57-72 (1980); J. Werchick, California Preparation and Trial §§1.2-1.6 (1981).

9. This is required in any event by Rule 11's "reasonable inquiry" duty.

a.   Liability

Facts bearing on the liability of all parties must be developed fully. Details are critical. Here a chronology of events usually works best. For example, in an automobile accident case, you will need to explore how the accident happened step by step. You need to get a detailed description of the scene of the collision. Diagrams and charts are very helpful. You need to establish the location of each car involved before the collision occurred, at the point of impact, and after the accident had run its course. You need to get details on speed, distance, time, and relationship to road markings.

b.   Damages

Damages information must be obtained, for both your client and all other parties, for each possible claim. For example, in an automobile collision case, damages should include out-of-pocket expenses, lost income, future expenses, and future lost income, as well as intangible damages such as permanence of injury, and pain and suffering. Find out if the client suffered an injury, the extent of it, how she was treated, how she felt then and feels now, and how the injury has affected her life. Find out if she had a preexisting condition that could affect damages. You should also explore insurance coverage for all parties, as well as collateral sources such as health insurance, employer benefits, and government entitlements (e.g., Social Security and Veterans Administration benefits). In contract and commercial cases, and cases in which equitable relief is sought, you need to determine if the injuries to the client can be measured in monetary terms.

You must determine if the defendant has the ability to pay a judgment. Find out if the defendant has insurance, the amount of the policy's coverage, and if the policy covers the event or transaction. Determine the defendant's income sources and assets, particularly those that can easily be attached to collect a judgment.

c.   Client background

Your client's background is important for several reasons. The client's personal background—education, employment, family history—is important for assessing the client's credibility as a trial witness. His financial background—income and assets—is important for assessing damages. Finally, the client's financial picture bears on a mundane but obviously important question: Does he have the ability to pay you? You need to get this background information from the client early on, but be sure you let the client know why this personal information is important for your evaluation of the case.

d.   Parties

It is frequently difficult to ascertain who all the parties to an event or transaction are and, if businesses are involved, their proper legal identities. Often the client does not know and has given little thought to this aspect of the case. Now is the time to begin obtaining the facts that will help you identify those parties. Once again, Rule 11 requirements must be kept in mind. For example, in an automobile accident case you will need to know not only who the other driver was, but also who owns the other vehicle and whether it is a business or rental vehicle, or was loaned or stolen. You will also need to know where the accident occurred and need to determine who owns, or is in control of, the accident location, since that entity may be responsible for designing, building, and maintaining the roadways. If a workplace accident is involved and state law bars bringing an action against the employer because of the workers' compensation act, look for other potential defendants, such as manufacturers of equipment or independent contractors.

From your fact investigation you will usually be able to identify the parties you will want to name in your lawsuit. However, identifying parties is not the same thing as learning the proper technical identity of parties. For example, just because the truck that ran into your client had the name "Johnson Gas" on its side does not necessarily mean that the Johnson Gas Company is a properly named party. The potentially liable party may be a sole proprietorship or a corporation with a different name entirely. You need to find this out.

For individuals, learn their correct full names. For corporations, partnerships, unincorporated businesses, and other artificial entities, you must not only learn the proper names, but also whether they are subsidiaries of other entities that should be brought in as parties. Each state's Secretary of State or Corporation Commission usually has a list of domestic and foreign corporations licensed to do business within that state. Such lists usually show the state of incorporation and principal place of business, which is useful for determining if diversity jurisdiction exists, and state who the resident agent is for service of process. If the party is an unincorporated business operating under an assumed name, you may be able to determine the true owners and properly named parties by consulting an assumed-name index, required by many jurisdictions.[10]

e. Defenses, counterclaims, and third-party claims

Plaintiffs and defendants alike must look closely at a frequently overlooked area: What do they have on us? And who else can be brought into the case? Cases are legion where a plaintiff has filed an action only to be hit with a much larger, previously dormant, counterclaim. Think expansively, particularly in the commercial area, since the parties usually will have had previous dealings that could give rise to counterclaims or third-party claims. You should look at both related and unrelated transactions, since liberal joinder rules may permit raising unrelated claims in the same action.

10. The capacity of individuals, corporations, and unincorporated associations to sue is governed by Rule 17, which refers to state law. Hence, you must always check state law to determine whether a party has capacity to sue or be sued, and what the technically proper party is.

f. Witnesses

The client must be questioned on all possible information sources, whether eyewitnesses, experts, or anyone else who possibly has useful information. Get names and information that will help to identify and locate people with information. Think expansively here, and don't be concerned with the admissibility of testimony at this point. Find out who your client has already talked to about the case, what he has said, and whether he has signed any written statements, reports, or claim forms.

g. Records

The client should bring to the interview all paperwork in her possession, such as accident reports, insurance claims and policies, bills, checks, personal records, medical records, tax records, business records, and correspondence. If the client does not bring them, have her do so as soon as possible. You should keep these records; if the client needs them, make photocopies for her. Learn what other records may exist and who has them, so that these can be obtained now, or later through discovery.

h. Physical evidence

Does the case involve objects such as vehicles, machinery, or consumer products? While most common in negligence and products liability cases, such evidence can exist in other cases as well. How to locate, obtain, and preserve physical evidence is discussed in §2.4.

i. Other lawyers

Clients often shop around for lawyers. While a client has a perfect right to talk to more than one lawyer about taking a case, there are always clients who go from door to door until they find a lawyer willing to take it. It is important to find out if the client has seen other lawyers about the case. On the theory that lawyers turn down cases because the cases lack merit, you should be appropriately cautious.

j. Client goals

What does the client really want? In some cases, such as personal injury, the answer is often simple. The plaintiff basically wants money damages and the defendant wants to avoid paying them. But even then it is important to probe deeper. What does the client view as a favorable outcome? Does he want the case to go to trial, or is he willing to have it settled? Is he looking for vindication, revenge, or other satisfaction not related to money damages? In other cases, such as contract and commercial disputes involving businesses, the answer may be difficult to discern. Money for damages is not always what the client wants or needs. The dispute may be with another business with which the client has an ongoing relationship, and that relationship may be more important than the money damages. Perhaps relief such as specific performance is more important than money damages. Now is the time to find out what the client thinks he wants and begin assessing whether his expectations are realistic or need to be modified.

Avoid predicting what the case is "worth," or when the client will get any money. These are questions that all clients ask sooner or later, usually sooner. Explain that you cannot at this early stage make any such predictions and that it would be foolish to do so before you have gathered more information, researched the applicable law, and are then in a position to make an informed analysis of the strengths and weaknesses of the case.

k.   Next steps

Following a client interview, write a short memo evaluating the client and her story. It is easy to forget your specific impressions of a client, yet her credibility as a trial witness will often be critical to her case's success. This is particulary important where more than one lawyer will work on the file.

If you conclude from the initial client interview that you will take the case, you will need to discuss the details of a contractual relationship, including fees, and you should let the client know what steps you will take concerning her problem and what she will need to do to help you. These are discussed in §4.3.

4.   Follow-up client interviews

Many things should be done during the initial interview of the client. Some cases are relatively simple, and interviewing a well prepared client can take less than an hour. Many cases, however, will require more than one session to collect the basic information. Accordingly, you might use the first session just to build rapport with the client, get the client's story out, and compile a chronology of events. A second session could then be used to review the client's records and ask focused follow-up questions about problem areas. In more complicated cases, it may take several client interviews to acquire the necessary information.

Follow-up interviews will also be periodically necessary during the litigation process. Whenever you receive additional information, through informal fact investigation or during formal discovery, you should review it with the client. The new information may differ from what the client previously told you. Obviously the contradictory information must be evaluated, discussed with the client, and dealt with. In some cases the client may admit that what he previously told you was not entirely true, and change his story. In others, he may deny the new information and stick to his version of the facts. Whatever the client's position, the new information, if it is at odds with the client's story, must be dealt with. Is it true? Is it more accurate? What does the new information do to the client's story? This is an ongoing process, but the key point to remember is that the client must be kept informed as the fact-gathering process progresses.

§2.4. *Exhibits acquisition*

Your interviews with the client should also identify future exhibits. These include the scene, physical evidence, documents, and records. In addition, interviews with witnesses and your review of exhibits when you get them, particularly documents and business records, may disclose additional exhibits.

You need to acquire these exhibits, get copies of them, or protect them from being lost or altered. The order in which you do things will depend on how important it is to obtain the particular exhibits. For example, physical evidence, such as the condition of a vehicle, machine, or consumer product, should be acquired quickly, before it is repaired, altered, destroyed, or becomes lost. Some records, such as a police accident report, are essential for you to begin your investigation.

The basic types of exhibits are the following.

1. Scene

If a lawsuit involves an event, such as an automobile accident, investigating the scene is vital. Whenever possible, the lawyer should visit the scene, even if someone else will do the technical investigation. That should include taking photographs of all locations from a variety of perspectives and making all necessary measurements so that you can make scale diagrams. Photographs should be both in black and white and in color and be enlarged to 8 inches × 10 inches for courtroom use. Diagrams for courtroom use should be at least 30 inches × 40 inches. While photographic enlargements and courtroom diagrams need not be made until shortly before trial, the necessary preparations should be made now. You should visit the scene at the same time and day of week on which the event occurred, so your photographs will accurately show the relevant lighting, traffic, and other conditions. You might also find additional witnesses to the event—people who are there each day at that time.

If you are reasonably proficient in taking photographs and have the equipment to take photographs that can be processed and enlarged with sufficient quality to make effective courtroom exhibits, you can take them yourself. This will not create a problem for you, a lawyer in the case, becoming a witness, since any person familiar with how the scene looked at the relevant time is a competent qualifying witness. However, where you will be the only person who can qualify the admission of the photographs, obviously someone else must come along because the lawyer cannot usually be a witness in a case she is trying. If you are not a proficient photographer, hire a commercial photographer to accompany you. You must tell the photographer specifically what pictures you will need.

Numerous photographs should be taken from a variety of perspectives. For example, in an intersection collision case, you will normally want pictures of how the intersection looked to each of the drivers as they approached it. Accordingly, pictures should be taken, in the road from the appropriate lane, with the camera held the same distance above the road as the driver's head. Several pictures should be taken, starting from perhaps 300 feet away, then moving to 150 feet, and so on. The photographs will then show what each driver saw as he approached the intersection. In addition, photographs should be taken from where other eyewitnesses, such as other drivers and pedestrians, were when the crash occurred. Finally, if there are nearby buildings, it's always useful to have overhead, bird's-eye-view pictures taken that will show lane markings, pedestrian walkways, traffic signs, and signals in the intersection. You must review witness statements beforehand to know where the witnesses were, and what they saw and did, before you can know what photographs you will need.

Diagrams present a different problem. Since the person who took the measurements and made a scale diagram is often the only witness who can qualify the diagram for admission in evidence, it is better to have someone other than the lawyer do this.

2. Physical evidence

Physical evidence, such as vehicles, machinery, and consumer products, if not already in the possession of police, other investigative agencies, or your client, must be obtained and preserved for possible use at trial. This includes not only locating them, but also keeping them in the same condition and establishing chains of custody. This is particularly important if the evidence will be tested by experts before trial. When you cannot take or move evidence for safekeeping, take a thorough series of photographs and sufficient measurements so that you can make accurate diagrams and models for trial.

Preserving physical evidence often requires that you act quickly. In an automobile accident case, for example, skid marks and the condition of the vehicles involved will be lost as the skid marks wear off and the vehicles are repaired. In these situations you must take immediate steps to prevent the loss, destruction, or alteration of the evidence and ensure a chain of custody when such a chain will be an admissibility requirement.[11] Have someone such as an investigator do this, since he may be a necessary witness at trial.

How do you actually "preserve" physical evidence? Two concerns are involved. First, you must gain actual physical possession of the objects so that they are kept in the same condition until the trial. Second, you must either label the objects or, if they cannot readily be labeled, put them in a container that can be sealed and labeled. Both of these steps ensure admissibility at trial by establishing the two basic requirements—identity and same condition. The usual way to accomplish this is to have someone like an investigator, who can serve as a trial witness, get the objects from wherever they are, label or put them in a container that is sealed and labeled, and have them taken to your office for safekeeping. This label should de-

---

11. See McCormick on Evidence §212 (4th ed. 1992); T. Mauet, Trial Techniques, §5.3. (4th ed. 1996).

scribe the object, show where it came from, who obtained it, when it was taken, and who received it at your office.

Evidence is frequently in the possession of nonparties, such as police departments and repair shops. If the evidence does not belong to your client, the nonparties are probably under no legal obligation to preserve the evidence for you. However, most will be cooperative when they learn that what they have is important evidence. They will usually keep the evidence in an unaltered condition until you have had an opportunity to photograph and measure it. You should check if someone else, such as an investigator from the police department or insurance company, has already taken these steps. Finally, a nonparty will sometimes agree to preserve evidence until you can serve him with a subpoena, or have the court issue a protective order.

Many times, of course, a client comes to a lawyer too late to take these steps, and the evidence will be lost. If the client comes to you shortly after the event, however, you should always act quickly to preserve the evidence. Many cases, particularly in the personal injury and products liability areas, are won or lost on this type of evidence.

3. Records

You should obtain all available documents and records from your client. You may as well obtain everything your client has because once suit is filed the opposing party will be able to discover from your client anything that is relevant and not privileged. If important documents and records are in the hands of other persons, see if those persons will voluntarily turn them over or provide copies. Public records are usually available on request. In many jurisdictions persons have a statutory right to obtain certain records on demand, such as their own medical reports. A written demand on behalf of the client, coupled with her written authorization, will usually suffice. If not, contact the sources to learn the required procedure for obtaining the records. These records are, of course, usually available by subpoena after suit is filed, but it is better to get them as soon as possible, since the records may be essential to evaluate the case before suit is filed. For example, in a personal injury case, you will need to review police accident reports, doctor's reports, hospital records, employment records, and perhaps others.[12] In a contract action, you will need to get the contract itself, and records that bear on the performance and nonperformance of the parties, such as orders, shipping documents, invoices, and payment records.

If you can get these kinds of records from others, maintain them properly. Keep the records you receive together, in order, and do not mark them. Keep a record of how, from whom, and when you got them, since these persons may be necessary foundation witnesses if the case later is

---

12. Since some records, such as hospital reports, will be technical, get a good dictionary or encyclopedia to help you understand them or use a consulting expert to evaluate them for you.

tried. Make additional copies that you can mark up and use during client and witness interviews.

§2.5.   *Witness interviews*

After you have interviewed your client, and obtained the available exhibits, the next stage of your informal fact investigation is interviewing witnesses. Here a great deal of flexibility is possible, and it is particularly important to plan ahead.

1.   Who and when to interview

The more you know, the more accurately you can assess the strengths and weaknesses of your case. It makes sense, then, to interview every witness, favorable, neutral, and unfavorable, to find out what each knows. The benefits of interviewing everyone, however, are always tempered by economic realities. There are few cases in which you can simply interview everyone regardless of expense. On the other hand, every case has critical witnesses that you must try to interview regardless of the cost. In addition, once taken, the case must be handled competently regardless of cost constraints. Between these two extremes, you need to decide whether you should try to interview a particular known witness and attempt to identify and interview others. For example, suppose you represent a party in an automobile collision case. From your client and the accident reports, you learn what other persons were present. If a police report identifies an eyewitness, you need to interview him; but what else should you do? Should you interview the police officer who wrote the report and other officers present who did not write reports? Should you try to locate bystanders who were present but have not been identified?

How far you go is determined by three basic considerations. First, you need to interview all critical witnesses regardless of cost. A competent lawyer simply must always do this. The critical witnesses are the eyewitnesses to an event, the participants to a business transaction, and other persons such as the principal investigating officers. Such witnesses will probably be witnesses at trial. In the above hypothetical, this would mean interviewing the known eyewitness, the police officer who prepared the accident report, and other eyewitnesses whose identity you are able to learn. Second, with witnesses who are not critical, interviewing *is* influenced by your cost constraints. For example, canvassing homes and stores near the accident scene may turn up someone else who saw the accident; however, doing this is expensive and may produce nothing useful. Attempting to identify and interview such possible witnesses may be worthwhile in a $200,000 lawsuit in which liability is unclear, but cannot be done in a $20,000 case where liability is clear. Third, how far you go in locating and interviewing witnesses depends on what you have developed so far. For example, if your client and two solid eyewitnesses clearly establish liability, it may not make sense to find other eyewitnesses who can corroborate the client. On the other hand, if your client's version is contradicted by one eyewitness, it is obviously important to locate and interview other witnesses to see which version they support.

When you have decided on the witnesses you need to interview, you must decide the order in which to interview them. Here again flexibility is required. It is frequently better to interview favorable and neutral witnesses first, before you interview the unfavorable ones, since you will have better success in pinpointing the differences in their stories. Identifying and interviewing the favorable and neutral witnesses first will give you the basis for your side's version of any disputed events and will help you identify the areas of disagreement when you interview the unfavorable witnesses. These areas can then be explored in detail. Frequently, however, you won't know for sure whether a given witness will be favorable.

On the other hand, there are advantages in interviewing unfavorable witnesses early before their attitudes and recall have solidified. For example, in an accident case you know a witness will be unfavorable because that witness is quoted in a police accident report. It may be useful to interview that witness quickly. He may change his mind, or tell you that he "didn't really see it happen," or "isn't sure" about important facts. You may minimize the impact of the witness through an early interview.

Are there limits on who you can interview?[13] The ethical rules prevent a lawyer from talking about the subject matter of the representation with another party known to be represented by another lawyer in the same matter, unless the lawyer has the consent of the other lawyer or talking to the other party is authorized by law. For example, if you represent the plaintiff, you cannot talk to the defendant about the case if you know the defendant is represented by another lawyer.

When the represented party is an organization with employees, however, the ethical rules meet the proverbial gray area. It is clear that a lawyer cannot interview an opposing party's current employees if those employees have a managerial responsibility in the organization, or if the employees are those whose acts or omissions can be imputed to the party, or whose statements may be admissible as admissions of the party. Also clear is that, as a general rule, a lawyer may contact an opposing party's former employees on an ex parte basis. Not so clear, however, is the question of whether the prohibition extends to an opposing party's former employees who, while still employees, were privy to privileged communications with the party's lawyer or whose conduct while employees gives rise to the claim against the party. Cases can be found on both sides of this question, so thorough research will be necessary.

---

13. See Model Code of Professional Responsibility, Rule 7-104(A)(1); Model Rules of Professional Conduct, Rule 4.2; Wyeth, Talking to the Other Side's Employees and Ex-employees, 15 Litig. (no. 4, Summer 1989); J. Iole & J. Goetz, Ethics or Procedure? A Discovery Based Approach to Ex Parte Contacts with Former Employees of a Corporate Adversary, 68 Notre Dame L. Rev. 81 (1992).

2.   Who should do the interviewing?

Either the lawyer or an investigator should conduct the actual interviews. There are advantages and disadvantages with each approach. If the lawyer interviews, the advantages are that no additional investigator costs are incurred, and he can get a first-hand impression of the person as a trial witness. This is particularly important with key witnesses. On the other hand, lawyer interviews can create impeachment problems. If at trial the witness denies making a statement to the lawyer, which is inconsistent with his testimony, the lawyer will have to be a prove-up witness. This puts the lawyer in conflict with ethical rules that generally prevent a lawyer from being a witness in a trial in which the lawyer represents a party.[14] A common approach is to have the lawyer personally interview witnesses known to be favorable, but have another person present when interviewing neutral or unfavorable witnesses. That person can then prove up impeachment at trial if necessary.

If an investigator interviews witnesses, the advantages are economic and practical. An investigator's time will usually be less expensive than the lawyer's, so there may be cost savings for the client. However, the time saving may be minimal, since the lawyer must spend time educating the investigator about the known facts, the issues, and about what direction the interviews should take. The principal benefits of a properly experienced investigator are that she will probably be better at locating witnesses, and will be an available impeachment prove-up witness at trial.

When hiring an appropriate investigator, you should establish a contractual relationship and give her specific instructions. A contract with the investigator will prevent misunderstandings about what work will be required, what the cost limitations of the case are, and how the investigator will be paid. The contract should expressly state that the investigator will be an employee of the lawyer, and that everything the investigator learns and obtains during the investigation will be reported only to the lawyer and will otherwise be kept confidential. This will improve the chances that the investigative reports will be protected from disclosure by the attorney's work-product privilege.[15] As always, it is best to put the agreement in writing, either in a simple contract or in a letter to the investigator.

3.   Locating witnesses

Lawyers are perfectly capable of locating many witnesses. The client frequently knows the important ones. Records, such as business records and accident reports, will usually identify others. When their names are known, it is surprising how many witnesses can be located over the telephone or by checking basic, available sources. The telephone book, neighbors at a previous address, workers at a former job, friends and relatives are all good

---

14. See Model Code of Professional Responsibility, Rule 5-101(B) and 5-102; Model Rules of Professional Conduct, Rule 3.7.

15. See Rule 26(b)(3). A lawyer's notes summarizing a witness interview are usually not discoverable under Rule 26(b)(3).

sources in locating a known witness. It is often the case that a witness has merely changed a telephone number, moved to a different apartment, or changed jobs, and tracking her down is relatively simple. If these leads do not work, check with the post office, voter registration and motor vehicle departments, utility companies, and other government agencies such as the Veterans Administration, Social Security office, and unemployment and welfare agencies. If the witness is important to you and cannot be located through these types of leads, you may need an experienced investigator.

4.   Purposes of the interview

There are several purposes you should try to accomplish during a witness interview. These purposes usually should be pursued in the following order. First, learn everything the witness knows and does not know that is relevant to the case. Have the witness tell what he knows, by using open-ended questions. These can be followed later with specific, focused questions; however, you want details only of the critical events and transactions, not everything the witness knows that may possibly be relevant. When learning what the witness knows, make sure you pinpoint the admissible facts based on first-hand knowledge, separating them from opinion, speculation, and hearsay. With witnesses who have unfavorable information, you should try to limit the damage by limiting the witness' testimony. Find out what the witness does not know, is not sure of, is only guessing about, or has only second-hand information about.

Second, pin the witness down. This means going beyond generalizations and getting to specific, admissible facts. For example, "driving fast" should be changed to an approximation of speed in miles per hour. "He looked drunk" should be pursued to get the details underlying the conclusion, such as "staggering, glassy eyed, and smelling of alcohol." Getting only generalizations and conclusions makes it easy for a witness to change his testimony later.

Third, get admissions. With unfavorable witnesses, having the witness admit that he "isn't sure," "didn't really see it," "was only guessing," or "was told" all serve to prevent the witness from changing or expanding his testimony at trial.

Fourth, get information that might be used for impeachment. If an unfavorable witness says something that later may be useful to impeach him, pin him down. For example, if an unfavorable witness to an accident says he was 200 feet away when it happened, make sure you commit him to that fact. Use "200 feet" in other questions, and recommit him to that fact, since at trial he may claim that the distance was shorter.

Fifth, get leads to other witnesses and information. It is surprising how often a witness will name other witnesses or divulge information not previously mentioned in any report. For example, asking a witness if anyone else was present at an accident scene will sometimes get a response like: "Sure, Ellen, my sister, was standing right next to me and saw the whole thing."

Finally, try to record the interview or get some type of written statement. How to do this is discussed later in this section.

5. Arranging the interview

Often the most difficult part of witness interviews is getting witnesses to agree to be interviewed in the first place. With favorable witnesses this is not usually a problem, and selecting a convenient time and place for the interview is a routine matter. Unfavorable witnesses, however, are frequently reluctant. Here you can take either of two approaches: attempt to arrange an interview, or attempt a surprise interview. A reluctant witness may agree to be interviewed at a convenient time and place, where privacy is assured, and if the interview won't take too long. Let such a witness know that cooperating now may eliminate the need to be deposed later, and suggest that an interview at home would be both convenient and private. If the witness senses that the real question is where and when, rather than if, she is more likely to agree to an interview.

If a witness will not agree to an arranged interview, the only alternative is the unannounced interview. Frequently, a witness who doesn't want to be bothered will nevertheless agree to talk when an investigator "pops into" the witness' office or "stops by" the house. Again, it may help to reassure the witness that the questions won't take long and may eliminate the need for further involvement. However, a witness has a perfect right to refuse to be interviewed, and you cannot harass or badger the witness hoping to change her mind. The only alternative is to depose the witness later.

6. Structuring the interview

How do you go about structuring a witness interview? First, review the case file, which should contain client interviews, exhibits such as police reports, perhaps other witness interviews, and the developing litigation chart. Second, get copies of any diagrams, photographs, and records you may use during the interview. Third, decide if and how you will record the interview. Finally, prepare an outline for the interview. A frequently followed order for witness interviews is the following:

1. Witness background
2. Story in witness's own words
3. Detailed chronological story
4. Questions focused on your theory of the case

First, witness background is important for assessing witness credibility and determining if there is any bias, interest, or other facts that affect credibility. Most witnesses don't mind talking about their work, family, and home. Asking these background questions usually puts witnesses at ease. Some witnesses, however, may resent what they consider to be intrusions into their private lives. In such cases you may want to slip the background information later into the interview, or simply touch on it at the end. Second, let the witness tell her story in her own words, even at the price of hearing irrelevant facts. It gives you a good picture of the kind of witness she will be at trial, and you may discover important facts that would never have come to light. Third, go over the story in chronological order and in detail. Get specifics on what the witness saw, heard, and did at all important times, and what she saw others do and say. Find out what exhibits the witness knows of, and other witnesses she is aware of. Find out what the witness personally knows and what is only opinion, speculation, or hearsay. Find out to whom the witness has talked or given statements. Finally, ask focused questions based on your theory of the case. For example, if the witness gives information that contradicts your version of the events, see how you can minimize its effect. If the witness is "not sure," "guessing," "didn't see it myself," or says other things that lessen the damage, make sure you note it. In addition, see if the witness can corroborate something useful to your side. Witnesses are rarely completely unfavorable; a little searching will often turn up something positive.

7. Recording the interview

Regardless of the witness, you should make a record of the interview. There are several possibilities:

1. Use a court reporter
2. Make a tape recording, with the witness' consent
3. Obtain a written, signed statement
4. Take notes during the interview
5. Have another person take notes during the interview
6. Make notes after the interview

The approach you use depends on what will best serve your interests and what the witness will permit. If you expect the witness to give favorable information and be cooperative, a short, written and signed statement is often best. After interviewing the witness, simply type a summary of his story and ask him to sign it. The statement should be from the witness's point of view (e.g., "I was standing on the corner of Main and Elm when I saw . . .") Have the witness draw and label a diagram showing where he was and what he saw. Another method is to send the witness a confirming letter summarizing what he said, and ask the witness to sign and return a copy acknowledging its accuracy. This will lock a favorable witness into his basic story, and there is no damage if the opposing side obtains the statement during discovery.[16] With unfavorable witnesses, it is often advanta-

16. While a lawyer's notes summarizing a witness interview are usually not discoverable, under Rule 26(b)(3) even trial preparation materials are not absolutely protected from discovery. Upon a showing of substantial need and undue hardship, such materials are discoverable, except that "mental impressions, conclusions, opinions, or legal theories of an attorney or other representative of a party" are always protected from disclosure.

geous to get a detailed statement. This improves your chances of getting contradictions, admissions, and impeachment that may be valuable at trial. Using a court reporter or a tape recorder is probably the most reliable method. Get the witness' permission if you plan to tape record, since surreptitious recordings are illegal in some jurisdictions. Avoid later criticism that the recording does not include everything the witness said by being mindful of when conversation is off-the-record.

What is best, and what a witness is willing to do, are two different things. Many witnesses are reluctant to talk, and they are usually under no legal obligation to talk to anyone, unless compelled by legal process. Of those willing to talk, many are understandably reluctant to give a signed statement or to have their statements recorded or reduced to a writing. Hence, your priority should be to get the witness to tell what he knows so you will learn what his trial testimony is likely to be, and get leads on other witnesses and evidence. Only then should you try to get the most reliable type of statement the witness agrees to give. In short, it is usually better to conduct an interview without any recording than to have no interview at all. You can always dictate immediately afterwards what the witness has said.

Whether a record of a witness interview is discoverable depends on the kind of record involved. Under Rule 26(b)(3), a "statement" is discoverable if it is "a written statement signed or otherwise adopted or approved by the person making it, or a stenographic, mechanical, electrical, or other recording, or a transcription thereof, which is a substantially verbatim recital of an oral statement by the person making it and contemporaneously recorded." If what the witness says is helpful, taking a discoverable statement usually creates no problems if the other side obtains it later, and the statement can be used to refresh memory or impeach if the witness testifies inconsistently at trial. If, however, what the witness says is unfavorable, there is usually no point in creating a discoverable statement that will only educate the other side to the fact that a good witness for them exists.

8.   Interviewing techniques[17]

Every witness is influenced by both positive and negative factors that affect her willingness to be interviewed and disclose what she knows. An interviewer, therefore, should understand these factors and use them to accomplish his primary purpose of finding out what the witness knows. These factors bear on both friendly and hostile witnesses. Hostile witnesses may be unwilling to talk at all; friendly witnesses, although willing to talk, may be influenced by a variety of negative and positive factors.

Negative factors inhibit witness disclosure. Some witnesses feel that they are being judged by the interviewer. Others tell the interviewer what he apparently wants to hear. Still others become inhibited by emotions such as fear or embarrassment. The interviewer must learn to recognize

17. See D. Binder & S. Price, Legal Interviewing and Counseling (1993), which covers these basic concepts in great detail.

situations in which these factors exist and use interviewing techniques that reduce their effect.

Positive factors promote disclosure. Witnesses usually respond favorably when the interviewer shows a personal interest in them. Witnesses like to feel that they are doing the decent thing by talking to the interviewer. They tend to identify with the side that values their testimony. Witnesses enjoy feeling important and may be more likely to help if they feel that the information they can provide is important to resolve a dispute fairly. Positive reinforcement is a strong motivator.

Getting witnesses to disclose fully and accurately is best achieved by minimizing the negative factors and reinforcing the positive ones. Accordingly, pick a convenient time and place for the interview. When scheduling the interview, remind the witness that it's always better to talk when the events are fresh in her mind. Remind her that it is natural to want to help others, and that her disclosing information will help ensure a just and accurate result. Point out what other witnesses have said about the case so as to give her an opportunity to correct inaccuracies. Finally, show interest in the witness. Empathy is also a strong motivator; a witness naturally will want to please someone who appears interested in her.

An interviewer can use either open- or closed-ended questions to achieve desired results. Use open-ended, direct-examination questions to get the witness talking, to obtain the basic story, and to pursue leads. For example, questions in a "describe how" and "tell me" format will force the witness to give descriptive answers. But use closed, leading cross-examination questions to pin the witness down and develop potential impeachment. This question form can focus on specific, isolated facts. For example, ask: "You're sure the car was going 40 mph?" and "She couldn't have been going faster than that, could she?"

The content of questions can also effectively influence responses. Let the witness know your attitude on the matter being discussed, since she has a psychological interest in satisfying her listener's expectations. For example, telling a witness that you feel badly about your client having been cheated by the defendant may get a more sympathetic story from the witness. Second, word choices can influence responses. For example, it is well known that using the phrase "how fast" rather than "how slowly" will increase estimations of speed. Third, leading questions are more likely to get the kind of answer you want. For example, asking a witness "That car was going faster than the speed limit, wasn't it?" is more likely to elicit a "yes" response. Fourth, knowing what other people have said or what other evidence has already shown can influence witnesses, since witnesses prefer consistency and disdain conflict. For example, telling a witness that another eyewitness has already stated that the car was speeding will often influence the witness.

9.   Evaluating witnesses

Following a witness interview, write a short memo evaluating the witness and her information. It is easy to forget your impressions of the witness, yet witness credibility is frequently the critical component in case evaluation. The memo is particularly important if more than one lawyer will work on the file. The memo should evaluate the witness' credibility and effectiveness as a trial witness, note the witness' attitude toward the case, and summarize where the witness' anticipated testimony will help and hurt your case.[18]

§2.6.   *Expert reviews*

Wrongful death, medical malpractice, product liability, major negligence, and commercial cases almost always use expert witnesses at trial. The plaintiff's case will probably require expert testimony to establish a prima facie case on liability and causation and to make out a solid case on damages. The defense case will probably have opposing experts. Accordingly, your investigation is frequently incomplete unless you have the file reviewed by appropriate experts.

You may need two experts: one to review the file and consult with you in order to develop facts and theories for trial, the other to be a trial witness. Of course, one expert can and often does perform both roles. Remember, however, that under Rule 26(b)(4) the facts and opinions of a consulting expert are usually protected from discovery, absent exceptional circumstances, but the identity and substance of facts and opinions of experts expected to be witnesses at trial are discoverable. Hence, having a separate consulting expert will usually limit what is discoverable by other parties, and should be valuable in developing theories and evidence for trial. Make sure that your agreement with the consulting expert clearly shows her status, and requires that she communicate only with you, so that her work comes under the Rule 26 protection. Some lawyers require in the agreement that the client is responsible for paying the expert's fees. Doing this should not change the protection of the work-product doctrine.

If a case is complex and will involve substantial work, it may be advisable to insist that the case be reviewed by an expert before you agree to take it. The cost of the review should be paid by the prospective client. While the lawyer can usually advance the cost of the review, requiring the client to pay for the review in advance is often an effective way of weeding out clients who already know they have a weak case. Such clients will often refuse to pay for the review, which should make you think carefully about taking the case in the first place, particularly where the client has the ability to pay. This is a sensible approach whenever you have a case that will require expert witnesses. Regardless of how the review comes out, both you and the client will benefit. If the case is complex and will require expert witnesses, Rule 11 may require an expert's review before filing suit.

18. Such a memo should also be absolutely privileged as work product and therefore not discoverable. See Rule 26(b)(3).

Do not send out a file for expert review until you have collected the reports and records the expert will inevitably need. Make sure the written materials you send her give a complete and neutral picture of the case, but do not give the expert privileged materials. Keep in mind that an expert who becomes the testifying expert at trial can under Rule 26(b)(4) be deposed and forced during cross-examination to produce all materials she received for her review. Factual materials that the lawyer gives to the expert may not be protected by the work product privilege;[19] therefore, do not give an expert any materials that contain your mental impressions and thought processes. In addition, rather than have the expert review the file generally, direct the expert to specific areas where you see potential problems. This is best done in conversations with the expert, after you have sent her the necessary materials. For example, in a medical malpractice case you might tell the expert that your potential theory of liability is that the anesthetic was improperly administered, and ask the expert if the standard of reasonable care was breached. A focused review is usually more productive.

While Rule 26 makes important discovery distinctions between consulting and testifying experts, hiring an expert as a consultant does not prevent you from using her as an expert at trial. That decision may have to be made at the discovery stage, however, since a standard interrogatory asks that you identify all experts expected to testify at trial. Again, if you list the consulting expert as a trial witness, she can be deposed and forced to produce all materials she has reviewed.

Because an expert is so important, and because a consulting expert may later be the testifying expert at trial, you must be careful in selecting one. Perhaps the best way to select an expert is simply to ask litigators you know to recommend one who is knowledgeable in the subject area of your case, is willing to work with and educate you, and will be an effective trial witness. If this fails, or you need an expert in an extremely specialized area, some lawyers' groups, such as the American Trial Lawyers Association, maintain expert directories, and law libraries sometimes have directories for various specialties.[20]

§2.7. The "small" case

This book discusses how to organize and investigate a case using the litigation chart method. This approach integrates the legal and fact investigations so that you can intelligently plan the litigation before filing suit, or responding to one. These are steps that every litigator should take when handling any litigation matter.

---

19. See, e.g., Bogosian v. Gulf Oil Corp., 738 F.2d 587 (3d Cir. 1984); FRE 612.
20. See e.g., H. Philo et al., Lawyers Desk Reference, which lists experts by category and is revised periodically. TASA, the Technical Advisory Service for Attorneys, is one of several organizations that refers experts in numerous fields. Many legal newspapers and journals also contain listings and information about experts. Local universities are a good source as well.

When a case is sufficiently large, perhaps with over $50,000 to $75,000 in issue, it makes economic sense for the litigants to devote substantial legal resources to achieve the best possible result. In such cases, the lawyers representing the parties will usually be able to do all the things a conscientious litigator should do, without being seriously constrained by cost. However, consider the client with a "small" case, involving less than $10,000, who comes to you. His case, although appearing to have merit, involves so little money that it is not economically possible to handle it competently and receive adequate compensation for the work involved. What do you do?

This is hardly a theoretical question. The "average" case filed in courts today involves approximately $25,000.[21] If that is the typical case, there are obviously numerous cases involving smaller amounts. Automobile accidents involving a few hundred dollars in direct losses, and consumer contract matters involving similarly small sums, are common disputes, and some are litigated.

The inherent conflict can be stated simply. On the one hand, every lawyer has a professional obligation to represent each client competently. On the other hand, a lawyer needs to be compensated to stay in business. How do you resolve this conflict?

The very small cases present less difficulty. Most jurisdictions have small claims courts in which the litigants can represent themselves at trial. Many jurisdictions do not allow lawyers in small claims courts, and judges hear the cases informally without adhering to strict rules of procedure or evidence. They frequently have brochures that explain how to bring a claim in small claims court and how the case will be heard. In addition, some jurisdictions have special procedures for other small cases. These frequently include restriction or elimination of discovery. The intent of both types of procedures is to bring down the cost of trying a case so that it makes economic sense to bring a lawsuit to enforce a claim in the first place. The cases that are too large to be brought as small claims, yet too small to make normal litigation cost effective, cause the greatest problems. What can you do when presented with such cases? These small cases are particularly problematical, because a case that is small in dollar amounts may be just as legally and factually complex as a larger case. However, keeping several concepts in mind can at least reduce the concerns.[22]

First, screening small cases is particularly important. This involves carefully assessing liability, damages, and the other party's ability to pay a judgment. There is nothing more unproductive than taking a small case with questionable liability or filing an action against a party who is effectively judgment proof. Small cases must be screened quickly before any substantial investment in time is made.

21. See Trubek, et al., The Costs of Ordinary Litigation, 31 U.C.L.A. L. Rev. 72 (1983). The authors conducted a study of approximately 1600 civil cases in five federal districts in 1978; half were state cases, half federal. They found that over two-thirds of the cases involved tort and contract claims, and the average amount at stake was approximately $10,000 (in 1978 dollars). Over 90 percent of the cases settled before trial. The median amount of time a lawyer devoted to a single case was 30.4 hours.
22. See Adelman & Halderman, The Dog Case, 10 Litig. (no. 3, Spring 1984).

Second, the client must understand what you can realistically do given the size of the case, and agree to your approach. For example, if the case is not worth the filing of a suit, perhaps you can attempt to get a settlement or resolve it through an alternative dispute resolution method. If the case is large enough to bring suit, but formal litigation would be prohibitively expensive, perhaps you can handle this particular case without formal discovery or with limited discovery. Whatever your approach, make sure the client knows what it will be and the reasons for it, and also agrees to it in writing.

Third, make sure you get your costs covered in advance, and let the client know the overall anticipated costs. A client who has paid the anticipated costs in advance has a direct financial interest in the litigation and will usually be more cooperative and realistic. A client who understands how costs, such as a medical expert's fee, can devour any recovery will have a better grasp of what can realistically be done.

Fourth, get the client to do as much work as possible, such as obtaining documents and records and locating witnesses. This can substantially reduce costs. You can also tell the client that you will not take the case until he has done this kind of preliminary work. Again, this not only reduces expenses but also involves the client in the litigation.

Fifth, you can sometimes economize without seriously compromising the preparation of the case. The largest savings can be made in the area of formal discovery, particularly depositions. Sometimes depositions need not be transcribed. Sometimes you can avoid depositions of witnesses entirely and rely on witness statements. Sometimes the opposing lawyer will agree to reciprocal informal interviews of parties in place of depositions. These savings, of course, must be discussed with the client, and he must agree to the procedures you take.

Sixth, the paramount rule, regardless of the size of the lawsuit, is always the same: The client's case must be competently handled. This means that you must do whatever is necessary to uncover the important facts and witnesses, even if it is not cost effective. If the opposing lawyer will not agree to informal interviews of the parties and you do not know what the opposing party will say at trial, you simply must depose that party. If the case cannot be settled short of trial, you simply must try the case. Lawyers, wittingly or not, sometimes take cases that are uneconomic from the lawyer's point of view. Once taken, however, the lawyer has the same professional obligation to prepare that case competently as he has for any other case.

Finally, keep in mind that when lawyers take cases, they frequently do so for reasons other than the compensation they will directly receive from that particular case. In small cases, accept the fact that you simply will not be paid at your usual rate. However, that fact alone should not prevent you from taking certain cases. The case may be from a regular client, whom you want to ensure remains satisfied with your overall representation. The case may come from a new client who may become a regular client if he is satisfied with the way in which you handle a small matter. The case may be legally or factually challenging. The case may be a high profile case that will enhance your reputation among lawyers and in the community. The case may be a new type of case and involve an area you have become interested in. Finally, you may decide to take a case to meet your pro bono obligations as a lawyer.

The high cost of litigation is a serious concern in our society and has sparked considerable discussion among the public, government, and the organized bar. Litigation procedures have become more streamlined in small cases; the new federal discovery rules went into effect in 1993; additional proposals to curtail formal discovery — or to eliminate it altogether in certain types of cases — are frequently made; alternative dispute resolution is becoming common; judges are taking a more active role in litigation management and settlement discussions. If a lawyer decides to take a case, however, the cardinal rule is that he always has a professional obligation to represent a client competently. That the client's matter is a small case cannot serve as an excuse for the lawyer to avoid professional obligations. The realities of your professional life as a lawyer are that once you agree to take a case, adequate planning and preparation are required to resolve the matter, regardless of its size. Accordingly, the basic steps discussed in this book must be followed to ensure that your representation is adequate.

III

LEGAL INVESTIGATION

§3.1.   Introduction

As you conduct your informal fact investigation, you must also evaluate the various legal considerations that arise in every lawsuit. These include determining what jurisdiction's substantive law applies; what claims, remedies, or defenses to pursue; what parties must or can be joined; whether the court has subject matter jurisdiction over the claims; whether the court has personal jurisdiction over the parties; and where venue is proper. This chapter discusses the legal choices a plaintiff must make before filing a lawsuit, and a defendant must make before responding to one, as well as the interdependence of these legal considerations. While this discussion is based on federal district court litigation, the basic analytical sequence is also applicable to state court lawsuits.

A note of caution is in order. Issues dealing with choice of law, legal theories of claims and remedies, joinder, subject matter jurisdiction, personal jurisdiction, and venue can be complex and the literature about them is extensive. A single volume can hardly deal with these issues in depth, much less one chapter in a general text on pretrial techniques. This discussion's purpose is necessarily limited to getting the new litigator to think intelligently about these legal considerations in broad terms to avoid "missing the boat" on vital issues. Where a serious legal issue exists, it must always be researched thoroughly before filing suit. As always, remember that Rule 11 requires that a lawyer conduct a reasonable inquiry into the law and determine that the pleading has evidentiary support and is not frivolous before presenting the pleading to the court. The rule, in short, requires that you do your homework.

§3.2.   Choice of law[1]

Before you can determine what claims, remedies, or defenses you can raise
in your case, you need to know which jurisdiction's substantive law applies. In federal court, where plaintiff brings a claim under the court's federal question jurisdiction, the resolution is simple: federal substantive law
applies.[2] However, if plaintiff brings a claim under the court's diversity
jurisdiction, and the claim is based on a substantive right created by state
law, two types of choice-of-law questions arise.

1.   When will a state's substantive law apply in federal court?

The question of when state law will be considered "substantive" and be
applied in federal court is the so-called *Erie* problem, based on the land-
mark case of Erie R.R. Co. v. Tompkins, 304 U.S. 64 (1938). In *Erie* the
Supreme Court held that whenever a federal court applies state substantive law, it must apply not only its statutory law, but its case law as well.
The principal impact of *Erie* is on diversity cases, where a federal court
must apply the appropriate state's substantive law.

The question of what is substantive law, as opposed to procedural, is
unfortunately not always clear. For example, a state's basic negligence law
is clearly substantive, and its discovery rules in civil procedure acts are
clearly procedural. However, matters such as statutes of limitations, privileges, and burdens of proof can arguably be both. The Supreme Court
has periodically grappled with the substantive-procedural distinction since
deciding *Erie*.

In Guaranty Trust Co. v. York, 326 U.S. 99 (1945), the Court announced what has come to be called the "outcome determinative" test.
When a state law, if applied in federal court, would substantially affect the
outcome of the case, the state law is substantive and must be applied. In
later cases, however, the Court modified the outcome-determinative test.
For example, in Byrd v. Blue Ridge Rural Electric Cooperative, 356 U.S. 525
(1958), the Court held that the federal right to a jury trial on a claim prevailed over a contrary state rule; in Hanna v. Plumer, 380 U.S. 460 (1955),
the Court applied the federal service-of-process rules over a conflicting state
rule; in Walker v. Armco Steel Corp., 446 U.S. 740 (1980), the Court applied a state rule defining how an action is to be commenced for statute of
limitations purposes over the conflicting Rule 3 in the Federal Rules of Civil
Procedure; and in Stewart Organization v. Ricoh Corp., 487 U.S. 22 (1988),
the Court held that the federal change of venue statute governs whether a
federal court should give effect to a contractual forum selection clause.

It should be obvious that the question of whether a federal court will
apply a state's substantive law is a complex one with which the United
States Supreme Court continues to grapple. Accordingly, any lawyer faced

1. James & Hazard §§2.33-2.37; Friedenthal §§4.1-4.7; Moore's Manual §§3.01-3.05;
Moore's Federal Practice §§0.301 et seq.; Wright & Miller §§4501 et seq.
2. In some instances, as with the Federal Tort Claims Act, the federal substantive law
refers to the forum state's substantive law.

with an *Erie*-type question must thoroughly research the decided cases to determine how the issue is likely to be resolved in a particular case.

2. What is the state's substantive law?

The second choice-of-law issue deals with multistate events and transactions. If, for example, an Arizona driver is suing a California driver over an automobile accident in Nevada and brings a diversity action in federal court, which state's tort law applies? Does it matter where the action is filed?

The Supreme Court in Klaxon Co. v. Stentor Electric Manufacturing Co., 313 U.S. 487 (1941), held that in a federal diversity action the forum state's conflict-of-law rules govern in determining which state's substantive law will apply. In the above example, if plaintiff brings suit in federal district court in Arizona, then Arizona's conflicts of law rules govern. While the rule attempts to restrict shopping between federal and state forums, a plaintiff who can bring an action in more than one venue may still be able to acquire a more advantageous forum. For example, if the Arizona plaintiff can file suit in Arizona, the Arizona conflicts rules govern, which may result in Arizona substantive law being applied, since Arizona has an interest in applying its own law to its own citizens. If the Arizona plaintiff can file suit in Nevada, the Nevada conflicts rules govern and Nevada may apply its substantive law, since the accident occurred within its borders. If Arizona and Nevada tort law differ and the plaintiff has a choice of forums in which to bring suit, he will obviously pick the more advantageous one.

When the choice-of-law issue has been resolved, it is sometimes difficult to determine what the applicable state's substantive law actually is. State law, of course, is what a particular state's legislature and supreme court have declared it to be. What happens, however, if there is no controlling statute and the state's high court has not spoken on a particular question of law? How should a federal district court decide what the applicable state law is? The Supreme Court has held that in such cases a state appellate court decision will be highly persuasive, although not binding.[3] If there is no appellate court decision, the district court can certify the question to the state supreme court. If there is no such procedure, the district court can look at any available sources to determine what the state law is likely to be were the state courts presented with the question. Finally, if the district court feels that an antiquated state law would no longer be followed, the court may determine that it is not bound by precedent and can instead fashion a rule that the state courts would likely create if again faced with the issue.[4] In such circumstances, of course, thorough research is required.[5]

3. Commissioner v. Estate of Bosch, 387 U.S. 456 (1967).
4. Bernhardt v. Polygraphic Co. of Am., 350 U.S. 198 (1956).
5. See Friedenthal §4.6 for an excellent discussion of how a district court determines applicable state law.

§3.3. Legal theories for claims, remedies, and defenses

One or two theories for claims or defenses probably provided the initial direction for your fact investigation. Before filing suit or responding to one, however, you should always explore whether the presently available facts will support other legal claims or defenses. There are dangers in prematurely labeling a client's legal problems. Think expansively, so that all reasonably assertable claims are considered before deciding which ones to raise in your initial pleading. However, there are contrary considerations that must be remembered. Rule 11 provides sanctions for improper pleadings when the attorney has not conducted a "reasonable inquiry" of the facts and law, or has filed for any improper purpose.[6] In addition, more claims usually create a more complex and costly lawsuit, something that may not be appropriate in a particular case.

This discussion obviously cannot review the numerous legal theories on which claims and defenses can be brought. However, it is always useful to review checklists of potential theories for claims and defenses before filing the initial pleading. Doing so will at least get you to consider other similar theories, both statutory and common law; to review the required elements of each theory; and to analyze the advantages and disadvantages of each in light of the existing facts.[7] Each of these theories, with its required elements, should be put on your litigation chart.

When you have identified all possible theories of claims or defenses, how do you find the "elements" for each of them? Perhaps the best place to start is with the pattern jury instructions used in the applicable jurisdiction. These usually exist for common claims and defenses with the required elements of a prima facie case itemized. Additional research will usually be necessary, particulary if the claims or defenses are not based on routine tort or contract theories. For common law claims and defenses, the best starting point is usually a hornbook or treatise on the substantive area involved. For statutory claims, you should obviously start with the statute involved and check the case annotations for elements and jury instructions. After checking these basic sources, check the recent cases interpreting and applying the substantive law. Computer searches on LEXIS or Westlaw are frequently useful. Finally, many states have practice manuals that cover types of litigation that are common to the jurisdiction; frequently these prove to be excellent practical reviews. With this type of research, you should have enough to "mull over" the pros and cons of the various legal theories that can be supported by the available facts.

For example, assume you represent the plaintiff in a personal injury case arising out of an automobile accident. You consider, of course, a negligence claim against the other driver and a claim based on violating the "rules of the road." However, is there a claim based on negligent maintenance of the defendant's vehicle? If the defendant had been drinking, can the drinking support a negligence or statutory claim? Again, the point

---

6. See discussion of Rule 11 in §5.2(f).
7. See, e.g., Actions and Remedies (C. Friend ed. 1985).

is to think expansively so that you consider every theory of recovery that can be supported by provable facts.

What claims you decide to bring in a lawsuit is influenced not only by theories of recovery, but also by the remedies permitted under each legal theory. Your choice of remedies will significantly influence what proof is relevant at trial and the scope of discovery.[8]

Under the Federal Rules of Civil Procedure, a party is not usually limited to the relief requested, and pleadings can ordinarily be amended. Nevertheless, it is always preferable to frame your pleadings so that they accurately reflect all the types of relief to which your client may be entitled. In addition, the remedies you seek will, like all the allegations in the pleadings, determine what will be relevant for discovery purposes. The distinction between legal and equitable actions no longer controls what remedies are permissible, since federal courts, like most jurisdictions, have merged courts of law and equity and have power to order any appropriate relief. Hence, it is important to review all potentially available remedies, legal and equitable, and request all that are proper. The simplest way to look at remedies is to review first the general types of legal and equitable relief, then relate that relief to the specific claims you are considering, and finally review any statutes and court rules that permit additional relief.

First, legal remedies (historically, those remedies permitted for actions in a court of law) include money damages, restitution, and recision. Money damages, the most frequently sought relief, can be compensatory, consequential, or punitive. While compensatory damages are always permitted, consequential or punitive damages are usually permitted only where statutes or case law permit them. Equitable remedies (historically, those remedies granted by a court of chancery when legal remedies were inadequate or inflexible) include injunctions, specific performance, reformation, unjust enrichment, accounting, constructive trust, equitable lien, and reclamation. Any of these remedies should be requested if appropriate to the circumstances, regardless of the kind of claims brought.

Second, the precise measure of the allowable money damages, frequently controlled both by statute and case law, depends on the type of claim being asserted. For example, damages for breach of contract depend on whether the contract involves land, personal property, construction, or employment. Tort damages also vary considerably, depending on whether the claim is based on personal injury, survival, wrongful death, undue influence, fraud, defamation, intentional tort, or statutory actions. Where a claim is statutory, the allowable damages are frequently specified in the statute.

Third, you must check to see if there are any statutory provisions for allowing recoveries for other damages, court costs, and attorney's fees. This includes checking not only the statutes providing for specific causes of action, but also federal and state procedural rules.[9] State civil practice

---

8. The leading treatise on remedies is Dobbs, Law of Remedies (2d ed. 1993).
9. There are over 100 federal statutes that permit awarding attorney's fees and other costs to the successful litigant. Common examples include §1983 civil rights actions, em-

rules often have provisions for costs and fees that, if viewed as substantive, may be applied in federal diversity actions.

For example, assume you represent the plaintiff in a contract dispute over the sale of goods. The plaintiff delivered the goods but has not been paid. Certainly, the plaintiff can receive compensatory damages, but are other remedies possibly available? Can the plaintiff support a claim for consequential damages? Is the defendant guilty of bad faith, or is there some other basis for a punitive damages claim? Are there any statutory means by which you can recover the plaintiff's attorney's fees and other costs? Once again, the point is to think expansively so that you consider every remedy that the law provides in your case.

Remedies issues should always be researched carefully to learn the full measure of damages permitted for the claims involved. A good place to start is with the damages instructions in those jurisdictions that have pattern jury instructions.

§3.4. Joinder of parties and claims

Joinder-of-parties issues are best addressed by asking a series of questions that parallel the analytical sequence involved. These are:

1. Who is the real party in interest?
2. Does that party have capacity to sue?
3. Is joinder of parties required?
4. Is joinder of parties permitted?
5. Do any special pleading rules apply?
6. Is joinder of claims permitted?

1. Real party in interest[10]

Rule 17(a) requires that an action be brought "in the name of the real party in interest." That party is the one who, under applicable substantive law, has the right that the lawsuit seeks to enforce. The purpose of the rule is to ensure that the parties with the real interests are the ones actually prosecuting cases. Potential issues arise when personal representatives are named parties. For diversity jurisdiction purposes, the citizenship of the real party in interest is controlling.

Rule 17(a) also specifies exceptions to the general rule by providing that an "executor, administrator, guardian, bailee, trustee of an express trust, a party with whom or in whose name a contract has been made for

---

ployment discrimination actions under Title VII of the 1964 Civil Rights Act, consumer products warranty actions under the Magnuson-Moss Warranty Act, and actions under the Freedom of Information Act. See E. R. Larson, Federal Court Awards of Attorney's Fees, (1981); Dobbs, Awarding Attorney Fees Against Adversaries: Introducing the Problem, 1986 Duke L.J. 435.

10. Wright §70; James & Hazard §10.3; Friedenthal §6.3; Moore's Manual §13.01; Manual of Federal Practice §§3.106-3.110; Moore's Federal Practice §§17.07-17.15; Wright & Miller §§1543-1558.

the benefit of another, or a party authorized by statute" may sue in his own name. While the plaintiff has the burden of showing he is the proper real party in interest, the exceptions to Rule 17(a) have largely eliminated controversy in this area. The only areas where disputes still arise are assignments and subrogation. While a complete assignment makes the assignee the real party in interest, 28 U.S.C. §1359 expressly provides that such an assignment cannot be used to "create" diversity where it would otherwise not exist. If an assignment or subrogation is only partial, both parties to the assignment or subrogation are usually considered real parties in interest.[11]

If the wrong party is sued, Rule 17(a) provides that no dismissal should be entered unless after a reasonable time following an objection a proper substitution of parties is not made or the real party in interest ratifies the action.

2. Capacity to sue[12]

A lawsuit must be brought by and against parties that have a legal capacity to sue. Capacity to sue is governed by Rule 17(b), which in turn refers to state law. In the case of an individual, capacity to sue is determined by the state law of the individual's domicile. For corporations, capacity is determined by the law of the state of incorporation. In other cases, including those involving representatives, the law of the forum state controls capacity to sue. The forum state's laws control partnerships and unincorporated associations, except that, regardless of the forum law, partnerships and unincorporated associations always have capacity to sue over substantive federal rights. Finally, under Rule 17(a) an infant or incompetent can sue or be sued in the name of a representative. If no representative has been appointed, a guardian ad litem can bring suit or be appointed for the sued party.

If a defendant wishes to challenge plaintiff's claim of capacity to sue, the defendant must, under Rule 9, deny the claim "with particularity." Failing to make the denial in a responsive pleading will usually result in any error being deemed waived.

3. Required joinder of parties[13]

Joinder of parties is governed by Rules 19 and 20. The joinder rules address a basic question: What parties must, should, or may be, brought into the lawsuit so that the plaintiff's claims can be properly decided? What

11. Wright §70; James & Hazard §§10.4-10.5; Moore's Manual §13.01; Manual of Federal Practice §3.109; Moore's Federal Practice §17.05; Wright & Miller §§1545, 1546.
12. Wright §70; James & Hazard §10.7; Friedenthal §6.3; Moore's Manual §13.02; Manual of Federal Practice §§3.111-3.117; Moore's Federal Practice §§17.16-17.27; Wright & Miller §§1559-1573.
13. Wright §71; James & Hazard §§10.11-10.15; Friedenthal §6.5; Moore's Manual §§13.04-13.07; Manual of Federal Practice §§3.120-3.124; Moore's Federal Practice §§19.05-19.21; Wright & Miller §§1601-1624.

parties must, or should be, joined is governed by Rule 19; what parties may be brought in is governed by Rule 20.[14]

Needless to say, these esoteric distinctions have been the source of much debate and litigation over the years. The present joinder rules are an attempt to get away from rigid labels and move toward a pragmatic analysis of the competing interests involved. On the one hand, there are legal and social interests in giving every party an opportunity to litigate and at the same time avoiding multiple suits over the same issues. On the other hand, there are corresponding interests in permitting some claims to be adjudicated, rather than none. The modern approach to joinder, as represented by Rules 19 and 20, is to resolve joinder issues by focusing on those competing interests.

Rule 19, dealing with required joinder, is divided into two basic rules. Rule 19(a) governs what parties are to be joined "if feasible"; Rule 19(b) governs what the court should do if all required parties cannot be joined.

Under Rule 19(a), a party should be joined if that party's presence is (1) required to grant "complete relief," or (2) the party has an interest in the action so that the party's presence is, practically speaking, necessary to protect his interest, or the party's absence may expose other parties to double or inconsistent obligations. Such a party should be joined unless he cannot be served with process, or the party's joinder would defeat federal subject matter jurisdiction. While the rule appears complex, in practice its application is not particularly problematical. As a practical matter, a plaintiff should join any potentially liable party who can be served, if the party's joinder will not defeat subject matter jurisdiction (and, of course, the Rule 11 requirements are met).

Rule 19(b) governs the situation where a party who should be joined cannot be because the party cannot be served with process, or because the party's joinder would defeat federal jurisdiction. The issue before the court then is whether to proceed without the party or dismiss the action. Rule 19(b) states four factors the court must balance in reaching an equitable decision: (1) whether nonjoined and existing parties will be prejudiced, (2) whether an order can minimize any potential prejudice, (3) whether any judgment without the absent party can be adequate, and (4) whether the plaintiff will have an adequate remedy if the action is dismissed.

These practical concerns frequently compete with each other, but certain conclusions are likely. First, if the consequence of a dismissal is that the plaintiff is left without any state forum in which to pursue claims against all parties, it is highly unlikely that the court will dismiss the action. Second, if an absent party can be brought in as a third-party defendant, there is strong ground for rejecting a present defendant's claim of potential prejudice. The possibility of intervention is also a strong ground for rejecting the claim of prejudice to an absent party. Third, the possi-

14. The "must-should" categories roughly approximate the traditional "indispensable-necessary" distinction; the "may" category approximates the traditional "proper" label. These traditional terms are now considered outdated.

bility of incomplete relief to the plaintiff will usually be rejected as a reason for dismissal, since that result alone prejudices no one. In short, the judicial tendency has been to retain federal jurisdiction rather than dismiss the case.

In community property states, additional joinder issues arise because spouses may be liable as joint obligors since a spouse's activities that form the basis for the lawsuit are frequently viewed as benefiting the marital community. For example, a spouse who causes an automobile collision on the way to work is usually viewed as engaging in an activity that benefits the marital community because driving to work is part of earning money for the marital community. In such situations, the other spouse should be joined as an additional defendant in the complaint.

4. Permissive joinder of parties[15]

Permissive joinder, governed by Rule 20, resolves the question of who may be joined as a proper party. Rule 20 provides two tests, both of which must be met before joinder will be permitted. First, there must be a question of law or fact common to all parties arising out of the action. Second, each plaintiff must have a right of relief, either jointly, severally, or alternatively against each defendant based on the same occurrences or transactions, or series of transactions or occurrences.

The language of Rule 20 is broad, and permits joinder whenever there is a legal or factual relationship between the parties making it sensible to have all these parties present in one lawsuit. On the other hand, permissive joinder can operate to delay the litigation and make it unfairly expensive and burdensome on certain parties. For that reason, Rule 20(b) gives the court broad regulatory powers, including the power to order separate trials to prevent any unfairness.

Where there is improper joinder, Rule 21 provides simply that the case cannot be dismissed. Rather, the misjoined parties are dropped and nonjoined parties added by court order.

5. Special pleadings rules

Required and permissive joinder rules, set forth in Rules 19 and 20, are not the only rules that regulate whether parties can be joined in a lawsuit. There are several pleading rules that govern a number of special types of actions. These are:

Rule 13—counterclaims
Rule 13(g)—cross claims
Rule 14—impleader

15. Wright §71; James & Hazard §§9.7-9.8; Friedenthal §6.4; Moore's Manual §14.01; Manual of Federal Practice §§3.118-3.119; Moore's Federal Practice §§20.05-20.08; Wright & Miller §§1651-1660.

Rule 22—interpleader
Rule 24—intervention
Rule 23—class actions
Rule 23.1—shareholder derivative suits

These pleadings, and their special requirements, are discussed in Chapter 5.

6. Joinder of claims[16]

Joinder of claims, governed by Rule 18, is always permissive. Each party can bring as many claims as the party has against every other party. These include both present and contingent claims. Deciding what claims to bring against another party is principally a practical matter.[17]

§3.5. *Subject matter jurisdiction in district courts*

Subject matter jurisdiction refers to the power of a court to hear particular matters. Federal district courts are courts of limited jurisdiction and cannot hear a case unless it falls within their power, as defined in Article III of the United States Constitution, and Congress has extended jurisdiction over the particular type of case.

Because federal district courts are courts of limited jurisdiction, a party seeking to invoke the court's jurisdiction must affirmatively plead and demonstrate proper subject matter jurisdiction.[18] The basis for jurisdiction must appear on the face of a well-pleaded complaint and cannot rest on counterclaims, defenses, or anticipated defenses. On the other hand, any party or the court can raise lack of subject matter jurisdiction. Although most commonly raised in the defendant's answer or by a Rule 12 motion to dismiss, it can be raised at any time, even after judgment or on appeal. If the court has no jurisdiction over the subject matter, the case must be dismissed.

1. "Case or controversy"[19]

The court must have an actual "case or controversy" that is ripe for adjudication. Put another way, the court will not hear moot or collusive cases, render advisory opinions, or hear controversies that are essentially

---

16. Wright §78; James & Hazard §9.4; Friedenthal §6.6; Moore's Manual §10.06; Manual of Federal Practice §§3.163-3.166; Moore's Federal Practice §§18.03-18.11; Wright & Miller §§1581-1594.
17. See §4.5.
18. See §5.2.
19. Wright §12; Moore's Manual §1.01(1); Manual of Federal Practice §1.4; Wright & Miller §3529.

political or administrative issues. This requirement limits cases to those involving real controversies in which parties have a direct stake in the outcome and will actively represent their interests.

A party must also have "standing" to sue. The standing doctrine is derived from the "case or controversy" requirement and limits the kinds of cases that can be brought in federal courts. To have standing, a plaintiff must show that the challenged conduct has caused an "injury" in fact and that the interest which the suit seeks to protect is within the "zone of protection" guaranteed by the statute or constitutional provision in question. The Supreme Court has considered the standing issue many times, and has not yet articulated a test that will easily resolve standing issues in particular circumstances.[20]

The question of whether there is an actual case or controversy, and the related issue of standing, arises frequently in public interest, constitutional, and administrative litigation. For example, a suit to enjoin enforcement of a city regulatory code provision, brought by a local resident, will raise both issues. In private litigation, there will ordinarily be an obvious controversy, with the parties having obvious standing. In public interest litigation, on the other hand, these issues are common as well as complex and must be researched thoroughly.

2. Federal question jurisdiction[21]

28 U.S.C. §1331 provides that "district courts shall have original jurisdiction of all civil actions arising under the constitution, laws, or treaties of the United States." Section 1331 is generally referred to as conferring "general" federal question jurisdiction. This distinguishes §1331 from other "specific" grants of jurisdiction found in §§1333 et seq. and from other non-Title 28 grants.

The general-versus-specific distinction is important because of the requirement that a party invoking the court's jurisdiction must affirmatively show the basis for jurisdiction. Issues over jurisdiction seldom arise when the basis is a specific grant in a statutory provision. Problems frequently exist, however, when the basis for jurisdiction is the general grant under §1331.

20. See Wright §13; Friedenthal §6.3; the standing test comes from Association of Data Processing Service Organizations v. Camp, 397 U.S. 150 (1970), and its companion case, Barlow v. Collins, 397 U.S. 159 (1970). See also Sierra Club v. Morton, 405 U.S. 727 (1972); United States v. Students Challenging Regulatory Agency Procedures, 412 U.S. 669 (1973); and Warth v. Seldin, 422 U.S. 490 (1975) on the "injury" part of the standing test. Recent Supreme Court cases include Raines v. Byrd, 521 U.S. — 1997; National Credit Union Admin. v. First National Bank & Trust Co., 522 U.S. — (1998); and Federal Election Commission v. Akins, — U.S. — (1998).

21. Wright §§17-22; James & Hazard §2.5; Friedenthal §2.3; Moore's Manual §§5.02-5.05; Manual of Federal Practice §§1.59-1.66; Moore's Federal Practice §0.62(2.-1); Wright & Miller §§3561-3567.2.

a. "Arising under"[22]

Jurisdictional issues occur under §1331 because its "arising under" language is so general. Section 1331 creates jurisdiction over civil actions "arising under the Constitution, laws or treaties of the United States." The constitutional provisions are contained in Article III, §§1 and 2. However, §1331, which contains the same language as Article III, §2, has been interpreted much more narrowly than the parallel constitutional language.

The basic requirements for jurisdiction under §1331 are that the claim be based on federal law, which must be demonstrated in the complaint, and that the federal claim be substantial rather than frivolous.[23] For example, plaintiff brings an action for patent infringement. This raises federal question jurisdiction because it is brought under the Patent Act. Another plaintiff brings an action for an unlawful search of his house. This raises federal question jurisdiction because it is brought under the Fourth Amendment of the U.S. Constitution. Where federal law expressly creates a remedy, jurisdiction will be found. However, where a federal statute, although declaring rights, does not expressly confer a remedy, complex issues exist, and they center on whether an implied remedy exists that is recognizable under §1331. On these issues the courts are frequently divided; therefore, the law must be thoroughly researched.

b. Specific grants of jurisdiction

There are several other sections of Title 28 that grant federal courts jurisdiction to hear particular matters. These include:

§1333—admiralty
§1334—bankruptcy
§1336—ICC/commerce
§1337—commerce/antitrust
§1338—patent, copyright, trademark, unfair competition
§1339—postal
§1340—IRS/customs
§§1341-1364—miscellaneous provisions

Finally, there are numerous statutory provisions outside of Title 28 that also confer jurisdiction on district courts. The more important ones are:

Jones Act, 46 U.S.C. §688
Federal Employer's Liability Act, 45 U.S.C. §56
Securities Act, 15 U.S.C. §77
Civil Rights Act, 42 U.S.C. §1983

22. Moore's Manual §5.02-5.03; James & Hazard §2.6; Friedenthal §2.3; Manual of Federal Practice §§1.60-1.66, §§1.80-1.108; Moore's Federal Practice §0.62(2.1); Wright & Miller §3562.

23. Since the complaint must affirmatively show that federal jurisdiction exists, it follows that raising a defense based on federal law cannot create jurisdiction.

Where jurisdiction is based on these specific grants, the same pleading requirements apply: A plaintiff wishing to invoke the court's jurisdiction must always affirmatively plead a proper jurisdictional basis.

Keep in mind that these federal grants of jurisdiction can be exclusive or concurrent with state courts. In several areas, notably admiralty, bankruptcy, and patent and copyright cases, the district courts have exclusive jurisdiction.

c. Pendent jurisdiction[24]

A claim can properly be brought in federal court if the basis for jurisdiction is a federal question. What happens, however, if plaintiff has other claims, not based on federal question jurisdiction? Can these be brought with the federal claim? If the other claims each have a separate proper basis for federal jurisdiction, such as diversity jurisdiction, no problems arise. However, if there is no such basis for the claims, the question arises of whether the other claims can be "joined" to the federal claim.

The concept of "pendent jurisdiction" addresses this question and strikes a compromise between the usual requirement that federal jurisdiction must be strictly construed and the obvious advantage of hearing at one time all claims that can be brought by one party against another. A simple solution is to deny federal jurisdiction on the non-federal claims, the result being that a plaintiff who wants to pursue all claims in one action must do so in a state court. However, this option is not available when the federal claim is one over which federal courts have exclusive jurisdiction. In this situation the options are to try all claims in federal court or to split the claims between federal and state courts.

The term "pendent jurisdiction," and the closely related term "ancillary jurisdiction," have been replaced by a comprehensive statute, 28 U.S.C. §1367, enacted in 1990, which controls what is now called "supplemental jurisdiction." Supplemental jurisdiction and the statute are discussed in subsection 1 below.

d. The United States as a party[25]

When the United States is a plaintiff, no special jurisdictional problems arise. However, the United States cannot be sued unless it has waived its sovereign immunity and consented to be sued. A plaintiff suing the United States, therefore, must expressly demonstrate the statutory basis under which the government has consented to be sued. The most fre-

---

24. Wright §19; James & Hazard §2.7; Friedenthal §2.13; Moore's Manual §5.15; Manual of Federal Practice §§1.109-1.112; Moore's Federal Practice §18.07(1.2); Wright & Miller §§3567, 3937.

25. Wright §22; James & Hazard §2.5; Friedenthal §2.10; Moore's Manual §13,078; Manual of Federal Practice §§1.128-1.135; Moore's Federal Practice §17.24; Wright & Miller §§3651-3660.

quently used grounds are the Court of Claims Act,[26] Tucker Act,[27] and Federal Tort Claims Act.[28]

Frequently, however, a plaintiff may wish or need to sue a federal official or federal administrative agency, rather than the United States directly. In this situation there must be a specific statute that permits suit against the agency or a named federal official. Such statutes frequently permit suits brought to challenge administrative agency decisions. For example, suit is frequently brought against the Secretary of Housing and Urban Development for denial of claimed Social Security benefits.[29] Where there is no statute permitting suit against a federal official or agency, it is still sometimes possible to sue an official individually for an alleged improper act. Finally, there are a number of federal entities, which may be incorporated or unincorporated, of which the United States is whole or part owner. Examples include the Federal Deposit Insurance Corporation and Federal Housing Authority. Whether such quasi-governmental entities can be sued in federal court is heavily regulated by statute and, sometimes, by case law.

3. Diversity jurisdiction[30]

Section 1332 provides for the jurisdiction of federal courts in civil actions involving diversity of citizenship, and parallels the constitutional grant of power found in Article III, §2 of the Constitution. Section 1332 sets out four categories of actions for which diversity jurisdiction is proper:

1. Between citizens of different states
2. Between citizens of a state and citizens or subjects of a foreign state
3. Between citizens of different states and in which citizens or subjects of a foreign state are additional parties
4. Between a foreign state as plaintiff and citizens of a state or of different states

Of these four categories, the first is the predominantly used section. The other three are usually referred to as the alienage sections. Diversity jurisdiction does not apply to domestic relations and probate matters, which are considered local matters properly raised only in state courts.

---

26. 28 U.S.C. §1491.
27. 28 U.S.C. §1346(a).
28. 28 U.S.C. §1346(b).
29. 42 U.S.C. §405.
30. Wright §§23-31; James & Hazard §2.5, Friedenthal §§2.5-2.7; Moore's Manual §5.06; Manual of Federal Practice §§1.19-1.58; Moore's Federal Practice §§0.71-0.85; Wright & Miller §§3601-3610.

a. "Citizenship" requirement[31]

Section 1332 is based on "citizenship," an imprecise term. The citizenship of natural persons is the state of domicile, and no person can have more than one domicile at a time. The citizenship of corporations is both the state where incorporated and the state where it has its principal place of business, which is usually defined as where a majority of its business is conducted or, if that is unclear, where the corporate headquarters is located. The citizenship of the legal representative of a decedent, infant, or incompetent is deemed to be the same state as the decedent's, infant's, or incompetent's citizenship. A permanent resident alien is deemed to be a citizen of the state where domiciled. (Other legal representatives, not mentioned in the 1988 amendments to §1332, presumably retain their own citizenship for diversity purposes.) In direct actions against liability insurers, the insurer is considered a citizen of the state where the insured is domiciled,[32] as well as the state where incorporated and where its principal place of business is located. Unincorporated associations present particular difficulties. If the association is not an entity entitled by state law to sue or be sued in its own name, its citizenship is that of each of its members. If the association is an entity entitled to sue or be sued, the prevailing rule is that here also the association is considered to be a citizen of each state of which a member is a citizen.

Needless to say, what constitutes citizenship for diversity purposes when artificial entities are involved can be a complex issue involving law that is frequently unsettled; thorough research is essential.

b. Complete diversity requirement[33]

The requirement that diversity must be "complete" in order for the federal district courts to have jurisdiction means that each plaintiff must have a different state citizenship from each defendant. Stated another way, if any plaintiff and any defendant are citizens of the same state, diversity will not be complete. For example, if citizens of Illinois and California sue citizens of Maine and Vermont, complete diversity exists. If citizens of Illinois and California sue citizens of Maine, Vermont, Connecticut, and California, complete diversity does not exist.

The complete diversity requirement applies to every party that is actually joined, regardless of whether that party is required or permissive. To retain the required complete diversity, a plaintiff can dismiss all but indispensable parties from the action. In addition, a plaintiff may manipulate the parties to create complete diversity. Because of this, a party's characterization as a plaintiff or defendant in the complaint is not controlling.

---

31. Wright §§24, 26; James & Hazard §2.5; Friedenthal §2.6; Moore's Manual §5.06; Manual of Federal Practice §§1.24-1.33; Moore's Federal Practice §0.74; Wright & Miller §§3601-3642.

32. Some states have so-called direct action statutes that permit suits to be brought directly against an insurance company. The typical situation is an automobile accident involving the insured.

33. Wright §§23-31; James & Hazard §2.5; Friedenthal §2.6; Moore's Manual §5.06; Manual of Federal Practice §1.34; Wright & Miller §3605.

Parties will be realigned as plaintiffs or defendants, and nominal or formal parties will be ignored, to determine if complete diversity actually exists. In the case of legal representatives of decedents, infants and incompetents, the citizenship of the representative is deemed to be the same state as the decedent's, infant's, or incompetent's citizenship. Where the legal representative is nominal, such as with a guardian ad litem, the citizenship of the represented party is also determinative for diversity purposes. Collusive assignments, made solely to create diversity, are also ignored.[34]

The complete diversity rule is somewhat misleading because it applies to the original plaintiffs' claims against original defendants and does not apply to many other situations. The concept of ancillary jurisdiction, which applies to counterclaims, cross-claims, impleader, and interventions as of right, significantly modifies the complete diversity requirement.

Complete diversity is determined according to the citizenship of parties at the time the initial complaint was filed. Later changes in citizenship by a party will not defeat jurisdiction.

c. Jurisdictional amount requirement[35]

Section 1332(a) requires (as of 1996) that the "matter in controversy exceeds the sum or value of $75,000, exclusive of interest and costs." The plaintiff's complaint is the sole basis for determining if the requirement has been met. The allegations are controlling unless there is a "legal certainty" that the jurisdictional amount cannot be obtained. This will occur only when plaintiff requests damages, such as punitive damages, to which he is not entitled under the applicable substantive law, and those damages are necessary to reach the jurisdictional amount.

The principal issue in this area involves the problem of valuation, particularly where equitable relief is requested. With injunctions, where this problem most frequently occurs, the measure of damages is the value of the right sought to be enforced or the value of the avoided injury. The value may be different, depending on whether it is measured from the plaintiff's or the defendant's perspective. The courts are divided on which view of the measure of damages is appropriate, although more appear to use the plaintiff's loss approach. For example, suppose the plaintiff brings suit to enjoin the enforcement of certain statutes, such as zoning ordinances or health regulations, and to have them declared unconstitutional. The court must look to see what the amount of the loss to the plaintiff would be if the statutes continue to be enforced.

Another issue involves aggregation of claims to meet the jurisdictional amount. Here there are four basic situations. First, where there is one plaintiff and one defendant, the plaintiff can aggregate all claims against the defendant to meet the jurisdictional amount requirement. For

34. See 28 U.S.C. §1359.
35. Wright §§32-37; James & Hazard §2.5; Friedenthal §2.8; Moore's Manual §§5.07-5.14; Manual of Federal Practice §§1.72-1.79; Moore's Federal Practice §§0.90-0.99; Wright & Miller §§3701-3712.

example, a plaintiff has two claims, each involving $40,000, against one defendant; the claims involve two separate, unrelated contracts. The plaintiff can properly aggregate the claims. Second, where there is one plaintiff and multiple defendants, plaintiff can aggregate claims only if the claims are joint rather than several and distinct. For example, a plaintiff has two claims, each involving $40,000, against two defendants; the claims involve two separate, unrelated contracts. The plaintiff cannot aggregate these claims. However, if the liability is joint, as would be the case if the defendants are partners jointly liable on a partnership obligation, aggregation is proper. Third, where there are multiple plaintiffs and one defendant, the plaintiffs cannot aggregate separate and distinct claims. The plaintiffs can aggregate only if the claims are undivided and a single title or right is involved. For example, two plaintiffs each have a $40,000 claim against one defendant; the claims involve two separate, unrelated contracts. The plaintiffs cannot aggregate these claims; however, if the two plaintiffs are partners suing to recover a debt owed to the partnership, aggregation is proper. Finally, where there are multiple plaintiffs and multiple defendants, the above analysis applies to the individual claims.

Interest and costs raise fewer questions. Costs include attorneys' fees only if a contract or statute permits them. Interest, which is ordinarily incidental to the action, is included for purposes of determining if the jurisdictional amount is met only if the interest itself is the basis of the action.

4. Supplemental jurisdiction[36]

Because federal courts are courts of limited jurisdiction, the question arises of whether a federal court can have jurisdiction over claims for which no federal jurisdiction exists. The concept of "pendent jurisdiction" principally addresses the question of what happens when a plaintiff, properly in federal court because one of the claims has federal question jurisdiction, also brings other claims, based on the same conduct, not having independent grounds for federal jurisdiction. The closely related concept of "ancillary jurisdiction" principally addresses the question of what happens when a plaintiff is properly in federal court because the claim has a proper federal jurisdictional basis, and another party wishes to bring a counterclaim, cross-claim, or third-party complaint, but this new claim does not have an independent federal jurisdictional basis.

The concerns in both situations are similar. On the one hand, both the litigants and the court have an interest in avoiding piecemeal litigation, in which some claims between the parties can be brought in federal court, while others must be brought in state court. On the other hand, allowing state claims to be brought in federal court, through the concepts

---

36. Wright §9; James & Hazard §2.7; Friedenthal §2.14; Moore's Manual §5.15; Manual of Federal Practice §§1.109-1.112; Moore's Federal Practice §8.07(5); Wright & Miller §§3523, 3567.

of pendent and ancillary jurisdiction, must be consistent with Article III of the U.S. Constitution as well as statutory grants of power to the federal courts.

The concepts of pendent and ancillary jurisdiction, being judicial creations, enjoyed a rich judicial history, producing leading cases such as United Mine Workers of America v. Gibbs, 383 U.S. 715 (1966), and Owen Equipment & Erection Co. v. Kroger, 437 U.S. 365 (1978). Following the much criticized case of Finley v. United States, 490 U.S. 545 (1989), Congress in 1990 enacted a statute which codifies pendent and ancillary jurisdiction under the new name of "supplemental jurisdiction" (and overrules the holding in *Finley*). While retaining most of the former concepts, the statute modifies them in certain respects.

The new statute, 28 U.S.C. §1367, has three principal provisions

(a) Except as provided in subsections (b) and (c) or as expressly provided otherwise by Federal statute, in any civil action of which the district courts have original jurisdiction, the district courts shall have supplemental jurisdiction over all other claims that are so related to claims in the action within such original jurisdiction that they form part of the same case or controversy under Article III of the United States Constitution. Such supplemental jurisdiction shall include claims that involve the joinder or intervention of additional parties.

(b) In any civil action of which the district courts have original jurisdiction founded solely on section 1332 of this title, the district courts shall not have supplemental jurisdiction under subsection (a) over claims by plaintiffs against persons made parties under Rules 14, 19, 20, or 24 of the Federal Rules of Civil Procedure, or over claims by persons proposed to be joined as plaintiffs under Rule 19 of such rules, or seeking to intervene as plaintiffs under Rule 24 of such rules, when exercising supplemental jurisdiction over such claims would be inconsistent with the jurisdictional requirements of section 1332.

(c) The district courts may decline to exercise supplemental jurisdiction over a claim under subsection (a) if—

(1) the claim raises a novel or complex issue of State law,

(2) the claim substantially predominates over the claim or claims over which the district court has original jurisdiction,

(3) the district court has dismissed all claims over which it has original jurisdiction, or

(4) in exceptional circumstances, there are other compelling reasons for declining jurisdiction.

Under the new statute, subsection (a) confers on the district court mandatory supplemental jurisdiction over all other claims that are so related to the original claim that they form part of the same case or controversy, unless the court exercises its discretion under the circumstances set forth in subsection (c) and declines supplemental jurisdiction. The use of the phrase "case or controversy" is intended to extend to the constitutional limits of federal court power.

Subsection (b) creates several exceptions to deal with situations in which a plaintiff in diversity cases might otherwise bring into the case claims against certain other parties that it would not be able to bring because of the lack of subject matter jurisdiction. This section does not restrict the use of supplemental jurisdiction by defendants in recognized and accepted circumstances, such as compulsory counterclaims, cross-claims, interpleader, intervention of right, and impleader. Such pleadings commonly involve indemnity. For example, consider a plaintiff who properly brings a claim in federal court that has proper subject matter jurisdiction. The defendant wishes to bring in a third-party defendant on an indemnification theory. Indemnification raises no federal questions, however, and since the defendant and third-party defendant are citizens of the same state, diversity is lacking. Yet, in this situation the court will have ancillary jurisdiction over the third-party claim.

5. Removal jurisdiction[37]

The right to remove cases from state to federal courts protects nonresident parties from perceived local prejudices. The removal jurisdiction of federal district courts is governed by 28 U.S.C. §§1441-1452. Since it is a jurisdictional statute, it is strictly construed and its requirements must be followed closely to ensure that removal is properly made.

Removal is the procedure in which a case, already filed in a state court, is transferred to the federal district court for the same district in which the state action is pending. The first requirement, then, is that the case has already been filed in state court. To determine if removal is proper, you must look to the complaint at the time the removal petition is filed. The removal cannot be based on defenses or counterclaims.

The removal statute permits the removal of otherwise nonremoveable claims if those claims are joined with other claims over which the federal court has proper jurisdiction under §1331, the general federal question jurisdiction statute. In addition, a federal court can retain a removed case over which it has proper subject matter jurisdiction, even if the state court did not have proper personal jurisdiction over the defendant.

Second, all defendants—except nominal, unknown, or fraudulently joined ones or ones who were not served with process prior to the filing of the notice—must join in the notice of removal. Since removal is for the benefit of defendants, each must agree to the removal; a "defendant" for removal purposes is each party against whom the original plaintiff brought a claim in state court.

Third, under §1446(b), the notice of removal must be filed within 30 days of the time the defendant receives a copy of plaintiff's initial pleading in state court, or within 30 days of receiving summons if the initial pleading under state practice is not required to be served on the defendant, whichever is shorter. If a case is not initially removable but later becomes so (such as by dropping a nondiverse defendant), defendant may

---

37. Wright §§38-41; James & Hazard §2.9; Friedenthal §2.11; Moore's Manual §§8.01-8.13; Manual of Federal Practice §§1.149-1.173; Moore's Federal Practice §0.155; Wright & Miller §§3721-3740. The mechanics of the removal procedure are discussed in §7.6.

file a notice of removal within 30 days of receiving a court paper that first reveals that removal is now proper. There is also an absolute one-year limitation on removing cases based on §1332 jurisdiction. The time period, like all the removal requirements, is strictly enforced. Once the petition is filed, it operates as a stay on any state court proceedings.

Fourth, removal is generally proper if the federal district court could have had jurisdiction over the action had it been filed originally in federal court. For this reason you must determine if the federal district could have had proper subject matter jurisdiction over the plaintiff's original complaint.

There are three basic grounds for removal: diversity, federal question, and special removal statutes. Under §1441, removal jurisdiction can be based on diversity; this is usually proper when each plaintiff has a different citizenship from each defendant. The complete diversity rule for removal has one important exception: §1441(b) prevents removal if any proper defendant is a citizen of the state where the action was brought. (The citizenship of defendants sued under fictitious names is disregarded.) This exception is based on the notion that a principal reason for permitting removal in diversity of citizenship cases is the possibility of local prejudice against noncitizen defendants, which fails if a defendant is a citizen of the forum state. Accordingly, the diversity jurisdiction for removal is narrower than diversity for original diversity jurisdiction purposes. In addition, complete diversity must exist both when plaintiff's original action was filed in state court and when the removal petition is filed.

Removal can also be based on federal question jurisdiction. If an action could have been brought in district court on federal question grounds, it can ordinarily be removed, and the citizenship of the parties is disregarded. Removal generally cannot be allowed unless the claim could be brought as an original action in federal court.

The removal sections also provide for removal in certain special circumstances. These include:

§1441(d) — civil actions against foreign states
§1442 — federal officers or agencies sued or prosecuted
§1442a — members of armed forces
§1443 — civil rights actions
§1444 — foreclosure against the United States

Section 1445 makes certain actions nonremovable. These include actions under state workers' compensation acts; actions against railroads, their receivers, or trustees; and actions against a common carrier, its receivers, or trustees, arising under specific federal statutes.

A case removed to federal court may be remanded back to the original state court under §1447. A motion to remand based on defects in the removal procedure must be made within 30 days of the filing of the notice of removal. A remand based on lack of subject matter jurisdiction may be made at any time before final judgment.

A plaintiff who wishes to file and keep a lawsuit in state court can use certain strategies to defeat removal. First, where diversity would otherwise permit removal, plaintiff can add a defendant who either is not diverse from the plaintiff or is a citizen of the forum state. So long as such a joinder is not fraudulent in the sense that plaintiff does not really wish to prosecute a claim against that party, it will defeat removal. Second, where diversity does not exist, plaintiff can draft the complaint to avoid pleading a claim that would permit removal based on federal question jurisdiction. Where plaintiff has decided that a state forum is preferable, it is often possible to structure the claims and select the defendants to prevent removal.

The mechanics of the removal procedure are discussed in §7.6.

§3.6. Personal jurisdiction[38]

Personal jurisdiction refers to the power of a court to bring a party before it. A judgment is not enforceable against a party unless that party can lawfully be brought into court and has received notice of the lawsuit. Thus, constitutional concepts of due process underlie this requirement.

Jurisdiction to adjudicate can be in personam, in rem, or quasi in rem. An in personam jurisdiction over a party is necessary for full enforcement of a judgment against a party and for the concepts of res judicata and collateral estoppel (now called claim preclusion and issue preclusion) to operate. An in rem action is one that involves property over which the parties have some dispute, and jurisdiction over the party exists by virtue of the party's ownership of the property. Finally, a quasi in rem action refers to an action brought to subject only certain property to the claims asserted. This is frequently done by seeking to attach property of a known party to satisfy a future judgment. These distinctions have less significance today at the federal court level, where the critical concerns involve the constitutional limits of personal jurisdiction and the issue of whether service was properly made. Hence, issues surrounding personal jurisdiction involve two separate questions:

1. Can the defendant constitutionally be subject to the court's jurisdiction?
2. Was service of process on the defendant proper?

The first question involves the due process limitations on personal jurisdiction, and the second involves the service-of-process requirements of Rule 4.

1. Due process requirements

Due process issues do not arise for plaintiffs, since by initiating suit a plaintiff is considered to have voluntarily submitted to the court's jurisdiction

---

38. Wright §§64-65; James & Hazard §§2.14-2.25; Friedenthal §§3.1-3.28; Moore's Manual §§6.01-6.19; Moore's Federal Practice §§0.219-0.229; Wright & Miller §§1061-1075.

for all purposes, including being required to respond to counterclaims and other claims brought in that action. Where a defendant is a resident of the forum state, due process problems do not arise, since by virtue of residency it is fair to require the defendant to defend against an action in the forum state. When a nonresident defendant, however, is sued in the forum state and does not consent to the jurisdiction of the court, due process problems may prevent that defendant from being required to defend there. Determining what the due process limitations are is a difficult question that the Supreme Court has frequently considered. The question is raised with increasing frequency as more businesses engage in national and international commerce.[39]

The leading constitutional cases include International Shoe Co. v. State of Washington, 326 U.S. 310 (1945), Hanson v. Denckla, 357 U.S. 235 (1958), and World-Wide Volkswagen Corp. v. Woodson, 444 U.S. 286 (1980). Recent significant Supreme Court cases are Burger King Corp. v. Rudzewicz, 471 U.S. 462 (1985), Asahi Metal Industry Co. v. Superior Court, 480 U.S. 102 (1987), and Burnham v. Superior Court, 495 U.S. 604 (1990).

In *International Shoe* the Court addressed the question of what activities by a corporation within a particular state will subject it to suit within that state consistent with due process concepts. It held that where a corporation's "minimum contacts" in the forum state were such that being forced to defend a suit in that state would not offend "'traditional notions of fair play and substantial justice,'" jurisdiction was proper. Many subsequent decisions, of course, expounded on what minimum contacts satisfied due process. In *World-Wide Volkswagen*, the Court rejected the argument that an out-of-state seller should be subjected to suit in another state simply because it was foreseeable that the vehicle sold might be involved in a collision in another state. Instead, the Court stressed that minimum contacts protect a defendant from being sued in a remote or inconvenient forum, and that foreseeability does not by itself create such contacts as would satisfy due process requirements. Requiring a defendant to defend in the forum state, the Court held, must be fair and not impose unreasonable burdens on the defendant.[40]

In *Asahi Metal* a divided court held that merely placing a product into the stream of commerce is not an act that will subject a party to the forum state's jurisdiction, even if the party was aware that the stream of commerce would sweep the product into the forum state. Minimum contacts requires some action purposely directed toward the forum state.

Personal jurisdiction issues are common, particularly in lawsuits involving defendants engaged in interstate business activities. The most recent issues center on commercial activities on the Internet. Businesses are increasingly using their web sites for a range of activities, from advertising

---

39. The issue rarely arises in tort litigation, because a tort is usually seen as an event caused by a defendant that subjects him to the court's jurisdiction, and because state automobile statutes usually impose a "consent to be sued" fiction on out-of-state motorists.

40. In *Burnham* the Court held that personal service within a forum state satisfies Due Process requirements.

and informational purposes to conducting commercial transactions and transmitting products. When litigation, whether based on contract or tort claims, springs from such uses, the question also arises whether these kinds of activities can subject a nonresident defendant to in personam jurisdiction in the state to which its web site activities reach. In due process terms, are these business uses of the Internet adequate "minimum contacts," did the defendant "purposely avail" itself of the privilege of conducting business in the state, or did the defendant "purposely direct" its activities to residents of the state, so that the nonresident defendant can "reasonably" be required to defend itself in the forum state? Case law, not surprisingly, is hardly uniform, as courts grapple with applying the Supreme Court's personal jurisdiction jurisprudence to doing business on the Internet.[41]

The minimum-contacts analysis applies with equal force to in rem and quasi in rem actions.[42] Because of this, distinctions such as in rem or quasi in rem have no direct bearing on the due process question of a defendant's amenability to suit in a particular forum. However, the distinctions are still important for determining the enforceability of judgments.

2. Service-of-process requirements

It is important to keep in mind that amenability to process is different from, and independent of, the adequacy of service of process. If a party is not constitutionally amenable to process, any service on that party will have no effect unless the party waives objections to the service. If a party is amenable to process, service of process on that party must still be properly made.

Service must be properly made because due process considerations require that service be made in a manner that will reasonably put a defendant on notice that he has been sued.[43] Since Rule 4(e) now permits service by any method allowed by the state law in which the district court is sitting, this means, in practical terms, that an out-of-state defendant can be served under the forum state's long-arm statutes. Alternatively, a defendant can be served pursuant to the law of the state in which service is effected.

Service of process under Rule 4 is discussed in §5.3.

41. See Robert W. Hamilton and Gregory A. Castanias, Tangled Web: Personal Jurisdiction and the Internet, 24 Litigation 27-35 (No. 2, Winter 1998); Ira S. Nathenson, Showdown at the Domain Name Coral: Property Rights and Personal Jurisdiction Over Squatters, Poachers and Other Parasites, 58 U. Pitt. L. Rev. 911 (Summer 1997); Marie D'Amico, A Survey of the Current Cases of Personal Jurisdiction and the Internet, 1 J. of Internet Law 8 (1998).

42. The Supreme Court so held in Shaffer v. Heitner, 433 U.S. 186 (1977), deciding that a defendant's ownership of property by itself did not establish such contacts as would create proper personal jurisdiction over the defendant, where the claims were not related to the property.

43. See Mullane v. Central Hanover Bank, 339 U.S. 306 (1950).

§3.7. Venue[44]

A lawsuit must be filed in a proper place. Where a lawsuit can be filed is governed by venue statutes. Those statutes determine the geographic districts where the case can properly be heard.

Since venue provisions are designed in part to protect a defendant from being forced to litigate in an "unfair" forum, it follows that a defendant can waive the benefits of the venue rules. Hence, a defendant must raise improper venue in a timely manner, either by a Rule 12 motion or in the answer, otherwise objections will be deemed waived.

Because a plaintiff may sometimes have more than one available venue, the question of which venue to choose may arise. This question involves both practical and legal considerations. On the practical side, convenience and the cost to the plaintiff, the plaintiff's lawyer and witnesses will frequently dominate the decision. The plaintiff's own district will often be the choice, if it is available. If the plaintiff's principal witnesses are in another district, that should be considered. On the legal side, choice-of-law decisions may be critical, since applicable substantive law may differ for such matters as statutes of limitations, elements of claims, and allowable damages. Further, since the subpoena power of a district is generally limited to its geographical boundaries, if uncooperative witnesses are out-of-state, you may need to choose another available forum to reach these witnesses. Finally, considerations such as the choice of judges, the desirability of prospective jury pools, and length of time until trial should all be considered.

1. Determining venue[45]

The general venue statute for federal district courts is §1391. Under §1391(a), if jurisdiction is based solely on diversity, venue is proper in

> (1) a judicial district where any defendant resides, if all defendants reside in the same state, (2) a judicial district in which a substantial part of the events or omissions giving rise to the claim occurred, or a substantial part of property which is the subject of the action is situated, or (3) a judicial district in which any defendant is subject to personal jurisdiction at the time the action is commenced, if there is no district in which the action may otherwise be brought.

Under §1391(b), if jurisdiction is based other than solely on diversity, venue is proper only in

> (1) a judicial district where any defendant resides, if all defendants reside in the same state, (2) a judicial district in which a substantial part of the events

44. Wright §§42-44; James & Hazard §§2.10-2.11; Friedenthal §§2.15-2.17; Moore's Manual §§7.01-7.15; Manual of Federal Practice §§2.1-2.78; Moore's Federal Practice §§0.140-0.148; Wright & Miller §§3801-3868.
45. Wright §42; James & Hazard §2.10; Friedenthal §2.15; Moore's Manual §§7.02-7.11; Manual of Federal Practice §§2.1-2.12; Wright & Miller §3801.

or omissions giving rise to the claim occurred, or a substantial part of property that is the subject of the action is situated, or (3) a judicial district in which any defendant may be found, if there is no district in which the action may otherwise be brought.

However, there are numerous special venue statutes, both in the Title 28 venue section and elsewhere, that control venue in special kinds of cases. The special provisions begin with §1394. Other venue provisions are scattered throughout the United States Code, usually as part of the substantive statute that creates a cause of action.[46] Consequently, you must always check whether a special venue statute exists that overrides the general provisions of §1391.

In addition, §1392 governs venue in "local" actions that are actions involving property. Whether the action is in rem, so that §1392 applies, is controlled by the nature of the remedy sought. Ordinarily, if the remedy is specific to the property, the action will be local, and §1392 makes the venue that of the res involved.

Once the applicable statutes are determined, the question of a party's residence arises, since §1391 is based on residence. An individual's residence is where the individual is domiciled. A corporation under §1391(c) is considered a resident of any district "in which it is subject to personal jurisdiction at the time the action is commenced." Unincorporated associations, if they have no capacity to sue under state law, are residents of each district in which any member of the association resides. If the association is an entity entitled to sue under state law, the association is a citizen of the district where it conducts its business. Aliens under §1391(d) can be sued in any district. Finally, where a defendant is the United States, its agencies, officers or employees, §1391(e) controls and provides that venue is generally proper—unless law provides otherwise —in a district where the defendant resides, where a substantial part of the events or omissions giving rise to the claim occurred, where a substantial part of property involved in the action is located, or where the plaintiff resides if no property is involved.

The venue provisions control where a plaintiff files the initial complaint against the original defendants. They do not apply to counterclaims, cross-claims, or third-party claims, since these are seen as ancillary to the initial suit and hence raise no additional venue issues.

2. Change of venue[47]

A change of venue can be based on three grounds: improper venue, governed by §1406; inconvenient venue, governed by §1404; and the doctrine of forum non conveniens. Under §1406, the court has discretion either to dismiss or to transfer to a proper venue any case that has been

46. For a list of such venue statutes, see Moore's Federal Practice §0.142.
47. Wright §44; James & Hazard §2.11; Friedenthal §2.17; Moore's Manual §7.12; Manual of Federal Practice §§2.52-2.74; Moore's Federal Practice §§0.145-0.148; Wright & Miller §§3841-3855.

filed in an improper venue. Since the statute encourages transfers "if it be in the interest of justice," this is the usual approach. Keep in mind that proper venue is a personal right. A plaintiff, by filing an action in an improper venue, waives the right to object to it. A defendant must raise any venue objection either by a Rule 12 motion or in the defendant's answer, otherwise objections will usually be considered waived.

Under §1404(a), the court may transfer a case from a proper venue to another venue, "where it might have been brought," "for the convenience of parties and witnesses, in the interest of justice." This section recognizes that a plaintiff frequently has venue choices, and that the plaintiff's choice, while proper, may not be the most convenient forum for the case seen as a whole. If this situation exists, the court can transfer the case to the more convenient forum, the only restriction being that the new forum must be in a district in which the plaintiff could have filed the action and where the court could have obtained personal jurisdiction over the defendants.

When a case is transferred from one venue to another, the substantive law follows the case. This is important in diversity cases, where the forum state's substantive law, including its conflicts of law rules, is applied. When a case is transferred to another district, in another state, the original substantive law is still applied to the case. This rule avoids forum shopping by the defense in an attempt to get more favorable law applied to the case.

The doctrine of forum non conveniens recognizes that there may be instances in which a court may dismiss an action because the selected forum, while proper, is inconvenient. The leading case is Gulf Oil Corp. v. Gilbert, 330 U.S. 501 (1947). Today most cases are decided under the venue transfer rule, §1404(a). However, the forum non conveniens doctrine is still used, particularly in cases in which the events on which the action is based occurred in a foreign country.[48]

---

48. See In re Union Carbide Gas Plant Explosion, 809 F.2d 195 (2d Cir. 1987).

IV

CASE EVALUATION AND STRATEGY

§4.1. Introduction

Case evaluation requires that you gather enough facts and consider sufficiently the legal issues to decide intelligently whether to take the case. Then, if you decide to take it, the evaluation requires that you devise a realistic, cost-effective litigation plan. This chapter discusses making the initial decision to take a case, establishing the attorney-client relationship, developing a litigation strategy, and completing prefiling requirements.

§4.2. Taking the case

You should take those cases that have factual and legal merit and are economically feasible, and you should usually decline the others. But just how and when do you decide if you should take a case?

First, always check for conflicts of interest with existing and former clients. A lawyer's relationship with a client is based on two key duties: loyalty and confidentiality. Both duties may be breached in the litigation environment if a lawyer represents multiple clients on the same matter if the interests of the clients are directly adverse, or represents a client against a former client on a substantially related matter in which the client's interests are materially adverse to the interests of the former client. A law firm and its lawyers are generally viewed as a single entity, and for conflicts purposes lawyers generally carry their former clients from former firms and government offices to their present firms. Hence, a conflict of interest may disqualify an entire firm, not just a lawyer within the firm. The bigger the firm, the more likely conflicts of interest will arise with present and former clients. The time to determine if a conflict of interest exists, and whether it bars representation of the client, is now, not when an opposing party moves to disqualify you or your firm.[1]

Law firms must have conflicts procedures to screen new matters for potential conflicts. These procedures include circulating a new client or new matter memorandum to all lawyers in the firm, using a docket or conflicts clerk to check for potential conflicts with existing or former clients in the firm's client data base, and having new lawyers list all former clients and matters they worked on at previous firms or government offices so that these can be entered into the conflicts data base. Developing a conflicts search procedure and following it carefully for every new client and matter will identify possible problems so that they can be analyzed and resolved before litigation is underway.

A conflict of interest situation in litigation arises when, simply stated, a law firm (1) represents a new client against another current client in the same or an unrelated matter, (2) represents a new client against a former client in the same or a substantially related matter, or (3) represents two clients in the same matter. When such a situation arises, it must be resolved under the applicable ethics rules.

If representing a client will be "directly adverse" to another client, the law firm cannot undertake the representation unless, following the requirements of Model Rule 1.7(a), the lawyer reasonably believes the representation will not adversely affect the relationship with the other client, and each client consents after consultation.

If representing a client "may be materially limited" by the lawyer's responsibilities to another client, a third person, or the lawyer's own interests, the law firm cannot undertake the representation unless, following the requirements of Model Rule 1.7(b), the law firm reasonably believes the representation would not be adversely affected, and the client consents after consultation. If multiple clients in a single matter are involved, that consultation must include explaining the implications of the common representation and the advantages and risks involved.

The question of whether a conflict exists and, if so, whether and how it can be resolved can be complicated and requires knowledge of all the applicable ethics rules, opinions, and case law in that jurisdiction. Because of this, most law firms, as part of their conflicts-check procedures, have an experienced partner available to review all new matters in which a possible conflict of interest may exist. In difficult situations, outside counsel may be necessary to review the question of whether a conflict exists and whether it can be waived.

Consider, for example, the common situation in which a driver and passenger in a car, involved in a collision with another car, seek a lawyer to sue the driver of the other car. Since the passenger could potentially sue the driver of the car in which she was riding (if there is any evidence of that driver's negligence), as well as the driver of the other car, a conflict of interst may exist between the passenger and her driver. In this situ-

---

1. The controlling conflicts rules are Rules 1.7 through 1.12 of the Model Rules of Professional Conduct, and DR5-101 and DR9-101 of the Model Code of Professional Responsibility.

ation, the passenger must be fully informed of her right to sue her own driver and the consequences if she decides not to sue, and must have the opportunity to consult further about the situation. If the passenger waives her right to sue her driver, the conflict disappears, and the lawyer can represent both the passenger and her driver in a lawsuit against the driver of the other car. (Note, however, that other conflicts may arise, such as whether to accept a proposed aggregate settlement, in which case Model Rule 1.8(g) must be followed.)

Second, your litigation chart, which sets out the potential legal claims and required elements of proof for each claim, provided the direction for your factual and legal investigation. This provides the framework from which to analyze the case. In addition, keep in mind Rule 11, which provides that an attorney's signature on a pleading constitutes a verification that the attorney has conducted a "reasonable inquiry" into the facts and law.[2] Hence, you cannot plead claims, remedies, or defenses that you have not adequately investigated to determine whether they are well grounded.

As the lawyer for a prospective plaintiff, you should take a case only if you can realistically expect to prove a prima facie case on at least one theory of recovery. You should already have some admissible proof for each element of each asserted claim or have a reasonable basis for believing you will get such missing proof during formal discovery. In addition, the potential recovery must be large enough to justify the work and risks of litigation. Many lawyers, for example, refuse even a simple case on a contingency fee basis unless a realistic recovery is at least in the $10,000 to $20,000 range because the fee, usually one-third of any recovery, will simply not provide reasonable compensation for the work and risks involved. In a complex case, such as a medical malpractice claim, the realistic damages have to be at least in the $50,000 to $100,000 range to make it economically feasible to take the case.

When to decide, as a plaintiff's lawyer, to accept or decline a case depends on the type of case and the factual and legal issues involved. For example, you might accept a simple automobile collision case not involving a serious injury after merely interviewing the client and reviewing the police accident report. Sometimes such a limited investigation will be enough to assess whether the client "has a case," whether, economically speaking, the damages are substantial enough to make it worth pursuing, and whether a judgment can actually be collected. In more complex matters, however, such as serious personal injury, medical malpractice, products liability, or commercial cases, you may need to do substantial legal research, extensive factual investigation, and have an expert review the case before you can make this decision. The basic question is always the same: Do I know enough from my fact investigation and legal research to conclude that the client has a provable case with substantial damages that can be collected? If the case appears weak on liability or damages, involves a great deal of work, and would be taken on a contingency fee basis, the best time to turn it down is now. Cases rarely look better than when

2. See discussion of Rule 11 in §5.2.4.

they first walk in the door. Every lawyer has taken cases and later regretted it. The best way to avoid this is by rejecting the marginal cases early.

There are exceptions. First, where a plaintiff is in imminent danger of having an applicable statute of limitations run, your first obligation is to file a claim to prevent the statute from running, even though you have not had an opportunity to investigate the facts and research the law. Protecting the plaintiff's claim from a limitations bar must take precedence over other considerations.[3] Second, keep in mind that lawyers frequently take cases for reasons other than the income that the case will produce.[4]

If you decide to take a case, you need to enter into an agreement with the client. If you turn down the case, you need to send out a letter declining representation. These steps are discussed in the following sections.

As a defendant's lawyer, the decision whether to take a case is in one way easier and in another way more difficult. It is easier from the economic point of view, since defendant's cases are not taken on a contingency basis. So long as the defendant agrees on how to pay the lawyer for the legal services, and the defendant is able and willing to pay, there are no economic risks in taking a weak case. However, the decision is more difficult in the sense that the lawyer and the defendant must agree on how best to defend the case. If the client realizes the case is not defensible on the merits, the client may try to pressure the lawyer to drag out the case or file unfounded defenses, counterclaims, or third-party claims. But a defense lawyer has the same obligations, under ethics rules as well as under Rule 11, as the plaintiff's lawyer. Such conflicts are best handled at the outset by letting the client know what you can and cannot do in defending the case, and by reaching agreement on how you plan to defend.

§4.3.   Establishing the terms of the attorney-client agreement

The attorney-client relationship should be formally established with a written agreement. There are several reasons for this. First, any contractual relationship is best established by a written instrument. Second, the agreement will prove the existence of an attorney-client relationship for privilege purposes. Third, it will establish the work to be done, what will not be done, and the basis for compensation, all of which are necessary for a good working relationship with the client. Fourth, ethics rules require that a client be informed of how the fee is set and of all the material facts concerning the representation. Although a written agreement is required only in contingency and referral cases, good practice dictates its use in all cases. For all these reasons, you need a written agreement with the client.

Unless your client is sophisticated and has experience working with lawyers, the client will have little understanding of the legal work involved in litigation and the various fee arrangements that can be made. It is in

---

3. Protecting the plaintiff's claim under these circumstances should not constitute a Rule 11 violation. See Boone v. Superior Ct., 145 Ariz. 235, 700 P.2d 1335 (1985).
    4. See §2.7.

everyone's best interests that the client be educated on these matters. You should discuss how you set your fees, and the expected costs, with the client.

Lawyers most commonly incorporate the terms of the representation in a letter from the lawyer to the client, usually called an engagement letter. The letter and a copy are sent to the client, who signs the copy to show approval of the terms and returns it to the lawyer. Written contracts are sometimes used, particularly with institutional clients. Regardless of which method is used, it should be sufficiently detailed to cover all aspects of the relationship. Unfortunately, disputes between lawyers and clients are common, but they can largely be avoided by making sure that the agreement is drafted in clear and simple English, covers all likely issues, and specifies what is not covered. In disputes between lawyers and their clients, ambiguities and omissions in attorney-client agreements will usually be strictly construed against the lawyer.[5] The agreement should cover the following basic subjects.

1.   Work covered

The agreement should specify what work will be performed and what will not be. For example, the agreement might be to prosecute a negligence claim arising out of a car accident through settlement or trial. If you will not handle any appeal or post-judgment proceedings to collect a judgment, or if there will be an additional charge for any such work, the agreement should specify this. If you will not handle a workers' compensation claim, insurance claim, or other related matters, the agreement should say so. In general, you must guard against a client thinking that you would do more than you agreed to do. Spelling out what is not covered should prevent this from happening. It is also a good idea, especially as the plaintiff in personal injury cases, to state explicitly that you have not guaranteed any particular outcome.

2.   Who will do the work

The agreement should specify who will do the work, unless the lawyer is a solo practitioner or it is clear that the entire law firm will collectively do the work. Clients usually think that they are hiring a particular lawyer to do all the necessary work on their problem. Clients today will not tolerate a bill that shows several other lawyers in a firm working on their problem, when they have never met these lawyers and were never told they would be involved. Consequently, particularly when the client is sophisticated and the matter complex, the agreement should specify who the supervising lawyer will be and how the matter will be staffed with other lawyers, paralegals, and support staff.

---

5. See R. Rossi, Attorney's Fees (2d ed. 1995).

3. Lawyer's fee[6]

A lawyer's fee is the compensation the lawyer will receive for professional services rendered on behalf of the client. The amount of the lawyer's fee, the way it will be determined, and when it will be paid must be spelled out. The total fee must be reasonable in light of the work to be done, the difficulty of the work, the amount of time it will involve, and the customary range of fees for similar work in your locality.

The agreement should specify how the fee will be determined. Three approaches are commonly employed: an hourly rate (common in corporate, commercial, and insurance defense cases), a fixed flat fee (common in criminal defense and family law cases), and the contingency fee (common in plaintiff's personal injury cases). Obviously the agreement can specify any number of combinations or modifications of these basic approaches, unless the fee is regulated or set by rule or statute. For example, agreements frequently specify a minimum retainer fee, paid up front, that is credited against an hourly billing rate. The agreement might use more recent approaches such as capped fees, or incentive billing and defense contingency fees, which base the fee in part on obtaining favorable results. When the fee is based on an hourly rate, the client must understand that what is being paid for is the lawyer's expertise and time. Hence, any time expended on a client's case will be billed to the client, regardless of whether the time is spent on court appearances, conferences, research, on drafting documents, or on making telephone calls.

The agreement should define how the fee amount is determined and when it should be paid. For instance, in personal injury cases where the plaintiff's attorney's fees are usually a percentage of any recovery, the agreement must specify whether the percentage is computed before or after expenses are deducted and that the fee is due when any judgment is actually collected. If the fee is on an hourly basis, it's a good idea to estimate the fee range, since a common misunderstanding with clients is what the total fee is likely to be.

If a fee will be shared with another lawyer outside the principal lawyer's firm, you must disclose this fact to the client and obtain his consent. The division of fees must be proportionate to the work done by each lawyer, or each lawyer assumes joint responsibility for the representation and the client agrees in writing.[7]

A lawyer has an ethical duty to make the fee reasonable. This may mean that the lawyer must review the fee, even in a contingent fee situation, to make sure it is in fact reasonable before submitting it to or collecting it from the client.[8]

Many statutes and rules regulate and limit attorney's fees. For example, statutory causes of action frequently either limit attorney's fees or

6. See Model Code of Professional Responsibility, Rule 2-106; Model Rules of Professional Conduct, Rule 1.5.

7. See Code of Professional Responsibility, Rule 2-107; Model Rules of Professional Conduct, Rule 1.5(e).

8. See, e.g., In the Matter of Schwartz, 686 P.2d 1236 (Ariz. 1984).

make them subject to court approval.[9] Make sure that your agreement complies with any applicable statutes and rules.

An attorney's lien, the right of a lawyer to hold or retain money or property until all proper charges have been paid or adjusted, can usually be imposed on a judgment to ensure payment of the fee. This is frequently done in contingent fee situations. In some jurisdictions an attorney's lien is only enforceable if the client expressly agrees to it. Hence, it is good practice to discuss the lien with the client and have the written agreement state that the client agrees to it.

4. Retainers

In some situations a lawyer should insist on a retainer to ensure payment of the fee and other costs. A retainer is simply a cash payment of a sum of money to the lawyer before work begins on the client's case. This makes sure that the lawyer will get paid for the work and that costs the lawyer advances will be reimbursed. A common arrangement is to insist on a retainer, and then periodically deduct fees and costs as they are incurred. Regardless of the precise arrangement, the agreement must specify the amount of the retainer, when it must be remitted, and what fees and costs will be deducted from it.

Whenever a lawyer receives advanced funds from a client, the funds must be put in a separate client trust account. Under no circumstances can any client's funds be commingled with the lawyer's funds.[10] Funds of all of a lawyer's clients can be held in one trust account; however, a separate ledger must be kept for each client showing receipts and disbursements. Most states have adopted, through statutes or court rules, the Interest on Lawyer's Trust Accounts (IOLTA) system, which requires holding client funds in interest-bearing accounts.[11]

5. Costs

The agreement should distinguish between fees due the lawyer for professional representation and the costs and expenses incurred during the course of that representation. The agreement should note anticipated costs, such as filing fees and other court costs; expert witness fees and expenses; court reporter fees; travel expenses; photocopying, mailing, and long distance calls. It is sometimes a good idea to estimate the usual costs for the type of case involved. In some cases, such as commercial, medical malpractice, and products liability cases, the costs of paralegals, experts,

9. See, e.g., Federal Tort Claims Act, 28 U.S.C. §2678; M. F. Derfner & A. D. Wolfe Court Awarded Attorney Fees (1983).
10. See Model Code of Professional Responsibility, Rule 9-102; Model Rules of Professional Conduct, Rule 1.15.
11. The Supreme Court, in Phillips v. Washington Legal Foundation, —U.S.— (1998), did not decide the questions of whether the IOLTA system is an unconstitutional Fifth Amendment "taking" of the interest earned on pooled client funds, and, if so, whether compensation was required. The Court, in a 5-4 decision, remanded those issues.

travel, and other expenses can exceed the lawyer's fee. The agreement should also specify when the costs will be paid; customarily the client is billed at regular intervals, such as monthly or quarterly. The agreement should make clear that costs are the client's obligation, even if no recovery is obtained.

Plaintiff's personal injury cases present a special situation. The reason for permitting a contingency fee arrangement—that the client is otherwise unable to pay for legal representation—also bears on the propriety of advancing costs. A lawyer may advance costs, such as court costs, deposition expenses, investigator fees, and expert witness fees; however, the client ultimately is still responsible for paying those costs. The most common approach is to reimburse costs to the lawyer when a judgment is actually paid. If there is no recovery, the client is still responsible for paying the costs, although a client without money will probably not be able to reimburse the lawyer. For this reason, some lawyers accept contingency fee arrangements for cases that will have substantial costs only if the client advances a sum of money sufficient to cover the expected costs. Requiring a client to advance expected costs has another benefit: It tends to weed out weak cases. A prospective client who knows his case is weak often will refuse to advance costs for an expert review before filing suit or will refuse to pay a retainer. Clients who, though able, refuse to invest in their lawsuits are often clients to avoid.

6. Billings

The agreement should specify when fees and costs will be billed. While monthly billing is normally best for both lawyer and client, less frequent billings are sometimes appropriate, particularly for regular business clients, or if little work is done in any given month.

If the client is new, or has a spotty payment history, consider advising the client of your intent to stop work on the case if your bills are not paid and charging interest on late payments. You should also obtain the client's consent to withdraw in the event of non-payment, regardless of the status of the case.

7. Authorization to file suit and withdraw

The agreement should contain a statement that authorizes the lawyer to file suit on behalf of the client or, if a defendant, authorizes the lawyer to defend the suit. The client should also be told that you have a right to withdraw from the case in case of non-payment of fees, or if later developments show that the matter has no merit.[12]

The terms of the agreement should then be put in writing, either in a letter to the client or in a written agreement. If a contingency fee agree-

---

12. See Model Code of Professional Responsibility, Rule 2-110(C); Model Rules of Professional Conduct, Rule 1.16(b).

ment, it must be in writing. As with any legal document, it should be written in plain English, not legalese.

Example (hourly fee agreement letter):

Dear Mr. Jones:

As we discussed in my office yesterday, I have agreed to represent you in the divorce proceedings recently started by your wife Joan. I will handle all negotiations necessary to attempt a property settlement before trial. If a trial becomes necessary, I will represent you to the conclusion of the trial and until the court enters a final divorce decree.

Fees for representing you will be based on the time expended on your case. My present hourly rate is $100 per hour. You have agreed to provide a retainer of $1,500 within one week. Based on what you have told me, I estimate the fee in your matter will be in the $3,000 to $5,000 range, although circumstances may change this estimate. The total fee will depend on the particular facts and circumstances of your situation and the time necessary to represent you to the conclusion of your divorce.

In addition to my fee, there will also be certain costs expended on your case, such as court filing fees, court reporter fees, long distance telephone and photocopying charges. You will be responsible for paying all such costs. Costs in divorce cases vary but usually fall in the $200 to $400 range.

I will send you an itemized statement each month showing the time I have spent on your case and the other costs that have been incurred. I will subtract each monthly statement from the $1,500 retainer until it has been used up. I will then bill you directly, and you have agreed to pay those monthly statements in full when you receive them. In the event that my bills are not paid promptly, you agree that I may withdraw from representing you in this matter.

Please confirm that this letter correctly reflects the terms of our agreement by signing and dating the enclosed copy of this letter on the spaces provided and returning the copy to me. If any of this is unclear, or you have other questions about this agreement, please call me as soon as possible.

Upon receipt of the signed letter and a check for the $1,500 retainer, I will begin to represent you and work on your case. If I do not receive the signed letter and check within ten days, I will assume that you have decided to retain another lawyer to represent you in this matter.

Sincerely,

/s/ *John Smith*

Agreed: _____

John Jones

Dated: _____

Example (contingency fee agreement):

AGREEMENT

Date: _____

I agree to employ the law firm of Smith & Smith, P.C., as my attorneys to prosecute all claims for damages against Frank Johnson and all other persons or entities that may be liable on account of an automobile collision that occurred on June 1, 1998, at approximately 3:00 P.M., near the intersection of Maple and Elm Streets in this city. I authorize you to file suit on my behalf.

I agree to pay Smith & Smith, P.C., a fee that will be one-third (33⅓ percent) of any sum recovered in this case, regardless of whether received through a settlement, lawsuit, or any other way. The fee will be calculated on the sum recovered, after costs and expenses have been deducted. The fee will be paid when any moneys are actually received in this case. I agree that Smith & Smith, P.C., has an express attorney's lien on any recovery to ensure that their fee is paid. I agree that no representations or guarantees of a recovery, or amount of any recovery, have been made.

I agree to pay all necessary costs and expenses, such as court filing fees, court reporter fees, expert witness fees and expenses, travel expenses, long distance telephone costs, and photocopying charges, but these costs and expenses will not be due until a recovery is actually received in this case. I understand that I am also responsible for paying these costs and expenses, even if no recovery is received.

I agree that this agreement does *not* cover matters other than those described above. It does not cover an appeal from any judgment entered, any efforts necessary to collect money due because of a judgment entered, or any efforts necessary to obtain other benefits such as insurance, employment, Social Security and Veteran's Administration benefits.

If in the opinion of Smith & Smith, P.C., the claims no longer appear to have merit, or a change in circumstances occurs, Smith & Smith, P.C., has the right to cancel this agreement and withdraw from representing me.

Agreed: _____
        John Jones

I agree to represent John Jones in the matter described above. I will receive no fee unless a recovery is obtained. If a recovery is actually received, I will receive a fee as described above.

I agree to notify John Jones of all developments in this matter promptly, and will make no settlement of this matter without his consent.

Agreed: _____
        John Smith for
        Smith & Smith, P.C.

8. Next steps

Once you have decided to take the case and have reached an agreement with the client, there are several steps you should take to get the new relationship started on the right track and make sure that it stays on that track. First, if your agreement includes an express attorney's lien, send a notice of your attorney's lien to the opposing party's lawyer and any insurance companies. Some jurisdictions have standard attorney's lien forms used in litigation. Sending out the notices will ensure that your fee is paid when any judgment is paid.

Second, you should have the client sign authorization forms that will allow you to obtain certain records before filing suit. Depending on your jurisdiction's laws and practice, you may need signed authorizations to get police reports and motor vehicle records; hospital, doctor, employment, and insurance records; Social Security, Veterans Administration, and other governmental records. Find out what type of authorization is necessary, and become familiar with the statutes requiring that such documents be made available to the client or his lawyer on request. You can also call the particular agency to learn its requirements and procedures. Some agencies have standard authorization forms.

Third, your client needs advice on what he should and should not do. He should be told not to talk to anyone other than you about the matter. Explain that persons may try to interview him or get him to make or sign statements. He should tell such persons that he is represented by a lawyer and cannot talk to them, and he should notify you of all such attempts. Explain that he is generally not required to talk to anyone unless required through the formal discovery process; he should direct all requests for information to you. He should not sign anything without first discussing it with you. Other persons may try to give him money. He should refuse any such attempts, and report them to you. He should be told to save and collect all relevant records, documents, bills, checks, and paperwork of any kind in his possession and deliver them to you; he should send records and documents that subsequently come into his possession to you as well.

Fourth, your client needs a blueprint for the future, since he may have little idea how civil litigation is actually conducted. He should be told what needs to be done before suit is filed, what happens during the pleadings, discovery, and motion practice stages of the litigation process, and what his role in this process will be. He should have some idea of how much time each of these stages takes and how far in the future any trial is likely to be; at the same time he should be aware that most cases are settled before trial. He also needs to be reminded of the risks and costs of any lawsuit, including the risk of an adverse verdict after trial. A well-informed client will understand the process he is a part of and will be likely to assist you throughout. Many lawyers use a follow-up letter or brochure that repeats this advice and contains a chronology of likely events. This is a sound practice that can easily be tailored to your litigation practice.

This is a good time, particularly for the defense side, to have a serious talk with the client who likely will, and probably ought to, lose. Such a client needs a dose of reality early, before he develops an unrealistic set of expectations about what you can do and about how the case will probably turn out. Such a client needs to be told clearly and regularly what you can do, as well as what you cannot do, to defend the case. It is difficult enough defending a weak case; a difficult client, with unrealistic hopes and expectations about litigation, only compounds the problems.

Finally, maintain communication with your client. Litigation goes in spurts; a period of activity is often followed by weeks, even months, of inactivity. If your client has not heard from you recently, he may erroneously conclude that you don't care about him or have lost interest in his case. Accordingly, make sure you maintain contact. Send him copies of all pleadings, discovery, motions, and other court papers, as well as copies of correspondence. Write him periodically to let him know what is going on in the case. If nothing is happening, let him know and explain why. A well-informed client will usually be a cooperative, satisfied client.

§4.4. Declining representation

A lawyer may not always be able to take a case. The matter may not be within the lawyer's expertise. It may not have merit or be large enough to justify a suit, or the defendant may not be able to pay a judgment. The lawyer may be too busy or have a conflict of interest. Or the lawyer may be unable to agree with the client on a fee. Whatever the reason, when a lawyer declines a potential case, it should be put in writing, usually in a letter to the prospective client.

Where a lawyer represents one party but cannot represent a related party because of a potential conflict of interest, the related party, who may be expecting representation, should be sent a letter in which the lawyer declines employment. Also, if an attorney withdraws from representing a client, an appropriate letter should be sent. It is important to make a decision and send the notification promptly, since a person's rights may be affected by any delay.

The letter declining the case ensures that the party clearly understands that you will not be representing her, and can help resolve any question about whether the attorney had a duty to protect the party's interests even though she was never a client.[13] If you decide not to represent a party, you nevertheless have an obligation to warn her if a statute of limitations or other notice statute may run shortly, so that she can get another lawyer in time.[14]

13. See J. M. Smith and R. E. Mallen, Preventing Legal Malpractice 4-5 (2d ed. 1996).
14. See, e.g., Togstad v. Vesely, 291 N.W.2d 686 (Minn. 1980).

Example (letter):

Dear Mr. Jones:

As we discussed in my office yesterday, I will not be able to represent you for any claims you may have based on an automobile collision that occurred near the intersection of Maple and Elm Streets in this city on June 1, 1998, at approximately 3:00 P.M.

Since I cannot take your case, you may wish to see another lawyer about handling this matter for you. As we discussed yesterday, if you wish to have another lawyer represent you, you should do so promptly. If you do not, there may be legal problems, such as a statute of limitations bar, that might prevent you from pursuing your claims. Since your accident happened on June 1, 1998, and the statute of limitations for tort claims in this state is two years, if you wish to file a lawsuit you must do so *before* June 1, 2000. To avoid such problems, I recommend that you find another lawyer promptly, so any rights you have can be protected.

Enclosed are the originals of the police reports and insurance claim forms you brought to my office.

Sincerely yours,

/s/ *John Smith*

Make sure that the statute of limitations computation is correct and, if there is a shorter statutory or contractual notice requirement which applies, that this is stated and computed correctly as well. If you are not sure of the computation period, do not state the date, since an incorrect statement could subject you to liability.

The letter should be sent by registered mail, return receipt by addressee only requested. When you get the signed return receipt, staple it to the copy of your letter. This will be persuasive evidence to rebut any later claim that you never actually declined the case.

§4.5. *Planning the litigation*

Assume you have accumulated the facts available through informal discovery; researched the possible legal claims, remedies, defenses, and counterclaims; put them on your litigation chart; researched other procedural questions; reached an agreement with the client to represent him; and have no timing problems. Now is the time, before filing your initial pleading, to structure a litigation plan.

A litigation plan consists of defining the client's objectives and developing a strategy to achieve those objectives. Once you develop a strategy in broad terms, you can then divide the strategy into its component, chronological parts.

Even if you think a litigation plan can't be developed, your client will think it can, and he's right. Sophisticated commercial clients, such as insurance companies and corporations, usually require a litigation plan before authorizing a lawsuit or, if a defendant, after receiving the complaint. The litigation plan requirements usually include an explanation of what claims, remedies, or defenses you will raise; a description of the basic facts, including the anticipated factual issues; an explanation of the planned discovery; a description of anticipated legal issues; an assessment of settlement possibilities; an assessment of the likely trial outcome; and cost projections for each stage of the plan. If sophisticated users of legal services have found that a detailed litigation plan promotes cost-effective representation, doesn't it make sense to make such a plan in every kind of case?

After you have completed your informal investigation, the basic steps in developing a litigation plan are the following:

1. Reevaluate the client's objectives, priorities, and cost constraints
2. Define the client's litigation objectives
3. Develop a "theory of the case"
4. Plan the pleadings
5. Plan the discovery
6. Plan the dispositive motions
7. Plan the settlement approach
8. Develop a litigation timetable

1. Reevaluate the client's objectives, priorities, and cost constraints

When the client first came to you for legal advice, he had one or more "problems" he told you about. One of your first steps was to identify his legal problems and objectives, and develop a scale of priorities for those objectives. Now is the time to reassess those problems and objectives. You will have the benefit of your partially completed litigation chart showing the fruits of your research and informal fact investigation. You will also know the client's cost constraints. Finally, time has passed. All of these may influence what the client's current objectives and priorities are. You need to sit down with the client, review what you have done to date, determine if the client's thinking is the same or has changed, and analyze those objectives and priorities to see if they still make sense in light of what you now know about the case.[15]

2. Define the client's litigation objectives

If the client's thinking is unchanged and the dispute cannot be resolved short of litigation, you next need to decide on broad litigation objectives that serve the client's overall objectives and priorities. Always remember that the client controls the objectives of the litigation, and the lawyer de-

---

15. Model Rules of Professional Conduct, Rule 1.2(a), provides that the client decides the objectives of the representation, subject to certain limitations.

cides on the means to achieve those objectives. For example, suppose that your plaintiff-client wants to settle early in the case and to keep expenses at a minimum. Your strategy may be to keep the pleadings simple, to push for focused discovery, and then to start early settlement discussions. On the other hand, suppose that you anticipate that a trial will be necessary. Your strategy may be to use broad pleadings with alternative theories of recovery, to engage in extensive discovery, and to prepare thoroughly for trial. Your litigation objectives will then form the basis for the remainder of your litigation plan.

3. Develop a "theory of the case"

Your side's "story" is a critical part of the litigation plan. You need to review what you presently know about the uncontested and contested facts, and ask some basic questions. Is your side's story complete or are there significant missing pieces? Are your witnesses reliable? Do their stories make sense? Is your side's story one that has jury appeal? Where does your side's version and the other side's version of the facts clash? How do you plan to win the credibility battle over the disputed facts?

Trial lawyers frequently call their side's position the "theory of the case."[16] Those with experience know that most trials are won on the facts, not the law. The winning side usually organizes credible witnesses and exhibits into a believable story, and wins the war over the disputed facts by presenting more persuasive evidence on its side of the dispute. This will only happen if you take the time to develop a coherent, persuasive theory of the case before drafting the pleadings.

4. Plan the pleadings and jury demand

Pleadings are the vehicle by which you bring your theory of the case to court. Seen this way, you will not make the mistake of (and violate Rule 11 by) raising a number of allegations in your pleadings and then wondering how you can find facts that fit into the theories of recovery.

What claims, remedies, or defenses should you assert? Inexperienced litigators often "throw the book at them" and plead every conceivable claim, remedy, or defense that meets Rule 11 requirements. This illusion of safety can come at a high price. By adding claims, a case becomes more complex, with its additional costs and time requirements. Adding claims frequently results in adding parties, again making the litigation more involved. Adding claims also broadens the scope of discovery with the danger that discovery, always expensive and time consuming, may escalate out of control. While you must protect the client's legal interests by advanc-

---

16. See T. Mauet, Trial Techniques §10.6 (4th ed. 1996). See also D. Binder & P. Bergman, Fact Investigation: From Hypothesis to Proof ch. 9 (1984); J. McElhaney, "The Theory of the Case," in Trial Notebook (3d ed. 1994).

ing essential claims, you should also consider the costs and disadvantages of pursuing every supportable claim against every proper party.

The better approach is to begin with your theory of the case. What claims, remedies, or defenses are reasonably supported by the facts that you have obtained through informal discovery or that you reasonably can expect to support with the fruits of formal discovery? Beyond that, do you have a realistic ability to prevail on each legal theory?

Once you have determined which legal theories can be supported, it's time to decide which ones to raise in a pleading. You again need to reflect on your overall litigation objectives. For example, if an objective is to hold down litigation costs, it may make little sense to raise numerous legal theories. Simplicity in the pleadings will better serve your objective.

What do your proposed pleadings do to your discovery plan? The more complex the pleadings, the more expansive and expensive the permissible discovery. The scope of the pleadings controls the scope of discovery, and often its costs, because anything relevant, that is not privileged, is discoverable; so the more things that are raised by the pleadings, the greater the areas that are now relevant for discovery purposes. There is little point in pleading a variety of legal theories, just to be "safe," only to have the litigation get out of control. For example, consider a plaintiff who wishes to bring a negligence claim against a trucking company because of a vehicle collision. The plaintiff is considering whether to plead a claim for punitive damages. Doing so, however, will greatly expand the relevant scope of discovery, since the defendant's financial and safety history will now be discoverable. If the likelihood of getting punitive damages is small, does it really make sense to push such a claim? You may well be undertaking substantial additional work without a corresponding benefit to your client. On the other hand, plaintiffs frequently want broad discovery, at least compared to defendants. By adding peripheral parties, consistent with Rule 11 requirements, you make discovery easier, since discovery can be more broadly applied to parties than nonparties.

When you have decided which of the possible legal theories to raise in the initial pleading, you will still need to consider the related legal issues. The plaintiff must appreciate how the choice of claims will affect such issues as the choice of parties that must be brought into the suit, whether subject matter jurisdiction exists for each claim, whether personal jurisdiction exists for each defendant, where venue is proper and, if more than one venue, where the best place to file suit is. These questions are all interrelated, and substantial legal research will be necessary when the issues are complex. The time to research is now, not when you are suddenly faced with a motion to dismiss for lack of subject matter jurisdiction or for failure to join an indispensible party.

A plaintiff must always balance the pros and cons of adding additional parties as defendants. This is particularly true when the potential additional party is an employee of a named defendant. The typical situation arises when a plaintiff, suing a trucking company or other commercial entity, must decide whether to name the company's driver as an additional defendant. The advantages are that discovery is easier if an employee is a named defendant and an employee is usually happy to testify to agency and scope of employment issues favorable to the plaintiff. The disadvantages are that the case becomes more complex, with more parties, sometimes more lawyers, and more work, and that the idea of driving a wedge between the driver and company will usually fail because both will probably be represented by the same lawyer (unless a conflict arises). In many cases, there is no point in naming the driver as an additional defendant, particularly where employment and scope of employment are not in dispute, although plaintiffs sometimes name the driver as an additional defendant to obtain discovery advantages, then dismiss the driver as a named party before trial. On the other hand, if there is an issue as to whether the driver is an employee or an independent contractor, or was acting outside the scope of his employ, the driver must be named as a defendant.

Finally, decide if you want a jury trial.[17] If so, a jury demand must be made with a party's first pleading, either the complaint or answer, or else under federal practice the right to a jury trial will be deemed waived. No hard and fast rules exist. Decisions must be made on a case-by-case basis, in consultation with the client. On the plus side, cases that have emotionally compelling witnesses and stories, where the client is sympathetic or the underdog, where the jury will want to do what's fair despite the law, and where the jury pool is favorable for your side, should be tried to a jury. On the other hand, not requesting a jury should always be considered. A bench trial will usually be cheaper, faster, simpler, often get an earlier trial date, and be preferable if your side involves dry, technical evidence and has a client and witnesses with little jury appeal.

5. Plan the discovery

The discovery stage is usually the largest part of the litigation process, the one that consumes the most time and money. Hence, it is particularly important to plan discovery to serve your client's overall objectives and cost considerations. Without planning, discovery usually becomes unfocused and expensive—two disasters you should avoid.

Planning discovery is essentially a seven-step process:

1. What facts do I need to establish a winning case on my claims (or to defeat the opponent's claims)?
2. What facts have I already obtained through informal fact investigation?
3. What "missing" facts do I still need to obtain through formal discovery?

The answers to the above questions should already be established on your litigation chart. You must consider four other questions:

---

17. See T. Mauet, Trial Techniques, §2.2 (4th ed. 1996); P. Taskier, Judge or Jury?, 24 Litigation (No. 1, Fall 1997).

4. What discovery methods are the most effective for obtaining the missing facts?
5. What facts and witnesses, that you already know through informal investigation, do you need to "pin down" by using formal discovery methods?
6. What restrictions does your litigation budget place on your discovery plan?
7. Finally, in what order should you execute your discovery plan?

These questions obviously require some time to think through. When you have decided on what discovery methods to use for particular information, exhibits, and witnesses, put them on your litigation chart and your litigation timetable.[18]

6. Plan the dispositive motions

What dispositive motions, such as summary judgment, should you plan? Will your planned discovery provide the basis for succeeding on those motions? On the other hand, if the other side will be making the motions, what discovery have you planned that will defeat them? The motions stage of the litigation process will only be successful if you have coordinated your discovery with your motions plan. This means that you must look down the road before filing the pleadings to see what motions will be realistic, and use discovery to obtain the facts necessary to prevail when the motions are later made.

7. Plan the settlement approach

Your sense of when to discuss the possibility of settlement with the opposing party must be part of your overall litigation plan. When the client's objective is to settle quickly and keep costs down, you might consider discussing settlement early, such as before filing suit, after the pleadings have been closed or after a critical witness has been deposed. Otherwise, you will probably want to consider settlement after discovery is closed, after dispositive motions have been ruled on, or when you are preparing for the final pretrial conference. At these later stages you will have a better grasp of the case's strengths and weaknesses, but you will have incurred substantial litigation expenses.

8. Develop a litigation timetable

After developing and coordinating each of the preceding steps in your litigation plan, you should draw up a realistic timetable. For this you need to consider the case's complexity, the likely responses of the opposing

18. This process is discussed in detail in §§6.3 and 6.4.

party, and the usual time between the filing of a complaint and trial date in the jurisdiction where the case is brought. You can then put the steps into a chronological sequence, and include them on your master calendar to remind yourself of the due date for each step in this particular case. Keep in mind that the court under Rule 16(b) will usually enter a scheduling order that will control that timetable.

The master calendar for this case, and all other open cases, becomes the firm's docket control system. Although a few lawyers still use a paper calendar system, nearly all firms today use docket-control software. The software system contains each date for each case in which some activity is scheduled or planned, such as court hearings, depositions, trial dates, and filing deadlines. It also contains reminders that important deadlines are approaching, such as the due date for serving interrogatory answers or expert witness reports. The system generates a daily schedule of events for all open cases, noting the time, location, and assigned lawyer for each scheduled event. For example, the daily activity printout would show that Smith v. Jones, Case No. 98 C 4332, office file number 98-121, assigned to John Burns, has a deposition of the defendant scheduled in Burns' office at 2:00 P.M. When court, deposition, or other dates change, it is your responsibility to make sure that the docket system reflects the changes. Keep in mind that such a system is only as good as the information with which it is provided. Such a docket control system is also essential for conflicts of interest checks, quality control, and malpractice prevention.

The planning of litigation must be an integrated, creative, flexible, continuing process. The plan needs to be integrated because each step should be tailored to achieving your client's litigation objectives while keeping in mind that each step influences the other steps. It should be creative because every case is different and must be planned out to account for the conditions of the particular case, rather than plugging the conditions into a standard formula. Finally, it must be flexible and continuing because developments invariably occur during the litigation process that require changes in your plan.

§4.6. *Example of litigation planning:* Novelty Products, Inc. v. Gift Ideas, Inc.

The following example illustrates the thought process that is involved in each step of a coordinated litigation plan.

Facts

Novelty Products, Inc. ("Novelty") is a corporation that manufactures novelty items that are sold to gift shops throughout the United States. Its corporate headquarters and manufacturing plant are in Buffalo, New York. Gift Ideas, Inc. ("Gift") is a corporation that owns a chain of gift shops located throughout California. Its corporate headquarters is in Los Angeles.

Over the past five years Gift has periodically ordered products from Novelty under an established procedure. Gift's purchasing department places orders over the telephone, and Novelty sends a written confirmation of the order before delivering it. Gift then pays for each shipment within thirty days of receipt.

One of the items Gift has ordered from Novelty during that time is a patented tabletop electric cigarette lighter called the "Magic Lite." Gift has ordered the lighter, in increasingly large shipments, approximately every six months. The lighter now accounts for about half of all sales from Novelty to Gift. The latest lighter order, for $80,000, was made the usual way, and was shipped last month.

A few days ago Gift notified Novelty that the latest shipment of lighters would be returned unpaid. Gift has just decided to make and market a tabletop electric cigarette lighter itself, and from now on its shops will only carry its own lighter. The Gift lighter, called the "Magic Flame," is almost identical in appearance and design to the Novelty lighter. A few months ago Novelty's design chief left the company and began working for Gift.

The shipment of lighters has been returned to Novelty, but Novelty has been unable to find another buyer for the lighters. Since Novelty will soon be marketing an improved version of the lighter, finding a buyer seems unlikely.

The president of Novelty now comes to you for help.

Assume you have researched potential claims against Gift, determined the elements of those claims, identified the sources of proof, and completed an informal fact investigation. You have interviewed your client and appropriate employees, and have reviewed your client's records and correspondence along with what you could obtain from other nonparty sources. At this time your litigation chart (for the contract claim) appears as follows:

LITIGATION CHART

Elements of Claims	Sources of Proof	Informal Fact Investigation	Formal Discovery
1. Contract			
(a) contract executed	pl.'s records pl.'s witnesses def.'s records def.'s witnesses	obtained from client interviews	request to produce depositions, interrogatories, request to admit

(b) pl.'s performance	pl.'s records pl.'s witnesses def.'s records def.'s witnesses	obtained from client interviews	request to produce depositions, interrogatories, request to admit
(c) def.'s breach (nonpayment & return of goods)	pl.'s records pl.'s witnesses def.'s records def.'s witnesses shippers	obtained from client interviews	request to produce depositions, request to admit subpoenas
(d) pl.'s damages	pl.'s records pl.'s witnesses 3d parties who rejected lighters	obtained from client interviews interviews	subpoenas

If your district follows Rule 26(a), the required initial disclosures and expert disclosures should be added to the formal discovery section of your litigation chart.

The litigation chart would be continued for every other potential claim you have been considering. In Novelty's case, these would include:

2. Bad faith
3. Theft of trade secret
4. Trademark infringement
5. Patent infringement
6. Unfair competition

Now is the time to develop the litigation plan. The steps are:

1. Reevaluate the client's objectives, priorities, and cost constraints
2. Define the client's litigation objectives
3. Develop a "theory of the case"
4. Plan the pleadings
5. Plan the discovery
6. Plan the dispositive motions
7. Plan the settlement approach
8. Develop a litigation timetable

1. Reevaluate the client's objectives, priorities, and cost constraints

From your interviews with Novelty's president, the company's objectives have become clear: Novelty wants to be paid the $80,000 due under the contract, yet it also wants to maintain its other ongoing business with Gift. It wants to accomplish these dual objectives quickly at a minimum cost. After your demand that Gift pay the contract amount has been rejected, Novelty's president agrees that litigation will be necessary. The president still hopes that litigation, if kept simple, will not destroy Novelty's ongoing business relationship with Gift. These client objectives remain unchanged.

2. Define the client's litigation objectives

Since Novelty's president has authorized litigation, you need to decide on the basic litigation objectives and then get the client's approval. In this case Novelty has three possible approaches: it can keep the case simple and bring only a contract claim against Gift; it can bring the former design chief in as a defendant by alleging theft of a trade secret; or it can expand the case against Gift by alleging bad faith, copyright, trademark, and unfair competition claims. Which one of these litigation objectives will best serve Novelty's overall objectives?

You first recommend not pursuing a case against the former design chief, since he was not under contract with Novelty, and you have no proof that he helped Gift design its new lighter. Pressing a theft-of-trade-secrets claim against him has Rule 11 problems and runs counter to the client's preference for handling the case simply, quickly, and cheaply.

You next recommend not pursuing the complex case involving the patent, trademark, and unfair competition claims. You have doubts that Novelty will prevail on these claims on both legal and factual grounds. In addition, such claims would undoubtedly destroy the continuing business dealings between Novelty and Gift, which remain important to Novelty. The claims would also create lengthy, expensive, and publicity-generating litigation, all things Novelty needs to avoid. Novelty could always decide to bring a separate suit on these claims if circumstances require it, since joinder of claims is always permissive and there are no statute of limitations that are about to run.

This leaves the basic contract claim against Gift, based on common law and the UCC sales provisions. The advantages of taking this approach are that you have an excellent chance of winning on the merits, and the case can be handled relatively quickly and inexpensively. The disadvantages are that damages may be low since a party has a duty to mitigate damages. However, to date Novelty has been unable to resell the returned lighters, so damages near the contract price may be appropriate. You also consider adding a bad faith claim, which, if permitted under the applicable jurisdiction's substantive tort law, might permit compensatory or punitive damages. Your thinking is that Gift is more likely to settle the case for the contract price when faced with a bad faith claim. However, your research of current bad faith law, under both New York and California law, reveals that such a claim probably cannot be brought in a contract case under your facts. Bringing such a claim probably would violate Rule 11 and destroy Novelty's hopes of preserving its business relationship with Gift.

You then develop a litigation budget for the proposed contract claim against Gift. You project the following amounts of time will be necessary:

Fact and legal investigation	15 hrs.
Pleadings	5 hrs.
Discovery	50 hrs.
Motions	15 hrs.
Pretrial conference	15 hrs.
Trial and trial preparation	50 hrs.

The total projected time remaining, without a trial, is about 100 hours; with a trial, the total time will be about 150 hours. Your hourly rate is presently $100. Accordingly, the legal fee to the client for resolving the dispute through a trial should be around $15,000. Since the case will not require experts, and the only significant costs will be deposition expenses, litigation costs should be in the $2,000 to $3,000 range. Since you feel the contract claim is strong and that under the circumstances getting $80,000 in damages is realistic, bringing the case — and trying it if necessary — still makes economic sense to the client. This holds even though Novelty will have to bear its own legal expenses, based on your research finding that no applicable law permits the recovery of attorney's fees in this situation.

You meet with Novelty's president and present the above analysis and litigation budget to him. He agrees with it, and authorizes you to file suit against Gift on the contract claim. He again reminds you of his wish to settle quickly if possible and to keep the tone of the litigation as a simple dispute between two businesses over which one will bear the loss for an improperly canceled order.

3. Develop a "theory of the case"

Before dealing with the pleadings, you need to consider what Novelty's theory of the case should be. You decide to portray Novelty as a small company that had ongoing business dealings with Gift, a larger corporate chain. The specific transaction was a routine one where Gift made an oral order and Novelty sent a confirming letter, shipped the lighters, and sent a bill. Gift refused to pay for the lighters, but had no valid reason to do so. Gift simply changed its mind after agreeing to buy because it was going to market its own lighter. When the lighters were returned, Novelty could not resell them because it was preparing to market an improved version of the original lighter. In short, according to your theory, Gift welshed on the deal, and therefore owes Novelty the full $80,000. You feel that this theory will both be simple and have jury appeal.

4. Plan the pleadings

So far, you have decided to bring a contract action against Gift; however, many important questions must still be answered. First, what substantive law will apply? Novelty, the plaintiff, is in Buffalo, New York; Gift is based in Los Angeles, California. The offer was made from Los Angeles and accepted in Buffalo. Since the contract was completed in New York and the place of contracting under the standard interests analysis usually controls the choice of the applicable substantive law, New York law will probably be applied, regardless of whether the action is filed in New York or California. Filing the action in New York will also help, since it is the plaintiff's home state.

Since you have decided to sue only Gift, proper parties are not a concern. However, if you file in federal district court, will the court have subject matter jurisdiction over the claims? In this case, jurisdiction can properly be based on the court's diversity jurisdiction under 28 U.S.C. §1332; since the plaintiff is a citizen of New York and the defendant is a citizen of California, complete diversity exists, and the claim is in excess of the required jurisdictional amount of $75,000.

Can you get personal jurisdiction over Gift? If suit is filed in California, service of process on Gift will be easy, since Gift's corporate headquarters is in Los Angeles. If suit is filed in New York, can Gift be forced to defend a lawsuit there and can Gift be properly served with process? Your research indicates that Gift's dealings with Novelty are adequate "minimum contracts" such that Gift can be required to defend in New York. Moreover, since provisions of Rule 4 of the Federal Rule of Civil Procedure allow for service under the forum state's long-arm statute, you should be able to properly serve Gift if suit is filed in New York.

Finally, where is venue proper? Under 28 U.S.C. §1391, New York (the Western District) is a proper place to bring suit. Since the Western District of New York has such obvious advantages to Novelty, suit, if brought in federal court, should be brought there.

The other possibility, of course, is to file the complaint in state court. New York (Buffalo) is the obvious choice, and you should be able to serve Gift under the state long-arm statute. However, because the federal court will get the case to trial sooner, and because federal judges are more actively involved in the settlement process, you decide to file in federal court.

5. Plan the discovery

The client has two basic objectives: keep it simple and inexpensive, and try to settle it quickly. The first objective was served by keeping the pleadings simple. The second objective must be remembered when planning the discovery, as well as in the later steps of your litigation plan, since your litigation budget allocates just 50 hours to discovery.

Consult your litigation chart. At this stage the facts you have gathered came principally from Novelty's employees and business records.

In a contract case, this is to be expected. The untapped sources, then, Gift's employees and records, must be reached through formal discovery.

Since a basic objective is an early settlement, you don't want to get mired in lengthy discovery. You decide to ask for limited and accelerated discovery at the planning meeting and the Rule 16 pretrial conference. In addition, you have decided to move for partial summary judgment on liability as soon as possible. These objectives — getting the missing information, getting evidence for your summary judgment motion, and pushing for early settlement — can be served by a carefully designed discovery plan.

For example, you decide to use discovery only to get Gift's records and witness testimony that deal with the specific transaction involved. You decide that the evidence of an established course of dealings between Novelty and Gift, which would be necessary at trial to prove the contract terms, can be established by Novelty's records and witnesses. Second, you decide to focus on the contract and its breach, not contract damages, which you can again prove through Novelty's records and witnesses. This will give you the information necessary for your motion for partial summary judgment on liability.

What remains to be decided is which discovery methods to use to execute the plan and what order to use them in. You decide to send a set of interrogatories to Gift dealing with the basic chronological events involved in the transaction. You also decide to send Gift a request to produce all records dealing with the specific transaction. These should, among other things, identify the Gift employees who handled the transaction and were involved in the decision to return the lighters. Finally, you decide to depose those same essential Gift employees in succession, during one or two days, to minimize their contact with each other. When this is done, you will send a request to admit facts that covers the liability facts of the case.

The last decision is when to take these steps. Ordinarily you will want to move quickly to stay ahead of the other side. Here you decide to send out the interrogatories and requests to produce records at the earliest permitted time, and to send out the deposition notices for the necessary depositions as soon as you receive adequate answers to your interrogatories and documents requests. The request to admit facts can then follow on the heels of the depositions.

6. Plan the dispositive motions

Your overall litigation objective is to seek an early settlement, preferably after pleadings are filed or discovery has begun. If this does not work, you plan to move for partial summary judgment on liability as soon as discovery is completed. You will then have the information necessary to support your motion and to create additional pressure for a settlement.

7. Plan the settlement approach

Early settlement has always been a priority in your case. Accordingly, you plan to make settlement overtures, if Gift does not initiate them, after the pleadings are filed, after discovery is well under way and also when completed, after the motion for partial summary judgment is heard, and at the final pretrial conference.

Your approach has been to use focused discovery, particularly the request to admit facts, and the partial summary judgment motion to eliminate liability from the settlement discussions and put pressure on Gift. Since Novelty has been unable to resell the lighters, there is no mitigation of damages problem and damages are likely to be the full contract price. You decide that, with Novelty's consent, you will agree to settle for an amount close to the contract price, minus your total litigation expenses. This puts the settlement "value" of the case in the range of $65,000 to $80,000, depending on how early the case is settled.

8. Develop a litigation timetable

Now that you have developed a litigation plan that will realistically serve the client's objectives and priorities, you need to put the basic components on a timetable. Your basic timetable for Novelty is:

LITIGATION TIMETABLE

1/1 (today)	Complete litigation plan
by 2/1	File complaint
by 3/1	Initial disclosure
by 4/1	Interrogatories, production requests to def.
by 5/1	Deposition notices to def. witnesses
by 6/1	Depose def. witnesses (same day if possible)
by 7/1	Requests to admit facts to def.
by 9/1	Motion for partial summary judgment on liability
by 10/1	Prepare pretrial memorandum
by 11/1	Pretrial conference
12/1	Initial trial date

You plan to recommend this schedule to the lawyer for Gift when you meet to develop a discovery plan under Rule 26(f), and propose it to the trial judge when you meet for the pretrial conference under Rule 16. These dates can then be put on your general docket calendar to remind you when the basic steps in this case should be completed.

§4.7. Prefiling requirements

Are you finally ready to begin drafting the pleadings? Not quite. There are still a few matters you need to consider before plunging ahead.

1. Statutory notice requirements

Some actions, primarily claims against governmental bodies such as municipalities, often have statutory notice requirements that must be complied with or else suit will be barred. These statutes usually have time limitations substantially shorter than the applicable statute of limitations, often as short as six months or less, and usually have detailed fact requirements. These statutes are usually strictly construed, so each statutory requirement must be closely followed.

2. Contract requirements

Many contracts, particularly insurance and employment contracts and contracts with governmental bodies, have notice and claims provisions that are drafted as conditions precedent. These provisions usually require notice of intent to sue, or presentation of claims before filing suit, and require that notice be given within a short period of time, usually much shorter than the applicable statute of limitations period. Make sure you comply with the conditions precedent required by the contract before filing suit.

3. Mediation, arbitration, and review requirements

By statute or contract, many disputes must be submitted to binding or nonbinding mediation or arbitration before suit can be brought. For example, construction contracts frequently have arbitration clauses, and many states require by statute that medical malpractice claims must first be presented to a medical review panel.

4. Administrative procedure requirements

Claims against governmental bodies usually cannot be brought in court until administrative procedures have been followed and exhausted. Sometimes this exhaustion requirement is statutory; sometimes it is judicially created. For example, claims for benefits from the Social Security and Veterans Administrations must ordinarily be pursued through the administrative process before resort to the judicial system is permitted.[19] Accordingly, determine what applicable administrative procedure statutes and case law apply to your claim, and make sure that they have been followed and exhausted before filing suit.

---

19. See 42 U.S.C. §421(c); Administrative Procedure Act, 5 U.S.C. §§551 et seq.

5. Appointment of legal guardian

Some individuals are incompetent to sue in their own name and must have a legal representative or specially appointed guardian litigate for them. Capacity to sue is governed by Rule 17, which generally defers to state law in determining both capacity to sue and the appropriate representative party.[20] Minors and incompetents, for example, can only sue through their legal guardians or conservators. Appropriate state court appointments of guardians, or other legal representatives, must be obtained before suit can properly be brought. When the statute of limitations will run shortly, this is a serious concern since obtaining such appointments may take time.

6. Lis pendens

Some jurisdictions require the filing of a lis pendens notice and service on all interested parties whenever a suit involves an interest in real property or tangible personal property. The notice is filed in the public records, usually property and title records. This gives notice of the pending litigation to parties having an interest in the property. Once notified, any interest in the property they acquire is subject to any judgment that may be entered in that particular litigation. Where your suit involves real or personal property, you should always check to see if any lis pendens rules apply; if so, follow them so that a judgment will be valid and enforceable against such parties. State lis pendens notice requirements are applicable to federal cases involving real estate.[21]

7. Attachment

Attachment is the legal process in which someone's property is seized to satisfy a judgment not yet rendered. While there are no federal attachment statutes, Rule 64 makes available the attachment procedures allowed under the forum state's law. State statutes often provide for attachment of a debtor's property interest under certain defined circumstances and usually specify the procedures, including service of process and bonds, that must be followed. Some jurisdictions also provide for prefiling attachment or garnishment procedures that may be used to freeze assets that may satisfy any future judgment. There are remedies for wrongful attachment, however, so caution is obviously in order.

8. Temporary restraining orders

If you are seeking injunctive relief, you may be able to obtain a temporary restraining order (TRO) to prevent immediate irreparable injury to your

20. See §3.4.
21. See Rule 64; 28 U.S.C. §1964.

client's interests. A TRO may be obtained under specified conditions for a strictly limited period of time, until a hearing for a preliminary injunction can be scheduled.[22] While it is difficult to obtain a TRO, there will be times when seeking a TRO is essential to preserve a client's rights.[23]

9.   Discovery before suit

Upon filing a verified petition that complies with Rule 27's requirements, you may depose a person before suit is filed to perpetuate that person's testimony. This should be considered in two situations. First, if you cannot get enough pre-filing factual information to comply with the Rule 11 requirements, using Rule 27 may be your only recourse. Second, if an important witness is old, sick, or is about to leave the jurisdiction, Rule 27 can be used to depose that person to perpetuate the testimony.

10.   Demand letters

While not legally required, demand letters, which state a party's claim against another party, are frequently used, particularly in tort, contract, and commercial cases. For instance, in anticipatory breach situations it is advantageous to send a demand letter asserting that the other side appears to be in breach and requesting assurances of performance. Such letters, if not responded to, may constitute admissions by silence.

Demand letters also serve practical purposes. In small disputes, where a compromise is possible, a demand letter that notifies the other side of your intent to sue unless an acceptable settlement is reached can often trigger settlement discussions. Including a draft of your proposed complaint shows the other side that you are serious. A demand letter will often generate a denial letter stating the basis for rejecting your claim, and is sometimes a good indication of what defenses will be raised if suit is brought later.

In some cases, where your ability to get the facts is limited because the important records are all in your opponent's possession, it may also be appropriate to send a draft of your complaint to your opponent and await a response. The opponent may respond by giving you information that will affect your decision to file the lawsuit or will affect the claims that you ultimately bring.

11.   Physical examinations

As plaintiff in a personal injury case, consider offering to have your client examined by a defense doctor before filing suit. There are several reasons to consider this. First, the defense is entitled to such an examination after

22. See Rule 65.
23. Obtaining a TRO or preliminary injunction is discussed in §7.5.

suit is filed, under Rule 35. Second, the plaintiff's injuries will be more apparent at this time. Third, such an offer lets the defense know you're prepared and confident about your case. Fourth, it may pave the way to an earlier settlement of the case.

Part B
CONDUCTING THE LITIGATION

V

PLEADINGS

§5.1.   Introduction

Pleadings get the lawsuit started, usually stop the running of the statute of limitations, and frame the issues involved in the lawsuit. However, modern pleading rules essentially limit the purpose of pleadings to notice of claims and defenses. Former purposes that included discovering facts, sharpening issues, and disposing of frivolous claims are now controlled by discovery and motion practice. Under modern rules, claims and factual issues will rarely be resolved at the pleadings stage. Hence, don't expect the pleadings to accomplish more than what they are designed to do.

Federal pleadings rules are principally contained in the Federal Rules of Civil Procedure, although other sources exist and must always be kept in mind. Under Rule 83 district courts can create local rules governing litigation in that district. Most have done so. Local rules generally do not affect the substance of pleadings, but ordinarily control mechanics such as the number of copies filed, size of paper, format, bindings, and whether papers can be filed by facsimile or other electronic means. Particular federal statutory actions, such as bankruptcy and copyright, may also have special procedure rules. Finally, specialized federal courts, such as magistrates, bankruptcy, and claims courts, may have special statutory and local procedural rules. Hence, you should always check procedural statutes and local rules in addition to the Federal Rules of Civil Procedure to determine what rules apply to your particular case.

Good pleadings practice is a combination of two things: a solid litigation plan and technically precise drafting. The litigation plan, which you have already developed, will control the claims and remedies (if a plaintiff), or the defenses and counterclaims, cross-claims, or third-party claims (if a defendant). The drafting of pleadings then becomes the primary concern, since pleadings that are technically precise will avoid attacks by motions and eliminate the need to file amended pleadings to cure defects that should have been avoided in the first place.

§5.2.   *General pleading requirements*

The Federal Rules of Civil Procedure have made simplicity and limited purpose the touchstones of the pleadings stage of the litigation process. Under Rule 2, all actions are "civil actions," and under Rule 7(a) the only basic pleadings allowed are complaints, answers, and replies.

1.   General "notice" requirements for claims[1]

Rule 8(a) permits four forms of claims:

1.   complaint—claim brought by plaintiff against defendant
2.   counterclaim—claim brought by defendant against plaintiff
3.   cross-claim—claim brought by one defendant against another defendant
4.   third-party complaint—claim brought by an original defendant against a new party (third-party defendant)

All forms are actually complaints, since each asks for relief of some kind, but the various labels designate which party is bringing the claim. Since they are all complaints, however, their requirements are the same. Rule 8 requires only a "short and plain statement of the claim showing the pleader is entitled to relief." This commonly, although perhaps inaccurately, is labeled "notice pleading."

Under "notice pleading," the only requirement is that the pleading contain enough information to fairly notify the opposing party of the basis of the claim. It does not require an elaborate narration of facts, nor does it require that a legal theory of recovery or relief be set forth. Previous distinctions about whether a pleading was of fact, law, or conclusion of law now have no significance. Hence, for most allegations the only requirement is a "short and plain statement" that gives fair notice of your claims to the opposing side. Forms 2 through 23 in the Appendix of Forms to the Federal Rules of Civil Procedure contain a variety of legally sufficient pleadings. The safest pleadings approach is to use the forms and modify them to meet the specific requirements of your case. The standard drafting technique is to state enough facts to identify the events or

1. Wright §68; James & Hazard §3.8; Friedenthal §5.7; Moore's Manual §901; Manual of Federal Practice §3.5; Wright & Miller §§1182-1192; Moore's Federal Practice §§8.02-8.06. The leading case on the simplified pleading requirements of Rule 8 is Conley v. Gibson, 355 U.S. 41 (1957).

transactions that your claim is based on and the legal theory of recovery. These techniques are detailed in §5.3.

The only exception to the simple notice pleading requirement is Rule 9, which requires that certain matters, including capacity and authority to sue, fraud, mistake, and special damages, be alleged specifically and particularly. This type of pleading is also discussed in §5.3.

The 1993 amendments to the federal rules included the new Rule 26(a), which provides for automatic initial disclosure of basic information that is "relevant to disputed facts alleged with particularity in the pleadings." Under Rule 26(a), a party may have some discovery benefits by alleging specific facts in the pleadings, to make it harder for the opposing party to avoid making the required initial disclosures. This is discussed in §§5.3 and 6.4.

2. Alternative and inconsistent pleadings[2]

Rule 8(e)(2) allows a party to plead multiple claims or defenses in alternative or hypothetical form, either in one or in separate counts or defenses. In practice, each claim is usually put in a separate count and each defense is designated separately. Keep in mind, however, that since pleadings can be used during trial, alternative or inconsistent pleadings may cast the party in a poor light. Hence, drafting must also be done with an eye toward the impression the pleading will have on the jurors.

3. Format requirements[3]

Format requirements are set forth in Rules 10 and 11. There are several that must be followed for every pleading. Local rules may also specify additional requirements.

a. Caption

The caption of a case refers to the names of the parties, the court in which the case is being filed, and the case number. Every pleading must have a caption containing this information.

b. File number

The file number is the case number that is stamped on the complaint when it is first filed with the clerk of the court. It must appear on all successive pleadings and other court papers. Although not required, the designation "Civil Action" is usually placed below the file number.

---

2. Friedenthal §§5.12-5.13; Moore's Manual §§9.05-9.06; Manual of Federal Practice §3.72.
3. Friedenthal §5.14.

c. Parties to action

The complaint caption must list all the parties to the action. Subsequent pleadings need only list the first plaintiff and first defendant, with an appropriate reference to additional parties, such as "et al."

Make sure that your caption correctly states the proper name and legal description of each party. Under Rule 17, every action must be brought in the name of the real party in interest; and, according to this Rule, the capacity to sue or be sued is controlled by the law of domicile, incorporation, or forum.[4] You must always check Rule 17(b) and (c) to see if a party has capacity to sue or be sued and that the correct person or entity is designated as a party. Common designations include the following:

- John Smith
- Sharon Jones, as guardian of the Estate of Robert Jones, a minor
- Robert Smith, as conservator of the Estate of Ellen Smith, an incompetent
- Frank Watson, as executor of the Estate of James Morley, deceased
- Barbara Myers, as trustee in bankruptcy of the Estate of Robert Jackson, bankrupt
- R. J. Smith Company, a corporation
- Johnson Hospital, a not-for-profit corporation
- Robert Smith, d/b/a Smith Cleaners
- Barnett and Lynch, a partnership
- Western Ranches Association, an unincorporated association

Where a party is being sued both individually and in a representative capacity, it should be spelled out.

Example:

John Smith, individually and as administrator of the Estate of Franklin Smith, deceased

The caption, then, simply lists each party and what side of the action each is on.

4. See §3.4.

Example:

UNITED STATES DISTRICT COURT
FOR THE NORTHERN DISTRICT OF NEW YORK

John Smith, and J. W. Smith Company, a corporation, Plaintiffs	
v.	No. _____
Randolph Construction, a corporation, and William Johnson, d/b/a Solar Consultants, Defendants	Civil Action

Sometimes it is impossible to identify a proper party by name before filing. In many state courts you can designate a party as "John Doe, the true name being presently unknown," and pursue the identity of the party through formal discovery. This sometimes happens when a plaintiff has been able to identify some but not all liable parties. The advantage of doing this is that plaintiff can get the case started against the known defendants and amend the complaint to add the additional parties when their identity is discovered (and the statute of limitations has not yet run as to the additional parties). However, in federal court the use of fictitious parties is prohibited, although some local rules provide for permitting the use of fictitious parties if ordered by the court.

Keep in mind, however, that naming John or Jane Doe defendants, when permitted, to attempt to toll the applicable statute of limitations under the concept of relation back will probably be ineffective, unless the person properly named later as a defendant had actual notice of the suit before the statute of limitations ran.[5]

d.   Designation

Each pleading should be labeled to show what type it is, such as a complaint, counterclaim, cross-claim, third-party complaint, answer, or reply. Where multiple parties are involved, it is useful to show against whom the pleading is directed.

---

5. See §5.13; Schiavone v. Fortune, Inc., 477 U.S. 21 (1986).

Examples:

COMPLAINT

DEFENDANT SMITH COMPANY'S
ANSWER TO CROSS-CLAIM OF DEFENDANT
FRANKLIN CORPORATION

THIRD-PARTY COMPLAINT AGAINST
JONES CONSTRUCTION COMPANY

e. Signing pleadings

Every pleading, or other court paper, must be signed by one of the party's lawyers. The signing must be by an individual, not a law firm, although in practice the lawyer's firm is frequently shown as "of counsel." The pleading must also contain the lawyer's address and telephone number.

Under the federal rules pleadings are not "verified" — that is, signed by the parties and notarized — although this remains proper procedure in many state jurisdictions. Verification is still appropriate in a few special circumstances, most commonly in applications for a TRO under Rule 65(b).

4. Rule 11[6]

Under Rule 11, a lawyer's presentation to the court of a pleading, motion, or other court paper (except discovery disclosures, requests, responses, objections, and motions, which are covered under the certification sanctions of Rule 26(g) and Rule 37) automatically constitutes a certification that to the best of the lawyer's knowledge, information, and belief the pleading has evidentiary support or is likely to have evidentiary support after reasonable investigation, is supported by existing law or can be supported by a nonfrivolous argument for a change in law, and is not being filed for delay, harassment, or some other improper purpose.[7] A presentation to the court means signing, filing, submitting, or later advocating a paper. The 1993 amendment broadened the scope of a lawyer's obligations, but limited the imposition of sanctions. Under Rule 11(b), "later advocating" a position in a previously presented paper is considered a presentation to the court.

Rule 11(a) requires that every pleading, written motion, and other paper be signed by an attorney of record or by the unrepresented party filing it. Each paper must provide the address and telephone number of

---

6. Friedenthal §5.11; Moore's Manual §3.70; Moore's Federal Practice §11.02; Wright & Miller §§1331 et seq.

7. Rule 11 parallels the applicable ethics considerations. See Model Code of Professional Responsibility, Rule 7-102; Model Rules of Professional Conduct, Rule 3.1.

the signer. If not signed, the paper "shall" be stricken unless corrected promptly after being called to the signer's attention.

Rule 11(b) imposes significant obligations on the lawyer. A subjective good faith belief that the pleading is well founded is no longer sufficient; a lawyer must make a "reasonable inquiry" into the law and facts, and have concluded that there is a sound basis in law and fact for each allegation against each party in the pleading. Rule 11(b) also imposes the same obligations on the client, since a party, even if represented by counsel, can incur penalties if the party presents a paper to the court by signing, filing, submitting, or later advocating in violation of the rule's standards.

What is a reasonable inquiry depends on the facts and circumstances that existed at the time the pleading was made.[8] Among the factors to be considered are the amount of time available to investigate the law and facts, the reliability of the client as a source of facts, and the extent to which an investigation could corroborate or alter those facts.

Can you rely on your client as the sole source for critical facts? This depends on whether it is reasonable under the circumstances. You must consider whether the client's story can be corroborated by information available from other independent sources, the cost of seeking such corroboration, whether the client has actual firsthand knowledge of the critical facts, how well you know the client, how reliable the client has been in the past, and whether the client's story is inherently plausible.[9] The reasonableness of the pleading or other court paper is measured at the time of its filing; Rule 11(b) does not impose a requirement to amend on discovering errors, although other practice rules do. However, if evidentiary support for a claim or defense is not obtained after a reasonable opportunity for investigation, Rule 11(b) calls upon the litigant not to advocate such claims or defenses.

Can you allege facts without first having evidentiary support for those allegations? Rule 11 does not prohibit filing a pleading or other court paper simply because the information you have may not yet be in admissible form. On the other hand, a mere hunch that the client may have a good claim is inadequate. You must have some reasonably reliable information that the client has a proper claim. The court can also consider whether you were on notice that your investigation, both legal and factual, was inadequate or incorrect. Arguments for the extension, modification, or reversal of existing law, or for the establishment of new law, are not violations of the rule so long as the arguments are "nonfrivolous."

If a pleading is signed in violation of Rule 11(b), the court "may" impose sanctions against the lawyer who signed the pleading, the law firm for whom the lawyer works, the party, or all three. A law firm is generally jointly responsible for the conduct of its partners, associates, and employees. Rule 11(c) does not provide factors a court should consider when de-

---

8. See Stempel, Sanctions, Symmetry and Safe Harbors: Limiting Misapplication of Rule 11 by Harmonizing It with Pre-Verdict Dismissal Devices, 60 Fordham L. Rev. 257 (1991); Ward, Rule 11 and Factually Frivolous Claims—The Goal of Cost Minimization and the Client's Duty to Investigate, 44 Vand. L. Rev. 1165 (1991).

9. See Lyles v. K Mart Corp., 703 F. Supp. 435 (W.D.N.C. 1989).

ciding to impose sanctions, but gives considerable discretion to the court. Sanctions can include costs and attorney's fees where they are directly incurred as a result of the violation, as well as nonmonetary sanctions such as striking the challenged paper or requiring participation in educational programs. Sanctions are limited to what is sufficient to deter repetition of the conduct or similar conduct by others in the same situation, and are proper even though there was no subjective bad faith or harassment.[10]

The court can impose sanctions in response to a formal motion for sanctions.[11] Such a motion is to be served separately from other motions and must describe the specific conduct alleged to violate the rule. However, under Rule 11(c) a motion for sanctions cannot be filed or presented to the court unless the challenged paper, claim, defense, contention, allegation, or denial is not withdrawn or corrected within 21 days of service of the motion. This is the so-called "safe harbor" provision; a timely withdrawal of a contention will protect the party against a motion for sanctions. The court can shorten or alter the 21-day rule.

The court can also act on its own, but only after notice and an opportunity to respond. The court will issue an "order to show cause" specifically describing the conduct in question and directing an attorney, law firm, or party to show why it has not violated Rule 11(b). When the court acts on its own, there is no "safe harbor"; there is no opportunity for the litigant to withdraw or correct a challenged paper, but such a withdrawal or correction is a factor that the court may consider in determining whether to impose sanctions. In addition, monetary sanctions against a represented party for frivolous legal positions may not be awarded on the court's own initiative, and monetary sanctions generally may not be awarded unless the order to show cause is issued before a voluntary dismissal or settlement of the claims made by or against the litigant. When awarded, a monetary sanction will usually be limited to a penalty payable to the court; a monetary award to an injured party will be allowed only in unusual circumstances.

Sanctions should be no more severe than necessary to deter the same or similar conduct in the future. Factors the court will consider include whether the misconduct was willful or repeated, its effect on the pleadings and the litigation, and what amount will serve to deter this person, as well as other litigants, in the future. The court can impose sanctions without holding a hearing in every instance. However, the pleading or other court paper must be signed before the court can impose sanctions on the signer.

Rule 11 is not self-enforcing. It is the responsibility of the bench and bar to ensure that sanctions are imposed where appropriate. Rule 11 is not to be used as a tactical weapon or a vehicle for fee-shifting. In fact, a motion for sanctions improperly brought is itself subject to Rule 11 sanctions.

---

10. See Cruz v. Savage, 896 F.2d 626 (1st Cir. 1990); Cabell v. Petty, 810 F.2d 463 (4th Cir. 1987).
11. See In re Itel Sec. Litig., 791 F.2d 672 (9th Cir. 1986).

To avoid Rule 11 problems, conduct an adequate prefiling inquiry. Personally interview the client, critically analyze the client's information, interview corroborating witnesses, obtain and review relevant documents, and research the applicable law. Make sure that each allegation, against each defendant, meets the "reasonable inquiry" standard. In short, do your homework first, then file.

The message of Rule 11 should be abundantly clear: Gone are the days when a lawyer could, with little preparation, file an action containing a variety of claims against a multitude of defendants and later simply dismiss those claims and defendants that never should have been raised or brought into the case in the first place. Rule 11's reasonable inquiry requirement has teeth, and judges now impose significant sanctions for violations.[12]

Rule 11 has spawned substantial satellite litigation, and the Supreme Court has decided several cases in this area in recent years. These include Pavelic & LeFlore v. Marvel Entertainment Group, 493 U.S. 120 (1989); Cooter & Gell v. Hartmarx Corp., 496 U.S. 384 (1990); Business Guides, Inc. v. Chromatic Communications Enterprises, Inc., 498 U.S. 533 (1991); Chambers v. NASCO, Inc., 501 U.S. 32 (1991); and Willy v. Coastal Corp., 503 U.S. 131 (1992).

In *Pavelic*, the Court held that because Rule 11 requires that pleadings and other papers shall be signed in the individual attorney's name, sanctions for violations of the rule could only be imposed on the individual lawyer signing, not on the lawyer's law firm. This holding was modified by the 1993 amendments to Rule 11. If a motion for sanctions is filed under this rule, Rule 11(c)(1)(A) makes it clear that a law firm is held jointly responsible when one of its partners, associates, or employees is determined to have violated the rule, absent exceptional circumstances. This is because such a motion can only be filed if the offending paper is not withdrawn or corrected within 21 days after service of the motion. Since the law firm is on notice of an alleged violation, sanctions may be appropriate. The court may consider whether other attorneys in the firm, co-counsel, or other law firms should be held accountable for their part in causing a violation. In *Cooter & Gell*, the Supreme Court ruled that a voluntary dismissal of an action does not deprive the court of jurisdiction over a Rule 11 motion, since a Rule 11 violation is complete once the improper court paper is filed. In *Business Guides*, the Court held that Rule 11 applies to parties who sign pleadings, even if they are represented by counsel. In *Chambers*, the trial court imposed sanctions on the defendant for bad faith conduct under the court's "inherent power" to control the conduct of parties who appear before it. The Court upheld the trial court, noting that the availability of Rule 11 or other sanctions do not preclude imposing sanctions under the court's inherent powers. Finally, in *Willy*, the Court held that Rule 11 sanctions can be imposed on lawyers and their clients even if

12. See Brandt v. Schal Assocs., 960 F.2d 640 (7th Cir. 1992), where the court upheld the imposition of a $443,564.66 sanction.

the trial court is later found not to have had proper subject matter jurisdiction over the case when the offensive conduct was committed.

5. Service and filing

Whenever a pleading is created—whether a complaint, answer, or reply—two things must happen. First, it must be properly served on the other parties. Second, it must be filed with the court.

How service is accomplished depends on which pleading is being served. Service of an original complaint and summons on a defendant must be done in accordance with the provisions of Rule 4. If a served defendant decides to bring a third-party complaint against a new defendant, the new defendant also must be served with the third-party complaint in accordance with the provisions of Rule 4. In these situations, the formality of service under Rule 4 is necessary to put the new defendant on notice that he has been sued and to obtain a lawyer and defend against the lawsuit. Service under Rule 4 is discussed further in §5.3.

After the complaint has been served, service of any subsequent pleadings—an answer, reply, or an amended pleading—on existing parties must be done in accordance with the provisions of Rule 5. When a party is represented by a lawyer, service is made on the lawyer. If a party is not represented by a lawyer, service is made on the party. Although Rule 5 permits several methods of service, the common ones are personal delivery, mail, or delivery to a lawyer's office to a person in charge. Under some local rules, service can be made by fax.

Pleading must, in addition to being served on the parties, also be filed with the clerk of the court. Unless local rules provide otherwise, pleadings must be filed with the clerk of the court either before service or within a reasonable time after service. The original complaint, of course, must be filed with the clerk of the court before service of the complaint and summons can be made. Filing of later pleadings is usually done at the same time the pleading is being served on the parties or lawyers. The usual practice is to take the original and an appropriate number of copies of the pleading to the clerk of the court for filing. Make sure you get a copy stamped "filed" and dated as proof of filing for your own files.

Finally, whenever service is made, you should attach a "proof of service" to the pleading. Proof of service of the complaint is made on the summons form. Local rules usually specify how proof of service of other pleadings is made. The usual practice is to have a certificate or affidavit of service attached to the end of the answer, reply, or amended pleading that shows when and how service was made, which includes the signature of the lawyer or the notarized signature of a member of the lawyer's staff.

§5.3. *Complaints*

The complaint is the plaintiff's initial pleading, which, when filed with the clerk of the court, starts the litigation. There are three essential components of every complaint required by Rule 8(a):

1. Statement showing subject matter jurisdiction
2. Statement of claims
3. Statement of relief requested

In addition, the complaint should contain a jury demand, if plaintiff wants a jury trial, must be signed by the lawyer, filed by the clerk of the court, and served with summons on the defendant. Beyond these requirements, how the complaint is organized is largely a matter of logic and clarity. Many lawyers organize a complaint by using introductory headings, such as "jurisdictional allegation," "parties," "facts common to all counts," "demand for relief," and "jury demand."

1. Subject matter jurisdiction[13]

Since federal courts are courts of limited jurisdiction, jurisdiction must be alleged in the complaint; and since jurisdiction cannot be assumed, it must be affirmatively demonstrated. Care as well as particularity is required. The jurisdictional allegation is usually the first part of a complaint and is customarily labeled as such. There are two principal ways that subject matter jurisdiction can be acquired in federal court.

a. *Federal question jurisdiction*[14]

Federal jurisdiction can be based on a federal statute, constitutional provision, or treaty. The general federal question statute is 28 U.S.C. §1331. To establish jurisdiction in this way, the complaint should cite the particular statute, constitutional provision, or treaty, and perhaps quote the operative wording or paraphrase it. Failure to do so is not fatal, since jurisdictional allegations can be amended[15] ; however, citing a federal statute, constitutional provision, or treaty will not conclusively confer jurisdiction, since facts alleged in the complaint can contradict and disprove the jurisdictional allegation. As always, the safest pleading approach is to track the language of the Appendix of Forms to the Federal Rules of Civil Procedure.

---

13. Wright §69; James & Hazard §3.24; Friedenthal §5.14; Moore's Manual §10.03; Manual of Federal Practice §3.6; Moore's Federal Practice §§8.07-8.11; Wright & Miller §§1206, 1208-1209.
14. See §3.5 supra.
15. See 28 U.S.C. §1653.

Example:

[Caption]

COMPLAINT

Plaintiff Ralph Johnson complains against Defendant Wilbur Jackson as follows:

Jurisdictional Allegation

1. Jurisdiction in this case is based on the existence of a federal question. This action arises under [the Constitution of the United States, Amendment _____, §____] [or the Act of _____ ____ , ____ Stat. ____, ____ U.S.C. §____] [or the Treaty of the United States _____], as is shown more fully in this complaint.

b.   *Diversity jurisdiction*[16]

Federal jurisdiction can also be based on diversity of citizenship. The diversity statute is 18 U.S.C. §1332. The jurisdictional allegation must affirmatively show complete diversity of each plaintiff and each defendant (and allege the required amount in controversy). The essential requirement is citizenship, not residence. An individual has only one state of citizenship. A permanent resident alien is treated, for jurisdictional purposes, as a citizen of the state where domiciled. (A nonresident alien is presumably still treated as if a citizen of the foreign country of which he is a national.) A corporation, for jurisdictional purposes, is deemed a citizen of both the state where incorporated and the state where it has its principal place of business.

Example (individuals):

Jurisdictional Allegation

Jurisdiction in this case is based on diversity of citizenship of the parties and the amount in controversy. Plaintiff is a citizen of the State of California. Defendant is a citizen of the State of Oregon.

Example (corporations):

Jurisdictional Allegation

Jurisdiction in this case is based on diversity of citizenship of the parties and the amount in controversy. Plaintiff is a corporation incorpo-

16. See §3.5.

rated under the laws of the State of Delaware having its principal place of
business in the State of New York. Defendant is a corporation incorporated under the laws of the State of Georgia having its principal place of
business in the State of Florida.

Where the party is a legally recognized unincorporated association,
such as a labor union or service organization, it is a citizen of every state
of which any of its members is a citizen. Partnerships are considered citizens of each state where a general partner is a citizen. For legal
representatives—such as a guardian of a minor, executor or administrator of an estate, and representative of an incompetent—the minor, deceased, or incompetent's citizenship is controlling for diversity purposes,
although there may be exceptions in special circumstances.[17]

Diversity jurisdiction under 28 U.S.C. §1332 also requires that the
"matter in controversy exceeds the sum or value of $75,000, exclusive of
interest and costs."[18] Since the jurisdictional amount must be alleged in
the pleadings, it is customary to simply paraphrase the statute at the end
of the jurisdictional allegation.

Example:

Jurisdictional Allegation

. . . The amount in controversy exceeds the sum of seventy-five thousand dollars ($75,000), exclusive of interest and costs.

Where a statute makes notice of a claim a prerequisite to suit, some
courts have held that the fact that notice was given is a jurisdictional requirement that must be alleged in the complaint.[19]

Because state trial courts are usually courts of general jurisdiction, a
specific jurisdictional allegation in complaints brought in state courts is
usually unnecessary.

2. Statement of claims[20]

Rule 8(a) merely requires that a pleading contain a "short and plain statement of the claim showing that the pleader is entitled to relief." Rule 8(e)
states that each allegation in the pleading shall be "simple, concise and
direct"; only a few claims, principally fraud and mistake, must be pleaded

17. See Wright §29; Wright & Miller §3606.
18. See §3.5. The $75,000 matter in controversy requirement applies to diversity cases
under 28 U.S.C. §1332; since 1980, it no longer applies to federal question cases under 28
U.S.C. §1331.
19. See Manual of Federal Practice §3.6.
20. Wright §68; James & Hazard §§3.14-3.20; Friedenthal §5.15; Moore's Manual §10.14;
Manual of Federal Practice §3.17; Moore's Federal Practice §§8.12-8.17; Wright & Miller
§§1215-1254.

with particularity. In short, technical requirements have been discarded, the sole requirement now being that enough be pleaded that the other party has fair notice of the claims presented sufficient to defend itself.

Since the requirements for the statement of claims are minimal, great latitude in drafting exists. Hence, the more significant drafting questions are: What is the most effective way to make a statement of the claim in a complaint? Are there any general drafting "rules" that apply?

a.   Use plain English

In recent years the trend in legal drafting has been away from legalese in favor of plain English. The same approach should be applied when drafting pleadings. Commonly used words, short sentences of simple construction, active verbs, and a preference for nouns and verbs over adjectives and adverbs create clear and forceful language. This benefits everyone in litigation — parties, lawyers, judge, and jury.

b.   Keep it simple

Pleadings are not the place to disclose the detailed facts on which you base your claims, nor the place to elaborate on your theories of recovery. The Rules require only a "short and plain statement." You need only allege enough to put the opposing party on fair notice of what your claims against him are. While this must be read in the light of the complexity of the case, with complex cases requiring more detailed allegations, the preference should still be for simplicity. Adding more than the pleading rules require is usually surplusage that does not improve the legal adequacy of the complaint.

Two sources should always be consulted when drafting complaints. First, check the wording of the elements instruction for each theory of recovery that will be given to the jury if the case goes to trial. Second, the official Appendix of Forms gives excellent examples of complaints in common situations that, by virtue of Rule 84, are legally adequate, yet use simple English. The safest approach in drafting pleadings is to modify these forms to your claims whenever practical.

Example (negligence):

1. On August 1, 1998, at approximately 3:00 P.M., plaintiff Jones and defendant Smith were driving automobiles on Elm Street, near Maple Avenue, in Chicago, Illinois.

2. Smith negligently crossed the center lane of Elm Street with his automobile, striking Jones' automobile.

3. As a result Jones received facial injuries, a broken arm, and other injuries, experienced pain and suffering, incurred medical expenses, lost substantial income, and will incur more medical expenses and lost income in the future.

Example (contract):

1. On August 1, 1998, plaintiff Jones and defendant Smith entered into a contract. A copy of the contract is attached to this complaint as Exhibit A.

2. Jones paid Smith $80,000 and has performed all of her obligations under the contract.

3. Smith failed to repair Jones' house as he was required to do under the contract.

On the other hand, there are times when making detailed or specific factual allegations can be effective. First, specific factual allegations are harder for the defendant to deny. Second, a specific allegation can be used to support a later specific discovery request. If the defendant denies the allegation in the complaint, she can hardly object to discovery methods that are directed to uncovering the denied fact. The enactment of Rule 26(a) in 1993 makes this substantially more important. Rule 26(a) requires automatic initial disclosure of facts and documents "relevant to disputed facts alleged with particularity in the pleadings." Hence, alleging specific events such as meetings, conversations, and transactions and referring to specific records and documents in a pleading will make it more difficult for the responding party to deny those allegations and to avoid disclosing facts and documents relevant to the pleading. Seen in this light, the complaint can be plaintiff's first discovery device, since detailed allegations will trigger the automatic disclosure requirements. Third, if plaintiff has a compelling story to tell, setting that story out in the complaint for both the judge and later the jury to read can be an effective approach, particularly if you are seeking an early settlement or other disposition of the case.

The preference for using simple English should also apply to naming parties. Use names rather than the pleading's designations, such as plaintiff, defendant, cross-claimant, or third-party defendant or other legal designations, such as trustee, drawer, or obligor, unless a local pleading rule requires the designation of the party. Using names keeps things clear, particularly where multiple parties are involved.

A common practice is to set out the full name of each party the first time it is used, then show in parentheses how you will refer to that party from then on.

Examples:

Defendant William B. Jones (hereafter "Jones") . . .

The International Business Machines Corporation ("IBM") . . .

c. *Plead "special matters" with particularity*

Rule 9 is an exception to the liberal "notice pleading" approach of the federal rules. Under Rule 9, certain allegations must be pleaded "specifically" and "with particularity." These include fraud, mistake, and special damages.[21] While capacity and authority to sue and conditions precedent can be pleaded generally, denials must be made specifically and with particularity.

What constitutes appropriate specificity and particularity in pleading these special matters is unclear.[22] While the particularity requirement should be viewed in light of Rule 8's liberal pleading standards, it is safer as well as proper to set forth the specific elements of the special matter being pleaded. This will ensure that the requisite particularity has been established.

Example (fraud):

1. On August 1, 1998, plaintiff Jones and defendant Smith entered into a contract. A copy of the contract is attached to this complaint as Exhibit A.

2. Under the contract, Jones agreed to pay Smith $80,000, and Smith agreed to sell Jones a parcel of land in Atlanta, Georgia. The precise location and description of the parcel are set out in the contract, attached as Exhibit A.

3. Before executing this contract, Smith represented that he had legal title to the parcel, that the parcel had no encumbrances of any kind, such as mortgages, tax liens, or judgment liens, and that Smith would be able to have the property rezoned to a B-2 zoning.

4. Those representations were false and fraudulent, Smith knew they were false and fraudulent when made, and Smith made them to induce Jones to enter into the contract.

5. Jones relied on Smith's representations and was damaged.

d.   Use separate paragraphs

The rules require a separate paragraph for a ''single set of circumstances'' whenever practicable — admittedly an imprecise standard. When in doubt, it is probably better to use paragraphs liberally, since this usually makes the pleadings simpler to follow. Keep each paragraph to a simple point, and avoid colorful characterizations. More important, it makes the complaint easier to answer and will minimize the likelihood that an answer will admit part and deny part of a single paragraph. As a result the positions of the parties will be clearer, benefiting everyone.

Example:

1. On June 1, 1998, plaintiff Jones and defendant Smith entered into a contract, a copy of which is attached as Exhibit A.

2. On June 15, 1998, Jones paid Smith $80,000 as required by the contract.

3. Jones has performed each of her obligations under the contract.

21. Subject matter jurisdiction must also be pleaded specifically. See §3.5.
22. See Moore's Manual §9.07.

4. Smith failed to deliver 1,000 folding chairs to Jones by June 30, 1998, and has failed to perform his obligations under the contract.

In some jurisdictions the practice is to number the paragraphs with Arabic numbers; others use Roman numerals.

e. Use separate counts

Although not required by the rules, it is customary to state each claim involving a separate theory of recovery in a separate count, even if all are based on the same general occurrence or transaction. This has the advantage of setting out clearly each legal theory that forms a basis for recovery.

Since setting out different theories of recovery in different counts usually requires restating some allegations, it is efficient and proper under Rule 10(c) to incorporate into the later count by reference those allegations made in earlier counts.

Example:

Count II

1-15. Plaintiff adopts Par. 1-15 of Count I as Par. 1-15 of this Count.
16. . . .
17. . . .

It is better to number all the paragraphs in all the counts of the complaint sequentially, rather than to begin each count with a Par. 1. This avoids confusion and makes it easier for the defendant to respond to each paragraph in the answer.

It is also useful to label the legal theory for each count and, where different counts are against different parties, show which parties are involved in each count.

Example:

Count I — Contract
(against defendants Jones and Roberts)

1. . . .
2. . . .
3. . . .

Count II — Implied Warranties
(against defendant Roberts only)

7. . . .
8. . . .
9. . . .

If the complaint alleges several theories of recovery, but the facts are common to all the counts, lawyers frequently set out the common facts separately and label them appropriately.

Example:

Factual Allegations

    1. . . .
    2. . . .
    3. . . .

Example:

Allegations Common to All Counts

    1. . . .
    2. . . .
    3. . . .

When this approach is used, the common allegations will immediately follow the jurisdictional allegation section.

f. Use exhibits

Rule 10(c) permits attaching exhibits to pleadings. This is most commonly done in contract cases, where a copy of the contract that forms the basis for the claim is attached to the complaint. When attached to the pleading, the exhibit becomes an integral part of it. This is sometimes a more efficient way of stating a claim than setting out the exhibit's contents in the body of the complaint.

Example:

1. Plaintiff Jones and defendant Smith entered into a contract on June 1, 1998. A copy of this contract is attached as Exhibit A.

Example:

8. The employee manual sets forth some of the terms of the employment contract entered into by Jones and Smith. A copy of this employee manual is attached as Exhibit B.

If the exhibit is lengthy, however, it may be easier to set out the key language in the pleading, rather than attach the exhibit to the pleading. Courts dislike lengthy attachments to pleadings.

3.   Prayer for relief[23]

Rule 8(a) requires a pleading to make a "demand for judgment for the relief the pleader seeks. Relief in the alternative or of several different types may be demanded." The Rule makes no distinction between legal and equitable relief.

Care in pleading relief is important for two reasons. First, since under federal law the nature of the remedy sought is often controlling on the question of the right to a jury trial,[24] the demand for relief should be drafted to ensure the right to a jury trial, or to avoid it, as the case may be. Second, where a default judgment is requested, the method under which default can be obtained is affected by the type of relief sought, and the relief granted is limited to that requested in the pleadings.[25] Since default is always a possibility, you should always draft the prayer carefully. Third, if jurisdiction is based on diversity, make sure the prayer for relief asks for a sum in excess of $75,000, exclusive of interest and costs, as required by 28 U.S.C. §1332.

The demand for relief should specify the types of relief sought, including legal and equitable remedies, interest, costs, attorney's fees, and any special damages, with sufficient detail. Where several specific types of relief are sought, the better practice is to itemize and number them.

Examples:

WHEREFORE, plaintiff demands judgment against defendant for the sum of $80,000, with interest and costs.

WHEREFORE, plaintiff demands a preliminary and permanent injunction, an accounting for all damages, and interest and costs.

Example:

DEMAND FOR RELIEF

Plaintiff demands:

1. That defendant pay damages in excess of the sum of $80,000;

2. That defendant be specifically ordered to perform his obligations under the contract;

3. That defendant pay interest, costs, and reasonable attorney's fees incurred by plaintiff.

Do you need a prayer for relief for each claim, or only one prayer for the complaint as a whole? Rule 8 does not specify, and local practices vary, so practical concerns should provide the answer. If each claim raised has

---

23. Wright §68; James & Hazard §§3.21-3.22; Friedenthal §5.15; Moore's Manual §10.15; Manual of Federal Practice §3.8; Moore's Federal Practice §8.18; Wright & Miller §§1255-1260.

24. See §3.3.

25. See Rules 54 and 55; Sec. 7.9.

different allowable damages, you may want to have a prayer for relief after each count for clarity's sake. However, if your claims all have the same allowable damages—when all claims seek negligence damages, for example—have one prayer for relief at the end of the complaint.

4. Jury demand[26]

Under Rule 38, a party may demand a jury trial, on any claim triable as of right by a jury, in writing at any time after the complaint is filed and "not later than 10 days after the service of the last pleading directed to such issue." To be effective, the jury trial demand must be served on the other parties and filed with the court. The party may specify in the demand which claims he wishes tried to a jury. The rule permits the jury demand to be placed on the pleading itself, and this is the customary method of making the demand. A common practice is to place "JURY TRIAL DE-MANDED" below the case number, and "PLAINTIFF DEMANDS TRIAL BY JURY" at the end of the complaint. Another common practice is to use a separate heading for the jury demand.

Example:

JURY DEMAND

Plaintiff demands a trial by jury on all claims on which she has the right to trial by jury.

Local rules usually have additional requirements, such as the filing of jury demand forms and the payment of fees.

If one party makes a jury demand, the other parties are entitled to rely on it. However, if a party makes a jury demand on only some counts, the other parties must make a timely jury demand on other counts. Failure to make a timely demand for a jury trial constitutes a waiver of the right under Rule 38(d), and courts have taken a strict view on waiver and only rarely exercise their discretion and permit a belated demand.[27]

5. Signature

Under Rule 11, every complaint must be signed by the lawyer preparing it, and that lawyer must be authorized to appear in the court in which the case is being filed. Signing the complaint triggers the Rule 11(b) certification about the complaint. The rule also requires that the lawyer's address and telephone number be shown. Since the rule requires the signature of an individual lawyer, a common practice is to show the law-

---

26. Wright §92; Friedenthal §11.9; Moore's Manual §9.10; Manual of Federal Practice §§7.20-7.21; Moore's Federal Practice §§38.07-38.46; Wright & Miller §§2318-2322.
27. See Wright §92.

yer's firm as "of counsel." Finally, a complaint in a federal court need not be verified or supported by affidavit. Verification is still a common requirement in some state jurisdictions for certain kinds of complaints.

Example:

Dated this 3rd day of June, 1998.

Jane Smith Johnson
Attorney for Plaintiff
Suite 1400
100 Madison Avenue
Chicago, IL 60601
(312) 807-9000

6. Common problems

The complaint is one of the most important documents in the litigation process. A complaint, in addition to getting the litigation started, sends messages to the defense about you: how well you have researched the facts and law, how well you have analyzed and made decisions about them, and how knowledgable you are about litigation. A well planned and drafted complaint sends a clear message that you are competent and prepared to move the litigation ahead. Accordingly, unless there is a pressing need to file quickly, usually because of a statute of limitations deadline, it makes sense to draft the complaint carefully, have others review it, and make revisions before filing.

Problems in preparing complaints usually fall into two categories. First, the complaint is not well thought out. Many lawyers make complaints unnecessarily complex, having too many parties and alternative theories of recovery. Remember that complex complaints usually generate complex, lengthy, expensive litigation, which may not be in the client's best interest. Most plaintiffs want a speedy, inexpensive, and favorable outcome. A good general rule is to file the simplest complaint that will serve the client's litigation objectives.

Second, the complaint is not well drafted. Remember that a complaint should be factually and legally clear. Use headings to break the complaint into its logical components, such as jurisdiction, parties, facts, counts, and relief. Make sure that the jurisdictional allegation properly alleges the basis for federal jurisdiction and that the facts demonstrate it. Make sure the allegations show that venue is proper. Keep the factual paragraphs simple, limited to a single point, and avoid unnecessary characterizations. Decide if you want a "bare bones" approach or whether you want more specific and detailed factual allegations, which will trigger the automatic disclosure requirements of Rule 26(a). Make sure that the counts clearly set forth the required elements of each of the legal claims. Make sure that the prayer for relief contains all the kinds of relief to which you may be entitled, and avoids requesting unsupportable dollar amounts. Finally, if you want a jury trial, make sure that the complaint contains a jury demand.

7.   Filing and service of summons[28]

Under Rule 3, a federal action is commenced when the complaint is filed with the clerk of the court, and commencement is significant for statute of limitations purposes. In federal question cases, the filing of the complaint tolls the statute of limitations. In diversity cases, however, state law controls, and if state law requires something more than the mere filing of the complaint—usually actual service of summons on the defendant—state law must be complied with fully before the statute of limitations is tolled.[29]

After the action is commenced, the complaint must be served on each defendant. Under Rule 4, detailed service of summons rules control how the complaint and summons are to be served on defendants. There are several steps involved, and you should check local rules for any additional filing and service-of-summons requirements. For example, most districts require designation or civil cover sheets and appearance forms to be filed with the complaint and summons.

a.   Issuing the summons

Under Rule 4(b), the plaintiff must prepare the summons and present it to the clerk after filing the complaint. If the summons is in proper form, the clerk is directed to issue it to the plaintiff. In practice, the summons form, which is available from the clerk's office, is usually filled out in advance and taken to the clerk's office when the complaint is filed. To assist in service it is useful to list on the form where and when service on each defendant can most likely be made. For example, if the service is to be made at the defendant's work address, it is useful to put down the working hours and where on the premises the defendant actually works. The clerk then "issues" the summons by signing and stamping it with the court seal, the date, and the case file number. In the case of multiple defendants, the plaintiff has two options: he can secure issuance of a separate original summons for each defendant or he can serve copies of a single original that names all of the defendants. Make sure you have enough copies of the complaint and summons for the clerk's administrative needs, for service on each defendant, and for your own files.

b.   Summons content

Rule 4(a) controls the summons content. The following example contains the standard elements of a summons.

28. Wright §§64-65; Moore's Manual §§6.01-6.19; Manual of Federal Practice §§3.80-3.94; Moore's Federal Practice §§4.02-4.46; Wright & Miller §§1061-1153.
29. See Wright §64.

Example:

SUMMONS

To: _____ *(defendant)* _____

You are hereby summoned and required to serve upon _____
_____, plaintiff's attorney, whose address is _____
_____, an answer to the complaint that is hereby served
upon you, within 20 days after service upon you, exclusive of the day of
service.

If you fail to do so, judgment by default will be taken against you for
the relief demanded in the complaint.

_____

Clerk of Court

[Seal of the U.S. District Court]

Dated _____

If there is a technical defect in the summons, such as the misspelling of
the defendant's name, the court, in its discretion, may allow an amendment of the summons.

The federal summons is used even if service is effected under state
service rules. (There is no longer a requirement that the summons conform to state law requirements where service is effected by state statute or
court rule.)

c. Persons who may serve the summons

As a general rule, the complaint and summons can be served by any
person who is not a party and is at least 18 years old. Service by the U.S.
Marshal is now required only in limited circumstances specified in Rule
4(c)(2) — for actions brought in forma pauperis and for actions brought
by a seaman. On motion of a plaintiff, the court may appoint a process
server.

d. Methods of service

How service of summons may be made depends on the entity being
served, and is governed by Rule 4(c)-(j).

i. Individuals

An individual under Rule 4(e) can be served a summons in several
ways. First, service can be made by personally giving the individual a copy
of the complaint and summons. Second, it can be made by leaving a copy
of the complaint and summons "at the individual's dwelling house or

usual place of abode'' with a person of suitable age and discretion residing there. Third, service can be made on an agent authorized by appointment or law to receive process. Fourth, where the individual is out of state, service may be made when any federal statute authorizes out-of-state service, pursuant to the laws of the state in which service is effected, and when a statute of the state in which the district court sits permits out-of-state service. These are the state long-arm statutes, which provide for extraterritorial service on any defendant who has had constitutionally sufficient contacts with that state.[30]

Finally, Rule 4(d) allows the plaintiff to request that the defendant waive formal service of the summons. Individuals, corporations, and associations that receive such a request for waiver of service then have a duty to avoid unnecessary service costs. The rule contains an incentive for a defendant to comply with the request by signing and returning it in a timely manner: additional time to answer the complaint. If defendant does not comply, he becomes responsible for the costs of formal service. This request and waiver, coupled with mail service has become the predominant method under which individuals (and domestic and foreign corporations, partnerships, and unincorporated associations) are served. Its effect has been to eliminate the U.S. Marshal's office from the substantial bulk of process serving which that office had historically done.

Under Rule 4(d)(2), valid service is accomplished by using first class mail or other reliable means such as messenger or fax to deliver to the defendant two copies of a notice of commencement of the action and request for waiver of service, a copy of the complaint, notice to the defendant of the duty to avoid unnecessary costs of service and the penalties for non-compliance, and two copies of a waiver form and prepaid means of compliance (such as a return envelope, postage prepaid). The request must state the date on which it was sent. Forms 1A and 1B in the Appendix of Forms to the Federal Rules of Civil Procedure illustrate the text of the requirements for this rule. The person served then completes and signs one copy of the notice and waiver and returns it to the sender, who is ordinarily the plaintiff's lawyer. Note that sending the summons and complaint by registered or certified mail does not eliminate the requirement that the sender receive a signed acknowledgment of service from the person served. This method of service can be used for those defendants who reside in the forum state, those who reside outside the forum state, and even those who reside in foreign countries.

If the sender does not receive the completed waiver of service within 30 days (60 days in the case of foreign defendants) of the date the request is sent, service of the complaint and summons must be made under Rule 4(e), (f), or (h), which, in the case of individuals, is effected by the means mentioned above. If this method of service becomes necessary, the court shall order the costs incurred in effecting service, and the costs (including attorney's fees) of any motion to collect the cost of service to be paid by the person served.

---

30. See §3.6.

The intent and effect of the service by mail and waiver of formal service rules are clear. Service by mail is easier, quicker, and less expensive, and the requirement of the signed waiver returned to the sender eliminates the need for the traditional proof of service. Only if the person served by mail refuses or fails to return the signed waiver within the 30-day period is the sender then obligated to use other methods of service and the person served obligated to bear the actual cost of service.

The waiver of formal service rules is attractive, but it has one important caveat. If the case is in federal court based on diversity jurisdiction, state law will control what needs to be done to toll the running of the statute of limitations. Some states require not only filing of the complaint, but also require actual proper service of the complaint and summons on the defendant. If the defendant refuses to sign the waiver of formal service and return it to the plaintiff, and the statute of limitations runs before the plaintiff properly serves the defendant through one of the other methods permitted by Rule 4, the lawsuit will be time-barred. Accordingly, a plaintiff should always serve the defendant with the complaint and summons through another method when faced with an imminent running of the statute of limitations.

ii.   Infants and incompetents

Service on infants and incompetents is made in the same manner as service would be made under the law of the state in which service is to be made. While state laws vary, they usually require service on a parent or a legal guardian of the infant or incompetent.

Service can also be made upon infants and incompetents in foreign countries under Rule 4(g). In such a case, service would be made according to the law of the foreign country or as the court directs.

iii.   Corporations, partnerships, and associations

Service on domestic and foreign corporations, partnerships, and unincorporated associations that can be sued in their own name can be made several ways under Rule 4(h). First, service can be made by personal delivery to an officer, manager, or general agent. Second, service can be made to an agent authorized to receive service of process; the list of domestic and foreign corporations, usually compiled by each state's Secretary of State or Corporation Commission, should show the authorized agent for service of process. Third, when the corporation is out of state, service can be made under any federal statute providing for service or under any method permitted by a statute of the state in which the district court sits—principally the state's long-arm statute—or service can be made pursuant to the law of the state in which service is effected. Finally, service can be made by mail using the procedure set forth by Rule 4(d)(2). This mail service procedure, which is the same as permitted for individuals, described above, is now the most common way corporations are served with a complaint and summons.

iv.   Officers and agencies of the United States, foreign, state and local governments

Rule 4(i) details the requirements for service on the United States and its federal agencies and employees, and Rule 4(j) details the requirements for foreign, state and local governments. The requirements are technical, and the Rule should always be reviewed before attempting service.

e.   Territorial limits of service

The geographical scope of service is governed by Rule 4(k). There are four basic precepts.

i.   Statewide service

Summons may be served anywhere within the state in which the district court sits.

ii.   The 100 mile "bulge" rule

The 100 mile "bulge" provision provides for some service within 100 miles of the place where the original action commenced, even if state lines are crossed. However, this rule applies only to parties brought in as third-party defendants under Rule 14, or as additional necessary parties to a counterclaim or cross-claim under Rules 13 and 19.

The purpose of the rule is to permit service of process on additional parties that are brought into the action after the original suit is filed and are necessary for a fair and complete disposition of the action. This is an important rule for multi-party litigation in large metropolitan areas such as New York, Chicago, and Washington, D.C., which cover several jurisdictions, since otherwise it would often be difficult to serve every party in the suit.

iii.   State long-arm statutes

Rule 4(e) provides for service on parties outside the state in which the district court sits whenever that state permits out-of-state service. The Rule refers, of course, to state long-arm statutes and attachment procedures that create quasi in rem jurisdiction.[31] It puts federal and state process on essentially the same footing as far as territorial limits are concerned

iv.   Federal statute or court order

Whenever a federal statute or court order authorizes service on a party outside the state in which the district court sits, service may be made in accordance with the statute or order.

31. See §3.6.

If the Rule 4(k) requirements are met, proper service of summons or filing a waiver of service is deemed to establish personal jurisdiction over a defendant. Under Rule 4(k)(2), if the exercise of jurisdiction over the defendant is constitutionally proper, service of summons or filing a waiver of service is also effective to confer personal jurisdiction over a defendant as to any federal claims, even if the defendant is not subject to personal jurisdiction in any state courts.

Finally, keep in mind that under Rule 4(d)(1) a waiver of service of summons does not constitute a waiver of objections to the jurisdiction of the court over the defendant or to venue. A defendant can waive service of summons and thereafter contest personal jurisdiction and venue in a Rule 12(b) motion or in the answer.

f. Timeliness of service

Under Rule 4(m) service of the complaint and summons must be carried out within 120 days after filing of the complaint. Unless good cause can be shown for not having carried out service in time, the action will be dismissed without prejudice as to the unserved defendant.

The complaint, of course, may be refiled against that same party. Refiling after the statute of limitations has run should not create a problem, so long as the original action was properly filed within the limitations period. The reasoning for this is similar to the "relation back" analysis for amended and supplemental pleadings.[32] However, when a state cause of action is asserted and state law requires more than the mere filing of the complaint to satisfy the state statute of limitations, such as actual service of summons, these additional requirements must be met within the limitations period.[33]

g. Proof of service

As discussed above, the complaint and summons are served most commonly today by mail service under the waiver rules of Rule 4(d). The proof of service will be the Notice and Waiver of Service of Summons (Forms 1A and 1B in the Appendix of Forms) that the served party signs and returns to the sender, who is usually the plaintiff's lawyer.

When the complaint and summons are served through a process server, Rule 4(l) requires that the person serving process establish proof of service promptly and in any event within the time during which the party served has to respond to the process. If process is served by anyone other than the U.S. marshal, proof must be in affidavit form. In practice, the proof-of-service affidavit is usually found on the summons form.

---

32. See §5.13.
33. See Wright §64; Wright & Miller §1057. The leading case is Ragan v. Merchants Transfer & Warehouse Co., 337 U.S. 530 (1949).

Example:

AFFIDAVIT OF SERVICE

I, _____, having been first duly
sworn, state that I served a copy of the summons and complaint on
_____ by _____ at
     (defendant)   *(method of service)*
_____ on _____ .
     (address)   *(date)*

_____
                           (signature)

Signed and sworn to before me
on: _____

_____

Notary Public

My commission expires on _____

h. Informal service

Sometimes you will know the lawyer who will represent the defendant in the lawsuit. You may have already had contact with the defendant's lawyer before filing suit, or you may know the lawyer who regularly handles the defendant's legal matters. In such instances, a good practice is to call the lawyer and let her know you are about to file suit. Ask her if she will accept service of process on behalf of the defendant. If so, simply deliver or mail the complaint and summons to her. However, because Rule 4 requires that the defendant sign and return the notice and waiver of service of summons within 30 days of service (60 days for foreign defendants), make sure that the defendant's lawyer gets the signed waiver from her client and delivers it to you within that time period. Mail service is not deemed effective unless the defendant signs and returns the waiver form.

If you think the defendant will try to avoid service of process, or will contest the validity of service, serve the defendant formally under one of the methods permitted by Rule 4. Otherwise, informal service can be a convenient approach; it is frequently used in commercial litigation with corporate parties.

§5.4. Rule 12 responses[34]

When a complaint and summons have been properly served on a defendant, he can respond in two basic ways. First, he can answer the com-

---

34. Wright §66; James & Hazard §4.2; Friedenthal §§5.22-5.24; Moore's Manual §§11.01-11.07; Manual of Federal Practice §§3.38-3.44, 4.2-4.34; Moore's Federal Practice §§12.05-12.23; Wright & Miller §§1341-1397.

plaint. Ordinarily, the defendant must answer within 20 days of service. If service was timely waived by the defendant, the defendant has 60 days from the date the request was mailed to serve an answer (90 days in the case of foreign defendants).

Second, before filing an answer the defendant can make any of three motions attacking claimed defects in the complaint.[35] These are a motion to strike, a motion for a more definite statement, and a motion to dismiss, all of which are governed by Rule 12. Where a defendant decides to attack the complaint with a Rule 12 motion, he must do so within the time permitted for his answer, ordinarily within 20 days of service of the complaint.[36]

1.   Motion to strike[37]

Under Rule 12(f), if the complaint contains "any redundant, immaterial, impertinent or scandalous matter," it can be stricken upon motion. While such a motion is not frequently made, it should be considered where there is a possibility that the complaint will be read to the jury during trial.

Example:

[Caption]

MOTION TO STRIKE

Defendant Johnson Corporation moves under Rule 12(f) for an order striking certain immaterial and scandalous matters from the complaint. In support of its motion defendant states:

1. Par. 2 of the complaint alleges that the "Johnson Corporation had gross receipts of $102,436,000 for fiscal year 1998." This allegation is immaterial to a contract action and should be stricken.

2. Par. 7 of the complaint alleges that the "Johnson Corporation is an international cartel that dominates the furniture polish industry." This allegation is impertinent and scandalous and should be stricken.

WHEREFORE, defendant Johnson Corporation requests that the court enter an order striking these parts of plaintiff's complaint and requiring plaintiff to file an amended complaint that deletes the stricken matter within 10 days.

---

35. See §5.3 for the requirements of a complaint.

36. If a Rule 12 motion is denied, a defendant generally has 10 days from the denial of the motion to answer the complaint.

37. Wright §66; James & Hazard §4.2; Friedenthal §5.24; Moore's Manual §11.05; Manual of Federal Practice §§4.20-4.22; Moore's Federal Practice §12.21; Wright & Miller §§1380-1383.

2. Motion for a more definite statement[38]

Under Rule 12(e), if the complaint is "so vague or ambiguous" that the defendant cannot respond to it, the defendant may move for a more definite statement. The motion must point out the defects and specify the details that are needed. However, since the complaint need only be a "short and plain statement," and pleadings generally should be "simple, concise and direct," and because discovery is the preferred method for flushing out details, such motions are disfavored and infrequently granted. A more commonly used approach is to move to dismiss under Rule 12(b)(6) for failure to state a claim on which relief can be granted.

On the other hand, this motion may become more frequently used in districts that follow Rule 26(a)'s automatic disclosure requirement. Since that rule requires initial disclosures for "disputed facts alleged with particularity in the pleadings," lawyers may use the motion to try to obtain more details about the pleadings before attempting to make the initial disclosures.

Example:

Caption

MOTION FOR A MORE DEFINITE STATEMENT

Defendant Johnson Corporation moves under Rule 12(e) for an order requiring plaintiff to provide a more definite statement. In support of its motion defendant states:

1. Par. 3 of the complaint alleges that "plaintiff and defendant and others entered into an agreement in 1998 under which defendant was obligated to deliver such amounts of furniture polish as plaintiff may from time to time request."

2. Nowhere else in the complaint is greater detail provided, and no copy of any contract is attached to the complaint. Without additional details, defendant cannot respond to this allegation.

WHEREFORE, defendant Johnson Corporation requests that the court enter an order requiring defendant to serve and file a more definite statement within 10 days showing what date this alleged contract was entered into, where it was entered into, every party to it, the requirements under the contract, and, if in writing, a copy of the alleged contract.

---

38. Wright §66; James & Hazard §4.2; Friedenthal §5.23; Moore's Manual §11.07; Manual of Federal Practice §§4.18-4.20; Moore's Federal Practice §§12.17-12.19; Wright & Miller §§1374-1379.

3. Motion to dismiss under Rule 12(b)[39]

Under Rule 12(b), the defendant may raise certain defenses either in the answer or by a motion to dismiss. This is the predominant motion for attacking the complaint, and it has several important characteristics.

a. The one motion requirement

If you decide to respond to the complaint with a motion to dismiss on Rule 12(b) grounds, the Rule requires that you present all defenses that can be raised in one motion to dismiss. In other words, you must consolidate all available Rule 12(b) defenses into one motion. This requirement prevents attacking the complaint on a piecemeal basis.

b. Rule 12(b) defenses

The following defenses may be raised in a motion to dismiss:

1. Lack of subject matter jurisdiction
2. Lack of jurisdiction over the person
3. Improper venue
4. Insufficiency of process
5. Insufficiency of service of process
6. Failure to state a claim upon which relief can be granted
7. Failure to join a party under Rule 19

In addition, there is some case law holding that affirmative defenses in Rule 8(c) may be asserted in a Rule 12(b) motion to dismiss.[40]

Federal practice has eliminated the need for special appearances to contest personal jurisdiction, since under Rule 12(g) the joinder of defenses does not create a waiver of any of them. Hence, a defendant can raise any of the Rule 12(b) defenses by motion and is not held to have waived the right to assert lack of personal jurisdiction.[41]

c. Waiver

Under Rule 12(g) and (h), defenses not consolidated into one motion to dismiss may be waived, but the waiver rules depend on the defense involved. Lack of jurisdiction over the person, improper venue, insufficiency of process, and insufficiency of service of process are all waived if not included in a motion to strike or, if no motion is made, in the answer. Hence, if any of these grounds are raised in a motion to dismiss, the others must be raised then as well, or they will be waived. Failure to state a claim and failure to join an indispensable party, however, may be raised

39. Wright §66; James & Hazard §4.2; Friedenthal §5.22; Moore's Manual §11.06; Manual of Federal Practice §§3.38-3.44, 4.23-4.30; Moore's Federal Practice §§12.07-12.14, 12.22-12.23; Wright & Miller §§1347-1366.
40. See Moore's Manual §1606(3); Manual of Federal Practice §3.41.
41. See Manual of Federal Practice §3.41.

in the answer, in a motion for judgment on the pleadings, or at trial. Finally, lack of subject matter jurisdiction is never waived and can be raised at any time.

The waiver rules create two categories of defenses to a claim. The procedural irregularity defenses are waived unless timely presented, while substantive defenses to a valid judgment cannot be so waived.

d. Practice approach

The underlying theory of Rule 12 must be kept in mind when deciding whether to present Rule 12(b) defenses in a motion to dismiss or in the answer. The Rule permits certain defenses that may terminate the litigation to be presented and heard early in the litigation process. This is obviously an efficient way to deal with a defective or meritless complaint. If you decide to assert a defense in a motion to dismiss, you should raise the other Rule 12(b) defenses available and assert them in one consolidated motion, because most of those defenses are waived if not raised then.

Second, consider the types of defenses that can be raised. Three of the grounds, lack of jurisdiction over the person, insufficiency of process, and insufficiency of service of process, are essentially procedural defects that usually can be cured. Since the plaintiff can ordinarily file an amended complaint or serve process on the defendant again, there may be little point in raising these defenses if the plaintiff can easily cure them. For example, where there is no proper personal jurisdiction over the defendant because of a defect in the process, but it is obvious that the defendant can be properly served later, there may be little point in raising these defenses even though they are technically available. On the other hand, where personal jurisdiction over the defendant does not properly exist, and probably cannot be obtained, the motion should be made.

If the defense is improper venue, the defense is waived if not included in a motion to dismiss that raises other 12(b) defenses.[42] Hence, if venue is in fact improper under venue rules, and the present venue is a logistically inconvenient location for the defendant, the motion should be made. If granted, the probable result will not be dismissal, but transfer to a proper venue.[43]

Finally, where the defenses are lack of subject matter jurisdiction, failure to state a claim upon which relief can be granted, and failure to join an indispensable party, the defendant has more flexibility since these may be made either in the answer or by a motion for judgment on the pleadings, even if a motion to dismiss based on other Rule 12(b) grounds has been made. Hence, the defendant has the option of including these grounds in a motion to dismiss or raising them later. Raising them by motion to dismiss, of course, will get the issue resolved sooner than by including them in the answer. Regardless of which approach is taken,

42. See §3.7 supra; 28 U.S.C. §§1391 et seq.
43. See §3.7 supra; 28 U.S.C. §§1404, 1406.

however, the plaintiff is on notice of a possible defect in his
can usually file an amended complaint correcting the defe

The history of Rule 12(b) shows that motions to dismis
in the final disposition of a lawsuit.[44] Indeed, federal plea
signed to frame issues, not resolve disputes. Hence, the tren
practice has been to make fewer motions under Rule 12, and
defenses instead in the answer; that is, to raise those defense........ a ...o..o..
to dismiss only when there is a clear strategic reason to do so, not simply
because the Rules permit it.

A motion to dismiss based on Rule 12(b) should clearly set out the
defenses being asserted in separate paragraphs.

Example:

[Caption]

MOTION TO DISMISS

Defendant Jones moves under Rule 12(b) for an order dismissing the
complaint. In support of his motion defendant states:

1. The court lacks jurisdiction over the subject matter of this action
because it appears from the complaint that the alleged claim does not
arise under the Constitution of the United States, any Act of Congress,
or treaties of the United States.

2. The court lacks jurisdiction over the subject matter of this action
because the controversy is not between citizens of different states, and
because the amount in controversy between the plaintiff and this defendant is less than $75,000, exclusive of interest and costs.

3. The court lacks jurisdiction over the defendant because the defendant is a corporation incorporated under the laws of the State of
Delaware, has its principal place of business in Delaware, and is not subject to service in the State of Maryland where service was attempted.

4. This action has been brought in an improper district, since the
complaint alleges that jurisdiction is based on diversity of citizenship,
plaintiff is a citizen of the State of California, defendant is a citizen of
the State of Nevada, and the claims arose in the State of Nevada. Venue
in the district of Arizona is therefore improper.

5. Service of process on the defendant was insufficient because service was made on the defendant's business partner at his place of business, as shown by the proof of service for the summons.

6. The complaint fails to state a claim against this defendant on
which relief can be granted.

7. The complaint fails to join all indispensable parties as required
by Rule 19 because the Phillips Corporation is an indispensable party,
has not been joined as a party, and if brought within this court's juris-

44. See Wright §66.

diction would destroy this court's jurisdiction since complete diversity would be lacking.

WHEREFORE, defendant Jones requests that the court enter an order dismissing the complaint.

The basic allegations of Rule 12(b) grounds should be developed both factually and legally. Where facts are necessary, statements in affidavit form and exhibits should be attached to the motion, although the court under the Rule can then treat the motion as one for summary judgment. If case law is pertinent, it should be contained in a memorandum of law accompanying the motion.

The most commonly raised ground for dismissal, of course, is Rule 12(b)(6), failure to state a claim upon which relief can be granted. The motion should be granted if, based on facts alleged and applicable law, there is no possible set of facts that could support the claim under any available legal theory.[45] The motion is conceptually limited to matters alleged in the complaint. If facts outside the pleadings are presented at a hearing on the motion, the court should treat the motion as one for summary judgment and proceed in accordance with Rule 56. If the motion is granted, plaintiff will routinely be given leave to file an amended complaint. However, if the plaintiff is acting in bad faith, has repeatedly failed to amend properly, or obviously cannot amend properly, leave to amend should be denied.[46]

Service of the motion must be made in one of the ways permitted under Rule 5 on every other party presently in the case. The most common methods are service by mail or personal service.

§5.5. Answers[47]

When the plaintiff's complaint has been properly served on a defendant, that defendant must respond, either by filing a Rule 12 motion, discussed in the preceding section, or by answering the complaint. The answer, like any other pleading and court paper, must comply with the requirements of Rule 11, under which a lawyer signing the answer thereby certifies that the denials of factual contentions are warranted on the evidence and that there are no frivolous legal arguments.

1. Timing

As a general rule, under Rule 12(a) the defendant must serve an answer within 20 days of service of the complaint and summons. Different deadlines may apply if the U.S. government is a defendant, or if a specific

45. See Conley v. Gibson, 355 U.S. 41 (1957).
46. Foman v. Davis, 371 U.S. 178 (1962).
47. Wright §66; James & Hazard §§4.4-4.8; Friedenthal §§5.17-5.20; Moore's Manual §11.08; Manual of Federal Practice §§3.28-3.44; Moore's Federal Practice §§8.21-8.29, 12.05-12.07; Wright & Miller §§1261-1279, 1347-1348.

federal statute applies. In addition, if service was timely wai
fendant, the defendant has 60 days from the date the requ
to serve an answer (90 days in the case of foreign defendan
tional time is an added inducement to defendants to waive
lowing the waiver provisions of Rule 4(d). Where the de
responds with a Rule 12 motion, the answer is due within 10
defendant receives notice of the court's action on the mot~~ion or within~~
10 days after service of a more definite statement.

2. General requirements

There are several rules that regulate the form and content of the answer.
Rule 8(b) requires that an answer shall "state in short and plain terms"
the defenses asserted. It must either admit or deny the allegations, or state
that the defendant is without knowledge or information sufficient to form
a belief as to their truth. Under Rule 8(c), affirmative defenses must be
set out in the answer, and under Rule 12(b), the specified defenses may
be set out as well. The defenses may be set out alternatively, inconsistently, and hypothetically. A hypothetical defense can be raised to an allegation in a complaint if it is found to be true, thus permitting a response
that both denies the allegation and raises a hypothetical defense to it.

Since a complaint must be answered, failing to answer will constitute
an admission of all facts alleged in the complaint; this does not apply, however, to the prayer for relief. Answering with a simple "admit," "deny," or
"no knowledge or belief" is usually sufficient. Under Rule 9(a), however,
where the answer raises an issue as to the "legal existence of any party or
the capacity of any party to sue or be sued or the authority of a party to
sue or be sued in a representative capacity," the denials must be made
with particularity.

To parallel the complaint, the answer must be organized in paragraphs and by counts, setting out separate defenses in separate counts.
Where there is only one defendant the answer is simply titled "ANSWER."
If there are multiple defendants, however, the title should specify the party
answering, for example, "ANSWER OF DEFENDANT ACME TOOL COR-
PORATION." If a defendant demands a jury trial, the "JURY TRIAL DE-
MANDED" notice should appear in the caption of the answer, and the
words "DEFENDANT DEMANDS TRIAL BY JURY" at the end of the answer. Finally, the answer, like every pleading, must be signed by the lawyer; this signature constitutes a certification that the pleading is made in
accordance with Rule 11.

The answer, therefore, may have three parts: responses to the complaint's allegations, affirmative defenses, and Rule 12(b) defenses. A well-
drafted answer will set out each part clearly.

3. Responses

Rule 8(b) permits three types of responses to the complaint's allegations.
The answer may either admit or deny the allegations, or state that the

party is without knowledge or information sufficient to form a belief as to their truth. The format, whether informally brief or more formal, is largely a matter of local custom, although the trend is toward brief responses. Instead of referring to the "defendant," use the defendant's name after the introductory statement. This personalizes the party in the answer.

Example:

[Caption]

ANSWER

Defendant Jones answers the complaint as follows:

Count I

1. Admits.
2. Jones admits the allegations in Par. 2.
3. Denies.
4. Jones denies the allegations in Par. 4.
5. No knowledge or belief.
6. Jones states that she is without knowledge or information sufficient to form a belief as to the truth of the allegations in Par. 6, and therefore denies them.

If the response is "no knowledge or belief," this must be based on good faith. Such a response should not be available on matters that are common knowledge or that can easily be learned by the defendant.[48] For example, if the complaint alleges that the defendant corporation had "gross receipts during 1998 in the amount of $6,450,000," the defendant's lawyer cannot answer "no knowledge or belief" since the lawyer can easily find out if the allegation is true or not.

The answer may admit only part of an allegation and deny the remainder, or may admit having no knowledge or information as to the remainder, as the case may be. Each paragraph of the complaint must be responded to individually, unless the defendant can in good faith collectively deny every allegation of the complaint.

Example:

1. Jones admits he is a citizen of the State of California, but denies the remaining allegations in Par. 1.
2. Jones admits he entered into a written contract with plaintiff on June 1, 1998, but denies that the contract was modified by agreement on August 1, 1998, or on any other date.

---

48. See Moore's Manual §11.08(2).

3. Jones denies he owned and operated a business known as Jones Excavating in 1998 or any other year. Jones does not have sufficient knowledge or information to form a belief as to the truth of the other allegations in Par. 3, and therefore denies them.

Within these guidelines the rules permit considerable drafting flexibility. The modern trend is toward brevity and conciseness. The standard approach is to simply have counts and numbered paragraphs corresponding to the counts and paragraphs of the complaint. However, it is just as effective to set out admissions, denials, and no-knowledge-or-information responses collectively when the situation is appropriate.

Example:

Count I

1. Jones admits the allegations of Pars. 1, 2, 3, 4, 5, and 6 of the complaint.
2. Jones denies the allegations of Pars. 8, 9, and 10 of the complaint.
3. Jones states she does not have sufficient knowledge or information to form a belief as to the truth of the allegations in Par. 7, and therefore denies them.
4. Jones denies all other allegations of Count I not specifically admitted.

Count II

1. Jones incorporates her answers to Pars. 1-3 of Count I.
2. Jones denies all other allegations of Count II.

Denying all allegations not specifically admitted is a safe practice, since this prevents a typographical error in the answer from prejudicing the defendant.

Claims under Rule 9(a) of no capacity or authority and claims under Rule 9(c) that conditions precedent have not been performed are raised by denials, but must be particularly specified.

Example:

1. Jones denies that plaintiff is a legal entity that has capacity to sue in its own name, and specifically denies that plaintiff has any legal existence that permits it to pursue this action in the name of "John Smith Corporation."
2. Jones denies that plaintiff has performed all conditions precedent as required under the contract, and specifically denies that plaintiff delivered a copy of the contract to Jones within 30 days of execution, although plaintiff was required to do so before the contract would be in force.

Not every allegation in the complaint must be responded to, since not every count, or every paragraph in a count, will contain an allegation directed at your defendant. Where you represent one defendant in a case that has multiple defendants, and some counts or paragraphs do not apply to your defendant, the usual practice is to point this out in your answer. This avoids the possibility of "silence" in your answer being interpreted as an admission.

Example:

Count II

The allegations in this count are not directed to this defendant.

Example:

12. The allegations in Par. 12 of plaintiff's complaint are not directed toward this defendant, so this defendant makes no answer to the allegations.

4. Rule 12(b) defenses

As discussed previously,[49] the defendant can raise Rule 12(b) defenses in a pre-answer motion to dismiss or can include them in the answer. If the defenses are raised in the answer, each should be labeled separately to refer to the specific defense being asserted, preferably by tracking the language of Rule 12(b) and elaborating where necessary.

Example:

FIRST DEFENSE

The complaint fails to state a claim against the defendant on which relief can be granted.

SECOND DEFENSE

This court lacks jurisdiction over the subject matter of this action, since the complaint alleges that jurisdiction is based on diversity of citizenship and there is no allegation that the amount in controversy exceeds $75,000, exclusive of interest and costs.

What is a "defense"? The safe approach is to list as a defense anything that might defeat part or all of any claim or request for damages in the plaintiff's complaint. For example, in a contract case the answer might

49. See §5.4.

list as a defense that plaintiff is not entitled to any damages that are not consequential damages. There is no penalty for incorrectly characterizing something as a defense; there is a risk that something not raised as a defense in the answer will be deemed waived because it is a defense that should have been raised.

5. Affirmative defenses

Rule 8(c) sets forth what it characterizes as affirmative defenses:

> accord and satisfaction, arbitration and award, assumption of risk, contributory negligence, discharge in bankruptcy, duress, estoppel, failure of consideration, fraud, illegality, injury by fellow servant, laches, license, payment, release, res judicata, statute of frauds, statute of limitations, waiver, and any other matter constituting an avoidance or affirmative defense.

Keep in mind that other defenses have also been characterized as affirmative defenses.[50] An affirmative defense is generally one in which a defendant has a burden of raising in the answer, and on which a defendant has a burden of proving at trial, unless in diversity cases applicable state law holds otherwise. When answering the complaint, the usual practice is to label each affirmative defense separately, and clearly describe the affirmative defense being asserted, preferably by using the language of Rule 8(c) and elaborating where necessary.

Example:

FIRST AFFIRMATIVE DEFENSE

Plaintiff's claim set out in the complaint did not occur within two years before commencement of this action, and is barred by the applicable statute of limitations.

SECOND AFFIRMATIVE DEFENSE

Plaintiff's claim is barred by defendant's discharge in bankruptcy.

Affirmative defenses are usually considered substantive. In diversity cases, therefore, the trial court will apply the substantive law of the state in which it is sitting.[51] That forum state's law must be researched for the substantive law that will apply under its conflict of law rules and for the recognized defenses. However, under state law an affirmative defense may not necessarily be one that the defendant has the burden of pleading. The danger in asserting such a defense as an affirmative defense in the answer

50. See Manual of Federal Practice §3.35.
51. This is the rule of Erie R.R. Co. v. Tompkins, 304 U.S. 64 (1938). See §3.2.

is that the defendant may be held to have undertaken the burden of proof. On the other hand, failing to raise in the answer all affirmative defenses mentioned in Rule 8(c) runs the risk that the defenses will be waived.[52] The safer course is to raise the defense and make it clear that you do not intend to assume a burden of proof not existing under state law.

Example:

THIRD AFFIRMATIVE DEFENSE

Plaintiff was contributorily negligent in sustaining the injuries complained of in her complaint. By raising the defense of contributory negligence, however, defendant expressly does not assume any burden of proof that applicable substantive law may place on plaintiff.

6. Practice approach

Drafting answers to complaints involves two basic considerations. First, make sure you respond to every allegation in every paragraph of every count of the complaint, since any allegation not responded to is deemed admitted. A safe practice is to deny all allegations not specifically admitted or otherwise answered. Where the allegations are admitted in part and denied in part, make sure the answer clearly states the facts being admitted and clearly denies all remaining allegations. Clear, simple language is critical here.

There may be times, however, when you may wish to admit an allegation even though you are not required to admit it. Remember that pleadings are always interrelated with discovery. If a fact alleged is denied, a plaintiff will invariably focus some of his discovery efforts on the denied fact. On the other hand, admitting a fact may have the effect of preventing further discovery of information that would prove the fact. When that information contains harmful or embarrassing facts, it may make sense to simply admit the allegation in your answer, although you could have—consistent with Rule 11—denied it.

Second, set out all Rule 12(b) defenses and affirmative defenses that you can raise in good faith; it is best to list and label them separately. There is no penalty for raising inconsistent, hypothetical, or alternative defenses. If you are in doubt whether a defense is considered an affirmative defense, the safer course is to raise it in the answer. The real danger is that you will fail to raise a defense with the result that it will be waived. If you need additional time to study potential defenses, it is better to move for additional time to respond than to serve a hastily considered answer.

If the plaintiff has not made a jury demand with the complaint and you want a jury trial, you must make an appropriate jury demand on the

---

52. See Manual of Federal Practice §3.37; Moore's Manual §11.08(4).

answer. If the plaintiff has made a jury demand on the complaint, you need not make one, although the safer approach is to make the demand on the answer as well. The jury demand is usually made by putting the words "JURY TRIAL DEMANDED" below the case number and the words "DEFENDANT DEMANDS TRIAL BY JURY" at the end of the answer. Local rules usually have additional requirements, such as jury demand forms and fees.

Service of the answer must be made in one of the ways permitted by Rule 5 on every other party presently in the case. The most common methods are service by mail or personal service on each party's lawyer.

The answer must have a proof of service showing that the answer was actually served on each party's lawyer. While local rules usually specify how proof of service should be made, the usual practice is to have a certificate from a lawyer or an affidavit from a nonlawyer state how and when service was actually made. The signed certificate or signed and notarized affidavit on the original is then filed with the clerk of the court.

Example:

CERTIFICATE OF SERVICE

I, ___*(attorney)*___ , state that I served the above by mailing a copy to the attorneys for ___*(plaintiff/defendant)*___ at ___*(state address)*___ on ___*(date)*___ .

Dated: _____   _____
                                     Name of attorney
                                     Address
                                     Tel. No.

AFFIDAVIT OF SERVICE

I, _____*(name)*_____ having been first duly sworn, state that I served the above by mailing a copy to the attorneys for the other parties at their addresses of record in this case.

                                     _____
                                     Name

Signed and subscribed to before me on ___*(date)*___ .

_____
Notary Public

My commission expires on ___*(date)*___ .

§5.6. *Counterclaims*[53]

In addition to Rule 12 motions and the answer, both of which are responses to the complaint, a defendant can also counterclaim. This is a pleading brought against a plaintiff within the time the defendant has to answer. The counterclaim is functionally identical to a complaint, and is made part of the answer. As such, the analytical approach and the pleading strategy for the counterclaim are the same as for a complaint. The plaintiff must respond to the counterclaim, either with Rule 12 motions or a reply, within the usual time limits. Counterclaims are either compulsory or permissive, and substantially different rules apply to each.

1. Compulsory counterclaims

Compulsory counterclaims, governed by Rule 13(a), are claims that a defendant is required to bring against the plaintiff. The purpose of the compulsory counterclaim rule is clear: If the court already has jurisdiction over the plaintiff, the defendant, and the subject matter of the lawsuit, it makes sense to hear and adjudicate at one time all claims related to the occurrence or transaction involved.

A claim is compulsory if four requirements are met:

1. the claim must already exist when the defendant is required to answer the complaint;
2. the claim must arise out of the same transaction or occurrence on which the complaint is based;
3. the court must be able to obtain jurisdiction over any necessary additional parties; and
4. the counterclaim must not be the subject of a pending action.[54]

No jurisdictional dollar amount is necessary. The court has ancillary jurisdiction over the counterclaim even if the plaintiff voluntarily dismisses the complaint. However, if the complaint is dismissed for jurisdictional defects, the counterclaim will be dismissed unless it has an independent jurisdictional basis.

The principal difficulty with compulsory counterclaims is in determining if the defendant's claim involves the same transaction or occurrence that gave rise to the plaintiff's claim. While this is often easy to determine in tort claims, such as an automobile accident, it is often a difficult question in the corporate and commercial area where numerous lengthy transactions are often involved. Courts have devised several approaches for determining whether the "same transaction or occurrence" is involved. These include deciding whether the legal or factual

53. Wright §79; James & Hazard §4.8; Friedenthal §6.7; Moore's Manual §11.09; Manual of Federal Practice §§3.45-3.50; Moore's Federal Practice §§13.02-13.41; Wright & Miller §§1401-1430.
54. See Moore's Manual §11.09(2).

issues are the same, whether the trial would involve the same proof, and whether the complaint and counterclaim are logically related. The purpose of Rule 13(a) is to promote fairness and efficiency by having related claims heard in one trial with consistent results. Accordingly, the phrase in general has been broadly interpreted. The "logical relation" test, the most flexible approach, has the support of most of the treatises on the topic.[55]

Keep in mind that where there is proper jurisdiction over the plaintiff's complaint, the court will also have ancillary jurisdiction over the compulsory counterclaims. In addition, since the plaintiff selected the venue by filing the original complaint, the plaintiff cannot complain about the same venue for the defendant's counterclaim. Hence, there are no basic jurisdiction or venue problems associated with bringing compulsory counterclaims.[56]

2. Permissive counterclaims

Permissive counterclaims, governed by Rule 13(b), are claims that a defendant may bring, but is not required to bring, against a plaintiff in the pending lawsuit. A counterclaim is permissive if it does not arise out of the transaction or occurrence on which the plaintiff's complaint is based.

A permissive counterclaim, because it is a claim asserting different grounds than the complaint, must have a separate jurisdictional basis. The reasoning behind the requirement is that a defendant cannot use a counterclaim to bring another claim into federal court that could not have been filed there as an original claim. A permissive counterclaim, in other words, cannot enlarge federal jurisdiction. If the permissive counterclaim has an independent jurisdictional basis, but no proper venue exists in the district where the plaintiff's complaint was filed, it also cannot be brought.[57] Both independent jurisdiction and proper venue must exist before the defendant can bring a permissive counterclaim.

The concept behind the permissive counterclaim rule is fairness. Since a plaintiff has total freedom to bring unrelated claims against the defendant, the defendant should have the same freedom, restricted only by the independent jurisdiction and venue requirements. If the counterclaims make the case too complex, the court can order separate trials on the counterclaims.

3. The United States as plaintiff

When the United States is a plaintiff, Rule 13(d) applies special rules. As a sovereign power, the United States has immunity from suit unless it has waived that immunity and has consented to be sued. No procedural rule

---

55. See Manual of Federal Practice §3.46; Moore's Manual §11.09(3); Wright §79.
56. See Moore's Manual §11.09(5); Wright §79.
57. See Manual of Federal Practice §3.47; Moore's Manual §§11.09(9) and (10).

can enlarge the types of suits that can be brought against the United
States. Accordingly, no counterclaim can be asserted against the United
States unless the government has expressly consented to be sued on that
type of claim. The only exception is recoupment, which can be asserted
as a counterclaim to reduce or defeat a claim.[58] This rule does not work
the other way around; when the United States is a defendant, there is no
equivalent restriction on its right to bring any proper counterclaim against
the plaintiff.

4.   Statutes of limitations

Statutes of limitations are usually considered substantive law. Federal statutes of limitations apply to federal claims, and state statutes apply to state
claims brought under diversity jurisdiction. A counterclaim, like a complaint, must be filed within the applicable statutory period, or it will usually be barred.[59]

5.   Waiver and amended pleadings

Failure to plead a compulsory counterclaim bars the defendant from asserting the claim later in another action. Rule 13(a) operates like a statutory bar in both federal and state courts.[60]

If a counterclaim was omitted through "oversight, inadvertence or
excusable neglect, or when justice requires," the court may permit an
amended answer to include the omitted counterclaim. However, the
court cannot allow such a counterclaim if the statute of limitations has
run because the concept of relation back applies only to amended
pleadings, and a new counterclaim in an amended answer is viewed as a
new pleading.[61]

Under Rule 13(e), a counterclaim that matures or accrues after the
defendant serves his answer may, in the court's discretion, be raised
through a supplemental answer. If the court denies it, no prejudice should
occur because such a counterclaim by definition cannot be compulsory
and the defendant can always assert it later as an independent claim. Of
course, where the defendant requests leave to file a supplemental pleading early in the litigation process and the counterclaim is based on the
same transaction or occurrence as the plaintiff's complaint, leave will usually be granted.

---

58. See Moore's Manual §11.09(20); Manual of Federal Practice §3.49.
59. See Moore's Manual §11.09(18); Wright §79. An exception is recoupment, which
only diminishes or defeats the plaintiff's claim and is usually viewed as arising out of the
same transaction.
60. See Wright §79; this bar is frequently characterized as res judicata, waiver, or estoppel.
61. See Moore's Manual §11.09(17).

6. Practice approach

A counterclaim is simply a complaint brought by a defendant against a plaintiff in a pending suit. In format, content, and signing the counterclaim should be drafted like a complaint.[62] The only difference is that the counterclaim is made part of the defendant's answer and is served on the plaintiff's attorney like any post-complaint pleading, motion, or discovery. It is usually titled "ANSWER AND COUNTERCLAIM," with separate headings and sections for each. If there are several plaintiffs against whom counterclaims are brought, the titles should be specific.

If the counterclaim is not included in the answer, it may be waived. To set it off from the answer, it should be clearly labeled a counterclaim; if you are unsure whether the claim is in fact a counterclaim, the safe course is to label it as such, since there are no penalties for an incorrect designation. If you are unsure whether your counterclaim is compulsory or permissive, the safe course again is to assert the counterclaim to avoid a possible waiver. Finally, since a counterclaim is analogous to a complaint, you should make a jury demand on those counterclaims that you want tried to a jury, since failure to do so may constitute a waiver. The plaintiff's demand for a jury trial will not extend to the defendant's counterclaims.

Example:

COUNTERCLAIM

Defendant Acme Manufacturing complains of plaintiff Wilbur Johnson as follows:

1. [If the counterclaim is permissive, you must allege the jurisdictional basis for bringing the claim in federal court.]

2. [Draft the pleading in the same manner as any complaint.]

7. Plaintiff's responses

The plaintiff must consider how best to respond to the counterclaim and answer. If the answer merely admits or denies the complaint's allegations, the plaintiff ordinarily need do nothing. However, if the answer contains redundant, immaterial, impertinent, or scandalous matters, you as plaintiff can move to strike. If the answer contains Rule 12(b) defenses or affirmative defenses, you may move to strike "any insufficient defense." In short, you can make any of the Rule 12 motions that are available when responding to a complaint. The plaintiff's responses to an answer that includes a counterclaim are discussed in the next section.

---

62. See §5.3.

§5.7. Replies[63]

The plaintiff under Rule 7(a) must reply to a "counterclaim denominated as such." There must be a counterclaim in fact, and it must be labeled a counterclaim on the defendant's answer. Only if both requirements are met must plaintiff reply. These requirements relieve the plaintiff of the burden of correctly guessing if the defendant's pleading is a counterclaim or an affirmative dcfense, since the distinction as a matter of substantive law is not always clear. However, a careful plaintiff will reply to any responsive pleading that may be a counterclaim, even to those not so labeled, since pleadings may be read to the jury during trial.

Since a counterclaim is the functional equivalent of a complaint, the plaintiff in responding is in the same position a defendant is in when responding to the original complaint. Hence, the plaintiff can respond to the counterclaim with any Rule 12 motions or may respond with a reply. The reply itself can answer the counterclaim, assert Rule 12 defenses, and raise Rule 8(c) affirmative defenses.[64]

Because a reply is simply an answer to a counterclaim, the reply should be drafted in the same manner as an answer[65] and should be titled "REPLY." When a plaintiff must respond to more than one counterclaim, the reply should show in the title which counterclaim is being responded to.

Example:

[Caption]

REPLY

Plaintiff Wilbur Johnson replies to Defendant Acme Manufacturing's counterclaim as follows:
1. Johnson admits the allegations in Par. 1 of the counterclaim.
2. . . .
3. . . .
WHEREFORE. . . .

§5.8. Cross-claims[66]

A cross-claim is essentially a complaint brought by one codefendant against another codefendant. Rule 13(g) permits a cross-claim if the claim

---

63. Wright §66; James & Hazard §4.9; Friedenthal §5.21; Moore's Manual §12.03; Manual of Federal Practice §3.55; Moore's Federal Practice §7.03; Wright & Miller §§1184-1188.
64. There is some case law permitting a compulsory counterclaim in the reply as well. See Moore's Manual §12.04.
65. See §5.5.
66. Wright §80; James & Hazard §9.12; Friedenthal §6.8; Moore's Manual §14.04; Manual of Federal Practice §3.51; Moore's Federal Practice §§13.34-13.35; Wright & Miller §§1431-1433.

arises out of the same transaction or occurrence that is the subject matter of the original complaint, or relates to any property that is the subject matter of the original action. If a counterclaim has been brought against two or more plaintiffs, those plaintiffs may cross-claim against each other. Also, if a defendant has brought third-party complaints against additional parties, those third-party defendants may cross-claim against each other.

There are several cross-claim rules that must be understood.

1. Discretionary pleading

Cross-claims are always discretionary. A cross-claimant may, but is not required to, bring his claim in the pending action. The cross-claimant can always bring the claim as a separate action. Hence, there are no waiver dangers involved in this decision.

2. Subject matter

A cross-claim must be based on the subject matter of the original complaint, a counterclaim, or property involved in the original complaint. This restriction is designed to protect the original plaintiff from being unfairly forced into litigation that involves a matter totally different from the matters raised in the original complaint, and one in which he may not have any interest. Requiring the cross-claim to arise out of the same transaction or occurrence as the complaint, or counterclaim, or the property involved in the complaint involves the same test and analysis used for compulsory counterclaims.[67]

The rule allows both matured and contingent cross-claims. Accordingly, claims that the coparty "is or may be liable" for all or part of plaintiff's claim against him are properly raised in the cross-claim. In fact, most cross-claims raise just such issues, usually based on active-passive negligence, indemnity, or contribution.

3. When made

Rule 13(g) requires that the cross-claim be made in a party's responsive pleading, usually the answer. Accordingly, just as a counterclaim must be made when answering a complaint, a cross-claim also must be made at that time. This promotes efficient and orderly pleadings.

4. Jurisdiction, venue, and joinder

Since cross-claims must involve the same subject matter as the original complaint or of a counterclaim, jurisdiction over the cross-claim is considered

---

67. See §5.6.1.

ancillary and venue is considered already established by the original pleading. Hence, there are no jurisdiction or venue problems relative to cross-claims. If the original complaint is dismissed, however, the cross-claim will also be dismissed, unless it has an independent jurisdictional basis.

Difficulties may arise in a related area, however. Rule 13(h) applies the joinder requirements of Rules 19 and 20 to cross- claims as well as to counterclaims. While Rule 13(g) requires that a cross-claim be brought against a coparty, usually a codefendant, additional parties that are indispensable to the cross-claim must be joined. Where an indispensable party cannot be brought in because jurisdiction over the person cannot be obtained, the cross-claim must be dismissed, although the dismissal will necessarily be without prejudice. The cross-claim can always be brought as an independent action later. Further, if the addition of cross-claims makes the trial too complex, the court can order separate trials under Rule 13(i).

5.   Cross-claims against the United States

Cross-claims against the United States cannot enlarge the scope of claims on which the United States as a sovereign power has consented to be sued. The cross-claim, like counterclaims, must be based on a claim that could have been independently brought against the United States. This result appears required by the concept of sovereign immunity, although Rule 13 explicitly requires this only for counterclaims, not cross-claims.

6.   Practice approach

The cross-claim, like a counterclaim, must be part of the defendant's answer. It must be served with the answer on existing parties in the same way any pleadings, motions, or discovery are served.

The cross-claim, like a complaint,[68] counterclaim, or third-party complaint, is a pleading that asks for relief. Hence, it should be drafted like a complaint. The prayer for relief will ordinarily reflect the contingent liability position of the cross-claiming party.

Example:

CROSS-CLAIM AGAINST DEFENDANT JONES

Defendant John Smith cross-claims against Defendant James Jones as follows:
    1. . . .
    2. . . .
WHEREFORE, in the event that Defendant Smith is liable to Plaintiff, Defendant Smith demands judgment against codefendant Jones in the same amount, plus interest and costs.

68. See §5.3.

7. Responses to cross-claims

When a cross-claim has been served on a coparty, that party can respond with any of the responses permitted to a complaint. The party can make any of the Rule 12 motions or can answer the cross-claim and raise Rule 12(b) defenses and affirmative defenses. The party responding to the cross-claim must do so by motion or answer within the required time for answering, normally 20 days.

§5.9. Impleader (third-party practice)[69]

Impleader, also called third-party practice, is governed by Rule 14. It is a method for bringing into the action new parties who may be liable to a defendant for some or all of the judgment that the plaintiff may obtain against the defendant. The original defendant becomes a "third-party plaintiff" filing a complaint against a new party, the "third-party defendant."

Impleader must be distinguished from the filing of counterclaims and cross-claims, both of which involve new claims between original parties to the action. Impleader, by contrast, is a procedure by which new parties, the third-party defendants, are added to the action. The process helps carry out one of the principal purposes of federal pleadings: Whenever possible, consistent with jurisdictional limitations, a court should hear all related claims in one action because this is an efficient way to resolve multi-party disputes and obtain consistent results.

There are several rules for impleader actions that must be understood. The terms usually employed to identify the parties in impleader situations are the original plaintiff; the original defendant, who is now also a third-party plaintiff; and the third-party defendant.

1. Discretionary pleading

Under Rule 14(a), an original defendant can serve a third-party complaint on a third-party defendant without leave of court so long as it is done within 10 days of serving the original answer to plaintiff's complaint. After that time the defendant must obtain the court's permission to do so. The original plaintiff, if served with a counterclaim, may under Rule 14(b) also bring in a third-party defendant.

The court retains discretion to allow or deny impleader, and any party may move to strike a third-party claim.[70] In deciding whether to allow impleader, the court must balance the preference for complete resolution of all related issues with any possible prejudice to the plaintiff. Ordinarily the court should permit impleader; if the case then becomes too complex, it can simply order separate trials on the third-party claims. If the

---

69. Wright §76; James & Hazard §10.18; Friedenthal §6.9; Moore's Manual §§14.02-14.03; Manual of Federal Practice §§3.125-3.134; Moore's Federal Practice §§14.02-14.37; Wright & Miller §§1441-1465.
70. See Wright §76.

court denies impleader, the third-party claim can usually be brought as an independent action.

2.　Subject matter

An original defendant, as a third-party plaintiff, may include in his third-party complaint any claim that asserts that the third-party defendant "is or may be liable to him for all or part of the plaintiff's claim against him." However, the original defendant's right to bring third-party claims is broader than would first appear from Rule 14. There are four types of claims that can be brought under the impleader rule.

First, and most commonly, an original defendant can bring an impleader action based on indemnity, contribution, active-passive negligence, subrogation, or any other theory that passes part or all of the defendant's liability to one or more new parties. Second, the defendant can bring a contingent claim against the third-party defendant. The "is or may be liable" language in the Rule permits accelerated contingent liability claims. Third, the original defendant may be able to bring an independent claim against a third-party defendant, since under Rule 18(a) any party can join claims against another. So long as the defendant has one claim against a third-party defendant that is proper under Rule 14(a), any other independent claims proper under the joinder rules can be added. Finally, the defendant can bring a claim against the third-party defendant that the original plaintiff could not bring directly against the third-party defendant.

3.　Jurisdiction and venue

Impleader necessarily involves two related questions: whether the new action is proper under impleader rules, and whether there is proper jurisdiction and venue over the new action. Although an impleader action may be proper under Rule 14, this does not necessarily mean that jurisdiction and venue properly exist.

Where impleader is based on an indemnity type of claim, for instance, ancillary jurisdiction exists and there will be no jurisdiction or venue problems. This situation is much like that which exists with the filing of compulsory counterclaims. Where impleader is based on a claim that is independent of the original plaintiff's claim against the original defendant, however, there must be an independent basis for jurisdiction.[71] This situation is much like that involving permissive counterclaims.

4.　Statutes of limitations

As with any complaint, a third-party complaint is subject to all applicable statutes of limitations. In addition, if the original plaintiff files an

---

71. The leading case is Owens Equip. Co. v. Kroger, 437 U.S. 365 (1978). See Wright §76.

amended complaint directly against a third-party defendant, it is considered a new cause of action to which the relevant statute applies. The concept of relation back, applicable to amended pleadings, does not apply here.[72]

5. Practice approach

A third-party complaint under Rule 14 is the fourth type of complaint permitted by the federal rules, in addition to complaints, counterclaims, and cross-claims. As such, it should have the three basic parts of any complaint: a jurisdictional allegation, a statement of claims, and a prayer for relief. In short, the approach to drafting a third-party complaint is essentially identical to that of the original complaint, although it should recite the circumstances of the already pending original complaint. The document itself is entitled "THIRD-PARTY COMPLAINT." The caption should clearly show the status of the various parties.

Where leave of court is required, the defendant must move for permission to bring the third-party complaint against the new party. The usual procedure is to attach the proposed pleading to the motion.

Since a third-party complaint brings new parties into the suit, each new third-party defendant must be served with the third-party complaint and summons, as required by Rule 4.

Example:

[Caption]

DEFENDANT JOHNSON'S MOTION TO BRING IN THIRD-PARTY DEFENDANT

Defendant Thomas Johnson requests permission to proceed as a third-party plaintiff against Frank Jones. A copy of the proposed third-party complaint is attached to this motion as Exhibit A. In support of his motion Defendant Johnson states:

1. . . .
2. . . .

WHEREFORE, Defendant Johnson requests that an order be entered permitting him to proceed as third-party plaintiff against Frank Jones, file the third-party complaint (Exhibit A), and to have that complaint and summons served upon Frank Jones as third-party defendant.

_____
Attorney for
Defendant Johnson

72. See §5.13.

Example:

UNITED STATES DISTRICT COURT
FOR THE DISTRICT OF VERMONT

Rebecca Smith,
      Plaintiff

    v.

Thomas Johnson,   No. 98 C 100
      Defendant and Third-Party
      Plaintiff   Civil Action

    v.

Frank Jones,
      Third-Party Defendant

THIRD-PARTY COMPLAINT

Defendant Johnson complains of Third-Party Defendant Frank Jones as follows:

1. Plaintiff Smith has previously filed a complaint against defendant Johnson. A copy of that complaint is attached as Exhibit A.

2. . . .

3. . . .

WHEREFORE, Defendant Johnson demands judgment against Third-Party Defendant Jones for all sums that Plaintiff may receive in judgment against Defendant Johnson.

6. Third-party defendant responses

A third-party defendant who has been served with a third-party complaint can choose any of the responses of any party served with a complaint. He may make Rule 12 motions, or he may answer the third-party complaint. He can also assert any defenses the original defendant may have against the original plaintiff. This protects the third-party defendant who might otherwise be prejudiced by the original defendant's failure to assert all available defenses against the original plaintiff.

Further, a third-party defendant can counterclaim against the original plaintiff directly, so long as that counterclaim involves the same transaction or occurrence that is the basis for plaintiff's claim against the original defendant. The court will have ancillary jurisdiction over such a counterclaim. He can also assert cross-claims against other third-party defendants under Rule 13.

Finally, a third-party defendant can also bring a third-party complaint against a new party who in turn may be liable to him for all or part of the original third-party complaint filed by the original defendant.

The approach for drafting each of these responses is essentially identical to the approach for responses discussed earlier in this chapter. Make sure that the particular response chosen bears a title that makes clear what type of response it is and identifies the pleading to which it is responding. Where ancillary jurisdiction does not attach to a third-party claim, an independent jurisdictional basis must exist, and there must be personal jurisdiction over the new parties.

While the pleading possibilities under Rule 14 appear complex, its underlying philosophy is simple: The federal rules broadly permit adding parties and claims so that all parties and all aspects of a dispute can be disposed of in one consolidated proceeding that produces consistent results. If the pleadings make the case too complex, the court can always order separate trials. This in fact is frequently done. The court will try the claims between the original plaintiff and original defendant first. The third-party claims can then be tried later if necessary. Ordering separate trials for the original claims and the subsequent third-party claims will also protect the original plaintiff from any unfairness that might be caused by the addition of the third-party claims.

7. Original plaintiff responses

Under Rule 14(a), after a third-party complaint has been filed, the original plaintiff can file an amended complaint directly against a third-party defendant. This in effect allows the plaintiff to do what could have, and perhaps should have, been done in the first place. However, there must be an independent jurisdictional basis for the amended complaint. If a third-party defendant has counterclaimed directly against the original plaintiff, that plaintiff must reply to the counterclaim within the usual time limits.

§5.10. Interpleader[73]

Interpleader is the procedure that allows a party, called a "stakeholder," who is or may be subjected to double liability because two or more claimants are making competing claims on a fund or property, to ask a court to determine proper ownership of or interest in the disputed fund or property. The standard situation involves multiple claims on the proceeds of an insurance policy. If the insurance company does not know who should get the proceeds, it may pay the wrong person and later be forced to pay a second time. In an interpleader action the stakeholder is the plaintiff, and the competing claimants become the defendants.

There are two types of federal interpleader: Rule 22 interpleader, and so-called statutory interpleader under 28 U.S.C. §1335. Each must be considered separately, since substantial differences exist.

---

73. Wright §74; James & Hazard §10.19; Friedenthal §§16.10-16.13; Moore's Manual §14.06; Manual of Federal Practice §§1.98, 3.135; Moore's Federal Practice §§22.02-22.17; Wright & Miller §§1701-1721.

1. Rule 22 interpleader

Rule 22 interpleader is in some respects broad, in others restrictive. It is broad because it allows interpleading claims that "do not have a common origin, or are not identical but are adverse to and independent of one another." It also allows the defense that the plaintiff-stakeholder is "not liable in whole or in part to any or all of the claimants." Accordingly, the plaintiff need not deposit the fund in issue with the clerk of the court or post an equivalent bond. The rule allows a defendant in a pending suit to plead interpleader in a counterclaim or cross-claim.

On the other hand, Rule 22 interpleader is restrictive since the usual jurisdiction and venue rules apply. This means that where federal jurisdiction is based on diversity of citizenship under 28 U.S.C. §1332, there must be complete diversity between a plaintiff-stakeholder and each defendant-claimant, a situation that in interpleader cases will rarely exist. The amount in controversy must also exceed $75,000, a determination based on the amount of the fund or value of the property involved. Proper venue is determined under the general venue statute, 28 U.S.C. §1391.

2. 28 U.S.C. §1335 interpleader

Statutory interpleader under §1335, while conceptually identical to Rule 22 interpleader, has significant procedural advantages. First, §1335 relaxes the diversity requirement by requiring that only two of the defendant-claimants have diverse citizenship. Plaintiff's citizenship is not considered. This relaxed diversity requirement allows most interpleader actions to be filed in federal court. Venue under §1397 is proper in any district where one or more of the defendant- claimants resides. Second, the amount in controversy need only exceed $500. Third, under §2361 the court may issue an injunction against any defendant-claimant pursuing another action involving the same fund or property in state or federal courts. Finally, statutory interpleader under §2361 permits nationwide service of process.

Section 1335 requires that the claims be "adverse to and independent of one another," but the claims need not have a common origin or be identical in type. However, the plaintiff must deposit the fund or property with the clerk of the court or post a bond in the amount of the fund or property.

Further, while §1335 itself is silent on whether to allow a statutory interpleader to be asserted in a counterclaim or cross-claim, most courts permit it.[74]

---

74. See Wright §74.

3. Practice approach

An interpleader complaint based on either Rule 22 or §1335 should have all the components of an ordinary complaint: a jurisdictional statement, a statement of claims, and a prayer for relief. Under §1335, the jurisdictional statement should state whether the fund has been deposited with the court or a bond has been posted in the appropriate amount payable to the clerk. The prayer for relief should ask for all relief that is appropriate, including a determination of the amount of liability, if any; a determination of which claimants are entitled to the fund or property and in what amounts; an injuction against any claimants pursuing other actions in state or federal courts based on this claim; and fees and costs, including attorney's fees where permitted.[75]

Example:

Whole Life Insurance Co., a corporation, Plaintiff	
v.	No. _____
Thomas Smith and James Smith, Defendants	Civil Action

COMPLAINT FOR INTERPLEADER

Plaintiff Whole Life Insurance Co. complains of defendants Thomas Smith and James Smith as follows:

Jurisdictional Allegation

1. Jurisdiction in this action is based on 28 U.S.C. §1335. Defendant Thomas Smith is a citizen of the State of Maine. Defendant James Smith is a citizen of the State of Vermont. The amount in controversy exceeds the sum of $500, exclusive of interest and costs.

or

1. Jurisdiction is based on Rule 22 of the Federal Rules of Civil Procedure and 28 U.S.C. §1332. Plaintiff is a citizen of the State of New York. Defendant Thomas Smith is a citizen of the State of Maine. Defendant James Smith is a citizen of the State of Vermont. The amount in controversy exceeds the sum of $75,000, exclusive of interest and costs.

---

75. Attorney's fees are permitted where the plaintiff is a passive litigant not disputing that it owes a set amount to someone. See Moore's Manual §14.06(2).

2. On June 1, 1998, plaintiff issued a life insurance policy on the life of Franklin Smith. A copy of that policy is attached as Exhibit A.

3. . . .

4. . . .

5. By reason of the defendants' conflicting claims, plaintiff cannot determine with certainty which defendant [, if either,] is entitled to any proceeds of the policy [or, if either is entitled, in what amount].

6. Plaintiff has deposited the face amount of the policy, $80,000, with the clerk of the court. [Required only under §1335 interpleader.]

WHEREFORE, plaintiff requests that the court enter a judgment finding that:

(1) Neither defendant is entitled to recover any money from the policy [permitted only under Rule 22 interpleader];

(2) Each defendant is permanently enjoined from pursuing any other actions or claims on this policy [permitted only under §1335 interpleader];

(3) If this court finds the policy in force at the time of Franklin Smith's death, that the defendants be required to interplead and settle their claims on the policy between themselves, and that plaintiff be discharged from any liability except to any person in such amount as the court adjudges plaintiff is liable;

(4) Plaintiff is entitled to costs [and reasonable attorney's fees if a passive litigant.]

§5.11.   Intervention[76]

Intervention, governed by Rule 24, is the procedure by which a nonparty having an interest in a pending action can protect its rights by becoming an additional party and presenting a claim or defense. The Rule closely parallels the joinder rules by allowing two types of intervention, intervention of right and permissive intervention.

1.   Intervention of right

Rule 24(a) permits two bases for intervention of right. The seldom-used basis is if "a statute of the United States confers an unconditional right to intervene."[77] The frequently used basis is Rule 24(a)(2), which sets forth three requirements for intervention of right.

First, the intervenor must claim "an interest relating to the property or transaction which is the subject of the action" pending. What is a sufficient "interest" remains unsettled, since Rule 24 in its present form was enacted in 1966 and the case law is hardly uniform. Various courts have

---

76. Wright §75; James & Hazard §10.17; Friedenthal §6.10; Moore's Manual §14.05; Manual of Federal Practice §§3.148-3.155; Moore's Federal Practice §§24.02-24.20; Wright & Miller §§1901-1913.

77. A list of such statutes is found at Moore's Federal Practice §24.06.

held that the intervenor's interest must be "direct," "substantial," or "significantly protectable."[78] An analysis of the intervenor's claimed interest, of the relief sought, and of the nature of the claims and defenses asserted in the pending action is required.

Second, the intervenor must be "so situated that the disposition of the action may as a practical matter impair or impede his ability to protect that interest." The critical term "as a practical matter" was included to make clear that this determination should not be limited to legal bars such as res judicata, but should include any substantial functional difficulties that might adversely affect the intervenor's interests.

Third, the intervenor must not be "adequately represented by existing parties." This requires a comparison of the interests of the existing parties with the claimed interests of the intervenor to determine how closely they are related. If the intervenor's interests are essentially identical to those of an existing party, so that the existing party will necessarily assert the same positions as the intervenor would, intervention should be denied.

2. Permissive intervention

Rule 24(b) permits two bases for permissive intervention. The seldom-used basis is if "a statute of the United States confers a conditional right to intervene." The usual situation for such a basis is where the federal or a state government can intervene in a case involving the constitutionality or interpretation of a statute.[79]

The frequently used basis for permissive intervention is Rule 24(b)(2), which permits intervention "when the applicant's claim or defense and the main action have a question of law or fact in common." This involves an analysis similar to that made for the permissive joinder of parties under Rule 20(a). This request to intervene is addressed to the court's discretion, and the court may deny it where the intervenor's request would "delay or prejudice" the rights of the pending parties or inject unimportant issues into the case. If a court denies intervention, there are no adverse legal consequences since res judicata will not apply to the unsuccessful intervenor. The common situation where intervention is permitted is where the intervenor has a claim against the defendant that is factually and legally similar to the plaintiff's pending claim against the defendant.

3. Timing

A prospective intervenor must move to intervene in a timely fashion, regardless of whether the intervention sought is of right or is permissive. Both Rule 24(a) and (b) require a "timely application," but where inter-

78. See Wright & Miller §1908.
79. See Moore's Federal Practice §24.10.

vention of right is requested, it will ordinarily be permitted, regardless of when the application is made, since the intervenor's right might otherwise be adversely affected. Despite this, it is possible to seek intervention of right so late in the pending action that it is considered untimely and is therefore denied.

When permissive intervention is sought, the court must consider "whether the intervention will unduly delay or prejudice the adjudication of the rights of the original parties." This requires analyzing the relief the intervenor wants, whether the intervenor will be an active or passive party, and particularly the stage that the pending action is in. Intervention obviously will be more favorably viewed when sought early in the pleading stage than if substantial discovery has already been taken.

4. Jurisdiction

The intervenor's addition to the pending action must meet jurisdiction and venue requirements. Where intervention of right is requested, the intervenor's claim is necessarily closely related to the original action and ancillary jurisdiction will attach. On the other hand, if intervention is not based on Rule 24(b)(1), independent jurisdictional grounds must exist.[80]

Venue should not be an issue, since it is viewed as a personal right and the intervenor is generally held to accept the venue that has already been established.

5. Practice approach

Rule 24(c) requires that the intervenor make a timely motion to intervene in the district in which the original action is pending. It must attach an appropriate pleading to the motion. The motion, which must be served on all existing parties, should state the reason why intervention is appropriate under the circumstances.

Example:

Frank Johnson, 　　　Plaintiff	
v.	No. 98 C 100
Wilma Smith, 　　　Defendant, Jacob Franklin, 　　　Intervenor	Civil Action

80. See Wright §75.

MOTION TO INTERVENE AS A DEFENDANT

Jacob Franklin moves for leave to intervene as a defendant in this action. A copy of his proposed answer is attached as Exhibit A. In support of his motion Franklin states:

1. Intervention is appropriate because. . . .
2. . . . .

WHEREFORE, Jacob Franklin requests that he be permitted to intervene as a defendant, file his answer to the complaint, and participate in this action as a party defendant.

ANSWER OF DEFENDANT-INTERVENOR FRANKLIN

Defendant Franklin answers the complaint as follows:

1. . . . .
2. . . . .

If the motion to intervene is granted, the intervenor becomes a party and has the rights of any party. The intervenor usually cannot contest past orders, but can counterclaim and cross-claim, present any appropriate motions, and fully participate in discovery. Keep in mind, however, that the court has power to limit intervention to certain matters if permissive intervention has been granted.

The denial of a motion to intervene raises the difficult issue of whether the ruling is final and appealable.[81] While there is a split in authority on this question, it appears that a motion for intervention of right is appealable if denied, but the denial of a motion to intervene permissively is appealable only where an abuse of discretion is shown. If the motion to intervene is granted, it is not an appealable order.

§5.12. Class actions[82]

The topic of class actions by itself can fill volumes, and literature on the subject in treatises, cases, and journals is extensive. It is obviously a complicated area, one in which the inexperienced litigator should tread cautiously if at all. Hence, this section is limited to a brief overview of the class-action requirements and the initial considerations and steps in such suits. The principal concern of the inexperienced litigator should be determining whether a case can be pursued as a class action. (The initial fight is usually over class certification and the scope of discovery that will be permitted on the certification question.) Assistance from someone with experience in class action litigation should be sought.

81. See Moore's Manual §14.05(6); Moore's Federal Practice §24.15.
82. Wright §72; James & Hazard §§10.20-10.23; Friedenthal §§16.1-16.19; Manual of Federal Practice §§3.138-3.147; Moore's Manual §14.07; Moore's Federal Practice §§23.01-23.97; Wright & Miller §§1751-1803.

1. General class requirements

Rule 23(a) sets out four class requirements that must be met before the action can proceed as a class action. These are frequently referred to as the requirements of numerosity, commonality, typicality, and adequate representation. These apply regardless of whether the class involves the plaintiff or the defendant.

First, the class must be so "numerous that joinder of all members is impracticable." The Rule itself does not define what a class is or how its members should be determined. Impracticability depends on the type of claims asserted and the persons asserting those claims. Because of this, the numbers necessary for a class action are quite flexible, and the ultimate decision whether a class action is the preferred method of dealing with a claim is left to the discretion of the trial court. While it is usually clear that hundreds of potential plaintiffs or defendants make the action suitable for class-action treatment, and that fewer than 30 ordinarily is not enough, the case law on class numbers in the middle range—perhaps 30 to 50 members—shows no particular pattern. Some of such classes have been held to be of an appropriate number, others not.[83] The outcome is as dependent on other considerations as it is on the number of class members.

Second, there must be "questions of law or fact common to the class." This requires the same type of analysis required for joinder and intervention requests.[84]

Third, the "claims or defenses of the representative parties" must be "typical of the claims or defenses of the class." Also, the representatives must be actual members of the class. In addition, the claims or defenses of the class must be reviewed, and there must be enough representative parties to ensure that each claim or defense is represented fairly. This obviously requires that the lawyers closely analyze the facts before selecting actual parties and initiating suit.

Finally, the representative parties must "fairly and adequately protect the interests of the class." This requirement is directed to both the representative parties and their lawyers. The interests of the representatives must be scrutinized to determine if conflicting interests exist. If they do, a possible solution is to certify separate classes. In addition, the lawyers must have sufficient ability and experience to represent the class competently. It may be useful to ask other members of the class to authorize the named parties and their lawyers to represent their interests.

2. General facts requirements

Rule 23(b) sets out three fact situations in which a class action is appropriate.

---

83. See Moore's Manual §14.07(1); Wright & Miller §1762.
84. See §3.4.

First, it is appropriate where separate actions would "create a risk of inconsistent or varying adjudications" that would "establish incompatible standards of conduct" for the party opposing the class, or where separate adjudications would "as a practical matter be dispositive of the interests of the others" in the class who are not parties to that adjudication. The former is commonly relied upon in actions against governmental entities to declare actions invalid, such as expenditures and bond issues. The latter is frequently relied upon in shareholder actions against corporations, such as to compel declaration of a dividend.

Second, a class action is appropriate where the party opposing the class has "acted or refused to act on grounds generally applicable to the class." Many of the cases brought on this basis are civil rights actions in which a party is asking for injunctive or other equitable relief under Title VII of the 1964 Act, and some employment discrimination cases.

Third, a class action is appropriate where "questions of law or fact common to the members of the class predominate over any questions affecting only individual members" and a class action is the best method for handling the entire controversy. This has become the most common basis for class actions, and one that is frequently relied upon in antitrust and securities fraud cases. However, a class action under this Rule — Rule 23(b)(3) — is rarely permitted in mass tort cases, such as airline crashes, because the plaintiffs' claims are usually seen as too diverse to justify class action treatment.[85]

3. Jurisdiction

In a class action based on diversity of citizenship, the usual requirement of complete diversity between any plaintiff and any defendant is relaxed. Only the citizenship of the named representatives of the class is considered.[86] Hence, through the simple device of selecting as named class representatives persons who are diverse in citizenship to the nonclass party, diversity for class action purposes can ordinarily be established.

The jurisdictional amount requirement is more problematical and often arises in a Rule 23(b)(3) class action. For a long time the courts have barred aggregating claims to meet the required jurisdictional amount.[87] In a diversity action each plaintiff must have a claim that exceeds $75,000; in a class action, therefore, the claims of the plaintiff class members cannot be aggregated, nor can the claims of the named representatives be aggregated.[88] This means that each named representative of the class must have a claim that exceeds the jurisdictional amount. In many potential class actions, of course, there are numerous members of the class with

85. See Amchem Products v. Windsor, 117 S. Ct. 2231 (1997), holding that a class for settlement purposes only was not appropriate in an asbestos exposure case brought under Rule 23(b)(3).

86. See Moore's Manual §14.07(6). The leading case is Stewart v. Dunham, 115 U.S. 61 (1885).

87. See Moore's Manual §14.07(6).

88. See Wright §72; Zahn v. International Paper Co., 414 U.S. 291 (1973).

individual small claims. In these situations the jurisdictional amount requirement in diversity cases cannot be met, and the claim cannot be presented in federal court. However, this problem does not exist when the claim is based on federal question jurisdiction since there is no jurisdictional amount requirement. Therefore, the common approach is to raise a federal question as the basis for jurisdiction whenever possible.

4. Procedure

Rule 23(c) governs the initial procedures in a class action. The first two steps are critical. First, the court must determine "as soon as practicable" if the action can be brought as a class action. This necessarily requires an evaluation of the Rule 23(a) and (b) requirements, a determination of what issues can be tried as a class action, and a determination of what the class or classes will be.[89]

Second, in an action under Rule 23(b)(3), the predominantly used section, the court must direct the "best notice practicable under the circumstances," which includes "individual notice to all members who can be identified through reasonable effort." Aside from related concerns, such as the actual technical requirements for notice, the "opt-out" provision, and res judicata issues, the immediate concern is a practical one. Notice can be an expensive undertaking, sometimes prohibitively so. For class members whose identity can be ascertained with reasonable effort, notice by first class mail is usually required; for unknown class members, some form of notice by publication is required. Since each side must bear its costs of litigation, the expense of actually notifying the individual class members can effectively prevent a claim from being pursued as a class action.[90]

§5.13. Amendments of pleadings and supplemental pleadings[91]

The principal concepts behind the federal rules' pleading requirements are that pleadings should accurately notify the parties of the claims involved and that enough flexibility should be permitted so that substantial justice is achieved in every case. Rule 15, the amendments rule, reflects these concerns. Amended pleadings should be freely allowed when fairness requires it; that is, whenever an amendment would create a more accurate or complete pleading and the opposing parties will not be substantially prejudiced. The Rule applies to all pleadings—complaints, answers, and replies.

89. A proposed amendment to Rule 23 adds a new subsection (f) that authorizes interlocutory appeals of district court orders granting or denying certification of a class. Rule 23(f) will become effective December 1, 1998, unless Congress enacts contrary legislation.

90. The Supreme Court has held that in class action suits brought under Rule 23(c)(2) the party seeking the class action must bear the costs of actual notice to the reasonably identifiable class members. Eisen v. Carlisle & Jacquelin, et al., 417 U.S. 156 (1974).

91. Wright §§66, 68-69; James & Hazard §§4.11-4.17; Friedenthal §§5.26-5.28; Moore's Manual §§9.09-9.11; Manual of Federal Practice §§3.58-3.65; Moore's Federal Practice §§15.02-15.16; Wright & Miller §§1471-1510.

1. Amendments as of right

Any party has a right to amend a pleading once, at any time before a responsive pleading is made. If no responsive pleading is permitted, an amendment by right can be made within 20 days after service, unless the case is already on the trial calendar. A motion that attacks a pleading is not considered a responsive pleading. If an amendment is by right, it is simply served on the other parties and no court action is needed.

When the amended pleading seeks to add new parties, Rule 15(a), permitting timely amendments of right, seems to conflict with Rule 21, which permits additions of parties only by leave of court. Courts have gone both ways on this issue, some holding that leave is always required, others not.[92]

There is also some conflict between Rule 15(c) and state statutes of limitations, which apply in diversity cases. In circumstances where the federal rule would permit an amended complaint but the complaint would be barred by the applicable state statute, courts have held that Rule 15 controls and permits the amendment.[93]

2. Amendments by leave of court

Rule 15(a) permits amendments by leave of court. The Rule expressly provides that "leave shall be freely given when justice so requires." The amended pleading can change the jurisdictional allegations, factual claims, legal theories of recovery, events and transactions involved, and even parties to the action.[94] Yet the courts have been indulgent in permitting amendments, and grounds such as oversight, error, or delay by themselves are generally held insufficient to deny leave to amend.[95]

Courts may exercise their discretion and deny leave to amend when, in addition to delay or neglect, there is some actual prejudice to the opposing party. In other situations, the court may grant leave to amend while restricting it to particular matters so that prejudice to an opposing party is minimized. Obviously the amending party should seek leave to amend as early in the litigation process as possible to minimize prejudice. A motion during the pleading stage will in all likelihood be granted. One made after discovery is underway, however, may well encounter difficulties.

When a motion for leave to amend is made after a motion to dismiss for failure to state a claim on which relief can be granted, some courts will not grant leave if it appears certain that plaintiff cannot, under the existing facts, state a proper claim.[96] Courts often look to see if the proposed amended complaint properly states a claim before granting leave to amend. If it does not, leave can properly be denied.

92. See Moore's Manual §909(2).
93. See Wright §59.
94. 28 U.S.C. §1653 provides that "defective allegations of jurisdiction may be amended, upon terms, in the trial or appellate courts."
95. See Moore's Manual §9.09(3).
96. See Manual of Federal Practice §3.60.

3. Statutes of limitations and "relation back"

An important concern in amending pleadings is whether the statute of limitations applies to amended pleadings. This question exists only if the amended pleading is filed after the applicable statute of limitations has run on a particular claim. Whether the statute will bar the amended pleading depends on whether the concept of "relation back," set out in Rule 15(c), will apply. The two principal types of amendments—changing facts and legal theories, and changing parties—must be considered separately.

a. Changing facts and theories

Rule 15(c) states that if the amended pleading's claims or defenses "arose out of" the same "conduct, transaction or occurrence set forth or attempted to be set forth" in the original pleading, the amendment will relate back to the date the original pleading was filed so that the statute of limitations will not operate as a bar. When the amended pleading alleges an entirely new claim, the concept of relation back will not apply. Whether the claims or defenses in the amended pleading "arose out of the same conduct, transaction or occurrence set forth or attempted to be set forth" in the original pleading is an imprecise standard, but courts have been reasonably lenient in permitting amendments, particularly when only a change in legal theory is involved.[97]

b. Changing parties

The more difficult situation concerns changing parties with an amended pleading. Rule 15(c) permits relation back to avoid a limitations bar where the new party added by amendment either actually knew of the suit and would not be prejudiced, or knew or should have known that, but for a mistake in identifying the proper party, he would have been sued.

The first situation involves actual knowledge of the action by the new party. The second involves a misnomer of a proper party, where the proper party knew or should be held to know that it was the target party all along. This is a common problem when commercial parties or the United States government is involved, where determining the technically proper defendants is difficult and sometimes impossible prior to discovery. Cases that have dealt with the question of when a party "should have known" he was the intended party are hardly uniform and should be thoroughly researched.[98]

97. See Wright §66.
98. See Manual of Federal Practice §3.61; Schiavone v. Fortune, Inc., 477 U.S. 21 (1986), is a recent leading case on the "identity of interest" exception. However, Rule 15(c) was amended in 1991 to change the result of the holding in *Schiavone*. Rule 15(c)(3) provides that relation back is proper when the amendment of a pleading adds a new party if that added party received notice of the institution of the action within the time provided for service under Rule 4, and knew or should have known that, "but for a mistake concerning the identity of the proper party, the action would have been brought against the party."

4. Supplemental pleadings

Under Rule 15(d), a party may move to file a supplemental pleading alleging transactions, occurrences, and events that have occurred since the time the original pleading was served. Permitting the motion is discretionary with the court, which can impose any reasonable terms to protect the other parties.

Since a supplemental pleading by definition raises new matters that have arisen since the original pleading was filed, statute of limitations and relation back issues will rarely be involved.

5. Practice approach

A motion for leave to amend, like any other motion, must meet the Rule 7(b) requirements. The motion must state with particularity the grounds for the motion and the relief sought. Timely notice must be sent to other parties. The better practice is to attach the amended pleading as an exhibit to the motion. In addition, it is both more convenient and a safer practice to have a complete amended pleading, rather than incorporate by reference parts of the original pleading. It is simply easier to deal with a complete pleading, and responses will likely be more accurate.

Example:

[Caption]

MOTION FOR LEAVE TO FILE AMENDED COMPLAINT

Plaintiff moves for an order permitting plaintiff to file an amended complaint. A copy of the amended complaint is attached to this motion as Exhibit A. In support of this motion plaintiff states:

1. Plaintiff's original complaint was against one defendant, William Smith, and alleged one theory of liability based on negligence.

2. New information, based on both informal fact investigation and discovery, has revealed that another party, Acme Motors, may be liable to plaintiff and that a valid claim against Acme may exist, based on products liability and implied warranty.

WHEREFORE, plaintiff requests that an order be entered permitting plaintiff to file the amended complaint attached as Exhibit A, which adds Acme Motors as a defendant and alleges two additional counts, based on products liability and implied warranty, against Acme Motors.

_____

Attorney for Plaintiff

If the motion is allowed, or the amended pleading is of right, a party that is required to respond to the amended pleading must do so either within the time remaining to respond to the original pleading or within 10 days of service of the amended pleading, whichever is greater.

Many motions to permit an amended pleading are made after an opposing party has been granted a motion to dismiss under Rule 12. Here the dismissed party should move for leave to file an amended pleading within 10 days of dismissal.[99] The better and more common practice, however, is to move for leave to file an amended pleading and have the motion granted at the hearing on the motion to dismiss, if that motion is granted. In this way the order granting the motion to dismiss will also contain an order permitting the amended pleading.

99. See Moore's Manual §9.09(5).

VI
DISCOVERY

§6.1. Introduction

Discovery is the principal fact-gathering method in the formal litigation process. In today's litigation environment, the discovery stage is where most of the battles are fought and where the war is often won or lost. Consequently, understanding discovery so that you can effectively and efficiently use the permissible discovery methods as tactical and strategic tools is critical for every litigator.

Federal discovery has several principal characteristics. First, it is largely a self-executing process. For the most part, lawyers conduct discovery without prior judicial approval, although in recent years courts are increasingly supervising and even dictating the order and timing of discovery. Second, the discovery rules are flexible and usually permit any order, and sometimes repeated use, of the various discovery methods subject only to the court's approved discovery plan and court protection against abuse. Third, orders regulating discovery are usually not final appealable orders. Since discovery issues will often be moot by the time a final judgment is entered in the case, appeals are relatively infrequent. This means that issues concerning discovery are principally resolved at the trial court level.

Recent years have seen numerous changes to the discovery rules, principally brought about by increasing pressure for discovery reform. Many judges, litigators, legislators, and the public see civil litigation as unnecessarily complicated, slow, and expensive; and Rules 26 through 37, the discovery rules, are usually identified as the worst offenders. Hence, the past 10 years have seen repeated efforts to simplify discovery and impose effective sanctions for discovery abuse.

In 1993, the most significant changes to the discovery rules in decades went into effect. The most important of the changes were the addition of Rule 26(a), which imposes automatic disclosure duties on the parties, and changes to the depositions and interrogatories rules. The details of these changes, and how parties use the new discovery rules, are discussed throughout this chapter.

Keep in mind that ethics rules apply to discovery, particularly Model Rule 3.4(d), which commands that a "lawyer shall not . . . make a frivolous discovery request or fail to make a reasonably diligent effort to comply with a legally proper discovery request by an opposing party."

§6.2. Scope of discovery[1]

Rule 26(b), the basic discovery rule that controls the scope of discovery, provides that a party may discover "any matter, not privileged, which is relevant to the subject matter involved in the pending action." This section discusses what "relevance" means in the discovery context and reviews the specialized areas now expressly regulated by Rule 26: insurance, statements, experts, privileges, and work product.

1. Relevance

Relevance for discovery purposes is exceptionally broad. Under Rule 26(b)(1), information sought need not be admissible at trial nor need the information itself be relevant. If the information sought to be discovered "appears reasonably calculated to lead to the discovery of admissible evidence" on the subject matter of the lawsuit, it is discoverable. In short, a "fishing expedition" is proper if it might unveil probative evidence.[2]

Rule 26(a)(1) expressly permits the discovery of three categories of information: (1) the identity of persons "likely to have discoverable information relevant to disputed facts"; (2) a copy or description of documents and tangible things in the control of a party that are "relevant to disputed facts"; (3) a "computation of any category of damages claimed" by a party and the underlying documentation.

The identity of trial witnesses and trial exhibits is now governed by and made expressly discoverable by Rule 26(a)(3), although this information is generally disclosable shortly before trial in the pretrial memorandum.[3]

1. Wright §81; James & Hazard §5.8; Friedenthal §7.2; Moore's Manual §15.02; Manual of Federal Practice §5.1 et seq.; Moore's Federal Practice §26.55; Wright & Miller §2007.
2. Wright §81; Moore's Manual §15.02; Manual of Federal Practice §5.24; Moore's Federal Practice §26.56(1); Wright & Miller §2008.
3. Wright §81; Moore's Manual §15.02; Manual of Federal Practice §5.27; Moore's Federal Practice §26.57; Wright & Miller §2013.

Rule 26(a)(3) excludes from disclosure trial witnesses and exhibits that will be used "solely for impeachment purposes." Previously courts had been divided on whether impeachment materials were discoverable.[4]

2.   Insurance Agreements[5]

Rule 26(a)(1)(D) makes discoverable any insurance agreement held by any person which "may be liable to satisfy part or all of a judgment," or "indemnify or reimburse for payments made to satisfy the judgment." This information is critical for assessing the "value" of the case and the defendant's ability to pay a judgment.

3.   Statements[6]

A "statement" for discovery purposes is defined by Rule 26(b)(3) to include "(A) a written statement signed or otherwise adopted or approved by the person making it, or (B) a stenographic, mechanical, electrical, or other recording, or a transcription thereof, which is a substantially verbatim recital of an oral statement by the person making it and contemporaneously recorded." This means that if a witness has been interviewed, but nothing tangible was produced, such as a written statement, recording, or transcript, there is no "statement" in existence that can be discovered. It also means that if a lawyer, after interviewing a witness, later makes notes summarizing the interview, but the notes are not substantially verbatim, the lawyer's notes of the witness interview are not discoverable, and fall within the Rule 26(b)(3) work-product doctrine.

A party is entitled to obtain a copy of his prior statement in the possession of anyone else upon demand, without a court order or a showing of need. A party is considered to have a right to his own written or recorded statements. Statements made by a party to his own lawyer are not discoverable, principally because the attorney-client privilege will apply to such communications.

A witness is also entitled to obtain a copy of his prior statement. Note that the rule does not expressly allow discovery of a witness's statement. Only the witness himself has a right to obtain a copy of his own statement. A lawyer, however, can always urge a witness to ask for a copy of his own statement and then obtain it from the witness. Because it is so easy to obtain the statement indirectly, many lawyers, and some courts, view witness statements as being discoverable directly.

4. Wright §81; Moore's Manual §15.02(1); Wright & Miller §2015.
5. Wright §81; James & Hazard §5.7; Friedenthal §7.2; Moore's Manual §15.02(1)(c); Manual of Federal Practice §5.37; Moore's Federal Practice §26.62; Wright & Miller §2010.
6. Wright §82; James & Hazard §5.8; Friedenthal §7.5; Moore's Manual §15.02(4); Moore's Federal Practice §26.65; Wright & Miller §2027, 2028.

4. Experts[7]

There are three basic kinds of experts: testifying experts, consulting experts, and informally consulted experts. Different rules govern the discoverability of their identity, opinions, reports, and background information. There are also experts who are employees of a party and were involved in the events on which the litigation is based, but they are treated like any fact witness.

Rule 26(a)(2) governs the disclosures of expert witnesses expected to testify at trial. Required to be disclosed are the "identity of any person who may be used at trial to present evidence" as an expert under the Federal Rules of Evidence. Also required to be disclosed is a signed written report of "a witness who is retained or specially employed to provide expert testimony in the case, or whose duties as an employee of the party regularly involve giving expert testimony." The report must contain "a complete statement of" all opinions to be expressed and the reasons for those opinions, the data and other information considered to form those opinions, exhibits to be used to support the opinions, the expert's qualifications, including all publications within 10 years, the expert's compensation, and a list of all cases in which the expert has testified at trial or by deposition within four years. Rule 26(b) now allows a party to depose such an expert as of right. Since Rule 26(a)(2) is so explicit, it should substantially reduce the arguments over the extent of discovery of testifying experts.

Rule 26(b) also governs consulting experts, those who have been retained or employed to help the lawyer during the litigation process, but are not expected to be witnesses at trial. Such experts ordinarily cannot be subjected to the discovery process, unless a requesting party can show "exceptional circumstances under which it is impracticable . . . to obtain facts or opinions on the same subject by other means." The rule in effect establishes a qualified privilege for the work of a consulting expert, one akin to that for a lawyer's trial preparation materials. The only exception is Rule 35(b), which makes the reports of a suitably licensed or certified examiner's mental or physical examination of a party discoverable in certain circumstances.[8]

Informally consulted experts, those experts who have not been employed or retained by the lawyer but have provided information, are not governed by the discovery rules. Therefore, neither the existence, identity, nor opinions of such an expert is discoverable. This prevents experts with minimal or incidental contact with the lawyer from being drawn into the discovery process.

---

7. Wright §81; James & Hazard §5.11; Friedenthal §7.6; Moore's Manual §15.02(5); Manual of Federal Practice §5.36; Moore's Federal Practice §26.66; Wright & Miller §2029-2034.

8. See §6.10.

5.   Privileges[9]

Rule 26(b)(1) excludes privileged matter from being discoverable. Federal privileges are controlled by Rule 501 of the Federal Rules of Evidence, which continue the development of privileges by case law, statutes, and constitutional provisions.

The first question to ask regarding this aspect of discovery is, What privilege law applies? Rule 501 provides that federal privileges, as developed by the courts, will apply. The exception is that in civil cases for which state law "provides the rule of reason" as to an element of a claim or defense, state privileges will apply. This essentially means that in federal criminal cases and federal civil cases based on federal question jurisdiction, federal privilege law will apply. However, in federal civil cases based on diversity jurisdiction, state privileges rules will apply. Which state's privileges rules will apply is determined by the forum state's choice-of-law rules. Where a privilege is based on the U.S. Constitution, such as the Fifth Amendment's self-incrimination clause, it applies regardless of the type of federal case involved.

The second question that must be asked is, What is the applicable federal or state privilege law? When the Federal Rules of Evidence were enacted, Congress chose not to codify federal common law privileges, preferring to let federal privileges continue to develop in the courts. Therefore, care must always be taken to research the law of the appropriate jurisdiction, because privilege law can vary.

State privileges, by contrast, are developed by both the courts and the legislatures, although in recent years the trend has been to codify privileges. Keep in mind that state jurisdictions vary widely in their privilege law. While all states recognize frequently used privileges such as marital, attorney-client and doctor-patient, they vary substantially in their recognition of others such as the privilege for accountants, reporter's informants, and governmental secrets. The scope of any privilege, and whether it applies in civil or criminal cases, also varies significantly. This is an area of evidence law that, when joined with choice of law issues, always requires substantial research.

The third question that must be asked is, What is the proper procedure for asserting a privilege claim? Rule 26(b)(5) requires that when a party wishes to withhold discoverable materials based on a claim of privilege, the claim must be made expressly, and the party claiming the privilege must describe the nature of the documents, communications, or things "in a manner that, without revealing information itself privileged or protected, will enable other parties to assess the applicability of the privilege or protection." Failure to comply with the notice requirement may be viewed as a waiver of the privilege.

This collection of descriptions and documents for which a privilege is claimed is commonly called a "privilege log." The documents themselves,

9. Wright §81; James & Hazard §5.9; Friedenthal §7.4-7.5; Moore's Manual §15.02(2); Manual of Federal Practice §5.30-5.34; Moore's Federal Practice §26.60-26.61; Wright & Miller §2016-2020; T. Mauet & W. Wolfson, Trial Evidence §8.8–8.14 (1997).

of course, must be segregated from other discoverable documents and may later need to be presented to the court for an in camera inspection if the requesting party moves to compel the production of those documents.

6. Trial preparation materials[10]

Ever since the Supreme Court decided Hickman v. Taylor, 329 U.S. 495 (1947), federal courts have recognized a two-tier privilege rule applicable to an attorney's work product; that rule, with some changes and added details, is now incorporated in Rule 26(b)(3).

The attorney's work product, now called "trial preparation materials," is protected by a qualified privilege. Trial preparation materials include "documents and tangible things" that were "prepared in anticipation of litigation" by another party or that party's "representative." A representative includes not only the lawyer but may include the lawyer's employees and agents such as an investigator. The party must expressly claim the privilege under Rule 26(b)(5).

If the privilege attaches, it is only a qualified privilege. The rule permits a party seeking discovery to obtain protected documents and tangible things upon a showing of "substantial need" because the party cannot obtain the "substantial equivalent" by other means without "undue hardship." Under the provisions of the rule, it is clear that undue hardship cannot be shown simply by demonstrating added expense or inconvenience. With witness statements, the area where this issue most frequently arises, there must be some demonstrable reason why the requesting party cannot get the substantial equivalent of the statement himself before production can be ordered.[11]

§6.3. Discovery strategy

The discovery rules in the Federal Rules of Civil Procedure are both broad and extensive, and in most cases they permit more discovery than either party will wish to make. Consequently, your overriding concern at the discovery stage is, What will be an effective discovery strategy for this particular case? As outlined previously, discovery planning is essentially a seven-step process.[12]

---

10. Wright §82; James & Hazard §5.10; Friedenthal §7.5; Moore's Manual §15.02(4); Manual of Federal Practice §5.35, 5.175; Moore's Federal Practice §26.57(2); Wright & Miller §§2021-2028; E. Epstein, The Attorney-Client Privilege and the Work-Product Doctrine, Section of Litigation, ABA (3d ed. 1997); see United States v. Adlman, 134 F.3d 1194 (2d Cir. 1998) for an expansive view of the "prepared in anticipation of litigation" requirement.

11. Wright §82; Manual of Federal Practice §5.35, 5.175; Moore's Manual §15.02(4); Moore's Federal Practice §26.64(3); Wright & Miller §2025.

12. See §4.5.5.

1. **What facts do I need to establish a winning case on my claims (or to defeat the opponent's claims)?**

2. **What facts have I already obtained through informal fact investigation?**

These questions should already be answered in your developing litigation chart.

3. **What "missing" facts do I still need to obtain through formal discovery?**

Discovery is the vehicle you use to force other parties, and nonparties, to disclose information they have which is relevant to the litigation. Your first question, therefore, should be, What information do I need to know, that I do not already know from my informal investigation and have not been admitted in the pleadings, so that I can properly prepare the case for a possible trial? While the answer will vary with each case, it will usually include most of the following:

1.   Identity of proper parties
2.   Defendant's ability to pay a judgment (insurance coverage and fiscal condition)
3.   Identity of agents and employees
4.   Opponent's factual basis for legal claims
5.   Opponent's position on factual issues
6.   Identity and location of witnesses
7.   Prospective testimony of adverse parties, agents, and employees
8.   Prospective testimony of witnesses
9.   Identity, opinions, reasoning, and backgrounds of experts
10. Prospective testimony of experts
11. Tangible evidence
12. Documents
13. Records
14. Statements of parties and witnesses
15. Deposition testimony of favorable witnesses that may become unavailable for trial

Not all of this information is necessarily discoverable. However, you should always compile a similar roster for each case — using your litigation chart — since it will control the information you will try to discover. Think in terms of evidence, not just in terms of information, and think how the formal discovery rules can be used to create evidence that later will be admissible at trial.

4. What discovery methods are most effective for obtaining the "missing" facts?

There are six methods of discovery permitted under the federal rules: initial disclosures, interrogatories, requests to produce documents, depositions, physical and mental examinations, and requests to admit facts. Although there is some overlap, each method is particularly well suited for certain kinds of information.

Initial disclosures, the new discovery method created by Rule 26(a)(1), is the automatic discovery method by which parties must disclose, early in the litigation, basic information they have about the case, including identity of witnesses, identity or disclosure of documents and tangible things, computation of damages and the sources of those computations, and insurance agreements which may pay part or all of any judgment. However, Rule 26(a) has an "opt-out" provision, and a number of districts have opted out of the rule.

Interrogatories are most effective for obtaining basic factual data from other parties, such as the identity of proper parties, agents, employees, witnesses, and experts, and the identity and location of documents, records, and tangible evidence. They are also useful in obtaining other parties' positions on disputed facts, and experts' opinions and bases for opinions. On the other hand, interrogatories are not usually effective instruments for getting detailed facts, impressions, or versions of events.

A request to produce documents and tangible things is the discovery method by which one obtains from another party copies of records, documents, and other tangible things for inspection, copying, and testing. Such a request also permits an entry on another person's land or property to inspect, photograph, and analyze things on it. This is the only discovery device that forces another party actually to produce records and things, and to permit entry onto someone else's property to copy, photograph, or study evidence. A subpoena to a non-party can obtain the same information.

Depositions are most effective in tying down parties and witnesses to details, and in discovering everything they know pertinent to the case. It is the only discovery vehicle that permits you to assess how good a witness a person is likely to be at trial. It is an excellent vehicle to secure admissions or other evidence favorable to your side. Further, a deposition is the only method to preserve testimony if a witness will become unavailable for trial.

A physical and mental examination of a party can be obtained by court order when the physical or mental condition of that party is in issue, a situation most common in personal injury cases. While other discovery methods can be used to get records of past examinations, this is the only means of forcing a party to be examined and tested prospectively. For that reason it is the best method for evaluating a party on such damages elements as permanence and extent of injury, and medical prognosis.

Finally, requests to admit facts is the discovery method that forces a party to admit or deny facts or a document's genuineness. An admitted fact is deemed conclusively admitted for the purpose of the pending trial. This discovery method is effective if limited to simple factual data, such as someone's employment on a specific date, or the genuineness of signatures on a contract. It is not a good method for dealing with opinions or evaluative information.

There are two more areas where, upon motion and court order, you may obtain additional discovery: consulting experts and trial preparation materials.

Under Rule 26(b)(4)(B), you can obtain discovery of your opponent's consulting expert only on a showing of "exceptional circumstances under which it is impractical . . . to obtain facts or opinions on the same subject by other means." While this is obviously a difficult standard, the Rule contemplates those rare cases where relevant expert information is solely in the possession of one party's expert, such as where a consulting expert has engaged in destructive testing of a product.

Under Rule 26(b)(3), trial preparation materials, which are protected from disclosure by a qualified privilege, can be obtained from an opponent "only upon a showing of substantial need." The party seeking production must also be "unable without undue hardship to obtain the substantial equivalent of the materials by other means." This exception to the attorney's work product rule arises most often in regard to non-verbatim memos of witness interviews, which are not usually discoverable. Where one side has interviewed a witness who now refuses to talk to other lawyers, who cannot be subpoenaed, or who has a lapse of memory, and the substantial equivalent of the statement cannot be obtained, the court may order the production of the memorandum.

5. What facts and witnesses, that I already know of through informal investigation, do I need to "pin down" by using formal discovery?

There is little point in using formal discovery methods with your favorable witnesses, unless those witnesses are old, sick, or are likely to move away. If this is the case, you will want to take the witness' deposition to preserve the testimony for trial, since the transcript will usually qualify as former testimony.[13]

With unfavorable, hostile, or adverse witnesses and parties, however, there are good reasons for deposing them, even if you already know from your informal fact investigation what they will say at trial. First, there are always benefits in learning in detail what those witnesses will say. Second, witnesses may testify inconsistently with their previous statements, or inconsistently with each other. Third, you may be able to limit the witnesses' trial testimony by getting the witnesses to admit to topics they have no first-hand knowledge of, are not sure of, or are only approximating or guessing at. All of these are good reasons for deposing important, unfavorable, or adverse witnesses you expect will testify for the opposing party at trial.

---

13. FRE 804(b)(1).

6. What restrictions does my litigation budget place on my discovery plan?

Information gathering, especially formal discovery, is expensive, and any discovery strategy must necessarily consider the expenses involved. While your litigation budget, which you have already prepared, will have analyzed the amount of time you will allocate to discovery, at this point you should give the discovery portion a second look. This should be done for three reasons. First, the pleadings, now completed, may force changes in your discovery strategy. Second, since discovery will usually consume the majority of your pretrial time allotment, it is particularly important to review it. Third, discovery can easily escalate out of control, so staying with your game plan is essential.

Most formal discovery methods are expensive, and responding to discovery, particularly interrogatories and documents requests, can become expensive because of the time involved in researching and preparing responses and reviewing the necessary documents. Depositions are an expensive discovery method, and it is here that cost effectiveness is particularly important. Deposition costs include the lawyer's time, witness fees, the court reporter's attendance fees, and transcript costs. Assuming a one-hour deposition, the witness, reporter, and transcript costs will probably exceed $200. A lawyer may need two hours to prepare for the deposition and one hour after the deposition to make a summary of her impressions. Even a short deposition, then, will cost the client several hundred dollars.

Deposition costs, therefore, require that you use this discovery method cautiously. You will probably need to depose your adverse party and critical witnesses in every case. However, you can often postpone depositions of experts and rely on initial disclosures, interrogatory answers and various records for settlement purposes, deposing your adversary's experts only when a trial becomes a realistic possibility. In some situations, such as the plaintiff's medical expert in a personal injury case, you may not always need to depose the doctor if his written report, required to be disclosed under Rule 26(a)(2), sufficiently details his opinions, bases for the opinions, supporting records and other background information. Similarly, consider moving for a physical examination of the opposing party only when a trial becomes likely. Also, use investigators to interview nonparty witnesses who are not central to the case. There are often other ways of getting the essence of a witness' testimony short of a deposition, and you must always balance the additional benefit of depositions with their cost in all cases where litigation costs are a concern.

Example:

Consider a typical automobile accident case, in which you represent the plaintiff. You previously estimated the "value" of plaintiff's case at $90,000, of which you will earn about $30,000 with a successful conclusion. You have made various estimates of time requirements, and have allocated 60 hours to preparing and responding to discovery. How do you estimate how much time you should plan spending on the various discovery methods?

Start by breaking down formal discovery into its component parts to consider what discovery is essential. First, you will need to meet with your opposing counsel to develop a proposed discovery plan, attend a pretrial conference with the judge, and prepare initial disclosures required under Rule 26(a)(1). You estimate these steps will take five hours.

Second, you will need to submit interrogatories to the defendant and answer the defendant's interrogatories. In automobile cases involving simple negligence claims, many jurisdictions use standard interrogatories. Sending interrogatories to the defendant, answering the defendant's, and reviewing the defendant's answers for sufficiency will probably take only a few hours, particularly if you have done your informal fact investigation before filing suit. You estimate interrogatories will take five hours.

Third, you will need to depose the critical witnesses: These will include the parties and occurrence witnesses. You will need to depose the defendant and one bystander, and to prepare your plaintiff for deposition, since the defendant will certainly depose him. In a simple automobile case, the plaintiff's deposition will probably take two hours, the defendant's and bystander's will perhaps take one hour each. Preparation for each deposition will probably take at least as long as the deposition itself. In addition, you will need to prepare a summary of each deposition immediately afterward and review the transcript of the plaintiff's testimony for accuracy before he signs it. Accordingly, you estimate that these depositions will take approximately 20 hours.

Fourth, you will need to send requests to produce documents to the defendant and nonparties, and answer the defendant's production requests. You will also need to organize and review all the documents and records you receive. These will include hospital records, physician records, employment records, vehicle repair records, police reports, and insurance reports. You estimate that this work will take 10 hours.

Fifth, the defendant may want to have the plaintiff medically examined, particularly if plaintiff is claiming any permanent physical injuries. You will need to review the information that is developed through that examination, which is usually disclosed through interrogatory answers and the report of the examining doctor. You estimate this will require 5 hours.

Sixth, plaintiff and defendant will probably depose each other's medical experts. Defendant will want to depose plaintiff's treating physician and plaintiff will want to depose the defendant's examining physician. Preparing, taking, and summarizing these medical-expert depositions will take substantial time. You estimate this will take 15 hours.

Finally, you may want to send a request to admit facts to the defendant, and you may have to respond to the defendant's. You estimate this will take four hours.

Notice that this time estimate already adds up to over 60 hours, and not all the variables that exist have been taken into consideration. On the positive side, both parties may agree not to depose each other's experts, or the case may settle early. On the negative side, you may need to depose additional witnesses or depose someone a second time, and you may need to file motions to enforce or protect your discovery rights. The point, however, is to analyze the cost considerations as you develop your discovery strategy, because the two must be consistent with each other.

7. In what order should I execute my discovery plan?

Formal discovery should be used as a progressive device in which each discovery method is used as a sequential building block. Under the Rules, there is no required sequence, except that before any discovery requests can be made, you must first meet with the opposing lawyer to develop a proposed discovery plan and make the initial disclosures required by Rule 26(a). After this point, the parties can engage in discovery to the extent permitted by the Rules, and consistent with the court's scheduling order setting forth the discovery plan. Under Rule 16, the judge may, and many do, hold a scheduling conference with the parties to decide how to regulate and expedite the case, particularly the discovery phase. At the conference, the judge will have the report of the parties on their Rule 26(f) discovery plan meeting. After the conference, the judge will enter an order that will control the remainder of the litigation. For example, the court may order that any interrogatories and documents requests be served within 60 days, answered within 30 days of service; that depositions of nonexperts be completed within six months; and that experts be deposed within nine months. The court will probably set a discovery "cutoff" date, when all discovery must be completed.

The only limitations on discovery should not be confining, and if the facts of the case make the limits imposed by the Rules unrealistic, the court has discretion to modify them. In addition, the court has power under Rules 26(c) and 37 to issue protective orders for failure to comply with the required disclosure rules and for other abuse of discovery. Finally, under Rule 29 the parties may, and frequently do, stipulate to modify certain discovery procedures without court approval, unless the stipulation would interfere with other court-ordered time limits and schedules. In that event, court approval is necessary.

Because the discovery process is so flexible, the relevant questions are, When should I start discovery? In what order should it be carried out?

The initial question can be answered simply. You should start discovery as soon as the Rules permit and as soon as practical. If you have done your prefiling investigation and preparation work, you should be able to begin discovery as soon as you have met with your opponent to develop a proposed discovery plan. Although the parties may agree to begin, or the court or local rules may permit, discovery prior to this meeting, the meeting may help eliminate some unnecessary discovery and provide a clearer focus for the discovery plan.

The following is a common discovery sequence:

1. discovery planning meeting and pretrial scheduling conference
2. required initial disclosures
3. interrogatories

4. requests to produce documents and subpoenas
5. depositions of parties, witnesses, and experts
6. physical and mental examinations
7. requests to admit facts

This sequence utilizes the building block approach to discovery. Once the initial disclosures are received, you can serve interrogatories and requests to produce on parties and subpoenas on nonparty witnesses in order to obtain the additional information and documents, records, and other evidence identified in the interrogatory answers. After you have received this information you are ready to take depositions of parties, witnesses, and experts. In personal injury cases the physical and mental examinations of parties are ordinarily conducted later in the litigation process, since these examinations usually focus on such issues as permanence of injury, prognosis, and loss of earning capacity. Once these steps have been completed, notices to admit can further pinpoint areas of dispute and eliminate the need to prove uncontested facts at trial.

This sequence, of course, can be and often is modified. Amended, supplemental, or additional pleadings may be filed that will necessarily alter the course of discovery. In addition, there may be tactical benefits in changing the usual sequence or in serving more than one discovery device at the same time. Keep in mind that the discovery process educates your opponents as well as yourself. Lawyers sometimes take the deposition of an adverse party early, before interrogatories or notices to produce have been sent out, on the theory that the adverse party will have neither the time nor the inclination to prepare thoroughly by collecting and reviewing all the pertinent records beforehand. Lawyers frequently couple interrogatories requesting the identification of documents with a request to produce the documents identified, and use early requests to admit facts in order to narrow the scope of discovery.

There is no magic formula for deciding on the best sequence for discovery. This should be tailored to the specific needs and circumstances of each case. An important point to remember, however, is that discovery should not be used simply because it is available. Each step must have a specific purpose and be part of an overall discovery strategy.

In addition to this basic seven step process, there are two additional considerations you should always keep in mind.

8. How can I conduct discovery informally?

The federal rules prescribe how discovery should be conducted, and a procedurally safe approach to discovery is to always do it "by the book." However, life doesn't always go by the book, nor does discovery in the litigation world. Litigation lawyers usually try to arrange things between themselves informally. This applies to all phases of the litigation process and is permitted and encouraged under Rule 29.

What aspects of discovery can be handled informally? The simple task of scheduling depositions can be. Instead of simply serving notice on your party opponent for his deposition, why not contact the other party's lawyer and try to arrange a mutually agreeable date and time? This will probably avoid any motions to reschedule the deposition, and will usually result in the same courtesy being extended to you in the future. Serve a notice of deposition after you have worked out the arrangement.

With nonparty deponents, whom you must subpoena and usually depose in the location convenient to that deponent, informal accommodations can be made. Serve the subpoena first, then see if the deponent is willing to come to your office. Offering to pay the witness' reasonable, legitimately incurred expenses in coming to your office, rather than following the formal Rule 45 procedures, frequently benefits everyone.[14]

It is also common to work out the mechanics of documents production informally. Why not call the other party's lawyer and work out how, when, where, and in what order each party will produce the requested documents, along with how they will be photocopied and who will pay for the charges. Another area where "working it out" informally is a common practice is in arranging to depose each other's experts.

While there are many other areas where the informal resolutions of problems are common, the point is the same: Whenever possible, it makes sense to try to work out the mechanics and details of discovery with the other side and with nonparties. Courtesy and reasonableness somehow make the world work better, and discovery in the litigation process is no different.

9.   How can I limit discovery against my party?

As the lawyer for a party, you often have an interest in limiting the discovery of your case, unless your case is so strong that you don't want to limit it, or where early complete disclosure will force a favorable settlement. There are three basic areas where you can affect whether information can be discovered.

First, if your client is a business entity, take immediate steps to control the paperwork generated in the business that has any bearing on the litigation: If it is not written down, it cannot be turned over under a request to produce. Have the business' employees communicate directly to you about the pending litigation, rather than to supervisors, since this may afford the advantage of bringing the communications under the attorney-client privilege protection.[15]

Second, again, if your client is a business entity, make sure that employees notify you if anyone tries to interview any of them about the case. Since any statements made by the employees may be admissions that are

---

14. See §6.9.1(c).

15. See Upjohn Co. v. United States, 449 U.S. 383 (1981). *Upjohn* rejected the "control group" test for determining which corporate employees' communications with corporate counsel will be protected by the attorney-client privilege. Any employee who has information necessary for the corporate counsel to evaluate will have those communications to corporate counsel protected by the privilege. However, state laws on the scope of the attorney-client privilege for corporate employees vary widely, so thorough research of the applicable jurisdiction's law is always necessary. T. Mauet & W. Wolfson, Trial Evidence §8.12 (1997).

admissible against the business employer under FRE 801, you are probably entitled to treat such an employee as a party. This means that no one can interview the employee without your permission, and you can represent the employee at his deposition. It also means that communications between the employee and you may be protected by the attorney-client privilege.[16]

Third, obtain statements from witnesses that bring the statements under the qualified trial preparation materials doctrine or, better yet, under the absolute attorney's mental impressions privilege. Verbatim signed statements from adverse witnesses are useful, since they can be used to impeach. They may be dangerous, however, when taken from favorable witnesses, and so it is safer to have your investigator — or for you yourself to — interview the witness, then prepare a summary of the witness' information with observations on how strong or weak the witness is, what kind of witness she will make at trial, and how her testimony fits into the theory of the case, along with other pertinent mental impressions. You will then have a useful record of the witness, which will probably be protected from disclosure. Even if the other side does obtain it through a showing of substantial need, it will not include any verbatim statements usable to impeach. The observations about the witness, however, should be absolutely protected as the lawyer's work product.

Finally, consider ways in which you can protect your testifying expert during the discovery process.[17] Rule 26(a)(2) now requires that each party disclose the identity of each expert expected to testify at trial, and a report containing a "complete statement of all opinions to be expressed ," the "data or other information considered by the witness in forming the opinion," and other background information about the expert.

How detailed should your disclosures be? While you may frequently want to minimize discovery, remember that the opposing party can always move to compel more detailed information. It is often a sound strategy to provide broad disclosure to other parties. This can provide substantial benefits in the future. First, it can forestall motions to compel full and complete disclosure. Second, it gives you a stronger position from which to resist motions for discretionary discovery. You can object on the basis that your existing disclosures are fully adequate to inform other parties and to allow them to adequately prepare for cross-examination of your experts at trial, which is the standard inquiry in deciding whether additional discovery should be ordered. Hence, the usual discretionary discovery requests — supplemental interrogatory answers, production of the experts' reports and working papers, and expert depositions — should not be granted. Third, providing complete responses puts you in a stronger position if you are seeking more expert discovery from other parties. Courts quite naturally are inclined to look at scope-of-discovery issues as a two-way street. Fourth, providing detailed disclosures may sometimes cause your opponent to forego taking the expert's deposition before trial.

---

16. See §2.5 discussing the rules that govern interviews of employees and former employees of a party.

17. See §2.6, discussing expert review of cases before filing suit.

Finally, maintain a professional relationship with your testifying expert to minimize the danger of disclosing matters that might otherwise be protected by the attorney-client and work product privileges. Allowing your experts to communicate directly with your client is dangerous. Disclosing information to your expert that is work product runs the danger that it may end up being discovered. But since the expert must have sufficient information on which to evaluate the case and develop opinions, the question becomes how to best convey the necessary information to your expert. The safe approach is to divulge only those materials that are discoverable by other parties anyway, and use caution when transmitting additional information to the expert. This will minimize the danger of having your case hurt or of your being embarrassed at trial.

§6.4. Discovery planning meeting and pretrial scheduling conference

Before formal discovery can begin, the parties must complete three steps: attend a discovery planning meeting, submit a written report of the meeting to the court, and attend a pretrial scheduling conference with the judge. These are controlled by Rules 26(f) and 16(b).

1. Law[18]

Rule 26(f) requires, unless the district has opted-out, that the parties that have appeared in the case meet "as soon as practicable" and in any event at least 14 days before a scheduling conference is held or scheduling order is due, to discuss the pleadings and the possibility of settlement, and to develop a proposed discovery plan. This is the "meet and confer" requirement. The discovery plan should contain the parties' views on the following topics:

1. changes to and timing of initial disclosures;
2. the subjects of and timing for discovery;
3. whether discovery limits should be modified;
4. need for protective orders or pretrial conference orders.

The parties are under an obligation to make good faith efforts to agree on a proposed discovery plan. Within 10 days after the meeting, the parties must submit to the court a written report outlining the discovery plan.

Rule 16(b) requires that the court enter a scheduling order, after receiving the parties's written report of their planning meeting. The order shall be issued "as soon as practicable but in any event within 90 days after the appearance of a defendant and within 120 days after the complaint has been served on a defendant." The usual procedure is that the

---

18. Wright §83A; Manual of Federal Practice §5.2; Moore's Federal Practice §26.01 et seq.

district judge, or a magistrate judge, sets a scheduling conference with the parties and receives the parties' written report at least four days before the conference. (The judge may also have the parties' initial disclosures, since these are also due at the same time as the parties' written report of their proposed discovery plan, unless the date is extended by stipulation of the parties or court order.) At the scheduling conference, the judge will discuss the case with the lawyers and fashion a sequence and timing for discovery and other matters, such as amending pleadings, scheduling expert disclosures, dispositive motions, pretrial disclosures, and settlement conferences.

2. Practice approach

a. Timing

When should the lawyers hold their discovery planning meeting? Rule 26(f) merely provides that it be held "as soon as practicable" and at least 14 days before the pretrial scheduling conference or order. Hence, you need to know when the judge has, or probably will, set a date for the scheduling conference and work backwards from that date.

Most judges will hold the scheduling conference shortly after the defendants have appeared and answered the complaint. At this time, the judge, and parties, can get a general picture of the case, what's in issue, how "big" the case is, and accordingly what the discovery needs are.

Complications can arise. What happens if not all defendants named in the complaint have been served? What happens if defendants file Rule 12(b) motions? What if defendants bring in third-party defendants? In these situations, the "as soon as practicable" language controls. Since the principal purpose of the parties' planning meeting and the court's scheduling conference is to set a realistic discovery plan, this cannot be accomplished when the pleadings are still substantially incomplete. Accordingly, most judges will wait until all parties have appeared and answered the complaint. On the other hand, if all but one defendant have appeared, and the unserved defendant is either not a critical party, or may never be served, the judge will probably still set an early scheduling conference date. Every judge has her own preferences; many have standing orders on when the conference will be held. Check with the judge's clerk after the case has been assigned if you don't know the judge's practice.

Since you must meet with the other parties to develop a proposed discovery plan, contact the other lawyers after they have appeared in the case. Rule 26(f) holds each party responsible for arranging and being present at the planning meeting, and "attempting in good faith to agree on the proposed discovery plan." Hence, you must attempt to schedule and hold the meeting, even if the other side is uncooperative.

At the meeting the parties should discuss amending the pleadings, the possibility of settlement, the details of the proposed discovery plan, and other matters such as the preservation of physical evidence and electronic data from inadvertent or intentional destruction, and the need for protective orders for trade secrets and other proprietary or confidential information. Aside from these matters, the meeting often accomplishes another intended purpose: getting the lawyers to meet in an informal setting. The reality is that if lawyers actually communicate, face to face, early in the litigation, to discuss their needs and concerns, the litigation process, particularly discovery, will be more efficient and less contentious.

b. Written report of proposed discovery plan

Rule 26(f) requires that the parties submit a written report of their meeting and proposed discovery plan to the court within 10 days of the meeting. This requirement gives the judge time to review the report before meeting with the parties at the scheduling conference.

The report should itemize the decisions, and disagreements, of the parties on each of the major components of the litigation process: pleadings, discovery, dispositive motions, settlement, and trial. Form 35 in the appendix of forms is a useful guide for what the court expects the written report to contain. Keep in mind that the judge may have a standing order on how the written report should be organized and what it should contain.

Example:

[Caption]

REPORT OF PARTIES' PLANNING MEETING

The parties submit the following written report, pursuant to Rule 26(f):

1. <u>Meeting.</u> A meeting was held on June 1, 1998, at the offices of Johnson & Barnes, 100 Main Street, Boise, Idaho. Present were William Johnson, plaintiff's attorney, and Sarah Anton, defendant's attorney. The parties jointly propose to the court the following:

2. <u>Scheduling conference.</u> The parties request a scheduling conference before the entry of a scheduling order.

3. <u>Pleadings.</u> Plaintiff should have until July 1, 1998, to add additional parties and amend pleadings. Defendant should have until August 1, 1998, to add additional parties and amend pleadings.

4. <u>Discovery.</u>
a. Initial disclosures under Rule 26(a)(1) will be exchanged by June 15, 1998.

b. Discovery will be needed on the following subjects: plaintiff's and defendant's conduct before, during, and after the collision; plaintiff's medical treatment, plaintiff's future medical needs, plaintiff's present and future lost income, and other claimed damages.

c. Interrogatories will be limited to 20 by each party to another party, and will be served by July 15, 1998. Responses are due 30 days after service.

d. Documents requests will be limited to 20 by each party to another party, and will be served by September 15, 1998. Responses are due 30 days after service.

e. Depositions of non-experts will be limited to 8 by each party, and will be taken by December 1, 1998. Each deposition will be limited to 3 hours, unless extended by agreement of the parties.

f. Written reports from plaintiff's retained experts under Rule 26(a)(2) are due December 15, 1998. Written reports from defendant's retained experts are due January 15, 1999.

g. Depositions of experts will be limited to 2 by each party, and will be taken between December 15, 1998 and February 15, 1999. Each deposition will be limited to 4 hours, unless extended by agreement of the parties.

h. Requests to admit will be limited to 15 by each party to another party, and will be served by March 1, 1999. Responses are due 30 days after service.

i. Supplementation under Rule 26(e) is due by April 1, 1999.

j. Discovery cut off date is April 1, 1999.

5. Dispositive motions. Dispositive motions will be served and filed by April 15, 1999. Responses are due by May 15, 1999.

6. Settlement. Settlement cannot be evaluated until after the experts' reports have been received. The parties request that the court schedule a conference to discuss settlement after February 15, 1999.

7. Trial.

a. Witness and exhibits lists under Rule 26(b)(3) should be due from plaintiff by May 1, 1999, and from defendant by May 15, 1999.

b. Parties should have 15 days after service of witness and exhibits lists to specify objections under Rule 26(a)(3).

c. The case should be ready for trial by July 1, 1999. The trial is expected to take approximately 4 days.

Respectfully submitted,

_____

William Johnson, attorney
   for plaintiff

_____

Sarah Anton, attorney for
   defendant

If the parties cannot agree on certain matters, the written report should state what the disagreements are and the basis for them.

Example:

6. Settlement. The parties cannot agree on when a conference to discuss settlement should be held. Plaintiff prefers a conference after initial disclosures have been served. Defendant prefers a date after experts have been deposed.

Finally, if the other party has failed to participate in the planning meeting, this must be reported to the court, since the failure to meet can subject that party to sanctions under Rule 37(g).

c.   *Scheduling conference*

Under Rule 16(b), the court is required only to enter a scheduling order. A scheduling conference is optional, although many judges hold scheduling conferences in all cases, or delegate it to a magistrate judge. Some judges, however, will not hold a conference if the case appears routine, and the parties' written report shows no serious disagreements and proposes a reasonable chronology of events. At the conference, the judge will have the parties' written report containing their proposed discovery plan, the pleadings, and perhaps the parties' initial disclosures under Rule 26(a)(1).

Your purpose at the scheduling conference is two-fold: convince the judge to accept the agreed parts of the written report, and your side of the matters on which the parties disagree. Remember that the judge will have attitudes about how litigation should be handled and about the pace and discovery complexity that is appropriate to certain kinds of cases. A diversity personal injury case or simple contract dispute is different from, and has different needs from, an antitrust or multiparty building construction case. Hence, the judge may routinely ratify the parties' written report without much discussion in routine cases, but go over the report in detail in large or complex cases. The more complicated the case, and the more contentious the parties, the more likely the judge will actively control the litigation, beginning with the Rule 16 scheduling conference. In some districts, cases are divided into routine and complex cases. If routine, the judge may put the case on a "fast track," and schedule discovery so that it is completed within a few months.

After the scheduling conference, the judge will enter a scheduling order, which will usually cover the same subjects as the parties' written report. The order controls what discovery will take place and when it will be completed, unless the judge later modifies the order.

Because the scheduling order is so important, make sure you "get it right" the first time. This means that your meeting with other parties to make a discovery plan must be candid and realistic and achieve a compromise between the parties' preferences and the likely attitude of the judge. This also means that the lawyers must "educate the judge" about the unusual circumstances that justify a discovery schedule different from what the judge will expect in this kind of case. Only when there is candid, open communication among the parties and judge will the result be mutually beneficial: a scheduling order that realistically and efficiently regulates the remainder of the litigation process.

§6.5. Law of Required Disclosures

In 1993, significant amendments to the Federal Rules of Civil Procedure became law. Among the many changes was the amendment of Rule 26. New Rule 26(a) established three categories of required disclosures: initial disclosures, expert disclosures, and pretrial disclosures. Initial disclosures are a new discovery method. Expert disclosures, while previously required, have been significantly expanded. Pretrial disclosures remain essentially what was previously required. Disclosures must be in writing, signed and filed with the court, unless a local rule or court order directs otherwise. There is a continuing duty to supplement disclosures when a party learns that they are materially incomplete or incorrect. A court by local rule or order can require that additional information be disclosed, and the parties may, of course, obtain this and other information through the other discovery methods.

Rule 26 also permits local district courts to "opt-out" of subsections (a), (d), and (f), and many have.[19] Districts can opt-out for all civil cases, or can choose to opt-out of only certain kinds of civil cases, such as Social Security reviews. However, in some of the opt-out districts local rules similar to Rule 26(a) may apply. Hence, you must always check the status of Rule 26 and applicable local rules in the district in which your lawsuit is pending.

1. Initial disclosures[20]

Under Rule 26(a)(1), each party must make initial disclosures to the other side, without a discovery request, in four categories of "core" information:

1. The name, address, and telephone number, if known, of each individual "likely to have discoverable information relevant to disputed facts alleged with particularity in the pleadings."
2. The description and location of documents, data compilations, and tangible things, or copies of them, in the possession, custody or control of the party that are "relevant to disputed facts alleged with particularity in the pleadings."
3. The computation of damages, making available for inspection and copying the documents on which the damages are computed.

19. See Moore's Federal Practice, §26, which contains a grid showing which districts have "opted-out" of Rule 26(a) and in what way. (Note that, while some districts have opted-out of Rule 26(a), some states are beginning to adopt versions of automatic disclosures, although the coverage of the state rule may be different.)
20. See Wright §83A; Manual of Federal Practice §5.2; Moore's Federal Practice §26.01 et seq.

4.   Insurance agreements, which may be liable for all or part of any judgment, making them available for inspection and copying.

A party must make the disclosures based on the information "then reasonably available to it" and cannot fail to make disclosures because its investigation of the case is not complete or it is challenging the adequacy of the other party's disclosure. Disclosures must be made about "disputed facts alleged with particularity in the pleadings," not just the party's own pleadings. This means that a party must list these witnesses and exhibits that other parties might reasonably be expected to use if the party knows of their existence. A party is under a duty to supplement and correct disclosures (including expert disclosures) if it learns that the disclosure was in "some material respect incomplete or incorrect."

The timing of the initial disclosures is controlled by Rule 26(a) and (f). The parties must meet to develop a discovery plan "as soon as practicable" and at least 14 days before the pretrial conference. No discovery can be done until after this meeting. Initial disclosures are due within 10 days of the parties' meeting, unless the parties stipulate otherwise, or a court order or local rule provide otherwise. This means that the judge will have the parties' initial disclosures at the pretrial conference, unless the parties have stipulated to a later disclosure date.

Initial disclosures have three basic consequences. First, this discovery is automatic, requiring no triggering request or action from the other parties, and will occur sooner than initial discovery under the previous rules. Second, initial disclosures should replace the first set of interrogatories and documents requests that invariably sought the same basic information now required to be disclosed automatically. Third, judges at pretrial conferences may have more information on which to base a realistic discovery plan, since the judge will ordinarily have the pleadings and the parties' written report of their Rule 26(f) meeting at the pretrial conference, and may have the parties' initial disclosures.

Initial disclosures, being automatic, are a departure from traditional discovery, which required a party to produce information only when served with a specific request. Initial disclosures may trigger significant changes in how lawyers litigate. First, since a lawyer is now required to disclose information automatically to the other side, if it is "discoverable information relevant to disputed facts alleged with particularity in the pleadings," the scope of the required initial disclosures may be influenced by the specificity of the allegations in the pleadings. This may cause lawyers to make their complaints and answers more fact-specific, although not required under "notice" pleading. Rule 26 does not further define "with particularity." The "particularity" requirement in Rule 9(b) is not analogous, although the "reasonable particularity" requirement of Rule 34 may provide some guidance. Second, lawyers may more frequently move for a more definite statement under Rule 12(e) to identify what the case is about and hence what is required to be disclosed in the initial disclosures. Third, Rule 26 requires a "reasonable investigation" before disclosures are made, an imprecise standard. Reasonableness is probably a function of how particular the pleadings are, how complex the case is, and how much time exists before disclosures are due. Fourth, and probably the most problematic, some litigators feel that the automatic disclosure requirement may put them in conflict with their duty of undivided loyalty to the client. Lawyers may be less than zealous in getting information from the client, and clients may become less zealous in telling their lawyers "everything," knowing that the lawyer may be required to immediately turn around and disclose damaging information to the other side.

These uncertainties will undoubtedly become resolved over time. However, keep in mind that the sanctions for violating Rule 26(a) can be severe. The court may exclude from trial a witness or information not listed or produced in the initial disclosure, if the failure to disclose was "without substantial justification" and was not "harmless."

2. Expert disclosures

Under Rule 26(a)(2), each party must also make expert disclosures. The disclosure includes the "identity of any person who may be used at trial to present evidence" as an expert. Also required is disclosure of a written signed report of "a witness who is retained or specially employed to provide expert testimony in the case, or whose duties as an employee of the party regularly involve giving expert testimony." The report must contain a "complete statement" of all opinions and bases; the data used to reach the opinions; summary exhibits; witness qualifications; all publications within 10 years; compensation; and other cases in which the witness has testified at trial or deposition within 4 years.

Expert disclosures are due at least 90 days before trial, or 30 days if the expert is solely a rebuttal witness, unless the court directs or the parties stipulate otherwise. The 90-day rule can create problems, since there will be no information provided to the other parties about the testifying experts until that time. (Under the old approach, expert information was provided through interrogatories, which are usually served early in the discovery phase.) When expert disclosures should be due must be taken up at the Rule 16 scheduling conference.

Expert witness discovery has been significantly broadened. Rule 26(a)(2) requires a "complete statement" of all opinions and bases for the opinions, the data relied on, and the background of the expert. Rule 26(b)(4) now provides for depositions of testifying experts as of right. Between the two provisions, parties can now get essentially unlimited information about, and from, the other party's experts.

However, note that an "expert" is someone who will give testimony under Rules 702, 703, and 705 of the Federal Rules of Evidence. Accordingly, someone who may be an expert in terms of background but who will not give opinion testimony at trial may not be considered an expert for the purposes of this rule. In that event, the witness should be disclosed under the initial disclosures section.

3. Pretrial disclosures

Under Rule 26(a)(3) each party must make pretrial disclosures in the following categories of evidence:

1. witnesses who are expected to testify at trial
2. witnesses who may be called "if the need arises"
3. witnesses who are expected to be presented through depositions (and a transcript of pertinent portions of the testimony)
4. each exhibit expected to be offered at trial
5. each exhibit that may be offered "if the need arises"

Pretrial disclosures are due at least 30 days before trial, unless the court directs otherwise. Objections to depositions and exhibits must be made at least 14 days before trial. Failure to object will be deemed a waiver of all objections except relevance.

The pretrial disclosures contain some of the information that has usually been included in the pretrial memorandum. The requirement of disclosing witnesses called and exhibits offered "if the need arises" presumably includes rebuttal witnesses and exhibits.

The times provided under Rule 26(a)(1), controlling the initial disclosures, can be modified by agreement of the parties or by court order. The times provided under Rule 26(a) (2) and (3) for expert disclosures and pretrial disclosures can be modified only by court order.

§6.6. *Practice approach to initial disclosures*

A lawyer preparing initial disclosures should ask four basic questions: Must I make initial disclosures in this district? When must I send initial disclosures to the other parties? What must I disclose? How should I organize and draft my initial disclosures?

1. Applicability of initial disclosures

Rule 26(a) permits districts to "opt-out," and many have. Hence, you need to find out if the district in which the case is pending has opted-out and, if so, whether a local rule substitutes another form of initial disclosure.

2. Timing

If your district follows Rule 26(a), you need to determine when the initial disclosures are due. Under Rule 26(f) the parties must meet to develop a discovery plan as soon as practicable, and in any event at least 14 days before the court holds a pretrial conference under Rule 16.

The logical time to have this meeting is shortly after the defendant has answered the complaint or, if the answer contains counterclaims, cross claims, or third party complaints, when the plaintiff has replied or other parties have responded to the defendant's claims. At this time, the claims and defenses will be reasonably clear, and the parties should be able to meet to develop a realistic discovery plan and schedule they can recommend to the court.

However, keep in mind that many judges are becoming increasingly active in managing cases and may schedule an early pretrial conference. The Rule requires that the parties meet at least 14 days before the pretrial conference and make initial disclosures within 10 days of the parties' meeting. This means that the court should have the initial disclosures at the time of the pretrial conference.

3. Topics

Rule 26(a)(1) clearly sets forth the required topics and the details within each topic. Required are:

1. The name, address, and telephone number, if known, of each individual "likely to have discoverable information relevant to disputed facts alleged with particularity in the pleadings."
2. The description and location of documents, data compilations, and tangible things, or copies of them, in the possession, custody, or control of the party that are "relevant to disputed facts alleged with particularity in the pleadings."
3. The computation of damages, making available for inspection and copying the documents on which the damages are computed.
4. Insurance agreements, making them available for inspection and copying, which may be liable for all or part of any judgment.

4. Drafting the initial disclosures

Drafting the initial disclosures requires that you make disclosures based on the information "then reasonably available." A party cannot avoid disclosures because its investigation is not yet complete, a situation that will more frequently apply to defendants. A party must make disclosures based on "disputed facts alleged with particularity in the pleadings," not just the party's own pleadings. A party must therefore look at both the complaint (including any cross-claims and counterclaims), the answer, and reply, see what facts are in issue, and make the appropriate disclosure. Keep in mind that a threadbare disclosure will probably result in motions to compel as well as follow-up interrogatories and documents requests, creating more work for you. Full disclosure of "core" information, based on the apparent factual issues and the information on hand, is required by the rule. It also sends a message to the opponent that you have done your homework, understand the issues and facts, and are fully prepared to litigate the case. This is an important message to send early in the litigation process, and sending a detailed initial disclosure does just that.

a. Heading

An initial disclosure, like any court document, must contain a caption showing the court, parties, and civil case number. It should contain a heading that identifies which party is making the initial disclosure.

Example:

[Caption]

PLAINTIFF'S INITIAL DISCLOSURES

Plaintiff Johnson makes the following initial disclosures, pursuant to Rule 26(a)(1) of the Federal Rules of Civil Procedure:

b. Content

Rule 26(a)(1) requires four categories of information, and drafting the actual information is simply a matter of carefully following the rule so that you provide what is required.

i. Witnesses

The first category is the name and, if known, the address and telephone number of each individual "likely to have discoverable information relevant to disputed facts alleged with particularity in the pleadings," and "identifying the subjects of the information."

Example:

A. The following individuals are likely to have discoverable information relevant to disputed facts alleged with particularity in the pleadings:

1. William Dawes (occurrence witness)
    483 Bright Street
    Wilmington, NC
    677-4123
2. Ellen Johnson (occurrence witness)
    address and telephone unknown
3. Mary Wilson, RN (nurse at emergency room)
    Mercy General Hospital
    Wilmington, NC
    447-7000

ii. Documents

The second category is a description and location of documents, data compilations, and tangible things, or copies of them, in the possession, custody, or control of the party that are "relevant to disputed facts alleged with particularity in the pleadings." While an itemized list of each document is not required, enough of a description is required to allow the other parties to make informed decisions about which documents to inspect and copy, and to draft a documents request directed to those documents. An adequate description of the documents should probably include the type of document, its date, and the general subject matter of its contents. The disclosing party can always decide to provide actual copies of the documents with the initial disclosure.

Example:

The following records, data compilations, and tangible things are in the possession, custody, or control of the plaintiff and are relevant to disputed facts alleged with particularity in the pleadings:

1. 1998 Honda Civic automobile, presently in possession of plaintiff at plaintiff's residence.
2. Mercy Hospital medical records, in the possession of both Mercy Hospital and plaintiff's attorney (copy attached).
3. Wilmington Police Department accident report, in the possession of both the Wilmington Police Department and plaintiff's attorney (copy attached).

iii. Damages

The third category is a computation of damages, making available for inspection and copying the documents on which the damages are computed. The disclosing party can always decide to provide copies of the documents with the initial disclosure.

Example:

Plaintiff's present damages are as follows and are based on the following records, which are in the possession of plaintiff's attorney and can be inspected and copied at any mutually convenient time:

1.	hospital expenses (Mercy Hospital)	$2,498.71
2.	doctor's expenses (Dr. Albert Rosen)	3,433.80
3.	drugs (Walgreen's Pharmacy)	126.00
4.	vehicle repair (Dobbs Honda)	2,135.00
5.	rental vehicle (Hertz Car Rental)	288.39
6.	lost wages (Montgomery Ward Co.)	3,122.00
7.	past pain & suffering	50,000.00
8.	future pain & suffering	10,000.00

iv. Insurance

The fourth category is any insurance agreements that may be liable for all or part of any judgment, making them available for inspection and copying. The disclosing party can always decide to provide copies of the agreements with the initial disclosure.

Example:

Defendant was insured under a general casualty insurance policy issued by Allstate Insurance, Policy No. 4522147. A copy of the policy is attached.

c. Signing, serving, and filing

The initial disclosures must be signed by a lawyer and served on every other party. Service is made by any permitted method under Rule 5, most commonly by mailing a copy to the lawyers for the other parties. The original disclosure, with an attached proof of service, is then filed with the clerk of the court, unless a local rule directs, as some do, that discovery is not filed until a need arises.

5. Effect of initial disclosures

Initial disclosures are likely to have several effects on how litigation is conducted in federal courts. First, initial disclosures will replace the boilerplate interrogatories and documents requests that customarily sought the basic information now required to be automatically disclosed under Rule 26(a)(1). This basic information will be available sooner than was previously the case. This means that interrogatories and documents requests will be used as supplemental steps to get missing information and to pin down the other party to specific facts and positions. Second, since the rule refers to "disputed facts alleged with particularity in the pleadings," parties may draft their complaints, answers, and replies with more factual detail, since a denial of a claimed fact in a responsive pleading will trigger the automatic disclosure of witnesses and documents relevant to the denied fact. Third, since the rules now also contain limits on the number of depositions and interrogatories, parties are more likely to move to compel more complete responses to the initial disclosures before pursuing the information through other discovery devices. Fourth, parties may be able to depose witnesses and parties sooner, if the initial disclosures have provided an adequate factual and documentary setting. Finally, initial disclosures may result in more motions for sanctions and other relief for failing to make adequate timely disclosure of required information. Lawyers will undoubtedly ask that witnesses and exhibits be precluded from trial if they were not properly and timely disclosed.

§6.7. *Practice approach to expert disclosures*

A lawyer preparing expert disclosures should ask four basic questions: Must I make expert disclosures? When must I make the disclosures? What must I disclose? How should I organize and draft the disclosures?

1. Applicability of expert disclosures

Rule 26(a) permits districts to opt-out, and many have. Hence, just as with initial disclosures, you need to find out if the district in which the case is pending has opted-out and, if so, whether a local rule substitutes another form of initial disclosure.

2. Timing

If the district in which your case is pending follows Rule 26(a), you need to determine when the expert disclosures are due. Under Rule 26(a)(2), expert disclosures are due at least 90 days before trial, or 30 days if the expert is solely a rebuttal witness, unless the court directs otherwise. Keep in mind that the court may have entered a pretrial order under Rule 16 establishing shorter time limits for the expert disclosures.

3. Topics

Under Rule 26(a)(2), each party must disclose "the identity of any person who may be used at trial to present evidence" as an expert. It also requires a written signed report for a "witness who is retained or specifically employed to provide expert testimony, or whose duties as an employee of the party regularly involve giving expert testimony." The latter category includes witnesses such as design engineers for manufacturers and research chemists for pharmaceutical companies. The written report must contain:

1. a complete statement of all opinions to be expressed and the basis and reasons therefor;
2. the data or other information considered by the witness in forming the opinions;
3. any exhibits to be used as a summary of or support for the opinions;
4. the qualifications of the witness, including a list of all publications authored by the witness within the preceding 10 years;
5. the compensation to be paid for the study and testimony;
6. a listing of any other cases in which the witness has testified as an expert at trial or by deposition within the preceding 4 years.

An expert witness can now be deposed as of right under Rule 26(b)(4), but only if the expert has first provided his written report.

4. Drafting the expert disclosure

Drafting the expert disclosure is just a matter of following the language of the rule and making sure that you provide all the required information.

a. Heading

The expert disclosure must contain a caption showing the court, parties, and civil case number. It should contain a heading that identifies which party is making the expert disclosure.

Example:

[Caption]

PLAINTIFF'S DISCLOSURE OF EXPERT TESTIMONY

Plaintiff Johnson makes the following disclosure of expert testimony, pursuant to Rule 26(a)(2). The following experts are expected to testify on behalf of the plaintiff at trial:

b. Content

By tracking the requirements of the Rule, making the required disclosure is simple.

Example:

1. Emily Lieberman, M.D.
a. Dr. Lieberman's opinions, the bases for her opinions, and the data she used to reach her opinions are contained in her signed written report dated June 1, 1998, a copy of which is attached.
b. Dr. Lieberman will use no summary exhibits during her testimony.
c. Dr. Lieberman's professional qualifications, including her publications within the last 10 years, are contained on her current curriculum vitae, a copy of which is attached.
d. Dr. Lieberman is being compensated for her study and testimony at the rate of $250 per hour.
e. Dr. Lieberman has testified as an expert at trial or deposition a total of 6 times within the last 4 years. A list of those 6 cases is attached.

c. Expert report

Rule 26(a)(2) requires disclosure of a signed written report from an expert who may testify at trial, and the report must include a "complete statement of all opinions to be expressed and the basis and reasons therefor." How do you get such a report from the expert that meets the requirements of the rule?

It goes without saying that the report should be prepared and written by the expert, who must sign it and who is responsible for its content. On the other hand, the expert needs to know the requirements of the rule, and the topics on which the expert will be asked to give opinions. The usual practice is that the lawyer and expert meet to discuss the issues; the lawyer explains the issues on which he needs expert opinions; and the expert explains whether he can give opinions on those issues and what the opinions will be. Sometimes the lawyer may ask the expert to assume certain facts as true and provide a factual summary with, preferably, the underlying source of the facts. The expert later drafts a written report of his evaluation of the issues, his opinions, and the reasons for them, and submits it to the lawyer, who reviews it for completeness and notes any errors and omissions. The expert then submits the final report to the lawyer.

How the expert's report looks when complete varies according to the circumstances, but most are organized along the following lines:

Example:

EXPERT REPORT

by

Mary G. Smith, M.D.

Case: Williams v. Johnson
         No. 98 C 1287

1. Introduction
    I have been retained as an expert by counsel for the plaintiff in the above-captioned litigation.
    I have been asked to express opinions on . . .
2. Professional qualifications
    I am a medical doctor and have been licensed to practice medicine since 1980 . . .
    Attached is a curriculum vitae detailing my professional background.
3. Matters considered
    As part of my review I have requested, received, and reviewed the following materials:
    I have also conducted an examination of the plaintiff . . .
    I have ordered and received the following tests . . .
4. Factual background
    On June 1, 1998, . . .
5. Opinions
    I have reached the following opinions:
6. Bases for the opinions
    My opinions are based on the following:
7. Conclusion
    For the foregoing reasons . . .

Date: _____   _____
                                       Mary G. Smith, M.D.

Keep in mind that instructions, conversations, letters, and any other communications between the lawyer and expert, records and documents sent to the expert, and earlier drafts of the expert's report are usually discoverable and admissible at trial. This is because there is no work-product doctrine protection between the lawyer and the testifying expert. Conduct yourself accordingly. Make sure you send to the expert only those things that would be discoverable anyway. Make sure the report is the expert's work. Lawyers who actively participate in creating and drafting an expert's report make themselves, their experts, and their case vulnerable at trial.

5. Effect of expert disclosure

Rule 26(a)(2), controlling expert disclosure, and Rule 26(b)(4), permitting expert depositions as of right, have substantially changed discovery practice directed to experts. First, expert discovery is often likely to be sooner, because expert disclosure is required at least 90 days before trial. This rule change should reduce the expert disclosure delaying games some lawyers played as the case moved closer to trial, and no disclosure was made until just before trial. However, expert disclosure may also come later, since no expert discovery is required until 90 days before trial. Most lawyers will probably ask the court to accelerate the expert disclosure date during the Rule 16 scheduling conference. Second, pre-deposition discovery of experts is significantly expanded, now requiring a "complete statement" of the opinions, basis, and data, as well as a complete biographical picture of the witness. This is much more than was previously required under the interrogatory rule governing experts. Since expert disclosure must be made before the expert can be deposed, there may be more motion practice directed to the completeness of the disclosed information. Third, not taking an expert's deposition, which is now of right, will be a realistic option in some cases, saving the lawyers time and the clients money. For example, the defense may not always need to take the deposition of plaintiff's emergency room treating physician, if expert disclosure is complete and the emergency room records have been obtained, particularly since the party taking the deposition of an adversary's expert is required to reimburse the expert "a reasonable fee for the time spent responding to the discovery." Even when the expert is deposed, the actual deposition should be significantly shorter because of the required expert disclosure.

What will be the extent of expert discovery if a district opts-out of the Rule 26(a)(2) expert disclosure rules? The enactment of Rule 26(a) coincided with the amendment of Rule 33, which refers to Rule 26(b)(1) providing that parties may discover "any matter not privileged." Hence, the probable result will be that the parties will be able to obtain the same expert discovery, only through the traditional vehicle of interrogatories.

§6.8. *Practice approach to pretrial disclosures*

Pretrial disclosures, governed by Rule 26(a)(3), are discussed in §8.2.

§6.9. *Interrogatories*

Interrogatories are frequently the second step in the discovery process because they provide the best method for getting basic facts about the other side's case not already obtained from the other party's initial disclosures. If your district has opted-out of Rule 26(a), interrogatories are usually the first discovery method employed. Further discovery can develop the information received in the interrogatory answers.

1. Law[21]

Although interrogatories are governed by Rule 33, that Rule is often supplemented by local rules. Some districts have approved pattern interrogatories for common cases such as automobile personal injury suits. Hence, you should always check the local rules for the particular jurisdiction.

Interrogatories may be used to learn basic facts; identify witnesses and experts; and identify documents and other tangible things. Also, they can be used to inquire about any claim or defense, and about any relevant matter that is not privileged, since the scope of discovery is defined by Rule 26(b). However, Rule 33(c) also permits interrogatories that ask for "an opinion or contention that relates to fact or the application of law to fact." The line between what is "opinion" and what is a question of "pure law" is admittedly imprecise and has generated substantial litigation.[22] Because such issues usually become either clearer or moot as discovery progresses, the court may order that such interrogatories remain unanswered until a later time.

Interrogatories can be served by any party on any other party at any time after the parties have met to develop a discovery plan as required under Rule 26(f). In practice, interrogatories are frequently served after the parties have served their initial disclosures and reviewed the other party's initial disclosures.

The role of interrogatories in the discovery process was significantly changed by the amendments to the Rules in 1993. First, initial disclosures under Rule 26(a)(1) have, as they were intended to, substantially replaced the boilerplate pattern interrogatories that asked for basic information from the other parties (unless, of course, the district in which the case is pending has opted-out of Rule 26(a)). Interrogatories in federal court are now used in a more focused way: to target information not revealed, and to clarify information revealed, in the initial disclosures.

Second, any party can serve on any other party interrogatories "not exceeding 25 in number including all discrete subparts," unless the parties stipulate in writing or the court orders otherwise. The parties can ask

---

21. Wright §86; James & Hazard §5.4; Friedenthal §7.9; Moore's Manual §15.09; Shepard's Manual §§5.10, 5.126-5.144; Moore's Federal Practice §33; Wright & Miller §§2161-2182.

22. Moore's Manual §15.09; Shepard's Manual §5.137; Moore's Federal Practice §33.17; Wright & Miller §2167.

for leave of court to serve more interrogatories. The question of whether an interrogatory is a single interrogatory or whether it is a compound interrogatory that attempts to get around interrogatory limits frequently arose, because many districts have had local rules limiting the number of interrogatories.[23] The Committee Notes to Rule 33 make it clear that the "including all discrete subparts" language bars a single interrogatory that requests information about discrete separate subjects from counting as one interrogatory. On the other hand, an interrogatory that seeks information about one subject but asks that information about the subject be broken down into categories should be considered one interrogatory. As always, you need to know how your judge will count interrogatories, since it will affect how you draft them.

Third, objections to interrogatories must be stated and the answering party must answer any part of an interrogatory to which there is no objection. Objections must be stated "with specificity," and grounds not stated in a timely objection will generally be deemed waived.

Answers are due within 30 days of service of the interrogatories, unless a different time is set by court order or by written stipulation between the parties. The answer must respond to each interrogatory separately with either an answer or an objection. An answer must be a "full" answer that fairly meets the substance of the interrogatory. The answering party has an obligation to find the information if it is within the party's possession, even if not within the personal knowledge of the actual person answering.[24]

Under Rule 33(d) the answering party may specify business records from which an answer may be derived or ascertained, instead of giving a direct answer, if the "burden of deriving or ascertaining the answer is substantially the same for the party serving the interrogatory as for the party served." Where this is the case, the answer need only specify the records in sufficient detail to allow the requesting party to locate and identify the records, and to give the requesting party a reasonable opportunity to inspect and copy them.

An answer must be signed under oath by the party making it. If any interrogatories are objected to, the lawyer making the objection must sign as well.

Finally, an answering party has a continuing obligation to supplement certain answers. Rule 26(e) requires supplementation of responses, even though complete when made, if "the party learns that the response is in some material respect incomplete or incorrect and if the additional or corrective information has not otherwise been made known to the other parties during the discovery process or in writing." Hence, unless the other parties have obtained the corrective information through other discovery or have been provided with that information in writing, the answering party must amend its answers within a reasonable time. Failing to do this will, on motion, subject the answering party to Rule 37 sanctions.

---

23. See Wright & Miller §2168.
24. Moore's Manual §15.09; Shepard's Manual, §§5.141, 5.155; Moore's Federal Practice §33.26; Wright & Miller §2177.

2. Practice approach

A lawyer preparing to send interrogatories to another party must ask three basic questions: When should I send out interrogatories? What kind of information should I seek? How should I organize and draft interrogatories to get the desired information?

a. Timing

The timing of interrogatories depends in part on whether the district follows Rule 26(a) or has opted-out of the rule. If Rule 26(a) is followed, interrogatories can be served on any other party once the parties have had their discovery planning meeting required under Rule 26(f). However, the better approach is to wait until you have received the other party's initial disclosures and attended the pretrial conference under Rule 16. These will both normally occur within 14 days of the discovery planning meeting. This will give you an opportunity to review the other party's initial disclosures and learn how the judge intends to schedule and regulate the discovery process in this case. This will allow your interrogatories to be more focused, an important consideration since interrogatories are now limited to 25 without leave of court or written stipulation of the parties.

If the district has opted-out of Rule 26(a), interrogatories are commonly sent out as soon as the initial pleadings have been made. For example, plaintiffs usually serve interrogatories on the defendant shortly after the defendant has answered the complaint; defendants frequently serve interrogatories on the plaintiff with their initial response (an answer or Rule 12 motion) to the complaint.

Sending interrogatories out quickly accomplishes two important things. First, it gets the discovery process started, which is particularly important since using the other discovery methods often depends on the interrogatory answers. With court imposed discovery cut-off dates increasingly a part of the litigation process, efficiency is important. Second, it lets other parties know that you intend to litigate actively, an important message to send to your adversaries early on.

b. Topics

Before drafting the interrogatories, ask yourself, What information do I want now so that I can use subsequent discovery methods to develop the information more fully? If you have thought through your discovery strategy,[25] you should know what information you need that is well suited to obtaining through interrogatories. If the district follows Rule 26(a), the other parties should have provided much of this information in their initial disclosures. However, even if you have received the initial disclosures you should be sure that you always know or, if you don't know, get the following information.

25. §6.3.

i.   Identity of parties, agents, and employees

Frequently in commercial litigation, you will not know the proper formal names of parties, parent corporations, or subsidiaries; where they are incorporated or licensed to do business; or the type of legal entities they are or their relationships to other parties. You need to know this information for a variety of purposes, relating to jurisdictional and joinder issues, for instance. You will also need to learn the identity of all agents and employees, and their relationships to the party. Interrogatories are the best method for getting this information.

ii.   Identity of witnesses

Most every lawsuit will have witnesses to the events and transactions on which the claims are based. Interrogatories are a good method for obtaining the witnesses' identities, locations, and relationships to the parties.

iii.   Identity of documents and tangible things

Similarly, most every lawsuit will have certain documents, records, and other tangible things on which the claims are based, or that are relevant to the claims. Interrogatories are the best method for identifying and locating these and for determining who has custody or control of them.

iv.   Identity of experts, facts, and opinions

Under Rule 26(a)(2), the expert disclosure rule, the other parties should have disclosed the identity and written report of their testifying experts. The report should contain a complete report of the expert's opinions, bases and supporting data for the opinions, and information about the expert's background. If the district follows Rule 26(a), expert disclosures will be the normal vehicle to obtain information about experts. If the district has opted-out of Rule 26(a), interrogatories will be the usual method to obtain this information.

Keep in mind, however, that the court under Rule 16 will probably have entered a pretrial order that controls when expert disclosures must be made. At this early stage in the litigation process, the parties may not yet have selected the experts who will ultimately be the testifying experts at trial. If you seek this information through interrogatories, the response will frequently be "not yet known." Nevertheless, many lawyers ask for expert disclosure early, because it makes an early record of the request. Keep in mind that Rule 26(e) requires that a party "seasonably" amend a discovery answer if the party learns it is incomplete or incorrect and the requesting party has not been provided with the additional or corrective information during the discovery process or in writing. Some lawyers, however, ask for expert information in a later interrogatory, after a substantial amount of discovery has been taken, the theory being that a useful answer is more likely to be received at that time.

v.   Details and sequences of events and transactions

Interrogatories are a useful method for obtaining concrete facts underlying vague or generalized claims. For this reason they are particularly useful in the commercial litigation area where lawsuits are frequently based on a series of events and transactions spread out over time, but are not detailed in any way in the pleadings.

vi.   Technical and statistical data

Interrogatories are a good method to identify and obtain technical and statistical data, such as financial statements, accounting information, sales data and similar information.

vii.   Damages information and insurance coverage

The plaintiff's complaint will often contain only a general request for damages "in excess of $75,000," the minimum jurisdictional amount. Damages interrogatories to the plaintiff are useful for drawing out the specific legal theories of recovery the plaintiff is asserting, the dollar amount claimed for each element of damages, and the basis for each claim.

Since it is vitally important for a plaintiff to determine the defendant's ability to pay a judgment, a standard interrogatory should ask about insurance policies that may cover the event or transactions on which the lawsuit is based, and for the details of the coverage. Rule 26(b)(2) expressly makes this information discoverable. If the pleadings, such as a punitive damages claim, make the defendant's financial condition relevant, this information should also be requested. Defendant, however, will usually object to any discovery of its financial condition or ask that such discovery be stayed until the court has heard and ruled on a summary judgment motion attacking the punitive damages claim. If you suspect that the defendant's insurer may be defending under a reservation of rights, you should try to obtain this information through an interrogatory because this fact will influence how you, and the defense, conduct the litigation.

viii.   Identity of persons who prepared answers and of sources used

Where interrogatories are served on a corporate party, they should ask for the identity of each person who participated in preparing the answers, and ask for the identity of the documents used to prepare each answer. This information will be important in deciding whom to depose and what documents to request.

ix.   Positions on issues, opinions of fact, and contentions

Interrogatories that ask for "opinions," "contentions relating to facts," or the "application of law to facts," are usually proper. On the other hand, interrogatories that ask for matters of "pure law" are objectionable. The dividing line is unclear, and a great many discovery motions deal with this problem.[26] Where a pleading is vague, however, a proper interrogatory can prove to be a useful request. For example, it is proper in a negligence action to ask what specific conduct plaintiff claims constituted the negligence, just as in a contract action it is proper to ask what conduct plaintiff claims constituted a breach.

The court has the power under Rule 33(c) to postpone answering such interrogatories. Accordingly, many lawyers avoid such requests in the initial interrogatories, since it may trigger objections and delay receiving answers to the more basic interrogatories.

Keep in mind that interrogatories, while important, can be a "low yield" discovery method. Interrogatories take time to prepare and answer, and the answers frequently try to limit the amount of information disclosed. The amount of information actually produced through interrogatories is frequently low. Therefore, focused interrogatories, which ask only for basic factual data, are usually more effective. If the district follows Rule 26(a), interrogatories should be used in a more selective and focused way: to target the "missing gaps" in the opposing party's disclosure statement or to pin down the opposing party on specific facts that may be used at trial for impeachment if the party that signed the interrogatory testifies inconsistently at trial.

c. Drafting the interrogatories

The drafting lawyer's principal task is to prepare a set of interrogatories that will successfully elicit the desired information. The questions must be drafted so as to force the answering party to respond to them squarely and to eliminate the possibility of evasive, though superficially responsive, answers. (Always ask yourself: If I received this interrogatory, could I avoid giving a meaningful answer because of the way the interrogatory is worded? If so, redraft the interrogatory.) Also, the questions must be organized sequentially to make sure that all desired topics are covered. Basic interrogatories for recurrent types of actions are frequently stored in a law firm's computer data base, making them easy to modify for a specific case. In addition, many jurisdictions have approved pattern or uniform interrogatories which, if appropriate for the case, should be submitted verbatim to the other side.

i. Headings

An interrogatory, like any court document, must contain a caption showing the court, parties, and civil case number. Further, the interrogatories should include a heading that identifies which party is submitting the interrogatories to which other party. It is also a good practice to label them "First Set," "Second Set," and so on, and to number them sequentially with a later set picking up where the previous set left off. This avoids confusion when references are later made to interrogatories and answers.

---

26. Moore's Manual §15.09; Manual of Federal Practice §5.137; Moore's Federal Practice §§33.12, 33.17; Wright & Miller §2167.

Example:

[Caption]

PLAINTIFF JOHNSON'S INTERROGATORIES TO DEFENDANT ACME CORPORATION

(First Set)

Plaintiff Johnson requests that defendant Acme Corporation, through an officer or authorized agent of the corporation, answer the following interrogatories under oath and serve them upon plaintiff within 30 days, pursuant to Rule 33 of the Federal Rules of Civil Procedure:

1. . . .
2. . . .
3. . . .

Example:

[Caption]

PLAINTIFF JOHNSON'S INTERROGATORIES TO DEFENDANT ACME CORPORATION

(Second Set)

Plaintiff Johnson requests that. . . .

15. . . .
16. . . .
17. . . .

Consider using headings for related sections of the interrogatories, such as "parties," "collision," "medical history," "contract," and "damages," particularly in more complex cases. These make the interrogatories easier to understand and answer.

ii.   Definitions and instructions

A common practice in more complex interrogatories is to have the actual interrogatories preceded by a definitions and instructions section. Terms used repeatedly in the interrogatories can be defined, making the interrogatories easier to follow, while deterring evasive answers. Terms commonly defined in interrogatories include "record," "agreement," "document," "communication," "witness," "participate," "transaction," "occurrence," "collision," "state," "knowledge," "describe," and "identify." Use broad descriptions of these basic terms so that the answering party cannot give a superficially accurate but effectively unresponsive answer.

Example:

DEFINITIONS

The following terms used in these interrogatories have the following meanings:

1. To "identify" means to (a) state a person's full name, home address, business address, and present and past relationship to any party; (b) state the title of any document, who prepared it, when it was prepared, where it is located, and who its custodian is.

2. A "document" means all written or printed matter of any kind, including but not limited to legal documents, letters, memoranda, business records, interoffice communications, and data stored electronically, which are in the possession or control of the answering party.

3. A "communication" means all oral conversations, discussions, letters, telegrams, memoranda, e-mail, facsimile transmission, and any other transmission of information in any form, both oral and written.

It is sometimes useful to have an instruction section detail how interrogatories should be answered. Again, it makes the particular interrogatories easier to understand.

Example:

INSTRUCTIONS

In answering each interrogatory:

(a) state whether the answer is within the personal knowledge of the person answering the interrogatory and, if not, identify each person known to have personal knowledge of the answer;

(b) identify each document that was used in any way to formulate the answer.

Finally, in cases where a series of events or transactions is involved, it may be useful to state the time frame the interrogatories are intended to cover.

Example:

Unless expressly stated otherwise, each interrogatory relates to the time period beginning June 1, 1998, through and including the date on which answers to these interrogatories are signed.

Keep in mind, however, that such preambles are useful only in more complex interrogatories. For instance, they are frequently employed in commercial cases. In other cases, such as simple contract or personal injury actions, they are usually unnecessary because they make the interrogatories more complex than they need to be. If interrogatories are drafted in clear, plain English, there should be no need to add definitions and instructions.

In addition, keep in mind that clear, simple interrogatories are more likely to yield clear, simple answers that will provide information that is actually useful. This makes the questions and answers much more effective if they are used during trial, such as admissions and impeachment. The more complex the interrogatories, the more complex and less useful the answers are likely to be. Accordingly, it is usually better to err on the side of simplicity.

iii. Interrogatory style

Interrogatories must be clear and must adequately cover the necessary subjects. The interrogatories are usually drafted as imperatives, not as actual questions, since the imperative form affirmatively requires the answering party to supply information.

The first purpose of interrogatories is to identify parties, witnesses, documents, and experts.

Example (parties and agents):

1. State the full name of the defendant, where and when incorporated, where and when licensed to do business, where it has its principal place of business, and all names under which it does business.

2. Identify each officer and director of the defendant during the time period of June 1, 1998, through the date answers to these interrogatories are signed.

3. Identify each company, subdivision and subsidiary in which the defendant has any ownership, control, or interest of any kind for the period referred to in Interrogatory #2 above.

Example (witnesses):

1. Identify each person who was present during the execution of the contract that forms the basis of Count I of plaintiff's complaint.

2. Identify each person who participated in or was present during any of the negotiations of the contract executed by plaintiff and defendant on June 1, 1998.

3. State the full name and address of each person who witnessed, or claims to have witnessed, the collision between vehicles driven by the plaintiff and defendant occurring on June 1, 1998.

4. State the full name and address of each person who was present, or claims to have been present, at the scene of the collision during and after the collision, other than the persons identified in Interrogatory #3 above.

5. State the full name and address of each person who has any knowledge of the facts of the collision, other than those persons already identified in Interrogatories #3 and 4 above.

Note that rather than ask for witnesses in a general way, the interrogatories first focus on witnesses to a particular transaction or event, then expand the scope in subsequent questions to ensure that all possible known witnesses are identified. This organizes the information into useful categories.

Example (documents):

1. Identify each document that relates to the shipping of the machinery by plaintiff to defendant on June 1, 1998.

2. Identify each document in your possession and control that refers to the plaintiff's employment termination that is the basis for plaintiff's complaint.

3. Identify each document that you contend put the defendant on notice of a dangerous condition existing on the roadway at the intersection of Main and Elm Streets on June 1, 1998.

A common practice is to combine an interrogatory that asks for the identity of documents with a request to produce all documents identified in the interrogatory answer. This has the advantage of getting copies of the identified documents more quickly.[27]

Interrogatories can also obtain information about experts expected to testify at trial. The use of a basic imperative with subsections is recommended.

Example (experts):

1. As to each expert expected to testify at trial, state:

a. the expert's full name, address, and professional qualifications;

b. the subject matter on which the expert is expected to testify;

c. the facts and opinions to which the expert is expected to testify; and

d. the grounds of each opinion.

However, remember that Rule 26(a)(2) now provides for disclosure of expert witness testimony and information that is substantially broader than what Rule 33 formerly permitted. Hence, unless the district has opted-out of Rule 26(a), expert disclosures, not interrogatories, should be the preferred method for obtaining information about the other party's testifying experts.

The above interrogatories are all directed toward obtaining the identity of parties and agents, witnesses, documents, and experts, and are a part of almost every interrogatory set. These questions obtain the hard data that will provide the springboard for further investigation and discovery.

Interrogatories should also ask for the specific facts on which the pleadings are based. This is particularly important since, due to the minimal requirements of federal "notice pleading," the pleadings frequently contain general conclusory language that gives little information about

---

27. See §§6.6 and 6.7 on drafting documents requests.

the facts on which claims, defenses, or damages are based. Interrogatories should develop the basic facts so that the parties can focus on specific facts underlying the legal claims.

Example (facts underlying complaint in personal injury action):

1. Describe the personal injuries you received as a result of this occurrence.

2. If you were hospitalized as a result of this occurrence, state the name and address of each such hospital or clinic, the dates of your hospitalization at each facility, and the amount of each facility's bill.

If a single interrogatory asks for several categories of information, it is more effective to set out those categories in lettered subsections. This makes it clear what information you want, and makes it more likely that you will elicit complete answers. Since each subpart relates to the same subject, it should count as a single interrogatory under Rule 33, an important consideration since the rule limits interrogatories to 25 unless more are permitted by court order or written stipulation of the parties.

Example:

3. If you were treated by any physicians as a result of this occurrence, state:
    a. the name and address of each such physician;
    b. each physician's areas of specialty;
    c. the dates of each examination, consultation, or appointment; and
    d. the amount of each physician's bill.

4. If you were unable to work as a result of this occurrence, state:
    a. the dates during which you were unable to work;
    b. your employers during those dates;
    c. the type of work you were unable to do; and
    d. the amount of lost wages or income.

5. State any other losses or expenses you claim resulted from this occurrence, other than those already stated above.

6. During the past 10 years, have you suffered any other personal injuries? If so, state:
    a. when, where, and how you were injured;
    b. the nature and extent of the injuries;
    c. the name and address of each medical facility where you were treated; and
    d. each physician by whom you were treated for those injuries.

7. During the past 10 years, have you been hospitalized, treated, examined, or tested at any hospital, clinic, or physician's office for any medical condition other than personal injuries? If so, state:
    a. the name and address of each such medical facility and physician;
    b. the dates such services were provided; and

c. the medical conditions involved.

These kinds of questions serve to systematically discover the facts on which the plaintiff's case is based, and the answers will point to the areas that need to be explored in greater detail.

Finally, interrogatories should be used to identify the facts on which specific claims are based. Complaints commonly allege in conclusory fashion that the defendant "breached the contract" or "negligently operated a motor vehicle." An interrogatory is an effective means of developing the facts that the other party claims support the legal contentions. These are commonly called "contention interrogatories." Keep in mind, however, that such contention interrogatories are frequently objected to on the ground that they are overly broad, so particular care must be used in drafting them. In addition, the court may order that such contention interrogatories need not be answered until a later time, when more facts are known to the answering party.

Examples:

1. State the basis upon which you claim that defendant acted negligently.

2. State the conduct by the plaintiff and any of its officers, employees, or agents that you claim constituted a breach of the contract.

3. Do you contend that Samuel Jones lacked authority to enter into a contract on behalf of the defendant corporation? If so, state the basis for this contention.

What are the common problems that arise when drafting interrogatories? Remember that the skill in drafting interrogatories is in finding a clear, simple way to elicit the information you need, and are entitled to get, without making the interrogatories unduly burdensome. A common problem is interrogatories that are overly broad. For example, interrogatories that ask "Identify in detail each and every fact that relates to your claim in Count I," "Identify all documents that relate to your complaint," "State in detail everything you did on May 1, 1998," and "State every fact on which you base your denial that the defendant was negligent" are probably overly broad. The answering party will either object or provide a summary of the relevant facts. Remember that interrogatories are effective in obtaining basic information. They are not usually effective in obtaining details of events, descriptions, or mental impressions.

Another common problem is interrogatories that are premature. For example, interrogatories that ask "Identify each witness that you expect to call at trial," and "Identify each exhibit you intend to introduce at trial" are premature. These ask for information that is probably not yet known or has not yet been decided, and is usually disclosed when the pretrial memorandum is due. The answering party will usually object or answer, "Not known at present; investigation continues," or give a partial answer to the extent it can, such as "Other than the plaintiff, plaintiff's employer, and treating physician, plaintiff has not yet determined who her trial witnesses will be.''

A third common problem is interrogatories that ask for facts only, rather than also request the identity of documents that contain the facts. For example, an interrogatory that asks ''Identify all persons who attended the May 1, 1998, meeting'' is proper, but should also be combined with an interrogatory that asks ''Identify each record, memorandum, and document of any kind that states the persons who attended the May 1, 1998, meeting.'' Asking for facts and documents, while obviously overlapping, is the better approach, since you later will want to send a request to produce the documents identified in the interrogatory answer, or combine documents requests with your interrogatories.

Finally, a common problem is interrogatories that are drafted so that the answer can give literally true but misleading answers. For example, asking ''Identify each eyewitness to the collision other than the plaintiff and defendant'' may get a literally true answer that none are known. A broader interrogatory asking ''Identify each person who was at or near the scene during or after the collision'' or ''Identify each person who has knowledge of the collision'' may yield more useful information.

iv.   Signing, serving, and filing

The interrogatories must be signed by a lawyer and served on every other party. Service is made by any permitted method under Rule 5, most commonly by mailing a copy to the lawyers for the other parties. The original interrogatories, with an attached proof of service, are then filed with the clerk of the court unless a local rule directs that discovery is not filed until a need arises.

d.   *Responses to interrogatories*

A party must usually answer interrogatories within 30 days of service of the interrogatories. Since they frequently require a substantial amount of work, information necessary to prepare the answers must be obtained reasonably quickly. If the client is out of town and unavailable, or the interrogatories are lengthy, move for additional time to answer. It is usually a good idea to call the opposing lawyer, explain your problem, and ask the lawyer to agree not to oppose your motion for additional time.

i.   Researching and preparing answers

A common procedure in answering interrogatories is to send the interrogatories to the client and ask her to respond to the request for information from her own records and from personal recall and to then return the information to you, her lawyer. You then draft the actual answers. After the client reviews the answers for accuracy and completeness, the client must sign the answer and notarize her signature and return it to you. This procedure works well with individual clients. When the interrogatories are complicated, the client and lawyer must work together on preparing the answers.

Corporate parties and other artificial entities, however, present special considerations. First, the lawyer representing the corporation must decide who in the corporation should answer the interrogatories. Ordinarily a corporate officer who has personal knowledge of the transactions involved, or who has knowledge of the corporate record-keeping system, is an appropriate choice. The selection of the person is not as significant as might first appear, however, because although whoever provides the answer will be bound by it, the answer will also be imputed to and be binding on the corporate party.

Second, the corporate party has an obligation to investigate files that are in its possession or control, to collect the requested information, and to put that information in the answer. Records are considered in a party's possession or control if they are records that are kept at the company's offices, or if they are physically in the possession of another, like an accountant or a storage company, but the party has the power to get the records returned. The corporation's duty to investigate is limited only by the extent of its own records, but there is no duty to conduct an independent outside investigation.[28] A corporate party cannot avoid answering a proper interrogatory through the device of selecting someone to answer the interrogatories who has no personal knowledge of any relevant facts.

Third, under Rule 33(d) a party can answer an interrogatory by specifying the business records from which the requested information can be derived if the burden of obtaining the desired information from those records is substantially the same for either party. This is a most useful device, because it avoids "doing the homework" for the requesting party and permits answers to be made more quickly.

ii. Objections

A party on whom interrogatories have been served has two possible responses: an answer or an objection. If the response is an objection, simply state the objection as your answer to a particular interrogatory. All grounds for the objection must be stated "with specificity." If part of an interrogatory is objectionable, the part not objected to must still be answered. There are several bases for objecting.

First, a party may object on the basis that the information sought is irrelevant. However, since the Rule 26(b)(1) definition of relevance for discovery purposes is quite broad, such an objection is difficult to make successfully. In addition, the court can impose sanctions for frivolous objections. Second, a party may object on the ground of privilege, relying on either the privilege for qualified trial preparation materials and absolute mental impressions under Rule 26(b) or on the privileges under Rule 501 of the Federal Rules of Evidence. Rule 26(b)(5) requires that a claim of privilege be made expressly and shall describe the nature of the matters claimed to be privileged in a manner that, "without revealing information itself privileged or protected," will enable other parties to assess the applicability of the privilege. Third, an objection can be made to in-

---

28. Moore's Federal Practice §33.07; Wright & Miller §2171.

terrogatories that ask for information that cannot be obtained by interrogatories, such as an interrogatory that demands the production of records. Fourth, an objection can be made on the basis that the interrogatory is annoying, embarrassing, oppressive, or overly broad, unduly burdensome and expensive. This is probably the most frequently raised objection, one that has generated a substantial body of case law. Where such an objection is raised, the answering party should also move for a protective order under Rule 26(c).[29] The claim that an interrogatory is unduly burdensome requires under Rule 26(b)(2) that the court balance the burden of collecting the information requested with the benefit to the requesting party. Where the work involved in obtaining the information is enormous and the benefit to the requesting party is small in light of the issues in the case, an objection to the interrogatory should be sustained.[30]

Where an objection exists, it should be made on the interrogatory answer. Draft the objection so that the opposing lawyer (and the judge, if there is a later motion to compel) knows that you are serious and have a well-founded basis for your objection. This will frequently cause the opposing lawyer not to file a motion to compel answers.

The usual practice is to repeat the interrogatory and then state your answer.

Example:

Interrogatory No. 8: State which officers were involved in the sale of forklift trucks to the XYZ Corporation on August 1, 1998.

Answer: Defendant objects to Interrogatory No. 8 on the ground that it asks for information that is irrelevant because it pertains to a transaction with a nonparty, the XYZ Corporation, that has no relevance to the controversy between the plaintiff and defendant.

Interrogatory No. 9: Identify all conversations between defendant's employees and defendant's corporate counsel between August 1, 1998, and the present date.

Answer: Defendant objects to Interrogatory No. 9 on the ground that it asks for material that is privileged under the attorney-client privilege.

Interrogatory No. 10: Identify all witnesses you have interviewed or from whom you have taken statements.

Answer: Defendant objects to Interrogatory No. 10. While plaintiff has a right to ask for the identity of all witnesses to the collision, asking for the identity of witnesses interviewed, or from whom statements have been taken, asks for work-product of the attorney and is protected from disclosure under Rule 26(b)(3).

If a proper objection exists, consider making the appropriate objection but also answering the interrogatory to the extent appropriate.

29. See §6.9.1.
30. See Wright & Miller §2174.

Example:

<u>Interrogatory No. 10:</u> Identify all witnesses you have interviewed or from whom you have taken statements.

<u>Answer:</u> Defendant objects to Interrogatory No. 10, since it asks for work-product of the attorney and is protected from disclosure under Rule 26(b)(3). However, since an interrogatory asking for the identity of all witnesses to the collision would be proper, defendant in the spirit of cooperation answers as follows:

The only known witnesses to the collision, other than the plaintiff and defendant, are Jennifer Jones, 200 Elm St., Dallas, Texas, and Wilbur Johnson, 400 Maple St., Ft. Worth, Texas.

Answering in this way should not be deemed a waiver of an otherwise proper objection, and again often results in the party not moving to compel answers. If the answer contains any objections, Rule 33(b) requires that the lawyer making the objections must sign the answer.

iii.   Answers

The other possible response is to answer the interrogatory. There are three basic types of responses.

First, the party can answer the interrogatory by supplying the requested information if it is either known or ascertainable from the party's personal knowledge or records. The answer should be brief, since you ordinarily don't want to volunteer information that has not been requested. On the other hand, you must answer with the essential facts at your disposal, since failing to disclose can subject you to serious sanctions. In addition, if you have a strong case and are looking toward a favorable settlement, you may want to volunteer information. You need to ask yourself: What message do I want to send to the other side? Full answers say that you have good evidence to support your claims or defenses and that you are confident in the merits of your case. Finally, keep in mind that interrogatories and answers can be read at trial, since a party's answers are admissions or, if the party testifies, can be used as impeachment. The lawyer's task in answering interrogatories is to strike an appropriate balance between the advantages of brevity and a full, detailed answer.

Example:

<u>Interrogatory No. 2:</u> Identify each person who was present during the execution of the contract that forms the basis of Count I of plaintiff's complaint.

<u>Answer:</u> John Marlowe and Phillip Johnson.

<u>Interrogatory No. 3:</u> Identify each physician who treated you as a result of this occurrence.

<u>Answer:</u> Dr. William Jackson, Mercy Hospital, Seattle, Washington; Dr. Erica Olson, 3420 Cascades Highway, Seattle, Washington; possibly other

physicians at Mercy Hospital, whose names are unknown; investigation continues.

Interrogatory No. 4: State the name and address of each person who was present or claims to have been present during the collision.

Answer: Mary Jones, 2440 Congress St., Tucson, Arizona; Frank Wilson, 1831 N. Campbell Ave., Tucson, Arizona; Abby Jones, 2440 Congress St., Tucson, Arizona; Jennifer Jones, 2440 Congress St., Tucson, Arizona; in addition, there were several other pedestrians in the vicinity, but the names and addresses of such persons are presently unknown; investigation continues.

Where the interrogatory asks for information on which the answering party has some personal knowledge but not to the detail requested, and no records exist that can supply those details, the answer should accurately reflect this situation.

Example:

Interrogatory No. 6: Identify each communication between John Marlowe and Phillip Johnson that relates to the contract that forms the basis of Count I of plaintiff's complaint.

Answer: There were several telephone conversations between Marlowe and Johnson during a period of approximately four weeks preceding the execution of the contract. The exact dates and substance of each of these conversations are unknown.

This type of answer is satisfactory when the answer cannot state facts that are not within the knowledge or recall of the answering party and no records exist to supply the details. The better practice is to follow up on this type of response through depositions, which allow the extent and details of the party's recall to be explored and developed.

Where an interrogatory asks for a party's contentions, a more complete answer is called for since the answering party does not wish to limit its proof or theories of liability.

Example:

Interrogatory No. 4: State the basis on which you claim that defendant acted negligently at the time of the collision.

Answer: Defendant (1) drove in excess of the posted speed limit; (2) drove in excess of a reasonable speed under the existing conditions and circumstances; (3) failed to keep a proper lookout to ensure the safety of others; (4) failed to keep his vehicle in the proper lane; (5) failed to yield the right of way; and (6) failed to obey traffic signals, markers, and "rules of the road." Investigation continues.

In this type of answer the "investigation continues" response is important because additional investigation and discovery may develop additional facts to support the negligence claim.

A second type of response is simply to state "no knowledge" where this is accurate. Keep in mind that an answering party must search his own records to determine if the information exists, and, if it does, use the information to answer the interrogatory.

Example:

Interrogatory No. 4: State if any witnesses to the collision prepared written reports of any kind regarding the collision.

Answer: No knowledge of any such reports.

Rule 26(e) imposes a continuing duty to supplement answers at appropriate intervals regarding witnesses, documents, testifying experts, damages, insurance, and answers that were incomplete or incorrect when made. A common response in such instances is to answer based on present knowledge and acknowledge the continuing duty under the Rule.

Example:

Interrogatory No. 2: Identify each person who saw or heard the collision.

Answer: Other than plaintiff and defendant, none presently known; investigation continues.

Interrogatory No. 3: Identify each person who was present at or near the collision when it happened, other than the persons already identified in your answer to Interrogatory No. 2.

Answer: None at present; plaintiff is aware of her continuing duty to supplement responses under Rule 26(e).

The third type of answer is to identify business records that provide the answers. Rule 33(d) requires only that the answer specify the records and give the requesting party a reasonable opportunity to examine and copy them. Actual production with the interrogatory answer is not required; however, such records are always discoverable through a request to produce under Rule 34. For this reason, many lawyers simply attach copies of the pertinent documents as exhibits to the interrogatory answers.

Examples:

Interrogatory No. 5: Identify each communication between Phillip Johnson and Jane East between June 1, 1998, and August 4, 1998, relating to the contract that forms the basis of Count I of plaintiff's complaint.

Answer: Any such communications are kept in the defendant's telephone logbook, the pertinent dates of which may be examined and copied at a reasonable time at the defendant's place of business.

Interrogatory No. 6: Identify each sales transaction entered into between plaintiff and defendant for the period of January 1, 1998, through August 4, 1998.

Answer: These transactions are recorded on the defendant's Sales Records, which are computerized after sales transactions are completed. A printout of these transactions is attached as Exhibit A.

Interrogatories are frequently coupled with a document request directed to any records identified in the interrogatory answers.

Example:

Interrogatory No. 4: If any witnesses to the collision prepared written accounts of any kind regarding the collision, identify each witness and the location of the written account. If your answer to this interrogatory identifies any such written accounts, pursuant to Rule 34 you are hereby requested to make available for copying, within 30 days of service of this interrogatory and documents request, any such written accounts within your possession, custody and control.

Answer: The only witness known to have prepared a written account of the collision is William Morris, 123 Elm Street, Boston, MA. A copy of his written account is in the possession of plaintiff's attorney, and a copy of which is attached as Exhibit A.

The standard approach in drafting interrogatory answers is to draft the shortest answer that fairly provides the information requested. Keep in mind, however, that, as with all court papers, your answers send messages to your opponent and the court. If your own answers to interrogatories are threadbare, the court will hardly be responsive if you complain that the other side's interrogatory answers are inadequate. Sometimes answering interrogatories more fully than expected sends positive signals about your case, signals that you are well prepared, know the facts, and have a winning case.

iv. Signing, serving, and filing

The format for interrogatory answers, like any other court document, should have the case caption and title of the document. The answers must be signed and sworn to by the party making them. If any interrogatories are objected to, the attorney must sign them as well.

The completed interrogatory answers must then be served on each party. Service is made by any proper method under Rule 5, most commonly by mailing a copy to the lawyers for the other parties. The original answer, with an attached proof of service, is then filed with the clerk of the court, unless a local rule directs that discovery is not filed unless a need arises.

Example:

[Caption]

DEFENDANT ACME CORPORATION'S ANSWERS TO PLAINTIFF'S INTERROGATORIES

Defendant Acme Corporation answers the first set of interrogatories put forth by plaintiff as follows:

Interrogatory No. 1: ....

Answer: ....

                                    Acme Corporation

                                    By _____
                                    William Phillips
                                    Vice President for Adminis-
                                    tration of Acme Corporation

State of Arizona | SS.
County of Pima |

    William Phillips, after being first duly sworn, states that he is an officer of Acme Corporation and is authorized to make the above interrogatory answers on behalf of Acme Corporation, that the above answers have been prepared with the assistance of counsel, that the answers are based either on his personal knowledge, the personal knowledge of Acme Corporation employees, or on information obtained from Acme Corporation records, and that the answers are true to the best of his knowledge, information and belief.

                                    _____
                                    William Phillips

Signed and sworn to before me on this _____ day of _____, _____

_____
Notary Public
My commission expires on _____

[Seal]

§6.10.   *Requests to produce documents and subpoenas*

After answers to interrogatories have been received you will usually have enough detailed information to ask for copies of identified documents, not already obtained as part of the other party's initial disclosures under Rule 26(a)(1), through a request to produce. Hence, requests to produce are usually the next step in the discovery process, although requests to produce documents are also frequently served with interrogatories.

1.   Law[31]

Requests to produce documents and things for inspection and copying and for entry upon land to inspect tangible things are governed by Rule 34. A request to produce can only be served upon parties. The scope of the request, like other discovery, is controlled by Rule 26(b), which permits the discovery of any relevant matter that is not privileged. The rule expressly requires that the items to be inspected must be set forth with "reasonable particularity."

Under Rule 34(c), a non-party's books, documents, and tangible things can also be subpoenaed for production, inspection, and copying. This process, controlled by Rule 45(a), is discussed later in this section.

Rule 34 permits requests to produce for three things:

1.   Documents (including writings, drawings, graphs, charts, photographs, phono records, and other data compilations) for inspection and copying
2.   Tangible things for inspection, copying, and testing
3.   Entry on land or property for inspection and testing

Of these, production of documents is the principal use of Rule 34 requests. The Rule requires a party to produce all documents that are in that party's "possession, custody or control." This obligates a party to produce all relevant documents, even those not in the party's actual possession, if the party has a lawful right to get them from another person or entity.[32] In short, a party cannot avoid production through the simple device of transferring the documents to another person or entity such as the party's lawyer, accountant, insurer, or corporate subsidiary. When this avoidance device is used the party is deemed to have retained "control" of the documents and is required to get them returned in order to comply with the production request.

A request to produce may be served at any time after the parties hold the meeting to develop a discovery plan required under Rule 26(f), and must describe each item or category to be produced with "reasonable par-

---

31. Wright §87; James & Hazard §5.5; Friedenthal §7.11; Moore's Manual §15.10; Manual of Federal Practice §§5.161-5.194; Moore's Federal Practice §§34.01-34.22; Wright & Miller §§2201-2218.

32. Moore's Manual §15.10; Manual of Federal Practice §5.172; Moore's Federal Practice §34.17; Wright & Miller §2210.

ticularity." This is usually read to require that, in the context of the case and the overall nature of the documents involved, a responding party must reasonably be able to determine what particular documents are called for.[33]

Rule 34 requires that the documents produced for inspection must be produced in either the same order as they are normally kept, or in the order, with labels, that corresponds with the categories of the request. The producing party cannot purposefully disorganize documents and records to make them more difficult to comprehend. The producing party must make the originals available for inspection and copying. Most courts take the view that the producing party has the choice of complying either by producing the records in the same order as they are ordinarily kept, or by producing them in the order that corresponds to the categories of the request; the requesting party cannot insist on the method of complying. Some courts, however, take the position that a producing party cannot produce a mass of jumbled documents, even if that is the way they were ordinarily kept; they must be organized in a useful way.[34] Further, the request to produce must specify a "reasonable time, place, and manner" for the inspection. The responding party must serve a written response for each category requested, usually within 30 days of service of the request, stating whether he objects, with reasons for the objection, or will comply.

2. Practice approach

a. Timing

Before serving a request to produce documents or a request for entry upon land to inspect, you need to know what documents you want produced and what things you want to inspect. If you have received the other party's initial disclosures under Rule 26(a)(1), you will probably already have copies of some of those documents or descriptions of them. If you have drafted your interrogatories carefully, and have asked for descriptions of relevant documents and for the identity of those whose custody those documents are in, answers to the interrogatories should provide sufficient detail to meet the particularity requirement for production requests. Hence, requests to produce should normally be served as soon as possible after the answers to interrogatories have been received. Sometimes, as previously mentioned, production requests are served at the same time as interrogatories.

This timetable presumes that the party has adequately, and in a timely fashion, made initial disclosures and answered your interrogatories. If the answering party has objected, failed to answer, or served evasive or incomplete answers, you must resolve the problems through appropriate discov-

---

33. Moore's Manual §15.10; Manual of Federal Practice §5.168; Moore's Federal Practice §34.07; Wright & Miller §2211.
34. See Cagan, Rule 34(b): Who's Organizing this Production, 20 Litigation No. 2 (Winter 1994); Moore's Federal Practice, §34.05; Wright & Miller, §2213.

ery motions.[35] Doing this, however, will necessarily delay serving the requests to produce. In this situation you should consider serving a request to produce anyway, since you can ordinarily determine in a general way what documents the other party is likely to have and describe them sufficiently by topic or subject matter to meet the particularity requirement. It is easy for discovery to become sidetracked or to stall completely. In these situations you must weigh the benefits and liabilities of waiting or going ahead in light of your overall discovery strategy.

b. Organization

Before actually drafting the request to produce, you need to organize your thoughts on what you want from the other party. If you have intelligently thought through your discovery strategy, received initial disclosures, submitted your interrogatories to and received answers from that party, then the bulk of your work is already done. You will know in sufficient detail what documents you want, what documents the answering party admits having, how those documents are described or labeled, and who their custodian is. It is also useful to review your party's records and documents. This helps you identify what records and documents you will need from the other side, making it easier to respond to the other side's requests when you receive them.

If you have not yet received interrogatory answers but have decided to send out requests to produce anyway, you will have to evaluate what documents the other party is likely to have, how they are likely to be labeled and organized, and who their custodian is. If this is difficult or impossible to do, you should consider deposing that party at an early date in order to question the deponent about his records. In the case of a corporate party, you should also consider deposing the party's custodian of records. This will help you determine what kind of records the corporation generates and maintains, and will in turn help you make a more focused documents request.

Watch making overly broad requests. Copying, filing, and indexing documents can be expensive. If the case is a commercial or products liability case large enough to warrant using an electronic litigation support system that stores and cross indexes the documents, the cost of such a system can be several dollars per document. If you are not sure of the volume of documents you are requesting, use interrogatories or depositions to find out before plunging ahead.

c. Drafting requests to produce

i. Heading

A request to produce should be drafted like any other court document. It must have a caption showing the court, case title, and docket number and be properly labeled. Where a case has several parties, it is

---

35. See §6.14.

useful to designate which party is sending the request to which other party; otherwise, the simple title "REQUEST TO PRODUCE DOCU-MENTS" will suffice.

Example:

[Caption]

PLAINTIFF JOHNSON'S REQUEST TO PRODUCE DOCUMENTS TO DEFENDANT ACME CORPORATION

Plaintiff Johnson requests defendant Acme Corporation to produce the documents and things listed below, pursuant to Rule 34 of the Federal Rules of Civil Procedure:

1. . . .
2. . . .
3. . . .

ii. Definitions

Requests to produce present the same problems concerning definitions as interrogatories. Accordingly, terms and phrases frequently used, such as "document," "record," "relating to," "transaction," "communication," and "occurrence," should be defined if the complexity of the case warrants their use. If so, it is best to use definitions identical to those used in the interrogatories.[36]

Example:

DEFINITIONS

The following terms used in this request to produce have the following meanings:

1. A "document" means. . . .
2. A "transaction" means. . . .

Another method is to incorporate by reference definitions already used in interrogatories.

Example:

DEFINITIONS

Plaintiff incorporates by reference each of the definitions in plaintiff's interrogatories previously served on defendant.

---

36. See §6.4.

Yet another method is to incorporate by reference your opponent's definitions previously used in the opponent's interrogatories or documents requests. He will be hard pressed to object to your use of his definitions.

Finally, make sure your definitions of records, documents, and the like are sufficiently broad. They should always specifically include handwritten and electronically created and stored records.

iii.   Drafting requests

Rule 34 permits three kinds of requests: to inspect and copy documents, to inspect and examine tangible things, and to enter upon land to inspect and examine things.

The requests to produce must specify a reasonable date, time, and place for the production. Rule 34 requires only that this be "reasonable," which must necessarily take into account the volume and complexity of the records sought. Since the Rule requires a response within 30 days of service, the date set for the production should be a longer time period.

Example:

A. Plaintiff requests that defendant produce the following documents for inspection and copying at the offices of Mary Anton, plaintiff's attorney, 200 Main Street, Suite 400, Tucson, Arizona, on August 21, 1998, at 2:00 P.M.:

    1. . . .

    2. . . .

B. Plaintiff requests that defendant produce the following things for inspection, copying, and testing at the offices of Independent Testing, 2000 Main Street, Tucson, Arizona, on August 22, 1998, at 9:00 A.M.:

    1. . . .

    2. . . .

C. Plaintiff requests that defendant permit plaintiff to enter defendant's lumber yard located at 4000 Monroe Street, Tucson, Arizona, for the purpose of inspecting, photographing and measuring the premises on August 23, 1998, at 2:00 P.M.

Most requests to produce involve documents. There are several ways to draft requests that will meet Rule 34's particularity requirement.

First, you can use the other party's initial disclosures and interrogatory answers. If those answers have listed and described a variety of documents, referring to the descriptions should be adequate. The responding party will be in a poor position to claim that a description it furnished is now suddenly insufficient.

Example:

1. Each document identified in defendant's answer to Interrogatory No. 6 in plaintiff's first set of interrogatories.

Second, ask for all documents that relate to a specific transaction, event or date. By making the request specific, it should not be challenged on the grounds of being too vague.

Example:

2. All documents relating to the sale of the property located at 4931 Sunrise St., Tucson, Arizona, entered into between plaintiff and defendant on July 31, 1998.

Third, you can ask for specific types of documents that relate to a more general time frame or course of conduct.

Example:

3. All bills of lading, invoices, and shipping confirmation notices for all goods shipped from plaintiff to defendant during the period from January 1, 1998, through April 30, 1998.

In each of the above examples, the party responding to the request to admit should not have difficulty in either understanding the request or identifying the documents requested. In contrast, a request calling for the production of "all documents relating to the allegations in plaintiff's complaint," "all documents which support your claim in Count I," or similarly vague language, is probably defective and unenforceable since it does not meet Rule 34's specificity requirement. A request calling for the production of "all documents you intend to introduce at trial" is improperly premature, since you are not required to disclose this information until the pretrial memorandum is filed.

It is possible that the responding party will not object to a general request, but, regardless, it is usually not an effective approach for discovery. Requests to produce should balance the safety of inclusiveness with the utility of a more focused request. A request that is too broad may result in a huge volume of paperwork being deposited in your office; you may have neither the time nor assistance to review all of it in order to extract the few documents that are relevant to your case.

Fourth, it is always useful to ask for the identity of any documents that existed at one time but have since been destroyed. This prevents the literally true but misleading response that there are "no records" of the description requested.

Finally, consider sequencing your documents requests to progress from the more specific to the more general. For example, requests might seek (1) all medical records relating to plaintiff's treatment of her knees and all other injuries following the collision; (2) all medical records relating to plaintiff's treatment for any knee conditions before the collision date; (3) all medical records relating to plaintiff's treatment for any orthopedic conditions for a period of five years preceding the collision date; and (4) all medical records relating to plaintiff's treatment for any medical condition for a period of five years preceding the collision date. This strategy often obtains more useful information than does one generally worded request.

The electronic age has changed the way businesses conduct business. Business records, formerly created on paper, are regularly, perhaps even usually, now created and stored in computer data bases. Paper records, even handwritten ones, are routinely downloaded into computer databases and then destroyed. Consequently, documents requests should always include requests for computer generated records, memoranda, correspondence, and other similar documents. These should include not only common business records such as invoices, bills of lading, and the like, but also records such as e-mail or voice-mail, and documents that have been optically scanned and stored on CD-ROM.

A carefully drafted documents request for records that may be created and stored electronically should consider two principal things. First, the definition of a "record" in the documents request should expressly include "electronically stored information" including "e-mail, voice-mail, and other similar records." Second, the request should expressly request "deleted and erased" computer records—since documents that have been deleted from a directory may still be retrievable from the computer's hard drives, floppy disks, or back-up systems—and specifically request that the search include any such "hard drives, floppy disks, and back-up systems." Third, keep the request focused on specifically targeted matters. Searching through data bases and back-up systems is time consuming, and a judge may well rule that a broadly worded general request for electronically stored information is too burdensome and issue a protective order. However, a focused request for such electronic records can sometimes ferret out a "smoking gun" document, memo, or letter that the opponent forgot about or thought had been purged from its electronic data base.[37]

What are the common problems that arise when drafting documents requests? Remember that the skill in drafting documents requests, like interrogatories, is in finding a clear, simple way to get the documents you need, and are entitled to get, without making the requests overly burdensome and at the same time meeting the rule's "reasonable particularity" requirement.

A common problem is that documents requests are overly broad. For example, a documents request that asks to produce "all records relating to plaintiff's allegation that defendant breached the contract" is overly broad, and does not meet the particularity requirement. The rule requires that the documents be identified, either individually or by category, with sufficient particularity that the responding party can reasonably identify which documents are being requested. A good technique is using the responding party's answers to interrogatories in describing the documents. If the answering party described documents in its interrogatory answers, it will be hard pressed to claim that the same de-

---

37. See M. Miller and B. Griffin, Computer Databases: Forced Production versus Shared Enterprise, 23 Litigation (No. 4, Summer 1997).

scription in documents requests is now insufficient to understand what documents are being sought.

Another common problem is that documents requests that do not adequately define what is being sought, so that the responding party can give literally true but evasive responses. For example, asking a party to produce "all documents relating to the board meeting on June 1, 1998" may not get a fruitful response, unless "documents" is broadly defined to include all paper records, handwritten records, electronic records, and so forth. Documents requests should define commonly used terms such as "records," "documents," and "communications" expansively so that the responding party cannot evade the request.

Another common problem is failing to couple with a documents request an interrogatory asking about records that once existed but have been destroyed, discarded, lost, or sent to another party. Such an interrogatory should ask "If your response to any documents request is that none exist or none are presently in your possession, state whether such documents were ever in existence, where and in whose possession they are now, who prepared the documents, who was custodian of the documents, who made the decision to destroy or send away the documents, when that decision was made, and any other reasons and circumstances why such records no longer exist." Asking about destroyed records through a broadly worded interrogatory is a good way to begin tracking down possible "smoking guns."

Finally, documents request are sometimes premature. Asking a party to "produce all documents you intend to introduce as exhibits at trial" is premature, since such information is usually disclosed only in the pretrial memorandum. Asking for that information now will get either an objection or a response of "not known at present; investigation continues."

iv.   Signing, serving, and filing

The request to produce should be signed by the lawyer and served on each party. Service is made by any permitted method under Rule 5, most commonly by mailing a copy to the lawyers for the other parties. The original requests to produce, with an attached proof of service, is then filed with the clerk of the court unless a local rule directs that discovery is not filed until a need arises.

d.   *Responses to requests to produce*

A party served with a request to produce usually must respond in writing within 30 days of service of the request. Even though the lawyers for the requesting and responding parties frequently reach an informal agreement on how and when to produce documents and conduct inspections,[38] the responding party should serve and file a written response, since this is required by Rule 34.

38. See §6.3.8.

i. Researching and preparing responses

If the preliminary investigation has been done, and answers to interrogatories have been prepared and served, you already will have done most of the initial work involved in responding to requests to produce. In addition, you should always send the requests to your client and ask the client a couple of questions about the requests. First, does the client know what the requests actually call for? If not, you may want to object on grounds of vagueness. Second, how much effort will be required to collect the documents requested? If it is substantial and the case is not complex, you may be able to object on the grounds that the requests are unduly burdensome and move for a protective order, or at least for additional time to respond.

After your party has collected the documents, review the material to determine if all of it is relevant. If there are any privileged communications, now is the time to object, since privileges are waived unless timely asserted. Finally, make sure that those documents are in fact all the available documents your party has in his possession, custody, or control. You can be sure that your party, and other witnesses, will be questioned about the completeness of the tendered documents during their depositions. Now is the time to review the documents for completeness with your party.

ii. Objections

As with interrogatories, a party on whom requests to produce have been served has two possible responses: an answer or an objection. If the response is an objection, there are several possible bases. First, an objection may be made on the ground that the documents sought are irrelevant. However, since Rule 26 has such a broad definition of relevance for discovery purposes, this is a difficult ground on which to prevail. Moreover, this ground will probably have been ruled on if the same objection was made to the interrogatory that asked for the identity of the documents. Second, an objection can be based on a privilege, either the privilege for trial preparation materials and mental impressions under Rule 26(b), or the privileges recognized under Rule 501 of the Federal Rules of Evidence. Under Rule 26(b)(5), the privilege must be expressly asserted and "shall describe the nature of the documents, communications, or things not produced or disclosed in a manner that, without revealing information itself privileged or protected, will enable other parties to assess the applicability of the privilege or protection." In practice, lawyers usually prepare a "privilege log" containing a generic description of each document for which a privilege is claimed and the particular privilege being asserted for that document, and a copy of each document. If the requesting party later moves to compel production, the privilege log and accompanying documents can, if necessary, be tendered to the court for an in camera inspection. Third, an objection can be based on the request being annoying, embarrassing, oppressive, or unduly burdensome and expensive. Here the answering party should seek a protective order under

Rule 26(c); still, an objection to a request to produce should be made on the response.[39]

Example:

[Caption]

RESPONSE TO PLAINTIFF'S REQUEST TO PRODUCE

Defendant Acme Corporation responds to plaintiff's Request to Produce Documents as follows:

1. Acme objects to plaintiff's Request No. 1 on the ground that it requests documents the disclosure of which would violate the attorney-client privilege, since the request on its face asks for the production of "all correspondence from corporate officers to corporate counsel regarding the contract dated July 1, 1998."

Frequently a request may be objectionable in part. Where this is so, the response should make clear what part is being objected to and what the responding party agrees to produce. Such an objection is a common response to a broad request asking for a variety of documents, some of which may be privileged.

Example:

2. Acme objects to plaintiff's Request No. 2 to the extent it asks for privileged communications protected by the attorney-client privilege. Plaintiff's Request No. 2 asks for the production of "all memoranda by defendant's subsidiary, Acme Productions, relating to a bid on U.S. Government Contract No. 97-3287, commonly known as the 'Tristar Contract.'" These memoranda include documents prepared by Acme Productions officers and employees, documents prepared at the request of and sent to Acme Corporation's General Counsel, which relate to the pending litigation and are protected from disclosure by the attorney-client privilege. Acme will produce the nonprivileged memoranda at the requested time and place.

iii. Answers

If a request to produce is not objected to, it must be answered. An answer involves two considerations: the formal response, and the practical concerns involved in arranging for the actual production of the documents. There should be a formal answer even if, as is often the case, the production is worked out informally between the attorneys, since Rule 34 requires a written response.

39. See discussion in §6.4.2(d).

Example:

[Caption]

RESPONSE TO PLAINTIFF'S REQUEST
FOR PRODUCTION AND INSPECTION

Defendant Acme Corporation responds to plaintiff's Request for Production of Documents and Inspection as follows:

1-8. Acme agrees to produce the documents requested in plaintiff's Request Nos. 1 through 8 at the offices of plaintiff's attorney on or before August 15, 1998.

9. Acme agrees to permit the inspection of the items described in plaintiff's Request No. 9 at its manufacturing plant located at 9000 Main St., Tucson, Arizona, at a mutually agreed upon date and time, but not later than August 31, 1998.

_____

Attorney for Defendant
Acme Corporation

If the request is for documents that are already in the lawyer's possession, they can be attached to the response.

Example:

3. Acme agrees to produce the contract requested in plaintiff's Request No. 3. A copy is attached to this response.

If records requested do not exist, the response should clearly establish this fact.

Example:

3. There are no documents in the possession, custody, or control of defendant Acme Corporation requested by plaintiff's Request No. 3.

Most production requests are worked out informally between the lawyers, who usually call each other and agree on the mechanics of delivering and copying the pertinent records. This will usually include when and where the documents will be produced, how the documents will be organized, and who will perform and pay for the actual copying. The usual procedure is for the documents to be produced at, or delivered to, the requesting attorney's offices on an agreed upon date. The responding party has the option of producing the records either in the order in which they are ordinarily kept, or labeled to correspond to the categories of the request. Since most production requests overlap on particulars to ensure completeness, a common approach in responding is to produce the documents in their usual order since this is easier for the responding party.

Regarding an informal agreement on the mechanics of reproducing the records, the rule requires only production — not copying — by the responding party. However, it is usually desirable for the responding party to make copies so as to retain possession of the original documents. For this reason it is common for the responding party to make copies of the records that comply with the requests; the cost of reproduction is then paid by the requesting party. Make sure that the copies you receive are clear and show any handwritten notes legibly; if not, insist on examining the originals. As the lawyer for the answering party, make sure you keep a copy of everything submitted to the opposing side so that no issues arise later over what was actually delivered.

When the documents involved are so voluminous that copying all of them would be prohibitively expensive, a common solution is to have the lawyer for the requesting party review the documents at the offices of either the answering party or the answering party's lawyer. The requesting lawyer can then select the relevant documents for photocopying.

Always index, bind and "Bates" stamp (a stamped page number) every document you send or receive to create a clear record of what, when, and to or from whom, documents were sent or received. Disputes frequently arise over whether certain documents were sent or received, and clear, complete records are necessary to resolve these disputes.

iv.   Signing, serving, and filing

The response to requests to produce must be signed, and served on every other party. Service is made by any permitted method under Rule 5, most commonly by mailing a copy to the lawyers for the other parties. The original response, with an attached proof of service, is then filed with the clerk of the court unless a local rule directs that discovery is not filed until a need arises.

3.   Documents subpoenas to nonparties

Rule 45 now provides that subpoenas can be issued to command any person "to produce and permit inspection and copying of designated books, documents or tangible things in the possession, custody or control of that person, or to permit inspection of premises, at a time and place therein specified." Rule 45 and Rule 34(c) provide a vehicle for obtaining documents and things directly from non-parties, without also requiring the attendance of the non-party at a deposition. The subpoena must be issued for the court of the district in which the production will be made. If the subpoena is unreasonable or oppressive, the court can on motion quash it or require that the party issuing the subpoena pay in advance the reasonable cost of complying with the subpoena.

§6.11. Depositions

Depositions are usually taken after both interrogatory answers and responses to documents requests have been received, since those answers and documents will usually be necessary to plan an intelligent deposition. Although depositions are both expensive and time consuming, they are essential for assessing witness credibility, learning what witnesses know, getting details, and pinning witnesses down. They can be used on parties and nonparties, and are the only method in which the opposing counsel does not directly control the responses. For these reasons, depositions play a critical role in the discovery plan of virtually every case.

Rules 27 through 32 govern depositions. Rule 30, which regulates oral depositions, is the principal one, however, since oral depositions are the predominant way in which depositions are taken.[40] Rule 45 controls deposition subpoenas directed to non-parties.

1. Law[41]

a. Timing

Oral depositions may be taken of any party or nonparty, and can be taken after the parties meet to develop a discovery plan under Rule 26(f). Leave of court is not necessary to take a deposition before the meeting if the deposition notice certifies, and provides supporting facts, that the deponent is expected to leave the country and will thereafter be unavailable for examination. Court approval is required under Rule 30(a) if the person to be deposed is confined in prison.

b. Number of depositions

Each side—plaintiffs, defendants, or third-party defendants—has a presumptive limit of 10 depositions. Under Rule 30(a), that number can be enlarged by court order or written stipulation of the parties. This means that when a case has multiple plaintiffs or defendants, the plaintiffs or defendants must get together and decide how to use their 10 depositions most effectively. It also means that the court, under Rule 26(b)(2), will be more actively involved in determining the number and order of depositions. While a deposition is normally considered to be of one person, Rule 30(b)(6) permits a deposition to be directed to corporations and other entities, and the corporation or other entity must designate one or more persons to testify on its behalf. Under these circumstances, a single deposition may be taken of more than one person and still count as one deposition for purposes of the 10-deposition limit.

40. Depositions on written questions, governed by Rule 31, are rarely utilized.
41. Wright §84; James & Hazard §5.3; Friedenthal §7.7; Moore's Manual §15.06; Manual of Federal Practice §§5.55-5.117; Moore's Federal Practice §§30.01-30.64; Wright & Miller §§2071-2157; Henry L. Hecht, Effective Depositions, Section of Litigation, ABA, 1997.

No person can be deposed more than once without court order or written stipulation of the parties. While Rule 26 does not put time limitations on depositions, Rule 26(b)(2) gives the court discretion to impose limits, and some local rules impose them as well.

c. *Notice*

Whenever a deposition will be taken, the party taking the deposition must give "reasonable" notice to every party to the action. Rule 30(b) does not specify what is reasonable, although some local rules specify minimum requirements, frequently five days. Also, many courts have addressed the question, most finding that reasonable notice is a flexible standard that depends on the nature of the case and the deponent involved.[42]

The notice must state the name and address of each person to be deposed. If the name is not known, the notice must describe the person to be deposed in sufficient detail to identify that person individually or as part of a class or group. This is frequently the case with corporations and other artificial entities, where the actual name of the proper person to be deposed is unknown. In such a case the corporation, or other entity, must designate an officer, director, managing agent, or other person to testify on its behalf. The notice must also state the time and place for the deposition.

Notice to a party deponent can be accompanied by a document request. A subpoena to a nonparty can be a subpoena duces tecum, commanding the nonparty deponent to produce designated materials at the deposition. In this situation, notice to the parties must include a designation of the materials the nonparty deponent has been directed to produce at the deposition. The easy way to do this is to attach a copy of the subpoena duces tecum to the notices. You should, however, always have the necessary documents of the party or non-party witness before taking the deposition, unless you plan to catch the party or witness unprepared, before he has had time to collect and review the relevant documents and records.

The notice of deposition must designate how the deposition will be recorded, which includes sound and video recording as well as stenographic means. Any other party can designate by notice other means of recording, each party bearing the cost of its method of recording.

In addition to the notice to other parties, of course, the person to be deposed must also be notified. Where the deponent is also a party, the notice of deposition is sufficient. Where the deponent is a nonparty, he must be subpoenaed in accordance with Rule 45.

Subpoenas can be issued directly by the attorneys as officers of the court. The attorney simply fills out a blank subpoena form issued by the clerk of the appropriate court, or the attorney as an officer of the court can also issue and sign a subpoena on behalf of the court, if authorized to practice law in the court in which the case is pending. The subpoena shall

---

42. Wright §84; Moore's Manual §15.06; Manual of Federal Practice §5.82; Moore's Federal Practice §§30.56-30.57; Wright & Miller §2106.

issue from the court for the district in which the deposition is to be taken or the production or inspection is to be made. The subpoena can be served anywhere within the district from which it was issued, within 100 miles of the place of the taking of the deposition or production of documents if outside the district, or anywhere in the state if a state rule allows such subpoena service. If a federal statute provides for it, the court may authorize service of a subpoena in any other place. In short, by permitting attorneys to issue subpoenas directly, the administrative aspects of issuing subpoenas have been substantially eased.

The witness attendance fee and mileage costs must accompany the subpoena. These fees are set by 28 U.S.C. §1821. The common practice is to attach a check to the subpoena for one day's witness attendance fee and the mileage costs incurred by the deponent travelling to and from the place where the deposition is to be held.

If the terms of the notice of deposition or subpoena are unreasonable or oppressive, make your objection known to the other parties. If the dispute cannot be worked out informally, file a motion for a protective order or, if representing a non-party deponent, move to quash the subpoena or for a protective order.

d. Location

Rule 30 does not specify where a deposition may be conducted. Accordingly, the deposition of a party can be held anywhere. If for some reason the location is unreasonable, the deposed party must seek a protective order under Rule 26(c).[43] The deposition of a nonparty must meet the requirements of Rule 45, discussed above.

e. Persons present

Who may be present at a deposition? The usual persons are the person being deposed, the parties' lawyers, and the court reporter. If the deposition will be videotaped, a videotape operator will also be there.

Parties usually have the right to be present at any deposition, although they infrequently appear. However, if a party's appearance is for an improper purpose, such as intimidation or harassment of a deponent, you must seek a protective order from the court. Nonparties and members of the media are usually held to have no right to attend depositions, since a deposition, unlike a trial, is not considered to be a public forum.

f. Recording

Under Rule 28, a deposition must be taken in the presence of someone authorized to administer oaths. Invariably, a certified court reporter who will stenographically record the testimony is also a notary public and therefore able to perform both functions. Rule 30(b)(2) allows the deposition to be recorded by sound, videotape, or stenographically. Rule

---

43. See §6.14.1.

30(b)(7) also authorizes depositions to be taken by telephone or "other remote electronic means." While the predominant means of recording remains the court reporter, since this method produces a written transcript, the other methods are being utilized more as ways to reduce costs or to make a more vivid recreation of the deponent's testimony. These other methods, particularly videotaping, have become a common way of recording experts' depositions when the experts are not expected to testify at trial and their depositions will be introduced in evidence during the trial. Video depositions are also a good idea if the opposing counsel is unduly interfering when you are taking the deposition, such as by repeatedly making objections that serve no proper purpose and are made only to coach the witness on a desirable response.

g.   Signing, correcting, and filing

There is no requirement that a deposition be transcribed. Under Rule 30(e), the deponent or any party is entitled to a transcript of the deposition. The deponent has the right to review the transcript for accuracy and sign it; and any party may also request that the deponent review and sign, so long as the request is made before the deposition is completed. This is commonly called the "read and sign" right. The deponent has 30 days after receiving notice that the transcript is ready to review it and, if there are any changes, to make and sign a statement noting the changes and the reasons for them. That statement will then be appended to the deposition transcript.

The reporter must certify that the witness was sworn and that the transcript is accurate. The reporter should then seal the original, which should include any exhibits that were marked and used during the deposition, and file it with the clerk of the court, unless local rules provide otherwise.

h.   Objections

Rule 30(c) provides that the reporter shall note on the deposition all objections to the qualifications of the reporter or other officer, to the procedure, evidence, and conduct of parties, as well as any other objections. The Rule states that testimony objected to shall be "taken subject to the objections," the intent being that the witness should answer the questions asked with all objections being noted. This permits a judge to rule on the objections later, in the event that any party wishes to use the transcript at trial.

Rule 30(d)(1) governs the conduct of attorneys making objections during the deposition. Any objections must be "stated concisely and in a non-argumentative and non-suggestive manner. A party may instruct a deponent not to answer only when necessary to preserve a privilege, to enforce a limitation on evidence directed by the court, or to present a motion" to limit or terminate the examination.

Rule 32(d) provides that objections to a witness' competency, or the materiality or relevance of the testimony, need not be made during the taking of the deposition, unless the ground for the objection could have been eliminated if made known at that time. However, objections to the form of questions, and other errors that might have been cured if the objection had been made, are waived unless timely made.

Rule 30 addresses the special problems concerning privilege objections. The usual procedure of requiring answers "subject to the objection" will not work. If the answer is privileged, providing the answer will constitute a waiver of the privilege. Therefore, a timely objection must be made, and if the deponent is a party, the deponent's lawyer can instruct the deponent not to answer pursuant to Rule 30(d)(1).[44] The party taking the deposition then has the option of moving for an order to compel discovery under Rule 37.

If the examination is being conducted in bad faith to annoy, embarrass, or harass the deponent, then a party or the deponent can demand that the deposition be suspended so that the party or deponent can move for a protective order under Rule 30(d) to terminate or limit the examination.

2. Practice approach

Deposition rules are sufficiently broad that they rarely restrict the deposition process in any meaningful way. Since the rules permit such latitude, the principal concerns are the practical ones of using depositions effectively as part of your overall discovery strategy. There are several questions that you should always ask.

a. Should I take a deposition?

Depositions are probably both the most effective discovery vehicle when used properly and the most ineffective one when misused. You should consider the pros and cons of depositions in general and weigh these considerations when deciding if a particular witness should be deposed.

On the plus side, depositions are by far the most effective discovery device for obtaining detailed information, primarily since the deposi-

---

44. The problem is more complicated with nonparty witnesses who are not represented by counsel. Can a lawyer for a party make an objection for the witness? Under Model Rule 3.4(f) and DR 7-104(A)(2), the usual answer is no. Since a party's lawyer does not represent the witness, the lawyer ordinarily cannot give legal advice to the witness other than recommending that the witness get advice, particularly since the witness may have interests that are, or may be, adverse to the party's. However, there is nothing improper in objecting to a question on behalf of your client; state the basis of your objection, and suggest that the witness talk to a lawyer before answering the question. There is nothing wrong in suggesting to anyone that he ought to talk to his own lawyer and get proper legal advice.

The problem also arises with employees of business entities. The lawyer for the business will usually treat the employee as her client and represent the employee at the employee's deposition. The theory is that since the employee's statements may be admissible at trial as admissions against the business, the lawyer for the business has a right to represent him (unless, of course, the employee is also a party or has his own lawyer). In some situations a former employee may be treated as a client, particularly where the former employee was a management level employee and was involved in acts that are the basis of the lawsuit. See §6.3.9.

tion is taken in question and answer form, which permits follow-up questioning on promising topics. Second, a deposition commits the deponent to the details of his story. This will tell you what the witness is going to say at trial, and gives you an opportunity to investigate those facts to see if contrary evidence can be obtained to refute the testimony. Third, the deposition gives you an opportunity to develop specific facts that may be used as impeachment at trial. Fourth, a deposition is in many respects a trial simulation, so you can evaluate the deponent as a trial witness. Finally, opposing counsel has only limited objection rights, making depositions the only discovery method in which counsel does not prepare the responses.

On the minus side, depositions are expensive. Even a short deposition will cost hundreds of dollars in lawyer's fees, reporter's fees, video operator costs, transcript costs, and possibly the witness' lodging and mileage fees. Where the amount at issue in a dispute is modest, costs are usually the primary reason for limiting the use of depositions. Second, depositions can perpetuate unfavorable testimony. Taking a deposition simply to find out what a witness will say can come at a price, if that witness is unfavorable and later becomes unavailable for trial. Third, a deposition educates your opponents as much as it educates you. Where you believe your opponent will learn more from the deposition than you, or you can get the same information informally such as by having an investigator interview the witness, taking the deposition can be counterproductive. Fourth, taking depositions may motivate an inactive opponent to prepare and pursue discovery. Unless your opponent has been using delaying tactics, motivating an opponent rarely does you any good.

b.   Whose deposition should I take?

The cost-benefit factors discussed above must be used in deciding which witnesses to depose. In addition, keep in mind that each side under Rule 30(a) cannot take more than 10 depositions, or take a second deposition of a person, without a court order or written stipulation of the parties. There are three basic categories of witnesses you need to consider.

First, the opposing parties should always be deposed. You obviously will want to tie them down to the detailed facts and their versions of disputed events and transactions, and evaluate them as potential witnesses. The only exception might be nominal parties, such as a guardian or administrator of an estate. When the party is an artificial entity like a corporation, the officers and employees directly involved in the transactions and events at issue should be deposed.

Second, consider deposing the principal nonparty witnesses you have identified. In personal injury cases, this would include eyewitnesses to the event involved, as well as witnesses to the major damages elements. In contract and commercial cases, it would include the witnesses to the conversations, agreements, and conduct that are relevant to the transactions involved, and witnesses to any breaches and resulting damages.

The nonparty witnesses category obviously has the potential to be the largest one, and it is here that you need to consider how far to go in keeping with cost-effectiveness. While you obviously need to learn what the testimony of important witnesses will be, there comes a point at which the information obtained from witnesses who are merely corroborative and peripheral is not worth pursuing through depositions.

A good rule of thumb for depositions is that you should depose your opponent's witnesses, not your own, since there is usually no benefit in deposing witnesses you know will be favorable. However, where such a witness is elderly or in poor health, or may leave the jurisdiction and be unavailable for trial, you should always consider taking the witness' deposition to preserve the testimony. Hence, at the beginning of the depositions stage, lawyers will usually depose a favorable witness that is known to have strong testimony in order to guard against disaster. If the witness becomes unavailable, a deposition will usually qualify as former testimony under Rule 804(b)(1) of the Federal Rules of Evidence. If this is your purpose, make sure that the deposition is conducted so that the transcript is clear and complete. Consider taking a videotaped deposition, since this is probably the most effective method of presenting former testimony to a jury.

Third, consider what experts you need to depose.[45] Under Rule 30(b)(4), any party can depose any expert identified as an expert whose opinions may be presented at trial. If your district follows Rule 26(a)(2) and requires expert disclosure, you will have a substantial amount of information about the other party's experts, including their opinions, bases for the opinions, data relied upon, exhibits to be used, and background information about the witness. In some cases, it may not be essential to depose the other party's expert. For example, in a personal injury case the information you will have from the expert disclosure, medical records, and other information obtained through interrogatories, documents requests, and depositions of other witnesses will sometimes be adequate to know what the plaintiff's treating doctor will say at trial.

In most cases, an expert deposition will be essential. The district may not require expert disclosure, and the amount of information you receive about the other party's experts will be inadequate to learn what the witness will say at trial. If the case depends in large part on the relative persuasiveness of the experts, you will need to depose the other party's expert to get a good feel for the kind of witness she will make at trial. The point is that, particularly in districts where Rule 26(a)(2) expert disclosure is required, you need not depose every expert in every case. Deposing experts is expensive and time consuming, particularly since under Rule 26(b)(4)(C) the party deposing the expert must pay the expert's reasonable fees, and should be done only when there is a clear need in doing so.

Where the expert is outside the court's jurisdiction and the expert will not come forward voluntarily to testify at trial, the expert will usually be "unavailable" for the purposes of FRE 804(a)(5). Since the expert cannot be compelled to testify at trial, the expert's deposition can

___

45. See discussion of experts in §6.3.9.

be admitted at trial as former testimony under Rule 32 and FRE 804(b)(1). For this reason, the deposition of such an expert should be taken to ensure that the questions and answers will be available for admission at trial. It is particularly important that an "unavailable" expert's testimony be clear and complete. A videotaped deposition should be considered here for this purpose. A video deposition has the advantage of presenting a vivid recreation of the deponent's testimony to the jury. Its disadvantage is that taking the deposition and then editing out objectionable questions and answers is expensive. Nevertheless, a video deposition of an expert, if done carefully, is a vastly superior method of presenting the absent expert's testimony.

Keep in mind that taking a deposition can benefit your opponent as well as you. Once taken, if the witness later becomes unavailable, the deposition probably will qualify for admission at trial under Rule 804(b)(1). Where you suspect this may happen, and the witness is unfavorable, consider taking only a short deposition to learn the basics of what the witness has to say. If the witness is one of your opponent's expert witnesses, and you suspect the expert may be unavailable at trial, consider not asking background qualifications questions. (Of course, nothing will prevent your opponent from asking the qualifications questions.)

c.   When should I take depositions?

Since under Rule 30(a) oral depositions can be taken any time after the parties meet to plan discovery under Rule 26(f), the timing of depositions is determined primarily by tactical considerations.

First, depositions can be taken before an action has been commenced if Rule 27(a) requirements are met. Those requirements are technical and detailed; they include drawing up a verified petition that sets out the facts of the anticipated suit, the details expected from the witness, and the reasons a deposition is necessary. The petition must be served, with a notice of deposition, to each anticipated adverse party that can be found. The amount of work required under Rule 27(a) is at least as much as is required to prepare, file, and serve a complaint and summons. For that reason, Rule 27(a) is ordinarily used only in those circumstances where service on the adverse party cannot be made quickly.

Second, another possiblity is to depose your opponent as soon as permitted after the suit has been commenced. This may be necessary in certain situations, such as when you need facts to support a jurisdictional motion, or when you need to learn the identity of proper parties and officers and agents of such parties, or when you want to depose a custodian of records to learn about your opponent's records so that you can prepare a more focused documents request.

An early deposition may also catch your opponent unprepared, not yet having collected and reviewed records and documents, and result in a more useful deposition. The witness may disclaim knowledge of certain facts, or assert facts that can be disproved. These can be used as admissions and for impeachment at trial.

On the other hand, there are obvious risks. Without interrogatory answers and documents received through documents requests, your preparation cannot be nearly as thorough as it should be. Rule 30(a) bars a second deposition of a person without a court order or written stipulation of the parties. If any party objects, you may be prevented from taking a second deposition. In short, taking an early deposition with the idea of taking a second detailed one later involves risks.

Third, the usual approach is to take depositions after initial disclosures, interrogatory answers and documents have been received. Only then will you have the necessary facts and materials to prepare thoroughly and take the kind of detailed, complete deposition you will want to take. This is particularly important when deposing adverse parties, where the party can only be pinned down when you have the preliminary discovery on hand.

Deciding when to take a deposition can only be done on a case-by-case basis. Your decision must balance the benefits of an early deposition against a later one based on the extent of your knowledge from existing discovery. The important concept to keep in mind is that the question of when to take a particular deposition should never be a routine matter, but should always be decided by weighing the benefits, disadvantages, and risks of a particular course of action.

d. What order of depositions should I use?

There are several approaches to establishing the order of depositions, and the approach that will be effective in a given case depends on the issues, parties, and witnesses involved.

First, continuing with the concept that discovery should be a building process, a common approach is to depose neutral and unfavorable witnesses first, then adverse employees, officers, and parties to the action, and finally, the adverse parties' experts. Arranging the depositions in this order allows you to use information obtained from witnesses to prepare for depositions of parties to the action and, in turn, the experts. This approach, however, has built-in disadvantages, since every deposition educates both you and the other parties. Every witness deposition you take before taking the adverse party's deposition functions to prepare that party to be deposed.

The second approach, therefore, is to reverse the order and depose adverse parties first, then the nonparty witnesses. This has the advantage of pinning down the adverse parties to detailed testimony before hearing other witnesses, who may have conflicting testimony.

The third possiblity is to schedule a series of depositions back to back so that later deponents do not have time to review the transcripts of the earlier depositions. This works well with unfavorable witnesses and adverse parties, who might otherwise try to find out what an earlier witness said and then tell a consistent story. If you see a danger of this happening in a particular case, simply schedule the first deposition for the morning, the second for early afternoon, and so on, allowing enough time so that you can realistically keep to the schedule. For example, when deposing corporate employees, it is often effective to schedule them back to back, starting at the bottom and working up to management. You are more likely to get inconsistencies this way.

As with the decision on when to depose, a decision on the order of depositions can only be made on a case-by-case basis. Deciding on the order should not be a routine matter, but should always involve weighing the advantages, disadvantages, and risks of a particular approach.

e.   What must I do to schedule a deposition?

Scheduling a deposition involves two decisions: when and where. When has been discussed above. Where depends on your personal preference and what the Rules allow. Rule 30 does not deal with location, so it leaves the choice up to the party taking the deposition of another party. However, Rule 45 has specific location rules for deposing nonparty witnesses. Such witnesses can be deposed anywhere within the district from which the subpoena was issued, or anyplace within 100 miles of the place where the subpoena was issued, even if outside the district, or anywhere in the state if a state rule allows such subpoena service. In addition, under Rule 30(b)(7) a deposition can, by court order or written stipulation of the parties, be taken by telephone or other remote electronic means.

The usual location for deposing a party is in your own offices. You will be comfortable there, have your files with you, and have your deponent away from familiar surroundings. If you have previously obtained responses to your documents requests, there should be no need to be at the deponent's place of business.

To depose a distant nonparty witnesses, you will often have to go to the witness, unless you can get the witness to come to you. While the Rule is designed to convenience nonparty witnesses, it can have the effect of inconveniencing everyone else. Therefore, it is usually a good idea to try to have the witness come to you. If, in addition to the mileage and witness fees, you offer to compensate the witness for actual travel expenses and lost wages, the witness may be more likely to come to your offices to be deposed.

To depose experts, it is frequently better to visit the experts at their offices. It will be convenient for the expert, and you will have access to the expert's reports, records, and reference material. This will avoid what otherwise is a common problem: the expert who, for one reason or another, fails to bring all necessary paperwork, thereby making a thorough deposition impossible. Make sure, however, that you bring everything you need to the expert's office.

Regardless of where the expert will be deposed, make sure you have previously obtained, either from the opposing party or through subpoenas, all records you will need for the deposition. Before deposing a doctor, for example, make sure you have the relevant hospital records as well as the doctor's own medical records. In addition, under Rule 26(b)(4) you must obtain the expert's report from the testifying expert before you can depose the expert. It is simply impossible to take a good deposition of an expert without first obtaining and reviewing all relevant reports.

After you have selected a time and place for the depositions, you must do the following:

1. Send notices to parties
2. Serve subpoenas on nonparty witnesses
3. Reserve a suitable room for the deposition
4. Arrange for a court reporter and video operator
5. Reconfirm deposition date and attendance

The notices to parties and subpoenas to witnesses should be served with a reasonable lead time. Given the busy schedules of most people, 20 or 30 days' notice is certainly appropriate. When deposing a party, it is always a good practice to call that party's lawyer and select a mutually convenient time before preparing the notices. This avoids delays, avoids motions to reset deposition dates, and generally helps create good working relationships between lawyers, which benefits everyone. With nonparty witnesses, it is frequently a good idea to serve a subpoena first, and subsequently try to arrange for the witness to travel to your office.

The notices must be sent to every party to the action. If the deposition is for a party, nothing else need be done. If the deposition is for a nonparty, you also must serve a subpoena on that witness which complies with the requirements of Rule 45. Such subpoena forms are usually available from the clerk of the court. The notice must state how the deposition will be recorded. Other parties may choose to record the deposition by other means, at their expense.

Example:

[Caption]

NOTICE OF DEPOSITION

To: <u>   *(defendant's attorney)*   </u>

Please take notice that I will take the deposition of Rudolf Watson, defendant, before a notary public, or any other authorized officer, on August 30, 1998, at 2:00 P.M., at Room 201, 400 Elm St., Chicago, Illinois, pursuant to Rule 30 of the Federal Rules of Civil Procedure. You are required to have the deponent present at that date, time, and place for oral examination. The deposition will also be recorded by videotape.

———————————————
Attorney for Plaintiff

If you wish to have the party deponent produce records and documents at the deposition, the notice can be accompanied by a statement directing that certain records and documents be produced at that time. The documents and records should be described with reasonable particularity. However, the better practice is to get all the necessary records and documents from the party before noticing the party's deposition. It is also a good practice to send a copy of the notice to the court reporter who is scheduled to take the deposition. The subpoena for a nonparty will be on a standard form issued by the appropriate clerk's office. It also can command the production of documents and things at the deposition. Make sure you attach a check for the necessary witness and mileage fees.[46]

Example:

[Caption]

SUBPOENA IN A CIVIL CASE

To: _____
     (name and address of deponent)

YOU ARE COMMANDED to appear at the place, date and time specified below to testify at the taking of a deposition in the above case.

Place of deposition _____ *Date and Time* _____

YOU ARE COMMANDED to produce and permit inspection and copying of the following documents or objects at the place, date and time specified below (list documents or objects):

Place _____   *Date and Time* _____

_____   _____
Issuing officer signature and title (indicate   Date
if attorney for plaintiff or defendant)

Issuing officer's name, address, and phone number:

_____

(See Rule 45, FRCP, Parts C & D on Reverse)

After the notice and subpoena have been served, arrange for a suitable room in which to take the deposition. Make sure a court reporter is scheduled and told where and when the deposition will be held. Those who should be present include the deponent, the court reporter, the lawyers for the parties, and perhaps the parties themselves. A conference room or private office in your law office suite is usually the best place to take the deposition. You will be comfortable there and have all your files available. However, if you want to be particularly accommodating to a witness for tactical reasons, use a location convenient for the witness. If the

46. 28 U.S.C. §§1821 et seq.

deponent is required to produce documents and you are afraid she will not fully comply, depose her where the records are kept.

Finally, it is always a good idea to reconfirm the deposition with the parties, lawyers, witnesses, and court reporter involved shortly before the deposition date. Rule 30 allows the court to order the deposing party to pay reasonable expenses, including attorney's fees, to the other parties and lawyers if the party giving notice fails to attend the scheduled deposition, or fails to serve a subpoena on a witness and fails to notify the other parties of this fact. Hence, if your conduct causes another party or lawyer to attend a scheduled deposition, and those parties or lawyers were not notified of your failure to subpoena a witness, they are entitled to recover reasonable expenses incurred by attending that deposition. Whenever a scheduled deposition is canceled for any reason, notify everyone entitled to notice immediately.

f. How should I prepare for taking a deposition?

Taking a good deposition obviously requires preparation. You must collect all the documentation that has any bearing on the witness' anticipated testimony, review it, and have copies available for use during the deposition. A copy can be marked by the witness during the deposition, in which case it should be given to the court reporter to attach as an exhibit to the deposition transcript.

This documentation includes all documents and records where the witness is "down on paper" and includes any written or signed statements, oral interviews reduced to writing, police reports in which the witness is mentioned, and records created by or mentioning the witness. If the deponent is a party, this documentation should include the party's pleadings, the party's initial disclosures, interrogatory answers, responses to documents requests, and any affidavits that accompanied motions, since you will probably want to question the party about specific allegations and representations contained in the pleadings and discovery.

When you have reviewed the available material, you should begin to outline how you will take the particular deposition. This depends on several considerations: Is the deponent an adverse party, unfavorable witness, or friendly witness? What information do you need to obtain? What foundations for exhibits do you want to establish? What admissions or impeachment should you try to obtain? Are you taking the deposition only to discover information, or should you take it with an eye toward preserving the witness' testimony for possible later use? What are the risks involved in deposing this person? These considerations must be evaluated so that you have good answers to the fundamental question you must ask yourself: Why am I taking this deposition?

These considerations affect how you will take a particular deposition. Regardless of your approach, your questioning should be thorough, because a basic purpose for depositions is to find out what the deponent knows. It is usually a good practice to make an outline of your anticipated topics with suitable references to the exhibits you will want to use. While such an outline must obviously be tailored to the facts of each case, certain general topics should usually be explored. There are numerous books available that contain checklists for various types of cases and witnesses. These are useful for considering the types of topics that can be explored and a sensible order for them, but such checklists should never be a substitute for tailoring your outline to the particular deponent.

Example (preliminary matters):

1. Background
   a. Name and address
   b. Personal and family history
   c. Education
   d. Job history
2. Documents and records
   a. Notice to produce and subpoenas
   b. Record keeping
   c. Records search
   d. Identifying produced records
   e. Identifying any destroyed records
   f. Names and addresses of other persons and entities that may have records related to case
3. Identity of party
   a. Officers, directors, employees, agents
   b. Parent corporation and subsidiaries, licensees
   c. Incorporation and places of business
   d. Residence
   e. Place where licensed to do business
   f. Names used in business
4. Witnesses
   a. Names and addresses of persons witnessing events and transactions
   b. Names and addresses of persons deponent has communicated with
   c. Names and addresses of persons who may know something about case

These background topics should usually be pursued regardless of the deponent. When the deponent is a party, most of this information should already have been received in the interrogatory answers, but you should have the deponent reconfirm the information and explain them in greater detail where necessary.

On the other hand, these background topics need not be the first matters covered in the deposition. It is sometimes more effective to question the witness first, then ask about the background and documents later. In this way you will find out what the witness knows, then find out what the witness can say about the documents. This approach often works well if the case involves numerous documents. This approach also works well with experts, who can be questioned about their opinions first, then the bases for their opinions, and, last, about their professional backgrounds. Keep in mind that many jurisdictions set time limits on depositions, which means that you must make sure you get to the important matters quickly.

Once you have organized your preliminary matters, you should outline the substantive areas, which depend on the type of case, legal and factual issues, and the witness' relationship to them. The key to the deposition here is detail. You need to make sure that the outline covers all the topics and is logically organized—usually chronologically—which helps you to be thorough and avoid mistakes. Sometimes, however, it may be useful to vary your topics from a strictly chronological order so that the deponent cannot anticipate questions.

The deposition should extract from the witness what the deponent knows that is pertinent to the case. Remind yourself that you usually get only one opportunity to depose a person, so you must be prepared to get the most out of that opportunity.

On the other hand, keep in mind that the basic purpose of any deposition is to learn what the witness knows and did, and what his trial testimony will be. Endless questioning, particularly if repetitive and argumentative, accomplishes nothing positive and only serves to educate the opposing lawyer and witness on what the content and tone of the cross-examination is likely to be at trial. There is a difference between finding out what you need to know, and finding out everything you can possibly know. Good trial lawyers know the difference.

Example (plaintiff in personal injury case):

1. Background questions
   a. (Preliminary matters as outlined previously)
   b. Health history before accident
2. Vehicles involved
   a. Make, year, registration
   b. Insurance
   c. Condition, inspection, repair records
3. Scene of collision
   a. Neighborhood
   b. Roads
   c. Traffic markings and controls
   d. Lighting
4. Weather and road conditions
5. Events before accident
   a. Activities earlier in day
   b. Food, alcohol, drugs
   c. Physical condition at time
6. Events immediately before collision
   a. Location and direction of vehicles
   b. Passengers
   c. Traffic conditions
   d. Visibility
   e. Other distractions

f. Where first saw defendant's car
g. Marking diagrams and photographs
7. Collision
    a. Speed of cars before impact
    b. Traffic signals
    c. Braking and other conduct of plaintiff
    d. Braking and other conduct of defendant
    e. Point of impact
    f. Where cars ended up
    g. Marking diagrams and photographs
8. Events after collision
    a. Bystander activities
    b. Police activities
    c. What plaintiff and defendant did
    d. What plaintiff and defendant said
    e. Plaintiff's and defendant's condition after collision
    f. Ambulance
9. Medical treatment
    a. At hospital—diagnosis and treatment
    b. Doctors visits after discharge—treatments
    c. Medication, therapy
10. Present physical condition
    a. Any physical limitations
    b. Any mental conditions
    c. Medication
11. Damages
    a. Vehicle
    b. Hospital expenses
    c. Doctor's bills
    d. Lost wages
    e. Insurance payments
    f. Other claimed losses

Example (corporate plaintiff in contract breach case):

1. Background questions
    a. (Preliminary matters as outlined previously)
2. First contact with defendant
    a. Reasons—how came about
    b. Persons involved
3. Course of dealing up to contract
    a. Types of business conducted
    b. Business practices
    c. Specific contracts entered into
    d. Performance history
4. Negotiations leading up to contract
    a. Dates, times, places, participants
    b. All communications

5. Contract execution
   a. Date, time, place, participants
6. Conduct following execution
   a. Performance by each party
7. Breach claimed
   a. When, what
   b. Witnesses
8. Conduct following breach
   a. Attempts to mitigate
9. Damages claimed
   a. Breach damages
   b. Consequential damages

Example (physician in personal injury case):

1. Professional background
   a. Education
   b. Internship and residency
   c. Licenses and specialty boards
   d. Description of practice
   e. Experience in type of injury involved here
2. Physician's medical records and reports
   a. Identify them
   b. Treatises he relies on
   c. Consultations
3. First contact with plaintiff at hospital
   a. Where and when
   b. History
   c. Symptoms
   d. Examination and findings
   e. Tests
   f. Diagnosis
   g. Treatment
4. Subsequent contacts with plaintiff
   a. Where and when
   b. Symptoms
   c. Examinations and findings
   d. Tests
   e. Prognosis
5. Opinions and conclusions
   a. Extent of injuries
   b. Permanence of injuries
   c. Effect on plaintiff
   d. Causation
   e. Why physician disagrees with other experts
6. Fees
   a. How much
   b. Future fees

g.   *How do I prepare for a videotaped deposition?*

Rule 30(b) permits videotape depositions as of right. Rule 26(b) permits expert depositions as of right. Consequently, depositions of lay and expert witnesses by videotape are increasingly common. Videotaped depositions have benefits and costs. On the plus side, a videotape preserves deposition testimony much more vividly and has much more impact on a jury than a stenographic transcript. This is an important consideration if you plan to introduce the videotape during trial as former testimony under FRE 804(b)(1) or to use the videotape as impeachment with a prior inconsistent statement during trial. In addition, videotaping a deposition usually stops the kind of lawyer misconduct which has been all too common: improperly coaching a witness, making improper objections, and the like. This kind of misconduct will be recorded graphically on videotape. On the minus side, videotaping is expensive, involving a video operator and appropriate equipment, although many lawyers now have their own equipment and trained personnel.

Preparation for the deposition involves two principal concerns: preparing the setting for the videotaped deposition, and preparing your party for the deposition. The setting for the videotaping is important, particularly when you want the deponent to look and sound persuasive. The video equipment must be of professional quality. You must decide if one or two cameras are necessary. If you use only one camera, the usual procedure is to start with a wide angle shot showing all the participants and, after the deponent is sworn, the camera is brought closer and focuses on the head and upper body of the deponent, or the dependent and examining lawyer. This process is repeated after every break. If you use two cameras, one camera can be a closeup of the deponent, the other a closeup of the questioning lawyer or a wide angle of all the participants. You must also work out how the deponent will handle exhibits and conduct any demonstrations.

The lighting, background, and setting are also critical to create an attractive visual image. The lighting must be adequate to properly illuminate the participants, and should be diffused to avoid harsh shadows. The background should be a light, softly textured wall or curtain that will highlight the deponent and not provide any visual distraction. The setting should be either a courtroom or a conference room or similar setting. An experienced video technician will be familiar with how to create a good visual and sound environment for a videotaped deposition and should be consulted in advance.

Preparing your client for a videotaped deposition includes all the steps involved in preparing a witness to testify at trial. The client must understand that in most cases the deposition *is* the trial. He must be taught how to dress, how to maintain eye contact with either the camera or the questioner, how to project his voice to sound confident, how to avoid pauses that may suggest uncertainty, and how to control his body movement to develop reinforcing gestures and eliminate distracting mannerisms. This will obviously take time, and rehearsing on videotape is essential.

h. How do I start the deposition?

If all goes well, the parties' lawyers, the court reporter, video operator, and the deponent will all appear at the designated place, date, and time. You should also consider having your client attend, since this will educate the client. This is a particularly good idea when the deponent will testify to conversations and transactions with your client, in which case the deponent is more likely to be truthful and candid when your client is listening to the testimony. After routine introductions have been made, the participants have settled down in the deposition room, the court reporter has set up the stenographic equipment, and the video operator is ready. You are ready to begin the oral deposition. Start by giving the court reporter a copy of a pleading with a complete caption; also, the reporter should be given the correct spelling for the names of all persons present. Then proceed.

First, ask the court reporter to swear in the witness. Some lawyers have the transcript affirmatively show that the witness was sworn.

Second, make sure an introductory statement for the record identifies whose deposition it is, the date and place, and everyone present. Also, the statement should reflect that notice was given, that the deposition is being taken under the Federal Rules of Civil Procedure, and that the witness has been sworn. Rule 30(b) requires that the court reporter put these matters on the record, unless otherwise agreed by the parties. In many jurisdictions the lawyer taking the deposition makes the introductory statement on the record.

Example:

Q. This is the deposition of the plaintiff, Margaret Singer, being taken in the case of Margaret Singer v. Robert Johnson, Case No. 98C 483 in the United States District Court for the Northern District of Ohio. It is being held at the law offices of Marlyn Anders, 200 Main Street, Suite 400, Cleveland, Ohio. Today's date is August 15, 1998. Present in addition to Ms. Singer are myself, Marlyn Anders, attorney for defendant Johnson, Sharon Witts, attorney for plaintiff Singer, and Darlene Winters, a certified court reporter and notary public. Ms. Singer, you were just sworn to tell the truth by the court reporter, correct?

A. That's right.

When the deponent is a party, he will usually have been prepared for the deposition, will know what to expect, and will be familiar with the procedure. When the deponent is a nonparty, however, this may not be the case, and it is sometimes worthwhile to explain the deposition procedure and its importance. This prevents a witness from later claiming, if impeached from the transcript, that he was confused or was being pressed by the lawyer.

Example:

Q. Mr. Johnson, have you ever attended a deposition before?
A. No.
Q. Do you know how a deposition works?
A. Not really.
Q. Mr. Johnson, I'm going to ask you questions about this accident, and you'll have to answer them under oath. The other lawyers can also ask questions if they want to. Afterward the court reporter will type up everything said here today. That's called a transcript. Do you understand?
A. Yes.
Q. It's important that you understand the questions and give accurate answers. If there's anything you don't understand, or anything you don't know or aren't sure of, you let us know, all right?
A. Yes.

Where the deponent is a party that has also been served with a request to produce, or the deponent is a witness that has been served with a subpoena duces tecum, have the deponent produce the records or documents on the record, even if he voluntarily sent them to you in advance. Identify them for the record, make copies of them and give the court reporter a copy to attach to the transcript, and mark them as exhibits.

Example:

Q. Ms. Jones, you received a subpoena for certain records of your company along with the subpoena to appear, correct?
A. Yes.
Q. Did you comply and bring the records?
A. Yes.
Q. May I see them? (Lawyer obtains them from witness.) For the record, the witness has handed me photocopies totaling five pages. The court reporter will mark them Deposition Exhibit A. Page one is an invoice, page two is a bill of lading, page three is a shipping notice, and pages four and five are account ledgers. Each page bears the name of ABC Shipping Company. Ms. Jones, does that accurately describe these five pages?
A. Yes.
Q. These are all business records of ABC Shipping?
A. Yes.
Q. Did you search the company records for all records relating to the transaction described on the subpoena served on you?
A. Yes.
Q. These five pages are the only ones that exist?
A. Yes.
Q. Other than these records, does your company make other records for a transaction of this kind?
A. No.

If you anticipate the need to introduce the records in evidence at trial, it is always a good procedure to qualify the witness as a "custodian or other qualified witness" and establish a business records foundation under Rule 803(6) of the Federal Rules of Evidence. If the witness is a party or agent of the party, the testimony will qualify as an admission; if a nonparty, the testimony should qualify as former testimony if the witness is unavailable at trial.

When you are examining the witness about documents, make sure that you have a good exhibit marking system when the depositions will involve numerous documents. Practices vary. For example, plaintiff may use numbers 1 to 300; defendant may use numbers 301 to 600. In this way, all deposition documents will be marked "Deposition exhibit no. _____". In some jurisdictions, the practice is for each side to designate its own deposition exhibits. For example, plaintiff will call its exhibits "Plaintiff deposition exhibit no. _____", the defense "Defendant deposition exhibit no. _____". Still others designate exhibits by the witness name. For example, if a Shirley Williams is being deposed, the exhibits will be called "Williams exhibit no. _____". The key concept is to have clarity in the marking system. You can then use the witness to establish the legal foundation for admissibility at trial for particular deposition exhibits. At the end of the deposition, make sure the court reporter has all the marked exhibits, which will later be attached to the deposition transcript.

Example:

Q.   Ms. Williams, you work for the defendant, the ABC Corporation?
A.   Yes.
Q.   You're the secretary to ABC's president, Mr. Greenberg?
A.   Yes.
Q.   You've been working for ABC and Mr. Greenberg since 1990?
A.   Yes.
Q.   Ms. Williams, you've seen Mr. Greenberg write his signature before, right?
A.   Of course.
Q.   About how many times?
A.   Certainly hundreds of times, maybe thousands.
Q.   And you've seen him write things out in longhand, right?
A.   Certainly.
Q.   Ms. Williams, I'm showing you a check which has been marked "Plaintiff's deposition exhibit no. 7". It's dated June 1, 1998, and is filled out by hand. Take a look at it.
A.   All right.
Q.   Have you seen that check before?
A.   I don't think so.
Q.   But you recognize the signature in the lower right hand corner of the check, right?
A.   Sure. That's Mr. Greenberg's signature.
Q.   Any doubt about that?
A.   No. I know Mr. Greenberg's signature. That's his.

> *Q.* Look at the rest of the face of the check. Is that also Mr. Green-
>   berg's handwriting?
> *A.* Yes. It's all filled out by him.

Finally, good practice requires that you put any stipulations on the record and state expressly what they are. Parties frequently deal with the status of objections, sometimes stipulating that all objections are preserved or that all objections are preserved except those directed to the form of the question. This can be useful because it eliminates the need to make most objections during the deposition, allowing for a much clearer and shorter transcript. Objections can then be raised later if the transcript will be used during trial. However, agreeing to the "usual stipulations" is bad practice and should be avoided, particularly when you are outside your usual practice area. Find out what the usual stipulations are, and then decide whether to agree with them.

i. What questioning styles should I use?

The questioning style you employ during the deposition must be consistent with your purpose. Are you taking the deposition primarily to gather information from a witness? Are you taking a party's deposition to pin the party down on details, to obtain admissions, and to develop impeachment? Are you deposing a favorable witness to preserve the witness' testimony in the event he becomes unavailable for trial? The different purposes will affect how you conduct the deposition.[47]

Regardless of your purposes, you should always keep two concerns uppermost in your mind: Have I clearly and unambiguously stated questions and received answers? How will this sound if it is read to a jury during trial?

i. Getting information

When your principal goal during the deposition is to gather information, it is frequently a good approach to let the witness ramble on rather than control the witness with narrow, focused questions. You are more likely to have the witness volunteer useful information if you ask broad questions in a friendly, informal way. You can always steer the witness to the topics that need to be covered and use follow-up questions to tie down the details. Whether the questions and answers violate evidentiary rules, such as leading or hearsay, is unimportant, if your only goal is to get information.

Just as important as finding out what the witness knows is finding out what the witness does *not* know or has no firsthand knowledge about. This will prevent the witness from adding to his testimony at trial, since you

---

47. The actual questioning techniques for examining a deponent are much the same, and as varied, as conducting direct and cross-examinations of witnesses at trial. For a discussion of these techniques, see, e.g., T. Mauet, Trial Techniques (4th ed. 1996); P. Bergman, Trial Advocacy in a Nutshell (2d ed. 1989); K. Hegland, Trial and Practice Skills (2d. ed. 1994); J. Jeans, Handbook on Trial Advocacy (2d ed. 1993).

will be able to impeach the witness on these new points. If the witness says he doesn't know or doesn't remember and you want the information, use follow-up questions. Ask: Who does know? Where is the information? What would help the witness remember? Who has the witness talked to about the information?

Find out what materials the witness reviewed to prepare for his testimony. Under FRE 612, if a trial witness used records and documents to refresh his recollection "before testifying," the adverse party may be entitled to see those records and documents. Some courts have held that this right prevails over claims that the records and documents are protected by a privilege.[48]

ii.   Eliciting detail and pinning down specific facts

When deposing an adverse party, you usually have dual purposes: finding out what the party knows in detail, and pinning the party down to specific, hopefully useful, facts. Ask open, nonleading questions to try to get the deponent to talk and to fully detail what he knows. If the opposing lawyer has done his homework, of course, the party will be loathe to volunteer information not specifically asked for. However, it is always good to use this approach since even a well-prepared party may sometimes divulge something you would never have uncovered.

The second purpose, pinning the party down, is usually accomplished by using leading, focused, cross-examination type questions. One of the most common mistakes is to let the witness give ambiguous or qualified answers that do not make for effective impeachment at trial. If the party hedges, ask follow-up questions that pin him down. If the party refuses, try to get him to admit that he is only "guessing," "approximating," or that he simply "doesn't know." Parties have a predictable talent for improving their recall of facts and details at trial. Therefore, getting an "I don't know" or an "I can only approximate" response can be useful for impeachment purposes if the party at trial claims to know specifically.

iii.   Preserving testimony

When deposing someone to preserve testimony for later admission at trial as former testimony under FRE 804(b)(1), your principal concern is to create clear, progressive testimony that will not run afoul of evidentiary rules. Keep in mind that, absent any contrary stipulations, Rule 32(d) preserves all objections to questions and answers except those directed to form or others that could have been cured had they been made promptly. Therefore, unless the witness is an adverse party or hostile witness, use nonleading questions. Avoid objectionable forms of questions, such as those that can be considered leading, compound, argumentative, speculative, ambiguous, or narrative. Don't ask questions that call for hearsay or improper opinions.

Deposition purposes, of course, do not always separate out with such clear definition. For example, even when you are deposing a wit-

---

48. See Sporck v. Piel, 759 F.2d 312 (3d Cir. 1985)

ness and are trying to pin the witness down with leading questions, you may want to use that witness to establish the foundations for records, documents, and other exhibits for possible use at trial.[49] If so, you must establish that the witness is a qualified witness, and state questions and get answers that meet the applicable evidentiary foundation requirements for each exhibit.

Some lawyers, at the end of a deposition, ask the deponent if he would like to correct anything he has said, or whether he has any additional information pertinent to the case that he has not been asked about. If the witness answers no, you can use this answer to impeach him at trial if he testifies inconsistently or testifies to new facts not previously disclosed, suggesting to the jury that the new or different testimony is a recent creation.

iv.   Common problems

Inexperienced litigators frequently experience problems while taking depositions. First, their time estimates are too short. Even a simple deposition will probably take half an hour; an eyewitness to a car crash may take an hour or more. If the deponent is a witness to a series of commercial transactions, or is an expert or a party in a medical or products liability case, the deposition may take a few hours. Keep in mind, however, that under Rule 30(d) and local rules courts are increasingly putting time limits on depositions; limits of three or four hours are common.

Second, their purposes are unclear. Depositions can be taken for one or more of three basic reasons: discovering information, pinning down for admissions and impeachment purposes, and for preserving testimony. You need to determine which of these three purposes are involved in every deposition and conduct yourself accordingly. If the latter two, you are creating a document—the transcript—that you will later use at trial. How it looks and reads is important.

Third, their questioning forms are unclear. How you ask questions has much to do with what your deposition purposes are. If discovery, use nonleading questions that get the witness talking. If pinning down, use focused leading questions. If preserving testimony, use questions that you would use if you were conducting a direct examination of the witness at trial.

Fourth, necessary documentation is missing. You ordinarily cannot take a good deposition of a witness or represent your client at a deposition unless you have previously obtained all the documentation necessary for that deposition. If the party or witness was directed, by notice or subpoena, to bring such documentation to the deposition but doesn't, refuse to take the deposition under these circumstances and continue the deposition to another date.

Fifth, they explore unnecessary details. This is a common problem with litigators who have little trial experience. Since they don't know what will be important if the case is finally tried, they cover all the bases by ask-

---

49. See T. Mauet, Trial Techniques ch. 5 (4th ed. 1996) on establishing foundations for various types of exhibits.

ing everything they can think of, about every conceivable topic. This rarely accomplishes anything useful. The way to deal with this is to spend time beforehand planning the deposition and getting help from more experienced litigators who have trial experience.

j.   How should I handle objections?

When you are taking depositions, there are three basic types of objections.

First, an objection can be made to the form of the questions or answers; Rule 32(d) requires that unless an objection is made promptly, it is waived. Even after a timely objection is made, the witness must still answer the question "subject to the objection." If you are taking the deposition only to gather information, you can safely ignore the objection. If you may use the transcript later at trial, however, determine if the objection has possible validity. If it does, rephrase the question properly to overcome the objection. Remember that you can never be totally sure that you will not need to use the transcript during trial.

Second, an objection can be made on evidentiary grounds other than privilege. However, since it is not necessary to object if the grounds are relevance, hearsay, or if the objection is not based on form, the other parties can reserve objections until such time as the deposition is used at trial. That is, if such an objection is not made at the deposition, it can still be made at trial—and this is the customary procedure. If made at the deposition, the deponent must still answer. Again, however, if you plan to use the deposition at trial, and a proper objection is made, you should rephrase the question to eliminate the problem.

Third, an objection can be made on the grounds of privilege or harassment. If made on privilege grounds, the witness will probably refuse to answer, since the witness' lawyer will direct the witness not to answer the question.[50] If on harassment grounds, an objection can be made along with a demand under Rule 30(d) that the deposition be suspended in order to make a motion to limit or terminate the deposition. When objections are made on privilege or harassment grounds, the witness will probably refuse to answer, leaving you, the lawyer taking the deposition, with two options. First, you can terminate the examination and move to compel answers. Second, you can ask other questions not objected to and finish the examination to the extent possible.

Regardless of how you react to the witness' refusal, you must decide whether to seek an order compelling an answer. You can discuss the legal issue with the lawyer making the objection to learn the reason for it, and then either rephrase the question or ask the lawyer to withdraw the objection. If the witness persists in refusing to answer, the information you seek is important, and you wish to force the issue, you must make a clear record. The question, the witness' refusal to answer, and the grounds for the refusal should be clearly spelled out, since the court reporter must

---

50. See discussion in §6.2.

provide a transcript of that portion of the deposition that you will attach
to your motion to compel discovery.[51]

Example:

Q. Mr. Jones, you were the maintenance man at XYZ Leasing dur-
    ing this time, correct?
A. Yes.
Q. You talked to people about the problem, didn't you?
A. Yes.
Q. That included the company lawyer, Mr. Johnson?
A. Yes.
Q. Tell us what you told Mr. Johnson about the problem.
Jones' lawyer: Objection. Mr. Jones, don't answer that question. That
    question calls for the disclosure of attorney-client communica-
    tions, which are privileged.
Q. Mr. Jones, do you refuse to answer the question?
A. Yes.
Q. Your refusal is based on your assertion of the attorney-client privi-
    lege?
A. Yes.

In this way you will have made a clear record of the witness' refusal to
answer and the reason for it. Ask the court reporter to mark this part of
the deposition and transcribe it later so you can attach it to your motion
to compel.

Finally, it is an unfortunate fact in litigation that some lawyers misuse
objections to coach the deponent into making more desirable responses.
This conduct violates the express terms of Rule 30(d)(1), which provides
that "any objection to evidence during a deposition shall be stated concisely and in a non-argumentative and non-suggestive manner." The purpose of this rule is clear. Lawyers cannot use objections to frustrate an
otherwise proper deposition, such as by using objections to coach the witness on a desired response or to frustrate and impede the examining lawyer. Lawyers cannot instruct deponents not to answer a question unless
necessary to preserve a privilege or to make a motion to terminate the deposition because it is being taken in bad faith or is unreasonably annoying or
oppressive. Such improper lawyer conduct unfortunately had become common in recent years, and the 1993 amendments to Rule 30 were made to
clearly establish rules for lawyer conduct during depositions. Where this repeatedly occurs—such as a lawyer who makes constant "clarification" or
"if he knows" objections—you should note your objection to the opposing lawyer and make sure the court reporter records it. If this conduct
persists, you may want to terminate the deposition and bring the matter
to the court through a motion to compel discovery or for sanctions. If past

51. Asking the court reporter to "certify the question," while not necessary to raise the
matter in a motion to compel answers, lets the court reporter know that this question
should be on a list of questions the witness refused to answer that will be appended to the
end of the deposition transcript. This is a common practice in state courts.

experience with a particular lawyer suggests this may happen, it may be effective to take a video deposition, because it will graphically capture the lawyer's conduct and sometimes will even act as a deterrent to such conduct. The videotape will show the misconduct more vividly than a written transcript. Some courts limit consultation between the witness and her lawyer during questioning, requiring what amounts to a trial environment for the deposition. Make sure you know your judge's guidelines for taking depositions.

k. How should I prepare and represent a deponent?

When you receive a notice for deposition of your client, preparing the client for the upcoming deposition may well be the most important single event in the litigation process. The opposing lawyers will use the deposition to determine what your client knows, develop admissions and impeachment, pin your client down to details about what he does or does not know, and generally size up your client as a trial witness. If the deposition goes well, the settlement value of the case will rise as well. Hence, preparation for the deposition is critical.

Shortly before the deposition date, have your client come to your office with enough time allocated to prepare him thoroughly. Scheduling this for the early afternoon, as the last appointment for the day, is a good idea since you will not be rushed by other appointments. On the other hand, some lawyers prefer to schedule such interviews in the morning, when they and the clients are fresh.

First, have the pleadings, discovery, documents, records, reports, photographs, diagrams, and sketches available for the client to review. However, show the client only his statements, not those of others. Showing your client other persons' statements will always create the impression, particularly at trial, that your client has tailored his testimony to be consistent with other witnesses, or has used the other statements to acquire information he himself does not personally have. This may also make such statements disclosable at trial, since under Rule 612 of the Federal Rules of Evidence an adverse party may be able to obtain any documents used to refresh the witness' recollection, even if used before trial; the party may be able to use them during the witness' cross-examination and to introduce in evidence relevant portions of the documents. It is usually better to avoid this problem by not showing your client other witnesses' statements. You can always refer to reports and statements of other witnesses and still deal with any inconsistencies. Always assume that the opposing lawyer will ask the deponent what she did to prepare for the deposition and what materials she reviewed. Although your communications with your client are privileged, your communications with non-party deponents, and what you show your client and other deponents, are usually not.

Second, review what a deposition is, what its purpose is, why it is so critical, and what the procedure will be. Explain to the client that once the deposition begins, you will be relatively inactive, except to make objections to preserve error when necessary, or to instruct him not to answer if critical to do so.

Third, review the verbal and nonverbal considerations, particularly if the deposition will be videotaped. The nonverbal impression the client makes is as important as the words he says. He should be told to dress appropriately. For most witnesses this means a conservative suit or jacket and tie; if the witness usually wears a uniform, such as a police officer, he should wear the uniform if his testimony is based on his being a police officer. He should be told to maintain eye contact with the questioner, since looking down usually creates a negative impression. He should be instructed to sit comfortably in the chair, sit still, rest his hands comfortably and use them to gesture to emphasize his testimony when appropriate. Finally, he should be trained to use clear, simple, proper English and avoid speech forms that suggest hesitancy and uncertainty. Doing this will take time, but is necessary since preparing a witness for the nonverbal aspects of a deposition, particularly, if videotaped, is as important as his trial testimony.

Fourth, review how your client should answer questions accurately. Impress upon him that even though the atmosphere will probably be informal, he must answer carefully. Standard advice includes the following:

- Make sure you understand the question. If you don't, say so.
- If you know the answer, give it. If you don't know, say so. If you know but can't remember just then, say so. If you can only estimate or approximate, say so. However, give positive, assertive answers whenever possible.
- Don't volunteer information. Answer only what the question specifically calls for. Don't exaggerate or speculate. Give the best short, accurate, truthful answer possible.
- Answer questions only with what you personally know, saw, heard, or did, unless the question asks otherwise.
- Be calm and serious at all times. Avoid arguing with the lawyers or getting upset over the questions. I will be there to protect you from unfair questions and procedures by making objections and instructing you on what to do and say.

Fifth, discuss how objections will be handled. Explain that most objections are made "for the record," and that usually the witness must answer despite the objection, which is made for possible later use at trial. However, be sure the client knows not to answer when an objection is made and you tell the client not to answer. This will be the case if the objection is based on privilege or harassment grounds, where answering the question may waive any error.

Sixth, review with the client what questions the lawyers are likely to ask. This involves creating a short outline as discussed previously. Make sure that the client can accurately respond to those expected questions in a positive, convincing manner whenever possible. Let the client know that other lawyers present may ask additional questions, but that you will probably not ask questions unless necessary to correct a mistake or clarify something ambiguous.

Finally, explain that the client has a right to review the deposition if it is transcribed, noting any corrections and the reasons for them, and to sign it. Explain why that right to "read and sign" should not be waived, stressing the importance of correcting any errors in the transcript. Rule 30(e) requires the deponent to request a review of the transcript to record any changes, and the request must be made before the end of the deposition. The deponent has 30 days after being notified that the transcript is available for review to read, note corrections, and sign the transcript.

Lawyers use different methods to educate clients on what will happen during a deposition and on how important their depositions are. Many lawyers send the client a letter explaining the do's and don't's of depositions, which the client can then review before coming to your office for further preparation. Another common method is to send the client an audiotape or videotape containing the same advice and showing a deposition being taken. Some lawyers use commercially available videotapes; others make their own videotapes showing them representing a client at a deposition. Whatever approach is used, the client can and should be educated on her deposition before coming to your office for further preparation.

Above all, the client must understand that her deposition is a pivotal event in the litigation, one that will require time for preparation and practice. Many lawyers videotape the client's practice deposition, using another lawyer as the questioner, and play back the videotape for the client. This effectively demonstrates to the client the impression she is making during the deposition and sets the stage for further improvement.

l.   After the deposition

When the deposition is completed, there are four things that still need to be done. First, decide if you want to order a transcript of the deposition. The party taking the deposition usually orders it; usually the other parties will want a copy as well. How long it takes to get the transcript depends on the court reporter, but it sometimes can take weeks. However, there is no requirement that you order a transcript of every deposition in the case. Transcripts usually cost at least three dollars per page, and typically run 40 to 50 pages for each hour the witness is being deposed. If the deposition provided nothing useful, or you are on a tight litigation budget, don't order the transcript until you know the case is going to be tried.

Second, dictate a memo recording your impressions of the witness. Include a summary of the kind of witness she will make at trial and how she helps or hurts your case. This is important, since a transcript does not give a good picture of the impression the witness made. Furthermore, the lawyer taking the deposition may not be the same lawyer who will later try the case.

Third, prepare a deposition summary when you get the transcript. A deposition summary, frequently prepared by paralegals, records in summary form the witness' testimony and correlates it to the transcript pages. It can also show subject matter and be cross-referenced, which is particularly useful if the summaries will be put into a computer data base.

Example:

Ronald Smith	Case No. 98 C 1022
v.	File No. 98-153
James Woods	

<u>DEPOSITION SUMMARY OF MARIAN WELLS</u>
<u>JUNE 1, 1998</u>

Page/Line	Subject	Text	References
8: 7-22	Address	Wells lives at 231 Barton, Dallas, Texas with husband, 3 children	
9: 12-34	Job	Works at IBM as computer programmer in R & D Division	IBM
10: 6-18	School	Graduated from Southern Methodist University in 1980, B.S. degree, math major	

The deposition summaries make it much more convenient for lawyers to review the depositions of witnesses, evaluate the case for settlement purposes, and prepare for trial.

Fourth, if the deponent is your party, arrange to have the party review the transcript for errors, and note any errors on the correction page the court reporter will provide. After the party notes any corrections, she must sign the deposition and return it to the court reporter.

Local rules commonly provide that the deposition transcripts are not filed with the clerk of the court, since they are so bulky. If a motion requires the transcript, it can always be produced at that time.

§6.12. *Physical and mental examinations*

In some cases, primarily personal injury cases, the physical and mental condition of a party is a critical fact affecting both liability and damages. Under those circumstances, that party should be examined to evaluate the genuineness of the condition, its extent and causes, and to develop a prognosis. Rule 35 governs this process.

1. Law[52]

Rule 35 applies to physical and mental examinations of a party and of a "person in the custody or under the legal control of a party." The Rule

---

52. Wright §88; James & Hazard §5.6; Friedenthal §7.12; Moore's Manual §15.11; Manual of Federal Practice §§5.195-5.198; Moore's Federal Practice §§35.01-35.07; Wright & Miller §§2231-2239.

clearly applies to minors and other legally incapacitated persons who are not the actual named parties, but are the real parties in interest.

A court order is required for such examinations, unless the person to be examined voluntarily agrees to the examination, which is permitted under Rule 29 so long as there is a written stipulation. In other situations you must move for a court order and give notice to the person and all parties. For the court to order an examination, the physical or mental condition of a party or related person must be "in controversy," and you must show "good cause" for requesting it.

The good-cause requirement has sometimes caused difficulty. In most cases, however, typically personal injury cases or paternity cases where the physical condition of a party is important, there are few problems and the parties often informally arrange for the necessary examinations. In these types of cases the need for the examinations is apparent from the pleadings. However, issues such as testimonial competency will not be apparent from the pleadings; therefore, the moving party must make a sufficient showing of need in the motion to satisfy the good cause requirement.[53]

The court's order must specify the date, time, place, manner, conditions, and scope of the examination, as well as the person or persons who will perform it. The scope of the examination is determined by the nature of the claims, defenses, and facts and issues in controversy. Rule 35 provides only that the physical or mental examination be done by a "suitably licensed or certified examiner." In practice the moving party usually suggests a physician and the court ordinarily approves the selection unless another party, or the person to be examined, has a serious objection. The court has discretion to approve or disapprove, and some districts have local rules that provide for the selection of "impartial experts" from approved lists.[54]

The party moving for the examination must, upon request by the examined party, deliver to the examined party a detailed written report of the examining physician setting out findings, results of tests, diagnoses, and conclusions, as well as reports of all earlier examinations for the same conditions. The party moving for the examination can then, upon request, get any previous or future reports about the same person for the same condition, unless, where a nonparty is examined, the party shows he cannot obtain the report. This procedure essentially provides for reciprocal discovery when one side requests a report from the examining physician. When the party examined requests a copy of the report of the physician who examined him, this operates as a waiver of the doctor-patient privilege not only as to that physician, but also as to any other physician who has or may later examine him as to the same conditions.

These disclosure requirements and waiver effects apply regardless of whether the examinations are made pursuant to a court order or through agreement of the parties, unless that agreement expressly provides other-

53. Moore's Manual §15.11; Manual of Federal Practice §5.196; Moore's Federal Practice §35.03(5); Wright & Miller §§2232, 2234.
54. Note that FRE 706 also gives the court authority to appoint and compensate experts.

wise. In addition, the discovery permitted under Rule 35 does not restrict other permissible discovery. However, Rule 35 is the only rule that can compel discovery where otherwise the doctor-patient privilege would prevent disclosure.

2. Practice approach

Since the situations in which physical and mental examinations can be compelled are usually obvious, these examinations are frequently arranged informally between the parties. Even where there is an informal agreement, however, it is always a good idea to put it in a letter or, even better, in a stipulation under Rule 29 that is then filed with the court.

Where an arrangement cannot be worked out, you must move for a court order compelling the desired examination. To comply with Rule 35, the motion must (1) ask for the examination of a party or a person in the custody or control of the party, (2) allege a genuine controversy about that person's physical or mental condition, (3) demonstrate good cause for the examination, (4) request the date, time, place, manner, conditions, and scope of the examination, and (5) designate the examiner who should conduct it. In addition, the motion should reflect that the parties conferred and attempted to resolve their differences, but were unsuccessful, since Rules 26(c) and 37(a) require such a certification whenever discovery motions are brought.

Example:

[Caption]

MOTION FOR ORDER COMPELLING PLAINTIFF'S PHYSICAL EXAMINATION

Defendant moves under Rule 35 of the Federal Rules of Civil Procedure for an order compelling plaintiff to submit to a physical examination. In support of her motion defendant states:

1. Plaintiff's physical condition is genuinely in controversy, since plantiff's complaint on its face alleges that "as a result of this collision, plaintiff has suffered severe and permanent injuries to his back and legs."

2. Since plaintiff alleges that his physical limitations are compensable, there exists good cause for a physical examination to evaluate the plaintiff's current physical condition, physical limitations, and prognosis.

3. William B. Rudolf, M.D., a board certified orthopedic surgeon, has agreed to examine the plaintiff at his offices at 200 Main Street, Suite 301, Washington, D.C., on August 15, 1998, at 4:00 P.M., or at another time if directed by this court.

4. The parties have conferred but are unable to agree on a physician to conduct the appropriate examination.

WHEREFORE, defendant requests that this court enter an order directing the plaintiff to be examined on the terms set forth above.

_____
Attorney for Defendant

If the court grants the motion, an order must be entered. In federal courts the practice is for the court clerk to prepare orders, which the judge then signs. Where permitted, however, it is always a useful approach to draft an appropriate order in situations where a nonparty, here the physician, is involved because the physician will want a copy of the order before conducting the examination.

Example:

[Caption]

ORDER

This matter being heard on defendant's motion to compel the physical examination of plaintiff, all parties having been given notice, and the court having heard arguments, it is hereby ordered that:

1. Plaintiff John Williams be examined by William B. Rudolf, M.D., at 200 Main Street, Suite 301, Washington, D.C., on August 15, 1998, at 4:00 P.M., unless the plaintiff and Dr. Rudolf mutually agree to an earlier date and time.

2. Plaintiff shall submit to such orthopedic examinations and tests as are necessary to diagnose and evaluate the plaintiff's back and legs, so that Dr. Rudolf may reach opinions and conclusions about the extent of any injuries, their origin, and prognosis.

3. Dr. Rudolf shall prepare a written report detailing his findings, test results, diagnosis and opinions, along with any earlier similar reports on the same conditions, and deliver it to defendant's attorneys on or before September 15, 1998.

Entered:

Dated: _____   _____
United States District Judge

Finally, keep in mind the reciprocal discovery provisions of Rule 35(b)(1). If the examined party requests a copy of the examiner's report, the party moving for the examination has the right to receive from the examined party other reports dealing with the same conditions, regardless of when made; however, you must request those reports. Perhaps the safer approach is to send that party a document entitled "REQUEST FOR MEDICAL REPORTS," show that it is made under the provisions of Rule 35(b)(1), and file the request with the court. If the other party fails to deliver, or later attempts to use such reports, you have made a record of your request and can object to the introduction of those reports at trial because the party did not comply with Rule 35.

§6.13. Requests to admit facts

Requests to admit facts and genuineness of documents are not designed to "discover." Up to now the parties have been acquiring information, through informal and formal discovery, and the information acquisition phase of the litigation process is essentially complete. The next step is to sift through all this acquired information and begin planning what you will introduce at trial and how you will do it. A request to admit (along with the pretrial statement and motions in limine) is a basic tool that you can use to streamline your proof at trial.

1. Law[55]

Requests to admit facts and the genuineness of documents, governed by Rule 36, apply only to parties. Admissions made in response to the requests are conclusive admissions for the purposes of the pending action only and cannot be used for any other purposes. This encourages a party to admit facts without worrying about collateral consequences.

Requests may be served on other parties at any time after the parties meet to develop a discovery plan under Rule 26(f). Like other discovery provisions, requests can be employed essentially at any time during the litigation process.

A request can be directed to three categories: the truth of facts, the genuineness of documents, and the "application of law to fact." The general scope of these requests is the same as for discovery in general; they apply to anything that is relevant but not privileged. Each request must be separately stated.

After a request has been served on a party, that party must serve a response within 30 days or the matters requested will be deemed admitted, unless the court permits or a written agreement between the parties provides for a shorter or longer time. This automatic provision of Rule 36 makes it a formidable weapon because inertia or inattentiveness can have an automatic, and usually devastating, consequence. Hence, there is one

55. Wright §89; James & Hazard §5.7; Friedenthal §7.10; Moore's Manual §15.12; Manual of Federal Practice §§5.199-5.215; Moore's Federal Practice §§36.01-36.08; Wright & Miller §§2251-2265.

cardinal rule for practice under this provision: Make sure you respond and serve the response within the 30-day period.

There are four basic responses permitted. First, you can object to a matter in the request. Second, you can admit the matter. Third, you can deny the matter. Fourth, you can neither admit nor deny because the matter is genuinely in dispute, or because after reasonable inquiry you do not have sufficient information to determine if the matter is true or not.

How you respond, and whether your response is justified under the circumstances, determines whether Rule 37 sanctions can be imposed. Rule 37(c) provides that the expenses—including attorney's fees—incurred in proving a denied matter can be taxed as costs against the losing party. However, if you neither admit nor deny on the basis of there being a genuine issue for trial, or because of genuine insufficient knowledge, Rule 37 sanctions cannot be imposed.[56]

Once a response has been received, you can move the court to review the adequacy of the objections and responses. The Rule requires that a response must specifically deny the matter or set forth in detail why the answering party cannot admit or deny after making a reasonable inquiry. A denial must fairly meet the substance of the requested admission. The better practice is to make a motion under Rule 36(a) to determine the sufficiency of an answer and see if the court will deem the matter admitted. This will avoid surprises at trial. The court can enter an order compelling an answer or amended answer if appropriate, order that the matter be deemed admitted, or continue the motion to the pretrial conference or to another date.

2. Practice approach

Because the scope of Rule 36 is broad, using and responding to requests to admit are principally strategic concerns that must be coordinated with your overall trial strategy. Note the emphasis on trial strategy, not on discovery. Requests to admit do not "discover" additional information; they are used to sharpen trial issues, streamline the presentation of evidence, and eliminate the need to formally prove uncontroverted facts. Hence, the question is not what you can get the other side to admit; the better question is: What do you want the other side to admit that ties in to your overall trial strategy?

a. Timing

Rule 36 permits requests to admit at any time after the parties meet to plan discovery, so the decision on when to use it is controlled by practical considerations. However, the requests are most frequently used at the end of the discovery stage. When you have received initial disclosures, interrogatory answers, and records pursuant to document requests, have de-

56. See Wright §90; Moore's Manual §15.13; Manual of Federal Practice §5.229; Moore's Federal Practice §§36.03(7), 36.07; Wright & Miller §§2265, 2288, 2290.

posed the parties and necessary witnesses, and, where appropriate, have completed physical and mental examinations, discovery is essentially complete. Requests to admit are most commonly served at this point because the existing discovery will identify what still remains in issue. The requests should be served after other discovery has been completed but before the pretrial conference is scheduled or summary judgment motions are made. Requests to admit served at that time will help determine what facts the other side will concede, or contest if the case goes to trial.

Another approach is to serve requests to admit early in the discovery process, sometimes coupled with interrogatories and documents requests, to bring the potential Rule 37 sanctions into play. This forces your opponent to decide what facts and issues she intends to dispute and allows later discovery to become more focused. If a party denies a fact in a request to admit, without a substantial basis for the denial, and that fact is later proved at trial, the party proving the fact can receive as court costs the reasonable expense of proving the denied fact at trial, including attorney's fees. By making requests to admit early, you start the period for which you may be entitled to get Rule 37 costs. Where you think the opposing party will use dilatory tactics or avoid serious settlement discussions on a case that should be settled quickly, making a request to admit early raises the risks for the party using those tactics. This can be effective in forcing your opponent to admit facts.

b. What to request

To determine what to request, look first at the elements of your claims. Second, analyze each "fact" you will need to prove to meet your burden of proof at trial on each element. This is what every trial lawyer must do in preparing for trial. Third, review the pleadings, to see what has been admitted, and your discovery results, to see what facts are conceded. Reviewing the discovery is particularly critical, since a fact, when conceded in interrogatory answers or in a party deposition, is only an admission by a party opponent, which is *not* the same thing as a conclusive admission. The party admitting a fact can still present contrary evidence at trial. To avoid this, focus on matters opposing parties have admitted in previous discovery. Those parties are likely to admit the facts in a request to admit if they have previously admitted them. The advantage is that when a matter is admitted under Rule 36, it is deemed conclusively established for purposes of that pending action, which bars that party from introducing contrary evidence at trial, unless the court permits amendment or withdrawal.

Fourth, think through your trial strategy. What witnesses and exhibits do you need to prove your case at trial? Where are your strengths and weaknesses? Is some of your evidence technical and likely to bore the jury? Is some of it costly to present? Is some of your testimony dramatic or emotional? Do some of your exhibits have significant visual impact? In short, don't ask the other side to admit something just because it's there; ask the other side to admit it because it improves your case at trial. This means that you will *not* ask the other side to admit your most compelling, emotional, or dramatic evidence; that's exactly what you want the jury to hear and see. On the other hand, if the evidence is technical, boring but necessary, excessively expensive to present, or comes from a weak witness, that's the evidence you want admitted through requests to admit.

c. Drafting the requests

The cardinal rule for drafting requests to admit is to keep it simple and clear. A lengthy, complicated request practically begs to be denied, objected to, or responded to with a lengthy, equivocal response. This will merely generate further motions and probably achieve nothing.

Simplicity requires that a request be short and contain a single statement of fact. Such requests are difficult to quibble with, and they stand the best chance of being admitted outright. They should also comply with admissibility rules such as those concerning relevance, hearsay, and authentication.

Organize your requests into the three permitted categories:

1. truth of facts
2. genuineness of documents
3. opinions of fact and application of law to facts

When drafting requests to admit facts, ask that the facts be admitted as true.

Example (facts):

[Caption]

REQUESTS TO ADMIT FACTS AND GENUINENESS OF DOCUMENTS

Plaintiff Ralph Johnson requests defendant Marion Smith to make the following admissions, within 30 days after service of this request, for the purposes of this action only:
    Admit that each of the following facts is true:
    1. On May 1, 1998, plaintiff had a valid driver's license issued by the state of Colorado.
    2. On May 1, 1998, defendant was the owner of a Chevrolet sedan having a Colorado license no. BCD-437.

When drafting requests to admit the genuineness of documents, the usual request is to ask that attached documents are "genuine." Genuine means that the document is what it purports to be, that is, it was made by the person or entity it appears to be made by and, if signed, was signed by the person it appears to be signed by. Keep in mind, however, that a party admitting the genuineness of a document admits that and no more. That party may still raise other evidentiary objections, such as relevance or hearsay, to the document's admissibility at trial.

Example (genuineness of documents):

>   Admit that each of the following documents is genuine:
>   3. The contract, attached as Exhibit A.
>   4. The check, attached as Exhibit B.

You can do much better than merely asking that a document be admitted as genuine, however. Always think about the evidentiary foundation necessary to get a particular document or record admitted at trial, then get the opposing party to admit the foundation requirements.

Example (foundation for documents):

>   Admit that the following facts are true:
>   5. The contract, attached as Exhibit A, bears the signature of the defendant.
>   6. The defendant signed the original of Exhibit A on May 1, 1998.
>   7. The contract, attached as Exhibit A, is an accurate copy of the original contract signed by the defendant.
>   8. A bill of lading, attached as Exhibit B, is a business record of the XYZ Corporation under FRE 803(b).
>   9. The bill of lading, attached as Exhibit B, is an accurate copy (other than a possible change in size) of the original made by XYZ Corporation.

Keep in mind that a fact can be contained in a document, so you may want the other party to admit the fact, admit the genuineness of the document containing the fact, or both. Juries usually respond favorably to exhibits, so it's a sound idea to get the document before the jury at trial.

Requests to admit can also ask for "opinions of fact" and the "application of law to fact." This is a problematic area since questions of "pure law" cannot be asked. For instance, a request that asks a party to admit negligence or culpability is objectionable, and that will be a genuine issue at trial. Where the line is between "opinions of fact" and "application of law to fact," as against "pure law" remains unclear.[57] Regardless of where that line is, treading close to it will probably draw objections. Accordingly, it is usually better to be on the safe side and leave the legal disputes for resolution at trial. Common situations where the application of law to fact is raised are issues of title, ownership, agency, and employment.

Example (application of law to fact):

>   Admit that each of the following statements is true:
>   10. Defendant was the legal titleholder of a lot commonly known as 3401 Fifth Street, Tucson, Arizona, on August 1, 1998.

---

57. See Wright §89; Moore's Manual §15.12; Moore's Federal Practice §36.04(4); Wright & Miller §§2255, 2256.

11. On August 1, 1998, William Oats was an employee of XYZ Corporation.

12. On August 1, 1998, William Oats was authorized to enter into sales contracts on behalf of XYZ Corporation.

Consider coupling requests to admit with interrogatories asking for the facts on which any response that does not admit a request is based. When the opposing party is faced with an interrogatory asking why a request to admit was not admitted, it makes it more difficult to deny the request in the first place. If the request is not admitted and the follow-up interrogatory is answered, you may have a better understanding of how the opposing side will attempt to deal with this issue at trial.

What are the common problems that arise when drafting requests to admit? Remember that the point of using requests to admit is to streamline the presentation of your case at trial by eliminating the need to present boring but necessary or expensive witnesses. The most common problem, therefore, is that requests to admit are not coordinated with your trial strategy. Always ask: What are the interesting and exciting parts of my case that I want the jury to hear? What parts of my case have no jury appeal and consist of boring or technical proof, which I would prefer to prove through a request to admit? In addition, your overall strategy may include making a summary judgment motion. The requests to admit should be considered in light of what you need to prove to win the motion.

Another common problem is that the requests to admit contain characterizations that the other party will be loath to admit. For example, asking "Admit that there was no reason to believe that ABC Corporation would not deliver the goods by June 1, 1998," or "Admit that defendant harbored doubts about its denying the claim for benefits" will usually generate either a denial or a claim that this is a legitimate trial issue. Avoid characterizations—"quibble words"—in the requests. Simple requests, based on nouns and verbs, and avoiding adjectives and adverbs, are more likely to be admitted.

Another common problem is requesting that a fact be admitted, rather than asking that the foundation for the admissibility of a record or document containing the fact be admitted. Remember that visual exhibits have persuasive power. Jurors would much rather look at a key record or document, blown up as a courtroom exhibit, than listen to the judge instruct them that a certain fact will be deemed conclusively admitted.

Finally, keep in mind that requests to admit are designed to streamline the trial. Keep in mind that the request and response will be read to the jury during trial and that the judge will probably give a specific jury instruction based on the request and response. Always consider how the request will sound to the jurors. When using requests to provide the basis for admissibility of an exhibit at trial, always review what technical evidentiary foundation is necessary to get that particular exhibit admitted in evidence, and draft the request to admit accordingly.

The requests to admit should be signed by the lawyer and served on each party. Service is made by any permitted method under Rule 5, most commonly by mailing a copy to the lawyers of the other parties. The original requests to admit, with an attached proof of service, are then filed with the clerk of the court, unless a local rule directs that discovery is not filed until a need arises.

d. Choosing a response

A party on whom requests to admit have been served must respond, usually within 30 days of receiving the requests, or else the matters in the requests will automatically be deemed conclusively admitted. There are four basic responses to a request.

First, you can object to the request. As with discovery generally, you can object that the matter requested is irrelevant or privileged. In addition, you can seek a protective order if the request is unduly burdensome or harassing.

Second, you can admit the request. When you do so, you conclusively admit the matter for the purpose of the pending action only. Such an admission prevents you from presenting contrary evidence at trial.

Third, you can deny the request. The denial must be based on good faith. If the requesting party later proves the denied matter at trial, under Rule 37 that party may get reasonable expenses, including attorney's fees, involved in proving the matter. The response can, of course, admit some parts of a request and deny others.

Fourth, under certain circumstances you can "set forth in detail the reasons why the answering party cannot truthfully admit or deny the matter." This is allowed if the answering party has made a "reasonable inquiry" in an effort to acquire necessary information for responding to the request but is still unable to respond. In addition, if the answering party considers the requested matter to be a genuine trial issue, it can either deny or set forth reasons for neither admitting nor denying. In practice, lawyers deny such requests after detailing the reasons why the matter cannot be admitted or denied.

When you have decided what the appropriate response should be, actually drafting the response is very similar to drafting answers to complaints. However, the better format is that used for interrogatory answers, where the answers and interrogatories both appear together.

Example:

[Caption]

RESPONSE TO REQUESTS FOR ADMISSIONS

Defendant Marian Smith responds to plaintiff Ralph Johnson's requests for admissions as follows:

Request No. 1: A contract, attached as Exhibit A, is a true and accurate copy of the contract signed by plaintiff on August 1, 1998.

Answer: Admit.

Request No. 2: Plaintiff performed all his obligations under the contract.

Answer: Deny.

Request No. 3: On August 1, 1998, William Oats was authorized to enter into sales contracts on behalf of XYZ Corporation.

Answer: Objection. Responding to this request would disclose the substance of conversations between William Oats, an attorney, and the XYZ Corporation, which are protected from disclosure by the attorney-client privilege.

Request No. 4: Mary Doyle is the sole titleholder of a lot commonly known as 3401 Fifth Street, Seattle, Washington.

Answer: Defendant cannot truthfully admit or deny this request and therefore denies it. Public records neither confirm nor deny, and defendant has no access to any documents that could confirm or deny it.

The response to requests to admit should be signed by the party's lawyer and served on each party. Service is made by any permitted method under Rule 5, most commonly by mailing a copy to the lawyers for the other parties. The original response, with an attached proof of service, is then filed with the clerk of the court, unless a local rule directs that discovery is not filed until a need arises.

e.   Requestor's responses

When a party has made and served responses to requests to admit on the requesting party, the requesting party can do two things: move to review the sufficiency of an answer, and move to review the propriety of an objection. Both of these are directed to the court's discretion. The court can enter any appropriate order, such as deeming a matter admitted, requiring an amended answer, or continuing the issue to the pretrial conference or other time.

When the answering party denies a request to admit facts, a good approach is to send the answering party interrogatories that ask for the basis of the denial. Another approach is to send "contention interrogatories" along with the requests to admit, again asking for the basis of each denial of a request. This frequently causes the answering party to admit the request, rather than attempt to justify the denial in the accompanying interrogatory answer.

§6.14.   Discovery motions

Discovery under the federal rules is largely executed without judicial intervention. Except for physical and mental examinations, discovery before the parties have met to develop a discovery plan, discovery which would exceed the numerical limits on interrogatories and depositions, and discovery which would violate a court order regulating discovery entered under Rule 16, the parties can conduct discovery without prior judicial approval. Only when there is a dispute over discovery need the courts become involved.

Three points should be remembered. First, Rule 37(a) now requires the moving party's lawyer to certify what good faith efforts have been made to confer with the other party to resolve a discovery dispute informally before the courts will intervene. An appropriate certification must be signed by the lawyer and attached to the motion. The certification can also be made part of the motion, and this is the more common approach. Second, discovery abuse has probably been the subject of more controversy and proposals than any other aspect of the litigation process. Courts have responded to the problem by becoming more involved in discovery, particularly by having discovery plan conferences and by dealing more actively with abuses and imposing stiffer sanctions. Third, amendments to Rule 26 give courts additional powers to regulate discovery. Rule 26(b)(2) gives courts the power to limit discovery where it is unnecessarily cumulative or duplicative, or is obtainable from other sources with less effort and expense. Rule 16 gives courts power to hold discovery conferences and impose a discovery plan. Rule 26(g) parallels the Rule 11 requirements that the lawyer's signature is a certification that he has read the discovery document; has made a reasonable inquiry; and that the document is consistent with the rules and law, is not made for any improper purpose, and is not unreasonably burdensome or expensive. In today's climate, abusing discovery by filing frivolous, needless, or unduly burdensome discovery requests, responses, or motions can result in severe sanctions.

There are two principal types of discovery motions, those for protective orders and those for orders compelling discovery.

1.   Protective orders[58]

Rule 26(c) and, in the case of oral depositions, Rule 30(d) govern protective orders. Whenever an entity or person from whom discovery is sought feels that it is being subjected to annoying, embarrassing, oppressive, unduly burdensome, or unduly expensive discovery demands, the appropriate procedure is to move for a protective order. Both parties and nonparty deponents can seek protective orders.

The motion must usually be brought in the district where the action is pending. However, where a deposition has been terminated so that a protective order can be obtained, the proper jurisdiction under Rule 30(d) is either the district where the action is pending or the

58. Wright §83; James & Hazard §5.13; Friedenthal §7.15; Moore's Manual §15.02(1)(d); Manual of Federal Practice §§5.94-5.105; Moore's Federal Practice §§26.67-26.79; Wright & Miller §§2035-2044.

district where the deposition is being taken. The latter may well be proper where a nonparty deponent is seeking the protective order, since the deposition is often taken where the deponent resides or does business.

Under Rule 26(c), the moving party must show "good cause." While grounds for protection are obviously numerous, the most common grounds are that the discovery requested is so lengthy and detailed that it is unduly oppressive and expensive; for example, discovery involving lengthy or repetitive interrogatories and depositions, and overly detailed documents requests and requests to admit. Another common ground is the serving of notice for depositions on high corporate officers who have no firsthand knowledge of any relevant facts. If the dominant purpose of the discovery is not to develop information reasonably necessary to prepare for trial or settlement, but to harass the corporate officer or force the opposition into submission, Rule 26(b)(2) is violated and the protective order is appropriate. Other motions frequently seek to limit disclosure, such as restricting persons present at depositions and preventing the disclosure of business secrets to persons outside the litigation, to limit the discovery methods which may be used, and to seal depositions and other discovery and require that they be unsealed only by court order.

Rule 26(c) also requires that the motion be accompanied by a certification from the moving party's lawyer that he has made a good faith attempt to confer with the opposing party and resolve the dispute without court action.

Keep in mind that many discovery matters come up by motions to compel after a party has objected to discovery requests. Objections are permitted in answers to interrogatories, document requests, and requests to admit. In these circumstances the objection protects the responding party. The requesting party must move for an order compelling discovery, and there is no need for the responding party to move for a protective order.

However, if you plan to move for a protective order, make the motion early. Do not wait until the other side moves to compel discovery. The judge will wonder how serious your motion for a protective order is if it follows on the heels of your opponent's motion to compel discovery. Hence, the better practice is to object to the discovery request and immediately file your motion for a protective order.

If a protective order is appropriate, Rule 26(c) provides a variety of remedies that can protect a party or person from embarrassment, oppression, and undue burden or expense. These include barring the requested discovery; regulating the terms, conditions, methods and scope of discovery; limiting persons present at the discovery; requiring the sealing of depositions and documents; and regulating or barring disclosure of trade secrets and confidential information.

The motion for a protective order must be prepared like any other motion, and must include statements of the facts as well as a request for the relief sought.

Example:

[Caption]

MOTION FOR PROTECTIVE ORDER

Plaintiff Willard Johnson requests that this court enter a protective order pursuant to Rule 26(c) against defendant Clark Johnson, and in support of his motion states:

1. On August 8, 1997, defendant took plaintiff's first deposition. This deposition took approximately four hours and generated a transcript of 238 pages. The transcript has been filed with the clerk of this court.

2. On April 15, 1998, defendant again took plaintiff's deposition. This deposition took approximately three hours and generated a transcript of 181 pages. This transcript has also been filed with the clerk of this court.

3. On July 2, 1998, plaintiff was served with a third notice of plaintiff's deposition.

4. This pending action involves a simple intersection collision. The two previous depositions have exhaustively covered what plaintiff knows about the collision, what happened afterwards, his medical treatment, and all claimed damages.

5. The notice for a third deposition, under these circumstances, constitutes an attempt to annoy, oppress, and place undue burdens on the plaintiff, and has no proper purpose. Since plaintiff lives out of state, another deposition will again impose significant financial and time expenses.

WHEREFORE, plaintiff Willard Johnson requests that this court enter a protective order barring defendant Clark Johnson from taking further depositions of the plaintiff or, in the alternative, restricting this deposition to such matters as counsel can demonstrate are relevant and were not inquired into at the previous depositions.

_____

Attorney for Plaintiff

Each discovery motion must be accompanied with a certificate of compliance, either a separate document or contained within the motion. If a separate document, it should look like the following:

CERTIFICATE OF COMPLIANCE WITH RULE 26

I, Allen Smith, attorney of record for Plaintiff Willard Johnson, certify that I have complied with the requirements of Rule 26(c) by doing the following:

1. On July 3, 1998, I sent a letter to defendant's counsel asking why a third deposition of the plaintiff was necessary. I received no written or oral reply to my letter.

2. On July 10, I called defendant's counsel and personally spoke with him. He stated that he noticed the plaintiff's deposition a third time to "make sure he'd covered all the bases," and gave no other reason for wanting a third deposition.

3. I requested that defendant's counsel withdraw the notice for the plaintiff's deposition, but he refused. Consequently the bringing of this motion for a protective order is necessary.

Dated: _____   _____
                                                   Attorney for Plaintiff

Example:

[Caption]

MOTION FOR PROTECTIVE ORDER

Plaintiff Nancy Jones moves, pursuant to Rule 26(c), for a protective order against defendant XYZ Corporation, and in support of the motion states:

1. The pending case is a product liability case involving a rubber hose manufactured by defendant XYZ.

2. Plaintiff has previously served a motion to produce the rubber hose involved for the purposes of inspection and testing. Defendant's response stated that the rubber hose has already been shipped to ABC Laboratories for testing.

3. There is a substantial danger that any testing by ABC Laboratories will alter or destroy the rubber hose and forever prevent plaintiff from inspecting and testing it.

4. In compliance with Rule 26(c), I hereby certify that I telephonically conferred with the attorney for defendant XYZ Corporation. The attorney refused to delay the testing by ABC Laboratories, and specifically stated that the testing would go forward unless this court granted a protective order. Consequently, this motion for a protective order has become necessary.

WHEREFORE, plaintiff requests this court to enter a protective order against defendant as follows:

(a) prevent anything from being done with or to the rubber hose until plaintiff has had a reasonable opportunity to inspect and photograph it;

(b) prevent any tests that would destroy or affect the appearance and integrity of the rubber hose;

(c) if destructive testing is necessary, order that such testing be conducted at a time and place so that plaintiff's experts can be present, observe the testing procedure, and obtain a copy of all test results;

(d) award payment of reasonable expenses, including attorney's fees, to plaintiff incurred as a result of making this motion.

_____

Attorney for Plaintiff

A common practice is to prepare a proposed order and attach it to the motion. The proposed order should parallel the motion by setting out what information needs to be protected and how it will be protected.

After the motion is prepared and signed, a copy along with a notice of motion must be served on every other party under Rule 5. The original of the motion and notice of motion, with a proof of service, must be filed with the clerk of the court. Keep in mind that many federal district judges delegate discovery matters to magistrate judges, so make sure your notice of motion correctly specifies who will hear the motion.

2.   Compelling discovery[59]

Rule 37(a) governs motions for orders compelling disclosure or discovery. A party seeking to compel discovery must move for an appropriate order in the district where the action is pending, except if the matters relate to discovery from a nonparty, in which case the motion must be brought in the district where the discovery is being taken.

The attorney for the moving party must attach a certification to the motion showing what good faith attempts to confer and resolve the dispute were made before filing the motion.

A party can move for an order compelling discovery whenever a party fails to answer or gives evasive or incomplete answers to proper discovery. Frequently the issue arises when a party responds by objecting to an interrogatory, request to produce, or request to admit. A motion to compel must then be made to determine whether the objection is proper. The issue also frequently arises when a party fails to answer interrogatories, produce documents after being served with a request to produce, refuses to designate a deponent on behalf of a corporate party, or, in the case of deponents, refuses to appear, be sworn, or answer questions. It also arises when a Rule 26(a) disclosure is claimed to be inadequate or not in compliance with the rule.

Under Rule 37(a)(4), the court has authority to award reasonable expenses, including attorney's fees, to the prevailing party, when a motion to compel is granted and also when the discovery sought is provided after the motion has been filed. Even if your motion is granted, the court may deny a request for fees and costs if it determines that no good faith effort to resolve the dispute was made prior to seeking court intervention.

59. Wright §90; James & Hazard §5.13; Friedenthal §7.16; Moore's Manual §15.13; Manual of Federal Practice §§5.216-5.235; Moore's Federal Practice §37.02; Wright & Miller §§2281-2293.

Rule 37(c)(1) provides a self-executing sanction for failure to make the Rule 26(a) required disclosures. Unless you have substantial justification for failing to make the required disclosures, you will not be permitted to use at trial, at a hearing or in a motion, any witness or information that you did not disclose unless the failure to disclose was harmless. In addition to or in lieu of the preclusion sanction, the court may order other appropriate sanctions, including expenses or attorney's fees, and even informing the jury of the failure to make disclosure.

The most common motions to compel usually involve either a party's failure to respond to discovery at all, or responding with evasive or incomplete answers that do not fairly meet the substance of the request.

Example:

[Caption]

MOTION TO COMPEL DISCOVERY

Defendant Alfred Jenkens moves that this court enter an order compelling plaintiff Thomas Smith to answer interrogatories, and in support of his motion states:

1. On June 5, 1998, defendant served his first set of interrogatories on plaintiff.

2. On July 15, 1998, defendant by letter reminded plaintiff's lawyer that answers to interrogatories were overdue and had not yet been received. A copy of this letter is attached as Exhibit A. No response to this letter has been received.

3. Over 100 days have passed since defendant served interrogatories on plaintiff and to date no answers have been received.

4. Defendant's counsel has called plaintiff's counsel three times since July 15, 1998, each time reminding him that the answers had not been received, and, during the last call, told counsel that a motion to compel would be filed unless answers were received immediately. That last call was made one week ago.

WHEREFORE, defendant requests the court to order plaintiff to serve interrogatory answers within five days and award reasonable expenses, including attorney's fees, to defendant incurred as a result of making this motion.

_____

Attorney for Defendant

After the motion is prepared and signed, a copy along with a notice of motion must be served on every other party under Rule 5. The originals of the motion and notice of motion, with a proof of service, must be filed with the clerk of the court. Keep in mind that many district judges delegate discovery matters to magistrate judges, so make sure your notice of motion correctly specifies who will hear the motion.

A good practice is to ask the court to set out in its order compelling discovery what the sanctions will be if the order is not obeyed. This makes it more likely that the opposing party will comply with the order.

3. Sanctions for abuse[60]

Rule 37 provides for the enforcement of discovery orders by permitting a wide range of sanctions for discovery abuse. Sanctions can also be imposed under the broader authority of 28 U.S.C. §1927. In recent years courts have been much more active in imposing sanctions, a trend that has received support from the Supreme Court.[61]

Sanctions for discovery abuse are contained in Rule 37, and are of three basic types. The severity of the sanction should obviously be commensurate with the seriousness and impact of the abuse.[62]

First, under Rule 37(a)(4), sanctions "shall" be imposed, after a hearing, against the losing party or that party's lawyer, unless the moving party failed to make a good faith effort to resolve the dispute informally before bringing the motion, or other circumstances exist that would make the imposition of sanctions unjust. Sanctions against the losing party or lawyer can include the reasonable expenses incurred by the winning party in making or opposing the motion, including reasonable attorney's fees. If the discovery motion is denied, the court can also enter any appropriate protective order.

Second, under Rule 37(b), sanctions for discovery abuse can be imposed where a deponent or party fails to obey a previous court order regarding discovery. In this situation, the court can enter essentially any sanction appropriate to the level of misconduct involved. Such sanctions can include ordering that certain facts be deemed admitted, barring a party from presenting evidence, striking pleadings, dismissing all or part of the action, entering a default judgment, and treating a refusal to obey as a contempt of court.[63] Sanctions can also include awarding reasonable expenses, including attorney's fees, if appropriate under the circumstances.

Third, under Rule 37(c) the sanction for failure to make disclosures required under Rules 26(a) or 26(e)(1) without substantial justification will be that the party failing to disclose as required is barred from using the withheld witness or information at a trial or hearing, "unless such fail-

---

60. Wright §90; James & Hazard §5.14; Friedenthal §7.16; Moore's Manual §15.13; Manual of Federal Practice §§5.216-5.235; Moore's Federal Practice §§37.03-37.09; Wright & Miller §§2281-2293.

61. Roadway Express, Inc. v. Piper, 447 U.S. 752 (1980); National Hockey League v. Metropolitan Hockey Club, Inc., 427 U.S. 639 (1976); Societe Internationale v. Rogers, 357 U.S. 197 (1958).

62. Societe Internationale v. Rogers, 357 U.S. 197 (1958).

63. National Hockey League v. Metropolitan Hockey Club, Inc., 427 U.S. 639 (1976).

ure is harmless." The court can also impose other appropriate sanctions, including reasonable expenses and attorney's fees.

Motions to compel directed to parties must be filed in the district in which the action is pending. Motions directed to nonparties must be filed in the district in which discovery is sought to be conducted.

Rule 37(c) also permits the award of reasonable expenses, including attorney's fees, incurred as a result of proving matters that were denied in a Rule 36 request to admit, unless there was a good reason for the failure to admit. A party denying a proper Rule 36 request does so at the risk of being responsible for the expenses later incurred to prove it. Reasonable expenses would include the attorney's time and witness expenses, such as travel and lodging, that are necessary to prepare and prove the denied fact at trial.

Finally, Rule 26(g) gives the court power to impose sanctions against the lawyer or party who signs, without substantial justification, a Rule 26(a) disclosure that violates the requirements of that rule. The sanctions can be imposed after motion of a party or on the court's own initiative, and include any appropriate sanction, including reasonable expenses and attorney's fees.

With the sanctions permitted by Rules 26 and 37, it should be obvious that the court has the power and discretion to impose such sanctions as will be an effective response to discovery abuse. The difficult decisions, however, involve those situations where the discovery abuse was not caused by the party itself, but by the party's lawyer. Under these circumstances, it may be unjust that a party who may have a meritorious claim or defense should suffer adverse consequences due to abuse by his lawyer. For that reason, Rule 37(b) also allows, as an alternative or additional sanction, the imposition of reasonable expenses, including attorney's fees, against the abusing party or his lawyer, or both, unless there was a substantial justification for the noncompliance. This permits the court to fine the lawyer directly if the lawyer was the principal cause of the failure to comply.

Conversely, a lawyer must protect himself from the possible imposition of sanctions when the client is the reason for a failure to comply with a discovery order. The common problem involves a client who fails to provide documents or information necessary to respond to discovery, or a client who fails repeatedly to submit to a deposition. When this occurs, the lawyer must make it clear to the judge and the other lawyers that his client is the cause of the problem. This can be done orally in conversations with the other lawyers, and perhaps through letters to them explaining what steps you have taken to try to comply with their discovery. If you do this, the other lawyers will probably ask for discovery abuse sanctions only against your client. If the other lawyers ask for sanctions directly against you, you must, both in a written response to the motion and at the hearing on the motion, detail the efforts you personally have made to comply with the discovery. Of course, if the client continues to refuse to cooperate with the lawyer, the lawyer may need to withdraw from the representation.

§6.15. *Discovery review*

Under Rule 16, judges may enter scheduling orders for, among other matters, the completion of discovery. Since most judges now actively participate in case management, they commonly set a discovery cut-off date at the scheduling conference. A cut-off date means that all formal discovery must be completed by that date. (Keep in mind that a request to admit facts is not usually considered discovery for this purpose.)

About three months before the cut-off date is a good time to review the status of discovery. Among the things you should consider are the following:

1. Required disclosures (Rule 26)
   a. Initial disclosures, expert disclosures, and pretrial disclosures received?
   b. Supplemental disclosures necessary?
   c. Motions pending?
2. Interrogatories (Rule 33)
   a. Answers to all interrogatories received?
   b. Supplemental answers necessary?
   c. Experts and opinions disclosed?
   d. Motions pending?
3. Documents requests (Rule 34)
   a. Responses to requests received?
   b. Documents actually delivered?
   c. Supplemental responses necessary?
   d. Expert reports received?
   e. Motions pending?
4. Mental and physical examinations (Rule 35)
   a. Plaintiff's examination done?
   b. Medical report requested and received?
5. Depositions (Rule 30)
   a. All necessary witnesses deposed?
   b. Experts deposed?
   c. Ordered transcripts received?

Discovery in large part is making sure you get what you need and what you are entitled to. As the months pass, many loose ends appear. You never received all the documents you were promised. You have yet to depose one of the experts. The other side never supplemented its interrogatory answers. A motion has never been ruled on. These kinds of loose ends tend to get lost in the shuffle as more immediate matters capture your attention.

Hence, about three months before the discovery cut-off date is a good time to review the status of discovery. Mark this date on your litigation calendar and docket control system. Why three months? It takes time to tie up the loose ends. You need to remind your adversary, first by letter and then by follow-up calls, that you have not gotten all your discovery. If resolving discovery disputes informally fails, you need to move to compel answers.

Taking these steps early makes good sense. The last thing a judge wants to hear on the eve of the discovery cut-off date is a motion to extend the time to complete discovery. The judge will naturally want to know what you have been doing in the preceding months. If your discovery activity has been low, or nonexistent, don't expect the judge to help you now.

VII

MOTIONS

§7.1. Introduction

"Motion practice" is a significant part of the litigation process. Motions are used to regulate the routine "housekeeping" matters in litigation, such as the rescheduling of discovery, hearings, and other deadlines. Motions are also used to reach dispositive results, such as motions to dismiss or motions for summary judgment. Every litigated matter will involve motions, so knowing when and how to present appropriate, well-drafted motions is an essential skill for every litigator.

A motion is simply an application to a court for an order. Presenting an effective motion, however, involves both technical requirements, such as format and service rules, and substantive requirements, which control how the body of a motion should be organized and constructed so that the motion will be persuasive to the judge. This chapter discusses both routine housekeeping and dispositive motions. However, pleadings motions, principally governed by Rule 12, are discussed in §5.4; discovery motions, principally governed by Rule 37, are discussed in §6.9.

§7.2. General requirements for motions

Rules 5 through 11 govern how motions are made. However, local rules must always be checked because they often detail matters such as filing requirements, page size, page limitations, format, organization, supporting memoranda and exhibits, and special service times. While motions may present numerous matters and seek a wide variety of relief, their basic requirements are generally the same.

[handwritten annotations: "3 Parts"; "① Authority (Summ judge pursuant to R 56) General motions rule. But there are infinite motions that may not be in a rule - why in this case should this motion be granted"; "② Grounds"; "③ Relief Requested - what do you want • have proposed order you want signed"; "MD 2-311"]

1. Form

Under Rule 7(b), a pretrial motion must meet three basic requirements. It must be in writing, must "state with particularity the grounds therefor," and must state the relief or order requested. A written notice of motion, which states what the motion is for, can also satisfy the requirement of a written motion. Within these broad requirements a great deal of flexibility is allowed, and how a particular motion is structured is controlled primarily by tactical considerations.

The format requirements for motions are identical to those for pleadings. A motion must have a caption showing the name of the court, the names of the parties to the action, and a designation of the motion involved. Where there are multiple parties, the name of the first party on each side, with an "et al." designation, is sufficient.

Every motion must be signed by a lawyer representing the moving party. The signature also constitutes a certification that the written motion complies with the Rule 11 requirements. The motion must show the lawyer's name, address, and telephone number. While some lawyers put the original of all court papers on a blue-backed sheet, Rule 7 does not require it and local rules usually dispense with this formality.

Example:

UNITED STATES DISTRICT COURT
FOR THE DISTRICT OF IOWA

John Smith, Plaintiff	
v.	No. 98 C 100
Johnson Corporation, et al., Defendants	

MOTION TO RESET HEARING DATE

Plaintiff John Smith moves this Court for an order continuing the hearing on defendant's motion for discovery sanctions, presently set for July 1, 1998, for ten days.

In support of his motion, plaintiff states:

    1. . . .

    2. . . .

    3. . . .

WHEREFORE, plaintiff John Smith requests the Court to enter an order continuing the hearing, presently set for July 1, 1998, to July 11, 1998.

Attorney for Plaintiff
Address
Telephone

In some jurisdictions the practice required by local rule is to state only the motion itself and put all supporting points, legal authority and exhibits on an attached memorandum. Where they exist, these format formalities obviously must be followed.

2. Notice, service, and filing

Rule 6(d) requires that a written motion, any supporting affidavits, and notice of the motion and hearing be served on every party at least five days before the hearing date, unless the federal rules or a court order alters the time requirement.[1] As a practical matter, all documentation that accompanies a motion should be attached to and served with the motion. Service by mail adds three days to the notice requirement.

Example:

[Caption]

NOTICE OF MOTION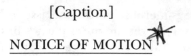

To: Alfred Jackson
    Attorney for Johnson Corporation
    100 Madison St., Suite 1400
    Chicago, Illinois 60602

Please take notice that on June 15, 1998, at 9:30 A.M., plaintiff will appear before the Hon. Prentice Marshall in Courtroom No. 2303, United States Court House, 219 S. Dearborn St., Chicago, Illinois, and present a motion to reset a hearing date. A copy of the motion, with supporting memorandum and exhibits, is attached to this notice.

_____
Attorney for Plaintiff
Address
Telephone

For the convenience of the court and other parties, it is good practice to give more notice than the minimum required by Rule 6 when possible under the circumstances.[2] It is also good practice to call the other lawyers to select a mutually agreeable hearing date, if possible, before sending out the written notices. This gives the court time to read the mo-

---

1. For instance, a motion for summary judgment must be served at least ten days before the hearing date. See §7.8.
2. Lawyers sometimes give only the required minimum notice, without prior contact, when the motion involved is routine or when the lawyer on the other side is using delaying tactics or other improper conduct.

tion, avoids disputes over whether notice was adequate, minimizes continuances, and fosters a good working relationship with the other lawyers in the case.

A motion can be served in any of the ways set out in Rule 5(b). The standard methods are to mail the motion and notice of motion to a lawyer for each party or have the motion and notice delivered to them or someone at their offices. Following service, the originals of the notice and motion should be filed with the clerk of the court along with a proof of service. In many jurisdictions the motion and notice of motion are filed with the clerk of the judge who will actually hear the motion, as well as with the clerk's office. Filing must occur "within a reasonable time" after service, but obviously must be done before the date set for the hearing. The usual procedure is to file the originals immediately after service. Be sure you get a copy of the motion, notice, and proof of service stamped "filed" and dated by the clerk to keep in your files. Filing by facsimile or other electronic means is proper if permitted by local rule.

Proof of service is merely a certificate, issued by a lawyer or a nonlawyer, that states that service on the other parties has been made in a proper way. The federal rules do not define certificate of service, but local rules usually do. These should be checked since some rules provide for a certificate from an attorney, while a nonattorney may be required to make a declaration under penalties of perjury or a notarized affidavit of service. The certificate of service is usually attached to the end of the motion.

Example:

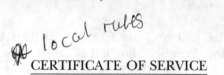

CERTIFICATE OF SERVICE

I, James Brown, served the above motion for a continuance by mailing a copy to Sharon Smith, the attorney for defendant Johnson Corporation, at 100 Madison St., Chicago, Illinois 60601 on June 7, 1998.

_____

Attorney for Plaintiff

How do you select the day for the hearing on the motion? Check with the clerk of the court to determine on what days the court hears motions, since practices vary widely. Some judges hold daily court hearings; others hear motions only on designated days. Find out what your judge's practice is so that the date you select will be one on which the motion can be heard. Finally, check with the clerk the day before the hearing to make sure the case will actually appear on the next day's motion calendar and to find out when you should be in the courtroom. Many judges arrange their court calendars to hear uncontested and routine cases first and contested matters afterwards.

3. Content of the motion

Under Rule 7(b), a motion must be in writing, must "state with particularity the ground therefor," and must state the relief or order requested. Since the Rule permits a great deal of flexibility, the content of a motion is principally governed by tactical considerations: What will be an effective way to present this motion?

The usual procedure is to draft a concise motion summarily setting out the matter and the relief requested, supplement it with a memorandum of law if appropriate, and attach any necessary exhibits and supporting documents. Some local rules require that the motion state whether the other party opposes, or will not oppose, the motion. Call the other side's lawyer to find out her position. In this way a judge can scan the motion quickly, then review the more detailed supporting materials. This format is required by many local rules.

The usual practice must be modified, however, for the relative seriousness and complexity of the motion and for local practice. For example, a motion to reset a hearing date because you will be on trial in another case should be brief. The motion need only point out when the hearing is presently scheduled, state where and when the conflicting trial is scheduled, and how long that case will take to try, and then suggest a new date for the hearing. In this situation the judge will want brevity, and the factual representations by counsel in the motion should be enough.

At the other extreme, a motion for summary judgment will usually be a thorough presentation of both law and facts. You will probably need to make a motion that sets out the background of the case, the relief requested, and incorporates by reference a memorandum that thoroughly discusses the applicable law and existing facts. The memorandum should also contain excerpts from the pleadings and discovery, exhibits such as documents and records, and witness statements in affidavit form. The motion and accompanying materials should be a self-contained package having everything the judge will need to decide the motion.

Learn what your judge's personal preferences on oral argument are and modify your written motion accordingly. Some judges dislike oral argument, and prefer to get everything in writing; others at best skim the written motions, preferring to have oral argument set out the details. While you must always comply with the Rule 7 and local rule requirements and protect your record by having the essential matters in your motion, there is no point in not acceding to your judge's preferences.

In short, drafting a motion requires a flexible approach. The relative complexity of the motion, local custom in presenting motions, and even the preferences of the judge all come into play. Motions that are specifically tailored to these considerations, which do not mechanically follow a set blueprint, have a much better chance of succeeding.[3]

---

3. The motion should be drafted with precision the first time, since no rule expressly allows amendments of motions; Rule 15 applies only to pleadings. In practice, however, amendments of motions are sometimes permitted.

4. Responses to motions

Once served with a motion, the respondent has two choices: oppose or not oppose the motion. If the motion is a routine one, a common practice, if you do not oppose the motion, is to notify the opposing lawyer of your position, who will tell the judge at the hearing on the motion that you have no objection to the motion. This will eliminate your having to come to court. However, you should file a statement that says you have no opposition to the motion, since it is good practice to have a written record of your position and this should eliminate the danger that your position is misrepresented.

Example:

[Caption]

STATEMENT OF NONOPPOSITION TO DEFENDANT'S MOTION FOR ADDITIONAL TIME TO ANSWER

Plaintiff John Smith does not oppose defendant's motion for 10 additional days to answer plaintiff's complaint, presently set before the Hon. Prentice Marshall on June 15, 1998, at 9:30 A.M.

_____
Attorney for Plaintiff

Another approach is to agree to a "consent order," in which both parties draft an agreed upon order that disposes of the motion. While this does not guarantee that the judge will sign it, in practice the judge usually will. This approach is common in state courts, but not in federal court.

On the other hand, if you decide to oppose the motion, serve and file your response in advance of the hearing. Rule 6(d) requires service at least one day before the hearing. The response should set out the reasons for your opposition and include case law and other authority you will want the judge to consider.

Example:

[Caption]

DEFENDANT'S OPPOSITION TO PLAINTIFF'S MOTION FOR LEAVE TO FILE A SECOND AMENDED ANSWER

Defendant Wilbur Johnson opposes plaintiff's motion for leave to file a Second Amended Answer, presently set before the Hon. Prentice Marshall on June 15, 1998, at 9:30 A.M., for the following reasons:

1. . . .
2. . . .

3. . . .

WHEREFORE, defendant Wilbur Johnson requests the Court to enter an order denying plaintiff's motion for leave to file a second amended answer.

Attorney for Defendant

5. Hearing and argument

On the date set for the hearing, check whether an order has already been entered. Many judges will enter orders granting routine and uncontested motions in advance of the hearing day. This is particularly likely where both parties jointly make the motion or the court has been notified in advance that the motion is unopposed. Check with the clerk before the motion calendar starts to determine if the motion has been ruled on. Some courts post a list of motions that have been ruled on outside the courtroom. If yours has already been decided, make sure you get a copy of the order from the court clerk. Most clerks mail copies of the order to the lawyers in the case.

If your motion is still pending, the case eventually will be called by the clerk. The usual practice is for the lawyers to approach the bench when their case is called, state who they are, and which party they represent. If the motion is a routine one, the judge will usually let the lawyers make brief comments, make a ruling from the bench, and immediately enter an appropriate order. If a significant motion is involved, the judge will probably permit lengthier arguments and take the case "under advisement," meaning the judge will research and consider the issues further before deciding the motion.

To prepare for oral argument at the hearing, it is critical to learn what your judge's practice is. Some judges disfavor oral argument and dispense with it altogether for routine motions or, for other motions, give the lawyers very little time to argue. In this situation you obviously must make all your points in the written motion. At the other extreme are judges who at best scan written motions and rely heavily if not exclusively on oral argument in deciding whether to grant a motion. Preparing for oral argument depends a great deal on knowing what the judge wants to hear. If you don't know, ask lawyers familiar with the judge, or watch a motion calendar in that judge's courtroom and see how the judge conducts hearings.

If the judge's practice is to allow substantial oral argument, you need to decide what will persuade the judge to rule in your favor. Sometimes the weight of prevailing law will be persuasive, at other times the facts. Whatever it is, don't repeat the contents of the motion unless the judge tells you he needs his memory refreshed. Many judges begin the hearing by telling the lawyers that they have read the motion and response, and then ask the lawyers if they have anything to add. Take heed of this request, since usually a motion has an important point that will persuade the judge. It may be the law, facts, basic fairness, or the result of a particular ruling. Basic fairness or the results of a ruling can frequently be argued more persuasively orally.

Regardless of what points you have selected to argue orally, act confident and professional. Address your comments to the judge, not opposing counsel. Above all, don't interrupt or argue with counsel. The judge will usually ask the movant to argue first, and then give the respondent an opportunity to argue. Nothing is as unprofessional and ineffective as two lawyers bickering with each other, yet unfortunately this is an all too common event during motion hearings.

As the movant, standard procedure is to approach the lectern positioned before the bench, or to stand at counsel table, introduce yourself, state what party you represent, give the other lawyers a chance to identify themselves and their parties, state what your motion is for, and then go immediately to the points you have selected to emphasize. When you are finished, the other lawyers can respond. When they are through, you may, depending on the judge's practice, have a short opportunity to rebut. Always be prepared to answer any questions the judge may ask.

Example:

> *Judge:* Call the next case.
> *Clerk:* Williams v. Louisiana Chemical Company. Defendant's motion to reset the trial date.
> (Lawyers for plaintiff and defendant come to the podium.)
> *Defense lawyer:* Good morning, your honor. Dominic Gianna for the defendant.
> *Plaintiff lawyer:* Lorna Propes for plaintiff Williams, your honor.
> *Defense lawyer:* This is our motion to reset the trial date for this case. We filed our motion, and plaintiff filed a written response.
> *Judge:* I've read the motion and response.
> *Defense lawyer:* Your honor, our motion to reset the trial date should be granted for three reasons. First, . . .
> *Judge:* Thank you. Plaintiff, do you wish to respond?
> *Plaintiff lawyer:* Yes, your honor. We oppose the motion because . . .
> *Judge:* Thank you, counsel. The trial date previously set will be vacated, and the trial will be rescheduled for April 1, 1998.

The key to making effective oral arguments is always remembering that the argument must be thought through in advance, coordinated with the written motion, and must supplement the motion by emphasizing the important points that, in your judgment, will present your side in its best light.

6. Order

Regardless of when the motion is decided, the court will enter an order. In federal court, routine motions are usually decided by a "minute order," which is merely a form on which the clerk makes an entry reflecting the ruling. The minute order is then signed by the judge or stamped with his signature, and a copy is mailed to the lawyers. If the motion is important, the judge may prepare a written opinion and order explaining the reasons for the ruling.[4] Make sure that every pending motion is ultimately decided by an order, that the order accurately reflects the court's ruling, and that you obtain a copy of the order.

The court may refer certain motions to a U.S. magistrate judge, since magistrate judges are empowered to hear routine civil pretrial matters.[5] In recent years it has become particularly common for magistrate judges to supervise the discovery process in civil cases. The motion procedure before a magistrate judge is identical to that before the district judge.

§7.3. *Extensions of time and continuances*

The kinds of motions that can be presented to the court are limited only by the movant's imagination. Practically, however, the routine housekeeping motions invariably deal with time and date modifications. These are the motions for extensions of time, continuances, and new hearing and trial dates.

Rule 6(b) governs extensions of time. If a motion to extend time is made before the expiration of the applicable time period, the court may grant the motion for "good cause." However, if the motion is made after the applicable time period had expired, the court may grant the motion only where the failure to act timely was caused by "excusable neglect."

What constitutes "good cause" or "excusable neglect" is addressed to the court's discretion, and must be evaluated in the context of the pending case. Courts have generally been realistic and accommodating in permitting extensions of time where the applicable period has not yet run. Usually any reason other than one involving bad faith and actual prejudice to an opponent will result in the court's granting a reasonable extension of time.[6]

Excusable neglect, on the other hand, is judged on a substantially higher standard. Courts have usually denied extensions of time where the failure to act within the required time limitations was caused by the lawyer's inadvertence or ignorance of the applicable rule or by a lawyer's busy case load and other work demands.[7] It is usually an extraordinary situation involving good faith, such as the death or serious illness of a lawyer or a member of her family, a delay by a client in forwarding a complaint

---

4. This practice may differ from state practice, where the prevailing lawyer sometimes prepares a draft order reflecting the court's ruling, which the judge then signs.
5. See Magistrate's Act, 28 U.S.C. §§631 et seq.
6. See Wright & Miller §1165.
7. See Wright & Miller §1165.

and summons, or difficulties in substituting proper parties or different lawyers, that must be present before a court will find excusable neglect and permit an extension of time.

Some time periods for post-trial matters usually cannot be enlarged. These include a motion for judgment after trial, motion for new trial (Rule 50(b)), motion to amend findings and judgment (Rules 52(b) and 59(e)), motion for a new trial (Rule 59(b)), motion to set aside a judgment for reasons such as mistake, fraud, or newly discovered evidence (Rule 60(b)), and appeals from magistrate judges' decisions (Rule 74(a)).

Make the motion and have it decided within the applicable time period. Give the court solid reasons why an extension is necessary, and ask only for such additional time as is reasonably needed. Above all, avoid missing a deadline. This is not a situation you want to find yourself in. The best way to avoid having these disasters arise in the first place is by creating, maintaining, and following a reliable docket control system, which will remind you of all significant dates for each case you are handling. These vary from simple calendars to sophisticated computer systems, but are critical for every litigation lawyer.

Routine motions for extensions of time or continuances should be structured simply. The pertinent information that forms the basis for the motion can ordinarily be put in the body of the motion.

Example:

[Caption]

MOTION FOR ADDITIONAL TIME
TO ANSWER OR RESPOND

Defendant Robert Johnson moves this court for an order granting defendant an additional 10 days to answer or respond to plaintiff's complaint. In support of his motion defendant states:

1. Defendant was served with the summons and complaint on June 1, 1998. Under the rules defendant's answer is due on or before June 21, 1998.

2. Defendant's attorney received the complaint from the defendant on June 13, 1998.

3. Plaintiff's complaint has five counts and is based on an alleged series of contracts with the defendant.

4. To answer the complaint, defendant's attorney will have to evaluate numerous business records, which the defendant is presently locating, and review them with defendant.

5. Defendant's attorney believes he can prepare and serve an answer or otherwise respond if an additional 10 days to answer or respond is granted.

WHEREFORE, defendant requests that this court enter an order extending defendant's time to answer or respond to July 1, 1998.

_____

Attorney for Defendant

Note that the motion asserts facts in the body of the motion that are based on the lawyer's own knowledge, or on information already contained in the court file. In this situation the facts do not need to be stated in affidavit form. Where the facts that are the basis of the motion are within someone's knowledge other than the attorney, the facts must be in affidavit form and attached to the motion.

§7.4. Substitution of parties

During the pendency of an action, occurrences may take place that will require that a named party be replaced by another. Such a substitution of parties can be required when a party dies, becomes incompetent, or loses all legal interest in the action. A public official, named as a party, can die, resign, or be voted out of office. In these situations Rule 25 provides for substitution with a successor party. Unless death abates the action, the court, upon notification and demonstration of the change, will order a substitution. In the case of public officials, the substitution is automatic.

The usual procedure is to make a motion for substitution of parties, state the reason for the substitution in the body of the motion, and attach any necessary documents as exhibits. For example, if a party dies and will be substituted by the administrator of the estate, attach a copy of the death certificate and the probate court order appointing the administrator of the estate.

§7.5. Temporary restraining orders and preliminary injunctions

Injunctions are of three types: temporary restraining orders, preliminary injunctions, and permanent injunctions. A permanent injunction is a final remedy that can be ordered only after a trial on the merits of the case. Temporary restraining orders and preliminary injunctions, governed by Rule 65, are provisional remedies. A temporary restraining order can be granted without notice to the other side, and can be granted only until a hearing for a preliminary injunction can be held. Its purpose is to avoid an immediate irreparable injury to the petitioning party. A preliminary injunction, by contrast, can be issued only after an adversarial hearing; it maintains the status quo until the case is tried.

Both temporary restraining orders and preliminary injunctions are forms of injunctions. Since an injunction is an equitable remedy, it can only be granted if the legal remedies are inadequate. Accordingly, make sure that the underlying complaint asks for injunctive relief and that such relief would be proper if the complaint's allegations are ultimately proved. While Rule 65 governs temporary restraining orders and preliminary injunctions, local rules often have additional requirements that must be met.

1. Temporary restraining orders[8]

a. Law

A temporary restraining order (TRO) is governed by Rule 65(b). Since this is an extraordinary procedure, the Rule's requirements must be followed precisely.

First, a TRO can be granted without notice to the opposing party, but only if three requirements are met. These requirements reduce the risk that a TRO will be granted in error and cause an injustice to the other party. The motion must be supported by affidavit or a verified complaint alleging specific facts that show that "immediate and irreparable injury, loss or damage will result" unless the order is issued before the opposing side can be heard. In addition, the attorney representing the applicant must file an affidavit stating the "efforts, if any, which have been made to give notice" and the "reasons supporting his claim that notice should not be required." Finally, the applicant for a TRO must post security in an amount the court deems sufficient to cover the costs and damages that may be incurred if the party restrained is found to have been wrongfully restrained. All three of these requirements must be met. Although Rule 65(b) expressly requires only that an applicant for a TRO show an "immediate and irreparable injury," case law generally holds that the applicant must make the same showing, at least on a preliminary basis, as that required for a preliminary injunction.[9] That is, the applicant must show, in addition to an irreparable injury, that there is a likelihood of success on the merits of the case, that the threatened injury to the applicant exceeds any foreseeable injury to the adverse party if the order is granted, and that any order will not be against the public interest. As a practical matter, a court will not enter a TRO unless these considerations, taken as a whole, appear to weigh heavily in the applicant's favor. Keep in mind that jurisdictions differ on the relative weight to be put on these considerations.[10]

Second, if a TRO is granted, the order must specify the injury, why it is irreparable, why it was granted without notice, and describe in reason-

---

8. Moore's Manual §10.07(2); Friedenthal §15.4; Manual of Federal Practice §7.101; Moore's Federal Practice §§65.05-65.08; Wright & Miller §§2951-2953.

9. Moore's Manual §10.07(2); Manual of Federal Practice §7.101; Moore's Federal Practice §65.06; Wright & Miller §2951.

10. See Gohn & Oliver, In Pursuit of the Elusive TRO, 19 Litigation (No. 4 1993)

able detail the acts that are enjoined. It is limited to the duration set by the court, which cannot exceed 10 days, although it can be extended for another 10 days for good cause.

Third, the court must set a date for a hearing on a preliminary injunction at the earliest possible time whenever a TRO is granted without notice. The party against whom the TRO was issued can, with 2 days notice, move to have the TRO dissolved.

b. Practice approach

Apply for a TRO only under appropriate circumstances. There is a great deal of work involved, and the court cannot properly issue a TRO unless an immediate and irreparable injury will occur without it. Since a TRO is a powerful and extraordinary judicial step, courts are necessarily reluctant to grant it except in the most compelling of circumstances.

Demonstrating an immediate and irreparable injury and an inadequate remedy at law is understandably difficult. The threatened harm must be both imminent and serious. Common situations involve threatened damage to unique property and proprietary interests. For example, if someone is about to cut down mature elm trees on another's property, if a magazine is about to release personal photographs of a private person without authorization, or if a former employee is about to sell trade secrets to a foreign competitor a TRO may be appropriate because in these situations the wronged party cannot be made whole through money damages. Make sure you know and can accurately describe both the threatened conduct and the persons and entities you seek to enjoin.

Second, make sure that the court has both subject matter jurisdiction over the claim and personal jurisdiction over the defendant. Lack of subject matter jurisdiction will result in dismissal of the complaint. Lack of personal jurisdiction will make any injunctive relief ordered unenforceable. Keep in mind that if you file in state court, the defendant may be able to remove to federal court if the requirements of 28 U.S.C. §1441 are met. If this happens, you may lose valuable time in actually obtaining the TRO, so it may make sense to file in federal court in the first place.

Third, moving for a TRO requires that you prepare, file, and ultimately serve several things at nearly the same time. These include:

- verified complaint, or unverified complaint with witness affidavits, and summons
- application for TRO and preliminary injunction
- attorney's affidavit of attempted notice
- witness affidavits
- security for costs and damages
- draft of proposed court order

i. Complaint and summons

Where a TRO is being sought, the allegations in the complaint will form the factual basis for the motion and must be coordinated with it. The relief requested should include a TRO, preliminary injunction, and permanent injunction. The factual allegations should, like any complaint, be specific enough to show that the pleader is entitled to the relief requested if the allegations are proved. Finally, although not required, the allegations should be verified by the party, since this has the same evidentiary effect as an affidavit. A complaint is verified when it contains a statement that the party has read the complaint, personally knows the facts, states that the facts are true, and the statement is sworn to before a notary public.

The complaint is usually filed at the same time as the application for the TRO. This means that the summons will not yet have been served. However, since the Rules require that the attorney state how notification on the adverse party has been attempted, you should always try to have service of the complaint and summons expedited, especially since Rule 4 permits service by private individuals.

The complaint, application, and supporting documents are usually filed with the emergency judge, an assignment that is usually rotated among the active judges. Find out who the present emergency judge is, and notify the judge's clerk of the situation.

ii.   Application for TRO and preliminary injunction

The application for a TRO should be combined with a request for a preliminary injunction, since under Rule 65(b) a hearing on a preliminary injunction must be scheduled as soon as possible after a TRO without notice is granted.

The application must allege that an immediate and irreparable injury will occur unless the TRO is granted. Since the application must be supported by facts, it usually refers to the verified complaint and accompanying witness affidavits for factual support. As with motions generally, the application itself is usually drafted simply and refers to the supporting material for the substance.

Example:

[Caption]

APPLICATION FOR TEMPORARY RESTRAINING ORDER AND PRELIMINARY INJUNCTION

Plaintiff applies, pursuant to Rule 65, for a temporary restraining order and requests that a hearing for a preliminary injunction be set. In support of his application plaintiff states:

1. Plaintiff will suffer an immediate and irreparable injury unless his application for a temporary restraining order is granted.

2. In support of his application for a preliminary injunction and a hearing date, plaintiff states:

(a) defendant will perform the threatened acts, as more fully set out in the complaint, unless enjoined;

(b) defendant's threatened action, if carried out, will result in irreparable injury to plaintiff;

(c) a preliminary injunction will not injure or inconvenience the defendant.

3. In support of his application, plaintiff incorporates by reference the allegations of his verified complaint and the facts as set forth in the witness affidavits attached as Exhibits A through C.

4. Plaintiff's attorney's certificate showing her efforts to give notice to the adverse party, and why notice to the defendant should not be required, is attached as Exhibit D.

5. Plaintiff is ready to provide security in such amount as the court determines is necessary to cover the costs and expenses incurred by the defendant in the event the defendant is found to have been erroneously restrained and enjoined.

WHEREFORE, Plaintiff requests that the court enter a temporary restraining order against defendant and set a hearing for a temporary injunction at the earliest practical time.

_____
Attorney for Plaintiff

iii.   Attorney's certificate regarding notice

Rule 65(b) requires that the attorney for the moving party certify in writing "the efforts, if any, which have been made to give the notice and the reasons supporting his claim that notice should not be required." Notice here includes informal as well as formal notice. Courts clearly prefer any notice over none at all, such as a telephone call to the adverse party, his lawyer if known, or an agent. Accordingly, the lawyer's certificate should show all the steps she took to give some advance notice to the adverse party. A sound approach is to notify the defendant by whatever means are available, unless there is a clear danger that any notice would create an even more immediate danger of irreparable injury.

Example:

[Caption]

CERTIFICATE OF ATTORNEY IN SUPPORT
OF APPLICATION FOR TEMPORARY RESTRAINING ORDER
WITHOUT NOTICE

I, Terry Anton, attorney for plaintiff, make this certificate, in accordance with Rule 65(b), in support of plaintiff's application for a temporary restraining order without notice to the defendant.

1. On June 1, 1998, at approximately 1:00 P.M., I was first informed of defendant's imminent conduct as set forth in the complaint. I immediately began drafting the complaint, this application, and the supporting documents.

2. At the same time I telephoned defendant at his place of business to advise him of this application, but could not personally contact him.

I left a message with his answering service, but have received no call from him.

3. I have attempted to locate the defendant's residence and present whereabouts without success.

4. I have no knowledge of any attorney who may presently represent the defendant, and have attempted to learn this without success.

_____

Attorney for Plaintiff

iv.   Witness affidavits

Rule 65 requires that the applicant for a TRO show specific facts, through a verified complaint or witness affidavits, that demonstrate the required "immediate and irreparable injury." Accordingly, you should review the verified complaint and determine what additional facts must be shown, and put them in affidavit form. The affidavit should show who the witness is and demonstrate that the witness has firsthand knowledge of all the facts recited in the affidavit.

Example:

AFFIDAVIT

I, William Jones, having been first duly sworn, state:

1. I am the plaintiff in this action. I live at 123 Maple Lane, Denver, and am the owner of that property.

2. On June 1, 1998, at approximately 8:30 A.M. I saw the defendant . . .

3. . . .

4. . . .

I hereby declare, under penalties of perjury, that the facts stated in this affidavit are personally known to me, and that they are true.

_____

Name of Affiant

Signed and sworn to
   before me on June 2, 1998.

_____

Notary Public

My commission expires on _____ .

Note that 28 U.S.C. §1746 sets forth a procedure for making and using unsworn declarations under penalty of perjury, which can be used for witness affidavits.

v. Security for costs

Rule 65(c) requires that a TRO cannot be issued unless the applicant provides adequate security to cover any costs and damages that may be incurred by the adverse party if the TRO is wrongfully issued. Accordingly, thought must be given to the likely security requirement. Ordinarily this means obtaining a bond from a surety or posting a cash bond with the clerk of the court, although the court can set any other security requirement. Since the court will not issue the TRO until the security has been set and met, you should always have the plaintiff prepared to deposit the likely cash bond immediately if the TRO is granted. Check with the clerk's office to determine its requirements for receiving bonds and other security. If you need a bond from a surety or fidelity company, call it immediately to find out what information and documentation it will require before issuing a bond. The cost of the bond is a litigation cost for which the client is untimately responsible, regardless of the outcome of the case.

vi. Hearing, order and service

The necessary papers need to be presented to the assigned judge or the emergency judge, who will review the papers to determine if the Rule 65 requirements and standards have been met. This will usually be done in the judge's chambers on an ex parte basis, since the other side will probably not have received notice of the application for the TRO. The judge needs to be convinced that an irreparable injury will occur unless the TRO is granted immediately, until a hearing, with both parties present, can be held.

It is the usual procedure in federal court for the judge or his clerk to issue orders, either minute or full written orders. However, since with a TRO time is critical, it is useful to prepare a draft order for the judge in advance so that it can be immediately signed if the judge grants the TRO. Rule 65(b) requires that the order specify the date and time issued, define the injury, state why the injury is irreparable, state why the TRO was granted without notice, specify the terms and duration of the order, and set a hearing date for the temporary injunction at the earliest possible time.

Example:

[Caption]

ORDER

This cause being heard on the application of plaintiff for a temporary restraining order and preliminary injunction, the plaintiff appearing ex parte without notice to the defendant, the court having considered the verified complaint, witness affidavits, and the attorney's certificate attached as exhibits to plaintiff's motion,

THE COURT FINDS:

1. Plaintiff's threatened injury as described in the verified complaint is irreparable because. . . .
2. This order is being granted without notice to defendant because. . . .

THE COURT ORDERS:

1. The defendant is hereby restrained from. . . .
2. This order shall remain in effect until June 4, 1998, at 5:00 P.M.
3. A hearing on plaintiff's motion for a preliminary injunction is set for June 4, 1998, at 2:00 P.M. and the defendant is hereby ordered to appear in this courtroom at that time.
4. A copy of this order, along with copies of the complaint, summons, motion, and supporting documentation, shall be served forthwith on the defendant.

SO ORDERED:

_____
Judge

Date: _____

Time: _____

Since the court's order is not enforceable until the defendant receives actual notice of it, you should attempt to notify the defendant by telephone of the court's order and arrange for immediate proper service of a certified copy of the order under Rule 4. Make sure the order is filed with the clerk of the court.

2. Preliminary injunctions[11]

a. Law

Preliminary injunctions are governed by Rule 65(a), which has several requirements. The procedure is simpler than that for a TRO, because the crisis atmosphere of a TRO is missing.

11. Moore's Manual §10.07(2); Friedenthal §15.4; Manual of Federal Practice §7.100; Moore's Federal Practice §65.04; Wright & Miller §§2947-2950.

First, the Rule requires notice to the adverse party. Although it does not specify the necessary time period, it is likely that the usual five-day notice period for motions under Rule 6(d) applies. Also, notice of the motion must include service of the complaint and summons.

Second, the movant must post security in an amount the court deems proper for the payment of costs and damages that may be incurred if the party is found to have been wrongly enjoined.

Third, the movant has the burden of showing, through verified pleadings or testimony and other evidence at the hearing, that: (1) if the injunction is not ordered, the movant will suffer an irreparable injury; (2) the movant will likely succeed on the merits of his claims at trial; (3) the threatened injury to movant exceeds any threatened injury to the adverse party; and (4) a preliminary injunction would not be against the public interest.

Fourth, if the court orders a preliminary injunction, the order must be specific and state in reasonable detail what acts are enjoined. The order granting a preliminary injunction remains in effect until the court has a trial on the merits, although the court can modify or vacate the order if warranted.

The court can consolidate the hearing on the motion for a preliminary injunction with a trial on the merits. If consolidation is not ordered, evidence presented at the hearing on the motion for a preliminary injunction need not be repeated at the trial on the merits. Consolidation is frequently ordered where injunctive relief is the principal remedy sought and the evidence at the hearing for the preliminary injunction would be largely the same as at the trial.

An order granting or denying a preliminary injunction and permanent injunction is appealable. An order granting or denying a TRO is not appealable.[12] Since the issuance of injunctive orders is addressed to the court's discretion, the order will be reversed on appeal only if it was erroneous as a matter of law or the order was improvidently granted.

b. Practice approach

A preliminary injunction can come before the court in two ways. First, it can be set by the judge as part of an order granting an application for a TRO. Second, the plaintiff can move for a preliminary injunction.

The critical point to remember is that the hearing on the preliminary injunction is, as a practical matter, often the determinative proceeding in an injunction case. Proof presented at the hearing need not be duplicated at a later trial. Furthermore, the court can advance the trial on the merits and consolidate the trial with the hearing. Where injunctive relief is the sole or principal remedy sought, the court will often accelerate and consolidate the trial and hearing. In practice, the hearing is the trial and is conducted essentially like a bench trial. The court will frequently order that discovery be expedited and state what discovery will be permitted under the circumstances. As the plaintiff's lawyer, you must be prepared to

12. See Wright §102.

go to trial quickly and present your entire case on short notice. This means that you must have live witnesses prepared to testify, and essential documents that can be qualified for admission in evidence, at the hearing on the preliminary injunction. When the hearing has been consolidated with the trial, if the court rules in favor of the plaintiff, it will enter a permanent injunction rather than only a preliminary injunction.

If you decide to present a motion for a preliminary injunction, it should be drafted both to allege the legal requirements for such relief and to specify precisely what acts are sought to be enjoined.

Example:

[Caption]

MOTION FOR PRELIMINARY INJUNCTION

Plaintiff moves for a preliminary injunction enjoining defendant, his officers, employees, agents and any persons working with him, until a trial on the merits is held and a final order is entered in this action. In support of his motion plaintiff states:

1. Defendant will act in the manner alleged in the complaint unless enjoined.

2. Defendant's threatened action if carried out will result in irreparable injury, loss and damage, as more fully alleged in the complaint.

3. The injury to plaintiff, if defendant is not enjoined, will substantially exceed any foreseeable injury to the defendant.

4. A preliminary injunction will not be against the public interest.

WHEREFORE, plaintiff requests that the court enter a preliminary injunction enjoining defendant from [specify and describe conduct sought to be enjoined].

_____

Attorney for Plaintiff

§7.6. Removal

1. Law

The right of a defendant to remove a case from state to federal court is a statutory right governed by 28 U.S.C. §§1441-1452 and the applicable law is discussed in §3.5 supra.

2. Practice approach

A defendant considering removal must ask several questions before preparing a petition for removal.

a. Should I remove?

Removal is nothing more than a change from a state to a federal forum. Consequently, there is no point in removing unless the defendants will benefit from the change. The potential advantages include a quicker trial date since federal courts frequently have less of a backlog than state courts. Federal districts, however, give priority to criminal cases and usually make diversity cases the lowest priority on the trial calendar. Another potential advantage is the procedural differences that may exist between the state and federal courts. For example, the pleading possibilities may be greater and the discovery rights broader in federal court. Also, the Federal Rules of Evidence may be more relaxed on admissibility issues than state evidence rules. Removing to federal court is also a way of getting the case away from an unfavorable state judge. Finally, federal jury panels are usually from a larger geographical pool and may have different characteristics than a state jury panel. These types of strategic possibilities must be carefully evaluated before proceeding further.

b. Can I get codefendants to remove?

Removal cannot be granted unless all defendants, except nominal or fraudulently joined ones, agree to remove. There is no point in filing a removal notice unless your codefendants agree to join in the removal. Defendants for this purpose includes only those defendants who have been served with the complaint and summons. Defendants named in the complaint who have not been served with the complaint and summons need not agree to removal, since they are not yet in the lawsuit.

c. Can I remove all claims?

The most common ground for removal is complete diversity between plaintiffs and defendants, and more than $75,000 in issue, so long as no defendant is a citizen of the state in which the action is brought, as provided by §§1332 and 1441(b). Also common is removal under federal question jurisdiction, as provided by §§1331 and 1441(b).

What happens if some, but not all, claims are explicitly removable under §1441? Under §1441(c) a defendant can sometimes have a nonremovable claim removed to federal court if such a claim is related to a removable claim. Such a determination is addressed to the discretion of the court, which can permit removal of the entire case or remand all matters in which state law predominates. However, §1441(c) now provides that if removal is based on a separate and independent claim, that claim must involve a federal question; separate claims based on diversity are no longer sufficient.

When fewer than all claims are removable, you must decide whether removing some but not all claims is strategically advantageous and economically feasible. The advantages are the potential benefits of removal that were discussed previously. The disadvantages concern the time and costs expended in litigating in two different forums.

d.   *What are the procedural requirements for removal?*

If after considering the relevant issues you decide that removal is the proper course, make sure you follow the procedure set out in 28 U.S.C. §§1446-1450, since case law requires that the procedures be closely followed. There are several basic steps that are requirements of the removal process.

i.   Timing

The notice of removal must, under §1446(b), be filed in the federal district court in the division in which the state action is pending within 30 days after the defendant receives a copy of the plaintiff's initial pleading, or summons if served without the complaint, whichever is shorter. If an amended pleading is the first indication that the case is removable, the defendant must file the petition within 30 days of the receipt of such pleading. Section 1446(b) imposes an absolute time limit of one year for removals based on diversity, measured from the commencement of the action.

ii.   Notice of removal

Each defendant in the case who has been served, except nominal or fraudulently named defendants, must sign and file a "notice of removal." The notice itself must contain a "short and plain statement of the facts" entitling the defendant to removal. This necessarily means that the jurisdictional requirements for removal must be alleged in the notice since plaintiff's state court complaint will not usually allege them. This is particularly important where diversity is the basis for removal, in which case the notice must allege the diversity jurisdiction requirements of both complete diversity and the jurisdictional amount. However, regardless of the jurisdictional basis, whether federal question, diversity, or actions against the federal government, it must be alleged accurately and completely since the appropriateness of the removal depends principally on this allegation. Where more than one ground for removal exists, each should be alleged.

Example:

[Federal court caption]

Mary Jones, Plaintiff	
v.	No. _____
John Smith, Defendant	

<u>NOTICE OF REMOVAL</u>

To: The United States District Court for the District of Arizona:

Defendant John Smith hereby gives notice that the above captioned case is being removed from the Superior Court of Pima County, Arizona, to the United States District Court for the District of Arizona. In support of this notice defendant states:

1. Plaintiff Mary Jones commenced this action against defendant John Smith in the Superior Court of Pima County under the caption of "Mary Jones, Plaintiff v. John Smith, Defendant," Docket No. 98 C 10478, by serving a copy of the complaint and summons on defendant on June 1, 1998.

2. The complaint alleges that [summarize each count]. A copy of the complaint and summons is attached. No other pleadings or other proceedings have been filed or taken to date.

3. This action is a civil action and is one over which this court has original jurisdiction under 28 U.S.C. §1331 [and/or §1332, etc.] and is an action that can be removed to this District Court pursuant to 28 U.S.C. §1441.

4. [If federal question:] This court has original jurisdiction over this action because it appears from plaintiff's complaint that this is a civil action that arises under the _____ Act, _____ U.S.C. §_____, [or Constitution or treaty] because plaintiff claims that. . . .

5. [If diversity:] This court has original jurisdiction over this action because it appears from plaintiff's complaint that this is a civil action, and:

(a) Plaintiff, both when this action was commenced and now, was and is a citizen of the State of California;

(b) Defendant, both when this action was commenced and now, was and is a citizen of the State of Nevada. Defendant was not, when this action was commenced, nor is he now, a citizen of the State of Arizona.

(c) The amount in controversy, exclusive of interest and costs, exceeds $75,000.

6. [If multiple defendants:] Each defendant served consents to the removal of this case.

7. [If no jury demand was made in the complaint, and you want one, add a jury demand and immediately comply with all federal jury demand requirements.]

_____
Attorney for Defendant

If the case has more than one defendant, the notice of removal should be signed by each defendant's lawyer, since each defendant must agree to remove.

iii.   Notice to adverse parties

Section 1446(d) requires that each adverse party be notified promptly of the filing of the notice of removal. This is done in the same way that notice is customarily given.

Example:

[Caption]

NOTICE OF FILING NOTICE OF REMOVAL

To: [*attorney for plaintiff*]

Please take notice that on June 10, 1998, defendant John Smith filed a Notice of Removal in the United States District Court for the District of Arizona. A copy of the Notice of Removal is attached to this notice.

_____

Attorney for Defendant

The original notice should be filed with the clerk of the court after copies of the notice have been sent to the attorneys of all adverse parties.

iv.   File notice of removal in state court

The final step in the removal process is filing a copy of the notice of removal with the clerk of the state court. This act terminates the jurisdiction of the state court.

v.   Further proceedings

Once the above steps are completed, removal is complete. There is no order required to effect removal. The federal district court retains jurisdiction, unless and until the case is remanded back to the state court, and can proceed as with any other case.

The usual state of affairs after a case has been removed is that the defendant who has been served has not yet responded to the complaint, and other defendants have not been served. The served defendant must, under Rule 81(c), answer or otherwise plead within 20 days of receipt of the initial pleading or summons, or within five days of filing the notice of removal, whichever is longer. The answer or other response must comply with the federal pleading rules. If plaintiff has not served all defendants before the notice of removal is filed, service must be made in compliance with Rule 4. In short, all action taken after removal must be taken under the federal rules.

vi.   Motion to remand

If a removal of the case from state to federal court is improper, it must be alleged in a timely motion to remand under §1447(c). If the motion is based on a defect in the notice of removal, it must be raised within 30 days of the filing of the notice of removal. If the defect is based on lack of subject matter jurisdiction, it can be raised at any time before final judgment. If the motion is granted, the order remanding the case may also order the payment of costs and actual expenses, including attorney's fees, incurred as a result of the improper removal.

§7.7. *Judgment on the pleadings*[13]

Motions for judgment on the pleadings are governed by Rule 12(c). After the pleadings are closed, but sufficiently before trial so that trial will not be delayed, any party can move for judgment on the pleadings. The motion determines if, based on the allegations in the pleadings, the moving party is entitled to judgment. For purposes of the motion, the movant's well-pleaded allegations that have been denied are deemed false, while the opponent's allegations are deemed true. In short, the pleadings are viewed in the light most favorable to the opponent of the motion. It is only when the undisputed facts as pleaded show that the movant is entitled to judgment that the motion should be granted.[14] If a party presents matters outside the pleadings and the court decides to receive them, the motion is treated as one for summary judgment.

The motion for judgment on the pleadings is usually made only in cases where "legal" defenses, such as the statute of limitations, are clearly shown to exist. Since under the federal rules answers need not be responded to, allegations in the answer cannot be the basis for judgment on the pleadings.

Example:

[Caption]

MOTION FOR JUDGMENT ON THE PLEADINGS

Defendant Johnson Corporation moves this Court to enter judgment on the pleadings in favor of the defendant. On the undisputed facts in the pleadings, defendant is entitled to judgment, under Rule 12(c), as a matter of law.

In support of its motion defendant states:

    1. . . .
    2. . . .
    3. . . .

---

13. James & Hazard §5.18; Friedenthal §9.1; Manual of Federal Practice §§4.31-4.34; Moore's Manual §16.01; Wright & Miller §§1367-1372; Moore's Federal Practice §12.15.
14. See Moore's Manual §16.01.

WHEREFORE, defendant Johnson Corporation requests the Court to enter judgment on the pleadings in favor of the defendant.

_____

Attorney for Defendant

Rule 15 provides that motions to amend pleadings should be "freely given when justice so requires." Therefore, if it appears likely that a motion for judgment on the pleadings will be granted, the plaintiff should move for leave to amend, if the defect can be cured. Under these circumstances the motion for leave to amend should attach the proposed amended pleading. Where the motion is made before substantial discovery has been conducted, it should ordinarily be granted, despite the pendency of a motion for judgment on the pleadings.[15]

The motion for judgment on the pleadings is closely related to the motion to dismiss under Rule 12(b).[16] Of the seven grounds for a Rule 12(b) motion, the most commonly asserted one is Rule 12(b)(6): failure to state a claim upon which relief can be granted. A Rule 12(b)(6) motion should be made after the defendant has received the plaintiff's complaint and before answering. If the motion is granted, the plaintiff will usually be given leave to file an amended complaint; usually the plaintiff can cure the defect. The litigation then continues.

By contrast, a motion for judgment on the pleadings is made after the pleadings are closed and it has become evident that there is a legal bar, such as an applicable statute of limitations, that will prevent plaintiff from recovering anything. For this reason, a motion for judgment on the pleadings should not be made unless it is clear from the facts in the pleadings, in light of applicable substantive law, that plaintiff cannot recover on his claim. Such motions are infrequently made.

§7.8.   Summary judgment[17]

Summary judgment is governed by Rule 56. It is designed to be an efficient method of deciding a case when there are no genuine disputes over any material facts. A motion for summary judgment can be made on any claim—complaint, counterclaim, cross-claim, or third-party claim—and on a complaint for declaratory judgment. Partial summary judgment can be granted on fewer than all parties, fewer than all counts, or on one of several issues within a count, such as liability.

15. See Manual of Federal Practice §4.33.
16. See §5.4.3.
17. Wright §99; James & Hazard §5.19; Friedenthal §§9.1-9.3; Moore's Manual §§17.01-17.19; Wright & Miller §§2711-2742; Moore's Federal Practice §§56.02-56.04; Manual of Federal Practice §§4.35-4.42.

1. When made

A complaining party may move for summary judgment on its claim 20 days after the action has been commenced or after an adverse party has moved for summary judgment. A defending party on whom any such claim has been asserted may move for summary judgment at any time. A motion for summary judgment must be served on all other parties at least 10 days before the hearing date.

Since Rule 56(a) allows motions for summary judgment early in the litigation process, when to bring such a motion is principally a matter of litigation strategy. While the Rule permits early motions, as a practical matter they have little chance of success before the pleadings have been closed. The motion is usually made after substantial discovery has been conducted, the important facts become known, and it becomes increasingly apparent that there are no serious disputes over the essential facts.

2. Standards and matters considered

A moving party is entitled to summary judgment only if "there is no genuine issue as to any material fact" and "the moving party is entitled to a judgment as a matter of law." The motion merely asks the court to decide if there are any material facts in issue and whether the substantive law entitles the moving party to judgment. It is not the court's function here to determine what facts are true. In deciding if material facts are in dispute, however, the court can consider the pleadings, discovery, exhibits, and witness affidavits.

What facts are material is determined by the claim involved and the allegations in the pleadings. The court will review the movant's motion and supporting matters and determine if any material facts remain disputed. The court will resolve any doubts against the moving party. Keep in mind, however, that the formal pleadings are not controlling. If the pleadings show a dispute, but the discovery and affidavits show that no dispute over any material fact exists, the motion should be granted.

If the motion fails to demonstrate that summary judgment should be granted, the opponent theoretically need do nothing. As a matter of practice, of course, the opposing party always responds to the motion with a memorandum and, if possible, affidavits showing why the motion should not be granted. However, if the motion with accompanying materials shows that the motion should be granted, the opponent ordinarily must, if able to, present a response and opposing affidavits to show that disputes over material issues still remain.[18] If the court then finds that disputed issues remain, the motion will be denied.

18. See Celotex Corp. v. Catratt, 477 U.S. 317 (1986), where the Court rejected the notion that the moving party must always support the motion with affidvits showing the absence of a genuine dispute over a material fact. Where a party has the burden of proof on an essential element and fails to make a sufficient showing to establish that element after an adequate time for discovery, there is no genuine dispute over a material fact and the other party may be entitled to summary judgment without a further factual showing.

3. Hearing, order, and appealability

At the hearing on the motion for summary judgment the judge will usually allow oral argument, and then ordinarily will take the case under advisement and enter a written order at a later time. The order will set out whether the motion is granted or, if partial summary judgment is requested, on what issues the motion is granted or denied. It will also set out the findings and reasoning that are the basis of the order.

Appealability of the order depends on whether the order disposes of all or only part of the case. When an order granting the motion disposes of the entire case, the order is final and appealable.[19] Where the order grants only partial summary judgment, either for some but not all parties or for some but not all claims, the order may be appealable, depending on whether the court makes it an appealable one under Rule 54(b). That Rule permits the judge to make the order appealable "only upon an express determination that there is no just reason for delay" and the judgment is expressly entered.

When the motion is denied, the usual reason is that material facts are still in dispute. An order denying summary judgment on that basis is not final and cannot be appealed.[20]

4. Practice approach

Summary judgment motions have three important characteristics. First, a summary judgment motion, if granted, will terminate part — and sometimes all — of the litigation. Second, a summary judgment motion is time consuming and expensive for the client. Third, the summary judgment motion frequently may not succeed or, even if successful, the losing party may successfully appeal. Therefore, the threshold question any lawyer contemplating bringing a summary judgment motion must ask is: Does it make legal, factual and economic sense for my party to bring the motion in this particular case?

a. Should I move for summary judgment?

Since summary judgment can only be granted under Rule 56 if "there is no genuine issue as to any material fact" and "the moving party is entitled to judgment as a matter of law," the first step is to determine if the case is the kind of case that is suitable for disposition through summary judgment. Small cases, those involving one or two issues, are suitable candidates. Contract cases, such as suits on promissory notes where the signatures are conceded to be either genuine or fraudulent, are also good candidates. Cases involving affirmative legal defenses, such as a statute of limitations or res judicata, should be considered. In these kinds of cases

---

See also the companion cases to *Celotex:* Matsushita Elec. Indus. Co. v. Zenith Radio Corp., 475 U.S. 574 (1986), and Anderson v. Liberty Lobby, Inc., 477 U.S. 242 (1986).

19. See Moore's Manual §17.19(1).
20. See Moore's Manual §17.19(2).

the legal issues are frequently clear, the facts may be simple, and the motion, if successful, may terminate the entire litigation. While both plaintiffs and defendants may bring summary judgment motions, it is the defense that more commonly brings them.

Certain kinds of cases may also be suitable for partial summary judgment motions. In a case having numerous parties or claims, a summary judgment motion may eliminate one or more parties or claims, thereby simplifying the case. A partial summary judgment motion can be directed at a specific part of the case such as damages issues. For example, the motion can attack punitive damages or consequential damages claims. Partial summary judgment may be sought on liability issues, so that the trial will be limited to the issue of damages. While partial summary judgment motions often make sense only in larger cases, it can be extremely beneficial in those cases.

What kinds of cases are usually not suitable for summary judgment motions? Cases involving mental state issues, such as fraud and intentional tort cases, cases involving circumstantial evidence, and those involving witness credibility issues, such as eyewitness testimony, are poor candidates. These cases invariably involve disputed facts and simply cannot be resolved by this motion.

There are other questionable reasons to pursue summary judgment. One reason frequently given is that the motion will expedite discovery. However, summary judgment is an expensive discovery vehicle, and motions to compel discovery are generally more efficient and effective. Another reason given is that the motion will force an earlier disclosure of the other side's experts. However, witness affidavits from experts are rarely from the experts who will testify if the case goes to trial. For example, the other side may obtain an affidavit from its consulting expert, and "save" its testifying experts for trial. Yet another reason given is that the motion will "educate the judge." However, there are usually easier ways to accomplish this, such as a good pretrial memorandum. Finally, some argue that a summary judgment motion increases the pressure on the other side to settle. While this may be true, a party reluctant to realistically explore settlement will usually feel pressure only when the trial date draws near.

Finally, there are good reasons not to file a summary judgment motion. First, the motion educates your opponent, since the motion is essentially a condensed trial. An early motion educates your opponent earlier. Second, the costs associated in bringing a serious motion are substantial, since the motion will usually require at least 10-15 hours to prepare, and may require much more time. The client must be advised what the expected costs are to bring the motion before the decision can be made. Third, most summary judgment motions fail. The client must also be advised of the likelihood of success or failure before an intelligent decision can be made to make the motion. You need to consider what will happen if you win the motion in the trial court, but lose it on appeal. This is principally a concern for plaintiff, who might be better off simply trying the case than winning a motion that might be reversed on appeal. Finally, you may decide not to present a motion for partial summary judgment because that part of the case has strong jury appeal, and it will improve your entire case if it goes to trial.

b.   When should I bring a summary judgment motion?

One possibility is to bring the motion early in the litigation process, soon after the right to amend pleadings has passed but before substantial discovery has been taken. This can be effective in simple cases such as suits on contracts or notes, involving simple issues such as whether payment was made or whether the parties executed the contract. However, keep in mind that the opposing party may ask for a delay in the hearing on the motion and the right to take additional discovery before responding to the motion, which the judge may grant under these circumstances.

Most summary judgment motions are brought after substantial discovery has been done, but well in advance of the trial date. This has the obvious advantage of using the other side's discovery responses to demonstrate that there is no factual dispute over any material facts. Be sure to make the motion well before the trial date, or before a trial date is even set. Summary judgment motions filed on the eve of trial are usually viewed as a desperate attempt to avoid trial and will be poorly received.

If you decide to make a summary judgment motion, file and serve the motion well in advance of the hearing date. While Rule 56 permits service to be made only 10 days before the hearing, or 13 days if service is by mail, the court will need time to evaluate a serious motion. In addition, the opposing party has a right to respond. Setting a hearing date well in advance will allow the opposing party to prepare and present a response and will minimize continuances.

c.   How should I organize a summary judgment motion?

Rule 56 has no technical requirements and states only that the movant show that she is "entitled to a judgment as a matter of law" and that there is no "genuine issue as to any material fact." Therefore, the movant must demonstrate that the law, and the facts, compel that the motion be granted. Hence, the two essential components of a summary judgment motion are:

1.   the memorandum of law, which discusses the applicable substantive law, and
2.   the statement of facts, which, with supporting exhibits, discusses the applicable facts of the case.

d.   How do I prepare the memorandum of law?

A good place to start is to get the pattern jury instructions used in your jurisdiction for the claims, or defenses, involved in the motion. The elements instructions will tell you what specific proof is necessary for each of those claims, defenses or counterclaims on which you are seeking summary judgment and is a useful blueprint for the specific contents of the memorandum of law. If your jurisdiction does not use pattern jury instructions, you must research the substantive law (which you should have already done before filing, or responding to, the lawsuit). Once you have done this, you can then easily draft a memorandum of law, which tells the judge exactly what must be proven to establish a prima facie case on each claim, or defense, involved.

Aim for brevity, both in the memorandum of law and the statement of facts. The motions most likely to be granted are usually the ones that can demonstrate that summary judgment is proper in a few pages. If it takes dozens of pages to accomplish this, the judge will usually find that the law is unclear or that some material fact is still in issue and deny the motion.

e.   How do I prepare the statement of facts?

Next, begin to organize your statement of facts that will show that there is no material fact over which there is a genuine dispute. The statement of facts will contain the material facts that are necessary to the motion and will be annotated to the factual sources that support it. A good method is to use the elements instructions to determine what facts are material, then organize and state those material facts in paragraphs much like the factual allegations in a complaint. Each material fact stated must then be cross-referenced to the sources that prove that fact.

Keep in mind the hierarchy of factual sources necessary to demonstrate that no material facts are in dispute. There are three basic sources:

1.   opponent's pleadings allegations and discovery responses
2.   records and documents (yours and opponent's)
3.   witness affidavits

Of these, your opponent's pleadings allegations and discovery responses will usually be the most persuasive, since it is more difficult for the opponent to contest the facts that come out of its own pleadings and discovery responses. Least persuasive are witness affidavits, since your opponent can usually attach contrary witness affidavits in its response, thereby creating a factual dispute over a material fact, and defeating the motion.

These factual sources need to be presented properly in the motion. Pleadings and discovery present no problems, since they are part of the record and copies of, or excerpts from, the pleadings or discovery responses can be appended to the statement of facts. However, records, documents, photographs, and other demonstrative aids presented as exhibits, and witness testimony presented by witness affidavits, must be prepared carefully to meet the Rule 56 requirements.

f.   How do I prepare exhibits?

The principal concern with exhibits is that they are properly qualified, since Rule 56 requires that any facts presented in support of the motion must be admissible in evidence. For example, merely attaching a business record as an exhibit to the statement of facts will probably be deemed inadequate. The sounder practice is to determine what evidentiary foundation would be necessary to get this exhibit admitted at trial, then prepare an accompanying witness affidavit that establishes the proper foundation for that exhibit. For example, most documentary exhibits can be properly introduced as either business records or, if signed instruments, by authenticating the signatures of the persons signing the instruments. Finally, make sure that the exhibit contents do not violate other evidentiary rules. For instance, double hearsay problems are common in business records. The key point to remember is that the judge need not consider "evidence" that supports the summary judgment motion if that evidence would not be admitted at trial. Hence, it is your responsibility to demonstrate that each exhibit would be admissible at trial, through a carefully drafted affidavit from an appropriately qualified foundation witness.

Since brevity is important, consider using summaries under Rule 1006 of the Federal Rules of Evidence to summarize voluminous records. Sometimes this information can be presented in graphs and charts and still meet Rule 1006's requirements.

g. How do I prepare witness affidavits?

Drafting witness affidavits must also be done carefully. Rule 56 requires that affidavits be based on "personal knowledge," state only "such facts as would be admissible in evidence," and "show affirmatively that the affiant is competent to testify" to the matters contained in the affidavits. The standard practice is for the lawyer to draft the witness affidavit in consultation with the witness. Hence, you need to plan what the witness would testify about if she were testifying at the trial of the case, and prepare the witness affidavit to recite that testimony. Accordingly, the affidavit should first show that the witness is competent to testify and has personal knowledge of the facts recited in the affidavit. The affidavit should then set out the events and activities of which she has firsthand knowledge and show how she has acquired that knowledge. If the witness will qualify records, documents, or other exhibits, the affidavit must set out the proper evidentiary foundation for each exhibit's admission in evidence, and the exhibit should be attached to the affidavit as an exhibit. Finally, the affidavit should be sworn to before a notary public, and a suitable attestation should be at the end of the affidavit.

Example:

AFFIDAVIT IN SUPPORT OF
MOTION FOR SUMMARY JUDGMENT

I, Gloria Patterson, having first been sworn, state under oath:

1. I am a resident of Tucson, Arizona, and have resided there since 1978.

2. Since January 1, 1980, I have been the president of Cross-Country Transportation, an Arizona corporation having its principal place of

business in Tucson, Arizona. As president, I have the overall responsibility for its operations, including entering into contracts on behalf of Cross-Country Transportation.

3. On June 1, 1998, at approximately 10:00 A.M., I was in the office of Smith Corporation at 100 Main Street, Tucson, Arizona, for a meeting with John Smith, the president of Smith Corporation, the defendant in this case. Also present was Adam York, the plaintiff in this case.

4. At that meeting, I saw John Smith sign his name to a contract, a copy of which is attached to this affidavit as Exhibit A. The signature at the bottom of page 5 of Exhibit A is that of John Smith, the defendant.

5. I have seen John Smith sign his name to various documents about 15 times over the past five years. Based on this previous experience, I recognize the signature on page 5 of Exhibit A as that of John Smith, the defendant.

I hereby declare, under the penalties of perjury, that the facts stated in this affidavit are personally known to me, and that they are true.

_____

Gloria Patterson

State of Arizona
County of Pima

Signed and sworn to before me on _____

_____

Notary Public

My commission expires on _____

Note that 28 U.S.C. §1746 sets forth a procedure for making and using unsworn declarations under penalty of perjury, which can be used for witness affidavits.

Expert witness affidavits, which should be prepared in the same way, do involve one additional problem. Rule 56 (requiring personal knowledge) and Rule 703 of the Federal Rules of Evidence (permitting expert opinion testimony without first admitting in evidence the facts or data the expert relied on to reach the opinion) are seemingly in conflict. The logical answer is that Rule 703 should control. Experts rely on many sources that are not within their personal knowledge in evaluating problems and reaching opinions and conclusions, yet may, under Rule 703, testify about their opinions and conclusions at trial. Furthermore, it is obvious that Rule 56 did not intend to make affidavit requirements more stringent than the evidentiary rules applicable to trials.

The basic rule on expert witness affidavits is not to use one at all unless absolutely necessary. In most cases, one expert's affidavit will usually generate an opposing expert's affidavit, thereby probably defeating the summary judgment motion. An expert's affidavit is usually useful only when it contains principally factual matter and basic, indisputable matter that the other side cannot contest by an opposing expert's affidavit.

h.   How does the summary judgment motion look when done?

Most effectively organized motions have several parts:

1. the motion itself, stating only what relief is being sought
2. memorandum of law, setting out the applicable law
3. statement of facts, annotated to the pleadings, discovery, exhibits and witness affidavits
4. excerpts from pleadings and discovery, marked and tabbed
5. exhibits, marked and tabbed
6. witness affidavits, marked and tabbed
7. table of contents, if useful

Finally, the overall impression your summary judgment motion should convey is simplicity, clarity, and confidence because a motion that is verbose, complicated, and muddled has no chance of success. From your memorandum of law the judge must quickly understand the elements of the claims, or defenses, involved in the motion. From your statement of facts the judge must be convinced that these are in fact all the material facts necessary to decide the motion. Finally, from your supporting pleadings, discovery, exhibits, and witness affidavits the judge must be convinced that there is clear, sufficient proof of each of these material facts.

Example:

[Caption]

MOTION FOR SUMMARY JUDGMENT

Defendant Albert Smith moves, pursuant to Rule 56, for an order entering summary judgment in his favor and against the plaintiff on:
   1. Count I of the complaint;
   2. Count II of the complaint on the issue of punitive damages only.
Defendant states that summary judgment is proper on these counts because there is no genuine issue as to any material fact in Count I, and no genuine issue as to punitive damages in Count II, and that defendant is entitled to summary judgment to the extent requested as a matter of law.
In support of his motion are the following attachments:

1. memorandum of law
2. memorandum of facts
3. excerpts from interrogatories and interrogatory answers
4. excerpts from depositions

5. excerpts from requests to admit facts and responses
6. three witness affidavits, marked Exhibits A, B and C.

WHEREFORE, defendant Albert Smith requests the Court to enter an order granting summary judgment on Count I of the complaint, and on Count II on the issue of punitive damages.

_____

Attorney for Defendant

However, not all summary judgment motions need to follow this itemized structure. Remember that effective summary judgment motions are clear and simple, and the simplicity must be appropriate to the circumstances. Therefore, if the motion can be made briefly, yet persuasively, so much the better.

For example, assume that defendant decides to move for summary judgment on the ground that plaintiff did not give the defendant, a municipal entity, proper notice of intent to sue within the required statutory period. Plaintiff's motion would only need to set forth the statutory notice requirement and cite the evidence, such as interrogatory answers or deposition transcripts, that shows that proper notice was not given within the required period. Such a summary judgment motion could probably be made in two or three pages and will be particularly effective because of its simplicity and brevity.

i. Common problems

What are the common problems that arise when drafting summary judgment motions? Remember that bringing a summary judgment motion takes time to do well and is expensive to the client. Therefore, the motion should not be made unless it has a realistic chance of success, is cost effective, and promotes the client's overall litigation strategy.

The most common drafting problem in bringing summary judgment motions is a lack of clarity and focus. Remember that the motion cannot be granted unless it demonstrates there is "no genuine issue as to any material fact and that the moving party is entitled to a judgment as a matter of law." This means that the motion must clearly set out both the applicable substantive law and the material facts that have relevance to the issues raised in the motion. Confusion, complexity, and verbosity are the enemies of successful summary judgment motions.

Another common mistake is inadequate references to the factual proof contained in the motion's statement of facts. The statement of facts, and its support, are usually the most important part of the motion. Remember that the motion must establish what every necessary material fact is, and show the source of proof of each of those facts. If the motion alleges material facts without showing the source of proof, the judge can ignore the claimed facts and deny the motion on that basis. This means that each claimed material fact needs a citation to its sources of proof, much the way that a statement of facts in an appellate brief needs constant cross-references to the trial transcript.

Finally, motions for summary judgment frequently contain defectively drafted witness affidavits. Remember that the judge will not consider any "facts" unless the motion affirmatively shows that the claimed facts are actually admissible at trial. This means that witness affidavits must demonstrate that the witness has first-hand knowledge of the facts recited in the affidavit and will be able to testify to those same facts if called as a witness at trial. It also means that, whenever the motion refers to an exhibit such as a document, record, or diagram, the judge cannot presume its admissibility. A witness affidavit from a competent witness must establish the evidentiary basis for the exhibit's proper admission in evidence at trial.

5. Opponent's responses

What should the opponent of a motion for summary judgment do? There are four basic things. First, if the summary judgment motion was brought early in the litigation, under Rule 56(f) the non-moving party can ask for a continuance to pursue discovery. This rule permits the non-moving party to "catch up" to the moving party as far as fact gathering is concerned, so that it will not be unfairly disadvantaged when the motion is heard. In this situation, the judge will probably order accelerated and focused discovery, and defer hearing the motion for an appropriate period.

Second, the opponent should consider making a cross motion for summary judgment. If such a motion can be made consistent with the requirements of Rule 11, it has the practical effect of opposing the original motion and frequently makes the judge inclined to deny both motions. This is frequently done in breach of contract cases.

Third, the opponent can actively respond to the motion. Rule 56(e) expressly states that an opposing party cannot rely on denials in the pleadings to resist the motion. Of course, if the motion on its face fails to show that the movant is entitled to relief, the opposing party theoretically need not do anything. In practice, however, the opponent must look at the motion, determine if it is defective on its face, and pinpoint the defects in its memorandum in opposition to the motion. If the motion incorrectly sets forth the applicable law, point it out. If the motion fails to state all the material facts necessary to decide the motion, point them out. If the motion fails to cite to the sources of proof of the material facts, point out where this occurs. If the witness affidavits are improperly drafted, fail to show the first-hand knowledge of the witness, fail to show the qualifications of the witness, or fail to establish an evidentiary foundation for the admission of exhibits relied on in the motion, point them out. In short, meticulously analyze the motion, statement of law, statement of facts, and supporting affidavits and exhibits to make sure that they are complete and proper.

Fourth, if there are no defects in the motion itself, you will need to oppose the motion by presenting exhibits and witness affidavits that contradict the movant's exhibits and affidavits on some material facts, thus creating factual disputes and issues of witness credibility. Since witness credibility issues and factual disputes over material matters can only be resolved at trial, the motion should be denied.

How the response is entitled and organized differs acccording to the lawyers and issues. The important point, however, is that the response clearly and efficiently demonstrates that summary judgment is inappropriate under the circumstances, either because of a fatal defect in the motion or because your response demonstrates that material facts necessary to the motion remain in dispute.

Example:

PLAINTIFF'S MEMORANDUM IN OPPOSITION TO DEFENDANT'S MOTION FOR SUMMARY JUDGMENT

Plaintiff Johnson submits this memorandum in opposition to Defendant Acme Corporation's motion for summary judgment on the claim for punitive damages. Since, as is demonstrated in this memorandum, there remain material facts in issue, defendant is not entitled to summary judgment as a matter of law, and the motion should be denied.

Law

Defendant incorrectly states the applicable law . . .

Facts

The facts essential to the question of whether a genuine dispute over material facts remain in issue are . . .

Argument

In this case, material facts are disputed by the parties . . .

Conclusion

Wherefore, Plaintiff Johnson requests that the court deny Defendant Acme Corporation's motion for partial summary judgment on the claim for punitive damages.

Dated: _____

_____
Attorney for Defendant

6. Hearing on the motion

The court will usually schedule a hearing on the motion. How you prepare for the hearing and how you present your strongest points are much the same as for any hearing on an important motion. As the movant, keep in mind that simplicity and brevity are the key to a successful hearing. If it takes a long time to demonstrate that you are entitled to summary judgment, the very length of your argument will help to defeat your motion. Plan on taking only a few minutes to demonstrate the key point: that since there are no material facts in dispute summary judgment should be granted. As the party opposing the motion, show how complex, convoluted, and contested the material facts are, so that the inevitable conclusion is that the dispute can only be resolved through a trial. How to argue at a hearing on a motion is discussed further in §7.2-2.

In most summary judgment motions the judge will take the motion "under advisement" after the hearing and issue a written order sometime later.

§7.9. *Dismissals and defaults*[21]

Dismissals are governed by Rule 41. There are two types of dismissals, voluntary and involuntary. While the Rule speaks only of plaintiffs, it is clear that the Rule applies to any claimant and therefore to any claim, counterclaim, cross-claim, or third-party claim. It permits dismissals of fewer than all claims against fewer than all parties.[22]

1. Voluntary dismissals

There are two ways to obtain a voluntary dismissal. First, if an answer or summary judgment motion has not yet been filed, a plaintiff can simply file a notice of dismissal with the clerk of the court. No court order is required. The rationale is that this Rule permits a plaintiff to withdraw a lawsuit that is ill-considered or prematurely brought without incurring penalties.

21. Wright §97; James & Hazard §12.14; Friedenthal §§9.4-9.5; Manual of Federal Practice §§7.5, 7.63; Moore's Manual §§19.01-19.11; Wright & Miller §§2362-2376; Moore's Federal Practice §§41.02-41.07.
22. Rule 15, governing amendments of pleadings, and Rule 21, governing joinder, overlap Rule 41 and should always be checked. See Moore's Manual §19.04.1.

Example:

[Caption]

NOTICE OF DISMISSAL

Please take notice that on June 15, 1998, plaintiff Wilbur Jackson filed this Notice of Dismissal to dismiss plaintiff's complaint without prejudice, pursuant to Rule 41, with the clerk of the Court.

_____

Attorney for Plaintiff

Second, if all parties who have appeared in the action agree on a dismissal, the plaintiff need only file with the clerk of the court a stipulation of dismissal signed by all parties. Again, no court order is required. This is the usual method for terminating a lawsuit following a settlement.

Example:

[Caption]

STIPULATION OF DISMISSAL

The parties, plaintiff Wilbur Jackson and defendant Frank Johnson, agreed on June 15, 1998, to dismiss the above-captioned action, with prejudice, and for each party to bear its costs of suit.

_____

Attorney for Plaintiff

_____

Attorney for Defendant

In all other circumstances, plaintiff may obtain a voluntary dismissal only by court order. The court has power to impose terms and conditions that are appropriate under the circumstances, which may include the payment of costs, expenses, and attorney's fees to the defendant. Under ordinary circumstances the motion should be granted, unless the defendant can show that some actual legal prejudice would result from a second lawsuit.

As a tactical matter, plaintiff should simply file and serve a motion for a voluntary dismissal of the action, stating reasons for granting the relief. If the court will only grant the motion upon terms that seem unduly harsh or expensive, plaintiff should consider withdrawing the motion and continuing with the action.

Regardless of whether the voluntary dismissal was obtained through a notice of dismissal or court order, the dismissal is without prejudice unless otherwise stated. The claim can then be refiled later. However, under Rule 41(d), if a plaintiff later files the same claim against the same defendant, the court can order the plaintiff to pay the costs of the previously dismissed action to the defendant, and can order a stay of the new action until plaintiff complies with the order for payment of costs.

Where the dismissal is made by notice of dismissal, the first one is without prejudice. However, to avoid abuse of this Rule by repeated filings and dismissals of actions, Rule 41(a)(1) has a "two dismissal rule." A notice of dismissal is with prejudice and constitutes an adjudication on the merits if the second dismissal is based on the same claim previously dismissed in any federal or state court.

The court ordinarily will not look into the plaintiff's motivation in seeking a voluntary dismissal. The only issues are whether a dismissal would create a legal prejudice to the defendant and what terms the order should include so that defendant's costs and expenses will be reasonably reimbursed. For instance, a plaintiff may dismiss an action that has been removed to federal court even if the only purpose of the dismissal is to defeat the removal and resulting federal jurisdiction, since a defendant has no absolute right to have a case tried in federal court.[23]

Under Rule 41(a)(2), a voluntary dismissal of a claim will not be allowed if a counterclaim has been pleaded before the plaintiff has served a motion for voluntary dismissal, if the counterclaim has no independent jurisdictional basis, or if the defendant objects to the dismissal. The reasoning behind this Rule is that the plaintiff, having previously decided to sue, cannot now use a voluntary dismissal to avoid the counterclaim. Where the defendant's counterclaim does have an independent basis for federal jurisdiction, the plaintiff may dismiss his complaint.

2. Involuntary dismissals

Involuntary dismissal provides a method for terminating a claim where a plaintiff has been guilty of misconduct. While the Rule mentions only a defendant's motion to dismiss, it is clear that the court may dismiss on its own motion.[24] There are several grounds for an involuntary dismissal.

First, a plaintiff's failure to prosecute a claim can result in dismissal. This depends on the nature of the case, but includes a plaintiff's lack of diligence in litigating, such as failing to respond to motions or to appear at hearings, and other repeated dilatory behavior. Involuntary dismissal is a drastic remedy and will normally not be imposed unless other remedies are inadequate. The difficult cases often involve situations where the plain-

23. See Moore's Manual §19.05.
24. See Moore's Manual §19.08.

tiff's inaction is a result of his attorney's misconduct, but the plaintiff may have a valid claim. In these situations the court will usually do something short of involuntary dismissal.

Second, the court can involuntarily dismiss where the plaintiff fails to comply with rules of procedure or with court orders. Keep in mind that most failures to comply involve discovery. The Supreme Court has held that only the discovery rules control sanctions for discovery abuse.[25] Hence, Rule 41 will govern situations involving failures other than in discovery.

Third, an involuntary dismissal may be entered at trial where the evidence presented by the plaintiff fails to demonstrate that the plaintiff is entitled to any relief. This is permissible only during a bench trial after plaintiff has rested his case in chief. This motion performs the same function as a motion for judgment as a matter of law in a jury trial. However, since the judge during a bench trial is also the trier of fact, the judge may evaluate the facts that the plaintiff has presented; while in a motion for judgment as a matter of law under Rule 50, the judge must consider the evidence in the light most favorable to the plaintiff.

An involuntary dismissal is with prejudice unless otherwise ordered. Hence, it is a final and appealable order.

3. Defaults

Closely related to dismissals are defaults, governed by Rule 55. This Rule allows a plaintiff to obtain a default judgment against a party that fails to plead or take any steps to defend against the pending action. The usual situation involves a defaulting defendant.

Defaults are allowed only when the claim seeks affirmative relief. If the claim is for a specific sum, or a sum that can be computed to a specific amount, a default judgment can be entered by the clerk of the court, provided the defendant is not an infant or incompetent. The plaintiff must present an affidavit to the clerk of the court setting out the facts showing default and the sum due. The affidavit should be in the same form as any notarized witness affidavit.[26]

In all other cases the claimant must make a motion for default at least three days before the hearing. If the defaulting party has appeared in the case, you must serve a notice of motion on that party at least three days before the hearing. Even if the defaulting party has never appeared in the case, it is a good practice to serve a notice of motion anyway. At the hearing the court will determine if the allegations of the claim are true and, if plaintiff is entitled to judgment, what the proper amount of damages is.

---

25. See Societe Internationale v. Rogers, 357 U.S. 197 (1958).
26. See §7.9.3.

Example:

[Caption]

<u>MOTION FOR DEFAULT</u>

Plaintiff Joan Franklin moves for an order finding defendant Thomas Johnson in default, finding that the defendant owes plaintiff the sum of $84,246.80 plus costs, and for judgment against defendant in that amount. In support of her motion plaintiff states:

1. On March 1, 1998, defendant Thomas Johnson was personally served with the summons and the complaint, as shown by the affidavit of service on the summons.

2. Defendant has failed to answer the complaint, has failed to make an appearance, or in any way respond or defend, although over 90 days have passed since service upon him.

3. Defendant has not responded to three letters sent to him by plaintiff's attorneys. Copies of these letters are attached as Exhibits A, B, and C.

4. Plaintiff is prepared to testify to her reasonable damages, which total $84,246.80.

WHEREFORE, plaintiff requests that the court find defendant Thomas Johnson in default, hold a hearing to determine the exact amount due plaintiff, and enter judgment for plaintiff and against defendant in that amount.

_____
Attorney for Plaintiff

Defaults are most commonly obtained in simple cases where a defendant who has been properly served fails to respond in any way to the lawsuit, and enough time has passed so that it becomes obvious the defendant does not intend to defend against the claim.

If the sum due is clear, such as in a contract action for past due rent or in an action for an unpaid bill for purchased merchandise, an affidavit to the clerk of the court is appropriate. In many cases, however, the full damages can only be determined at a hearing, requiring that a motion for default be made.

At the hearing on the motion, sometimes called a "prove up," you should be prepared to show that service on the defaulting party was proper, that the allegations of the complaint are true, and what the proper damages are. While judges vary on the formality of the prove-up hearing, you should have all your documentation available and any witnesses on hand that may be necessary to prove your case. For example, in an action on a contract, you should be able to prove proper service with the proof of service in the court file. If necessary, have the person who served the complaint and summons testify. You can prove the existence and execution of the contract by calling a witness who was present at its execution.

Another witness along with exhibits can prove performance by the plaintiff, typically payment of the contract price. Other witnesses and records can show nonperformance by the defendant and the extent of the plaintiff's damages. Although the court may not require them, or permit witnesses to summarize what they know in a narrative fashion, it is always safer to have all your witnesses available and prepared to testify as if the proceeding were a trial.

A defaulting party can only have the default judgment set aside if any of the reasons under Rule 60(b), principally excusable neglect, are shown.[27] For that reason, you should take certain steps to minimize the chances that a default will be vacated. First, serve the defendant by the most direct of the permitted service methods. Second, wait an appropriate period of time, at least 60 to 90 days, before seeking a default. Third, during this time you should send the defendant periodic letters asking for a response and spelling out the consequences of a default. Finally, send the defendant a notice of motion for the default motion, even though this is required only if the defendant has previously appeared in the case. Taking these steps now will support the motion itself and will make it less likely that the defaulted defendant will succeed in having the default judgment set aside later. The defendant will usually try to vacate the judgment only when you take steps to execute the judgment against the defendant's property, such as garnishing a savings account, and the matter suddenly becomes "serious."

Moving for a default judgment as soon as permitted under the Rules usually has the effect of stimulating action by the defendant. If you think the defendant really wants to defend, but is just dragging his feet, making a quick motion for default is frequently an effective technique for getting the lawsuit going.

§7.10. Consolidation and separate trials[28]

Under Rule 42 the court may consolidate separate cases for trial, or have parts of a single case tried separately.

1. Consolidations

Consolidation is governed by Rule 42(a) and has several elements. First, actions can be consolidated only when all actions are "pending before the court." This means that the cases have all been filed and are presently pend-

27. What constitutes "excusable neglect" under Rule 60(b) is unclear, since the term is not defined in the rule, and the case law is hardly uniform. Some courts require a showing of culpable conduct or bad faith; others require only a showing of carelessness or negligence. The Supreme Court has not resolved the issue, although in Pioneer Investment Services Co. v. Brunswick Associates, 507 U.S. 380 (1993) it considered what the term excusable neglect means under a bankruptcy rule. See Wright & Miller, §2851.

28. Wright §97; Friedenthal §6.2; Manual of Federal Practice §§7.3-7.4; Moore's Manual §20.01; Wright & Miller §§2382-2390; Moore's Federal Practice §§42.02-42.03.

ing in the same district court. Second, the actions must have "common questions of law or fact." Typical are personal injury actions by several plaintiffs arising out of a single accident. Third, the court may decide to consolidate only certain issues for hearing or trial, such as the liability issues. This is a discretionary matter for the court and is usually decided after discovery has been completed and the cases are scheduled on the trial calendar.

2. Separate trials

Under Rule 42(b), the court may also order separate trials. This is permitted where separation will create convenience, avoid prejudice, or permit a case to be tried more efficiently and economically. The court has broad authority to separate claims, counterclaims, cross-claims, and third-party claims and to separate issues in any claims, or to separate parties. The typical situation involves unrelated permissive counterclaims or third-party claims where it makes sense to try unrelated claims later or spin off third-party actions to keep the trials simpler. This decision is also usually made only when discovery is complete and the case is on the trial calendar. Frequently a decision to sever is made at the pretrial conference.

While the court has authority to separate issues, a problem often arises because the Rule expressly reserves a party's rights to a jury trial. The case law is still unclear as to when a court may order separate trials of issues before different juries.[29] Separate trials on liability and damages issues before the same jury cause no problems, but there is some dispute over different juries deciding the separate issues.[30]

§7.11. Interlocutory appeals[31]

Motion practice can be a significant part of any litigation, and the trial court may rule on numerous motions—discovery and summary judgment motions, for example—as the litigation proceeds. Can the party that loses a motion immediately appeal the order, or must it wait until after the case ends and the trial court enters a final judgment?

A "final judgment" is a judgment order that decides the case on the merits and leaves nothing else for the trial court to do. While the distinction of what is final—and what is not final—is obvious in most cases, in some situations, usually involving complex litigation, uncertainty can arise because Rule 54 does not itself define what a final order is. Merely designating an order as a "final order" is not determinative of that fact. Rule 54(b) does eliminate much of the uncertainty over what constitutes a final order by providing that the trial court may enter a final judgment as to fewer than all parties and claims, so long as the trial court expressly determines that there is no just reason for delay and expressly directs that judgment be entered.

29. See Wright §97.
30. See Wright & Miller §2390.
31. Wright §§101-104; Wright & Miller §§3920-3930; James & Hazard §§12.9-12.12.

As a general rule, parties can only appeal from a final judgment of the trial court. The benefits of the general rule are obvious: it prevents piecemeal appeals; it allows an appellate court to consider all appellate issues in the context of a complete trial record; and the trial court will be correct in its rulings most of the time. On the other hand, there are situations where an earlier appeal is sensible, and rules, statutes and case law have allowed interlocutory appeals in several situations.

First, interlocutory appeals may be taken as of right under 28 U.S.C. §1292(a) if:

> (1) the interlocutory order grants, continues, modifies or dissolves an injunction, or refuses to dissolve or modify an injunction.[32] ;
> (2) the interlocutory order appoints a receiver, or refuses to appoint a receiver or refuses to take steps to accomplish the purposes of a receivership;
> (3) the interlocutory decree determines the rights and liabilities of parties in an admiralty case.

Second, interlocutory appeals are discretionary under §1292(b). This section, which is infrequently used, provides for interlocutory appeals if the trial court certifies in its order that the case "involves a controlling question of law as to which there is substantial ground for difference of opinion and that an immediate appeal from the order may materially advance the ultimate determination of the litigation." If the trial court issues such an order, the appropriate appellate court has discretion whether to permit the interlocutory appeal.

Third, courts have recognized an additional narrow class of special cases, the so-called collateral orders doctrine, that may also be appealed immediately, although the principal litigation is not completed.[33] These involve situations where the trial court has decided one issue of a case that is entirely collateral of the main litigation but too important to deny review until the entire case is decided.[34] The issue must be independent of the principal action, the order must completely dispose of that issue, and it must be effectively unreviewable if an appeal is allowed only after final judgment. These are also infrequent and are principally involved in complex litigation.

Fourth, the extraordinary writs of mandamus and prohibition may also be used to appeal the trial court's rulings in limited circumstances. For example, writs of mandamus are most commonly used to enforce a right to a jury trial where the trial court has improperly denied that right.

If you can properly take an interlocutory appeal, make sure you follow the applicable Federal Rules of Appellate Procedure, particularly Rule 5, which governs appeals by permission under 28 U.S.C. §1292(b).

---

32. By case law a distinction has been drawn between preliminary injunctions and temporary restraining orders: an order granting or denying a preliminary injunction is appealable, but an order granting or denying a TRO is not.

33. See Wright §101.

34. The leading case is Cohen v. Beneficial Industrial Loan Corp., 337 U.S. 541 (1949).

VIII
PRETRIAL CONFERENCES AND SETTLEMENTS

§8.1.   Introduction

Approximately 95 percent of civil cases filed in court settle before trial. The law prefers settlement and has created several methods to accomplish it. Judges prefer settlement, and the trend has been toward greater judicial involvement, principally by using pretrial conferences to get the adversaries together to discuss settlement possibilities. Finally, most clients ultimately prefer settlement over the increased expenses and uncertainties of a trial. Small wonder, then, that lawyers settle most cases before trial.

This chapter discusses both pretrial conferences and settlement because the two are closely related in most cases. Judges are increasingly using pretrial conferences to force settlement discussions as a case nears trial. Although lawyers can and do discuss settlement at other times, once a case has been filed in court the most common point at which settlement is discussed seriously is after discovery has been completed but before trial preparations have begun. Since this is when pretrial conferences are commonly scheduled, it makes sense to discuss both pretrial conferences and settlements as interrelated parts of the litigation process.

§8.2.   Pretrial conferences[1]

1.   Procedure

Pretrial conferences are governed by Rule 16, which gives the trial court broad authority to hold pretrial conferences on a wide spectrum of matters and to enter comprehensive pretrial orders. Rule 16 is not mandatory, however, and trial judges vary widely in how they use the Rule. Many districts and individual judges have also adopted local rules and instruc-

---

1. Wright §91; James & Hazard §§5.16-5.17; Friedenthal §§8.1-8.3; Moore's Manual §§18.01-18.09; Manual of Federal Practice §§6.1-6.18; Moore's Federal Practice §§16.07-16.22; Wright & Miller §§1521-1530.

tions further regulating pretrial conferences, and specifying the organization and contents of the pretrial memorandum. Hence, in preparing for a pretrial conference, you must comply not only with Rule 16, but also with applicable local rules, and be aware of your judge's special instructions on, and attitude toward, pretrial conferences. Note that Rule 16(f) authorizes sanctions for failure to participate in good faith in pretrial conferences

There are three basic purposes for holding a pretrial conference. First, it is used early in the litigation process to develop a discovery plan. Second, it can be used to streamline the case for trial purposes. Third, it can be used to promote settlement of the case. This section discusses the second purpose; §8.3 discusses settlement conferences.

Under Rule 16(d), a final pretrial conference can force the parties to sit down with the judge and discuss settlement possibilities, force the parties to narrow the issues that will actually be tried, and streamline the presentation of evidence by obtaining stipulations, evidentiary rulings, and limitations on witnesses. The usual time contemplated by Rule 16(d) for the conference is a few weeks before trial. By this time pleadings will be closed, discovery completed and most motions will have been ruled on.

Judges vary widely in how they conduct pretrial conferences. Some will merely have an informal meeting in chambers, without the court reporter, to discuss the general nature of the lawsuit. At the other end of the spectrum are judges who will hold a formal conference, sometimes in open court, and conduct a detailed review of the pretrial memorandum, make all possible rulings, and detail them in an extensive pretrial order. Some judges actively encourage settlements, others do not. Also, some judges are flexible and let the lawyers participate in deciding what type of conference would be most productive in a particular case. Learn how your judge conducts final pretrial conferences and prepare accordingly. If you do not know your judge's practice, ask around. The judge's law clerk is usually a good place to start.

2.   Pretrial disclosures and memorandum

Rule 26(a)(3) requires that each party must disclose to the other parties certain information that it may present at trial other than solely for impeachment purposes. The information must be disclosed at least 30 days before trial, unless the court directs otherwise. The information required to be disclosed includes:

1.   witness who are expected to testify at trial
2.   witnesses who may be called "if the need arises"
3.   witnesses who are expected to be presented through depositions (and a transcript of pertinent portions of the testimony)
4.   each exhibit expected to be offered at trial
5.   each exhibit that may be offered "if the need arises"

Parties receiving the pretrial disclosures can, within 14 days of receipt, file objections to the designated deposition transcripts and the exhibits list. All objections other than relevance are waived by failure to object.

These pretrial disclosures are usually made as part of a pretrial memorandum. How detailed to make the memorandum depends on local rules and the particular judge's procedures; some require only a short, general memorandum, while others expect a detailed review of the case. Some vary the requirements, depending on the complexity of the case. The trend is toward requiring a pretrial memorandum that is prepared jointly by the parties. Keep in mind that many jurisdictions have local rules concerning the organization and contents of the memorandum. Many judges have standing orders that specify the content and organization of the pretrial memorandum. The following subjects are ordinarily included in a pretrial memorandum and discussed at the conference.

a.   Jurisdictional statement

Because federal courts are courts of limited jurisdiction and subject matter jurisdiction must be affirmatively shown by the plaintiff (and can be challenged at any time), the jurisdictional basis for the case is usually the first item in the pretrial memorandum.

b.   Issues of law

A principal purpose of the pretrial conference is to reduce legal issues to those that will actually be tried. Pleadings often assert many possible claims and defenses against every possible party. In the pretrial memorandum the judge will usually require each party to state the claims and defenses that will actually be presented at trial. Keep in mind that the pretrial order, which reflects the pretrial memorandum, amends the pleadings. Therefore, if you decide to waive certain claims in the memorandum, they will be deemed waived for trial. At this time the judge may also permit amendments to the pleadings so that the pleadings accurately reflect the disputed trial issues.

Where multiple claims are involved, the judge has authority under Rule 42(b) to order separate trials when it will promote the orderly and efficient presentation of evidence. In addition, as a trial strategy matter it is often preferable to pursue only the strongest claims without presenting alternative theories of recovery, particularly if they are factually or legally inconsistent.

c.   Uncontested and contested facts

To avoid unnecessary formal proof and to focus on disputed facts, the judge will usually require that each party state what facts it agrees to and what facts it contests. Where facts are agreed upon, they may be introduced at trial through stipulations. While a judge has no authority to force the parties to stipulate to facts, as a practical matter it is often in everyone's best interests to do so. Keep in mind that if you do not admit a fact, your opponent can then serve a request to admit. If you do not admit it in your response to the request and your opponent later proves that fact at trial, the court under Rule 37(c) may award costs and attorney's fees expended to prove it.

Some judges use the uncontested facts as an introduction to the case during jury selection. Therefore, a useful way to prepare the uncontested facts is to use storytelling to give a clear overview of the case, rather than to merely list the uncontested facts.

d. Witness lists

The judge will usually require a list of lay and expert witnesses that will be called in each party's case in chief. Be safe. List all witnesses you may call at trial, including the adverse party and the adverse party's witnesses. Remember that you are not required to call all the witnesses you list but you will be precluded from calling witnesses not listed. Judges also frequently require addresses and a summary of each witness's expected testimony and the qualifications of each side's experts. Under Rule 26(a)(3), this requirement does not extend to witnesses that are solely impeachment witnesses, but the rule covers witnesses "whom the party may call if the need arises," which should include rebuttal witnesses. Each party may be asked to state whether it intends to object to the subject matter of any witness' testimony or the qualifications of any expert; also, the judge may eliminate cumulative or repetitive witnesses.

e. Exhibit lists

Parties will usually be required to prepare lists of all exhibits they will introduce in evidence at trial. Again, be safe. You cannot introduce at trial an exhibit that was not listed in the pretrial memorandum. Pleadings and discovery usually are not considered exhibits, but deposition transcripts are. Under Rule 26(a)(3), the requirement extends to all exhibits the party expects to offer and exhibits the party "may offer if the need arises," and a "designation of those witnesses whose testimony will be presented through a deposition," unless the witness or deposition is to be used solely for impeachment purposes. The usual procedure is to list and describe each exhibit, and designate the sections of each deposition transcript by page and line number, and attach copies of the exhibits and the designated sections of each transcript to the memorandum. Opposing parties may be required to state whether they object to any of the exhibits and, if so, provide the legal basis for the objection. This requirement essentially operates as a motion in limine on objections to evidence. If there is no objection to an exhibit, the judge will usually treat the exhibit as admitted in evidence. Where objections exist, the judge may be able to rule on them before trial. Keep in mind, however, that some objections, such as foundation objections, cannot be ruled on in advance of trial. However, the judge is at least alerted to the objections that will be heard at trial and thus will be able to decide them more efficiently.

f.   Damages proof

In certain types of cases the judge may direct that evidence on damages issues be presented separately. Other parties will be required to state whether they object to the evidence or the amounts asserted. Certain special damages, such as lost wages and medical bills, are often not contested and can be admitted at trial through stipulations.

g.   Instructions of law

The judge usually requires that each party submit proposed jury instructions and state whether it intends to object to the opponent's instructions, and, if so, provide the basis for each objection. While the judge often cannot decide whether to give an instruction before evidence has been presented at trial, the judge can usually rule on the wording of proposed instructions. Since this can be a time consuming task, reviewing the instructions at a pretrial conference can often avoid substantial delay at trial. If the case is one in which special interrogatories or verdict forms will be submitted to the jury, the same procedure can be followed.

The usual practice is to put each instruction on a separate page, and show on the bottom of each instruction its number, which party requested it, and the legal basis for the instruction.

h.   Voir dire questions

The most common practice in federal court today is for the judge to ask the voir dire questions during jury selection. Where this is the practice, the lawyers are asked to submit proposed voir dire questions to the judge, who then decides whether to ask the questions during the jury selection process. Frequently judges will direct the parties to list their proposed voir dire questions in the pretrial memorandum.

i.   Trial briefs

Most judges today expect the parties to submit a trial brief discussing the applicable substantive law and likely evidentiary issues. Some judges want the parties to append their trial briefs to the pretrial memorandum; others ask for trial briefs only if settlement negotiations have broken down and a trial looks likely. The brief's complexity should reflect the relative complexity of the substantive and evidentiary issues. The trial brief alerts the judge and parties to anticipated procedural and evidentiary issues, reviews applicable law, and permits the judge to schedule hearings and make rulings on motions in limine. The advantage to both sides should be apparent, since each side has an interest in presenting its case in chief in a smooth, uninterrupted way. Jurors are annoyed by constant side bar conferences and recesses. Trial briefs, coupled with pretrial motions and motions in limine, will minimize trial interruptions and benefit everyone.

A simple joint pretrial memorandum is usually drafted by the lawyers for each of the parties, with each party contributing those portions that reflect its own witnesses, exhibits, and objections to the other side's evidence. This has the obvious benefit of putting all the necessary information in one document. However, it's always a good idea to volunteer to do the final drafting work to make sure that it accurately contains all your material.

Example:

[Caption]

JOINT PRETRIAL MEMORANDUM

Counsel for plaintiff Frances Johnson, defendant Robert Jones, and defendant Lisa Roberts submit the following Joint Pretrial Memorandum:

I

Jurisdiction

Jurisdiction is based on diversity of citizenship under 28 U.S.C. §1332. Plaintiff is a citizen of California, defendant Jones is a citizen of Arizona, and defendant Roberts is a citizen of Nevada. The amount in controversy exceeds the sum of $75,000, exclusive of interest and costs.

II

Uncontested Facts

The collision involving two cars occurred on June 1, 1998, at approximately 2:00 P.M. Plaintiff Frances Johnson was a passenger in a 1990 Honda Accord owned and driven by defendant Robert Jones. Jones was driving north on Kolb Road intending to turn left (west) on 22nd Street. As he was executing this turn, the defendant Lisa Roberts, who was driving her 1988 Buick Skylark southbound on Kolb Road, struck Jones' car.

Kolb Road has two lanes of traffic in each direction, a left turn lane at the intersection, and a median strip. Twenty-second Street has two lanes of traffic in each direction, a left-turn lane at the intersection, and a median strip. The intersection of Kolb Road and 22nd Street is controlled by several traffic lights.

The weather on June 1, 1998, was sunny and clear. The road conditions were dry.

Plaintiff Frances Johnson was injured as a result of the collision. She was taken to St. Mary's Hospital emergency room for treatment and was admitted to the hospital for continued care. Plaintiff was discharged from St. Mary's Hospital on June 4, 1998. Plaintiff's hospital and physician bills for this period totaled $4,471.04.

Plaintiff was absent from work between June 1, 1998, and July 5, 1998, when she returned to her job as a bank teller at First National Bank.

III

Contested Facts

1. Which car had the right of way at the time of the collision?
2. What color were the traffic lights at the time of the collision?
3. What was the extent of the injuries to plaintiff?
4. Does plaintiff have any permanent injuries or disabilities as a result of this collision?
5. Will plaintiff need further medical treatment in the future and, if so, what treatment?
6. What amount of money will reasonably compensate plaintiff for the damages incurred as a result of this collision?

IV

Contested Issues of Law

1. Was defendant Robert Jones negligent?
2. Was defendant Lisa Roberts negligent?
3. If both defendants were negligent, what is the degree of negligence of each defendant?

V

Exhibits

A. *Plaintiff Johnson's Exhibits:*   *Objections to Admissibility:*

1. Medical expenses totaling $4,471.04 as evidenced by vouchers in support of each expenditure contained in a blue brochure with a cover sheet listing the medical expenses.   None.
2. The Police Department official report of the accident.   Objected to by defendant Jones on hearsay grounds.

		Objections to Admissibility:
3.	St. Mary's Hospital emergency room records of the plaintiff.	None.
4.	Photographs of the plaintiff showing her shoulder deficit.	None.
5.	X rays taken of the plaintiff.	None.
6.	Photographs and diagrams of the intersection involved.	None.

B. *Defendant Jones' Exhibits:*　　*Objections to Admissibility:*

1.	Plaintiff's hospital and medical records.	None.
2.	X rays.	None.
3.	Plaintiff's employment records.	None.
4.	Bills concerning property damage.	None.
5.	Time sequence of signal lights.	None.
6.	Photographs of the vehicles.	None.
7.	The police report as far as it is admissible.	None.

C. *Defendant Roberts' Exhibits:*　　*Objections to Admissibility:*

1.	Police report of accident.	Objected to by plaintiff and by defendant Jones, for the reasons stated in the attached Memorandum of Law
2.	Photographs of vehicles involved.	None.
3.	Plaintiff's medical records.	None.

VI

Witnesses

A. *Plaintiff Johnson's Witnesses:*

1. Plaintiff.
2. Elizabeth Martin, M.D.
3. Ernest Jackson, M.D.
4. Philip Wigmore, a bystander.
5. Bernie Sullivan, plaintiff's supervisor at First National Bank.
6. Investigating police officer Frank O'Malley.
7. Defendants.

B.   *Defendant Jones' Witnesses:*

    1.   The parties to this action.
    2.   Investigating police officer Frank O'Malley.

C.   *Defendant Roberts' Witnesses:*

    1.   The parties to this action.
    2.   Doctors who have seen or treated plaintiff.
    3.   Richard Hollister, a bystander.
    4.   Officer Barbara Horn, Police Department.
    5.   Glenda Sylvester, accident reconstruction expert.

VII

Jury Instructions

Plaintiff and defendants' proposed jury instructions are attached.

1. Plaintiff Johnson objects to Jones' instructions numbers 4, 7, and 9, and objects to Roberts' instruction number 6 for the reasons stated in the attached Memorandum of Law.

2. Both defendants object to plaintiff Johnson's instructions numbers 6, 7, 8, and 13 for the reasons stated in the attached Memorandum of Law.

RESPECTFULLY SUBMITTED this 1st day of June, 1999.

By   _____
          Attorney for Plaintiff Johnson

By   _____
          Attorney for Defendant Jones

By   _____
          Attorney for Defendant Roberts

3.   Pretrial order

Rule 16(e) requires that the judge enter an order reciting the actions taken at the pretrial conference, and local rules frequently specify how, and by whom, the order will be drafted. Practices vary widely. Some judges prepare the order, either by stating the results of the conference in open court so the court reporter will record it, or by preparing a written pretrial order. Other judges have the parties draft an agreed order, which the judge then reviews and signs. Some judges ask the parties to estimate the number of trial days necessary to try the case; in lengthy trials, judges may impose time limitations on the parties. The estimated length of trial and any time limitations are then included in the pretrial order.

The content of the pretrial order is critical, since the order controls the trial. If the pretrial order incorrectly recites the disputed issues, witnesses, exhibits, or other matters, it must be promptly corrected. The best time to do this, when possible, is while the order is in draft form and not yet signed by the judge. Once entered, the order can be modified "only to prevent manifest injustice."

A simple pretrial order might look like the following.

Example:

[Caption]

FINAL PRETRIAL ORDER

The following are the results of pretrial proceedings in this cause held pursuant to Rule 16 and IT IS ORDERED:

I

This is an action for damages arising out of a collision involving vehicles driven by defendant Jones and defendant Roberts, which occurred on June 1, 1998, at the intersection of Kolb Road and 22nd Street.

II

Jurisdiction is based on diversity of citizenship under 28 U.S.C. §1332. Plaintiff is a citizen of California, defendant Jones is a citizen of Arizona, and defendant Roberts is a citizen of Nevada. The amount in controversy exceeds the sum of $75,000, exclusive of interest and costs.

III

The following facts are admitted by the parties and require no proof:

1. The collision occurred on June 1, 1998, at the intersection of Kolb Road and 22nd Street.
2. Defendant Jones was the owner and operator of a 1994 Honda Accord that was involved in the collision.
3. Defendant Roberts was the owner and operator of a 1992 Buick Skylark that was involved in the collision.

4. Plaintiff Johnson was a passenger in defendant Jones' vehicle at the time of the collision.

5. The weather on June 1, 1998, was sunny and clear. The road conditions were dry.

6. The intersection of Kolb Road and 22nd Street is controlled by several traffic lights.

7. Plaintiff was absent from work from June 1, 1998, through July 5, 1998.

8. Plaintiff was admitted to St. Mary's Hospital emergency room on June 1, 1998, and was discharged from the hospital on June 4, 1998.

9. Plaintiff's hospital bill was $2,492.83.

10. Plaintiff's doctor bills to date total $1,978.21.

IV

The following are the issues of fact to be tried and determined upon trial:

1. Whether the defendants used due care in operating their vehicles?

Plaintiff contends that both defendants were speeding, not driving safely, and not keeping a proper lookout.

Defendant Jones contends that he was driving within the speed limit and operating his vehicle safely.

Defendant Roberts contends that she was driving within the speed limit and operating her vehicle safely, and that defendant Jones failed to yield the right of way.

V

The following are the issues of law to be tried and determined upon trial:

1. Whether the defendants, or either one of them, were negligent?

Plaintiff contends that both defendants were negligent and that their negligence jointly and directly caused plaintiff's injuries.

Defendant Jones contends that he was not negligent, and that his conduct caused no injuries to plaintiff.

Defendant Roberts contends that she was not negligent, that she did not violate any statutes, and that her conduct caused no injuries to plaintiff.

VI

1. The following exhibits are admissible in evidence in this case and may be marked in evidence by the Clerk:

a. Plaintiff's exhibits: (see attached List number 1)

b. Defendants' exhibits: (see attached Lists numbers 2 and 3)

2. As to the following exhibits, the party against whom the same will be offered objects to their admission upon the grounds stated:

a. Plaintiff's exhibits: (see attached List number 4)

b. Defendants' exhibits (see attached Lists numbers 5 and 6)

3. The parties will offer the following deposition testimony and have the following objections:

a. Plaintiff deposition excerpts (see attached List number 7)

b. Defendants' deposition excerpts (see attached List numbers 8 and 9)

VII

The following witnesses will be called by the parties upon trial:

a. On behalf of plaintiff: (see attached list number 10)

b. On behalf of defendants: (see attached lists numbers 11 and 12)

VIII

A jury trial has been requested, and was timely requested. It is anticipated that the case will require three trial days.

APPROVED AS TO FORM:

_____

Attorney for Plaintiff Johnson

_____

Attorney for Defendant Jones

_____

Attorney for Defendant Roberts

The foregoing constitutes the Final Pretrial Order in the above case. All prior pleadings in the case are superseded by this Order, which shall not be amended except by consent of the parties and by order of this court.

_____

United States District Judge

Dated: _____

The pretrial order bars parties from raising any claims or defenses not permitted by the order, and restricts the witnesses, exhibits, objections, and any other matters to those contained in the order. While Rule

16(e) permits modification to prevent manifest injustice, the granting of such a motion is discretionary with the judge, and counsel must ordinarily present a persuasive reason for amending the order.

Since pretrial orders are not usually final orders, they cannot be appealed under 28 U.S.C. §1291 until the case is disposed of by a final judgment.[2] However, an appeal following a final judgment can raise errors in the pretrial order.

§8.3.   Settlements[3]

Settling a case involves three basic steps: determining the case's settlement value, selling your assessment to the opposing side, and having the client agree. While a case can be settled at any time, settlement possibilities are almost always explored when a case nears the pretrial conference stage and a trial is just around the corner. Discovery will be complete at this point, and there is sufficient information to accurately assess the case.[4] If settlement before or at a settlement conference does not occur, they can, and often do, occur just before or during trial, particularly just after the jury is picked, opening statements are made, or after the plaintiff has testified.

For this reason, you should take stock of your case again when the final pretrial conference is first scheduled. Preparing the pretrial memorandum necessarily will involve reviewing the pleadings, discovery, contested issues, witnesses, exhibits, and potential factual and legal problems. You might as well review the case for its settlement potential in the same systematic way.

1.   Case evaluation[5]

You need to evaluate the case in a clear, progressive way so that you reach an accurate and realistic assessment of its strengths and weaknesses. The sequence to use for your case evaluation should include the following, which parallel the way you have used a litigation chart to structure your litigation plan.[6]

a.   List elements of proof

Look at the elements instructions for liability, special damages, general damages, and defenses for every claim you intend to pursue at trial.

2. Under a few special circumstances an interlocutory appeal may be permitted. See §7.11; 28 U.S.C. §1292; Moore's Manual §18.08.
3. See G. R. Williams, Legal Negotiation and Settlement ch. 5, pp. 90-109 (1983); J. Jeans, Trial Advocacy 2d ed. ch. 20, pp. 425-465 (1993).
4. Obviously, settlement should be explored earlier as well, for instance just before or just after filing suit, or after the plaintiff's deposition has been taken, when the costs both in terms of time delay and litigation expenses can be held down.
5. See J. Jeans, Trial Advocacy 2d ed. ch. 20, (1993).
6. See §2.2.

The elements instructions will itemize exactly what facts must be proved. This, of course, should already be on your litigation chart.

b. List sources of proof

List all lay and expert witnesses, with a summary of their testimony; all exhibits; and any other anticipated proof, such as stipulations and judicial notice. Include only evidence that you reasonably believe will be admissible at trial.

c. Relate proof to elements

Now list the various witnesses and exhibits with the specific facts that must be proved for each claim and defense. Do this for your opponent's proof as well. This approach will organize the evidence and show what evidence there is to prove and refute for each element of the claims and defenses.

d. Review credibility of the proof

Once you have organized the evidence and related it to the elements of the claims and defenses, you must take the critical step of realistically assessing whether it will be considered credible to a jury. How persuasive will the witnesses be? How probative are the exhibits?

Assessing credibility of proof is largely a function of trial experience, but there are other ways to get a "feel" for your case. Do the witnesses have good personal, family, and employment backgrounds that will make them believable to a jury? Do they tell stories that make sense? What kind of impression did they make when they were deposed? Are their stories consistent with our common experience in life? Are the witnesses consistent with each other? A good practice for any lawyer, regardless of experience, is to try out your case, giving an objective summary of your side's proof as well as the other side's proof. This can be done before experienced trial lawyers, colleagues, friends, and spouses. Their reactions to the case and assessment of the case's strengths and weaknesses will usually be good indicators of how the proof will be viewed by a real jury.

e. Evaluate your case's jury appeal

Cases, of course, are not presented in a perfect, dispassionate world. A major consideration is whether your case, or your opponent's, has jury appeal. This must be assessed whenever any party has made a jury demand. Granted, "jury appeal" is an elusive concept, but it is extremely important to consider both before filing a demand for a jury trial with your initial pleading and before reviewing the case for settlement purposes. The basic components of jury appeal are the claims, the parties, and the lawyers.

The claims have much to do with whether a jury will be sympathetic to, or offended by, the conduct of either side. For the most part, juries are sympathetic to the unassuming individual who has been victimized. For example, a simple negligence case involving property damage or a routine contract action usually has little jury appeal. A negligence case against a drunk driver, however, or a contract action by a home owner against a home builder charging faulty construction will have substantial appeal.

Jury appeal is influenced by who the parties are. Similar cases can have widely varying verdicts, depending on the appeal of the parties. A plaintiff who is physically attractive, speaks well, and has a middle-class background will have considerable appeal. A trial involving a wealthy defendant, or a corporate or government defendant, will usually generate substantially higher verdicts for the plaintiff.[7]

Finally, the particular trial lawyer will obviously have some impact. Experienced trial lawyers with a proven record for obtaining good verdicts in similar types of cases can be expected to get better verdicts than other lawyers. Accordingly, you should always investigate your opponent's actual jury trial experience and reputation as a trial lawyer, and add this information to the overall analysis.

f. Review jury verdict reporters

Most jurisdictions, particularly those with large metropolitan populations, have jury verdict reporter services that periodically report the facts of cases tried and the verdicts obtained.[8] By researching these services, not only for your jurisdiction but similar ones, you can at least learn the range of verdicts realistically attainable in similar cases. Keep in mind, however, that verdicts can vary widely depending on the jurisdiction, judge, lawyers, and facts—factors not readily apparent in the reports.

g. Review the trial expenses

Trials are expensive, both emotionally and financially. The client must realize the emotional toll a trial can take, and must be aware of the significant demands a trial will make on his time, demands that must take priority over all other obligations. Give the client a projection of how much of his time you will need in order to prepare and try the case, and what he will be doing during those hours. Where a client is unwilling to make the necessary commitment, or is unprepared to handle the emotional stresses and uncertainties of a trial, settlement is the obvious course.

The client should also be aware of the trial expenses involved, because they can be substantial. This is a good time to review your litigation budget with your client.[9] If you are being compensated on an hourly basis, you should give the client a current estimate of the trial preparation

7. There are numerous psychological studies that have identified factors that affect witness credibility. See, e.g., Applying Social Psychological Research to Witness Credibility Law, in 2 Applied Social Psychology Annual (1980).

8. Frequently used national services are the ATLA Law Reporter and Jury Verdict Reports, which report the monetary range of successful plaintiff's verdicts.

9. See §2.2.5.

and trial time involved. Experienced trial lawyers usually need at least one day of preparation for each day of trial, and often more. With hourly rates frequently exceeding $100 per hour, a five-day trial, requiring five preparation days, can easily cost a client $10,000 in attorney's fees alone. Where a statute permits awarding attorney's fees to the winning party, this will significantly increase the costs to the losing side.

Witness fees, particularly for experts who expect to be compensated for their time and expenses, and travel and housing expenses, can be substantial since medical and other technical experts usually command an hourly rate comparable to that of lawyers. For example, doctors usually insist on being compensated at the same hourly rate they would receive in their practice; taking a doctor away from his practice for even half a day can cost several hundred dollars. Flying an expert in to testify at trial will obviously be substantially more expensive. Finally, court costs and other expenses cannot be overlooked, since they can add up during a protracted jury trial. Court costs, including the initial filing fees and the daily juror fees, can become substantial in any lengthy trial.

h. Consider preparing a settlement brochure

In recent years it has become fashionable among plaintiff's personal injury lawyers to prepare so-called settlement brochures in major cases. These brochures essentially set out the background of the plaintiff along with the evidence showing liability and damages. The fact summaries are usually supplemented by photographs and documents such as employment records, hospital and other medical records, bills, and medical and economic expert reports detailing the extent of injuries, the degree of permanent physical losses, and the plaintiff's economic future. Some lawyers believe that developing such a brochure is the most effective way of presenting the plaintiff's case before trial and obtaining a favorable settlement, since it can graphically show the nature and extent of the injuries, summarize the quality of the plaintiff's case, and demonstrate the jury appeal of the plaintiff. Even if you are not preparing a settlement brochure, consider bringing graphic exhibits to demonstrate your proof on liability and damages at the settlement conference.

i. Determine the settlement value

Your case evaluation is not complete, of course, until you have reached a dollar amount, or range, that represents a realistic settlement figure that you can recommend your client accept. This means that you must translate the case evaluation into a final dollar amount. Of course, there are many factors other than a monetary analysis that may affect the way a case is settled. These include the amount and coverage of the defendant's insurance, whether any of plaintiff's damages have been paid by other sources, the defendant's ability to pay a judgment if little or no insurance coverage is available, each party's ability to bear the costs of litigation, the willingness of the parties to go to trial, the effect of litigation on the parties' business and personal interests, the skill of the trial lawyers, and whether publicity surrounds the litigation. While these can significantly affect the settlement of any case, most cases are settled principally on an evaluation in monetary terms, and there are several steps in this process.[10]

First, you need to establish the dollar amount of a likely verdict if the plaintiff were to prove both liability and damages. In some cases, such as contract actions, it may be possible to reach a specific figure. In others, such as personal injury actions, it is probably better to use a dollar range for a likely verdict. Make the same determination for any counterclaims. The more common the facts are, the more accurately you will be able to assess a likely verdict range.

Second, you need to determine the probability that the plaintiff will succeed on the question of liability; this probability is expressed as a percentage. For example, if you conclude that the plaintiff is as likely to prevail on liability as lose on it, the likelihood of success is 50 percent. This means that the "value" of the case for settlement purposes is 50 percent of the probable damages. Make the same kind of analysis for any counterclaims. For example, if a personal injury case is being tried under comparative negligence, you need to determine the likelihood of the jury concluding that the plaintiff was also negligent, express it as a percentage, and reduce the value of the case by that amount.

Third, analyze the additional costs the client will incur if the case goes to trial. These costs will include lawyer fees and other trial expenses, such as the cost of having experts testify. Of course, if you are being paid on a contingency or flat fee basis, there will be no additional legal fees. When you are being paid on an hourly basis, however, you will need to estimate the hours required to finish preparing and to try the case and then multiply that number by your hourly rate. Those additional legal fees and trial expenses reduce the value of the case if it goes to trial and should be discounted for settlement evaluation purposes.

Fourth, you need to take into account the time value of money. Money received now is worth more than the same amount of money received one year from now. As the plaintiff in the case, you will need to discount the "value" of the case to reflect the benefit of receiving an amount of money now rather than after a trial. The discount, expressed as a percentage, depends on how much sooner the plaintiff will get the money and the increased value of getting it now. For instance, if the plaintiff would get a certain amount of money after a verdict but the case will not be tried for a year, and the investment yield on a prudent

10. During the past few years, litigation support firms have developed decision tree models to determine the settlement values of cases at various stages of the litigation process. A decision tree, a commonly used tool in the business world, divides the litigation process into its component parts and analyzes the risks that exist at each stage of the process. While assigning probabilities to each component of the process may be difficult — for example, what is the probability that summary judgment on plaintiff's punitive damages claim will be granted, or what effect will a ruling limiting expert testimony have on the trial? — this method does force you to analyze every possible influence on the settlement value of a case. In large and complex litigation, decision tree analysis is becoming common as lawyers increasingly understand that settlement analysis can, and should, be done systematically.

investment is currently 6 percent, that amount of money received next year is worth about 6 percent less than if received now. Plaintiff needs to discount the value of the case by these time value considerations; a defendant would add the same amount, since deferring payment of a judgment is a benefit.[11]

Fifth, see if the defendant's insurance coverage, or other ability to pay, will create a practical limit on what the plaintiff can realistically hope to recover. Where insurance coverage is low and the defendant has no substantial assets that could help satisfy a judgment, the policy limit may be the only amount the plaintiff can ever recover. In this situation the defense may simply "tender the policy" to settle the case.

Example:

You represent the plaintiff in a personal injury case on a contingency basis. The applicable state's law uses comparative negligence. Your settlement value analysis should go along the following lines:

1. Assuming liability, you assess the probable verdict range at $40,000 to $60,000.

2. You assess the likelihood of proving liability at 80 percent. However, you conclude that the jury will find the plaintiff 33 percent responsible for his injuries.

3. Since you are representing the plaintiff on a contingency basis, a trial will not create additional legal costs. However, you estimate that the plaintiff will have to pay $5,000 for trial expenses, principally expert fees and costs.

4. You estimate the case will not be tried for 18 months; the current rate of return for safe investments is 6 percent.

The value of the case computes as follows:

1. Median "value" of the case is $50,000 (the midpoint of your verdict range).

2. Your 80 percent recovery chances reduce the value to $40,000; the comparative negligence likelihood of 33 percent reduces the value to approximately $26,000.

3. Your estimated trial expenses of $5,000 reduce the value of the case to $21,000.

4. Finally, the 18 months to trial and investment rate of 6 percent per year reduce the value to about $19,000.

These figures show a current settlement value of approximately $19,000 to the plaintiff. In other words, plaintiff should consider accepting any settlement that exceeds $19,000. Since discovery has already revealed that the defendant has an applicable insurance policy with $50,000 coverage, collecting the judgment should not be a concern.

The defendant, of course, should be making the same type of analysis. Because the defendant will usually be paying legal fees on an hourly basis and can expect to pay several thousand dollars in lawyer's fees if the

11. This assumes that there is no prejudgment interest applicable.

case goes to trial, her settlement value may be higher than the plaintiff's. When the plaintiff and the defendant have analyzed the likely jury verdict in a similar fashion, a dollar range may be created that makes settlement attractive to both sides. Settlement is then likely to be reached on a figure that is higher than the plaintiff's settlement value but lower than the defendant's. For example, if plaintiff has valued the case at $19,000 and the defendant has valued it at $22,000, any settlement figure between these two extremes would be beneficial to both parties.

j.   Evaluate the tax consequences of settlement[12]

Finally, you must know the potential tax consequences of a settlement. The beginning point is 26 U.S.C. §104(a)(2), which excludes (as of the 1996 amendments) from income any damages received, through suit or settlement, for "personal physical injuries or physical sickness." This has been generally interpreted to mean damages received through a tort or tort-based claim. For example, a settlement of a negligence claim based on a vehicle collision in which the plaintiff received physical injuries will be excludable from plaintiff's income, even though part of the damages may reflect lost income.

Section 104(a)(2) makes clear that punitive damages received are taxable income. It also makes clear that compensatory damages for non-physical personal injury cases, such as defamation and wrongful discharge, are also taxable income.

What should a plaintiff do to fall within the exclusion of §104? At the complaint drafting stage, plaintiff should bring tort, not contract, claims and allege damages for personal physical injuries whenever possible. At the settlement stage, the settlement agreement should state that the settlement is for the plaintiff's personal injury claims whenever possible. If the complaint alleges both tort and nontort claims, it may be possible to settle only the tort claims and dismiss the nontort claims. The agreement should characterize the settlement amounts as compensatory, not punitive, damages. However, keep in mind that while the characterization in the settlement agreement may be influential, it is not dispositive, and the IRS may challenge it later.

A defendant should not have a tax reason to resist characterizing a settlement as excludable under §104, since whether the defendant can deduct the settlement on his tax return (as a business expense, for example) will not be controlled by how plaintiff treats the settlement on his return. However, defendant does benefit in having any possible settlement treated early as excludable under §104, since the settlement ultimately agreed on should be lower if both sides agree that it will be nontaxable to the plaintiff.

---

12. See L. Frolik, Federal Tax Aspects of Injury Damage and Loss, Bureau of National Affairs 1987; R. Wood, Taxation of Damage Awards and Settlement Payments, Tax Institute, 1991; see also O'Gilvie v. United States, 117 S. Ct. 452 (1996), holding that punitive damages awards are taxable income, the same result reached in the 1996 amendment to §104(a)(2).

In commercial litigation—involving such diverse claims as business torts, contract, antitrust, bad faith, and punitive damages—and in structured settlement agreement situations, the tax consequences of a settlement are complex, and a settlement should never be entered into unless you have determined the likely tax consequences to your client or have received the advice of an experienced tax specialist.

2. Negotiating a settlement with opposing counsel

The dynamics of negotiation, in the litigation arena as well as in other fields, has received increasing attention in recent years. This has occurred, in part, because litigation and trial costs have made settlement more desirable, but also because there is a growing awareness that learning negotiating methods can improve a lawyer's ability. The literature on negotiation methods for lawyers is rapidly expanding, and a number of books are particularly useful for litigators.[13] Although this text obviously cannot summarize this literature, some generalizations about negotiations may still be useful.

First, trying a case inherently involves risks, since neither party can ever predict with absolute certainty what a jury will decide in a given case. Settlements are simply the way in which lawyers eliminate the risks in the litigation process.

Second, since risks are at the core of the process, you need to do whatever you can to minimize them. This requires that you adequately prepare the case for trial, since the more you know about the case, the fewer the uncertainties and unknown factors, and hence the less risk. It also requires that you realistically evaluate the case for settlement purposes.

Third, the more relative uncertainty there is in your opponent's mind, the more flexible and compromising he is likely to be. Factors that increase uncertainty in your opponent's mind are your own thorough preparation of the case and willingness and ability to go to trial if necessary, and your client's willingness and preparedness for trial. In communications with your opponent, you need to stress the strong points of your case, probe for the weak spots in your opponent's case, and see if you can glean your opponent's true attitude about the case. Much of this can be accomplished through your contacts during the discovery and motions stages.

Fourth, negotiation styles are as varied as lawyers are numerous. They range from the "take it or leave it" approach to an approach that involves making an initial high demand or low offer that will be followed by protracted negotiations. Nevertheless, there are two basic approaches that are

13. G. Bellow & B. Moulton, The Lawyering Process: Negotiation (1981); H. Edwards & J. White, Problems, Readings and Materials on the Lawyer as a Negotiator (1977); R. Fisher & W. Ury, Getting to Yes (2d ed. 1991); W. Ury, Getting Past No (1991); X. Frascogna & H. Hetherington, Negotiation Strategy for Lawyers (1984); R. Haydock, Negotiation Practice (1984); K. Hegland, Trial and Practice Skills (2d. ed. 1994); G. Williams, Legal Negotiation and Settlement (1983).

commonly followed.[14] The first approach is competitive: the lawyer makes an initial high demand, keeps the pressure on the opponent, and makes as few concessions as possible. The atmosphere is entirely adversarial, and the projected attitude is one of strength. This approach, perhaps the traditional way in which settlement negotiations were conducted, has benefits, principally that any settlement reached will probably be a good one for the client of the more competitive lawyer. Its drawback is that probably a lower percentage of cases settle under this approach. A possible conclusion to draw is that this approach is effective where you have a strong case and don't need to compromise.

The other approach is more cooperative: the lawyer makes a more realistic initial demand, emphasizes the parties' shared interests, and shows a willingness to make concessions. The atmosphere is conciliatory. The benefit to this approach is that probably more cases get settled. On the negative side, the settlement may not be as good for your client, since the other side may try to take advantage of your attitude. Accordingly, this approach may be effective where both parties are equally strong.

The cooperative approach is becoming more accepted, probably because it seems to improve the possibilities of reaching an eventual agreement. While it has several characteristics,[15] the key to the cooperative approach is to avoid taking rigid "positions." Instead, the lawyers who are negotiating focus on the mutual interests of their clients, avoid personalizing the conflicts, and expand the possible solutions before objectively reviewing the possible solutions to settle on a resolution of the problem. This approach, by avoiding personalities and rigid posturing, becomes a joint effort to reach solutions. Where the parties have a complex set of interests, this approach may be useful.

Regardless of which negotiating approach you use in a particular case, the question of which side should first raise the possibility of settlement must be considered. Many lawyers avoid raising it first, on the theory that it suggests weaknesses in the case. Where you have obviously prepared your case thoroughly, however, and show a capacity and willingness to try the case if necessary, no such implication should arise.

Which side should make the initial offer? Frequently both sides are reluctant to state the first dollar figure, on the theory that since the initial figure will be the starting point for later compromises it is better to get the other side committed first. The result is often unrealistically high or low initial offers, which the other side can easily reject. The more effective approach usually is to make a realistic initial offer because this will put pressure on the opponent. The last thing the opponent wants is to get a serious offer, reject it, and end up with a less favorable result following a trial. A realistic offer puts pressure on the opponent to evaluate it seriously.

Finally, remember that the possibilities for settlement frequently track litigation stages. The opposing clients are often unwilling to compromise

14. See G. Williams, Legal Negotiation and Settlement (1983).
15. See R. Fisher & W. Ury, Getting to Yes (2d ed. 1991); W. Ury, Getting Past No (1991).

when litigation begins, the stage when emotions are high. As time passes, however, emotions subside and the costs of litigation become realities to the clients. Still, the lawyers are often unwilling to discuss settlement until discovery is complete, a point when the ability to evaluate the case is greater. Consequently, the pretrial conference stage is where most serious settlement negotiations occur. The clients are increasingly willing to settle, the lawyers are able to assess the case, and substantial cost savings can still occur if a trial is avoided. Finally, if the plaintiff's latest demand is reasonably close to the defendant's last offer, the judge can enter the picture and help the parties reach an agreement. For that reason, negotiation is more accurately seen as an ongoing process that can, and does, come into play throughout the preparation for litigation.

3.   Negotiating at a settlement conference

Under Rule 16(a), the court can direct that a conference be held to facilitate a settlement. The court may direct that parties, or representatives with settlement authority, attend the conference or be available by telephone. With consent of the parties, the court may engage in ex parte communications with the parties and their lawyers.

Settlement conferences with the court most commonly are held after discovery is closed but before final trial preparations begin. Settlement conferences may be held in conjunction with the final pretrial conference contemplated by Rule 16(d). A common practice is for a judge, other than the one before whom the trial will be held, to preside over the conference.

Settlement conference practices vary widely. Some judges actively promote settlement, others are passive about settlement. Some will meet with the lawyers only, others will insist that the clients be present. Some will meet collectively with the lawyers or parties, others will meet with each lawyer and party on an ex parte basis. Still others use both collective and ex parte meetings. Ex parte discussions with the judge can be important, particularly for parties involved in emotionally charged cases such as negligence and wrongful death, because it gives the parties a chance to express their feelings to the judge. Once they get the feelings off their chest, settling the case becomes possible. Some judges will review the court file before the conference, focusing on the pleadings and joint pretrial memorandum, while others expect the lawyers to tell them what the case is all about at the conference. Some judges require the parties to submit confidential settlement memoranda or letters containing the parties' positions on liability and damages, an assessment of their strongest and weakest facts, a justification of their settlement demands and offers, a history of their settlement negotiations, and their predictions of a likely verdict range if the case is tried. Because practices vary widely, you must know what the general procedures in your jurisdiction are, as well as what the specific practice of your particular settlement judge is. If you don't know, ask the judge's clerk or secretary, or talk to lawyers familiar with the judge. Be prepared for the unexpected. The judge may ask a lawyer to cut a legal fee to make settlement possible. The judge may ask the lawyer what the lawyer's fee is, or what the party's settlement authority is. The judge may want to talk to the client without the law-yer being present. The judge may propose settling the case using baseball arbitration rules. The important thing to keep in mind is that anything can happen at a settlement conference. Your job as the lawyer is to learn what you can expect from the particular settlement judge and to prepare your-self and your client appropriately.

What does the judge want to know at the settlement conference? There are two principal concerns. First, the judge wants to know what the likely outcome of this case will be if it were tried before a jury. Second, the judge wants to learn which party is prepared and eager to try the case. These two concerns will shape the judge's attitude and recommendations during the conference.

As plaintiff, you will usually have the first opportunity during the con-ference to tell the judge "what the case is all about." Be an advocate, and project a winning attitude. Show that you are eager to try the case, yet remain willing to be reasonable. Decide how you would present your case to a jury, how you would justify the amount you are asking for, and then argue it to the settlement judge. Consider starting with damages proof, using exhibits to make them clear. For example, summarize your out-of-pocket expenses with the exhibits that support them. In a personal injury case, those expenses exhibits would usually include all medical bills, pho-tographs of the plaintiff, and expert reports. This will give the judge a grasp of how "big" the case is and what proportion of the damages sought are concrete, out-of-pocket expenses, as opposed to intangible damages such as pain and suffering. Next, summarize your proof on liability, again using exhibits such as police reports, photographs, and diagrams to sup-port it. Some plaintiffs' lawyers put together a settlement brochure that contains the key damages and liability information and supporting exhib-its. As defendant, your job is to show that plaintiff's damages are overin-flated and will not be convincing to a jury, that liability is questionable, and that your offer to settle is therefore reasonable.

Each side usually will have only a few minutes to present its best points on damages and liability, so your presentation will essentially be like a short closing argument, but factually based and shorn of emotional rheto-ric. Expect the judge to question your positions. After all, the judge will see her role as showing that plaintiff's demand is unrealistically high, while the defendant's offer is unrealistically low. If the judge can get the plaintiff to come down, and the defendant to come up, a settlement may be possible. Hence, your role as an advocate is to convey to the judge that you are prepared, that your figures are realistic and supportable, and that you and your client are ready and eager to try the case if the other side refuses to be "reasonable." While the expectation at the conference is that both sides will be flexible, your aim is to get the judge to adopt your po-sition as the more reasonable, realistic one and then pressure the other side to accept it.

If the judge recommends that the case be settled for a certain amount, what should you do? Keep in mind that the decision to settle or go to trial is the client's. While you can, and should, advise the client whether the recommended settlement is reasonable, the client makes the final decision, and you must live with it. Be prepared for an unusual or creative settlement suggestion. For example, if the stumbling block in a medical malpractice case is the extent of future medical expenses, the judge might suggest settling for a given dollar amount coupled with a reservation of right to sue if a future medical contingency occurs.

Who should be the negotiator at the settlement conference? While traditionally the lawyer trying the case has also been the negotiator, in recent years lawyers have increasingly turned the job of negotiating a settlement, and attending the settlement conference, to a negotiating lawyer. The logic is that by getting someone else, other than the lawyer who has been managing the litigation, to negotiate, chances for a settlement are improved. This approach is becoming common in large commercial cases. However, if a settlement conference will be held as part of a final pretrial conference, Rule 16(d) requires that the lawyer trying the case attend the conference.

Finally, be patient. Experienced judges and litigators know that settlements often take time. A settlement may not be reached during the first settlement conference. However, the key concept is to get the parties talking about settlement. Once the ice is broken and the parties are talking, most cases seek their own pace, and most eventually settle.

4.   Client authorization

Before you begin negotiations on behalf of a client, you must have authority to settle. The law in almost all jurisdictions is that an agreement to represent a client does not confer authority to settle. Therefore, the client must expressly authorize his lawyer to settle.[16] A client cannot give a valid consent unless he is fully informed concerning the terms of the proposed settlement, understands the terms and the reasons for them, and expressly consents to them. The best way to accomplish this is to schedule a meeting with the client to discuss the upcoming settlement possibilities; candidly give the client your present assessment of his case, explaining what you believe a reasonable settlement would be and why. If the client agrees to settle the case on those terms, you should still obtain his written authorization for that settlement. This is best done by sending a letter that recites the terms of the settlement proposal to the client. He should sign and return a copy of the letter acknowledging and approving its terms. When time is short, authorization by phone will suffice, but this should be followed up with a letter reciting the details of the authorization, as in the example below.

Example:

Dear Mr. Johnson:

As we discussed yesterday, the defendant's lawyer in your case asked us to consider the possibility of settling your case without a trial. I am writ-

16. 30 A.L.R.2d 944 (1953).

ing to make sure you understand what is involved in a settlement and to obtain your permission to reach a settlement with the defendant.

Trials involve risks, and it is impossible to predict with certainty how your case will look to a jury and what verdict the jury will return. Nevertheless, based on the present state of your case, it is my judgment that if a jury were to find the defendant liable, it would return a verdict in the $30,000 to $40,000 range. However, I feel that there is perhaps an even likelihood that a jury would find no liability at all. In addition, we must consider that the expenses of going to trial will be in the $2,000 range, which primarily involves the costs of having the medical experts testify. Finally, keep in mind that my fee for representing you in your case is one-third of any recovery.

The "value" of your case for settlement purposes, then, is approximately as follows: a potential verdict of $30,000 to $40,000, discounted by 50 percent to reflect the possibility the jury will find that no liability exists, and reduced by the $2,000 trial expenses. This comes to a total in the $13,000 to $18,000 range. Of course, by settling the case, you will avoid having to pay the trial expenses.

Based on these considerations, I recommend that you settle your case for not less than the sum of $15,000, which, after deducting my fee, would result in your actually recovering $10,000. Each side will pay its own court costs, which for us have been approximately $150 to this date. Yesterday you told me to go ahead and try to settle your case for not less than $15,000. Of course, I will negotiate with the defendant's lawyer and try to get a higher settlement.

If you still authorize me to settle your case for not less than $15,000, please sign and date the copy of this letter in the spaces provided and return it to me as soon as possible. I will keep you fully informed of the settlement negotiations as they progress.

Sincerely,

_____

John Lawyer

Authorized:

_____

William Johnson

Date: _____

When representing a defendant where insurance coverage is involved, remember that your client is the party, not the insurance company. While insurance contracts customarily permit the insurer to select defense counsel and control the conduct of the defense, case law has increasingly upheld the client's right to authorize any settlement.[17] In short, you must represent the best interests of the insured, and the insurer usually cannot settle a case against the insured's wishes. If this occurs, the client can usually have the settlement set aside, since under these circumstances it is not binding.[18] Finally, keep in mind that when you represent more than one client, you have a professional responsibility to each client when settling the case.[19]

5. Settlement contracts

Since settlements are simply agreements between parties, general contract law principles apply. Good practice generally requires that the agreement be in writing and signed by each party, and some local rules require it.

Settlements are generally made using either a release, a covenant not to sue, or a loan receipt. When the agreement has been executed, the case can be dismissed with prejudice. It is extremely important to understand the legal differences between the various settlement methods. The choice of method is influenced by the types of legal claims and the number of parties involved, whether the settlement is intended to be complete or partial, the type of court action or approval that may be necessary, and the applicable law of contribution. You must know the law of the jurisdiction that governs the settlement contract because statutes and case law concerning releases, covenants not to sue, and loan receipts vary among the jurisdictions. Also, the drafting of the agreement is important, since you need to ensure that it is treated under the applicable law in the way you want it treated, and that it has the effect you intend. This is particularly important in cases with joint tortfeasors, where issues of contribution among the tortfeasors may arise.

a.   Releases, covenants not to sue, and loan receipts

A basic common law release operates as a discharge of all claims against the parties to the release as well as against any persons against whom the same claims are or could have been asserted. In short, a release is a complete discharge, or satisfaction, of an action. For this reason a release is used only when there is a settlement of the entire lawsuit involving every claim and every party.

A covenant not to sue does not discharge any parties. It is simply a contract between two or more parties in which the plaintiff agrees not to sue or to pursue an existing claim against one or more defendants. For

17. See §8.3.4(g) on insurer good faith requirements.
18. This conflict between a client and the client's insurer is a complex area of law and must be researched thoroughly. See, e.g., R. E. Keeton, Basic Text on Insurance Law ch.7 (1971).
19. See Model Rules of Professional Conduct, Model Rule 1.8(g) governing aggregate settlement of claims.

this reason a covenant not to sue is used when there is a partial settlement not involving every party.

The need for covenants not to sue has an historic basis. Since under common law a release was a discharge of all joint tortfeasors, a plaintiff could not use a release when he wished to settle a tort claim with fewer than all defendants. The covenant not to sue solved this problem. Today the effect of the common law release rule has been eliminated in those jurisdictions that have adopted the Uniform Contribution Among Joint Tortfeasors Act.[20] However, the laws of the states are not uniform, and the relevant laws must be understood to determine the effect on contribution whenever the settlement involves a tort claim having multiple joint tortfeasors. A simple covenant not to sue does not prevent a nonsettling defendant from later bringing a contribution claim against the settling defendant after a final judgment, unless a statute (like the Uniform Contribution Among Joint Tortfeasors Act) in the applicable jurisdiction prevents this result. Therefore, it is critical that you know how your jurisdiction deals with the question of contribution.

In recent years the loan receipt, sometimes called a "Mary Carter agreement,"[21] has been used to generate some contribution among joint tortfeasors. Under this settlement approach, one defendant agrees to "loan" a certain amount to the plaintiff. The plaintiff "settles" with that defendant, but that defendant remains in the case with his exposure limited to the loan amount, with a chance of recovering the loan amount if the plaintiff gets a recovery greater than a stated amount against the other defendants. Through the loan receipt approach a defendant can settle for a given amount, which might be recouped after trial. Plaintiff for her part gets an early partial recovery and a cooperative defendant. The legality of this basic settlement technique has been upheld in most jurisdictions over public policy objections, but courts have also generally required that the existence and sometimes the terms of a loan receipt be disclosed to the remaining defendants and have allowed it to be used to show the bias and interest of a witness who testifies at trial if the witness is associated with the settled defendant.[22]

Any number of variations of the basic loan receipt formula are possible. In some situations the loaning defendant is dismissed as a defendant. Sometimes the loaning defendant is dismissed with prejudice, sometimes without. The choices are numerous and are affected by the extent to which the details of such arrangements are admissible at trial, and whether the jurisdiction's law of contribution among joint tortfeasors is affected by any particular agreement's structure. The jurisdictions vary widely on the validity and enforceability of the numerous variations of Mary Carter agreements. It should be apparent that you should never en-

---

20. W. Prosser & P. Keeton, The Law of Torts §§49-50 (5th ed. 1984).

21. Booth v. Mary Carter Paint Co., 202 So. 2d 8 (Fla. App. 1967). See also Vermont Union School Dist. No. 21 v. Cummings Const. Co., 143 Vt. 416, 469 A.2d 742 (1983); City of Tucson v. Gallagher, 108 Ariz. 140, 493 P.2d 1197 (1972).

22. See Reese v. Chicago, Burlington & Quincy R.R., 5 Ill. App. 3d 450, 283 N.E.2d 517 (1972) aff'd, 55 Ill. 2d 356, 303 N.E.2d 382 (1973); held improper, see Elbaor v. Smith, 845 S.W.2d 240 (Tex. 1993); Dosdourian v. Carsten, 624 S.W.2d 241 (Fl. 1993).

ter into a loan receipt agreement unless you are familiar with the particular jurisdiction's applicable law.

b. Drafting the agreement

Regardless of which type of settlement is used, care obviously must be taken in drafting the agreement to ensure that it is specifically tailored to the case involved. First, the agreement should clearly state whether it is a release, covenant not to sue, or loan receipt, and state what matters it does and does not resolve. Second, the agreement should describe the events involved in the case, since the discharge will only be for those events. Third, the agreement should recite the claims of liability and damages and the defendant's denial of them, since it is the compromise of these disputed claims that constitutes the mutual consideration in the agreement. Fourth, the agreement should specify how the pending court case is to be terminated. Fifth, the agreement can contain a choice of law clause and specify the details of any contribution in a covenant not to sue, if appropriate and permitted under the applicable jurisdiction's law. Finally, if the terms of the settlement are to remain confidential, the agreement must expressly provide for confidentiality. Most defendants, faced with other plaintiffs having the same or similar claims, will insist on confidentiality as a condition for settling the case.

The following are simple examples of a release, covenant not to sue, and loan receipt. They should be modified to fit the facts of any particular situation and the particular law of the applicable jurisdiction.

Example:

RELEASE

In consideration of the sum of $ _____ , which Plaintiff acknowledges receiving, Plaintiff _____ agrees to release Defendants _____ and ____ _____ and their heirs, survivors, agents, and personal representatives from all claims, suits, or actions in any form or on any basis, because of anything that was done or not done at any time, on account of the following:

All claims for personal injuries, property damage, physical disabilities, medical expenses, lost income, loss of consortium, and all other claims that have been or could be brought, including all claims now known or which in the future might be known, which arise out of an occurrence on or about _____ *(date)* _____ , at _____ *(location)* _____ , when Plaintiff claims to have been injured as a result of a collision between an automobile driven by Plaintiff and automobiles driven by the Defendants.

As a result of this collision, Plaintiff has brought suit against the Defendants for damages. The Defendants have denied both liability and the claimed extent of damages. This release is a compromise settlement between Plaintiff _____ and Defendant ____ _____ and Defendant _____ .

    This agreement is a release and shall operate as a total discharge of any claims Plaintiff has or may have arising out of the above occurrence against these Defendants and any other persons.

    Plaintiff _____ and Defendant _____ _____ and Defendant _____ also expressly agree to terminate any actions that have been filed, particularly a claim by this Plaintiff against these Defendants currently filed as civil action no. _____ in the United States District Court for the District of _____ , in _____ . Plaintiff and these Defendants agree to execute a Stipulation of Dismissal, with prejudice, and file it with the Clerk of the above Court, thereby terminating that action in its entirety, within seven days of the execution of this agreement.

Date: _____

_____
Plaintiff

_____
Defendant

_____
Defendant

Example:

COVENANT NOT TO SUE

    In consideration of the sum of $_____ , which Plaintiff acknowledges receiving, Plaintiff _____ agrees not to institute, pursue, or continue any claim, suit, or action in any form or on any basis, because of anything that was done or not done at any time, against Defendant _____ and his heirs, survivors, agents, or personal representatives on account of the following:

    Any claims against Defendant _____ for personal injuries, property damage, physical disabilities, medical expenses, lost income, loss of consortium, and any other claims that have been or could be brought, including all claims now known or which in the future might become known, which arise out of an occurrence on or about _____*(date)*_____ , at _____*(location)*_____ , when Plaintiff claims to have been injured as a result of a collision between an automobile driven by Plaintiff and an automobile driven by Defendant.

    As a result of this collision, Plaintiff has brought suit against Defendant for damages. Defendant has denied both liability and the claimed extent of damages. This covenant not to sue is a compromise settlement between Plaintiff _____ and Defendant _____ _____ .

   This agreement is a covenant not to sue, and not a release or an accord and satisfaction. Nothing in this agreement shall operate as a discharge against any other persons, and Plaintiff _____ _____ expressly reserves the right to pursue any claims against any other persons other than Defendant _____ and his heirs, survivors, agents, and personal representatives.

   Plaintiff _____ and Defendant _____ _____ also expressly agree to terminate any actions between them, particularly a claim by Plaintiff against this Defendant currently filed as civil action no. _____ in the United States District Court for the District of _____ , in _____ _____ . Plaintiff and Defendant agree to execute a Stipulation of Dismissal, with prejudice, and file it with the Clerk of the above Court, to terminate that action against this Defendant only, within seven days of the execution of this agreement.

Date: _____

                                              _____
                                              Plaintiff

                                              _____
                                              Defendant

Example:

LOAN AGREEMENT

   Plaintiff _____ and Defendant _____ _____ enter into the following agreement:

   Plaintiff _____ has filed suit against Defendant _____ and other Defendants. This suit, civil action no. _____ , is pending in the United States District Court for the District of _____ in _____ . Defendant _____ and the other Defendants have denied the claims.

   Plaintiff's pending suit is based on a collision that occurred on or about _____*(date)*_____ at _____*(location)*_____ in which Plaintiff claims to have suffered injuries as a result of a collision between an automobile in which Plaintiff was a passenger and other automobiles. Defendant _____ was the driver of the automobile in which Plaintiff was a passenger. Defendant _____ has denied liability for Plaintiff's claimed injuries.

   Plaintiff wishes to compromise her claim against Defendant _____ _____ . Defendant _____ wishes to compromise Plaintiff's claim against him. Plaintiff _____

_____ and Defendant _____
agree to the following:

    Defendant _____ agrees to loan Plaintiff the sum of $_____ . This loan is without interest. Defendant _____ will remain a party in the suit. Plaintiff promises to repay the loan from any judgment or settlement Plaintiff actually receives and collects from any of the other Defendants in the above action. Plaintiff will be obligated to repay the loan only to the extent of any recovery actually collected from any of the other Defendants, and in any event Plaintiff shall have no obligation to pay Defendant _____ _____ any sum exceeding $ _____ *(loan* _____ *amount)* .

Date: _____   _____
                                               Plaintiff

                                             _____
                                             Defendant

    When drafting a settlement contract, you must research the law of the applicable jurisdiction to determine the validity and effect of these settlement devices,[23] and you must keep the following basic concepts clear. First, the effect of a release under common law terminates all of plaintiff's claims against all existing and potential defendants, not just the settling defendant. As a plaintiff, never agree to a release unless you intend to terminate all present and future litigation. Second, a covenant not to sue, first created to avoid the effect of the common law release rule, technically keeps the claims alive against the settling defendant since the plaintiff only agrees not to enforce the claims against that defendant. As a result, a settling defendant is still exposed to contribution claims by the other defendants who are still in the lawsuit. As a defendant, never agree to a covenant not to sue unless you have adequate protection against later contribution claims, either by statute or by the settlement agreement. Third, remember that contribution among joint tortfeasors is not the same thing as indemnification. Contribution does not affect valid indemnification claims against any parties. Fourth, many states by statute protect a settling joint tortfeasor defendant by providing that any judgment against the nonsettling defendants be reduced by the amount the settling defendant paid the plaintiff, and by discharging the settling defendant from any later contribution claims by nonsettling defendants and other joint tortfeasors (the Uniform Contribution Among Joint Tortfeasors Act so provides). However, not all states have such statutes, so the settling defendant must know the applicable jurisdiction's law to assess his exposure

_____

23. For an excellent discussion of this area along with illustrations of potential problems, see Dewey, Traps in Multitortfeasor Settlements, 13 Litigation (No. 1, Summer 1987).

to later contribution claims. Fifth, the settlement agreement can usually specify what jurisdiction's law will apply to the agreement. Such a choice of law clause can then apply more favorable law to the contribution issues. Sixth, jurisdictions vary in how they define a defendant's pro rata share of any judgment against joint tortfeasors. If the jurisdiction does not protect a settling defendant from contribution claims, the defendant should make sure that the settlement agreement adopts the applicable jurisdiction's definition of a pro rata share and insist that the defendant get a "credit" for either the amount paid to the plaintiff to settle or a pro rata share of any ultimate judgment plaintiff gets, whichever is greater. Finally, if the lawsuit involves both contract and tort claims, make sure you know how much of the settlement amount will be allocated to each type of claim. This is important, because contribution exists only in tort, not contract. Shifting the allocation of the settlement amount between the contract and tort claims will affect the amount of contribution the non-settling defendants may be entitled to later.

It should be apparent that the drafting of a settlement can be complex, particularly in situations involving joint tortfeasors. In general, every plaintiff wants a guaranteed dollar amount from the settling defendant, wants to keep claims alive against the nonsettling defendants, and wants no relief from contribution for the settling defendant. Every settling defendant, by contrast, wants to get out of the case with a guaranteed dollar amount to cap his exposure, and wants adequate protection from later contribution claims, if a statute does not already provide it. A careful lawyer must know the legal effect and validity of these settlement devices, the contribution law that applies to the tort claims, and must prepare a carefully drafted instrument that fits the particulars of the case so that the final agreement achieves what the lawyer needs in order to adequately protect his client.

c. Structured settlements

In recent years so-called structured settlements have become common, particularly in the personal injury area when plaintiffs have been seriously and permanently injured. A structured settlement is simply a settlement under which the plaintiff receives periodic payments rather than one lump sum. The benefit to the plaintiff is that she is assured of support over a period of years. Defendant's insurance companies are also benefited, since paying a settlement over a number of years reduces the true cost of the settlement. Socially, structured settlements help ensure that the plaintiff will not become indigent and depend on the state for support. Under §104(a)(2) of the Internal Revenue Code, periodic payments receive the same tax treatment as lump sum payments,[24] and some states have legislation regulating them, often based on the Model Periodic Payments of Judgments Act. Structured settle-

24. This change came about through the Periodic Payment Settlement Act of 1982, amending §104(a)(2).

ments are complicated, and involve both statutory regulation and tax laws. This is an area where advice from someone experienced in this settlement method is warranted.

The most frequently used approach in structured settlements is to provide for an initial lump sum and a series of periodic payments. The lump sum is large enough to cover the plaintiff's attorney's fee, other legal expenses, and the plaintiff's unpaid bills. The periodic payments cover either a fixed period of years or the lifetime of the plaintiff; the periods are either annual or a shorter time. If the payments may extend over a number of years, they may be tied to the inflation rate by providing for increases based on the Consumer Price Index or other measure of inflation rates. The defendant's insurer usually funds the periodic payments by purchasing an annuity from an established life insurance company that will automatically make the payments required under the agreement.

d.   High-low agreements

In recent years, high-low agreements have become common. While not a device that settles a case, it does have benefits for both sides. A high-low agreement is an agreement between plaintiff and defendant that establishes the maximum and minimum recovery to the plaintiff and thereby eliminates the risk of either a complete win or loss. It is frequently used in personal injury cases involving large potential damages.

For example, consider a personal injury case in which plaintiff is seeking damages in the millions, and defendant is contesting both liability and damages. Plaintiff's principal fear is that the jury may return a defense verdict on damages. Defendant's principal fear is that the jury may return a verdict in favor of the plaintiff on liability and award several million in damages. Accordingly, plaintiff and defendant agree that the case will proceed to trial, and that, regardless of the jury's verdict, plaintiff will not receive more than $2,000,000 and not less than $500,000. The $2,000,000 becomes the "high" and the $500,000 becomes the "low" in the high-low agreement. The agreement becomes a compromise eliminating the possibility of a catastrophic verdict for either side.

High-low agreements are negotiated much like a settlement agreement, but are usually made just before or during trial. This is because as the trial progresses, the parties have a greater sense of urgency in avoiding a disastrous result. Both sides have a mutual interest in reducing risk and achieving finality by avoiding an appeal. The parties' last demand and offer before settlement talks collapsed are a good starting point in reaching a high-low agreement, although the numbers will be modified by how the trial is progressing.

When negotiating such an agreement, be sure to consider all the possibilities that may arise and need to be included in the agreement. For example, will the agreement bar post-trial motions and any appeal? What happens in the event of a mistrial, caused either by events during the trial or by the jury's inability to reach a verdict on all or some counts? Who pays costs, and what are the included costs? Does the agreement cover pre-judgment and post-judgment interest? When should the judge be informed that an agreement exists, since the existence of the agreement may influence how the judge conducts the trial?

In most cases, the lawyers will advise the judge of the agreement and its terms at the end of the trial, when the jury is ready to deliberate, and put on the record the terms of the agreement. When the jury returns its verdict, the judge later enters judgment consistent with the terms of the agreement and the jury's verdict. The jury, of course, is not told about the agreement.

e.   *Terminating the suit*

After a settlement agreement has been reached, the lawsuit must be terminated. The standard method is to file a stipulation to dismiss with the clerk of the court. Under Rule 41 a court order is no longer necessary.

Make sure the stipulation to dismiss is with prejudice as to the settling defendant, since this bars the plaintiff from refiling the claim later. If the settlement is only partial, as is the case with a covenant not to sue or a loan receipt, the stipulation must clearly show which party is being dismissed and which parties remain in the case. The stipulation is signed by the lawyers for the parties who have agreed to settle.

Example (*complete dismissal*):

[Caption]

STIPULATION OF DISMISSAL

Plaintiff _____ , Defendant _____
_____ , and Defendant _____ agree to dismiss this action with prejudice, and each party will bear its costs and attorney's fees.

Date: _____

_____
Attorney for Plaintiff

_____
Attorney for Defendant

_____
Attorney for Defendant

Example (partial dismissal):

[Caption]

STIPULATION OF DISMISSAL

Plaintiff _____ and Defendant _____ _____ agree to dismiss this action with prejudice as to Defendant _____ only, and the action shall continue as to the remaining Defendants.

Date: _____   _____

Attorney for Plaintiff

_____

Attorney for Defendant

A simple stipulation of dismissal will be adequate when the case will not be dismissed until the settlement has actually been carried out. For example, in a personal injury case the stipulation of dismissal is routinely filed with the clerk after the plaintiff has received and cashed the settlement check. In this situation, there is no danger that the defendant will breach the settlement agreement.

However, if the settlement agreement requires future performance, you will want the court to retain jurisdiction for the purpose of enforcing the terms of the agreement, should that ever become necessary. For example, a settlement agreement may require the other party to make future periodic payments, or contain a noncompetition clause. In this situation, you will want the court to retain jurisdiction after the case is dismissed. The safe approach is to have the agreement expressly provide for it and to have the court enter an order of dismissal expressly retaining jurisdiction. The Supreme Court recently held that a district court retains jurisdiction over the case after a dismissal with prejudice only if the order of dismissal refers to and incorporates the settlement agreement or expressly reserves the court's jurisdiction to enforce the settlement agreement.[25] If the settlement agreement calls for continuing the court's jurisdiction, and the order of dismissal incorporates the terms of the settlement agreement, the court will retain jurisdiction. A party that violates the settlement agreement also violates the court order, and the district court will have ancillary jurisdiction to enforce the order.

Where you want the court to retain jurisdiction, make sure the settlement agreement has an appropriate clause.

---

25. See *Kokkonen v. Guardian Life Insurance Company of America*, 511 U.S. 375 (1994), which makes clear that Rule 41(a)(2) permits a dismissal order that retains jurisdiction for the purpose of enforcing the settlement agreement if the parties wish this to occur.

Example:

The parties agree that the court shall retain jurisdiction over this case and the parties for the purpose of enforcing the terms of the settlement agreement. The parties further agree that this case will be terminated only through an order of dismissal that expressly incorporates the terms of this agreement and expressly retains the court's jurisdiction over the case and the parties.

You will then need to prepare a draft order incorporating the agreement and retaining the court's jurisdiction and submit it to the court for signature.

In certain types of cases court approval is needed for any settlement. Settlements in class actions must have court approval under Rule 23(e). Also, settlements involving decedents' estates or incapacitated parties such as minors and incompetents usually require court approval. In these situations the action will be brought in the name of the representative party, such as a guardian, guardian ad litem, conservator, administrator, or executor. Local statutes and rules must always be checked to ensure compliance with technical requirements. The usual procedure is to present a petition to the court having jurisdiction over the party, usually a probate or family court, and to serve notice to all parties and other interested persons. A hearing is then conducted on the proposed settlement and, if approved, an appropriate court order authorizing the settlement will be entered.

f. Offers of judgment

Rule 68 provides that a party defending a claim can serve an offer of judgment upon the opposing party more than 10 days before the trial. The purpose of Rule 68 is to encourage settlements where reasonable offers to settle have been made. If the offer is refused and a judgment following trial is the same or less favorable to the plaintiff than the pretrial offer of judgment, the plaintiff becomes responsible for the defendant's "costs" incurred from the time of the offer. An offer of judgment can be made on any "claim," including the plaintiff's claims against the defendant, defendant's counterclaims against the plaintiff, cross-claims between defendants, or third-party claims against third-party defendants.

In recent years Rule 68 has become a prominent weapon in the settlement stage of the litigation process and has generated substantial case law. Rule 68 applies whenever a final judgment is in a plaintiff's favor but is the same or less favorable than the offer to settle made by a defendant.[26] The defendant's offer to settle must be reasonably certain in amount and must be unconditional, but there is no requirement that the settlement and cost amounts be itemized.[27]

The principal difficulty in applying Rule 68 has concerned the meaning of the term "costs." It is clear that costs include clerk and marshall

---

26. Delta Air Lines v. August, 450 U.S. 346 (1981).
27. Marek v. Chesny, 473 U.S. 1 (1985).

fees, witness fees, and court reporter fees,[28] but less so concerning attorney's fees. In Marek v. Chesney,[29] the Supreme Court held that "costs" refers to all costs that can be awarded under applicable substantive law. In that case, a 42 U.S.C. §1983 civil rights action, §1988 allowed attorney's fees to the prevailing party. However, the plaintiff's judgment was not as favorable as the defendant's pretrial offer of judgment. Therefore, plaintiff could not recover as part of costs any attorney's fees incurred from the date of the defendant's offer. Since this included the attorney's fees for the entire trial, plaintiff could not collect attorney's fees amounting to over $100,000.

Case law to date has generally rejected a similar argument, in attorney's fees cases, that the plaintiff who gets a judgment less favorable than a previous offer should also be required to pay defendant's post-offer attorney's fees.[30]

The present usefulness of Rule 68 to defendants depends largely on whether "costs" include attorney's fees. Where they include only court costs and the like, these are likely to be sufficiently small in most cases that they will not exert much pressure on a plaintiff to settle. Where costs include attorney's fees because a statute expressly so provides, Rule 68 affords substantial leverage against a plaintiff since, if the later judgment is less favorable than defendant's offer of settlement, the plaintiff will forgo recovering attorney's fees from the date of the offer. As Marek v. Chesney illustrates, this can be a substantial amount.

If a defendant wishes to make an offer of judgment to the plaintiff, this must be done more than 10 days before trial begins. Make sure the offer is actually delivered to the plaintiff's attorney within the permissible time. Make sure every offer of judgment has a reasonable time limit. Do not file the offer in court at this time; otherwise the trial judge may see it and be influenced by it.

Defendants usually make settlement offers under Rule 68 when settlement negotiations have broken down and a trial is to begin soon. However, the offer can be made at any time, and you should consider making it earlier if you can realistically assess the case's value, particularly where attorney's fees are included as costs. The offer can be made in a letter, sent by registered mail or hand delivered, or in a formal offer with an attached proof of service.

The offer of judgment should be tied to your settlement approach and your earlier offers to settle, so that it puts realistic pressure on the other side, and later demonstrates to the settlement judge that you have been realistic in evaluating the case. As plaintiff, your offer should be somewhat less than your evaluation of a likely jury verdict; as defendant, somewhat more. This will account for the elimination of risk, time, costs of trial, and an appeal.

28. See 28 U.S.C. §§1920 et seq.
29. 473 U.S. 1 (1985).
30. Crossman v. Marcoccio, 806 F.2d 329 (1st Cir. 1986).

Example:

[Caption]

OFFER OF JUDGMENT

To: _____ *(attorney for plaintiff)*
_____

Defendant Johnson Corporation, pursuant to Rule 68, offers to allow judgment to be entered against it, in favor of plaintiff Frank Jones, in the amount of fourteen thousand ($14,000) dollars, and costs of suit incurred to the date of this offer.

This offer is made under Rule 68 of the Federal Rules of Civil Procedure and Rule 408 of the Federal Rules of Evidence, is made as a settlement offer, and is not to be taken as an admission of, or any indication of, liability on the part of this defendant.

This offer shall remain open for ten days after service of the offer.

Date: _____   _____
                                                      Attorney for Defendant
                                                      Johnson Corporation

If the plaintiff elects to accept the offer of judgment, he simply sends a notice to the defendant that he accepts the offer. The acceptance must be made and written notice served within ten days of when the offer is served. Judgment can then be entered on the accepted offer.

g. *Evidence rules*

Under Rule 408 of the Federal Rules of Evidence, compromises and offers of compromise are not admissible to prove liability or damages. Rule 408 is broadly drafted to bar settlement discussions from being introduced at trial on those issues. The Rule, however, does not prevent admission of such evidence for other purposes, principally to expose bias and interest of a testifying witness. The law is clear that a party that has settled and later becomes a witness at the trial of the same case can be cross-examined on the existence and content of the settlement. The same Rule has generally been applied to Mary Carter agreements, since they usually show bias and interest.[31]

h. *Insurer good faith requirements*

In civil litigation a defendant will often have some insurance coverage. The insurance contract normally has language under which the in-

---

31. Johnson v. Moberg, 334 N.W.2d 411 (Minn. 1983); Hegarty v. Campbell Soup Co., 214 Neb. 716, 335 N.W.2d 758 (1983).

surer reserves the right to manage the defense and negotiate a settlement. However, courts have usually imposed a duty on the insurer to deal fairly and in good faith to protect the interests of the insured. This duty comes about because the interests of the insurer sometimes conflict with those of the insured. The insured naturally wants the company to stand behind her and defend vigorously or, if a settlement is reached, to settle within the policy limits. The insurer also has an interest in defending vigorously, but in a settlement situation only has a financial interest in settling the case under the policy limit. Hence, the insurer and insured's interests come most sharply in conflict where there is a risk of exposure over the policy limits since, once the policy limit is reached, only the insured has additional exposure. Because of this conflict, courts have imposed a good faith obligation on the insurer to defend the case fairly and to adequately protect the insured's interests. In other words, the insurer has a duty to defend and must conduct the defense in the best interests of the insured as though there were no policy limits.[32]

Any settlement offer from the plaintiff should be communicated to the insured, since the insured is the actual party. Case law is not uniform on whether failure to notify the party of a settlement offer is a breach of good faith, but some courts have so held.[33] It is obviously a good practice to notify your client of every settlement offer, regardless of how unrealistic it is. Where a duty to defend in good faith has been breached, the insurer is generally liable for the entire judgment, regardless of policy limits.[34]

For defense lawyers the message from case law should be clear. The defense lawyer's client is the insured, and the lawyer's professional and ethical obligation is to serve the best interests of the client. That the lawyer was selected, and will have fees paid, by the insurance company does not alter the professional obligations. Where settlement negotiations are in progress, both the insured and insurer must be kept informed of its progress. Whenever possible, the insured and insurer should both agree in writing to any settlement. Since the lawyer serves the client, not the insurer, the lawyer must accept a reasonable settlement, even when it involves the policy limits, if it is in the best interests of the client. Where exposure above the policy limits is involved and you, as lawyer, cannot get both the insured and the insurer to agree to a settlement, you must always research the status of the law in your jurisdiction to determine what the rights, duties, and liabilities of the insured and the insurer are in such circumstances.

i.   Enforcing settlements[35]

Although uncommon, a party may sometimes breach a settlement. Since a settlement agreement is a contract, the settlement can always be enforced in a separate contract action, but this is not the preferred

32. See G. Williams, Legal Negotiation and Settlement ch. 5, pp. 105-106 (1983).
33. See L. Russ & T. Segalla, Couch on Insurance (3d ed. 1995).
34. See 49 A.L.R.2d 711 (1956).
35. Wright & Miller §§2860 et seq.

method. Under Rule 60(b), the wronged party can move to enforce the judgment, provided that, as discussed above, the order of dismissal previously entered expressly retained the court's jurisdiction for purposes of enforcing the settlement agreement. The motion must be made in the same court, preferably before the same judge to whom the case had been assigned, and must cite a permissible reason for obtaining relief from a final judgment. You may need to have the case restored to the court's active calendar before you make the motion. At the hearing on the motion, be prepared to prove up the breach of the settlement agreement.

j. Settlement statement

When a plaintiff's lawyer has received a settlement check from a defendant or defendant's insurer in accordance with a settlement agreement, the check must be deposited in the client's trust account. The lawyer must then, if being paid under a contingency fee agreement, prepare a written statement showing what the outcome was, the amount to be remitted to the client, and how that amount was calculated.[36] This statement, commonly called a settlement statement or sheet, shows the gross amount received in settlement, costs, attorney's fees, and the net amount that goes to the client. The client needs to approve the accounting, and the funds are disbursed from the client's trust account in accordance with the statement.

Example:

SETTLEMENT STATEMENT

June 1, 1998

Settlement amount	$100,000.00
Costs (per attached itemized list)	$10,000.00
Net amount (settlement amount minus costs)	$90,000.00
Attorney's fees (33⅓% of net amount)	$30,000.00
Net amount to client (net amount minus attorney's fees)	$60,000.00

ACCEPTED AND APPROVED:

_____

[client's signature]

Date: _____

---

36. See Model Rules of Professional Conduct, Rule 1.5(c). Such a statement is required in every contingency fee case, whether the case is concluded by settlement, trial, or other means.

The statement should be modified to include other particulars of the case, such as other distributions for workers' compensation liens. It should also reflect, where pertinent, that the client is solely and completely responsible for any unpaid bills, such as medical bills.

APPENDIX

LITIGATION FILE: *JONES v. SMITH*

This appendix is part of the litigation file in Jones v. Smith, an automobile collision case. It illustrates each basic step in the pleadings, discovery, motions, and settlement stages of the litigation process.

FACTS

John Jones, a 23-year-old delivery truck driver, was involved in a collision with Susan Smith. The collision occurred on September 2, 1998, at the intersection of 40th Street and Thomas Road in Phoenix, Arizona. Jones injured his stomach, neck, back, a shoulder, and an ankle and was out of work for a month. His car was also damaged.

Jones brings suit in federal court in Phoenix, Arizona. He claims that Smith negligently ran a red light at the intersection and crashed into his car (he was not operating a delivery truck at the time). Jones is a citizen of Arizona; Smith is a citizen of Nevada. The lawsuit was filed on January 2, 1999.

UNITED STATES DISTRICT COURT FOR THE DISTRICT OF ARIZONA

The "Caption" includes the Court, the parties, and the case number.

John Jones,
         Plaintiff,
 	
   v.
 	
 Susan Smith,
         Defendant
	NO. _____
	
	 Civil Action
	
	 <u>JURY TRIAL</u>
	 <u>DEMANDED</u>

The court clerk will stamp the case number when the complaint is filed with the clerk.

The jury demand is usually put in the caption as well as at the end of the complaint.

COMPLAINT

Plaintiff John Jones complains of defendant Susan Smith as follows:

1. Jurisdiction in this case is based on diversity of citizenship and the amount in controversy. Plaintiff is a citizen of the State of Arizona. Defendant is a citizen of the State of Nevada. The amount in controversy exceeds, exclusive of interest and costs, the sum of seventy-five thousand ($75,000) dollars.

This is the standard jurisdictional allegation in diversity cases. It should be the first paragraph of the complaint.

2. On September 2, 1998, at approximately 2:00 P.M., plaintiff John Jones ("Jones") was driving a vehicle northbound on 40th Street toward the intersection of 40th Street and Thomas Road in Phoenix, Arizona. Defendant Susan Smith ("Smith") was driving a vehicle eastbound on Thomas Road toward the same intersection.

The factual allegations should be clear and simple. This makes it more likely that they will be either admitted or denied outright, making the pleadings easier to understand.

3. Smith failed to stop for a red light at the intersection of 40th Street and Thomas Road, and negligently drove her vehicle into Jones' vehicle.

4. As a direct and proximate result of Smith's negligence, Jones injured his stomach, neck, back, a shoulder, an ankle, and other bodily parts, received other physical injuries, suffered physical and mental pain and suffering, incurred medical expenses, lost income, and will incur further medical expenses and lost income in the future.

The negligence and causation claims are kept simple. This is adequate under "notice pleading" requirements.

The injury allegations are usually spelled out in some detail.

WHEREFORE, plaintiff John Jones demands judgment against defendant Susan Smith for the sum of $100,000, with interest and costs.

Many complaints simply ask for "a sum in excess of $75,000," the jurisdictional limit.

Dated: January 2, 1999

Anne Johnson
Anne Johnson
Attorney for Plaintiff
100 Congress Street
Phoenix, AZ 85001
882-1000

This avoids requesting
unrealistic damages.
The danger of exagger-
ated damages is that,
unless amended, the
pleadings can be read
to the jury at trial, making the plaintiff look
greedy.

PLAINTIFF DEMANDS TRIAL BY JURY

Most jurisdictions also
require submitting a
jury demand form and
paying a jury demand
fee to preserve the right
to a jury trial.

UNITED STATES DISTRICT COURT
FOR THE DISTRICT OF ARIZONA

John Jones,
      Plaintiff

    v.

Susan Smith,
      Defendant

NO. _____

SUMMONS

TO THE ABOVE-NAMED DEFENDANT:
Susan Smith
200 Palmer Way
Las Vegas, Nevada

    You are hereby summoned and required to serve upon Anne Johnson, plaintiff's attorney, whose address is 100 Congress Street, Phoenix, AZ, 85001, an answer to the complaint which is herewith served upon you, within 20 days after service of this summons upon you, exclusive of the day of service.

    If you fail to do so, judgment by default will be taken against you for the relief demanded in the complaint.

Thomas Barber
_____
Clerk of the Court

[Seal of U.S. District Court]

Dated: January 2, 1999

A good practice is to give the person who serves the complaint and summons any additional information about the defendant that may help make an effective service.

In this case service is made under the Arizona long-arm statute. Service could also be made using the mail and waiver of service provisions of Rule 4.

The person making the service must prepare an Affidavit of Service showing how service on the defendant was actually made.

The Affidavit of Service form is frequently attached to the summons form.

UNITED STATES DISTRICT COURT
FOR THE DISTRICT OF ARIZONA

John Jones,
       Plaintiff,

    v.   No. 99 C 1000

Susan Smith,
       Defendant

ANSWER

Defendant Susan Smith answers the complaint as follows:

1. Admit
2. Admit
3. Deny
4. Defendant denies plaintiff was injured as a result of any negligence by the defendant, and is without knowlege or information sufficient to form a belief as to the truth of all other allegations in Par. 4, and therefore denies them.

Simple responses are more likely to be made since the complaint's allegations are correspondingly simple.

First Defense

Plaintiff's claimed injuries and damages were caused by plaintiff's own negligence, which was the sole proximate cause of any injuries and damages plaintiff may have received.

WHEREFORE, defendant requests that plaintiff receive nothing, and that judgment be entered for the defendant, including costs of this action.

Each defense should be set out separately.

Dated: January 15, 1999

William Sharp

William Sharp
Attorney for Defendant
100 Broadway
Phoenix, AZ 85001
881-1000

AFFIDAVIT OF SERVICE

I, Helen Thompson, having been first duly sworn, state that I served a copy of defendant's Answer on plaintiff by personally delivering it to Anne Johnson, attorney for plaintiff, at 100 Congress Street, Phoenix, Arizona, on January 15, 1999.

Helen Thompson
Helen Thompson

Signed and sworn to before me on January
    15, 1999

Mary Ryan
Notary Public

My commission expires on December 31,
    1999

[Seal]

After the complaint has been served, every other court paper must be served on every other party in accordance with Rule 5. The usual service is personal delivery or mailing to the party's attorney of record.

An affidavit or certification of service should always be attached to every court paper showing how proper service was made.

All court papers must be filed with the court either before service or within a reasonable time after service.

In practice, court papers are usually filed with the court clerk the same day service is made.

UNITED STATES DISTRICT COURT
FOR THE DISTRICT OF ARIZONA

John Jones,
                Plaintiff

        v.   NO. 99 C 1000

Susan Smith,
                Defendant

PLAINTIFF's INITIAL
DISCLOSURES

Plaintiff John Jones makes the following initial disclosures to the defendant, pursuant to Rule 26(a)(1) of the Federal Rules of Civil Procedure:

(A) Individuals

The following individuals are likely to have information relevant to disputed facts.:

1. John Jones, plaintiff
2. Susan Smith, defendant
3. Caroal Brown
   42 East Cambridge Street
   Phoenix, AZ
   482-3737
4. Mary Porter
   42 East Cambridge Street
   Phoenix, AZ
   482-3737
5. Off. Steven Pitcher
   Phoenix Police Dept.
6. Lenore L. Lang, M.D.
   333 East Campbell Avenue
   Phoenix, AZ 85016
   482-6000
7. Frank Hoffman, M.D.
   222 West Thomas Road, Suite 100
   Phoenix, AZ 85013
   222-4000
8. J. Franks, D.C.
   55 North 27th Avenue
   Phoenix, AZ 85007
   881-9876

9. Diane Devo
    Devo Wholesale Florist
    3731 40th Street
    Phoenix, AZ 85007
    434-1000

10. John Jones, Sr., and Mary Jones
    1020 N. 50th Street
    Phoenix, AZ 85013
    332-8571

Witnesses #1-5 are occurrance witnesses; witnesses # 6-10 are medical and damages witnesses.

(B) Documents and tangible things

The following documents and tangible things, which are attached, are relevant to disputed facts:

1. Devo Wholesale Florist employment records
2. Doctors Hospital medical records
3. Dr. Lang office records and bill
4. Dr. Hoffman office records and bill
5. Dr. Frank office records and bill
6. Walgreen Pharmacy bills
7. Phoenix Police Dept. accident reports
8. X-rays
9. Photographs of accident scene

(C) Damages computation

The following is the present computation of known damages:

1. *Medical and related expenses:*
Doctors Hospital bill	$1,257.18
Dr. Lang bill	339.70
Dr. Hoffman bill	340.00
Dr. Franks bill	697.80
Walgreen Pharmacy bills	83.13
2. *Lost wages:*
Devo Wholesale Florist	700.00
3. Property damages:
Toyota vehicle repair	1,213.00
4. *Other expenses:*
Broken wristwatch	75.00
College books	162.00

5. *Pain and suffering:*

Past	over 40,000.00
Future	over 30,000.00

The documentation of these damages is contained in the documents identified in section (B) above.

(D) Insurance

Rule 26(a)(1)(D) does not apply to the plaintiff since defendant has filed no counterclaims in this action.

Dated: January 20, 1999

Anne Johnson

Anne Johnson
Attorney for Plaintiff
100 Congress Street
Phoenix, AZ 85001
882-1000

UNITED STATES DISTRICT COURT
FOR THE DISTRICT OF ARIZONA

John Jones,
        Plaintiff

        v.   NO. 99 C 1000

Susan Smith,
        Defendant

DEFENDANT'S INTERROGATORIES
TO PLAINTIFF

Pursuant to Rule 33 of the Federal Rules of Civil Procedure, defendant Smith requests that plaintiff Jones answer the following interrogatories under oath, and serve them on the defendant within 30 days:

1. Describe the personal injuries you received as a result of the occurrence described in the complaint (hereafter "this occurrence").

2. State the full names and present addresses of any physicians, osteopaths, chiropractors, and other medical personnel who treated you as a result of this occurrence, each such person's areas of specialty, the dates of each examination, consultation or appointment, the amount of each such person's bill, and whether each bill has been paid.

3. Were you confined to a hospital or clinic as a result of this occurrence? If so, state the name and address of each such hospital or clinic, the dates of your confinement at each facility, the amount of each such facility's bills, and whether each bill has been paid.

4. Have you incurred other medical expenses, other than these requested in Interrogatory Nos. 2 and 3, as a result of this occurrence? If so, state each expense incurred, the nature of each expense, when the expense was incurred, to whom it was incurred, and whether each expense has been paid.

5. Have you incurred any expenses as a result of this occurrence other than medical

Interrogatories will usually be the first discovery device the parties serve on each other.

In this example, the defendant served interrogatories on plaintiff two weeks after answering the complaint. (Many defendants serve interrogatories with the answer.)

Note how each interrogatory deals with a separate, defined category and asks for all relevant data for the category. This will usually generate more complete answers. It also gives the answering party the opportunity of answering the interrogatory by producing the relevant records that contain the answers.

expenses? If so, state the nature of each expense, the date incurred, the amount of each expense, the reason for incurring each expense, and whether each expense has been paid.

6. Were you unable to work as a result of this occurrence? If so, state the dates during which you were unable to work, each employer during these dates, the type of work you were unable to do, and the amount of lost wages or income from each employer.

7. Have you recovered from the claimed injuries that resulted from this occurrence? If not, state the claimed injuries from which you have not recovered and any present disability.

The plaintiff's current condition and medical history are important areas that should be explored thoroughly. This can then be verified during the plaintiff's deposition.

8. During the 10 years preceding September 2, 1998, have you suffered any other personal injuries? If so, state when, where, and how you were injured and the name and address of each medical facility where, and physicians by whom, you were treated for these injuries.

9. During the 10 years preceding September 2, 1998, have you been hospitalized, treated, examined, or tested at any hospital, clinic, physician's office, or other medical facility for any conditions other than those requested in Interrogatory No. 8? If so, state the name and address of each such medical facility and physician and the dates of such services and the medical conditions involved.

10. State the full name and address of each person who witnessed, or claims to have witnessed, the collision between the vehicles involved in this occurrence.

Occurrence witnesses are obviously important in this kind of case. It's a good practice to break them up by category in appropriate cases.

11. State the full name and address of each person who has any knowledge of the facts of the collision other than those persons already identified in Interrogatory No. 10.

12. Describe your vehicle involved in this occurrence, any damages to your vehicle as a result of this occurrence, the name and address of any firm repairing your vehicle, the amount billed for repairs, when such repairs took place, and whether the repair bills have been paid. If your vehicle has not been repaired, state where it is presently located and its condition.

13. Identify, by date, description, and source any medical records and any other records or documents of any kind in your or your attorney's possession or control that relate in any way to this occurrence and the injuries and damages you claim resulted from this occurrence.

14. For each expert expected to testify at trial, state:

(a)   the expert's full name, address, and professional qualifications;
(b)   the subject matter on which the expert is expected to testify;
(c)   the substance of the facts and opinions to which the expert is expected to testify; and
(d)   a summary of the grounds of each opinion.

Medical records are obviously critical in this kind of case. The descriptions you get will be used to send production requests to the plaintiff and subpoenas to third-party sources.

This interrogatory tracks the language of Rule 33. If the jurisdiction follows Rule 26(a), expert disclosures would be made in accordance with Rule 26(a)(2) and the timetable set by the court.

Dated: February 1, 1999

A proof of service must be attached.

William Sharp
William Sharp
Attorney for Defendant
100 Broadway
Phoenix, AZ 85001
881-1000

UNITED STATES DISTRICT COURT
FOR THE DISTRICT OF ARIZONA

John Jones,
        Plaintiff

    v.   NO. 99 C 1000

Susan Smith,
        Defendant

PLAINTIFF'S ANSWERS TO
INTERROGATORIES

Plaintiff John Jones answers Defendant's interrogatories as follows:

Interrogatory No. 1: Describe the personal injuries you received as a result of the occurrence described in the complaint (hereafter "this occurrence").

Answer: Cervical, dorsal and lumbar sprain and strain; cerebral concussion; multiple contraction headaches and concussion headaches; left hemiparesis with ataxia; ankle sprain; numbness; multiple contusions and abrasions.

Interrogatory No. 2: State in full the names and present addresses of any physicians, osteopaths, chiropractors, nurses, or other medical personnel who treated you as a result of this occurrence, each such person's areas of specialty, the dates of each examination, consultation, or appointment, the amount of each such person's bill, and whether each bill has been paid.

Answer:
Doctors Hospital
1947 East Thomas Road
Phoenix, Arizona 85016

Lenore L. Lang, M.D.
333 East Campbell Avenue
Phoenix, Arizona 85016

Frank Hoffman, M.D.
222 West Thomas Road
Suite 100
Phoenix, Arizona 85013

The usual way of answering interrogatories is to set out the questions and the answers, making it easy to correlate the two.

J. Franks, D.C.
55 North 27th Avenue
Phoenix, Arizona 85007

(Answer may be supplemented as discovery and investigation continues.)

Interrogatory No. 3: Were you confined to a hospital or clinic as a result of this occurrence? If so, state the name and address of the hospital or clinic, the dates of your confinement at each facilty, the amount of each facility's bills, and whether each bill has been paid.

Answer: No; treated, but not confined, at Doctors Hospital.

Interrogatory No. 4: Have you incurred other medical expenses, other than those requested in Interrogatory Nos. 2 and 3, as a result of this occurrence? If so, state each expense incurred, the nature of each expense, when the expense was incurred, to whom it was incurred, and whether each expense has been paid.

Answer:

Doctors Hospital	$1,257.18
Lenore L. Lang, M.D.	339.70
Frank Hoffman, M.D.	340.00
J. Franks, D.C.	697.80
Walgreen Pharmacy	83.13

Those bills have been paid.

(Answer may be supplemented as discovery and investigation continues.)

Interrogatory No. 5: Have you incurred any expenses as a result of this occurrence, other than medical expenses? If so, state the nature of each expense, the date incurred, the amount of each expense, the reason for incurring each expense, and whether each expense has been paid.

Answer:

Broken wristwatch	$ 75.00
College books	162.00

Wristwatch repair bill has been paid.

Here the plaintiff has prepared partial answers, and acknowledges that further information will generate supplemental answers later. However, these partial answers were prepared within the 30-day requirement of Rule 33.

Interrogatory No. 6: Were you unable to work as a result of this occurrence? If so, state the dates during which you were unable to work, each employer during these dates, the type of work you were unable to do, and the amount of lost wages or income from each employer.

Answer: Yes. September 2, 1998, to October 1, 1998. Devo Wholesale Florist. Delivery truck driver. $700—one month's salary.

This is a typical interrogatory answer. It provides all the facts requested, does so efficiently, and does not volunteer anything not asked for.

Interrogatory No. 7: Have you recovered from the claimed injuries that resulted from this occurrence? If not, state the claimed injuries from which you have not recovered and any present disability.

Answer: Plaintiff still experiences headaches, neck pain, and lower back pain.

Interrogatory No. 8: During the 10 years preceding September 2, 1998, have you suffered any other personal injuries? If so, state when, where, and how you were injured, and the name and address of each medical facility where, and physicians by whom, you were treated for these injuries.

Answer: No.

Interrogatory No. 9: During the 10 years preceding September 2, 1998, have you been hospitalized, treated, examined, or tested at any hospital, clinic, physician's office or other medical facility for any conditions other than those requested in Interrogatory No. 8? If so, state the name and address of each such medical facility and physician, the dates of such services, and the medical conditions involved.

Answer: No.

Interrogatory No. 10: State the full name and address of each person who witnessed, or claims to have witnessed, the collision between the vehicles involved in this occurrence.

Answer:

John Jones, plaintiff
Susan Smith, defendant

Carol Brown, 42 East Cambridge Street, Phoenix, AZ

Mary Porter, 42 East Cambridge Street, Phoenix, AZ

Officer Steven Pitcher, Phoenix Police Department

(Answer may be supplemented as discovery and investigation continues.)

Interrogatory No. 11: State the full name and address of each person who has any knowledge of the facts of the collision, other than persons already identified in Interrogatory No. 10.

Answer: See persons listed in answer to Interrogatory No. 4; John Jones, Sr., and Mary Jones, plaintiff's parents; Diane Devo, plaintiff's employer.

(Answer may be supplemented as discovery and investigation continues.)

Interrogatory No. 12: Describe your vehicle that was involved in this occurrence, any damage to your vehicle as a result of this occurrence, the name and address of any firm repairing your vehicle, the amount billed for repairs, when such repairs took place, and whether the repair bills have been paid. If your vehicle has not been repaired, state where it is presently located and its condition.

Answer: 1995 Toyota Corolla four-door sedan. Extensive damage to left and front side of car. Jack's Auto Repair, 2000 East Valley Road, Phoenix. $1,213. Repairs completed about September 30, 1998. Repair bill has been paid.

Interrogatory No. 13: Identify, by date, description, and source any medical records, and any other records or documents of any kind in your or your attorney's possession or control, that relate in any way to this occurrence and injuries and damages you claim resulted from this occurrence.

Answer:

Employment records of Devo Wholesale Florist

Doctors Hospital records

Dr. Lang's office records

Witness lists must frequently be supplemented over time, since the ongoing investigation will often uncover additional witnesses.

This is another typical answer. It provides the facts called for, yet does not volunteer anything.

Dr. Hoffman's office records
Dr. Franks' office records
Medical bills
X rays taken by the above health care providers
Phoenix Police Department Accident Report
Photographs of the scene of the accident

(Answer may be supplemented as discovery and investigation proceeds.)

Interrogatory No. 14: For each expert expected to testify at trial, state:

    (a)   the expert's full name, address, and professional qualifications;

    (b)   the subject matter on which the expert is expected to testify;

    (c)   the substance of the facts and opinions to which the expert is expected to testify; and

    (d)   a summary of the grounds of each opinion.

Answer:

Frank Hoffman, M.D.
222 West Thomas Road
Suite 100
Phoenix, AZ 85013

J. Franks, D.C.
55 North 27th Avenue
Phoenix, AZ 85007

Lenore L. Lang, M.D.
333 East Campbell Avenue
Phoenix, AZ 85016

(Answers may be supplemented as discovery and investigation continues.)

Dated: February 25, 1999

John Jones

John Jones, Plaintiff

The initial answer to this standard interrogatory is frequently "None known at present—investigation continues," on the basis that the answering party has not yet decided who its testifying experts will be.

Here the treating physicians will obviously be witnesses at trial, so their names are disclosed, with supplemental answers to follow.

State of Arizona
County of Maricopa | SS.

I, John Jones, being first duly sworn, state that:

I am the plaintiff in this case. I have made the foregoing Answers to Interrogatories and know the answers to be true to the best of my knowledge, information and belief.

John Jones

John Jones, Plaintiff

Subscribed and sworn to before me this 25th day of February 1999, by John Jones, Plaintiff.

Mary Ryan

Mary Ryan, Notary Public

My commission expires on
December 31, 1999

[Seal]

Interrogatory answers must be signed under oath by the party making them.

Like any court papers, the answers must be served on every party. A proof of service, showing how service was made, must be attached to the answer.

UNITED STATES DISTRICT COURT
FOR THE DISTRICT OF ARIZONA

John Jones,
      Plaintiff

    v.   NO. 99 C 1000

Susan Smith,
      Defendant

REQUEST FOR PRODUCTION OF DOCUMENTS

Pursuant to Rule 34 of the Federal Rules of Civil Procedure, defendant requests that plaintiff produce within 30 days, in the law offices of William Sharp, 100 Broadway, Phoenix, AZ 85001, the following documents for inspection and copying:

1. All medical reports, records, charts, X-ray reports, and all other records regarding any medical examinations and treatment received by plaintiff for the injuries claimed in the complaint.

2. All U.S. Income Tax Returns filed by plaintiff for the years 1993 through 1998.

Dated: February 1, 1999

William Sharp
William Sharp
Attorney for Defendant
100 Broadway
Phoenix, AZ 85001
881-1000

Note that this documents request was served at the same time as were the interrogatories.

Documents requests usually depend on interrogatory answers to identify the relevant documents. Here, however, what the defendant wants is both simple and obvious, so the defendant decides to serve the requests with interrogatories.

A proof of service must be attached.

UNITED STATES DISTRICT COURT
FOR THE DISTRICT OF ARIZONA

John Jones,
            Plaintiff

            v.   NO. 99 C 1000

Susan Smith,
            Defendant

PLAINTIFF'S RESPONSE TO REQUEST FOR PRODUCTION OF DOCUMENTS

Plaintiff responds to defendant's Requests for Production of Documents as follows:

1. Plaintiff will produce copies of all reports in plaintiff's possession regarding medical examinations and treatment of plaintiff for his injuries. These copies will be delivered to defendant's attorney on or before March 1, 1999.

2. Plaintiff herewith produces his U.S. Income Tax Returns for the years 1993 through 1998.

Dated: February 25, 1999

Anne Johnson
Anne Johnson
Attorney for Plaintiff
100 Congress Street
Phoenix, AZ 85001
882-1000

A response to a production request should be filed so there is a court record that shows how and when the request was complied with. If photocopying will be expensive, the requesting party will usually have to pay for the photocopying charges.

A proof of service must be attached.

UNITED STATES DISTRICT COURT
FOR THE DISTRICT OF ARIZONA

John Jones,
      Plaintiff

    v.

Susan Smith,
      Defendant

NO. 99 C 1000

SUBPOENA DUCES TECUM

TO: Diane Devo, President
      Devo Wholesale Florist
      3731 40th Street
      Phoenix, AZ 85010

YOU ARE HEREBY COMMANDED to appear and give testimony under oath at the law office of William Sharp, 100 Broadway, Phoenix, AZ 85001 on March 15, 1999, at 1:30 P.M. You are also commanded to bring the following:

All records relating to the employment of John Jones at Devo Wholesale Florist, from the first day of employment through the present date, including but not limited to records showing wages received, hours worked, and the condition of John Jones' health.

Dated: March 1, 1999

[Seal]

Thomas Barber
Clerk of the Court

A deposition subpoena that also requires the witness to bring specified records can be used to obtain records from nonparty witnesses. Under Rules 35(c) and 45, the records alone can now be subpoenaed.

Make sure that you serve a Notice of Deposition on every other party, because other parties always have a right to attend any deposition and question the deponent.

UNITED STATES DISTRICT COURT
FOR THE DISTRICT OF ARIZONA

John Jones,
      Plaintiff

    v.
                 NO. 99 C 1000

Susan Smith,
      Defendant

NOTICE OF DEPOSITION

TO: PLAINTIFF JOHN JONES

Please take notice that the undersigned will take the deposition of John Jones, Plaintiff, on March 15, 1999, at 2:00 P.M. at 100 Broadway, Phoenix, AZ 85001. You are hereby notified that the plaintiff is to appear at that time and place and submit to a deposition under oath.

Two weeks notice is appropriate in this type of case.

A subpoena is not necessary since the deponent is a party.

Dated: March 1, 1999

William Sharp

William Sharp
Attorney for Defendant
100 Broadway
Phoenix, AZ 85001
881-1000

A proof of service must be attached.

UNITED STATES DISTRICT COURT
FOR THE DISTRICT OF ARIZONA

John Jones, 　　　　Plaintiff 　　　　v. Susan Smith, 　　　　Defendant	NO. 99 C 1000

DEPOSITION OF JOHN JONES

DEPOSITION OF John Jones, taken at 2:13 P.M. on March 15, 1999, at the law offices of William Sharp, at 100 Broadway, Phoenix, AZ 85001, before Mary Ryan, a Notary Public in Maricopa County, Arizona.

Appearance for the plaintiff:

Anne Johnson
100 Congress Street
Phoenix, AZ 85001

Appearance for the defendant:

William Sharp
100 Broadway
Phoenix, AZ 85001

JOHN JONES

Called as a witness, having been first duly sworn, was examined and testified as follows:

EXAMINATION BY MR. SHARP:

Q. This is the deposition of the plaintiff, John Jones, being taken in the case of John Jones v. Susan Smith, Case No. 99 C 1000 in the United States District Court for the District of Arizona. It is being held at the law office of William Sharp, 100 Broadway, Phoenix, Arizona 85001. Today's date is March 15, 1999. Present in addition to Mr. Jones are myself, William Sharp, attorney for defen-

This is a standard introductory statement.

dant Smith, Anne Johnson, attorney for plaintiff Jones, and Mary Ryan, a certified court reporter and notary public. Mr. Jones, you were just sworn to tell the truth by the court reporter, correct?

A. That's right.

Q. It's important that you understand the questions and give accurate answers. If there's anything you don't understand, or anything you don't know or aren't sure of, you let us know, all right?

A. Yes.

Q. Please tell us your full name.

A. John J. Jones.

Q. How old are you?

A. I'm 23.

Q. Are you married or single?

A. Single.

Q. Where do you live?

A. 1020 North 50th Street, Phoenix, Arizona.

Q. How far did you go in school?

A. I graduated from high school—Central High, 1994.

Q. What did you do after high school?

A. I joined the army.

Q. Tell us about your army experience.

A. After basic training, I was sent to an infantry division, and did most of my three years in Germany. I was a corporal when I received my honorable discharge. That was in August 1997.

Q. What did you do after that?

A. I came back to Phoenix, moved into my parents' house, and started working for Devo Wholesale Florist.

Q. Where is that located?

A. It's at 3731 40th Street, Phoenix.

Q. What kind of work do you do there?

A. I started as a sales clerk, then I became a driver on one of their trucks.

Q. What do you do as a driver?

A. I deliver flowers from the store to customers in the Phoenix area.

Q. What were your hours in August and September 1998?

A. It varied, but it was usually 6:00 A.M. to 2:00 P.M.

a. Personal background.
Note the form of the questions and the tone of the examination. The principal purposes of this deposition are to acquire information and assess the plaintiff as a trial witness. Accordingly, the questions are usually open-ended, designed to elicit information and have the plaintiff do the talking. The questions are asked in a pleasant friendly way.

b. Work experience.

Q. Were those your hours the day of the accident?

A. Yes.

Q. Other than your job for Devo Florist, did you have any other jobs or activities in September 1998?

A. I didn't have any other job. I was a part-time student at Glendale Community College.

Q. Mr. Jones, were you ever involved in an automobile accident before September 2, 1998?

A. No.

Q. Did you ever have personal injuries of any kind before September 2, 1998?

A. No.

Q. During the past 10 years, other than for this accident, did you ever see a physician for any reason?

A. Well, our family doctor is Dr. Hoffman. I would see him from time to time for checkups, shots, and things like that. But I never had any serious injury or illness that I went to Dr. Hoffman for.

Q. Mr. Jones, tell me each injury you feel you've received as a result of the accident on September 2.

A. Okay. I hurt the left side of my neck, my lower back, my left ankle, my left shoulder, and my stomach.

Q. Let's start out with the left side of your neck. What injuries did you receive there?

A. I think I whipped my head to the side when the car crashed into me and I strained my neck. I had these shooting pains in my neck whenever I tried to move it.

Q. How long did that pain continue?

A. Well it was pretty severe for about a week, and then it started getting better. I still get pains there from time to time.

Q. Tell me about the injuries to your lower back.

c. Accident and health history must be explored, since preexisting injuries would affect the damages picture.

d. Each claimed injury should be explored in detail.

The "tell me" form of questions are used to get the witness to disclose everything.

If the plaintiff at trial tries to claim additional injuries, he can hardly say he didn't mention all his injuries during the deposition because the lawyer didn't give him a chance to do so.

Since pain and suffering will probably be the largest single element of damages, these questions are important to "pin down" the witness and prevent later exaggeration at trial.

A.   Well, that was sort of the same thing. I must have wrenched my back from the force of the collision. Just like my neck, it was stiff and hurt for a while. After about a week it started getting better, and today I only get the pain from time to time, especially toward the end of the work day.

Q.   Tell me about your left ankle.

A.   I sprained my ankle during the accident. That was probably the worst injury. I had to stay off my feet for about two weeks, and I really couldn't start walking on it for three or four weeks. That's the injury that kept me out of work for a month.

Q.   When did your ankle start getting better?

A.   About a month after this happened it was well enough so I could start working, although I was still limping for quite a while. It probably took about four months before the ankle healed up completely.

Q.   Tell me about the injury to your left shoulder.

A.   I got some cuts and scratches and bruises on my left shoulder when I crashed into the dashboard of the car. That hurt for maybe two weeks, and then went away.

Q.   Finally, tell me about the injuries to your stomach.

A.   I guess I injured my stomach when I smashed against the steering wheel. It was just painful inside of my stomach. That went away after a few days.

Q.   Other than these injuries to your neck, lower back, ankle, shoulder, and stomach, did you receive any other injuries?

A.   Oh yeah. I received a concussion on the left side of my head. That's what the doctor told me.

Q.   Mr. Jones, let's talk about the medical treatment you received for these injuries following the accident. First, how did you get to Doctors Hospital?

A.   An ambulance came to the intersec-

The "any other injuries" question is always useful. Again, it prevents later exaggeration.

e.   Medical treatment.

Note how this deposition is organized chronologically (with

tion and they put me on a stretcher and drove me to the hospital.

Q. What happened when you arrived at Doctors Hospital?

A. The ambulance attendants took me into the emergency room, and some nurses checked me over, took my pulse and blood pressure, and stuff like that. After a while one of their doctors examined me. I think her name was Dr. Lang. I told Dr. Lang where I hurt and about the accident.

Q. What kind of treatment did you receive at the hospital?

A. Well, they examined me, x-rayed, cleaned-up some of the cuts on my shoulder and chest, and put my ankle in a cast. It wasn't one of those big plaster casts, it was a cast that went around the back of my ankle and foot and was surrounded with an elastic bandage. I must have been there a couple of hours, and by that time my parents had come to the hospital, and they took me home.

Q. Did you receive any medication prescription?

A. The doctor gave a prescription for Tylenol with codeine, which my mother picked up at the drug store. The doctor told me to follow instructions on the bottle and take the medication if I needed it for the pain.

Q. Mr. Jones, tell us about the month you spent before you went back to work.

A. Well, the first week I pretty much spent in bed. Sometimes I got up and lay on the couch and watched TV. At that time everything was aching, my neck hurt, my head hurt, my stomach hurt, my ankle was swollen up. I spent all my time with my foot up to keep the swelling down, and I was taking the medicine to keep the pain down.

Q. How long was it before you were able to move around the house?

A. I'd say the first week or 10 days I pretty much spent on my back. After that period of time the pain in my head, shoul-

the exception of the accident itself). This is usually the best way to organize the questions, unless you have a specific reason for doing it another way.

f. Recovery period.

der and stomach started going away, and the swelling in my ankle was starting to go down. I got a pair of crutches and started moving around the house a little bit. I couldn't stay on my feet very long before the foot would swell up if I stood up for any length of time.

Q. At the end of September, 1998, what was your physical condition like?

A. The scratches and bruises had gone away. The pains in my neck, shoulder, stomach and leg, and back, had started to get better. The only places that really kept on hurting was my lower back and my ankle.

Q. Tell me about those.

A. Well my back would have these stabbing pains from time to time. It felt real stiff. My ankle was stiff. My ankle was still swollen, and I couldn't walk on it yet. Dr. Hoffman, my family doctor, had removed the cast about three weeks after the accident and I could start walking without crutches, but I was still limping and the ankle would get sore if I walked on it for any length of time.

Q. When did you see Dr. Hoffman?

A. My mom took me to Dr. Hoffman about three weeks after the accident. He checked me out, removed the soft cast from my ankle, and told me it was okay to start walking around without the crutches if I could stand it.

Q. When did you stop using the crutches?

A. I stopped using them when I went back to work at the beginning of October.

Q. What did you see Dr. Franks, the chiropractor, for?

A. Well, my mom thought that going to a chiropractor might help my back and ankle. My back still hurt, and my ankle was still sore. She thought that it might be a good idea to get some physical therapy to see if that might help. That's why I went to Dr. Franks.

Since the defendant's purpose is to minimize the extent and length of the pain, these questions are important. Again, they prevent later exaggeration.

The history of the plaintiff's treatments is, of course, available from the medical records, which the defendant will have before the deposition. Nonetheless, these questions test the witness' recall and propensity to exaggerate.

Q. How many times did you see Dr. Franks?

A. I went to him for the first time around October 1st. I went to see him maybe twice a week for the next couple of months.

Q. What kind of treatment did Dr. Franks perform?

A. He would give me physical therapy. That involved bending my back, stretching it, applying heat treatments, things like that. The same thing was true for the ankle.

Q. Did it help?

A. Yes. About two months later, maybe by Christmas, most of the stiffness and pain had gone away.

Q. From December 1998 to the present day, describe your physical condition.

A. It's better. I still have pain from time to time in my back and ankle.

Q. When do you get the pain there?

A. Well, it depends on how much or how hard I work. The more I work the more likely I am to get those pains.

Q. How often do you get those pains?

A. It's maybe once a week for an hour or two, usually at the end of the work day.

Q. When was the last time you took Tylenol with codeine?

A. I took that stuff for maybe six weeks.

Q. Did you ever take any painkillers other than Tylenol with codeine?

A. I sometimes take aspirin when I get these pains.

Q. Other than what you've told me about, do you have any other injuries or problems that you feel were caused by this accident?

A. No, you pretty much covered it.

Q. Mr. Jones, let's talk about some of the bills involved here. First the medical bills. Your interrogatory answers show that the bills from Doctors Hospital, Dr. Lang, Dr. Hoffman, and Dr. Franks have all been paid. Who paid those bills?

A. I'm not sure. I know they were paid

These questions effectively limit the damages.

g. Expenses and lost income.

by my health insurance. I think my mother paid the Walgreen pharmacy bill.

Q. Who paid for the wristwatch repair?

A. My mom paid that. I'm supposed to pay her back.

Q. You claim college books expenses in the amount of $162. Tell us about that.

A. Well, I was a part-time student at Glendale Community College. I had already bought the books for the two courses I was taking. When I got injured, I couldn't take the courses I signed up for.

Q. Did you lose any tuition money?

A. No. The College said since I got hurt it wouldn't charge me for the courses I signed up for.

Q. How much income did you lose as a result of this accident?

A. I get paid $700 a month salary from Devo Florist. I went back to work October 1, 1998. The way I figure it, I lost one month's salary, or $700.

Q. The $700 is your gross income, isn't it?

A. Yes.

Q. What's your take-home pay?

A. We get paid on the first and fifteenth of the month. My take-home for half a month is about $270.

Q. Mr. Jones, let's talk about how this accident happened. Describe the vehicle you were driving.

A. It's a 1995 Toyota Corolla four-door. I bought it when I got out of the service. It was in really good shape, because I took good care of it.

Q. Is the title to that car in your name?

A. Yes.

Q. The accident happened around 2:00 P.M.?

A. Yes.

Q. At the time of the accident, where were you coming from?

A. I was coming from work at the flower shop.

While the fact that most of the bills have been paid by insurance is not admissible at trial, it will have some effect on the settlement picture.

n.   The accident.

Note that here the questioner has saved the accident as the last topic. Some lawyers save the most important part of a deposition for the end, on the theory that the lawyer then has a better "feel" for the witness and the witness' guard will be down by that time.

These scene description questions are useful to see how effectively the plaintiff can describe

Q. Where is that flower shop located?

A. On 40th Street and Thomas Road.

Q. 40th Street is the north-south street, correct?

A. Yes.

Q. Where is the flower shop in relation to the intersection?

A. It's not right at the corner. It's on 40th Street maybe 300 feet south of Thomas.

Q. Which side of 40th Street is the flower shop on?

A. It's on the east side.

Q. Tell me how you went from the flower shop north on 40th Street.

A. My car was parked in the lot next to the flower shop. When I got out of work, I pulled out of the lot and started going north on 40th Street.

Q. Describe what 40th Street looks like.

A. It's a pretty wide street. It has three lanes of traffic in each direction. In addition, it has left-turn lanes at the major intersections.

Q. There are traffic lights at the corner of 40th Street and Thomas, right?

A. Yes.

Q. Where are they located?

A. I think there's one at each corner and on the median strips.

Q. How many lights face the northbound traffic on 40th Street?

A. Probably around three.

Q. When you pulled onto 40th Street, which lane did you pull into?

A. I got into the inside lane, right next to the median strip.

Q. Mr. Jones, when was the first time you looked at the traffic lights at the corner of 40th Street and Thomas?

A. When I first pulled onto 40th Street and got in the inside lane.

Q. How far were you from the intersection at that time?

A. I guess around 100 feet.

Q. How fast were you going at that time?

A. Maybe 20 or 25 miles per hour.

the scene, and are good questions to see how effective a trial witness he will make.

This is a useful answer since he was only about three seconds from the intersection before he looked at the lights.

Q. What was the color of the traffic lights at that point?

A. Green.

Q. What happened as you went northbound on 40th Street?

A. Well, it all happened really quickly. As I went north, the light turned yellow just before I got into the intersection. I was going through the intersection on the yellow light when suddenly I got smashed by another car from the driver's side.

This answer is also useful since it suggests that the plaintiff was not paying much attention as he entered the intersection.

Q. How long had the light been yellow at the time the other car collided with you?

A. It couldn't have been more than two or three seconds.

Note how the questions become more specific. The questioner's purpose now is to "pin down" the witness to specific facts.

Q. How fast were you going when you were hit?

A. Maybe 25 or 30 miles per hour.

Q. Did you ever see the car that hit you before the impact?

A. Not really. I first saw it just before it was about to smash into me. It couldn't have been more than 10 or 15 feet from me. Before I could even put on my brakes, the car hit me.

Q. Tell us what happened from the moment the two cars hit?

A. Well, I remember putting on my brakes, I kind of skidded in the intersection, and the other car seemed to be stuck against the side of my car. I can remember getting bounced around inside the car and smashing my head and chest against the inside of the car and the steering wheel.

Q. Were you wearing a seat belt at that time?

A. No.

Q. Did your car have seat belts?

A. Yes.

This is important, since in some jurisdictions this fact is admissible to show plaintiff's own negligence or failure to prevent damages.

Q. What happened when your car came to a stop?

A. I was pretty much numb. I can remember people coming up to me when I was in the car telling me not to move. I wasn't going to move anyway. I just hurt all over. I don't know how long it was, but after a while an ambulance came and they got me out of the car and put me on a stretcher.

Q. Mr. Jones, just before the impact, describe exactly what you were doing.

A. Well, I remember starting into the intersection. Since the light was yellow, I remember looking to the right to make sure that there weren't any cars taking a turn that might get in my way. I just looked to my right and then looked back up the road, then I saw the other car coming from my left just before it crashed into me.

Q. Did you ever put on your brakes before the impact?

A. No, I don't think so, there wasn't time to react.

Q. Mr. Jones, is there anything you remember about how this accident happened that you haven't told me about this afternoon?

A. No, nothing that comes to mind. I think I've pretty much told you everything.

Q. That's all the questions I have at this time. Do you have any questions, Ms. Johnson?

Ms. Johnson: No.

Mr. Sharp: Will you waive signature?

Ms. Johnson: No, we'll read and sign.

(The deposition was concluded at 3:06 P.M.)

John Jones
John Jones

Some lawyers always ask this kind of question, since it's potential impeachment if the plaintiff "remembers" more at trial.

The party deponent should not waive signature, since he should review the transcript for accuracy.

Note that the plaintiff's lawyer asked no questions. This is the usual practice, unless the party gave incorrect or confusing answers that need to be corrected or clarified.

Note also that the plaintiff's lawyer made no objections during the deposition. The questions were proper, so objections were unnecessary. The lawyer did not make objections for the purpose of coaching the plaintiff on desired responses, ethically questionable conduct some lawyers unfortunately engage in.

State of Arizona
County of Maricopa   SS.

The foregoing deposition was taken before me, Mary Ryan, a Notary Public in the County of Maricopa, State of Arizona. The witness was duly sworn by me to testify to the truth. The questions asked of the witness and the answers given by the witness were taken down by me in shorthand and reduced to typewriting under my direction. The deposition was submitted to the witness and read and signed. The foregoing pages are a true and accurate transcript of the entire proceedings taken during this deposition.

Dated: April 1, 1999

Mary Ryan
Notary Public

My commission expires on
    December 31, 1999.

The court reporter must arrange a meeting with the deponent so he can review the transcript, note any claimed inaccuracies, and sign the transcript. Any claimed inaccuracies are usually put on a separate sheet and attached to the transcript.

UNITED STATES DISTRICT COURT
FOR THE DISTRICT OF ARIZONA

John Jones,
     Plaintiff

  v.

Susan Smith,
     Defendant

NO. 99 C 1000

NOTICE OF MOTION

TO: Anne Johnson
     Attorney at Law
     100 Congress Street
     Phoenix, AZ 85001

PLEASE TAKE NOTICE that on June 10, 1999, at 9:00 A.M., or as soon as counsel can be heard, defendant in the above-captioned matter will present the attached Motion to Compel Discovery before the Hon. Joan Howe, Courtroom No. 4, United States Court House, Phoenix, Arizona.

Even with service by mail, this is adequate notice. As a professional courtesy, however, it's a good idea to call the opposing lawyer and let him know you're serving the motion.

Dated: June 1, 1999

William Sharp
William Sharp
Attorney for Defendant
100 Broadway
Phoenix, AZ 85001
881-1000

UNITED STATES DISTRICT COURT
FOR THE DISTRICT OF ARIZONA

John Jones,
          Plaintiff

          v.   NO. 99 C 1000

Susan Smith,
          Defendant

MOTION TO COMPEL DISCOVERY

Defendant moves for an order compelling plaintiff to answer in the full interrogatories previously served on plaintiff, pursuant to Rule 37 of the Federal Rules of Civil Procedure. In support of her motion defendant states:

1. Defendant served interrogatories on plaintiff on February 1, 1999.

2. Plaintiff partially answered these interrogatories on February 25, 1999. Many of the answers are incomplete and do not provide the facts called for.

3. Plaintiff's answers to Interrogatory Nos. 2, 4, 10, 11, 13, and 14 stated that "answers may be supplemented as discovery and investigation continues."

4. To date plaintiff has neither supplemented his interrogatory answers nor advised defendant that no additional answers will be forthcoming, although defendant has requested, by telephone and letter, that plaintiff submit supplemental answers.

WHEREFORE, defendant requests the court to order plaintiff to serve supplemental interrogatory answers within 10 days and award reasonable expenses, including attorney's fees, incurred by defendant as a result of this motion.

Since over three months have passed since plaintiff served incomplete answers to interrogatories, this motion should be brought.

In many jurisdictions local rules require that a motion must be supplemented by a memorandum of points and authorities. In other jurisdictions this is done only for complicated or contested motions, such as for summary judgment. You should always show what efforts you have made to get compliance before filing the motion.

Keep in mind that many jurisdictions require a lawyer to certify compliance with local rules that require that the parties first try to resolve discovery disputes informally.

Dated: June 1, 1999

William Sharp

William Sharp
Attorney for Defendant
100 Broadway
Phoenix, AZ 85001
881-1000

Note that Rule 37 allows the court to award the reasonable costs incurred in being forced to bring this motion. This includes attorney's fees. Asking for perhaps $100-250 here would be reasonable.

AFFIDAVIT OF SERVICE

I, Helen Thompson, having been first duly sworn, state that I have served a copy of the attached Notice of Motion and Motion to Compel Discovery on plaintiff's attorney by mail at 100 Congress Street, Phoenix, Arizona 85001, on June 1, 1999.

Helen Thompson

Helen Thompson

Signed and sworn to before me on June 1, 1999.

Mary Ryan

Notary Public

My Commission expires on December 31, 1999.

[Seal]

UNITED STATES DISTRICT COURT
FOR THE DISTRICT OF ARIZONA

John Jones,
            Plaintiff

                    v.   NO. 99 C 1000

Susan Smith,
            Defendant

REQUESTS TO ADMIT FACTS
AND GENUINENESS OF DOCUMENTS

Plaintiff requests defendant, pursuant to Rule 36 of the Federal Rules of Civil Procedure, to admit within 30 days the following facts and genuineness of documents:

1. Defendant was the owner of a 1995 Buick Skylark sedan on September 2, 1998.

2. Defendant was driving the 1995 Buick Skylark sedan when the collision occurred on September 2, 1998.

3. Defendant was a driver licensed by the State of Nevada at the time of the collision.

4. Each of the following documents, attached as exhibits to this request, is genuine and a business record of the entity it purports to be from:

Exhibit No.	Description
1.	Phoenix Police Dept. accident report.
2.	Title and registration documents from the Nevada Dept. of Transportation showing defendant to be the owner of a 1995 Buick Skylark sedan.
3.	Driver's license issued to defendant by the Nevada Dept. of Transportation.

Dated: June 1, 1999

Anne Johnson
Anne Johnson
Attorney for Plaintiff
100 Congress Street
Phoenix, AZ 85001
882-1000

If this case will go to trial, the plaintiff will need to establish basic facts. These requests cover facts that the defendant will probably not contest, and that will streamline the plaintiff's case during trial.

A proof of service must be attached.

UNITED STATES DISTRICT COURT
FOR THE DISTRICT OF ARIZONA

John Jones,
        Plaintiff

        v.   NO. 99 C 1000

Susan Smith,
        Defendant

DEFENDANT'S ANSWER TO PLAINTIFF'S
REQUESTS TO ADMIT FACTS AND
GENUINENESS OF DOCUMENTS

Defendant answers plaintiff's Requests for Admission of Facts and Genuineness of Documents as follows:

Request No. 1: Defendant was the owner of a 1995 Buick Skylark sedan on September 2, 1998.

Answer: Admits.

Request No. 2: Defendant was driving the 1995 Buick Skylark sedan when the collision occurred on September 2, 1998.

Answer: Admits.

Request No. 3: Defendant was a driver licensed by the State of Nevada at the time of the collision.

Answer: Admits.

Request No. 4: Each of the following documents, attached as exhibits to this request, is authentic and a business record of the entity it purports to be from:

Exhibit No.	Description
1.	Phoenix Police Dept. accident report.
2.	Title and registration documents from the Nevada Dept. of Transportation showing defendant to be the owner of a 1995 Buick Skylark sedan.

Like interrogatories, the usual practice in answering is to set out both the request and the answer. This avoids confusion.

3.   Driver's license issued to defendant by the Nevada Dept. of Transportation.

Answer: Admits.

Dated: June 20, 1999

William Sharp
William Sharp
Attorney for Defendant
100 Broadway
Phoenix, AZ 85001
881-1000

A proof of service must
be attached.

UNITED STATES DISTRICT COURT
FOR THE DISTRICT OF ARIZONA

John Jones,
             Plaintiff

       v.   NO. 99 C 1000

Susan Smith,
             Defendant

OFFER OF JUDGMENT

Pursuant to Rule 68 of the Federal Rules of Civil Procedure, defendant offers to allow judgment to be taken against her in the amount of EIGHTEEN THOUSAND and 00/100 DOLLARS ($18,000.00), and costs of suit incurred to the date of this offer.

This offer is being made under Rule 68 of the Federal Rules of Civil Procedure and Rule 408 of the Federal Rules of Evidence.

By this time defendant has sufficient facts to assess the case's settlement value. The offer of judgment will put additional pressure on the plaintiff to consider a realistic settlement.

Dated: August 1, 1999

William Sharp
William Sharp
Attorney for Defendant
100 Broadway
Phoenix, AZ 85001
881-1000

A proof of service must be attached.

UNITED STATES DISTRICT COURT
FOR THE DISTRICT OF ARIZONA

John Jones,
            Plaintiff

            v.   NO. 99 C 1000

Susan Smith,
            Defendant

MOTION FOR ORDER TO COMPEL PLAINTIFF'S PHYSICAL EXAMINATION

Defendant moves under Rule 35 of the Federal Rules of Civil Procedure for an order compelling plaintiff to submit to a physical examination. In support of her motion defendant states:

1. Plaintiff's physical condition is genuinely in controversy since the complaint alleges a variety of physical injuries.

2. Plaintiff during his deposition stated that he still suffers from the consequences of the accident that is the basis for his complaint. These include periodic pain in his back and ankle.

3. There exists good cause, in light of the above, for a physical examination of the plaintiff to evaluate the plaintiff's current physical condition and prognosis.

4. Rudolf B. Anton, M.D., a board certified neurologist, has agreed to examine and evaluate the plaintiff at his medical office located at 4401 North Scottsdale Road, Scottsdale, Arizona, on September 15, 1999, at 5:00 P.M., or at another time, as directed by this court.

WHEREFORE, defendant requests that the court enter an order directing the plaintiff to be examined on the terms set forth above.

Since plaintiff has not accepted the offer of judgment, defendant must continue her trial preparations. Getting a current evaluation of the plaintiff's medical condition and prognosis from a physician who has not previously seen the plaintiff is vital.

Keep in mind that many jurisdictions require a lawyer to certify that he has complied with local rules that require that the parties first try to resolve discovery disputes informally.

Dated: September 1, 1999

William Sharp
William Sharp
Attorney for Defendant
100 Broadway
Phoenix, AZ 85001
881-1000

A proof of service must be attached.

UNITED STATES DISTRICT COURT
FOR THE DISTRICT OF ARIZONA

John Jones,
          Plaintiff

          v.   NO. 99 C 1000

Susan Smith,
          Defendant

JOINT PRETRIAL MEMORANDUM

Pursuant to Local Rule, plaintiff and defendant submit the following joint pretrial memorandum:

Judges frequently have instructions on what the memorandum should contain and how it should be organized.

I

Jurisdiction

Jurisdiction of the court is based on diversity of citizenship under 28 U.S.C. §1332. Plaintiff is a citizen of Arizona. Defendant is a citizen of Nevada. The amount in controversy exceeds the sum of seventy-five thousand ($75,000) dollars, exclusive of interest and costs.

II

Uncontested Facts

Plaintiff Jones and defendant Smith were involved in a vehicle collision on September 2, 1998. The collision occurred at the intersection of 40th Street and Thomas Road in Phoenix, Arizona, at approximately 2:00 P.M. At the time of the collision Jones was driving his car, a 1995 Toyota Corolla four-door sedan, northbound on 40th Street; Smith was driving her car, a 1995 Buick Skylark sedan, eastbound on Thomas Road. The intersection is controlled by traffic lights.

These facts have all been admitted in the pleadings or during discovery.

On September 2, 1998, Jones was employed as a delivery driver by Devo Wholesale Florist and was being paid gross wages of $700 per month.

Jones received various physical injuries as a result of the collision. He missed one month's work and wages from his job. His medical bills to date total $2,717.14. His vehicle repair costs totalled $1,213.00. His other out-of-pocket expenses totalled $237.00.

III

Contested Issues of Fact and Law

1. Did Smith run a red light?
2. Did Jones run a red light?
3. Was Smith negligent?
4. Was Jones negligent?
5. If both Smith and Jones were negligent, what is the degree of negligence of each of them?
6. What were the extent of Jones' injuries as a result of this collision?
7. What are Jones' reasonable damages?

IV

Exhibits

A. *Plaintiff Jones'*   *Objections, if any*
    Exhibits
    1. Doctors Hospital
        records   None.
    2. Dr. Lang's office
        records   None.
    3. Dr. Hoffman's office
        records   None.
    4. Dr. Franks' office
        records   None.
    5. All bills for above   None.
    6. X rays taken by above   None.
    7. Devo Wholesale Flo-
        rist employment
        records   None.

8.	Phoenix Police Dept. reports	Objection, for reasons stated in attached memorandum.	If any evidence is objected to, the judge may rule on the objections, if possible to do so, during the pretrial conference.
9.	Accident scene photographs	None.	If objections are made, the objecting party should state the basis for the objection, with supporting citations if necessary.
10.	Jack's Auto Repair records and bill	None.	
11.	Watch repair bill	None.	
12.	Glendale Community College bills	None.	
13.	Walgreen pharmacy bill	None.	
14.	Accident scene diagrams	None.	

B.   *Defendant Smith's Exhibits*   *Objections, if any*

1.	Plaintiff's hospital and medical records	None.
2.	Rudolf Anton, M.D., medical records	None.
3.	Accident scene photographs	None.
4.	Accident scene diagrams	Objection, misleading.
5.	Phoenix Police Dept. reports to extent admissible	None.

V

Witnesses

A.   *Plaintiff Jones' Witnesses*
  1. Plaintiff
  2. Carol Brown, 42 East Cambridge Street, Phoenix
  3. Mary Porter, 42 East Cambridge Street, Phoenix

4. Dr. Lang
5. Dr. Hoffman
6. Dr. Franks
7. Diane Devo, Devo Wholesale Florist
8. John Jones, Sr., and Mary Jones, plaintiff's parents
9. Officer Steven Pitcher, Phoenix Police Dept.
10. Defendant
11. Personnel from Jack's Auto Repair, to qualify exhibits
12. Personnel from above hospitals and physicians, to qualify exhibits

B. *Defendant Smith's witnesses:*
1. All of plaintiff's witnesses
2. Dr. Rudolf Anton

VI

Jury Instructions

Plaintiff's and defendant's proposed jury instructions are attached.

1. Plaintiff objects to defendant instruction Nos. 6, 7, and 9, for the reasons stated in plaintiff's attached memorandum.

2. Defendant objects to plaintiff instruction nos. 2, 3, 4, and 6, for the reasons stated in defendant's attached memorandum.

RESPECTFULLY SUBMITTED,

Date: November 1, 1999

Anne Johnson
Anne Johnson
Attorney for Plaintiff

William Sharp
William Sharp
Attorney for Defendant

Pretrial memoranda frequently also contain a memorandum of law from each party that discusses any legal issues that the judge will need to resolve before or during trial.

The judge's final pretrial order will usually track the language and organization of the memorandum and contain all rulings on admissibility issues that were made at the conference.

RELEASE

In consideration of the sum of twenty-six thousand dollars ($26,000), which plaintiff acknowledges receiving, Plaintiff John Jones agrees to release Defendant Susan Smith and her heirs, survivors, agents, and personal representatives from all claims, suits, or actions in any form or on any basis, because of anything that was done or not done at any time, on account of the following:

All claims for personal injuries, property damage, physical disabilities, medical expenses, lost income, loss of consortium, and all other claims that have been or could be brought, including all claims now known or that in the future might be known, which arise out of an occurrence on or about September 2, 1998, at 40th Street and Thomas Road, in Phoenix, Arizona, when plaintiff claims to have sustained injuries as a result of a collision between an automobile driven by plaintiff and an automobile driven by defendant.

As a result of this collision plaintiff has brought suit against defendant for damages. Defendant has denied both liability and the claimed extent of damages. This release is a compromise settlement between Plaintiff John Jones and Defendant Susan Smith.

This agreement is a release and shall operate as a total discharge of any claims plaintiff has or may have, arising out the above occurrence, against this defendant and any other persons.

Plaintiff John Jones and Defendant Susan Smith also agree to terminate any actions that have been filed, particularly a claim by this plaintiff against this defendant currently filed as civil action No. 99 C 1000 in the United States District Court for the District of Arizona, in Phoenix, Arizona. Plaintiff and defendant agree to execute a Stipulation of Dismissal, with prejudice, and file it with the Clerk of the above Court, thereby terminating that action in its entirety, within five days of the execution of this agreement.

A release would be the standard way of settling this case, since it is a complete settlement by all the parties.

Date: <u>December 1, 1999</u>

<u>*John Jones*</u>
John Jones, Plaintiff

The parties, not their lawyers, must sign the release.

<u>*Susan Smith*</u>
Susan Smith, Defendant

UNITED STATES DISTRICT COURT
FOR THE DISTRICT OF ARIZONA

John Jones,
      Plaintiff

    v.
                        No. 99 C 1000

Susan Smith,
      Defendant

STIPULATION OF DISMISSAL

Plaintiff John Jones and Defendant Susan Smith agree to dismiss this action with prejudice, and each party will bear its costs and attorney's fees.

The stipulation of dismissal terminates the lawsuit. No court order is necessary.

Dated: December 2, 1999

Anne Johnson
Attorney for Plaintiff

William Sharp
Attorney for Defendant

INDEX